Shadows Over Kashmir — A Riddle

Shadows Over Kashmir

A Riddle

Biplab K. Mazumdar

Reference Press

New Delhi

Shadows Over Kashmir
A Riddle

ISBN: 978-81-8405-070-7

Rs.1450/-

First Published 2011

Published by:
Reference Press
4831/24, Ansari Road,
Darya Ganj,
New Delhi-110 002.
INDIA
Phones: 23260807, 41563444
Fax: 41563334
E-mail: info@essessreference.com
www.essessreference.com

Cover Design by *Patch Creative Unit*

Printed and bound in India at Salasar Imaging Systems.

Dedicated to

My MOTHER

CONTENTS

Author's Note

India has already attained sixty years of independence through the mires of a seething bubble of political lava in the midst of religious vanity and egotism, breaking through the thin crust of social volcano. Hidden away somewhere and locked in each other's religious fanaticism, the fumes of religious animosity between India and Pakistan are seen through a red mist of rage as the sole author and architect of all misfortunes in this sub-continent. Both the countries are in this ugly, dangerous and unpredictable mood. We look tired and strained and there are shadows under our eyes. We all laugh together helplessly, and are silent and short-tempered with fear of being struck down by religious fever and by monotonous routine of political handshakes. The innocent people of Kashmir look ill and weary by that fever, after the hot, restless nights of cross-border terrorism. Both the countries quarrel with regrettable frequency and get on each other's nerves to the point of desperation, and complain about each to the White House. The doors all along the valley were locked yesterday and will remain locked tomorrow, combined with uncertain temper of today. Anxieties are doubled. Why? Because the boom of the sound with the same savage regularity as the sound itself strikes through our throbbing head. Sixty years perhaps longer... And New Delhi thinks again of Kashmir problem. Recurrent fever of excitement and infinite diplomatic negligence go with the crackle of rifle-fire and the boom of guns. It sounds like a big attack that had been silent during the past night but had begun again with the dawn. We wait, pant and pray for 'PEACE' in the valley of Kashmir. But our neighbouring country, Pakistan, has lost her restlessness. There is a sharp and un-tigerlike yelp and Pakistan-sponsored infiltrators surreptitiously get away into the jungle of Pak-occupied Kashmir. The valley has witnessed these long, burning and breathless days of rasping and scratching sound of fires and fumes for over sixty years. Why? Because the whole Kashmir question is shrouded in the deepest mystery and only referred to in whispers. We are kept in complete ignorance of the matter. Our white faces are the same terror of the unknown that is on the people of Jammu & Kashmir. We have only the haziest idea of what happens when a child was born in the valley of mysterious diplomacy and shakehands.

The day Adam partook of the forbidden fruit and fell, man's ceaseless quest for the secret of life and recipe for longevity began. Throughout the medieval ages, alchemists burnt the midnight oil in attics and basements looking for the elixir of life and the philosopher's stone, and to their wide and unremitting research we owe the birth of the science of chemistry as well as many valuable inventions. And now man cowers under the new monster of nuclear weapons created by himself and so mankind blunders along.

And today, it is the third block, the uncommitted world or the area of peace, that has leapt into prominence, threatening to upset the calculations of the strategists of the cold war. The objector and the rebel who raises his voice against what he believes to be the injustice of the present and the wrongs of the past is the one who hunches the world along. And all the social illusions, on Kashmir issue, which we have raved about in religion serve only the purpose of deceiving and blinding the ignorant of this sub-continent. Communal bacteria is the back entrance of political chaos in this sub-continent.

There is no doubt that the people who invaded and committed aggression in Kashmir were aided and abetted completely with arms and transport and petrol by Pakistan. The Pakistani army was there in Nov. 1949 and we have the most absolute, hundred percent, foolproof of that. When the limited number of Indian armed forces... about a thousand or two .... had driven the raiders, who could not obivously resist an organised army. They came settling there. And that was the Pakistani army at Uri entrenched with guns and the like and it became a different problem. For the first time Mr. Nehru realised that Pakistan was not merely helping and aiding the raiders but was actually sitting there with its whole army. Nehru's realisation came too late. Truly speaking, Nehru's good words are a mask for concealment of bad deeds. His dry-water diplomacy makes the Kashmir problem. His diplomacy on Kashmir issue is fluid, soft and yielding. Behind that word 'partition', demons lurk. And Pakistan with that venomous word has done her fiercest fighting for Islamic doctrines in the valley, in favour of systematic hatred against India.

The vehicles that brought these raiders to Kashmir had rather curious inscriptions on them. One did not normally think of the Pathan raiders going about in large numbers of motor vehicles. But the inscriptions on these vehicles were often "To Delhi" and not merely Kashmir or Srinagar, but "To Delhi via Kashmir". These might have been the flight of imagination of the persons who had put it there. But they had put it for the sake of subordinate interests.

Now the question is : Why Pakistan invaded Kashmir? Because Pakistan justified it by what had happened in Junagadh and in other places, which had nothing to do with Kashmir. Pakistan brought in this argument about genocide. Genocide : There was genocide undoubtedly in Pakistan. It was a horrible affair. How a relatively simple issue was mixed up with other matters so as to produce confusion in people's minds. In every clause of partition, Pakistan shakes her fists in the face of constituted authority and thunders against India.

An interesting thing about the invasion was that in the beginning there was no Indian army in Kashmir, not a soldier was there for many days after the invasion. And the whole valley of Kashmir lay open to any invader. Srinagar was defended by the people of Srinagar, just volunteers. It was a remarkable period, when common people stirred by risk and danger, had got to defend their city and their valley. These broad facts have to be remembered. Kashmir is legally, constitutionally and practically correct.

If the law is thrust upon us we have the law and the aggressor is the guilty party. And the law is that Kashmir has acceded to and is a part of the Union of India. When devaluation of the Indian rupee took place and the Pakistan rupee was kept at the old level, there was a big exodus in 1949-50. Why? Because they saw no future for themselves in East Pakistan (now Bangladesh). One never knows himself till he has denied himself. Political sloth is the torpidity of the mental faculties; the sluggard of theology is a living insensible. Little does Pakistan realise into what maelstrom of suspicion, jealousy and intrigue, she is about to enter. She follows religious fanaticism anxiously into a hall of shame, hovering around and nipping green leaves and buds of Kashmir with careful devotion of being intoxicated with sham modesty.

High hopes mingle with grave apprehensions for the future among the people. There is much excitement and nervousness in the air. It is better to suffer wrong than to do it, and happier to be sometimes cheated than not to trust.

When India was reborn as an independent country, the world was already in the throes of the cold war and the progress of Asia towards national independence and reconstruction has proceeded amongst the global struggle for power. It is an historical misfortune that the renaissance of Asia should coincide with a ruthless struggle among the great powers for the mastery of the world. Pakistan, born in the shadows of midnight, has run with the same ruthless struggle, as the great powers, for the mastery over the valley of Kashmir with a babble of Jehadi Slogans and laughter of crude fanaticism, assuring the countrymen in a conspiratorial whisper.

The uncommitted world is a world of diversity. It includes ancient nations like India, Egypt, as well as modern nations like Sudan and Jordan. It includes tropical jungles, stony deserts and high mountains peoples of every race and of many cultures. In this sub-continent, there are many diversities and differences but there is unifying factor; desire for peace and freedom. Peace area in Kashmir does not spread. Day by day, month by month, year by year, as the threat of terrorism predominates over Kashmir and omnious presence of Pakistan in the valley grows, military alliances with China do not lose their teeth, bases of jehadi slogans become a wasteful drain on national resources and an unshakable faith on Islamic terrorism. Pakistan seems to remain isolated from the free world. And this isolation is spelling a greater danger for democracy than even the threat of global Islamic terrorism.

From the first pallid whisper of dawn in the valley in November, 1949 and when silence gave place to familiar sounds of the valley, Pakistan invaded Kashmir, both India and Pakistan have started out confronting each other, each trying to play a dominant role in Kashmir. Those who refuses to join the U.S. bloc are criticised as sitting on the fence. Peace is not merely an absence of war. Peace is a state of mind. The state of mind is completely absent from the valley today. If the whole world is divided into major nuclear powers and hostile camps, there is no hope either for the Kashmir issue, or for the world, and war becomes inevitable.

The man who will live above his present circumstances is in great danger of living much beneath them; or as the Italian proverb says, "The man that lives by hope will die by despair."

When nature of Pakistan indulges in theological hidebounds, there is always an odd quirk to it. She is now seen like a hurled-down tree lying in desolate abandoned grief with stark arms spread all along the provinces, including POK. A violent gust of religious extremism will, sooner or later, come and tear those poor flowers away. Her illogical claim over Kashmir is as cynical an old woman with a devastating sense of humour as ignorant enough she is to scoff at all agreements on Kashmir issue. A cease-fire which is not followed up with a reasonable argument by an adjustment of political differences remains potentially explosive and nothing but fond illusions can impel the Pakistani rulers to suppose that pending agreement the armistice can remain in force. She remains just a cynical old woman.

Oddly enough, it is possible to quote a proud imperialist in support of this view. In his "History of the English Speaking People", Sir Winston Churchill declares, "It is the primary right of men to die and kill for the land they live in, and punish with exceptional severity all members of their own race who have warmed their hands at the invaders hearth."

Terrorism, of course, is the primary evil of our times, and is dangerous to condone it in any circumstances. That is why people are usually careful as well as alive to disparage and denigrate the frightening gesture of Islamic terrorism that the jehadis have taken all over the valley. All treaties and agreements on Kashmir solution run afloat. Something is to be said for the view that violence of religious fanaticism is less deplorable in the hands of the nationalists than in the those of the imperialists. Feelings of religious strain and political tension have filled Kashmir with such sick despair that the familiar sense of safety in and around the capital is still silent, and this feeling of insecurity looks at our political leaders, abstracted face. But they don't feel embarrassed or shy or ashamed in their presence in parliament. Why? Do they have overcome everything with shame? Whereas the people of the battered Kashmir look as cluttered and untidy and forlorn as any desolated house of Kashmiri Hindu pundits. The sound of their footsteps died away in the darkness of nightmares and stretched back to the limitless distance.

'Azad Kashmir', under Pakistan's control, has been turned into forbidden territory. No one is allowed to visit the area and the world outside does not yet get a chance to know what is going on in 'Azad Kashmir'. There is no Govt. worth the name in the area, and each one is a law upto himself. Whenever a complaint is made about the dire conditions of life, the only answer one usually gets is that Pakistan has now become an Islamic Republic, and Muslims of Azad Kashmir must try and become a part of that Republic. This forbidden area is now the principle source of cheap labour and training camps of budding terrorist groups.

There has been a steady depletion in the population of 'Azad Kashmir' since Pakistan occupied that area in 1947. From a total of about 1,100,000 people, according to the 1941 census, the population of 'Azad Kashmir' has fallen by several thousands and thousands of people. They are now working as domestic servants in homes, all over West Pakistan, including Karachi. Karachi, Pakistan's largest city and most popular for its commercial hub, has a history of political, ethnic and sectarian violence. Any explosion causes a widespread panic in a very busy commercial and residential areas in the bustling city of about 16 million people. The new political maddrasas and radical mosques are born every month in Pakistan's tribal areas and in Afganistan. These maddrasas should be shut down and must be out of national curriculum. Pakistan, the petridish of the forces of terrorism and fanaticism, has suffered more victims of terror than any other nation on earth.

Mr. Nehru was not eminently practical on Kashmir issue. Did he want people to develop the nerve of failure and take risks? Today, the intellectual, like everyone else, faces a staggering problem of relating himself genuinely to other people on Kashmir issue and other problems than his own. On all sides, we see people succumbing to the social pressures. And the protagonists of liberation movement in Kashmir are the enemies of the starched uniformity and have an intense dislike for any collective life in the valley. They work like mad even when they know that the movement bores them.

If entire nation of Pakistan must be suspected of 'anti-India hymns of hate', it should surely be conceded that a readiness to 'take sides' is almost invariably a characteristic of political immaturity. So the Kashmir question can never be settled by the kind of 'taking sides' and 'ganging up' which has led to the formation of Islamic blocs committed to specific attitudes and ideologies. Indo-Pak political engagement is in war, a battle, in love, the salubrious calm all along the valley that precedes the real hostilities. Pakistan is of the masses and for the masses of anti-India propaganda. She has become alienated. Why? Because she has lost her creative role in Kashmir solution and become only a passive receptor of impressions, thoughts and opinions. She has become alienated because her frame of reference on Kashmir dispute and her concept of world peace are no longer adapted to human dimensions. Why? Because her tastes of democracy, opinions on theocracy and preference are exclusively manipulated by the big bosses of religious extremism ... a stormy petrel. Her alienation is her neurosis. This is her insanity. So, religious entertainment in the valley in the name of liberation movement in Kashmir is an industry of fanaticism. Actually, Pakistan eats a phantasy of religious extremism and has lost contact with the real thing we eat. Why? Because Pakistan seems to be a victim of persecution complex of partition. And she strives steadfastly with risks of terrorising the people of Kashmir.

This is undoubtedly one of the reasons why Islamic terrorism and fascism have found such fertile soil in Pakistan. People, preoccupied with under-nourished religious teachings, are quarrelsome, militants and easily led by unscrupulous leaders and confused by grandiose promises to free Kashmir from the clutches of India. Finally, a marked increased in mortality and grave danger of civil war are expected.

There are many that despise the half the world, but if there be any that despise the whole of it, it is because the other half despises them.

Pakistan is on the brink of an abyss, if she takes one step more in her old direction. There are two kinds of charity, remedial and preventive. The former is often injurious in its tendency; the latter is always praiseworthy and beneficial. The rebirth of the vast new nations in Asia represents the real revolution in the 19th century: And it has produced the greatest changes in the political map of the world.

When are individuals most truly individual? How do we know that their tastes are their own? In this sub-continent, we see that men of ten suffer a failure of nerve in the face of the prevailing economic, social and cultural pressures. The main danger to indvidualism today in India lies not in the desire of the majority of men to conform but in a system in which the individual in pursuing his own ends with the interest of others. The individual will continue to suffer, as he does today, neurosis and failure of nerves. Like a child in a bombed town of Indian States, he does not even see the enemy face to face. He finds himself in a trap and in his desperation, he digs deep for security like a rat in a cheese. It does not help to ask him to develop the nerve of failure which will enable to take his defence with good homour of our politicians. The prejudices of ignorance are more easily removed than the prejudicians. The prejudices of ignorance are more easily removed than the humour of our politicians. The prejudices of ignorance are more easily removed than the prejudices of interest : the first are all blindly adopted, the second wilfully preferred.

Terrorists seem to be mentally ill. Pakistan should pass a legislation to keep guns out of the hands of the mentally ill. Americans are among the world's most heavily armed people, and the country has one of the world's highest murder rates. Even Pakistan has long been reluctant to tackle the politically explosive of gun-control. Why? Because Pakistan is alive with felons, fugitives, drug addicts, wife beaters and hardliners of Islamic terrorism. The sectarian image of the Pakistani Govt. can only exacerbate the Shia-Sunni divide in Pakistan and fan out the civil war like situation there.

Partition : What is dishonourably got is dishonourably squandered. It is one of the merciless ironies of our history, even after sixty years of independence, many parliamentarians find themselves caught in the whirlpool of corruption, under the dark clouds of power politics in Kashmir. They are corrupted by pleasure. The towering character of George Washington enabled him to play the great role as a parliamentarian, that he did in America. He likes to give advice to his young ones : "Avoid gambling. This is a vice which ... the child of avarice, the brother of iniquity and father of mischief."

Whereas our parliamentarins are caught in the vulgarity of religion or racialism. They have not yet possessed the virtues of integrity to an abundant degree. When war breaks out, they will burst like a soap bubble. For their vitriolic passion for political gambling, Kashmir has cast upon Indian democracy a gloomy shadow of political insecurity and economic bondage. He who seeks all things, wherever he goes, only reaps, from the hopes which he sows, a harvest of barren regrets.

So many reasons are there for international terrorism sponsored by Pakistan.

1. The West uses the country for its short-term political objectives,
2. The West uses dollar diplomacy in her military rather than her people,
3. Pakistan was exploited under conlonialism,
4. Manipulated as a tool of cold war intrigue,
5. The West made Pakistan into a surrogate for a war against the Soviets in Afganistan,
6. At the end of the war, Pakistan and Afganistan were abandoned to the forces of extremism and fanaticism,
7. And now Pakistan plays with words of 'anti-India hymns of hate'.

The people of Kashmir are chattels to be shared with religious extremism; but are the people of religious groups in Pakistan to be shared between theology and Islamic terrorism? Why should the Muslim League .... the author of the partition of India on communal lines .... not accept the partition of Kashmir?

Each drum-beat of three-pronged propagandaism ... religious extremism, theology and Islamic terrorism ... is a heart-throbbing drama fully dramatised with a great theatrical performance around the valley of Kashmir. The Jehadi cancers enter the blood-stained stage of propagandaism all tensed up. They split, the jehadis on one side and the terrorists on the other. They advance with heavy energy towards each other. The drum-beat and the heart-throb get more insistent. The dancers warm up all along the valley. Both the jehadis and the terrorists with their blood-stained arms entwined against their backs surge forward and retreat. They form a circle opens and closes. This stage of propaganda is a magnetic field of Islamic globalisation. The tension is half-pain and half-joy. Soon it touches the breaking point of LoC. It cannot go on. It must come to a stop. It does. The dance is over.

They dance to appease the religious gladiators of terrorism as the Indian secularists try to appease the Indian Muslims to win over the ballot boxes.

Dancing to appease them is a part of communal life. It is also a living tradition of Indian political leaders. Even the jehadis have enough talent to make a begining in the way of building up a national ensemble of jehadi dancers, who will take the first step. Here is a challenge for Islamabad ... a sanctum sanctorum of Islamic terrorism. If they transgress this limit of propriety, public censure may well visit them with a world of chaos. Pakistan has forgotten that all extremes are error. The reverse of error is not truth, but error still. Truth lies between extremes.

Against whom Pakistan is so feverishly arming herself? A Pakistani journalist who specialises in foreign affairs points out his finger on a map across the Himalayas and the Karakoram range. But some cross-examination does yield two significant answers ... that Pakistan is afraid of 'aggression from India' and that wants Pakistan to hold a pistol against India's head.

Her links with America are only political, economic and matrimonial. Why matrimonial? President's Iskandar Mirza's son and U.S. Ambassador Hildreth's daughter were husband and wife ... but also accidental. For, as in the pioneering days of America, Pakistan, in her present pioneering period, is seized with an oil rush. Some of the world's richest deposits may be found along the Markan coast of Baluchistan, west of Karachi. It is fantastically rich in oil. The topography of the Marakan coast is ideal.

Even this progress in Pakistan, she, like all converts, is ruthlessly fanatical against India in holding to crude Islamic belief. Don't throw out your dirty water until you get in fresh. Pakistan does not know intelligence and application help in life. Islam elevates the soul. In this critical phase, Pakistan is inclined to doubt all the accepted truth of Christianity, Hinduism and all other religions. She accepts the philosophy of pyrrohonism. She is a holder of schismatic opinions owing to doctrinal and disciplinary differences with- in the country. Such religious schizophrenia is an incurable mental disease marked by religious breakdown in relation between religious dualism and diplomatic dualism accompanied by political delusions and retreat from democracy.

Pakistan's foreign policy on Kashmir : The policy is to say 'yes' to everything that America does. Therefore, all talk of following an independent foreign policy and of befriending India and other countries ... urged by some opposition members in the National Assembly ... is utterly bereft of reality. She just can't help following the policy which she does follow, if occasionally there is some talk of pursuing an independent foreign policy, it can be interpreted, charitably a wishful thinking, and uncharitably, as blackmail of America, on Kashmir problem. Crores and crores of rupees are parcelled out of Pakistan in the shape of foreign economic aid. Each and every minister of Pakistan looks like a perfect tailor's model, and that in a poverty-stricken country of banana republic, everyone has to see one wear the same three-piece suit twice over. Pakistan's hidden mask behind Kashmir question may become her credit card of Islamic terrorism. For every minute you are angry, you lose 60 seconds of happiness. From loss of reason, you go to complete ruin.

Telegraph messengers on scooters, and 2008 model American cars speed along Islamabad's broad, clean throughfares. They are, in a sense, symbolic of modern Pakistan. Camel and donkey carts and streamlined cars represent different ages altogether. Pakistan-sponsored terrorists and jehadis speed along the capital by modern American and Indian cars. Fine clothes are a craze with officialdom.

One often hears the remark in Pakistan that "We belong to the West, while India belongs to the East." Now one fails to understand whether the 'East' and 'West' are geographical or ideological terms. Pakistan's ideologies, on Kashmir issue, are gotten with pain, kept with care and lost with grief. It is a malicious enjoyment of author's misfortune.

In fact, terrorist society in Pakistan is far from being classless. They have become a class which works together in the words of Islamic jehad 'not so much from ideological and moral unanimity, but rather from the same way of living and similar interests, from the nature of crudely infatuated religious jingoism and the manner in which it attains. This new aristocracy of Islamic nation like Pakistan rests on the foundations of tremendous armed strength, complete state-sponsored terrorism, prison camps, an all-pervading secret organisation of ISI and a vast propaganda-fed anti-India slogans. Terrorism and religious extremism have nothing in common. The perverted theologians and mullocracy have merely perverted the very idea of democracy. Where they are in power, they have destroyed every freedom of people. Military dictatorship in Pakistan is internally aristocratic and externally militant. The method of Islamic philosophy under Gen. Musharraf involved a great departure from their own ideals. So theology in Pakistan is not merely a political doctrine but also a religion with elaborate dogmas and inspired scriptures. The roots of that go much deeper. By the dictatorship of a military ruler in Pakistan means the dictatorship of religious pyrrhonism. So, Pakistan talks to India on Kashmir without proper introduction.

The violence and indiscipline which India has witnessed during the last sixty years have been widespread. Why are we drifting? Why? Because our leaders are following new 'isms' ... crankyism and make-believeism ... and on top of it we are living in an atmosphere of suspense and uncertainty and suspicion. Why? Because of the indecisions of New Delhi. The ruling Congress rulers at the centre have so far adopted a policy of wobbly and weak attitude on Kashmir question. That leads to political disaster and social chaos. The so-called political fasting on Kashmir issue is nothing but a fraud and an act of coercion and blackmail.

If this single thing is not scotched sternly and immediately, the hydra-headed monster of anarchy must soon raise its head not only in the valley but all over the country. But there is evidence of a sense of defeatism and frustration which cannot but be deeply disturbing to every Indian concerned with the future of Kashmir. People give the name of zeal to their propensity to mischief and violence.

It is not a little paradoxical that the cult of personality should have reached its most dangerous heights in a country. But the debunkers of Nehru are accused on being half-hearted in repairing their earlier error on the Kashmir issue. They obviously feel no compunction in practising what they deplore in others. They did not do anything which was not liked by Nehru.

Kashmir tries with India born out of the will of the people is indissoluble and no power on earth would be allowed to break it. Kashmir is the spiritual home of India and the fact which is only reality. Why? Because it has an unbroken glorious history for the 2500 years.

Pakistan has no doubt murmured honeyd words in ISI's jaded ears. Kashmir seems to have been on these propagandists' platter. Her alternate melancholy and cheeriness have a crude Islamic flavour of a softening of the brain. Her rulers, on the Kashmir issue, set out with a begging bowl and return empty-handed. As every good newspaperman knows, nothing is so stale as yesterday's news. A good politician should know that an abortive conference is as dead as cold mutton.

Pakistan's attempts to warm up resuscitate the talks and serve these talks as a stew in U.N.O. The gesture has damaged her political reputation on the Kashmir debate. Hampered by heterogenous team of theology-based colleagues who did not see eye to eye with the rulers on all points of Kashmir, every ruler was manoeuvring from a position of weakness where Pakistan would remain to be seen as another Iraq. There is no greater sin that going back on one's promise.

'Parts of Pakistan' are identified as a separate component in the war on terror., distinct from Afganistan, with which it has hitherto been hyphenated. Extremists are increasingly using Pakistan as a base to destabilise Afganistan's young democracy.

G.Parthasarathy, former India's High Commissioner, said : "... in a recent poll in Afganistan, 80% of those polled expressed 'strong approval' of India and its assistance programme ... a development that the Taliban and its mentors in Rawalpindi evidently find unbearable. India's imprint in Afganistan is visible across the country. Over 400 Tata buses and 200 minibuses gifted by India ply in major town and cities ... The Taliban controls large areas of rural Pakistan ... The main worry for Afganistan is across the border. Tensions along Afganistan's borders with Pakistan are set to escalate as the Americans appear determined to hit at Taliban and Al-Quaida hideouts and bases in Pakistan's tribal areas. " (Times of India, Sept. 12, 2008).

Mr. Nehru was an incarnation of political dualism on Kashmir debate. Sad that this one-time patriot should today be a synonym for politi-persecution, more despotic than the shoguns of Japans and more curel than the Machus of China. Nehru's decision abounds in contradictions. At one time, he was the rising hope in Asia. Unfortunately, on the Kashmir issue, he is a source of danger in Asia and a drawback to the cause of peace in Kashmir throughout the world.

Jinnah's Pakistan was born in an atmosphere of defeat and disillusionment, when Jinnah's name was looked upon as the symbol for the self-contradictory and miscalculated political road disastrously followed by his Kashmir policy. Mr. Nehru could not pledge himself to the questionable game of Kashmir. From Jinnah down to the present leaders of Pakistan, they have never learned the restraints of manners, they express themselves meretriciously, but they are in no way odd or eccentric. Those outbursts of spiritual violence appear among men who live are cogged hour by hour to the counting victims after terrorism. Pakistan, a land of quixotism, walks out in the waking world, with all the liberty of the irrational, all the swagger and thrust of the released self. Visions, nightmares, hallucinations are paraded in the full daylight of consciousness; dreams of Kashmir liberation movement are spoken out loud. A whole class lays bare to the world its secret fantasies as does a patient to a psychonalyst.

Every age likes to think itself unique, our own with more justification than most. This is first the peaceful world before 1914, broken into by the First World War. There follows a post-war decade to 1929. Then the Second World War, and the uneasy pace that has followed it. The First World War began for Americans in 1917, the Second in 1941. Peace ended for the Chinese in 1931 and has never been restored. At the present time, we anticipate localised war rather than a new general conflict; and world history may be again drifting apart into distinct fragments. What enabled Jinnah to impose a double-whammy of totalitarian discipline with Jehadi songs in Kashmir was initially the numerical weakness and the physical and moral exhaustion of the remnant of Islamic extremism, and later the political illiteracy and social immaturity of a new and growing generation recruited forcibly from the poverty-stricken class. Pakistan's nationalism survived through the Jinnah era, but it survived only in a state of hibernation from which it has been violently awakened by today's Islamic terrorism. The religious superstructure has been inherited from the Jinnah era. Its problems and dilemmas are very different from those which preoccupied and oppressed Muslims sixty years ago. The bizarre orthodoxy of Pakistan's eschatological discourse, with its compulsive deformity and inconsistency, has become an anachronism.

This book is in every respect solid in the fabric of historical fact and critical analysis, ranging widely over the economic, social and political problems on Kashmir issue. Painstaking in research and critical analysis, and lucid in presentation. The pace of the narrative is more rapid than any other books, and the pages are not clogged by an accumulation of tedious detail. This book is presented with thumbnail detail. Readers should be impartial and unprejudiced in their honest outlok.

I am indebted to BBC World News, CNN, Times Now etc. I owe my indebtness to Mr. Sumit Sethi, Reference Press, for his heartiest and most richly satisfying cooperation to make this publication possible.

Dr. Biplab K. Mazumdar

JAMMU AND KASHMIR

A. 1. 1846 - 1947 in British India
   2. 1947 - 1952 a princely state within the Dominion of India
   3. 1952 - 1957 an independent Republic
   4. 1957 a constituent state of India

B. an object of contention between India and Pakistan since 1947

C. 98,780 sq. miles in all

D. 85,861 sq. miles under Indian control

E. the rest (12,919 sq.miles) under Pakistani occupation though claimed by both countries

F. Capital : Srinagar

KASHMIR

A. a province of Jammu and Kashmir

B. 8539 sq.miles

C. Capitals : Srinagar (in summer) and Jammu (in winter)

D. Containing the vale of Kashmir, a valley in the Himalayas in the Western Kashmir province

E. Formerly Cashmere

F. Was partitioned in 1949, the N.W. area becoming Azad Kashmir, (Free Kashmir), controlled by Pakistan

G. Partition brings political hazards over the valley, and the State administration.

IMPORTANT INDIAN PEAKS : (Twenty Peaks)

Peak	Height (in meters above mean sea level)
A. Peaks in Indian Territory	**(Twelve (12) peaks belong to India)**
1. Kanchenjunga	8,598
2. Nanga Parbat	8,126
3. Masher Brum E	7,821
4. Nanda Devi	7,817
5. Kamet	7,756
6. Saser Kangri	7,672
7. Chaukhamba (Badrnath peak)	7,138
8. Trisul West	7,138
9. Nankun	7,135
10. Pauchunn	7,128
11. Kangto	7,090
12. Dunagiri	7,066

B. Peaks in Pak-occupied Territory	**(Eight (8) peaks belong to POK)**
1. K2 (Godwin Austen)	8,611
2. Gasher Brum	8,068
3. Broad peak	8,047
4. Disteghil Sar	7,885
5. Masher Brum W	7,806
6. Rakaposhi	7,788
7. Skyang Kangri	7,544
8. Sia Kangri	7,422

PHYSICAL FEATURES REGARDING KASHMIR

A. The Himalayas

1. Almost a 2,500 km long continuous mountain wall on India's north
2. Extending from Indus in the West to Brahmaputra in the east
3. Divided into Western, Central and Eastern Himalayas

B. The Western Himalayas

1. Jammu and Kashmir
2. Himachal Pradesh

C. Central Himalayas

1. Uttaranchal
2. Nepal

D. Eastern Himalyas

1. Northern parts of West Bengal
2. Extend into Sikkim, Bhutan and Arunachal Pradesh

The Himalayas : (Three parallel Ranges of mountains) : The Himadri, The Himachal, and the Shiwaliks

A. The Himadri Range : (Known as the Greater Himalayas)

1. Northernmost range and lies on the edge of the Tibetan Plateau
2. The highest mountain range of about 6000 metres above the sea level
3. The world's highest mountain peak
   - (a) Mount Everest (8,848 metres) in Nepal belongs to Greater Himalayas
   - (b) Kanchenjunga (8,598 metres)
   - (c) Nanga Parbat (8,126 metres)
   - (d) Nanda Devi (7,817 metres)

   .... the highest peaks of the Greater Himalayas in India.

B. The Himachal Range (South of the Himadri Range) : Known as the Middle of the Lesser Himalayas)

1. A height varying between 3,700 and 4,500 metres above sea level.
2. Alternating ridges and valleys
3. Highly dissected uplands contain many of India's important hill stations
4. Kashmir, Kulu and Kangra valleys of India and Kathmandu valley in Nepal in this range.
5. The popular hill stations ... Shimla (Himachal Pradesh); Mussoorie and Nainital (Uttaranchal), Darjeeling (West Bengal) lie on the Himachal range of the Himalayas.

C. The Shiwalik Range

1. Southernmost range of the Himalayas
2. The lowest range of the Himalayas
3. A height of between 900 and 1,200 metres above the sea level
4. Made up of mud and soft rocks
5. A discontinuous range lying on the northern border of the Ganga plain extending towards east to merger with the main mountains.

D. PASSES : A road or way over through mountains)...An easy access to the foreign invaders (like Pakistani intruders and China) and greatly influenced the course of India's history.

1. Through the Himalayas with their loftiest mountain ranges, some gaps in

their ranges

2. Provide natural routes across these high mountains
3. These gaps are called 'Passes'
4. Traditional trade routes over the past centuries

E. Important 'Passes' in the Himalayas

1. The Jelap La
2. Nathua La
3. Bomdi La and etc. etc.

F. Mountains on India's north-eastern side : These mountain ranges are neither as tall nor as spectacular as the mighty Himalayas

1. Poorvanchal mountains
   - (a) Parkai Bum ... in the north
   - (b) The Naga Hills
   - (c) Mizo ... in the south
   - (d) Lushai Hills
   - (e) The Garo ... in the centre
   - (f) Khasi and Jaintia Hills

What is Pakistan-occupied Kashmir (PoK)

It refers to a *disputed region* between India and Pakistan in south Asia that is under the *de facto* administration of *Pakistan.* It borders the Pakistani *Punjab* and *North West Frontier* Provinces to the west, the *Wakhan Corridor* of *Afghanistan* to the north west, the Xinjiang Uyghur Autonomuous Region of *People's Republic of China* to the north and *Indian-administered Kashmir* to the east.

Strange to say, a part of this area of the *former princely state of Kashmir,* the trans-Karakoram tract was ceded to China. Why? And the remaining area was amalgamated into two regions *Northern Areas* and *the Azad Kashmir.* Both nations had a *war in 1947* over the former kingdom. India refers to this region as *"Pakistan-occupied Kashmir"* (or PoK). Most international agencies including U.N.O. and the Red Cross refer to this region as Pakistan-occupied Kashmir.

WHAT IS THE POSITION OF INDIA?

1. Maharaja Hari Singh, King of *the Princely State of Jammu and Kashmir* agreed to *Governor-General* Lord *Mountbatten's* suggestion to sign the *"Instrument of Accession"* India demanded accession in return for assistance.
2. After accession, India recovered part of the territory of *the Princely State of Jammu and Kashmir* east of the present *Line of Control* from the tribal invaders.
3. India claimed that the whole territory of the Princely State of Jammu and Kashmir had become Indian territory (India's official posture) due to the accession.
4. It claims the whole region including Pakistan-occupied Kashmir territory as its own.

   Pakistan has a different perspective on this interpretation.

WHAT IS PAKISTAN'S INTERPRETATION?

1. The *Pakistan Declaration* of 1933 has envisioned the princely state of Jammu and Kashmir as one of the "*Five Northern Units of India*" that were to form the new nation of Pakistan, *on the basis* of its Muslim Majority. India has a different perspective on this interpretation.

OCCUPIED DIVISIONS

The whole area of Pakistan-occupied Kashmir was administered as it was before independence :

a) *1947 to 1970 :* Additionally, a part of Hunza-Gilgit called *Raskam* and the *Shaksgam Valley* of *Baltistan* region, ceded by Pakistan to the *People's Republic of China* in 1963 pending settlement of the dispute over Kashmir. This ceded area is also known as the *Trans-Karakoram Tract.*

b) *Post 1970 :*
   1. Azad Kashmir
   2. *The Northern Areas :* Gilgit was an agency leased by the Maharaja to British Govt. Baltistan was western district of *Ladakh* province which was annexed by Pakistan in 1947. This area is part of the disputed Jammu and Kashmir Region.

c) *Aksai Chin :* Pakistan-occupied Kashmir does not include *Aksai chin,* the area of the former *princely state of Kashmir and Jammu* that is under *Chinese* since 1962. The cease-fire line that separates *Jammu and Kashmir* from the *Aksai Chin* is known as the *Line of Actual Control* (LAC).

Short Sketch of History behind Pakistan-occupied Kashmir (PoK)

(a) During the *partition* of *British India* into *the Dominion of Pakistan* and the Republic of *India,* the *Princely States* had the options of joining either *India* or *Pakistan.*

(b) The *Maharaja* of Kashmir wanted independence but a revolution by Muslims in the western part of the kingdom and the incursion of tribesmen from *Northwest Frontier Province* made him appeal for help from India.

(c) The tribesmen were sent in but British General *Douglas Gracey* of Pakistan refused to follow orders from *Mohammad Ali Jinnah* to attack kashmir.

(d) The tribesmen were equipped with light tanks and were almost at the doorsteps of *Srinagar* before Indian army stopped them.

(e) The raiders advanced to *Baramulla,* the biggest commercial centre of the region with a population then of 11,000, until they were only an hour away from Srinagar.

(f) Unable to prevent the advance, the Maharaja, on October 24, 1947, appealed for military assistance from the Govt. of India. The Indian Govt. argued that in order for assistance the state would have to accede to India.

(g) A simultaneous appeal for assistance and for the state's accession to the Indian Union was also made by *Sheikh Abdullah,* leader of the National

Conference, and the undisputed leader of the people, who had for his views been imprisoned by the Maharaja's Govt. into September 1947 and released only under pressure of India's Prime Minister.

(h) On receipt of the signed Instrument of Accession from the Maharaja, preparations were made to fly Indian troops to the State. The formal letter of acceptance of the Accession was signed by Lord Mountbatten on October 27 making Jammu and Kashmir an integral part of India even as Indian forces were airlifted to Srinagar.

(i) Jawaharlal Nehru, then Prime Minister of India asked the UN to intervene.

(j) The United Nations passed the *United Nations Security Council Resolution 47* asking Pakistan to withdraw all its forces from Kashmir. This was to be followed by plebiscite to determine the wishes of people of the entire state of Kashmir.

(k) However, the required withdrawal never happened. The area which remained under the control of Pakistan is called "*Pakistan-occupied Kashmir*".

India's Relations with neighbouring countries

The Himalayas have alway been the principal barrier to India and as the highest ranges lie mostly on the other side of Nepal, any new development in the border areas affects India's security. India is naturally anxious to see that peace and stability are maintained in the Himalayan states. Our country is anxious; whether our leaders have no qualms of conscience. Who are they? They are busy in the blackest billingsgate, the most ungentlemanly insolence and in the most perfidious arrogance in collision with a dogma of their own out-worn ideologies. Poisonous they are, whether they know it or not. Nepal, a remote land-locked and mountainous contry, is in sourthern Asia, bordered by China (Tibet) to the north and India to the south, dominated by the Himalayas including Mount Everest. The country was conquered by the Gurkhas in the 18th century and despite defeats by the British in the early 19th century has maintained its independence.

Ever since India became independent, she has been taking a great deal of interest in her neighbours. With an area of about 18,000 miles, Bhutan extends for a distance of approximately 190 miles, east and west along the sourthern slopes of the central Himalayas. The main instruments governing India's relations with Bhutan were the Sinchula Treaty of 1865 and the Treaty of 1910 between the former Govt. of India and the Govt. of Bhutan. On August 8, 1949 India entered into a new treaty of perpetual peace and friendship with Bhutan. Under the new treaty, the Govt. of India undertook not to interfere in the internal administration of Bhutan agreed to be guided by India in regard to her external relations.

Nepal

Compared to Nepal and Bhutan, Sikkim is a small state. It is in the hart of the eastern Himalayas and has an area of 2,818 sq. miles. Political relations between India and Sikkim dated from about 1817 and until the transfer of power in August, 1947 were regulated by a treaty signed in 1861. After the transfer of power, relations were governed by a Stand Still Agreement, which broadly speaking kept the old arrangements alive.

A provisional agreement was reached in March 1950 between the representatives of the Govt. of India and the Maharaj Kumar of Sikkim, who was authorized by the Maharaja to participate in the discussions on his behalf, embodying all the provisions of 1861.

A new treaty was signed with Sikkim on Dec. 5, 1950, whereby Sikkim will continue to be Protectorate of India, enjoying full autonomy in internal affairs. Defence, external affairs and communications are the responsibilities of the Govt. of India. The Govt. of India have the right to station troops anywhere within the state. Why? Feeling its mystery and grandeur, the Govt. of India have shouldered the full responsibilities of protecting Nepal and Sikkim from the falsehood of Islamic jehad and from the danger of Pakistan's double-barreled diplomacy and double-whammy of China's bare-faced dogmas.

Nepal is the bridge-head from which India can get forward to attack the enemy. Our military strategists in association with our foreign policy makers should be intelligent and quick to understand the geographical position of Nepal. Do they know a false tooth is held permanently in place of natural teeth? Are they fully aware of Chinese whispers passing from one person to another changing each time? Wait for the psychological moment to do something in order to be successful. Otherwise, every psychological moment will be like a lamb to the slaughter. Why? When any opinion of Pakistan or China on Nepal leads to absurdities, it is certainly false. But it is not certain that an opinion is false. Why? Because it is of dangerous consequence. Policy makers! Don't divide yourselves between right and expendience. Do you know miracles after miracles, since partition, have rolled down in political torrents either from Pakistan or China? Both China and Pakistan have a long chronicle of folly and crime. Had the Jews remained in palestine, they would long ago have lost their individuality in the process of their State's construction, like all other nations.

Nepal is the biggest and the most important of the three border States. A narrow tract of country extending for about 520 miles along the southern slope of the central axis of the Himalayas. It has an area of about 56,000 sq. miles.

Indo-Nepalese relations were governed by a treaty signed on Dec. 21, 1923, which confirmed all previous treaties, agreements and engagements, including the treaty of Sagauli signed in December, 1815. Earlier India and Nepal had a commercial treaty signed in 1792. These centuries-old cultural, racial and religious ties between Nepal and India were further cemented by two treaties signed on August 1, 1950.... one of peace and friendship and another of trade and commerce.

In this ever-changing whirligig of criss-crossing political situation in this sub-continent, the geographical position of Nepal is as vulnerable physically or emotionally as the Indian Ocean to India. Why? Because Pakistan's deliberately designed in-your-face aggressive attitude towards India's neighbouring countries may make jehadists and extremists react strongly against India's predominating influence over this sub-continent. Why? Because her name has always been invoked as a symbol of Islamic megalomania... an eponymous character of the present 'Pakistan.'

Tibet

Tibet is a mountainous contry (the highest plateau in the world) on the northern frontier of India. India is deeply concerned about happenings in another country, Tibet. Ever since the people's Govt. of China talked about Tibet and its liberation, the Govt. of India through their ambassador in peking, had expressed their desire for a peaceful settlement of the matter. Why? Because India was interested in her fifty-year old autonomy being maintained. The Suzerainty of China over Tibet was never denied. Besides, India is keen to preserve trade and cultural relations with Tibet. The advance of the Chinese army into Tibet on Oct. 25, 1950, came as a surprise, especially at a time when the Tibetal delegation, at the instance of India, was on its way for negotiations. In other note to China the following day, the Govt. of India expressed their deep regret that the Chinese Govt. should have decided to seek a solution for the problem of their relations with Tibet by force. It is an autonomous region of China since 1965.

This is China whose hypocrisy and lies have always been with her by her lateral thinking and expeditionary force to another country to fight in a war. To India, China is a sign of the times. What China does not know is that an incredible whammy of bad judgement and bad luck will have to strip off her well-designed communism.

India should be careful of any agreement or pact or treaty or deal with other countries. A lot of small words can meet your needs with a strength, grace and charm that large words lack. Why? Because small words cast a clear light on big problems like Kashmir issue or on big things: war and peace, life and death.

In agreements, short words are bright. Why? Because short words are bright like sparks that glow in the night. Short words are sharp like the blade of a knife. Short words are hot like salt tears that scald the cheer. Short words are quick like moths that flit from flame to flame. And short words are terse like the dart and sting of a bee. Short words only make a straight line between India and Pakistan on Kashmir issue or any other problems.

When asked to explain Britain's wartime policy to Parliament, Prime Minister Winston Churchill responded with these ringing monosyllables: "It is to wage war, by sea, land and air, with all our might and with all the strength that God can give us." In his poem "The Death of the Hirad Man". Robert Frost observes that "Home is the place where, when you have to go there, they have to take you in."

Caution : India should never be a Faust who was reputed to have sold his soul to the Devil. You should never be characterised by flippant and inopportune humour.

Kashmir issue has been greatly complicated by pride and prejudice. What Pakistan is very much afraid of is the verdict of the Kashmiri people. Nehru's voice was bound to be a cry in the wilderness. Like all other setellite countries our Islamic countries like Pakistan have made it their business to say 'yea' 'yea', and 'Nay', 'Nay' to every 'Yes' and 'No' of America in the U.N. Assembly. In such an eventuality, India will be in the awkward position to take side and be a part to world war III, for, was with China means war with Pakistan and other Islamic countries. The paramount need to India today is to stand aloof from the Armageddon.

Avoid the multitudinous tongue. Why? dishonour mangles true judgement. Seek the very way to catch them through agreement and short words. Otherwise you will make a monster of the multitude. Why? Monster is always ingratitude from the noise of their own drums.

Prior to thinking over India's neighbouring countries, you foreign policy-makers should always be with your own voice and own tongue. You have to lay your hands upon them where the disease is violent. The best of our country's happiness, honour and fortunes always keeps with your perfect decision in perfect time.

Listen more, talk less. Finally, I would like to end this chapter with an amusing story. American TV host Larry King tells this story. "I was a guest once on a morning show. The interviewer was the type who asks a question and then looks away, not listening to your reply. The third question she asked was 'what is your secret to being a successful talk-show host?'

"I saw she was not paying any attention to me, so I joked, 'I work for the CIA. They get me good guests, and then I in turn signal words every night for their agents."

"Without missing a beat, she fired off her next question. Meanwhile, her whole crew was laughing uproariously in the studio." If you talk too much, you may say the wrong thing.

ABOUT THE BOOK

The cold war between India and Pakistan on Kashmir issue has frozen into an equipoise of destructive strength on the part of two giants and their might will now be tested, not in war, but in a multi-front political contest. The sixty years that stand between India and Pakistan on Kashmir issue have been for the world years of conflict, hatred and bitterness and also of a great and sombre challenge. Many a time have nations gone to the brink of a general war : of localised wars there have been not a few.

Sorrow or suffering is the starting point of the Kashmiri people. Happiness over the valley is a passing show. Its very transience is a source of anxiety which causes a religious fundamentalism and social darkness that terrifies even the people of this sub-continent.

One of the many ideologies shoving and pushing for position on the political stage of Kashmir today is the ideology of multi-racialism; and of the several multi-racialisms being sponsored from the corridor of Islamabad to the corridor of fundamentalists is that of a wealthy and interesting Islamic organisation. Its aim is to develop in Pakistan a new local patriotism, transcending the distinction of Shia-Sunni racialism and overriding the loyalities of anti-India hymns of hate.

Never before has the Islamic world being convulsed by the kind of crisis of conscience which has overtaken it today. The Islamic terrorism is going on and no Orwellian fantasy can be an adjective to it.

Separatism ... casteism, communalism and provincialism ... glares and stares with bitterness at a neighbour who lives in another state or speaks another language. Linguistic fanaticism is getting deeper and deeper. Flabbiness, inconsistency and ambiguity amongst our rulers at the centre on the Kashmir issue have always been more and more rampant. Why? Because the Congress today is more than ever before bent on capturing power and retaining it even at the cost of all manner of compromises. A party of compromise even on the Kashmir issue.

We know there is no way out of the tortured paradox of love and hate policy. We know nothing can abolish Pakistan's private tragedy ... the suffering of a Hamlet or an Oedipus. But it is different with the tortured paradoxes of Pakistan's political strategy on Kashmir. We see freedom stifled in the name freedom and justice defiled in the name of justice we protest.

The crimes of Pakistan lie not in the fate of victims but in the silence of those who for sixty long years knew what was happening and said nothing. Political spoonerism, both in India and Pakistan, applauds the leaders they now condemn and they condon all they did. We know, we understand and even so we keep quiet.

For in the very process of confessing, our leaders seek to cover up the guilt on the Kashmir issue, delivering violent utterance of phillipics against one another. Truly speaking, Kashmir issue is a fantastic series of illusive images. Our leaders have not told the full story behind the political camouflage in the valley, either by an organised and extensive propaganda or by candid words full of dulcet phrases of Hindu-Muslim unity. They have not even asked the most pertinent question : Could one man do it by himself? Could the caprice of one man pervert the entire system of Kashmir solution? Is there nothing wrong in a system of conspiracy? Is there nothing wrong in a political system of appeasement in the face of much painful and pitiless cruelty of Pakistan-sponsored terrorist activities in India? Is there no connection between the terror and the pampered bureaucracy? Is not terrorism an adjective ingredient of Islamic rule in Pakistan? Are not Islamic thoughts debased by mixing inferior of spurious ingredients of political thoughts on the Kashmir issue? So peace in Kashmir is afloat.

Freedom always means freedom in specific circumstances and with the constraints implicit in those circumstances. We know best how external circumstances around Kashmir press on a man's inner world. An innocent Kashmiri Hindu Pundit knows where he feels exalted or humiliated, free or crushed. He knows our rulers waiver between shame and cynicism. They practise dishonestly. Is Kashmir issue a mere accident? They need not shrink from the dark side of the truth. Truth alone can redress the old wrongs. They must have the integrity to confront the truth of their own feelings. There is no room for make-believe. Sloth never arrives at the attainment of a good wish.

Inspite of having attained freedom from the numerous shackles which had tied down our aspirations, cramped our development and number our feelings, we thought that to talk of independence would itself be a blasphemy.

Political contacts between India and Pakistan have not yet been extensive. In their days, the British discouraged this. Pakistan, like Czarist Russia, has a hungry eye on the greatest gem in India... Kashmir. Even Hitler cherished a dream of reaching India through Turkey and Iran. While German scholars and intellectuals were attracted by India's rich ancient cultural heritage, German politicians regarded India as a priceless sub-continent in possession of a rival colonial power. Today neither that Germany nor that India exists any longer.

Every meeting of the commonwealth Prime Ministers sees Pakistan rattling the bones of the favourite skeleton in her cupboard of religious fundamentalism. Year after year, Kashmir has hovered like a pale baleful ghost over the commonwealth meeting led occasionally like a money on a lead to cut capers before the British public and press. Even Pakistan seems to have tired slightly of her deceitfully manoeuvred political gamesmanship. Since the birth of Pakistan, her allusions to Kashmir have been set pianissimo and not on the brass of fortissimo settlement of past years. Time brings its softening. Reason is the test of ridicule, not ridicule the test of truth.

Nationalism throughout the valley is for the most part confined to armchair politicians who ravel in marathon speeches and in the passing of resolutions. Somnolence goes with sonority.

Undue procrastination indicates that a man does not see his way clearly : undue precipitation, that he does not see it at all. The common practice of Pakistan's cunning on the Kashmir issue uses to cover the militants in one place, lay themselves open in another. Why? Because a wounded conscience is able to unparadise the paradise itself.

What is the difference between a women and a glass? The glass reflects without speaking, while a woman speaks, without reflecting. And the difference between Pakistan and a glass is that glass is polished and Pakistan quite unpolished.

For Kashmir solution : It does not help to pick new holes in a tattered argument. It is always more helpful to patch it up where the holes show our political debauchery, betraying the nation treacherously. Who are they? They are seasoned devils and regarded as the cheif of fallen leaders. They are held to preside over those condemned to eternal fire. They are mischievously energetic, clever and self-willed politicians. Cultures do not blend like tabacco. But different cultures do get mixed up somehow. Why don't our leaders try to find out how the mixing up has gone on in our Kashmir case?

It was Emerson who laid down the dictum that who so wishes to be a man must be a non-conformist. If there had been many 'no-men' at the time, there would have been World War I, much less World War II. And even now the World War III can be averted by the mere expedient of encouraging people to say exceptional; the wise man marvels at the common.

Truth and objectivity of Pakistan as the Islamic Republic become the first victims of propaganda and hate-campaigns, the blind, suicidal onslaught spread to the arena of dispassionate study and research and democracy in Pakistan was faced with a serious challenge to the superiority of her moral values over the totalitarian forces of thought-control and rationing of Islamic jehad. The cold war between India and Pakistan has been caused not by greed, but by fear.

In the initial stages of the cold war on Kashmir issue, statesmen of both countries were planning strategy of victory or retreat-without-loss and the politicians and the press were busy stirring up mass hysteria, few had the time, opportunity and even the perspective to 'ponder the real causes' of this tragic turn-out of Kashmir issue. These difficulties multiply tensions between East and West. And Pakistan has lost her name in a shrunken and haunted world of Islamic terrorism.

Today the sun over Kashmir has dipped down towards the horrizon and batched the terrorirised valley in its blackened and gaspings scares.

Pakistan should take a long-range view deliberately and straightaway. Because the memories over Kashmir are scattered over the years.

Pakistan is like a blind passenger with the dog on a lead to other secret places. Oppressively hot in religious passion and ill-tempered in between the starting place and the finishing point of her worthless promise, Pakistan is an un-predictable eccentric.

1

Introduction

There is no hitching post in the universe, which Einstein was supposed to have made in answer to a boat-train reporter's request for "a definition of relativity in one line." But so many hitching-posts are there happening suddenly and unexpectedly in between science and religion. When Einstein wrote the famous equation e-mc, could it possibly have foreseen that thirty-nine years later this equation would help to launch a new type of bomb which would kill more than 120,000. Japanese in a second? Had the scientists a right, or a duty, to advise the head of the State against using atom bomb? This is a political gesture outside the realm of science. Why? Revolts against the autocratic rule of the 'But' seldom succeed. The army of 'IFS' are increasing in numbers. The 'IFS' are full of promise. If the promise is not realised, it is because of 'Buts'. Today, the lives of the millions with the blessings of the Almighty 'But' have found a new slogan ... ISLAMIC TERRORISM. All the Islamic parties are desirous of implementing this new slogan with profit.

Pakistan has exorcised obstinate Islamic ghosts like Islamic Jehad and terrorism. To Pakistan, dead old things of peace and compromise always find it very difficult to live comfortably under changed roofs. They will not surrender without a show of force. Many more ghosts are as thick as the sands of the sea.

Good manners and a quiet demeanour are taboo to Pakistan on Kashmir issue. The most reserved human beings turn into loud extroverts, as though an overdose of anti-India slogans has gone into their heads. Today, Pakistan is what Churchill once said about Russia : "Russia is a riddle wrapped in a mystery inside an enigma." Stalin, the Red dictator, had marked Malenkov out as his successor. When Churchill asked the Red dictator who would follow him, Stalin grinned cheerfully and replied, "I have everything arranged in my country. I know exactly what will happen." Jinnah also knew exactly what would happen to Pakistan after his death.

Bulganin was in Moscow when Hitler's hordes descended upon it. Napoleon said that there was a baton in every private's knapsack. Bulganin unearthed his baton from a bank vault as Jinnah discovered his baton of Islamic jehad from the vault of Kashmir. Today, Pakistani leaders have lost a baton of veritable Niagara of speech. Alas! Political memories are not as short as some suspect.

Pakistan stands in the way of a smooth transition of a big 'But'. This big 'But' of Pakistan has descended from a double-whammy of the merchants of Islamic crusaders and the psychic activity of religious fanaticism. Without this double-whammy, Pakistan would be a maze without a clue. They are driven by a messianic urge to remake the world.

Pakistan should be free from vainglorious hopes and selfish thoughts over Kashmir issue. Do you know the explosion of a nuclear bomb kills in three ways .... by the force of explosion, by the intense heat and by the burst of radiation? The nuclear bomb does speak the doom of civilisation.

The Kashmir situation is just like a magician who plucks a rabbit out of a battered old hat. Unhappily, the hat is still what it always was and the rabbit is an illusion. In this case the hat is Pakistani aggression in India. In the General Assembly in 1951, Nehru declared : "The moral standard of both the Orient and the Occident are entirely different." He is absolutely right. Why? Because the choice between the good and evil is always clear. But the choice between the evils ... Pakistan and China ... is quite different. In the case of Pakistani aggression, our moral standards are clearly different. So, by an inversion of the facts and a broadening of the basis of discussion, we can arrive at the conclusion that the United States and its majority supporters in the United Nations are the real culprits on the Kashmir problem. In these extenuating circumstances, we cannot, however, blandly ignore and even reward misconduct over the Kashmir issue.

One of the truly disturbing features of the present U.N.O. is the implication on the part of the waverers that the principle or the moral issue is not vital. The United Nations will not collapse from military weakness, but it would lose its entire reason for its existence if it does not uphold or tries to uphold its principles. You cannot call a murderer unless you can catch and execute him. But whether you catch him or not he is a murderer and society ought to brand him as such. The basic difference in processes of thought and moral standards between Asians and Westerners is dangerous. We already have the two worlds ... totalitarianism and democracy. Are we to create or superimpose two more worlds of Orient and Occident and build another iron curtain of terrorism? The way the Chinese, with Indian encouragement, are appalling to the Asiatic and Arab countries against the so called white countries is one of the most frightening of recent developments.

Aggression is not determined by the size of the party or country. Concern over the contingency of provoking world war is legitimate but there is no surer way of inviting a situation where such a war becomes inevitable. Why? Because it becomes a matter of survival more than to condone aggression. Pakistan suffers from Jean Paul Sartre's first volume 'The Roads to Freedom'. Pakistan is afflicted with a tedious, sometimes disgusting nation of cruelty, perversion, vice and violence. China suffers from Jean Paul Sartre's 'Troubled Sleep' and is devoted to the psychology of defeat by her preconceived fear of western powers, the cynicism, despair and moral collapse. Why? Because 'Troubled Sleep' is shrouded with scenes of brutality and wrapt in morally vicious conduct. Such human baseness in Pakistan is a sickening syndrome. Some of the Chinese comrades are seeking to escape from the pleasant realities in stupefying drunkenness of theocracy. But Islamabad has confused the climate in a heat and dust of terrorism and allowed a morose and embittered approach.

The future of this sub-continent is at stake, and the Western powers should not commit themselves thoughtlessly to a disastrous policy. A swift military decision depends on many factors, some of which are unpredictable. Pakistan cannot write on a clean slate. She has been inflicted by corruption, inefficiency and selfishness. Would it be wise for the U.S.A. to take up the heavy responsibility of keeping Govt. in power in a vast and difficult country like Pakistan, Afganistan, and Iraq? The masses would be resentful. Pakistanis would be uncompromising. Across the undefined border, there would be Iran, Saudi Arabia and Syria, ubiquitous and inscrutable, ready to jump into the fray at the earliest opportunity. And all over Asia, Pakistan would portray Islamic thoughts for her own interests. And it would be for the Western powers to get heavily engaged in a war in Asia. Why? Because any attack on Pakistan or any Islamic country by the Western powers would raise nationalist feeling in the Arab world. A large scale war is considered to be engrossed in Asia, given the political aspect of the danger. These calculated dangers are likely to prove true, no one can say at present. Because they are all fundamentalists to a degree. The mountain is being robbed of its record of producing the mouse. Islamabad is expecting a happy event. It is now revealed the mouse. Islamabad is expecting a happy event. It is now revealed that Pakistan is in an advanced stage of pregnancy to produce the nuclear bomb. She is now going to join the nuclear motherhood. The birth certificate is not yet authoritatively available. China has already owned the motherhood of the atomic baby. North Korea has agreed to act as the midwife. Why? The baby will be delivered in North Korea. We do not know whether it would be non-violent bomb or not.

Since independence Pakistan has roped terrorist organisations to I.S.I with a logarithm of hypocrisy within the wheels of conundrum, putting down its roots to all theocratic institutions by her well-thought-out political camouflage. And the deep-seated rumblings of political crusaders have run deep into other Islamic nations. And the resultant effect is : Demolition of America's 'World Trade Centre'. Why? Because the Western countries have now become a shooting gallery for practices of winning prizes in Islamic globalisation. And Pakistan has been used to shooting up her prominence, camouflaging her ugly face on and off. It is better to be the widow of a hero than the wife of a coward.

The most disastrous consequences of twisting away the chronic message and the transcendent values and ethics of the great Koran get into an ogre of religious fanaticism and persecution. Such political sectarianism and religious bigotry sewed up with social ribaldry has only vitiated the very foundations of Islamic thoughts all over the world. Today a tinpot dictatorship in Pakistan tinged with colourful theocratic pundits makes the Islamic society dangerous and springs up the upper-crust on a high pedestal of administration run by an oligarchy. According to the 'Katha Upnishad' : "Fools dwelling in darkness, but thinking themselves wise and erudite, go round and round, by various tortuous paths, like the blinded by the blind." And the great Koran says in a superlative way : "They know an outward aspect of the life of this world but are heedless of the hereafter. As for those who believe and do right actions and humble themselves before their Lord, they are the companions of the Garden, remaining in it timelessly, forever." What the great Koran says is great and remains everlasting. Muslims should be free from the ideological preconceptions. In India, there is a preconstructed and well-furnished conspiracy between our politicians and mullocracy how to capture the Muslim vote-banks. A hollow bankruptcy of secularism. Is it not to be considered a question of separate identity?

Pakistan president Pervez Musharraf once pitched up a proposal for Kashmir solution. Musharraf's old proposal was :

1. Identify seven regions across Jammu and Kashmir, including Azad Kashmir, Gilgit, and Baltistan in Pak-occupied Kashmir.
2. Demilitaries the region
3. People from federal Govts. under joint supervision of India and Pakistan.

General Musharraf like his predecessors has always ignored the sentiments of the people of Jammu and Kashmir and even Laddakh and tried to canalise his old traditional hypocrisy after imposing his choice on the people of these regions. But the people of those regions are quite indifferent to his proposals.

General Musharraf has now given the 4 point formula. His new 4 point formula is :

1. Kashmir retains its current borders, but people move back and forth freely.
2. Region to have self-governance with India, Pakistan and Kashmir represented.
3. Troops be withdrawn in a staggered manner.
4. Joint supervision mechanism with India, Pakistan and Kashmir represented.

But his new 4 point formula has already been rejected by the Pakistan-based United Jehad Council ... a conglomerate of 13-terrorist groups operating freely in PoK and J & K. General Musarraf is really a tinpot dictator. According to some Kashmiris, this proposal is really a humbug. He is figured to be a leader of fun. He has been used to humming and hawing over a Kashmir solution. According to report of M Saleem Pandit in Times of India (27.12.2006), "Musharraf's ever new ideas on Kashmir confuse the people more than anything else." It was told by a Political Science teacher in Kashmir University. What lies behind the four-point formula? Kashmiris have suffered a lot due to

Pakistan-sponsored terrorism. They also suggest that General Musharraf should get back the portion of Kashmir to India, that Pakistan has gifted to China. Mark Twain, a great American novelist and essayist, says : "No tribe, howsoever insignificant, and no nation, howsoever mighty, occupies a foot of land that was not stolen." It is a befitting exemplary to the Pakistan-occupied Kashmir as well as to Pakistan's gifted land of India to China. According to Chandogya Upanishad, "As one not knowing that golden treasure lies buried beneath his feet may walk over it again and again ... " Little does Pakistan know that she walks daily over PoK stolen at midnight.

Mark Twain says in "Mark Twain in Eruption': "We are discreet sheep; we wait to see how the drove is going, and then go with the drove. We have two opinions : one private, which we are afraid to express; and another one ... the one we use ... which we force ourselves to wear to please ..." Please : whom? China, to be sure : This is Pakistan. The same countenance, the same voice, and the same stature. The uniformity of thought, feeling and action with the same interpretation of language is the fundamental error of Pakistan over the Kashmir solution. Sincere diplomacy is hardly possible for Pakistan. Why? Because her mental make-up is just like dry water or wooden iron.

Pakistani newspapers are to make the ignorant more ignorant and the crazy crazier, whereas, Indian newspapers are expected to be, like Ceasar's wife, above suspicion, especially on the Kashmir issue; it is accused by some of being, like Satan himself, dark, powerful and evil; it actually is ... newspaper men often suspect ... more like Dickens' Gummidge a "lone, Iron Creature" that feels things more than anyone else.

The press, both in India and Pakistan, are free in printed form. Sometimes they are the handmade of politicians. All of this brings to mind the fact that newspapers are under constant attack for real or fancied errors of omission or commission ... and still they survive. Whatever one's tastes in gardens or flowers, the show has something to satisfy them to a high degree, but, beyond that, it brings into the midst of our brick and mortar the undying message of survival or revival. This is the healing message to the media of both countries ... India and Pakistan ... to make the Kashmir to be tuned in with a good go of peace and harmony, forgetting all old scores of dissensions and bloodletting massacre. Most newspapers are not to be inflammatory these days.

General Musharraf's well-advertised latest book, "In the Line of Fire", represents the romanticism of his youth. And the fact he has cleverly portrayed with a great finesse is a half-ironic, half-sentimental melancholy yearning over the loss of youthful love, youthful dreams and youth itself. It also represents the disillusionment of his immaturity. He knows how to ring in false and ring out truth. But this time we have learned much about the complexity of his emotions and the frustration and unhappiness that so often accompany self-indulgence and misused privilege over the Kargil War and other bygone wars and battles. He has failed to battle out to control over his verbal exuberance as he did as a military ruler waving the flag of stratocracy. He has frittered away, like other predecessors, a plenty of opportunities to make peace in Kashmir. The majority of his writings are slight and inconsequential; expert craftsmanship of lies has lavished on second-rate material. If a ruler of a nation tells a lie, who will solve the Kashmir problem?

Mussolini was not quite technically dead, of course. It was not until the spring of 1945 that the pupil of Lenin and teacher of Hitler we can trace so much of the modern world's evil.

In the similar way, if every Pakistani ruler is really dead in everybody's mind, it is going to be difficult to appraise them. All they were a terrible character, all right. But if Musharraf and his predecessors were called to the bar "to answer for the damage they have done to Pakistan and the disgrace they have brought upon the people of Pakistan and of Kashmir" they might turn on the Pakistanis and ask them this tremendously disquieting question : "And you, why did you believe in us?" or why did they tolerate us? Why did they let them get where we got in the first place? It is a remarkably serene record of a spectacularly untidy time.

Totally oblivious of their duty, the Western powers suffer from infernal desire of Dante's Inferno of the Fire'. They are getting disenchanted at the feelings of others. Today power belongs to the free world. It must remain there. The United States has shown the Europeans that they are willing to fight and die regardless of the order in order to stop Islamic terrorism over the world and Chinese aggression over the Indian Sub-continent. That demonstration is coupled with a clearly expressed determination by the U.S.A. to commit sufficient strength in Europe to stop Pakistan's alliance with China and North Korea sinking herself into blatant rumour over the Kashmir problem. India must rely on her military men and not on her politician branded as the followers of opportunism and political dandyism.

Kashmir problem is the off-shoot of a long-continued squabble between the politically inspired meddlers and bureaucracy ridden service. The authors of independence were fighting a loosing battle. Why? Because they had put much faith in the loyalty of the top people they had inherited. And they were the victims of congressional whims of our foreign policy makers. So the Kashmir issue has been outrageously defrauded.

There were masked or unmasked dictators all over the world in those days. They are still a goodly in number, but the situation is much more complex and even the dictators have to be far more responsive to popular opinion than seventy or eighty years ago. In the case of Pakistan's deceitful attitude over Kashmir is dangerous not only to Kashmir but to the Islamic countries in Asia. Treading the footsteps of his predecessors, General Musharraf is responsive to the constitution. He is a centralist, or federalist, who believes in giving component states as little authority as possible. He is too, on his record, a demagogue whose appeal is directed to the under-privileged masses of Pakistan. He is supposed to be entitled with "Father of anti-India hymns of hate". His intention is praiseworthy to the under-privileged masses and to the Madrassa-based fundamentalists. This type of paternalism has its dangers. We who are hemispheric neighbours will watch the results with interests and with the same friendliness with Pakistan and its satellites as we have seen in Afganistan, Iraq, Lebanon and Palestine. Why? Because Pakistan is guilty of 'engaging in aggression' and guilty of 'engaging in hostilities against India' through the grapevine. His grasping megalomania is too powerful to be undeniable. It can be said in sober truth that the worst of all eventualities is terrorism. It is worse even than possible military defeat. As six decades of bitter history over the Kashmir problem have proved conclusively, and disastrously, it can be expected merely to encourage the successful aggressor to embark on new aggression. And it is the stark fact of the situation in Pakistan.

Pakistan has not ever reconciled herself to India's claim that Kashmir is an integral part of India. She had kept dilly-dallying with her voice-worn phrases of traditional thoughts and views. She has done everything deliberately. And Pakistan has rather executed the policy of 'Jehad' over Kashmir since 1965. According to Lt. Gen. (Retd) K.S. Brar : "A special task force called "Gibraltor Force' was raised for infiltration into the Kashmir valley, a force of approximately thirty thousand, consisting of regular army, Azad Kashmir Militia, Frontier scouts, Muzahids and Razakars, organised in company-strength groups, was infiltrated across the entire 490 kilometer belt into the valley on August 5, 1965, hoping to receive spontaneous support from the people of Kashmir. Pakistan believed, Kashmiris would welcome the infiltrators with open arms, and revolt against the Indian army thus achieving its aim of wresting Kashmir without having to go to war." Lt. Gen. Brar has categorically focussed on Pakistan's political depression, echoing an insincere and cynical sound of promises with much of her old traditional airs and graces against India on the Kashmir problem. Relying on the resounding comment of Lt. Gen. Brar, it can be worth-saying that a sunken economy and hollow-beaten foreign policy makes Pakistan cruder and cruder, indulging in riotous mirth. It is held to be self-evident truth. Lt. Gen. Brar says again : "This, however, did not happen. On the contrary the local population gave them a bloody nose and helped the army in rounding up the infiltrators in large numbers .... The army in Kashmir, during the years that followed, remained ever alert and was operationally deployed to carry out its traditional assigned role of safeguarding India's territorial integrity against any Pakistani misadventure." (The Role of the Army in Kashmir, Lt. Gen. K.S. Brar, in New Approach).

Lt. Gen. Brar's qualitative and quantitative analysis is comprehensively just and noble. Kashmir is the land of Pakistan-sponsored fanatics and is a holiday centre of mass-murdering bailiwick pitching up a holiday camp for having a tedious moralising discourse. Free of all honest-to-God messenger of peace and harmony over the valley, infiltrators-cum-terrorists of different groups keep honeymooning in the valley. A syndrome of a terrified and revolted shuddering for the horrors, in a fit of delirium tremens, has tried out to fool away the Kashmiris and the Indian Security Forces by permutation and combination of attacks.

Truly speaking, Pakistan is a resident evil ..... an apocalypse in South-East Asia. General Musharraf, writing a memoir of his life and experiences, "In the Line of Fire", with the hindsight of his immaturity, has painted a gloomy terrible picture of the twisted puritanism of modern Pakistan. Everyone seems to be cursed with a ferocious prudery not far from purulences. He, like his predecessors, deeply dyed in political hidebounds on Kashmir problem, in his private crusade for holiness, has piled up vicious scandal all over the world, through this book. He just shows that the gruesome Pakistan is an unhappy nation driven by her private furies well along the road to madness. In 'Home is an Island', Alfred Lewis says, "All countries are good. We can learn to live anywhere. Only the land of our birth we remember the best, somehow." Whereas Pakistan wants adventure, new horizon, problems more challenging than the tranquil routine of life in Kashmir. Truly speaking, Islamabad is trying hard to swim in the ocean of lies and cunning stratagem and at the same time slithering away for hunting octopuses in this sub-continent. Pakistan's rumblings over Jehad in Jammu and Kashmir are sixty years old. Nobody in Pakistan has dared to fix a specific date of the birth of terrorism. A few Muslims do not want to hear it. It is the cancer of Islamic philosophy. Jehadi slogans have rhythm, of course, but a cacophony corresponding to the exasperation of life in general. Like the crack of a whip, Jehadi slogans have awakened the indomitable passion of Islamic world. It has had a marked effect on all Islamic nations. It does not displease the barons of Fundamentalism, if it does not last too long and is not too tortured. Jehadi slogans are thought to be branded as 'familiarising catastrophe'. Who is to blame for its not being done?

Jehadis are not meant to be pawns on a chessboard of ideological conflict nor peons in a new collective slavery. Riyaz Punjabi says : "At the outset of the militant phase in Kashmir, the prominent and well-organized militant grouping, 'Hizbul-Mujahidden' (HM), the militant 'Jammat-i-Islam' (JL) had made it clear that HM stood for : "Islamisation of socio-political and economic set up, and unification of Ummah" (New Approach). Mr. Punjabi says also : "The real ideology to achieve the objective of an Islamic Caliphate was manifested in the year 1992, when Kashmiri society had already undergone the phase of military for two years. The militant groupings with pronounced Caliphate ideology made it clear that the present struggle in Kashmir was in fact, Jehad. These groupings rejected any dialogue, even tripartite talks on Kashmir, unless these resulted in the emergence of an Islamic Caliphate." But the HM asserted that "Our aim is the establishment of an Islamic Caliphate the world over. We do not believe in ideological or geographical boundaries." (The Daily Nida-I-Mashriq, 30th January, 1993). It is fact that Pakistan has originated the ideology of Islamic Caliphate. Whereas Murshid Hussain, a well-known columnist in Pakistan, writes in 'The Nation' : "For Pakistan, ECO (Economic Cooperation Organisation) is a convenient bridgehead for Central Asia, and this element is certainly a plus also for the struggle of Kashmir people as well, since Kashmir itself is an extension of Central Asia, both geographically as well as culturally."

So, through Islamic Caliphate, they are trying to find a place in a changing world that would preserve these inestimable qualities very damaging and camouflaging to the world now. The word 'Jehad' is old by some standards but the jehadis are alert, intelligent and highly individualistic. They are proud, loyal and brave. So many jehadis are there : communist jehadis, communal jehadis, imperialistic jehadis, bureaucratic jehadis and so on.

Pakistan is impregnated with jehadi process. She does not know the study of good relationship is a great pursuit, full of beauty and alive with intellectual as well as technical interest. It will bring Pakistan into intimate contact with life and offer unusual personal freedom. As an art of friendship, there is none greater, as a study, none more fascinating. And Pakistan, devoid of all moral catharsis in the art of relationship, hangs around the valley. It is very difficult to find a consonance among all these voices.

General Musharraf, like his predecessors, follows China's dual-track diplomacy, like Mammoth, on the Kashmir issue. Mammoths had two humps like a Bactrian Camel, one on their shoulders and one on their heads. Through his book, 'In the line of fire', he has had half so much passing his course. The book only portrays the views of an adventurer as a romantic terrorist.

Pakistan's policy over Kashmir issue is afflicted with muscular dystrophy, a progressive weakening and waxing of muscles of religious fanaticism that always ends in death. The disease is hard to diagnose in its early stage, if one diagnoses its family history dated back to partition, muscular dystrophy is hereditary.

An act of aggression is to be countered by international force. The action is meant the change of balance by the gathering strength of the free world. A democratic Govt. at Islamabad, timorously nervous, not to be motivated by the Western love of honour, is ready to tinker with New Delhi in a slip-shod way how to tide over the double tides or double track diplomacy by U.S. pressure or terrorist groups. The barons of terrorist organisations can know all that is yet known about spiral nebulae and know no more about conchology than you or I. The facts and theories of Islamic organisations are gathered by different men at different places.

Yet learn the time of day around the valley. Perhaps men today in Pakistan do not enjoy as much leisure as some of the prophets of sixty or so ago said they would. "What time is it?" is a question we hear asked in an anxious tone. One who seems to fear it is later than he thinks. Man encounters difficulties when he seeks to make use of it. It is time for Pakistan that today there are sixty seconds in the minute, sixty minutes in the hour, as there were yesterday; today difference may be that we are spending time faster than it used to be spent. Islamabad has squandered away a plenty of time after packing out the values of agreements and pacts on Kashmir issue either by a whooping lie or by a confused assemblage of arguments or by willing away much histrionic displays or by wild and woolly manners. So, Pakistan is guilty of heinous crimes over the Kashmir issue.

This is a clear lack of logic behind her sweeping as well as slithering away revisions in the agreements between India and Pakistan. Now the question is : what happens to the basic principle when Pakistan that has so clearly violated the code of civilisation is treated so generously? Which is the thief of time? : procrastination or punctuality?

India should stand on the old saying : If you want peace, prepare for war. Pakistan's earnest desire for peace, prepare for war. Pakistan's earnest desire for peace is just like a venomous snake in the grass in and around the valley. Why? In the country like Pakistan as a whole, literacy has been steadily declining, but there are many who are functionally illiterate ... that is, able to read but unable to make easy use of printed matter.

The contumely and scorn that is heaped on the large majority of U.N. members has caused the speculation that Pakistan may be laying the lie for playing up with Kashmir as she has done for long. General Musharraf was talking from strength ... a weakness, that he was threatening, pleading, warning and arguing.

The Great Powers once were having headache as to how to resist the spread of communism they were altogether unmindful of the racialism that was rearing its head. They forget that communism, with all apocryphal thoughts, is likely to profit by the racial war. Both terrorism and communism, in practice, are homologous to each other. The world should not forget Hitler's murder of 6 million Jews, which had such a disastrous effect on his own country. In all Muslim countries, racial segregation is a dangerous threat as well as a fell disease, and will arouse the strong emotions amongst the people of Asia. Such amorphous integration of Islamic communities, having an amphibious nature of fanaticism and a prejudiced world of opinion, would only amuse a pleasant diversion angling for ancien regimes. A good marriage happens to come between terrorism and fundamentalism. Why? Marriage has been described as giving half one's food to get other half cooked. With a precision of mind, Mark Twain, a great scholar, says, "It is your human environment that makes climate." Mark Twain perfectly delves into the matter. Why? Because when they shut themselves in social hidebounds and don't allow anybody else from that strait-jacketed framework of mind, to escape, no fresh air of human environment would get through that well-guarded gate of fundamentalism. So the Kashmir problem will remain the same as we have witnessed for over sixty years. We can magnify the present situation of Kashmir, through the eyes of the great poet, Kalidas, in his 'Ritusamhara' : "The bloom of tender flowers is past/And lilies droop forlorn,/ For winter-time is come at last,/ Rich with its ripened corn;/Yet for the wealth of blossoms lost/ Some hardier flowers appear/ That bid defiance to the frost/ of sterner days, my dear."

Why Kashmir problem today? Pseudo-communism is the most welcome guest to the congress. Such pseudo-communism as may threaten India will, paradoxically, be constitutional communism, exactly as such Democracy as dominates us today through the instrumentality of Congress, the generous given of the first constitution of India, is a dictatorial democracy.

After dictatorship is always dictatorship. When the Congress Govt. under the Nehru regime had to drive away British imperialism from India, how could it be cowed down to the Russian imperialism here? The Pseudo-Indian communists talked only of Moscow and wanted to listen to the Kremlin and not even to their leaders here in India. They are really a foreign element on the soil of India. They are credited with producing test-tube babies of imported isms. Besides they have involved their own parties in a mess of quibbling and doubtful logic on the Kashmir issue, in defence of the indefensible.

We now see that it is easier to appoint a Minister than a domestic servant. When the Kashmir problem was brewing up with a babel of babbling cacophony, the then Congress rulers at the centre looked like a group of disgruntled men who had kept on floundering ever since they left the Congress and were keeping themselves alive merely on a diet of violent criticism and outshadowing other anti-Congress groups. The Congress Govt, had swept off its fact by what promised to become an effective slogan. People who are privileged to run Govts. are like screen-lovers who are adored and idolised the world over but cannot retain their hold on their own wives for long.

Yesterday's hero is often today's villain is always tomorrow's angel. Hero-worship and devil-worship go in panoramic succession. A country like Pakistan is built up because the entire people unbeknown to their futurity are galvanized by the element of foot-loose and compulsion of fancy-free. Lt. Col. J.K. Dutta says : "... Nehru committed an unforgivable act ... he agreed to a Pakistani offer of cease-fire. There could not have been a greater sample of unpolitical attitude. He opted to pay heed to the unsolicited advice of his British mentors. Spear-headed by Mountbatten and egged on by General Douglas Gracie, the Pakistani C.in.C together with his Indian counterpart Gen. Robert Lockhart, Nehru dismissed Gen Cariappa's plea to continue the military operations and capture the Pakistan occupied Kashmir. Regrettably, neither India nor her valiant armed forces were given any succour towards this end. Nehru took the Kashmir case to the United Nations thereby not only defeating India's chance of settling the issue but allowing Pakistan an equally God sent chance to be one up on us. The period 15th August to 31st December, 1947 was indeed a glorious period for Pakistan and its founder : they got their independent Pakistan, got their part of Kashmir and what is more, elicited enough global support for their cause to keep the Kashmir issue into limbo. This was an impressive performance by a country hardly six months old. It has remained so ever since." (Kashmir : India and Pakistan). Owing to Nehru's tinpot diplomacy, Kashmir has now been under the mobrule of gangsterism and hired terrorist organisations sponsored by Pakistan's Inter-services Intelligence (I.S.I.). Comouflaged by hypocrisy, Kashmir is a hunted house of terrorism in Asia, owing to Nehru's misbegotten political airs and graces. Why? Superstition and hypocrisy die hard for the benefit of the politicians to live long. According to Jack London, "A bone to the dog is not charity. Charity is the bone shared with the dog, when you are just as hungry as the dog, "Nehru was a perfect mesmeriser of imperfect diplomacy for the creation of Kashmir problem and of our well-advertised secularism. His blunder is worse than cannibalism. What he had committed has not yet been repaired. Owing to Nehru, today's Kashmir is preoccupied with Pakistan's double-distilled propaganda from which all falsehoods, imbecilities and abominations body themselves, and from which no true thing can come.

Edger Snow was a well-known American journalist. His book "People On Our Side" (published in 1944), reveals out an interesting comparative study concerning Stafford Cripps, Gandhi and Nehru, revived by Stafford's death, in his negotiation with the Indian leaders in 1942. Edger Snow, who had met Cripps in London in 1943, gave in his book the following account of his talk with Sir Stafford on the failure of his mission :

"Gandhi was the real stumbling block," said Cripps, "For my proposals to have been accepted would have required the splitting away of Congress from Gandhi's control. It would have meant a revolt inside the party and a revolt requires a leader. It had counted on Nehru and told him : "Jawaharlal, if you will take up this offer, we two can decide the future of India, your position in the Council here, backed by my position in the cabinet, will give us such moral power that the Viceroy cannot dispute you here nor the cabinet challenge me in England. That was perfectly true, too, and there is no doubt in my mind that after the war Nehru and I could have got what I wanted. He seriously considered one night what it would make and came to the conclusion that he could not fight Gandhi for control of the Congress. I told him that Gandhi might hold on to the Congress but that he could carry the country with him. It is a tragedy Nehru could not see."

"Thus it became clear to me that Cripps had staked everything on reaching an understanding with Nehru ... And it was the little Mahatma, who did not want to fight anybody but the British, who had defeated him, he admitted."

Edger Snow's interview with Jawaharlal Nehru at Allahabad on the failure of the Cripps Mission, as related in his book, is also reproduced here :

"When I asked him why the talks had failed, he (Nehru) responded with unexpected acerbity; "Cripps is a terrible diplomat, simple terrible; He has done enormous harm to Britain in the eyes of Indians. He amazed me after all these years. Apparently, he never believed me when I said in the past that we wanted a complete independence. Now when it came down to it and he saw we were in earnest he was hurt and surprised when I spoke of matters formerly taken for granted between us. "You don't mean you really want to break away from us entirely, do you?" he asked me. Think of it after all I have said and written after all Cripps himself has written."

Margin stands in line more than a mile. Honesty may be the best policy, but the policy seems to have lapsed. Intoxication of power had seduced Nehru. Fair becomes foul and foul becomes fair. If Pakistan stands as an emblem of terrorism, India symbolises and ensures publicity at a proportionately low cost. After partition, on Kashmir issue, friends of congressmen intended to remain anonymous. All of them gave a hearty shake to the hidden hands that signed the transfer in invisible ink. This has needed the much-needed moral courage to Kashmiris and have-nots of Jammu and Kashmir to sleep on the pavements and dream for sixty years at a stretch.

Sheikh Abdullah, Kashmir premier, passed the following statement, on May 2, 1952, at Srinagar :

"Follow one leader, one organisation and one programme, and your efforts will be crowned with success." The above is not a quotation from any speech in Nazi Germany or Fascist Italy, like Mussolini, Sheikh Abdullah started his career as a school master. The differences could not be ironed out. They are vampires of the night over the valley with the claws and beaks bright, sucking the blood of Kashmiri Hindu pundits and pith of Kashmiris and marrow of natural beauty. The shrieking and pinching voice runs over the years, beguiling the slumbering nights of the valley either by New Delhi or by Islamabad, through a lofty idea of a high esteem over a number of agreements. We genuinely believe that prostitutes would be more honourable company than Indian politicians with whom Pakistani politicians demand to be linked. The former is hard-boiled egg and the latter a dehydrated potato.

In an article, 'Bogey of Kashmir Autonomy', Mr. Jagmohan says in 'New Approach' : "At the local level, all the eggs were placed in Sheikh Abdullah's basket. No lesson was learnt from the experience of the plebiscite front (1955-75), The Kashmir Conspiracy case (1958-64), the Moi-Maqadas agitation (Dec. 1963- Feb. 1964), and the underground subversive and terrorist activities of al-Kashmir, al-Jehad and al-Fatah (1965-71)." Mr. Jagmohan further says : "A historic opportunity to settle the issue permanently was missed at the time of the Simla Agreement (1972). The Kashmir Accord (1975) was another manifestation of the habit of nursing illusions. These illusions, too, were soon shattered by such events as the Resettlements Act (1982), India-West Indies Cricket Match (1983), and the Kidnapping and killing of Indian diplomat, Ravinder Mahatre, by JKLF at Birmingham (February 1984). "(Ibid) So, our foreign policy makers, unbeknown to Pakistan's camouflage hindering Indian diplomats from making any agreement, have so far misjudged their calculated move. Truths of Pakistan's hypocrisy are so old that our foreign policy is positively decrepit with age. Our foreign policy makers know Pakistan is the most daring liars. They know Pakistan is a model of immorality. Why? Because theocracy tells fanaticism that follows in its father's foot steps ... because its mother, Pakistan by name, is suspicious. There is an old saying that black will take no other hue. But black is, indeed, capable of taking the red hue ... blood-letting violence through Jehadis.

Such funereal prescription is generally prescribed not only by Pakistan but by other countries preoccupied with fundamentalism. We know fierce and poisonous animals were created for terrifying man.

The gravity of Kashmir situation gives one the impression that any negotiation with Pakistan on Kashmir will break down sooner or later. India Govt's apprehension is widely shaped in official circles in New Delhi.

The increasingly belligerent attitude Pakistan has been displaying at the negotiations over the exchange of thoughts hardly leaves any room for optimism about their final outcome. Fanatical crusaders ... from the Kashmir-based terrorist organisation to Al-Quaida ... have not been slow to utilise the continued disturbances over the Kashmir valley, whatever may be the underlying cause to serve their own purpose. Their warning that they will not sit idly by while their fellow-brethren are ill-treated in Indian jails will fill misgivings about their real intentions. And their hostilities remain localised. The secrets are more diplomatic than military. The only thing wrong with our parliamentarians is that they don't smart in the right place.

Life in Kashmir is 10 percent what you make it, 90 percent how you take it.

Every agreement, between Indian and Pakistan, is mere scrap of papers. It signifies nothing and is secured by noise and shouting, by complaints and denunciations. Pakistan sleeps no moment on an old past. Why? Because Kashmir, to Pakistan, is a fabulous land of warring fanatical crusaders and exciting opportunities, opportunities to die horribly or to acquire vast riches. For a long time, Pakistan's search for wealth is a failure. She met with disaster after disaster. She is beaten and flayed and imprisoned and enslaved in her religious hidebounds. Infiltrators have fought as mercenaries, often in the service of Pakistani rulers, often looting and killing even more ferociously than the countrymen. Those who buy peace with their souls are never free again.

Pakistan's old-fashioned romance with Kashmir is clumsy stuff, superficial and slavishly faithful to an ancient formula. It would be unfairly severe. Because crude fanaticism that Pakistan deals with Kashmir issue likes telling tales of violence, romance and general derring-do. There is a plethora of drafting and re-drafting of compromise on Kashmir issue that has been raised over the powers of New Delhi and Islamabad. Key words like 'consulting' and 'informing' and the phrasing which relates to the spirit vis-a-vis the 'text' of the treaty, are sure to be centres of controversy. Islamabad believes that the realisation of their ambitions for Kashmir domination is closer than ever. This is called the 'Battle of Words'. Each year the camp of war and reaction. This is evident from the frequency of Pakistan's accusations that the capitalist warmongers are preparing new plots and striking to unleash new wars. Hitler similarly prepared the way for his own moves by propaganda indictments of those who stood in his way. In the same way, Pakistan will take and embark on new adventures in the future to gain its objectives on the Valley. Why? Because every Pakistani ruler, descended from the date of partition to the present day, suffers from egoism, that plays with each other. Most of them are like an oak tree in a flowerpot. According to Swami Sukhabodhananda, "The flowerpot is like the ego and our being is like the oak tree ... A woodpecker was pecking at an oak tree. A lightning struck the tree and felled it. The woodpecker flew away and boasted, "I never knew I was so strong. I can make a tree fall. "(The Best of Speaking Tree: Vol. I, II, III). All of the rulers, and even Pakistan's present ruler, think so as the woodpecker does.

The White House effort to prepare its people for further worsening of the international situation is clearly shown by the 'Hate Islamic Mission of Fundamentalism' campaign, which has reached new peaks of virulence in U.S.A. during last few years. India believes that international tension will lessen if the policies advocated by the present ruler replace now being followed by this country.

Aggression all over the world ... aggression is carried on by a variety of means from open warfare to exploitation of national sentiment. The campaign of vilification and threats against India has been going on for long that it is difficult to diagnose timing of Pakistan's plans for un-seating the heretic. Very dangerous is the hotting-up campaign of vilification against India on the Kashmir issue. It would only heat several young Muslims of the Valley. Such heretical belief can only generate orthodoxy synonymous with ignorance of the concerned sect. George Bernard Shaw says in 'Man and Superman' : "Every genuine religious person is a heretic and therefore a revolutionist." Pakistan's heretical belief on Hinduism is alive and extremely perilous. And the tone of the Pakistani press suggests that Islamabad expects its major near-future gains to be made in Asia. It is an axiomatic truth that a lost dog is more likely to be found than a missing cat. Because dog that is man's best friend more likely to have identification and its owners are more prompt in searching for his missing pet. A lost dog is found after a call.

In this connection, Lord Birdwood says in his book, 'Two Nations and Kashmir', "If as I believe, Abdullah had then been confirmed as the people's leader, I would have risked the fate of the Kashmir Valley in his hands. In these circumstances all the indications were that Srinagar would at that time have turned to India. Poonch and the Frontier states breaking away to form Pakistan." Whereas M. Brecher writes in 'The Struggle for Kashmir' : "At the risk of being branded a communist, in 1949 the Sheikh initiated a series of land reforms. A century of Dogra rule had resulted in the ownership of the 2,200,000 acres of cultivable land in the hands of a small class of landlords-Chakdars. The owners were Hindu, the tillers Muslim. With the reforms, the maximum land holding was limited to 2.75 acres : the remainder was distributed among the peasantry. The vast majority of Kashmiris have benefited from these reforms and many of those interviewed expressed the fear that in Pakistan, where no comparable land reforms have taken place, the land given to them might be returned to the landlords ...".

From Brecher's point of view, it can be said that the sensations and the emotions of childhood to envy Kashmiri in the valley spiked with frozen fires of horrors are buried deep beneath the slit of every year's damaging slogans of the jehadis. We may say they are all imprisoned in solitary confinement for urging Pakistan's war of liberation in the valley against India, entangled by a succession of eccentric crusaders.

Depending on these land reforms, the disparity between Pakistan words and Pakistan deeds which first befuddled India as well as Kashmiris on the Kashmir issue and then alarmed the non Islamic western powers is illustrated again by the ever-increasing succession of extremists taking place all along the border. They have always drummed together another 'Kashmir Peace'. And the fellow Muslim travellers in the Valley are called upon to support the familiar propaganda line by proclaiming Pakistan's desire for peace. Why? 'Peace' is an alluring word to befuddle India on the Kashmir issue. The unwanted Muslims remained to be seen were intensifying their military and political preparations starting in a concerted movement. And they were purging the terrorist dominated political parties of all doubtful elements in order to make it a reliable fifth-column. The contrast between Pakistan professions and Pakistan actions has become so glaring that it has ever begun to trouble an increasing number of hitherto faithful jehadis, elsewhere in Europe, who were not yet ready to help turn their commitments into the Kashmir Valley. The New York Times, on Feb 23, 1951, summarises the issue in a pithy way : "Problems come and problems go, but the Kashmir dispute seems to go on forever. Few of any post-war problems have enlisted such persistent, disinterested carefully thought-out offers of assistance, and none has failed more dismally. Meanwhile a highly dangerous situation has developed." The paper has clearly pointed out the fact.

Pakistan is supposed to be an Islamic country of being a 'super-govt.' of a super-ruling group composed of alleged super-patriots, who are a disgrace to the ideals and principles of an Islamic country. Fawning flatteries over dollar diplomacy loom large over Pakistan.

Even after the sixty years of independence, the stakes are great and emotions have been running high. The Vale of Kashmir is the nearest thing to an earthly paradise, rich in products, lovely in its setting and temperate in climate. Why is the valley of Kashmir a significant factor to India? Because Indian trade routes to Central Asia pass through Kashmir. Strategically, Kashmir is a bulwark for India. There is a valuable timber and perhaps minerals. And for Pakistan? For Pakistan, Kashmir is equally important strategically and economically. Rivers that irrigate the Punjab start in or flow through Kashmir.

According to Surinder Singh Oberoi, "Kashmir, along with Laddakh and Jammu comprises the states of Jammu and Kashmir (J & K) which is situated in the lap of mighty Himalayan belt. The total area of the State is 222236 sq. km. Which includes 78114 sq. km. under Pakistan control. 37555 sq. km. area is occupied by China since 1962." (New Approach).

Kashmir always receives the freedom with a Joyous roar. We hope a sparkling in the sunlight of the valley. Her winning will survive, if mutuality of effort and mutuality of trust are imperative. Pakistan ought to know that terrorist organisation can have a positively harmful effect on the security of this sub-continent. Lincoln believed in a united nations and daily our nations are growing more and more disunited. Our great shrine of liberty and freedom, on the part of the world, would endanger the freedom of all nations and of all them. Lord Kemsley, the great British publisher, says : "I believe East and West can alongside each other ... but only if the British Commonwealth and the United States stand together." (The London Sunday Times, Feb. 1951). It is an undenying fact that we cannot protect ourselves by withdrawing from the rest of the world.

Some Jehadis are fiercely proud, stubbornly independent and corruptibly honourable, dithering about their own instinctive, confused emotions. But they are young, foolish, ignorant and violently emotional. How Islamabad getting to be spiked with highly explosive and destructive I.S.I. drives them into a pit of desperate and futile rebellion, and into becoming an alcoholic, deserts, murderer and finally terrorist. It is a powerful and brutally shocking mission of Pakistan personal meanness, intrigue and favourtism can be expected everywhere in life.

How this wily situation comes out? According to Joseph & Korbel, "... the recalcitrance and the suspicion that have characterized the Kashmir dispute is uncompromising and perhaps uncompromisable struggle of two ways of life, two concepts of political organisation, two scales of values, two spiritual attitudes, that find themselves locked in deadly conflict, a conflict in which Kashmir has become with symbol and battleground..." Mr. Korbel clarifies the dispute well, "To India the subcontinent is inescapably one nation. To Pakistan, it is just as inescapably two. The examination of the intensity of these two beliefs, their nature, their origins, and the events that were and remain the expressions of their conflict is essential to the full understanding of these conflicts present day symbol, Kashmir."

Another reason is that the proposal of a plebiscite was as ludicrous as unreasonable. Why? Because Kashmir is an integral part of India culturally, economically and politically. The fundamental reason is partition .... a Himalayan blunder. The then Congress leaders, seethed with unfathomable ambition-drunkard for power, had sown the poisonous seeds in a whispering atmosphere of communal tension and reaped the harvest of partition into the field of permanent dissension with political hiccups. Very much glacial is the relations.

The tricky game of turning the tables of agreements and treaties is always hysterical. Since partition, Pakistani rulers, sitting at the helm of tin-pot dictatorship, have stepped in the valley anticipating panic, shrill internal dissensions and exasperation with local non-Muslims. The fighting machine, when it is built up in the valley, has presented a terrible temptation. India stands ready to explore every approach to the honorable conciliation of outstanding difficulties between India and Pakistan on the Kashmir dispute.

But the country like Pakistan thinks exclusively in military terms and loses sight of other means .... even to the extent of concluding that war is the easiest way out.

India and Pakistan have so far covered many a conference. The result is : words ... but no decisions. The procedures are as usual as before. The meetings begin in an atmosphere of cordiality, both the countries exchange pleasantries and small talk with delegates. As soon as the handshaking and opening ceremonies are over, one of the rival countries makes propaganda sallies on every point, big or small. The diplomats of the counterpart make counter-arguments. There follows a period of waiting, punctuated by wrangling, and adjournment. The meeting breaks up with nothing ... except propaganda ... to show for it. But both are really interested in agreement to make peace in the valley. This hide-and-seek game has been running for over 60 years without qualms of conscience. But Kashmir remains a bed-ridden patient with protracted illness for unnecessary protracted delays. So the ebbing of the wave of war fears has left a sort of apathy. And there is much public resentment for this pre-emptive measure taken by the two rival countries. Aside from this invitation, the mood of Indian Parliament and the thinking of National Assembly are peacefully optimistic. Lawnmowers are as before claterring in the late afternoon, for having another conference to make peace in the valley. In Washington, the assesment is that the changed atmosphere hold both dangers and advantages for the West.

It is surely a tragic paradox. With a caustic tongue and a candid-camera eye, Pakistan, together with the help of theocratic rulers, has put together a lush story of propaganda that goes on the rocks around the valley ... but glamourously. Here is a Kashmiri soap opera costumed by terrorists. In totalitarian countries, the term 'brainwashing' has been coined to describe what happens when resistance fighters are transformed into meek collaborators. Ultimately, the victim doubts his own convictions and beliefs and gives way to hidden feelings of guilt. And finally, the victim believes his own false confessions and even bears false witness against others. This gamesmanship still goes invariably and successfully.

A military camp near the Afghan border is a hotbed of support for the Taliban and Al Quaida. It is in Zamzola in South Wazairistan so as to fight Afghan, NATO and U.S. forces. There is a cluster of many mud-walled compounds. North Waziristan is another area where Taliban sympathies run deep. A range of forest mountains, 60km. North of Wana, the main town in South Waziristan, and close to the boundary with Afganistan and North Waziristan. In trouble, they take shelter in mountain caves near the border with Pakistan. This area belongs to Taliban insurgents. Gomal district in Eastern Pakistan province is a dangerous hotbed of terrorists. In Jan, 2007, a Pakistani army air strike killed many Taliban insurgents. So, it is an unvarnished truth that terrorism is totally sponsored by Pakistan. The President Pervez Musharraf has acknowledged that Taliban backers in Pakistan are lending support to the extremists. Mr. Musharraf said : "There is the Al Quaida and Taliban in Pakistan, don't get me wrong." (Times of India, Jan 25, 2007). His following comment plays terror corporation card. He said, "The fight against Al Quaida can never succeed without Pakistan." He plays a hide-and-seek game with the world and threatens his country's participation in the war on terror. Truly speaking, Pakistan is a safe haven for the Al Quaida. They come into Pakistan to recruit Taliban. Pakistan feels loneliness in a bewildering labyrinth of virtue and vice. According to Aristotle : "Virtue is more clearly shown in the performance of fine actions than in the non-performance of base ones." What an ill-smelling whispering campaign of terrorism comes out from the windows of the I.S.I.'s head-quarters! A nation without intelligence leads to fanaticism. Appraising former President Truman in an article written in the New York Times, in 1964, Dean Acheson said : "Mr. Truman's natural modesty survived even the corrupting adulation which naturally seeps through every opening of the White House. The President's modesty came from a candid understanding of his own capacitites and limitations, which left him at peace with himself." Every ruler of Pakistan mutters vaguely and says in a theatrical voice, "I am pleased for India to meet Pakistan on the Kashmir issue." The heart of the complex. The rulers, will-o'-the-wisp movements made them a difficult man to find. And the present ruler is being purposely evasive.

The rumours swept Pakistan on 24th September, 2006, during a power outrage that blacked out large parts of the country, including the capital, Islamabad, the neighbouring garrison city of Rawalpindi and eastern city of Lahore. But Mr. Musharraf said : "I came to power in a bloodless military coup seven years ago" Given the rumours, he said, "I have been told the power breakdown was in Ghazi Barotha, and these rumours surfaced due to this. As if a power breakdown is needed to create such disturbance." Musharraf joked, standing alongside his wife, while visiting the United States in 2006. Scoffing at rumours that he had been overthrown in a coup. As the rumours were running wild in newspaper offices in Pakistan and the journalists were flooded with telephone calls and text messages inquiring about the rumours, General Musharraf, in New York, was due to launch his autobiography 'In the Line of Fire' on 25th Sept. 2006. He was scheduled to meet President Bush and Afghan President Hamid Karzai to discuss the war on terrorism. He had been out of the country for two and a half weeks. Musharraf has survived several assassination attempts since withdrawing Pakistan's support for the Taliban in neighbouring Afganistan in 2001, after the Islamic militia refused to surrender its guest, Osama bin Laden, in the wake of Al Quaida's September 11 attacks on the United States.

Having been apprised of the rumour, Musharraf had a heart trouble and had a routine medical check-up in Texes with a Pakistani-American doctor over the week end of his visit.

Musharraf's memories 'In the Line of Fire' betokening his evil days, after digging his own graveyard, for his disgusting hypocrisy with the western powers, and doing everything with a blistering pace of attacking the Christian community would bog him down in a quagmire of Himalayan blunder. He will be in a pathetically helpless state of negation and despair. The bogey of insecurity will hang over him. John Steinback, in 'The Short Reign of Pippin IV' writes : "The King said, 'Power does not corrupt. Fear corrupts, perhaps the fear of a loss of power." Musharraf suffered from a fear of a loss of power. So many fears are there : Fear of hunger, fear of wild beasts, fear of sickness and finally fear of death. And the basest of all fears is a fear of self-created Himalayan blunder that Musharraf has written in his memoirs, 'In The Line of Fire'. While fears of assassination remain, speculation about Musharraf's grip on power was seldom heard openly, as there was an overt political challenge to him. He always plays Islamic dogma in a wrong way. From the age of ten, the Islamic dogma has been the fundamental principle of every Muslim in Pakistan. They do not know other religion. They cannot enter into the idea of any other religion and do not know what they play with Islamic dogma is a mockery.

One letter writer in the Pakistani daily 'Dawn' has categorically lambasted Musharraf very severely on his memoirs 'In The Line of Fire', "It is very strange that a sitting president has written a memoir and is plugging it openly. Most presidents write books after they retire. President Musharraf should not use Pakistan to gain wealth."

The Times in Britain opened a serialisation on Musharraf's memoirs on 25th September, 2006, with the Pakistani leader's account of how the C.I.A. paid his government millions of dollars for handing over to America hundreds of Al Quaida suspects. After having had the rumour, Mahmoud Ahmed, from the Pakistani Embassy in Washington, phoned over to Musharraf about his reaction over the rumour, Musharraf said to him in Urdu "wo hamari eent se eent baja dey gain." It means .... they will take us apart brick by brick. And Richard Armitage, former Deputy Secretary of State has reprimanded with a threat to bomb Pakistan back to the Stone Age, if Pakistan refuses to help the U.S.A. in its war on terror.

Pakistan has now been caught in a dangerous matrix of being a Banana Republic.

The Mundaka Upanishad articulates it in a superlative way : "Two birds, united always and known by the same name, closely cling to the same tree. One of them eats the sweet fruit; the other looks on without eating ..." Seated on the same tree, the U.S.A. eats the sweet fruit of Banana Republic; and Pakistan eats the bitter but venomous fruit of being a Banana Republic.

Eric Hoffer, in 'The True Believer' says : "Self-righteousness is a loud din raised to drown the voice of guilt within us." Why? The author further positively takes it into beautiful account," A movement makes its greatest appeal by offering opportunities for united action and demanding self-sacrifice. True believers are ripe for action and even death."

The decline of basic democracy in Pakistan from its former high estate to its present near extinction is inescapably linked with the decline of the art of conversation. Like his predecessors, General Musharraf is a helpless individual, an onlooker. It would be mere conceit to regard his own faults as being half so serious in their consequences as theirs. Nice? They would never conquer their evil instincts over the Kashmir Valley. The present ruler hangs over the Kashmir issue with a whirlpool of worshipful attention upon the prejudices and reminiscences of his predecessors. Alas! the good listeners must be few indeed.

It is the business of the free world to maintain independent organs of information. We of the Indians cannot bear to see the colossal curtains of hypocrisy bungling around the valley in the name of 'liberation movement of the people of Kashmir'. With all its divisions, inequalities and petty tyrannies, we still think of the New World as a 'vast settlement' of young peoples, united in the search for it not yet in the realisation of a democratic society.

A comprehensive discipline must be needed to overcome Pakistan's negative qualities. The Dalai Lama Says, "A criminal gang may need discipline to perform a successful robbery, but that discipline is useless." Liberty is not procured only by a Roman holiday over the valley.

As a member of the New World Community, we care what happens to Pakistan and we care what happens to Kashmir. It is a thumping loss and a threatening danger to us all when Pakistan, a member of the banana republic, lowers the standard of liberty and turns back toward the dark and fatal road on which Hitler and Mussolini led their people to disaster. An attack on one is an attack on all. An attack on freedom of one people in the valley is an attack on the freedom of all in the world. Eric Hoffer in 'The True Believer' says, "We are less ready to die for what we have or are than for what we wish to have and to be. It is a perplexing and unpleasant truth when men already have something worth fighting for they do not feel like frighting."

But the people in Pakistan cannot be expected to curb their hot-blooded indignation easily becoming very excited to perform clever or dangerous tricks. The first impulse of would-be dictators the sure sign of the will to unquestioned power, is the attempt to control the sources and dissemination of news, to fulfil their cherished desire after a blood-curdling horror.

Iran's possession of a nuclear bomb would not be very dangerous. Instead, the danger lays in the chances of proliferation or an arms race in West Asia. Possessing the weapon would be useless for Iran, whose leader for Isreal to be 'wiped off the map'. On 29th January, 2007, French President Jacques Chirac, said of Iran and its nuclear programme : "Where will it drop it, this bomb? On Israel? It would not have gone 200 metres into the atmosphere before Teheran would be razed." Who is responsible for this situation in Iran? The answer is very simple. Pakistan. Why? Because Pakistan has supplied fissile material to fuel nuclear reactors. And Iran is secretly trying to develop nuclear weapons. According to President Chirac, "If Iran uses the weapon on Israel, Teheran would be immediately razed." 'New York Times on 30th Jan. 2007). Three days later, thousands and thousands of Iran's volunteer militia, including women, celebrated the anniversary ceremony of the country's Islamic revolution at the Khomeni shrine in the Behest Zahra century.

Iran is supposed to be a scape goat due to Pakistan. Pakistani rulers have been stuffed with a strong leaning towards the cynical materialists congenial to their thoughts. They have all committed buggery with Islamic thoughts since India was partitioned off. And the other essential elements of mass movements of Islamic ideology are : make-believe and play acting, the pageantry of crescent symbols and ceremonies, deprecation of the present and exaltation of the future programme over the Kashmir issue, glorification of fanaticism, idolization of jehadis in the crucible of blood-letting movement and hatred (always a popular emotion) propaganda backed by stern coercion and the release of violent action. Jehadi movements over the world are often incited by men of words, brought to a boil by fanatics, and if they survive long, organized by practical men of action.

American policy smiles on the invasion-occupation liberation cycle with all the concomitant death and horrors as it is found in Afganistan and Iraq. Everyone is to prevent the world's ideological conflict from deteriorating into open warfare. There is a risk involved, to be sure; but it is a day for sackcloth and ashes when the strongest nation on this planet lacks the courage to take such a risk.

Even our country, India, tosses off maxims and aphorisms with the aplomb of her traditional foreign policy. India glitters with icy wit. India should not run parallel with other countries' ill-concocted ideologies. Pakistan is thrusting up her staggering thoughts all over the world on Kashmir issue and at the same time littered up with a hypnotic inertia and vengeful ventrioloquists.

But it is hoped that there will no longer be gullibles in Kashmir to be fooled by the brazen piece of falsehood simmering away in various directions, stitching up the un-Koranic ideologies and principles in and around other Islamic nations. Propaganda over Kashmir is frisking away all the time. And Pakistan as Stalin did has just treated the Western powers to another super-duper piece of propaganda. Such vagaries of propaganda machinery locked in vacuous imagination might not be grasped in the outside world, but Pakistanis must be laughing themselves sick over it.

Pakistan lives on the veil of illusion. According to Bertrand Russell? "Fear is the main source of superstition and one of the main sources of cruelty." Pakistani rulers, on Kashmir issue, have been pierced with sharp arrows of bigoted Islamic thoughts. And cruetly obviously emerges on beaten track.

Under a strait-jacketed theocracy, besieged by hynotised fundamentalism, people in Pakistan, like Afganistan and Iraq, have got used to absorbing everything of tin-pot dictatorship. "The wind blows where it will, and you hear the sound of it, but you do not know whence it comes or whither it goes." (John 3.8). And the Atharva Veda gives out the same message, "Like a newborn child, freed from the womb, be free to move on every path."

Every Muslim is proud of being a Muslim, irrespective of caste or creed. The black market trade in arms is growing wider and wider. Iraq is one of the leading countries in black market trade in arms. Pakistan only is following that beaten track. Proud of being a fundamentalist, they plan to torture and kill Indian soliders. The word 'Negro' has no ethnographic significance. In Ethiopia, it is anathema for anyone to call any of the people regardless of their colour, 'Negroe'. In Bantu Africa, the people resent the name, and question why the most enterprising and intelligent group of people of African descent living in a most advanced part of the western world should accept a name which is a derogatory tag attached to them by others. It seems as if the perpetuation of the name 'Negro' to characterise the Africans who are forcefully taken to the west works as a weapon of division between him and the people who remained behind in the continent of Europe. The thought there is that the appellation strikes an unusal note, because it cuts these people from the glory and the background which is theirs. But the Muslims are proud of being a Muslim.

Indeed, there is still room about people who used to tell us that Mussolini was a great fellow. Why? Because he made the trains run on time. Now the question is : How have they been getting alone? The chickens have odd ways of coming home to roost. In Pakistan, the people who are used to go roaring around saving Pakistan by calling everything against the stratocratic rule of a timorous dictatorship by a tinpot dictator don't like a fascist beast.

If the Indian politicians today look back through the Indian history, to trace their connection with those days of blood, they find they have none, even in the turbulent days of Kashmir. They cannot carry themselves back into that glorious epoch. When they look into the history just after 60 years of independence, they find that those old men say, "All we say is self-evident truth." Our political parties, having no ideology or principle, lead such a kind of conspiracy that always goes against the rest of the nation. Leaders and conspirators are bedfellows. Shame does not keep them from getting out of it. They are the peculiar creatures of our land. So, the Kashmir problem runs through the doldrums of political camouflage as before, with an artificial and tedious discipline. In Indian politics, ignorance is strength, and freedom is slavery. So Kashmir issue remains silent. They discuss the problem with Pakistan for their own interest. Why? Because they try to forget those of humanity. They don't care to know that a man in Kashmir is a human being. So, the Kashmir problem has grown up with sap and juice of our leaders' camouflage. Of all the preposterous assumptions, they are well-fed, well-housed and well-warmed. Whenever a fellow-creature in Kashmir suffers, or the dignity of human nature is violated by falsehood or tyranny, our leaders are not ready to aid the unhappy.

A few years ago, the French magazine, 'Espirit' asked a hundred psychiatrists and psychologists, if it were possible to make a man accept our ideology that he loathed and to steal his spiritual freedom. 'Espirit' also wanted to know how far psychiatry had wittingly or unwittingly operated with tyrannical political systems. And finally it reaches the conclusion that even the strongest will can be broken down and that confessions of guilt are easy to extract and that psychiatrists may become the tools of commissars and of the secret police. This breaking down of mind is called 'menticide', a crime worse than genocide. It is listed as a new crime. So, Pakistan's planned mental torture over the Kashmiris are 'Pathological cravings'. Conditions change from time to time and from place to place but the fundamental principles remain the same as Pakistan does, suffering from 'menticide'. But we can be certain that the United States of America will as usual serenely survive all the hot-eyed yammers who have ever danced to any of the totalitarian tunes. And so will Islamabad. The era in the call-warriors in Pakistan has tuned up in fanaticism, fighting their doctrinaire way through the valley of Kashmir and through the christian-dominated countries of the world. It has been composed with a copy of 'Islamic globalisation' and Musharraf's 'In the Line of Fire'. It is an epoch of friendship with totalitarianism.

Pakistan and her master-minded theocratic rulers want to do in their fighting against the Trojan-horse ... the Shia and Sunni based communities ... led by the devious bureaucrats expert at building spurios front organisations of propaganda against India on Kashmir issue.

Every Pakistani ruler, wheedling out the crude Islamic terrorist groups, comes to power. For example, Zia-ul-Haq assumed the military regime in Pakistan with the help of 'Jamat' to strengthen his position. Mr. Jagmohan, former Governor of Jammu and Kashmir, writes in 'New Appraoxh' : "The Pakistani branch headed by Mudoodi ... became active in what can be called 'Islamic' politics, beginning in the 1950's with the instigation of riots against the Ahmadiya community. In the past three decades, the outfit has become the core of fanaticism and fundamentalism in Pakistan. It played an important role in the campaign against Zulfikar Ali Bhotto and then supporting the military regime of Gen. Zia-ul-Haq... Because of this relationship, the Jammat gained considerable influence in the officer corps of the Pakistan-armed forces, a factor that has in no small way affected Pakistani policy towards India."

Gen. Musharraf, Saddam Hussein, following their footsteps of their demi-gods, who stayed at home and moved into their jobs started getting those not-too-subtle-to recognise bits and pieces of pinkish propaganda all through the Line of Control (LoC).

We have been impressed over the past years by the freak, almost gloating emphasis upon the numbers of enemy killed, since the vivisection of India. In any previous wars, between India and Pakistan, on the Kashmir issue, have we sought primarily to kill our enemies? Has not our nation reached a new low in its ethical and moral standards?

We shuddered at the Nazi human incinerations which killed their victims quickly, while many of those we slaughtered are left to die lingering death on frozen fields of the valley. We do not forget the hideous concentration camps. But the Nazis did not advertise their atrocities and many Germans were ignorant of them, while we have published our policy.

One wonders what this is doing to our boys and young men who are forced to carry on this holocaust of human sufferings. Since partition, millions of people have been driven from their homes and are refugees. The untold plight of the civilians, very much scurrilous as well as damaging to our country's democratic ideals, is perhaps the greatest tragedy to which Asia has ever been subjected and our well-branded refugees have scouted around for a room and for food. But our leaders are responsible for this vast destruction.

We live in an ironic age, in which it is sometimes hard to tell when the battle of words is to leave off and some other kind of battle begin. We have to be prepared for both kinds of combat, hoping that words, plus a determination to resist if words will not suffice, will result in peace. This hope must be stronger because of the realisation ... perhaps on the both sides of India and Pakistan... that there is only one thing worse than victory in a world war, and that is defeat. The Russians enjoy a very convenient ambiguity of the Russian word 'mir' for peace. When Islamic extremists are parading down the roads of Islamabad, with AK-47 on the shoulder, in day-light, under the banner, 'We want peace and Kashmir', the same words proclaim all over the world 'We demand the world'. Reading such devious peace propaganda, one wonders for which peace they are going to fight ... whether for the preservation of the present situation all over the valley or for a future peace after a new catastrophe over the valley. They will stand in need be with arms in hand for the interests of Islam. The emphasis in the slogan 'Fight for Peace' is definitely on fighting. After all, a hidden manifesto is supposed to be there ... Do not wait for peace in the valley, you have to attain peace through fight and scuffles. Having had so much of these damaging views, the men ruling Pakistan are very far from being pacifists. Stalin said as early as 1928 : "Imperialist pacifism is an instrument for the preparation of war and for the making of these preparations by pharisaical talk about peace" (Witold Rudzinisk : A UNO delegate from Poland on 'Korean war' in 1959).

Historians cruelly but truthfully remark that Pakistan has already committed suicide. In suicidal note, only the political leaders are responsible for causing partition homeless and destitute. Our leaders failed to realise their own responsibility of leadership to straighten out this needless and potentially destructive tangle.

It is an undeniable fact that a strong western ground defence and continued development of the atomic bomb would avert world war III. Ground forces in India must be made as strong as in Europe. Why? It would be strong enough to hold back attackers while we strike by other means. India has got more effective missiles and bombs, today, than twenty years ago. This is to be used as a tactical weapon. Our country's defence should be such that an attack on us would be suicidal. There is no doubt, if we do, the attempt will not ever be made and we can live without world war III.

Life in Kashmir grows better and life in Kashmir grows worse. Who knows the sum of human happiness is greater, the sum of human misery less, than it was hundred years ago? Who knows we have lost or gained in human virtue ... in intelligence, in sympathy, in simple goodness? But hope survives. It survives in the religious celebrations of Hindus and Muslims. It survives whenever spring comes to any part of the world. It survives in children of both the countries, being born and grown up. To surrender hope is a kind of death. Civilisations that have lost hope have died and so have individuals. We may go farther. Doomsday is hope; and basic democracy is fruitless.

Both sides on the Kashmir issue...India and Pakistan are unhappy. Because both sides have found flaws in the compromise.

History of Pakistan is the unfolding of miscalculation. If Pakistan is successful over terrorism in Kashmir, she will win false friends and true enemies. Pakistan should think big anyway. Because the biggest people with the biggest minds can be shot down by the smallest people with the smallest minds.

Lines on the map of cross-border terrorism representing longitude and latitude are usually poor substitutes for natural boundaries, as the division of India has demonstrated. The first great effort to divide the world by such an arbitrary line was a prophecy of failure to come. The map of the world today has been very largely made by the competitive advanturers of Western Europe nations that look to the sea. The nations of Central and Eastern Europe had no part in this great era of growth and expansion. The difference of outlook and attitude towards world problems which began then is at the bottom of the division of Europe today.

Parallel and meridians and even natural boundaries ...sea, mountains and rivers ... put serious obstacles in the way of understanding between India and Pakistan on the Kashmir issue. The really serious obstacles are those recently invented and known as terrorism and fanatical crusade of Islamic organisations. There may be trouble over boundaries in Europe, in Asia, in South Africa in the future as in the past, and these may threaten wars. Terrorism simply stands as the 'symbol of the cold war', preventing other boundaries would not matter so much.

Freedom is hope. And the horrifying thing about all tyrannies of terrorism is that in stifling the individual's impulse to plan, change and improve his own life, they kill hope. We must believe that this murder of the human heart cannot long continue.

Men of goodwill everywhere can share in the faith that the Golden Rule is still the sum of all good laws, and will ultimately prevail; and that general aspirations beaten down they will triumphantly proclaim, for countless Hindu-Muslim religious celebrations to come, the divine and undying hope in the spirit of Hindu-Muslim unity over the valley.

Lawlessness among the Muslims in Islamic countries is largely a corrupt of politics and crime, in an unfettered way, has become Big Business in India also. When the youth has reached maturity, the effects of early disease become painfully apparent. The result of this fidelity to the spirit of a nation is the most rambling, meandering, diffuse and loosely thrown together the historical message of Islamic thoughts. Religious romanticism is gruesomely exciting and several are romantic and gallant. These ingredients include : press gangs, scurvy, desert islands, stranglings, attempted piracy, near madness.

Pakistan's claim over the valley is the knave-haunted double-talk of illegal documents as well as the stinging clarity of holier-than-thou attitude. It is the chained, stiffed-shirt cliches Pakistan uses to praise the liberation movement of the Kashmiris.. It is the voice of the bleaches in and around the POK warming up in a surreptitious way. Such a mystery of chemistry is the verbatim testimony given by malefactors of great stealth hiding in and out of National Assembly. It is a tribal chant of preponderant propagandists and bureaucratic cant. Jehadi slogans are the shouts of children bucketing out of schools. And Pakistan is branded as the ground zero of terrorism. President Bush said in the second week of Feb, 2007, "Taliban and Al Quaida figures do hide in remote regions of Pakistan. This is wild country, this wilder than the wild west. And these folks hide and recruit and launch attacks." The most senior administrative officials of White House point to Pakistan as a possible patron, sponsor, or the very least a sanctuary of terrorism. According to the report of C.Rajghata, "One military official, Gen. Karl Eikenberry, went so far as to suggest a 'steady direct attack' against terrorist command and control sanctuaries in Pakistan, days after another official, intelligence czar, John Negroponte, identified Pakistan as the nerve centre of international terrorist planning." (Times of India, Feb, 20. 2007).

In pursuit of terrorist outfits in the Kashmir valley, there are so many Islamic charities in Pakistan. All they are in cahoots with terrorists. For example, Al Rasheed Trust and Al-Akhtar Trust are dangerous. They have 21 offices particularly in the southern province of Sindh. Because of their suspected links with Al Quaida and Taliban, their assets have been declared illegal, in the name of welfare activities in hospitals and clinics. And there is an office of Hurriyat Conference in Islamabad. They are comprehensively dissociated from the ethics of the Koran. The Great Koran says "Bread feeds the body indeed, but flowers feed also the soul. "The Earth laughs in flowers but terrorists laugh in fanaticism. Pakistan wants to show how deep-seated her love is for terrorism. Pakistan is a safe haven as well as a sanctuary for the terrorists and fanatical crusaders as Argentina is for the criminals. Argentina has got a history of harbouring criminals and war ciminals charged with far more heinous crimes. Several Nazi leaders found refuge in Argentina after World War II. After World War II, Argentina became a leading haven for Nazi war criminals, with the protection of Juan peron. Most remembered and reviled of course was Adolf Eichmann whose last words were, "LONG LIVE ARGENTINA". Israeli researchers claim that German technicians were always welcome to the period after the war. Argentina's welcome to Nazi expertise and reticence to part company with wanted Nazi criminals was not unique but shared with several other countries. Joseph Schwammberger's extradition to Germany and Erich Priekbe's extradition to Italy seemed to be some acknowledgement of the country's dark past.

Pakistan is a good disciple of Argentina, harbouring terrorist criminals in Pakistan and sharing notorious laurels with infamous Taliban and Al Quaida leaders. The threat of a terrorist attack in India by the home-grown Islamic radicals has always been at the highest for over years. They are planning suicide attacks against soft targets and key infrastructure for mass casualty. The British document says Al Quaida's influence extends from North Africa, including Egypt, through to Lebanon, Turkey and Jordan, and into Somalia and Sudan. Al Quaida is resilient and effective in Iraq, its operating environment and financial position has improved. The task of countering Islamic terrorism is a daunting one. There will be more attacks in Britain. The secret report Al Quaida, which was behind the September 11, 2001 attacks in New York and Washington, had a foothold in almost every majority Muslim country. Truly speaking, Pakistan Govt. is mentally impotent, either by inconclusive statement over the Kashmir issue or by tinpot dictatorship to combat the very ferocious Al Quaida-Taliban venture. U.S. will have to change her policy on the question of making aid contigent to fight against terrorism. Because President Musharraf seemed to have an unwritten 'peace deal' agreement with Al Quaida-Taliban joint venture in a clandestine way to make his power of seat safe and intact from the insurmountable pressure of western powers. And Musharraf had surreptitiously given a wide space to the Al Quaida-Taliban joint venture to be regrouped to attack the western powers. It is a cat-and-mouse game of Pakistan over U.S. dollar diplomacy.

The oppressive shadows of Pakistan's holier-than-thou attitude on her peace making process over the valley is as alarming as harrowing to a banana republic. Everything is mysterious. Inexplicable Jehadi slogans sound across the hills. The Jehadis wearing strange dress make a charm and humour and imaginative appeal of fantasy. The general theme of extremism in and around the valley is confused and obscured by the many minor mysteries with which Pakistan has darkened the Paradise. The sword can stand for war or militlarism; but a sword embraced by a serpent of terrorism. What is the significance of a tramp and a thief, who bears the mysterious mask, reappearing as a corporal in the secret I.S.I.? Or are all these minor mysteries just part of the irrational atmosphere of a dream over the valley?

They can honestly say that they are defending the liberation of the Kashmiri people. Because Pakistan and National Assembly are confronted not alone with the armed might of the fanatics but also with their logic and their well-cooked-up religious dialects. Their unguarded words, their mistakes and contradictions, their fallacies in reason are hurled back upon them with devastating fury. The skillful protagonists of Pakistan have walled up their recognition of POK. Extreme necessity has made Pakistan bedfellows with China whose prejudices and practices over Aksai Chin and Tibet India can no more stomach than the ways of her avowed foes. Strange to say, all other religious institutions in Kashmir permit no suspicion of racial prejudice to enter into their policies over Kashmir. And the friendship of peoples of religious fanaticism all over the valley recommends that sort of wicked foolishness. Truly speaking, Pakistan is a Govt. by crony. The tent atmosphere of Islamic organisations all over the valley seems conducive to creating a carnival spirit for a mounting horror.

Kashmiri Hindu pundits are the by-standers in various degrees of innocence, who sometimes contributed some of the memorable observations that have been stolen by fanaticism, so seldom been lost. The murder of many Kashmiri Hindu pundits of Kashmir is one of those nefarious acts of religious madness which appear to punctuate our turbulent age in the Kashmir valley with increasing frequency, but which continue to shock and arouse the civilized world. Pakistan is a nation where anything can happen. When the surface of the smouldering violence is egg shell then, so it is in Pakistan, a shot fired in a mosque may start an eruption that can spread in many directions. The aftermath shows how Pakistan is using the shock and turmoil to serve their own purposes. What is done to fanaticism, they will do to society. Blaise Pascal, a French scientist and philosopher, says : "Cold words freeze people, and hot words scorch them, and bitter words make them bitter, and wrathful words make them wrathful. Kind words also produce their own image on men's souls; and beautiful image it is. They soothe, quiet and comfort the hearer." Terrorists have not ever heard of it except the words of Mullocracy on the Kashmir issue.

For the truth is that when one is not always easy to appreciate the real value and many issues of Kashmir problems. Why? Because he runs into so much intrigue and inertia. The Madrassa-based Islamic culture has outlawed the Govt. It will bring nearer the ever-present danger that Pakistan might suffer a similar fate as Afghanistan and Iraq. The Govt. is feared and hated by the big land-lords, the tribal chiefs and entrenched officeholders. Why? Because the Govt. has packed its cabinet with new men, pledged to carry through long overdue social reforms. The Govt. is opposed by nationalist blocs that stir up the passions of awakening people of telling them that the wealth of the country is being drained off by U.S. This sense of grievance, rooted in poverty and fed by the fanatical propaganda, has grown into a furious campaign. This violent episode is like a flashlight thrown into a crater where boiling and stagnant currents meet in the dark. Whispering peace criss-crosses the meadows of the Kashmir valley looking out the mock blank windows' spectral stare. It is like accepting defeat without having been defeated.

Before partition, Kashmir was the constant stimulant of having fresh air known to be the best tonic for the nerves. No backstair lobbies or secret deals : Historians cruelly but truthfully remark that the peace over Kashmir has already committed suicide. But peace frequently brings a renewal of hope and lessening of fears.

India is honestly interested in keeping peace over the valley. We deomonstrably do not have any aggressive interest or designs. We can afford to state the truth and to be patient. We can also insist on exposing falsehood. The Pakistani propoganda of the truth, if courageously presented, can outrun the propaganda of the big and little lie. The defenders of the valley can exact a heavy toll from any enemy attempt to destroy their liberties. But Islamabad may not be willing to pay this price nor to face the utlimate defeat that would surely come to the destiny of future Pakistan. Pakistan's fate of 'present tense' will be sealed for 'Future Imperfect Tense'.

Pakistan should propose a Kashmir settlement that seems to meet our terms .... gradual withdrawal of all occupation forces, unification of trade and commerce between two rival countries, demilitarization along the border. Such a solution would only favour the West more than the East. Such an offer of Pakistan would be a manoeuvre designed to lull this sub-continent, and ourselves into slowing down the military programmes. She will have a delicate craftsmanship and a personal outlook ... a combination of compassionate understanding a tough insistence on recognising human failings over the valley. Devoid of all notions, our neighbouring country is preoccupied with a lonely, imaginative, frustrated and adolescent Islamic country. She falls permanently in love with mullocracy and fanaticism. It would be magically wonderful to Islamic organisations ... a portray of a malicious egoist. Pakistan, truly speaking, is a moonig, hysterically emotional Islamic country, always loving and idealising someone, her teacher China, always filling Pakistan's life with tears and romantic drama over the valley. And Islamabad has become a 'political-grape-bag' of White House favourites. Even New Delhi can legislate honestly a good management over the valley. Communist China is ipso facto an imperialist and also implies totalitarianism and dictatorship. China is considered to be the deadly foe of Indian democracy, trying to distinguish between lower case communism and communism with a capital 'C'. China has confused one with the other in Asia.

Iran lives in the shadow of fear, and a glance at the map is enough to suggest the disastrous consequences to the world, if the creeping shadow becomes a reality. Pakistan's influence over Iran has grown and the Iranians are so terrified of offending the giant neighbout like Iraq that they have given in to some America's incessant demands. Saddam's death is a reminder that his unhappy country occupies a more important place in Afghanistan and Iraq, both are in political shambles and social marshes; Pakistan, painfully anxious to bring her country into industrial globalisation, is now caught like all rulers of under-developed lands, between the strong undertow pulling backward and currents racing ahead too fast. Restraint and humility in dealing with evil are necessary to human society.

And every allegation contributed by Pakistan against India is a malicious fiction not worthy of refutation. Why? It has been engineered by U.S.

imperialists and their accomplices. And it again proves that the United Nations has been tranformed by the manipulation of the American imperialist bloc into a tool for American imperialist aggression.

Is peace impossible over the valley? The hydrogen, after the atomic bomb and streamlined destructive missiles and weapons, has amplified but not created the question; peace is popular. A flood of letters and agreements between India and Pakistan on the Kashmir issue has deeply considered this realisation. Most of them have been written in no mood of sauve-qui-peut; they call for no flight from facts or compromise with evil. Most of them are addressed to the moral issues and political obligation which lie beneath the physical threat. This flood of letters and agreements has ultimately succeeded to mystery of chemistry, and then been succeeded by religious hypocrisy and political cant, straining the truth and swinging the lead. Such romance of make-belief has always trumped up the main issue. Double-dealing and political window-dressing have showed India that Pakistan is a past master in weaving and hatcheting a well-painted meritricious demad over the valley on the liberation movement of the Kashmiris. Most of them raise again, in one way or another, the place of peace or the policy of resistance.

Some time ago, a famous cartoonist drew a picture of some grim and symptomatic present day children playing in the street. They had written a rude word on the pavement. The word was 'peace', mis-spelt. Some even alleged that the cartoon was, unwittingly or wittingly, terrorist propaganda. The reaction was symptomatic. It is always for the free countries to makc unmistakably plain that the postulates of their adversaries in faith, in ideas, in mullocracy are making safe the peace. We arm to parley.

There has been no truer or briefer summary of what the western aims must always be. The readiness to 'parley' has been much misunderstood and deliberately misinterpreted. It has been called 'appeasement' of the kind calculated to hand over the citadel of human freedom to its foes without a strength. The final purpose of Pakistan's journey is quest of peace over the Kashmir valley has been, and is, to furnish the conditions of peace-making through Islamic strength. So that the would-be aggressor, whether by assault or by stealth, will know that Pakistan cannot get her way and so will talk of terms for a fair peace after blasting out bombs in the trains or in the congested cities of India or any other nation. To make a so-called peace on Islamic terms, it is pleaded, very rightly, is to surrender freedom and hope. So it is argued that since Islamic ideology of fanatical crusaders cannot change, parley is impossible. So if parley is impossible over the Kashmir issue ... though this is less often said ... peace between India and Pakistan is impossible, too. Readiness is the only resort while the other side will not make agreements or keep faith. The aim of policy over the Kashmir issue is to render it in the interests of foe as well as friend that the peace should be kept. This is the meaning of 'We arm to Parley'. And the culture of cronyism should be ironed out. According to Ashtavakra Samhita (1.9.10), "Burn down the forest of ignorance, with the fire of conviction..." If ignorance once dispelled, it is difficult to re-establish. Fabricated illusions and schizophrenics may have misspelt the Indo-Pak relations. Pakistan is worse still to be ignorant of her own ignorance. The popular will for peace may be indiscriminating; it may lack in knowledge; but it is natural and real. Countries at points very far removed from the central clash. The United Nations has failed to stamp out the embers of national conflict, smouldering in Kashmir, and flickering on the frontiers of Israel. These are all the faults of statesmen and politicians. Peace by cooperation is not half-pledged.

When a nation is numerically and geographically weak and economically endangered, one possible response is aggressiveness. He should never altogether ignore this possibility. An atmosphere of aggression is generally the result not of natural wickedness or of deliberate policy, but of fear. So, Pakistan takes the policy of aggression through terrorism, for her own existence in the world today. Western powers are knocking at the doors of Pakistan through the doors of Afghanistan.

Some say the infrastructure of society in Pakistan is not only nationalist but even racialist. Some say, Israel, like all civilised nations, is not racialist. Its nationalism harmonises with internationalism, and Israel is an enthusiastic member of U.N.O.

The Arab menace, of course, helps .... psychologically the Arab-boycott is a positive advantage to Israel ... and Israeli politicians are skillful in representing the needs of the country. Israel is based on U.S... One has only to look at the map to see the precarious nature of Israeli's territory. The frontier between Israel and Jordan ... an artificial frontier, the result of negotiation, not geography ... runs at places only miles from the sea; it cuts Jerusalem in half and leaves the Jewish half a salient in Arab territory; and it leaves historic Judah and Israel ... Bethlehem and Hebron, Jericho and Mount Ephrain ... in Arab hands.

Behind this wavering frontier, Israel has a population more than 58 lacs. Its immediate Arab neighbours have more 26 million, Iraq and Saudi Arabia more than 13 millions. India, Arabia and Africa are being scraped for Jews, but those who are brought into Israel now barely affect the number of European Jews who are re-emigrating or returning to their former homes.

Since 1948, some 70,000 Jews have been admitted to Israel. And in the same period, some 800,000 Arabs have been driven out of it, leaving behind them, as a windfall for the invaders, over 300,000 acres of land, together with houses, stock and other forms of wealth. The ingathering of exiles involved capital gain and capital expense to Israel.

It is worth considering if Asianism can be developed within the Commonwealth, thereby providing a strong barrier to any western power. Because Asianism is a psychological reality.

No doubt, God made Gandhi but Gandhi made Jinnah. And at so critical moment, between fanaticism and terrorism, British leadership, alas; proved most un-British and lost itself in mere emotion.

Apart from the heart-break of the process itself, partition, anywhere, can only create more problems. Then it professes to solve.

There is the political sphere the Indo-China war, which may set the East in flames at any moment. There is the Kashmir dispute, which Pakistan would dearly love to see put at the top of the agenda of today's world problems. There is the question also between India and Pakistan on terrorism. SriLanka and India have a migrant problem and a dangerous but damaging problem. Bangladesh has already been afflicted with a fell disease like crude fanaticism and anti-India hymns of hate. The Balkanisation of India, Pakistan took place with independence.. And nothing has been substituted for the bonds of colonialism ... a word which Asians have come to hate. All experiments are mysterious in their beginnings. And there is a danger that the fanciful statements may have caused some confusion among friends and foes and have blunted the effectiveness of Kashmir issue.

"Asianism" is a psychological reality and any calculation that leaves it out of account is a miscalculation. It is true that Pakistan seems to be turning away from Asia and seeking friendship and support from the Middle East; an economic and cultural pact has been signed with the Arab world. But whatever may be the reality of an assumed link between the Arab State and West Pakistan, the assumption is entirely unreal for Bangladesh ... and Bangladesh holds more than half the population and monopolises the country's most profitable asset, jute. Even in the West Punjab, even in the Mogul City of Lahore, where the old connection with the Arabic and Persian culture is most zealously preserved, the appeal to Asianism is potent.

There is something about budding leaves and about falling leaves which inspire the human race in the Kashmir valley to assemble the conferences either at Islamabad or at New Delhi, and pass strident resolutions for the cross-section of the public in Jammu and Kashmir, rich and poor, young and old students of Kashmir, city men and factory workers, and here and there a face well-known in picture papers. What is the explanation?

The mosques in Pakistan are puzzled. They had thought that materialism had so swamped the minds of the people that the majority had lost all interests in spiritual things. Now it has been demosnstrated that this indifference is only a veneer. Beneath the surface a Muslim is seen deeply concerned about his religion and to his own surprise he finds himself for the present moment at least talking about it naturally and without embarrassment. Religion now in Pakistan is a popular subject for conversation. Behind this there is revealed a longing in the heart of man, a sense of hunger for Kashmir he hardly knows that, a reaching out for that which can satisfy those hitherto uspoken yearnings deep within him. Thousands of such people have now found their hunger satisfied by their personal receiving of the present Islamic fanaticism into their hearts all over the valley.

Why has the preaching of the young Muslim done for them what apparently the Mosques have not done? It would be a million dollar question to other Islamic nations in future. It is important that an answer be found to this and similar puzzling questions. It has long been recognised by Muslim leaders of thought in Pakistan that the greatest need of the present time is terrorism in Kashmir and other western countries, in the name of spiritual revival. Will the Mosques be humble enough to learn the lessons of this fanaticism and be willing to apply them to themselves?

What are the lessons? The answer seems to lie somewhere in this direction. The people of the Islamic world want to know the truth. They want it declared with authority and conviction, dogmatically and without apology. The great Koran, which has meant so much to the people of Pakistan in past generations still has an astonishing appeal. Thousands and thousands of Islamic Jehadis have responded to its divine message but not in practice. In the same way, nineteen hundred years ago, men were puzzled by the preaching of St. Paul, preaching which swept away the Paganism of the Roman Empire and the dead ecclesiasticism of Judaism.

So the political situation in Kashmir today, ... Kashmir being a focal point ... is bedeviled by the irreconcilable rivalries of two Muslim sects. These, under their leaders, the ailing Lahore and the grim stately figure of Karachi, have carried their religious differences into the field of politics of reciprocal destruction. An example can be cited here; 'March 2007' is the bloodiest day to the Islamic world. When streams of Shia pilgrims were heading to Kerbala to commermorate Arbian, the end of a 40-day mourning period since Muharram, which marks the death of prophet Mohammad's grandson, Shia religious rituals had been targets for Sunni terrorists in a campaign that American and Iraqi officials say is meant to spark communal warfare. That attacks stepped up by the insurgents blamed on Sunni Al Quaida, unleashing a sectarian violence. In 2006, the same attack had happened to a Shia shrine in the city of Samarra. That Sunni insurgents are always ready to step up their recurring attacks over the Shia pilgrims in and around Baghdad. It was the bloodiest day demanding immediate action for the suppression of a crying evil of terrorism. In the spring and in the autumn, the delegates of both the countries coverage, banners are unfurled and trumpet calls are sounded, salvoes are fired which echo round the world and there is general agreement that there should be a law about it. Few days later, terrorism re-starts, holding out its various wings of hydra-headed monsterism. Blast in the train and proxy war shuffle on and off. Indian soliders are up and doing across the cross-border terrorism, extremists are arrested and courts are ready to pass their judgements. It has been the go of the Kashmir valley for over sixty years. Kashmir has now become a funeral parlour. Cenotaph is erected in different places. Parliamentarians get free of anxiety, giving forth an illusive and deceitful statement. And our political leaders start conjuring up the public with a bag of tricks or with tricks of the trade, spinning out a yarn of diplomatic charlatanism. But India believes in Czech proverb : "Do not protect yourself by a fence, but rather by your friends." The word 'friendship' bears a satire, making merry with our foolhardiness. Truly, fanciful meanings of all agreements make a dilemma. Whereas our neighbouring country, Pakistan is always tickling away the terrorists. To feed the terrorist movement, men and woment are recruited from the Madrassa-based Islamic institutions and are trained in POK and then smuggled across the frontiers. Pakistan is rapidly peopled with Jacks and Jills of all trades of extremism who are turning the side street into a self-sufficient community. Besides having this, military groups have given a pessimistic picture of Pakistan's administrative plight and risked having a bad influence on the men's morale.

In '1984' Orwell joins Aldous Huxley in a general warning against the cruelties in a scientifically planned totalitarian society, particularly in its attitude to country lovers. The emotional pattern of Pakistan's foreign policy is fear, recovery from fear, increased faith in it, suspicion, doubt, confusion and fear again. Pakistan is a land with a most painful sensation to the world. Totally inoffensive personality is created by the use of drugs of anti-India hymns of hate and unholy schadenfreude, auto-suggestion of fanciful dogmas, torture, flimsy analysis, and so forth. Waziristan, Baluchistan and Sind provinces are convulsed by quarrelling, spying, cupidities, jealousies and land-lubberly suspicions.

According to Ashtavakra Samhita, "It is bondage when the mind desires or grieves at anything, rejects or accepts anything, feels happy or angry at anything." Whereas W.Somerset Maugham says, "People ask you for criticism, but they only want praise."

The people in Kashmir are puzzled. The arrival of some Islamic leaders in Kashmir is greeted in some quarters either with ridicule and hostility or with contemptuous silence. But religion has become front-page news. Many go out of curiosity, expecting to find an exaggerated emotionalism or the raving of a hot-gospeller. Instead they hear a well-reasoned statement through forceful declarations of half-forgotten fundamental truths of Kashmir problem. To their surprise, they discover that these truths which they have imagined are out of date and irrelevant find a responsible echo in their own hearts and hold out a possible hope in this age of despair over the valley. Those who watch them go are puzzled. Here is an astonishing sectarian violence to the present history of Islamic world. More than 120 were dead and 200 injured. Islamic World should be alert immediately. Now the question is : who is responsible for the bloodiest day of sectarian violence? No doubt, Pakistan is a path-finder as well as torch-bearer unleashing a simmering wave of sectarian violence between Shia and Sunni in Pakistan. The consequences of such poisoning Pakistan have so far exercised in between Lahore and Karachi and have spread out like wild-fire all over other Islamic nations. It is poisoner's poison. Pakistan is very much obedient to the dishonest will of sectarianism and insurgence over the valley, bloting its beauty and confounding its fame, as whirlwinds shake fair buds. Shia-Sunni problem is a bitter clamour of two eager tongues. The blood that is hot must not be cooled. A perennial syndrome in Pakistan. They have been trying to bully the Kashmiri people into silence with their nerve-racking and frightening movement. They are devoid of all the feelings of man and heroic qualities.

This country, Pakistan, cannot afford to make light of the dangers arising form the shipments of arms from behind other Islamic countries, including China. It is all too easy to assume that Pakistan is poor, overpopulated, and with an 'exploitation' by U.S. business interests, blackmailing Pakistan on the Kashmir question. It is in some way a legitimate target for Pakistan being a Banana Republic. The 'Banana Republics', with their tempestuous parochialism and tropical torpor seem outside the harsh realities of the cold war. But, for the very reason, the Indian sub-continent is so vulnerable to Islamic and Chinese propaganda, it is necessary to look realistically and approachingly at the Pak-Chinese challenge there. The threat to India on the Kashmir issue is not so simply to western political philosophy but to peace is a vital region. Bachelors and spinsters of middle age in Kashmir .... whatever else they may have missed ... cannot escape the horrible and perennial tyranny of Jehadis. Slogans may be howling beneath a cloudy sky across the valley to make a Roman Holiday. Bernerd Shaw once described a perpetual holiday as a good working of hell. India can provide standards of judgement and Pakistan can provide myths which can cloud judgement altogether. Who will dare to say in Pakistan that terrorism is a sinful amusement? Because majority of them are reduced to shouting to the hangers on, terrorism will give a sovereign apiece to those who help to prey on the distressingly grievous situation.

If the Indian politicians have obligations towards us and the Kashmiri people, so do we have them towards our politicians. It is altogether too short a step from the changes being bandied now to charges not only of insincerity but of outright corruption. It is not perfectly obvious that our parliamentarians have approached the proposal of their pension increase with considerable only at the stage of stark reality. Failure to reach a settlement can open up untold dangers. And, most ominous of all, there is the pressure of wider intervention on both sides. Do they seek a settlement on terms which the western powers can possibly accept? Pakistan administration is pessimistic and sold to U.S. The country is in darkness at noon.

So far, so fantastic. The arithmatic of progress is notoriously delusive with the chemistry of political illusion. It is not ten times more wonderful to see terrorist outfits which happen 1000 miles away than to see them which happen 100 miles away. It gives unequivocal pleasure to many ... perfectly dangerous. In any consideration of Pakistani ruling class must rear its ugly head. They have become exquisitely prudish in this matter, turning a blind eye to facts too painful to face.

Not only Pakistan, but other Islamic countries today are facing a challenging task on the Shia-Sunni conflict. One of the outstanding facts in Pakistan is that crusade is the revelation of the spiritual hunger of large number of people; it would seem that the time is ripe for a real revival of religion in this country.

The need for this is evident to those of us who come into contact with the troubles created by broken human relationships and loveless homes, together with a pack of faith and hope.

In the present divided world ... Islamic and non-Islamic world ... the boundaries of political belief do not always coincide with national frontiers. This increases both the need for espionage and the means by which it can be carried out. It also encourages Govts. to make their secret organisations more active than would have been thought possible ... or necessary ... a generation ago.

Pakistan is always thinking, no doubt, of the system of stratocracy and informers like I.S.I., swayed by the Islamic despotism, but this system is taken over and expanded by the extremists like Al Quaida, Let, and other inscrutable terrorist organisations, that apply it to the prosecution of Islamic Jehad abroad as well as to the consideration of their own regime. Indeed, the very extent of Pakistani espionage over the valley creates its own weaknesses. So, bureaucracy in Pakistani, obviously, creates muddle, and universal suspicion paralyses its decision over the Kashmir question. And it is a fantastical trick of a tinpot dictatorship to steal from the basic democracy.

A nation that apprehends death is no more dreadfully but as a drunken sleep; careless in reality of Kashmir, reckless in terrorist outfits, and fearless of what's past, present, or to come; insensible of mortality, and desperately mortal. Agents are still formally disowned by his Govt., but modern statesmen and diplomats, both in India and Pakistan, on the Kashmir question, are not usually as innocent as they were during the freedom movement. Now a days we see how Embassies, both in India and Pakistan, are used by some powers as cover for their agents, and the field for mistrust is much wider than it has ever been. Diplomatists, journalists, scientists, colleagues and friends tend to be viewed askance. With a dire yell, the fire of fanaticism is spied in populous cities on India. Today, embassies all over the world are beset with knee-crooking knaves, dotting on their own obsequious bondage of suspicion. The offices of High Commissioners and Ambassadors are preoccupied with old fond of paradoxes to make people laugh for their own political interests, not to think over a comity of nations. Even the High Commissioners of both India and Pakistan swear against objects with strong shudders and heavenly arguments.

"Have you no rocks, no towns, no trees in your own countries? ... here in this place of democracy, preachifying priest-ridden Islamic thought and incommodo?" Espionage of Inter-Services Intelligence (I.S.I.) must be the answer. Only in these two rival countries where frontiers are uncertain or tension endemic is its hand to penetrate as wiser to leave the easel behind. Now vast tracts of Islamic surface are shut off from travellers of every description. In Islamic countries, particularly in Pakistan and Middle East, it is foolhardy for the citizen, let alone the foreigner, to show an interest in factories or bluebooks. Total espionage is one of the inevitable consequences of total war, and will only come to an end when nations are more humble in their ambitions and more open in their dealings with each other, even in Kashmir. Espionage is a great game.

Mr. Nehru had many talks at the dinner table with Md. Ali in 1954, but Kashmir was never mentioned. Why? Because Kashmir is a silent zone. Sign, resign, and again sign any political creed that suits our political leaders. Mr. Nehru once said : "The time is past for shouting." He is right. Now is the time for shouting a whispering campaign, making some reservations of our wrongs :

In 1955, President Oweight D. Eisenhower once dwelt at length on the State of the world at large and the 'free world' in particular, and concluded by saying, "Today the world is at peace." The question is : which is the peaceful part of the world, please? It is an insecure peace. Yet the lessons of terrorism and Islamic extremism, re-inforced by the bitterness and confusion created by Pakistan on Kashmir question should by no means be overlooked by any statesman who wants real peace, not the insecure peace which the world is enjoying today. From the American point of view, this insecurity can be converted into security only by maintaining countervailing military power to persuade the terrorist sponsored countries of the futility of seeking their ends through aggression. Pakistan's mission of peaceful co-existence runs afar and goes deep. There is a yiddish proverb : "He who can't endure the bad will not live to see the good."

The word 'aggression' has varying connotations to international controversies. There is no accepted definition of 'aggression'. In large parts of Asia, there is a growing conviction that the USA does not in all cases seek its ends through methods consonant with the true spirit of democracy and international good-will. For example, Indo-Pak conflict over the Kashmir question. It is an unfortunate that values of human life differ from continent to continent. The fear so candidly expressed on the basis of past experience and present tension is unequivocally shared by many Islamic militants scattered throughout not only in Asia but in western nations also. The USA shows no awareness of the dark cloud which American policy is creating over the East to fight out terrorism. The free nations have to meet united response. The two most important nations in Asia ... India and China (a surrogate mother fishing in trouble waters of Kashmir question) are not parteners in this plan of united response. So Asia has now become a free and accessible wide tract of land to America to do its best at its own cost. And the constructive use of Kashmir question is a camouflage to Pakistan familiarising the world with terrorism. If the atmosphere between India and Pakistan be really as good as it has never been before, a reverse method would probably be more fruitful. But Pakistan has always been in favour of whetting on its stone-hard heart of fanaticism and of sharpening its murderous knife dull and blunt to the dangerous success of bloody-war. King Richard, in Shakespeare's King Richard the third; says; "All unavoided is the doom of destiny." In 'From Underground', Dostoyevsky says : "Man only likes to count his troubles, but he does not count his joy." Pakistan's conflicting elements inside the country have already been exposed. And peaceful co-existence between India and Pakistan has become Don Quixotism. Pakistan's adventurous characteristics are summarised and compressed into alternative three : The Koran, Bottles and Islamic fanaticism. Today Pakistan is thickly populated with theocratic pundits, untutored and untutored young generation.

Inexhaustible vocabulary on meaningless issue over the Kashmir question and long-winded multiloquence in any symposium or seminar have exposed Pakistan's policy over the Kashmir question. She plays the hypocrite with sham modesty garbling away trickery and practical joke. The rulers should not lose their tongue or waste no words on the Kashmir question or save their breath. Even their tone of voice is as ungraceful as unpolished while wagging their tongue, on terrorism, confucious says : "Silence is the true friend that never betrays."

When persons serve machines, men and women suffer degradation. In most of the provinces in Pakistan, like Baluchistan, Paktoonistan, Sind, Karachi and others like POK, the people lose dignity, self-respect, the power of free choice and self-development. They begin to think and behave like slaves under an enthnocentric school of Islamic thought with a great influence of stratocracy. They are apt to forget that slaves were not always poor. Sometimes, as in ancient Rome, they lived a life of pampered pets. But they were still slaves, the victims of an evil system, and the modern world of Islamic fanaticism is bringing back slavery in Pakistan as it bringing back arbitrary arrest, the iniquisition, torture, and all the worst devices of tyranny, practising a bogey of sectarianism between the Sunni and the Shia.

Marriage of theocracy and mullocracy in Pakistan is a lottery in which theocracy stakes liberty of Kashmiri people and mullocracy their happiness. Linguism leads jingoism, amounting even to Hinduism ... becomes too audibly loud, ludicrous and vociferous Terrorism is a common language of Pakistan today.

So, Islamic fanaticism about Kashmir question is as tall as a palm tree with a head as big as a room, its eyes are like burning pans, two of its teeth ... theocracy and mullocracy ... are as long as tusks, its face is like that of a falcon, the belly is of many colours and its hands and the feet are stained with blood of terrorism. Its body is covered with long hairs of terrorist organisations. In a voice as loud as thunder, the Islamic fanaticism said to Kashmir, "Wait, I eat you," The valley replied, "What will happen to you? If you continue to wage a war of terrorism, you will degrade yourself more." Pakistan has spread out a political virus all over the world. Pakistan will gain nothing but shame. Sad hours seem long.

One of the leading newspapers in Pakistan, The Nation, said, in an editorial after the latest bombing against an anti-terrorist judge in Multan," Are these attacks isolated incidents of fanatic wrath, or is it some widespread coordinated effort to intimidate the State itself?" The Paper also raised a warning very much threatening as well as alarming to a tinpot dictator, "Coordinated or not, these are dangerous times to be seen as representatives of the State; the militants are driving home a point." A tractable obedience to Islamic priesthood is a slave ... most malignant stretching beyond moral ethics and philosophy. Moderate Muslims in Pakistan hate this mechanism of destructive policy. Truly speaking, Pakistani ruler is trying to build their evils on the graves of great men like the Poet Iqbal, Md. Ali Jinnah and others, leaving a thousand-fold un-Islamic devil-worshipping demonopathy. In Peshwar and other parts of North-West Frontier Province, residents say English language schools have received threats, school girls have been warned to veil themselves, music is being banned and men are told not to shave their beards. Then, there is the mounting toll of the suicide bombings. What a horrible scenario of crude fanaticism in Pakistan alive with demoniac possession : It is called home-bred terrorism stalking over Pakistan. The Times of India, dated March 15, 2007, says "Terrorist leaders have threatened to unleash scores more, in effect opening a new front in their war. Diplomats and concerned residents see the bombings as a proof of a spreading 'Talibanisation' as Pakistan's military ruler pervez Musharraf called it, which has seeped into more settled districts of the country from the tribal areas that the Taliban and Al Quaida have made a home." We know he cannot be a perfect man, not being tried and tutored in the world; experience by industry achieved, and perfected by the swift course of time. And Pakistan has sown the poisonous seeds of Talibanisation in her own country ... the breeding ground of another Kashmir. Pakistan's mad humour of love over the valley for over 60 years has now become a loving humour of madness in her own country, after setting up an industry of Talibanisation. Full of smiles has transformed into full of tears. So pungent and crude is the destiny that the lunacy is so ordinary. Gen.Musharraf had never expected it. He is a fool; he is a great quarreller.

Few cities in Pakistan are used as a logistic supply base for the propagation of Talibanisation in Pakistan. It is goint to be second Afganistan ... the venomous malice of their swelling heart against Pakistan's attempt to pitch up any sort of democratic process in Pakistan. These mischiefs may be returned with all mockeries of resolutions taken on the Kashmir issue. The daylight is sick. The joint mechanism to curb terrorism over the valley is based on Pakistan's erroneous promise. Why? Pakistan's view is "Jammu and Kashmir is a disputed issue and should not be mixed with the joint mechanism on terror. And the fundamental refusal of Pakistan to view Jehadi violence in Jammu and Kashmir as a terror activity has led the efficacy of the Havana deal ... which saw the joint mechanism being agreed upon ... being doubted by security and foreign policy experts.

Musharraf's January 2004 pledge to curb anti-India terrorism is erroneous and full of wickedness transported by his jealousies to bloody thoughts and to revenge on India over the Kashmir question. His deeds make all the resolutions black over the Kashmir issue. His tyranny on the Kashmiri Hindu pundits works with jealousies. He has used all his tongues to talk to the bitterest camouflaging the Indian politicians altogether. It is a silly cheat. Kashmir has always been counted by falsehood and servile accusations. Every accusation is unfathomably horrible and bloody. Pakistan's physical assault on Kashmiri people on the pretext of liberation movement must not be used for an aggressive or even a directly spiritual end; it may be an Islamic duty to use it. The shooting of one man in cold blood in the valley, as part of a campaign of terror, is far more repugnant to the Islamic mind, both in respect of its corrupting effect and of the attitude to human life which it reflects, that the destruction of a city for strategic purpose. The highest aim of temporal statesmanship in Pakistan must be to surround these new opportunities for destruction with safeguards against the weaknesses inherent in human nature. It is a task calling for patience and realism as well as faith. Mutinous winds of murderous fanaticism have already snowballed the Kashmir question.

Pakistan is always thinking, no doubt, of the system of stratocractic govt. and informers like I.S.I., swayed and sashayed by the fin de siecle ideology of factionalism that bolsters up the Islamic despotism, but this system is taken over and expanded by the extremists like Al Quaida, Let and other inscrutable logistics of terrorism, that applies to the prosecution of Islamic Jehad abroad. S.K. Singh says in 'New Approach' under the caption, 'Stray Thoughts on Kashmir', "In this confused state of national mind-set they have gone ahead and fought three wars with their closest neighbour and lately translated themselves into a nuclear weapon state. Their role of idealism was to demand Kashmir territory, simply because the state had a majority of Muslims. All these years they tended to ignore concepts of integrity, national cohesion, economic development, and political culture based on commonly defined and mutually shared evolution of the nation-state, in both our countries. Their army has convinced them that what they do not understand should not trouble them."

Pakistan has not yet seen her own faults. According to 'Sutra of Hui Neng 2', "He who treads the path in earnest sees not the mistakes of the world. If we find fault with others we ourselves are also in the wrong ..."

Kashmir is an invisible writing. Its thinking is so acute, its imagination so glowing, its hatred of injustice so peremptory, its courage so strenuous, its character as a whole so unenviable. But it is damaged by the deceitfulness and inhumanity of Pakistani extremists in the name of liberation movement in Kashmir. Pakistan's foreign policy makers in collaboration with I.S.I. are just as wicked as the Nazis were. Truly speaking, Pakistan's inferiority-complex forces her into the most aggressive self-assertation. She has been devoured from early childhood by anxiety and guilt and in a manic-depressive symptom and compulsive neurosis. So, her well-advertised Islamic country is an attack of progressive insanity. So, in the height and pride of her glory as an Islamic country, Pakistan is seated in a chariot of melancholy and her associates with all soliders' dance.

Centering on the hotbed of terrorism in Kashmir, this sub-continent rolls on with Islamic fanaticism. Why? The educational institutions in Islamic country like Pakistan are used as an invulnerable instrument of dwarfing their personalities. The Muslim child will be made to feel that he is inferior to the white child. In the interests of the survival of the white people, they will shirk at nothing to realise their goal of keeping non-white in a state of permanent inferiority and servitude. The forces of imperialism have received a shattering blow in Asia. Through the collosal juggernaut of crude Islamic thoughts all over the Kashmir valley, all of the Pakistani rulers, since partition, on the Muslims of Pakistan by retarding their full development, including their human personalities : to complete and seal their doom by enslaving their mental growth through the spiritual education, under the influence of a very regimented mullocracy, would vitiate and add poison to the permanent inferiority of Muslim children. Looking back from the Kashmir question, the growing generation of Pakistan should look for the ultimate victory in their campaign for freedom from oppression and tyranny, done at the behest of stratocratic rulers, police intimidation, mounting injustice, all oppression, all discrimination, all apathy, and from the legalised robbery of fanaticism all other countries. Don't bother about people, Doctor : You will be out of danger, if you are in the safe company of another Doctor. 'Hide us, or they kill us.'

If you know how to spend less than you get you have the philosopher's stone. Rudyard Kipling, in his 'Jungle Book', wrote that what monkeys think today, the rest of the denizens of the jungle would think tomorrow. Of course, that was not an original joke of Kipling. It was too obvious for even a joke, as it was a perverted parody of the earlier and sincere statement of G.K. Ghokale.

The growing youth of present Pakistan should get rid of these insurmountable crises only by a mounting pressure of mass revolution against the orgies of theocracy, mullocracy and even the religious fanaticism all over the Kashmir valley. They should not think of Kashmir question. They must think of how to prosper their country with industrial globalisation from the irrecoverable hidebounds of religious parochialism and gummings of all political trickery. They are all dogmatic, imperious and dictatorial on Kashmir issue.

Nehru once told pressmen at London airport, in June, 1955, that politics were a bit of nuisance, This is all right. Let each politician be assured at his nuisance value, on Kashmir solution.

Our political leaders need to learn that the purity of mind is the holiest pilgrimmage and that the soul can be purified without dips in the holy water of Dal Lake. Their internal filth is enough for 'washing' at home with spiritual soap.

Mr. Nehru used to fly a 'pigeon of Peace' on the Kashmir question. His pigeon and Md. Ali's dove co-fly in the common quest of peace ... though in different directions ... demonstrated, thereby, ornithologial co-existence in the sky of Kashmir. The Indian Prime Minister's cloud-messenger of peace, the pigeon, was, however, employed in the past for carrying secret messages on flying espionage missions, like many Pakistani infiltrators held prisoners in India as spies for entryism.

But our Prime Minister Mr. Nehru and Pakistan's premier, Md. Ali. were frittering away their energy and resources in meaningless quarrels. Today leaders of both the countries speak with a loud speaker in one hand and a gun in the other. Islamabad carries broom stick in one hand and a lantern of terrorism in another, signifying the understood slogan : clean the augean stable and enlighten. The disgraceful way in which Pakistan is being defeated daily by printer's Devil leaves Pakistan, at least, with no heart to strike a hard bargain with its cantankerous correspondents belonging to both theocracy and mullocracy.

What is the sum and substance of the co-existence of Hindu-Muslim unity in India in the economic field? It is not to make the rich richer and the poor poorer. Let them stay where they are. The former flourishing and the latter famishing in their respective spheres of continued co-existence without complaint. The neo-Mughals of New Delhi are more monarchial than the Great Mughals of old Delhi.

There exists in human nature a strong propensity to depreciate the advantages, and to magnify the evils, of the present time. 'What is Congress?' asked Congress President U.N. Dhebar in the course of his presidential address at the Avadi Congress. No reply was forthcoming as no patriotic translation into Hindi has been made hitherto of what is still called Congress in pre-independence language.

Unconsciously, but with magical effect, the people of Pakistan find a new life flowing in their hearts, new blood circulating in their veins, and a new spirit capturing their minds and a new hope welling up in their bosom. It simply takes possession. This is a gift of Islamic thought ... a foolish extravagant spirit, utilising terrorist outfits over the Kashmir valley as sports at such eruptions of crude fanaticism and sudden breaking out of mirth. George Orwell says on a sudden breaking out of mirth in sports : "It is bound up with hatred, jealousy, boastfulness, disreagd of all rules and saddistic pleasure in witnessing violence; in other words it is war minus the shooting ... ". Orwell continues, "there are quite enough real causes of trouble already, and we need not add to them by encouraging young men to kick each other on the shins amid the roars of infuriated spectators."

So, don't walk alone, like one that had the patience; to sigh, like a school boy that had lost his A. B. C.; to weep like a young wrench that had buried her grandmother, to watch, like one that fears robbing. Even the shuttle diplomacy between two rival countries has only generated fear-surprised eyes all over the valley.

It was terrible but siccipian task to any country of the world to solve unsurpassable problem after the partition. What is it? The problem of integration of over 600 Indian States was solved in a friendly way and almost incredible quickness. The question is : Is Kashmir problem more and more critical than that of the insumountable problem like the integration of over 600 Indian States? Certainly not. A lack of farsightedness lies in there. The most untaught knavery and crudest politics may have alienated them. Who is responsible for this vindictive situation? It has now got to be a game of hide-and-seek. Nevertheless, the clevage between the two principal powers in this sub-continent are too deep and fundamental on the conflicting viewpoints. But actually the causes have gone far deeper than any academic or ideological basis. Pakistan is a confirmed believer in armed strategy. And the suppressed masses are turning out more vocal in Pre-emptive tone and aggressive. The frustrated intellectuals of Pakistan and the unemployed youths have a stronghold on the illiterate masses of the country, marshalling towards religious fanaticism branded as Islamic nation, and the land is fertile for anti-India hymns of hate and malevolence. The people are poor and illiterate. But their poverty and illiteracy do not prevent them from seeking an answer to the prevailing anachronistic conditions. Finally, in the face of the threat from the Islamic organisations, the vested interests can hope to hold on to what they have only with the help of a power bloc which will agree to maintain the status quo of crude Islamic ideology over the valley. And the sectarianism stands divided with two groups pulling in two opposite directions with a sharp attack of mental anguish. Students are lured away by the so-called fin de siecle Islamic thoughts over the valley. The power rests with the feudal classes represented in the National Assembly. Their nerves have been shattered due to apprehension of theocracy and western powers and police pin-pricks.

Pakistan is the show window of Islamic terrorism and safe haven for terrorists in the Islamic world today. Each side is pouring millions into sectors of the city ... just to put on a better show than the other. No wonder, thousands and thousands of infiltrators flock from Pakistan in Kashmir just for a look and stay to see the bright lights of crescent flags of Jehadis. Pakistani people do not talk in terms of political parties ... they talk about leaders. Yesterday, it was Gen. Musharraf, a confirmed villain of Banana Republic. Tomorrow it will be somebody else. But it's always a leader, not a party. They still have a warm spot in their heart for a paroxysm of rage.

Politics are knavish professions. Political leaders settle in rouge. Like wolves and bears, the bastard - brains cast their savageness aside during their electioneering campaign over the valley. India has achieved political independence. Decades of life and death struggle with a ruthless alien rule has come to a close. But a far harder and more exacting struggle over the Kashmir question has been looming large. The associates and followers of the Father of the Nation have so far speeded up the Kashmir question very much inscrutable today. After partition, Mr. Nehru has given his sweet-heart-secularism-a lipstick as a birthday present on the occasion of the partition of India. Why? Because he knows that sweet-heart secularism would get most of it back. Secularism is a game of politics how to acquire power. According to Tulsidas, "It is tough to live in this jungle we call life." (Ram Charit Manas).

The hyphenated-terrorists like migrating birds display a remarkable ability to fly thousands of miles to return to a specific garden sponsored by Pakistan through grapevine or province after province. It is one of the most fascinating mysteries that how the hyphenated-terrorists like the bird, pigeons, find their way home far away they are taken; they almost return to their safe haven, Islamabad. Muslim terrorist-field around the Kashmir valley is much like a compass. Like a human baby, all of the terrorist organisations have become attached to their 'mother' .. Pakistan, and follow her around. It is the magnetic field of theocracy and mullocracy. They all react to the external magnetic field of other Islamic countries to plan and work out their precise location for further terrorism. So they have all been pre-occupied with the incredible abilities like pigeons. They all use hundreds and thousands of fake passports, making fraudulent applications.

Not only the hyphenated-terrorists but even the Bagladeshis are involved in a large scale immigration racket with fraudulent applications using also the identities of dead children or adults. India should not impose a blanket ban on veils at all Muslim institutions in India. Blanket ban on veils depends on circumstantial evidence whether they are involved in terrorism or not, to create carnage on a colossal and unprecedented scale in India. Under the prevailing constitutional position, it is a million dollar question to our Govt. South Waziristan, bordering Afghanistan, is believed to be an epicentre of all pitched battles, plunging Pakistan into the most bitter political row. There is a systematic detention, torture and killing of men, women and children. Dujail, like South Waziristan, was once a stronghold of the Shia Dawa Party, a group strongly opposed to Saddam and his war with Iran. Like Saddam, General Musharraf had visited there, praising those who had served Pakistan in the fight against India on Kashmir issue.

Deprived of all rights, women in Kashmir are now in a miserable condition. It is like Dante's 'Inferno of the fire'. Penalties are gone from the law books. Terrorists want more blood and more brutalities. Impatience is the mental disease of the present generation in Pakistan. Fanatical extremism, in the name of liberation movement, has swooped down upon the innocent women, even upon the Kashmiri Hindu women. Crusaders have drained away more blood, worn down the tissues of Hindu-Muslim unity, sold more houses, plunged more families into bankruptcy, armed more villains, slain more pregnant women and just-born child, snapped more wedding rings, deflowered more shcool-going and marriageable girls, blinded more eyes, hacked away more limbs, dethroned reasons, wrecked manhood, dishonored womanhood, broken more hearts, left them more in widowhood, blasted more lives and houses, driven more to suicide and dug more graves than any other scourge that has ever swept its death-dealing waves across the world. Perfect Hitlerism in the name of Kashmir solution : Truly speaking, a woman in Kashmir is just like a forbidden tree. Why? Because fanaticism is their true-telling friend. Deep shame does not strike the Islamic country. Hostility and tumult reign over the valley.

This is an age of duplicity in which the phonies have inherited the earth.

Pakistan's wonderful promise to stop terrorism signifies her nature as bloody as the hunter, full of respite. A missing link lies in Kashmir solution. That tyrannous heart does not think so. Pakistan is the churlish messenger of peace on Kashmir issue. Is Gandhiji considered to be a great on the partition of India? Ralph Waldo Enerson says, "... the great man is he who in the midst of the crowd keeps with perfect sweetness the independence of solitude." People will judge it in time. Whereas Oscar Wilde says: "It's not whether you win or lose, it's how you place the blame." And the Kashmir problem remains the same as it was before.

Besides having these leaders' hypocrisy over the Kashmir issue, the present furore has snowballed into Musharraf's most domestic political crisis since he seized power in a coup in 1999. Karachi, Pindi, Peshwar, Quetta, Multan, Sind, Waziristan have boiled up the cauldron of domestic politics with fires of indignation. Kidnapping the girls and housewives were Gen. Musharraf's nemesis. Kidnapping was the most serious crisis of his presidency. Many husbands disappeared, presumably kidnapped by Govt's security agents.The housewives have started organising other family members of the disappeared. The long bondage of womanhood in Pakistan is linked by treachery. This bondage is a perpetually constant and regular employment of violence. This is only one decisive victory of Gen. Musharraf's timocracy. They are women of a breed whose racial ideal was not Helan of Troy, passed passively from male hand to male hand, as men pass gold or lead. Housewives are desperate against the abruptness and lack of transparence in administration led by theocracy and mullocracy. A Peace deal has already been signed in between the pro-Taliban terrorist groups and Pakistani authorities. In some provinces, the schools were closed. Why? The terrorist groups are looking for children to prepare them for Jehad and for suicide attacks. It is reported. The terrorists had asked the school administrators to assemble them so they could address them. It is the Pakistan's policy over the Kashmir question. How ugly nights of ignorance came breathing at Musharraf's heels : Bastard instructs, bastard in mind, bastard in valour. So, bastard in everything is illegitimate, as if the son of a whore fights for a whore. Kashmir today haunts Pakistan like a wicked conscience.

Mr. Surinder Singh Oberoi says : "It is alleged that the Islamic twist by Pakistan is attracting muslim mercenaries, while Pakistan denies the charge and says that it is their moral duty to help them diplomatically." Mr. Oberoi also says : "Kashmiri separatist leaders are challenging the Instrument of Accession which was signed by the erstwhile Maharaja of Kashmir." (Kashmir : Now and Then in New Approach) And it is undeniable fact that Pakistan's political strategy over the Kashmir question is like a bikini. What they reveal is suggestive, but what they conceal is vital. Mr. Oberoi has given a statistics of the worst picture in the valley. He says : "More than 25,000 people, including security force personnel, armed militants and innocent have fled the valley and still the uncertainty prevails. The roaring of the gun continues." (Ibid).

Every beast of the wild knows the wild dog for what he is ... a ruthless slayer; he haunts by day and night. The most deadly and efficient destroyer of world peace is terrorism. It has speed and endurance that enable it run down the modern technology of western powers. Thus it is world's most dreaded and most deadly game killer. Nowadays, people know the price of everything, but the value of nothing. Why do they not create a new tradition instead of following the old?

Muslim fanaticism is like a silent bird like an eagle, but has a shrill, squealing cry, something between a bark and laugh, sounds decidedly uncanny. Like the eagle, terrorism drops straight down upon its prey, from which it squeezes out the life with its taloons of Jehadi slogans.

Like the extremely noisy bird, Pallas Fishing Eagle, common in Kashmir, the Pakistani-sponsored terrorist group, LeT, frequents rivers and marshes. It rests on the craggy peaks lying about the valley and POK. Like this eagle, LeT has an eye like a telescope which sees into the mysteries of the Kashmir question. It swoops down, like a flash, upon the innocent men, women and children with its invulnerable taloons of Islamic globalisation. Like the hawk-eagle, Taliban is reputed to be a fierce disposition.

Like the serpent-eagle, Al Quaida is spotted with large spots of its various organisations on its wings, when it soars, the wings are held well back; and its tail lying at Islamabad does not project very far. And Islamabad gives vent to a shrill successions of whistles when on the wings. And the leaders of theocracy and mullocracy make no world-wide protest. They like flying with a majestic sailing through the western nations with flapping of the huge wings of terrorist organisations only at intervals, riding upon the back loveable mother, Pakistan. Because they are trying to preserve the hard-won Islamic rule in Pakistan. Whereas freedom in India, like Pickle, can only be preserved by the rulers to be steady as a rock.

Those who are familiar with Congress political history in India, even in Kashmir problem, need not be told that a party split based on vital differences on Kashmir policy is a source of great weakness and may even render the party politically impotent for many years. The split in the Congress party caused by some geriatric but power-drunkard leaders belonging to feudalism has always amputed the Kashmir policy and snowballed the controversy off and on, for a generation. Not only that but Congress policy has handicapped the Jammu and Kashmir Govt. and made it politically impotent over decades. Partition has caused great damage. Even Mr. Nehru's well-deserved pseudo-reputation and statesmanship may not be able to create complete confidence in the minds of the Kashmiri voters. His fame naturally spread throughout the world and particularly to the secularists. His name was something to conjure with Kashmir question. The crowning event of his life, regarding Kashmir question, dedicated to communal flare-up, came when he invented RSS was the sole responsible for waging a colossal juggernaut of communalism in India. No other problem is probably so much today than that of communalism in India. But so many ailments are previously considered incurable. And Kashmir problem still stands there as it was before. Communalism is a wonder-drug to our so called pseudo-secularists to win over the Muslim votes. So communalism is a vote-catching weapon to our secularists. According to a very old song : "A young man's heart is full of love; get away, old men, get away :"

The Western powers sphearheaded by U.S. are ready to ratchet up international pressure on Gen. Musharraf to break up the old traditional friendship between Inter-Services Intelligence (I.S.I.) and Jehadis. ISI has married up with Jehadis since 9/11.Bajpur province bordering Afganistan is an invulnerable hunting ground of Islamic militants. Because Pakistan's military regime has already signed a peace deal process with the Salarazi and Utmankhel tribes so as to drive out the foreign terrorists' cross-border terrorism bordering Afganistan. The U.S. military strategies have succeeded in sowing dissension between the religious nationalist and Al Quaida elements. Why In Bajaur area? Because Bajaur is likely to be Al Quaida's headquarters ... a place of mapping out a master-plan for terrorist outfits all over the world, including Kashmir. This is the off-shoot of peace deal process.

At the centre of Islamabad, there is a brothel, a five-minute walk from the mosque. Aunty Shamin is its owner. In Islamic religion, prostitution is evil.

An uprising chaos has happened to create a confrontation between the dictatorship and the judiciary. The Centre for public Integrity (CPI) said : "Coalition Support Funds (CSF) money has continued to flow, despite growing U.S. concerns over Pakistan's assistance in the global war on terror." The Pentagon merely said in March, 2007, "This payment is based on the bills submitted from the Govt. of Pakistan for the support it provided to U.S. military operations during April through June related to the global war on terrorism." (Times News Network March 29, 2007). In this critically generated embarrassing situation, Pakistan, as a Banana Republic, is a confirmed stooge of the White House. Spoonerism and dictatorship run side by side to combat terrorism. Pakistan's chief enemy is her own unruly nature and the dark forces pent up within her. The rulers are vicious, and the Islamic passions may be operated upon. Pakistan is now in the crudest form of her existence as an Islamic nation.

In this well-integrated or half-organised world, Kashmir question has married up with Islamic firebrands and religious fanaticism, even with their harsh machinery and crudely motivated scorching arguments over the valley. Middle East produces a perilous derangement filling up the gap between Kashmir and the Middle East. The feuds and tangles of the Middle East back up the Kashmir problem year after year. The current dangers on the bloody frontiers between India and Pakistan, and between the Middle East countries and Israel, have been on the edge of the larger lunacy.

Using Kashmir as an invulnerable catalyst, Muslim fanaticism running wild over the Middle East, has started fighting against the western powers. Kashmir has ever been to them a safe haven. Israel remains in a condition of suspended, or cataleptic, war not only with Egypt but with palestine, Jordan, Iraq, Syria, Lebanon and Saudi Arabia. A resumption of the shooting invokes no new principle at all rather than that of humanity and sense. The State of Israel is still a turbulent island of millions of people surrounded by millions and millions of bitter and articulate enemies very much ideologues. Like the Kashmir problem, between India and Pakistan, the quarrel between the Middle East and Israel seems indissoluble. Like the frontiers of Kashmir, frontiers between the Middle East countries and Israel reach almost to everyone's backdoor ... armed, neurotic, irrational, a zealous adherent of an ideology and triumphalism, a symbol of the vicious, vitriolic and frustrating half-peace that turns decent people into thugs.

Like the Kashmir problem, the Middle East crisis makes a fundamental psychological rift ... the political sophistication and urgency of the Jews, the historic traditionalism of the Arabs, the mutually antipathetic qualities that make each so hateful to the other. The same backpedalling is going on in between India and Pakistan. Both are at the searing heat of dissension and estrangement. There are two kinds of people in the world : givers and takers. The latter may eat better, but the former sleep better. We know every political defeatism and every loss of political ideology contain in its seed of ignorance.

Like Pakistan's fundamentalist group jabbering out Jehadi slogans, the Arabs have never reconciled themselves even to the physical existence of the Jewish State as Pakistan to the physical existence of India's predominance over the Kashmir valley. The collective security pact is designed to serve as a shield against the Zionist peril, and against no other.

The King of Saudi Arabia once said : "Israel is a cancer that must be uprooted if it costs us ten million men." These things are a background to the sudden berserk furies of the Jews. In the same way, Pakistan-sponsored belligerent attitude of Jehadi slogans is a cancer not only to the solution of Kashmir question but to this sub-continent also. It is constantly jarring on the nerves of Kashmiri people.

But Why? The reason is not growing strength but in growing weakness. Like the ever-growing tension and confusion over the Kashmir question, both the Arab and Jewish solidarity under the pressure of overstrung world is collapsing. Chemicals in a condition of dissolution tend to explode.

Those of us who feel our own immediate world rather shaky and wambling around us might well consider the case of the Kashmir question and the Arab world, which at this moment rocks and thrashes around like a camel in a quicksand. It is fact.

The Kashmiri people like the Arab world have always a strong likeness to the United Nations being a collection of nationalist suspicion from Pakistan, dynastic rivalries of feudal lords and personal doubts hold together only by a common fear. Its instrinsic fallacies and flaws have come nearer to disintegrating completely.

To Pakistan, on the Kashmir question, one good hate is a necessary nourishment, but two are luxury. In an effort to canalise all her mutually contradictory passions and nefarious activities, Pakistan like Egypt finds it necessary to accuse India, with the extraordinary suggestion that Pakistan had not been invited by China to attack in Kargil. After Kargil, Pakistan has lost in a cul-de-sac of her own self-righteousness.

Jamal Juma, coordinator of the Palestinian Grassroots Anti-Apartheid Wall Campaign, said : "The Palestinian struggle could have been more successful if the Arab Governments were not allies of the U.S. and had put pressure on Israelis to end aggression and occupation." He told it in an international Conference on West Asia in New Delhi, in 2007. And the divisions between the Hamas and the Fatah have not helped either. Even the news of the Indian Army Chief's visit to Israel shocked the Palestinians. To Mr. Juma, it is definitely very frustrating. He also said : "The Palestinians are imprisoned in their own land." So, the Arab Governments like the foolish Pakistani rulers reject what they see, not what they think.

It is precisely at this point on Kashmir drama, our former Prime Minister, Mr. A.B. Bajpayee, turned up on the stage in Kashmir, with the slightly perplexing effect of a light comedy leading man who found himself to unexpected half-way through the last act of 'Macbeth'.

The time is past now for sentimentalising the strange State of Pakistan which has ceased to be a nation built on dreams of Islamic globalisation and is discovering that there are as many problems in the Kashmir valley as there are in the Diaspora, the outer world.

Pakistan has decided that in their anxieties with the militant groups, she can do nothing by argument. Opportunities multiply as she is seized. Gen. Musharraf, father of terrorism, has always been with Jehadis. Pakistan recalls from her hermitage in Beijing and arises her anxious thought. The poor old world prepares for another dose of cold war in a hot climate of Kashmir question. If the shadow of suspicioin hangs heavily on Islamabad, who will protect the fanatical crusaders?

It is an unvarnished truth that Pakistan's fate and political destiny is closely tied to U.S. dollar diplomacy.

The Western defence ring has already spread all along the southern border of Russia ... from Greece to Pakistan. Like the Kashmir problem, there has been violent disagreement among Arab states like Pakistan with other provinces. In fact, Western diplomats feel that Iraq's action will show to other Arab leaders that Arab society is nothing if its sole aim is to oppose the west and Israel. Arabs must be realistic as Pakistan has not been as yet.

Like Pakistan's politics over the valley, Arab league politics, since its very inception, has been anything but positive and constructive. Year after year, Pakistan's meetings on Kashmir question have produced nothing but resolutions never acted upon by Pakistan's promises when they returned to their capital from the meetings. No one should shed tears, if the Arab League or Pakistan now cracks down under the pressure of world events.

Arab politics is generally led by Egypt though based on non-cooperation with the west. Likewise, Pakistan's politics is primarily dictated by the fin-de-siecle religious shibboleth supervised by theorcracy and mullocracy and coordinated by the Sunni group ... a foreboding sign to any Islamic country. The Arabs have been holding back from the West as a bargaining counter as Pakistan from India on the Kashmir counter.

Israel, which the Arabs feel, came into existence with the West's help as the vivisection of India with the help of Lord Mountbatten, and Nehru & Co. And Pakistan holds POK as her own possession. It is as foolhardy for Arabs to insist on the return of refugees as it was for India to insist on the return of nearly 8 million refugees who came from Pakistan in 1947. It simply cannot happen.

The impracticability of Arab politics as Pakistan against India on Kashmir question is apparent. It is a vicious circle which the West has been trying to break its own advantage. And they seem to have succeeded by making a bargain with Iraq and Afganistan, and then with Iran and North Korea. This is the romance of Western politics on Islamic countries. Western diplomacy has shown remarkable success in the Middle East. India is a big concession to Arab sentiments.

Western statesmen have often warned against Pakistan's game of hide-and-seek politics to divide the allies and to stop terrorism. And it now appears that it is the allies and terrorist groups themselves are running at each other's throat. For every minute Pakistan is angry, she loses 60 seconds of happiness. "From anger arises infatuation, from infatuation, confusion of memory, from confusion of memory, loss of reason, and from loss of reason, one goes to complete ruin." (Bhagabhat Gita 2.63).

Truly speaking, the dropping of 'etc.' from the language of Indo-Pak agreement would necessitate a lot of thinking that is not being done at present.

What is the greatest problem today? Ambitious totalitarianism or terrorism? The greatest problem today is emotionalism in politics ... in place of reason; glands instead of cerebration.

Everyone feels a sense of puzzlement, frustration and dissatisfaction. There is a marked tendency to project it all to a scapegoat. For example, capitalism is the scapegoat of communism and vice-versa.

Hitler invented a race ... the Aryans ... and made the Jews the scapegoats. We may call it 'escapegoatism'. It means the resort to a scapegoat is an escape from the real facing of a problem ... and by its very nature, it is an emotional, not rational, mental mechanism.

Look at McCarthy or at Bush or at Saddam or at Hitler or at Mussolini, or at Gen. Musharraf. How men like that could flourish so long.

This is a very dangerous situation. Why? Because the military mind believes in getting its blow in first ... in attack as the best form of defence. Anger, irritation, the collective passions that mark nationalism ... unless these can be restrained. The Third World War will destroy us. Why? Because it will undoubtedly be an atomic one.

We teach our children dull, dead language like Hindi, Arabic, Pustu, Latin, and other, instead of the rudiments of politics, and stuff them with a lot of other unecessary things instead of educating them to citizenship. If freedom and democracy can't stand up clearly to everyone, we should have something to be worried out. We have to clear the air of misconceptions, prejudice and emotionalism.

Making the Kashmir problem worse, a notable scrimmage between the Shia and the Sunni societies over the valley blazes up among the variously embattled theologians in every way. It is a second rate mind with a first rate ambition. Some of the wheels within wheels so adroitly engineered are still turning in Pakistan on the Kashmir question, and even on the militant groups. Idle hands of New Delhi clutch trouble, and insubordination leads to punishment and to shouts and to heavy war on the nervous system. It is a dreadful affair, so certified by the neighbouring country.

Pakistan, at intervals, it seems, turns savage, utters a loud bubbling roar of fanatical crusade and engages in fierce contest with India on the settlement of Kashmir issue. Hundreds and thousands of portraits of Laden hang on in the houses of Pakistan as their demi-god or as a messiah. It is an identification parade of Rogue gallery ... a camouflaged instrument of power of crude Islamic cultural propaganda and an excellent source of fin de siecle society for the extremism. It is considered to be the personification of everything evil and most of them regard it as indestructible. The whole Islamic school of fanaticism in and around the valley is designed to produce men of the strongest will-power and unscrupulous energy for whom mental problems are a waste of time but who understand human beings and how to rule them ruthlessly. The moderate Muslims in Kashmir and Pakistan appear puzzled and rather irritated. Embarrassed in a bewildering labyrinth of political criss-crosses, Gen. Musharraf has written his memoir 'In the Line of Fire' afterwards nervously apologising, lest his exuberant spirits to be a tinpot dictator should betray him into talking too much and too heedlessly. His passion for self-advertisement has embarrassed him, and he is a passionate, giddy, dangerous imprudent ruler of Pakistan. He confides to I.S.I. Quietly, gracefully, composedly, he takes leave of Islamic culture. Composedly, too, he settles to the new phase of life ... terrorism. This is natural. Pretty well everyman minds losing a portion of power and eminence if he had held it for any length of time. He is conceited to trust his own judgement.

The Kashmir dispute always plays its part in hardening sentiment against India. Of all the knotty problems that disturb the peace in Asia, none has roused more passion that the conflict between India and Pakistan for possession of the fertile valley and green forests of the beautiful land that lies between

Afganistan and Tibet. The U.N. has been trying for a peaceful settlement since 1948 to demilitarise the province. But Mr. Nehru had a special feeling for the vale of Kashmir, the homeland of his family, and had repeatedly declared that he would never surrender it to Pakistan. His uncompromising, together with Pakistan's unwarranted destructive campaigns on this issue, had considerable effect in the world.

India is not a well-matured nation in foreign policy learning that national independence is not merely a matter of throwing off foreign rule. The conflict over Kashmir adds to her danger, but in her position next door to two pushing communist empries, though well-advertised, quality is cheap, ... India has to steer a dangerous course in any event. Pakistan is not willing to leave Kashmir on the anxious seat while the lesson of the present crisis does not sink in.

India must be aware of the old slogan : The people can't eat the constitution. Terrorism over the valley sings in and out in different tunes. The Chinese communists have resorted to terrorism as a weapon to keep land-lords and bourgeios elements in power. The agrarian reforms are conducting a nation-wide blood purge in which they themselves announce the execution of hundreds, though the real number of their victims is preserved to run into the thousands and is put by the Chinese Nationals at more than a millions but terror, once started, is hard to stop as Pakistan does today over the vale of Kashmir. In future, China, in the name of revolution, will soon begin to eat its own children as Pakistan is rolling down over the vale of Kashmir and the rest of the world. Islamabad does not tell a terrorist who's making the noise in the vale of Kashmir.

The slow kettle is beginning to simmer. Dr. Farooq Abdullah was lost in the Byzantine politics of Kashmir and in a general atmosphere of political as well as mental slavery. He tuned over the Kashmir question at different times. India Today, in 1994, says about Dr. Farooq Abdullah's different tunes : "It is India that is responsible for what has happened in Kashmir..." And even the political gregariousness of Mir Qasim, former Chief Minister, with egotistic manner, was fully incapable of inspiring the Kashmiri people. The magazine 'Life and Time' 1991, says about his conclusive remark:" If I dump petrol in my house ... and my opponents set a match to it, it is largely my fault ... wherever the entire people rise up in one voice, you cannot suppress it by force ..." Truly speaking, Kashmir is fed on illusions. Kashmiris believe whatever they want to believe. Ved Bhasin in 'Creative Approach To Kashmir Problem' says : "The people of India, unfortunately, have been fed with lies by the rulers in New Delhi, about the actual situation in Jammu and Kashmir. What happened in the State since 1990 need not be enumerated. "Now the question is : May prejudice boast of her fascination and tyranny exult in his claims? May delusion over the Kashmir question continue to practise her clever and magical stratagem over the people of Kashmir? May Muslim dogmatism administer the slumbering opiate? To my country, India, be true to yourself; you cannot then be false to others.

And to my neighbouring country, Pakistan, be true to yourself; those who everyday barter away other men's liberty will soon care little for their own. Leave the legacy of your dishonest name. Because you have acquired treachery by arms, over the vale of Kashmir.

The world, seen from Islamabad, has a sword hanging over it, a sword jerked up and down with the recurrent blasts of alarm and reassurance issuing on alternate days from the National Assembly or the capital; but it can hardly be equable enough to justify the snail-like pace of the Kashmir debate. If it takes all this time to wrangle over the one-two-threes of the agenda, how long will it take the Foreign Ministers to argue out the actual issues over the Kashmir question?

The question is : Does either side really want a conference? So far both sides seem to be stalling. The Pakistan delegates have come up after every deadlock with a revised version of the text over Kashmir question, a shade nearer the Indian position than the one before, and this is taken as a sign that Pakistan wishes to delay but not close the door. India attempts to sound out Pakistan's intentions, but the main thing the long-drawn out haggling has accomplished to date is to lessen interest in the outcome. But her attitude and actions have communicated so roughly that it stands like a wall between us and and spreads like a pall over the world.

The harping on the words of talkathon either in Islamabad or in New Delhi is merely pettifogging and political monoeuvre. The suspicion it expresses is a profound and dangerous fact. But though this is terribly real, the argument over the agenda has become unreal to the general public. What is the good of it? Whereas terrorism is gaining ground even among the angriest critics of our policy.

Tempers are getting too frayed for the slow processes on which the prevention of war depends. All the political weather prophets have predicted that this will be stormy beyond anything we have experienced to date. Inspite of everything, another circus comes and with it the circus, ever changing and ever the same.

Political witchcraft and Islamic priestcraft go on, hand in hand together. They are like the two sides of a coin, overlapping each other. So, mothers, wives and children in Pakistan are tools of priesthood. Religious priesthood in Pakistan is regarded as a superior type of human being. How does the priestcraft look at the people? James Gibbons says : "To the carnal eye the priest looks like other men, but to the eye of faith he is exalted above the angels, because he exercises power not given even to angels." (The Faith of our Fathers, XXVIII, 1876). The mysteries of religious fanaticism, ... an unvarnished truth ..., in Pakistan are kept in the hands of the priests, and even the govt, whatever its colour, is dictated by the priests. They are patient to martydom to the cause of Kashmir question. Public life gradually dies. Clique-ism develops into an authoritarianism of handful political leaders believing in priestcraft. So the whole body of people within the nation is in fear of untold pangs of anxiety and awe. Such strong but delicate fabric is made up of many threads of religious passions and anti-India hymns of hate and malevolence.

No military rulers in Pakistan, since independence, have ever been concerned with their times, concerned with life and liberty of the people of Pakistan, and even for the freedom of the individual and of his world. And every military ruler has been basking in cooling showers for thirsting powers and beholding a rainbow of ecstasy on the terrorist activities over the vale of Kashmir. All they have filed stale historically humourous accusations against India. And General Musharraf is a little Napoleon and trying to start an Islamic Jehad over the vale of Kashmir as his predecessors did. He is regarded as a spokesman for Jehad in Kashmir. Even so he has transgressed both the written and unwritten dimensions of military propriety. He has not only advanced his ideas of crusaders' views over the valley in private and through proper channels of all Islamic thoughts, but he has deliberately set out to swing public opinion and political passion of all Arab world to his concepts and to use his domestic and international political prestige to force a change in Govt. policies over the Kashmir question off and on. His lip has trembled at one point as he feels for the words over the Kashmir debate. Twice he has tried to cover up with sardonic military humour but it does not help much in concealing his emotions. Under his patronage, Pakistan has already jeopardized the future of Muslims as an Islamic nation. Why? Because she has continued to follow a vague policy of hazy altruism over the Kashmir question. Kashmir issues have so far been handled with such ineptness that the fundamental issues involved are being obscured. So Pakistan's political triumph is a victory of extremism for Jehadi slogans and for religious fanaticism. This is why the silencing of General Musharraf on Al Quaida, LeT, and Taliban is necessarily dangerous. Benazir Bhutto, former Prime Minister of Pakistan, wrote in her revised autobiography, "Benazier Bhutto ... Daughter of the East" : "I realise that like the assassination of philippines Senator Benigne Aquino in Manila in August 1983, I can be gunned down on the airport tarmac when I land. After all, Al Quiada has tried to kill me several times. Why would we think they wouldn't try again as I return from my exile to fight for the democratic elections they so detest?" In the fall of 1993, Benazir said her assassination was ordered and the "chosen assassin was a Pakistani with ties to the I.S.I. during the Afghan Jehad. His name was Ramji Yusef. He had participated in the first attack on the World Trade Centre that same year. After the February bombings, Yusef returned to Pakistan. Seven months later, he was assigned my assassination. He attempted to kill me on two separate occasions during the election campaign of 1993."

According to Mrs. Bhutto, when Yusef was captured by her government in 1995, he had in his possession plans for hijacking US commercial aircraft and using them as weapons against buildings." Al Quaida had similar plans to hijack several commercial jets on the same day over the Pacific as a mass terrorist attack". It is the greatness of Benazier Bhutto that consists in her saying what is true of her country. Her commnet is so sound and so dangerous to the present ruler as well as to the I.S.I.

In the new Chapter, "Prime Minister And Beyond" that she has added in the revised autobiography. Benazier said that during her tenure as Prime Minister in the first term in February, 1989, when she asserted authority over the I.S.I. in May, Osama bin Laden was aksed by the ISI ... with whom he had long and close relations ... to help overthrow the democratic government and install a theocratic rule in Pakistan.

Pakistan has totally forgotten the principles of basic democracy. In Pakistan, basic democracy is substituted by some incompetent bureaucrats, by some ministers corrupted to heart, making themselves as if by fixing upon a stake over Kashmir question, and by thrusting a sharp stake through the body of theocratic rulers to wage a war of terrorism. Emphasizing that democracy in Pakistan, Benazier Bhutto said : "In this age of the exploitation and radical interpretation of my beloved religion, we must always remember that democratic governments do not empower protect and harbour terrorists. A democratic Pakistan, free from the yolk of military dictatorship, would cease to be the petri dish of the pandemic of international terrorism." So, insurgence, sectarian killings, sporadic vòlleys of gunfire across the border, extremism, and the united state-backed Jehadi groups are the flashing points all over the vale of Kashmir. Flummoxed by the ever-increasing fluidity of censurable comments over the Kashmir issue, Pakistan should remember the Swedish proverb: "Fear less, hope more; eat less, chew more; whine less, breathe more; talk less, say more; love more, and all good things will be yours." Don't stand on the foundation of falsehood. Because falsehood and its ingredients are born of greed, anger and delusion. And fruits of all these ingredients are endless ignorance and suffering that Pakistani rulers see today.

Nawaz Sharrif and Benazier Bhutto's dismissal from the power has divided Pakistan into warring camps of those who would impeach their president for dismissing so honourable public servants and chief justice of the Supreme Court, and those who praise their president for his courage in stamping insubordination in their armed forces. As a result of this controversy, Pakistan stands before the world as a divided nation, and this obvious lack of united purpose can only give comfort to India on the Kashmir question.

They are now at war of terrorism with internal acrimonious bickering. They already have over a quarter of a million of their sons in the field of battle against non-Islamic world. Each day their casualty lists grow, but there is no honourable way of stopping this war, of justifying their supreme sacrifices their sons are making. They are spending the billions in their fight on the Kashmir question. They show India their weakness of purpose, and their newspapers, radio and television tell the world of their internal conflict. Pakistan is the copy-writer of Hitlerism to sell out thousand colourful militant slogans swiftly to the hearts of their co-religionists. She is allergic to orthodoxies of politics as much as those of religion. She is also allergic to Islamic dogmas and religious doctrines and partisan passion. So, Pakistan seems to be of a decidedly divided mind about her philosophy over this sub-continent.

Since independence, Pakistan, on Kashmir issue, has compiled a fine catalogue of her hypocrisy, lies and folly as expressed in widely prejudices about racialism, sectarianism, crude religion, sex, superstition and self-opinionated political bigotry. Bertrand Russell, a philosopher and mathematician, says in his 'Unpopular Essays', "Politics is largely governed by sententious platitudes which are devoid of truth." The quintessence of Russellism as expounded in these essays is expressed in the following two sentences : "The most savage controversies are those about matters as to which there is no good evidence either way. Persecution is used in theology, not in arithmetic, because in arithmetic there is knowledge, but in theology there is only opinion."

Perhaps to keep his franchise as an elderly sage, Bertrand Russell has included a chapter of prophetic speculation in 'Unpopular essays'. Before the end of the present century, unless something quite unforeseeable occurs, one of three possibilities will have been realised. These three are :

1. "The end of human life, perhaps of all life on our planet"
2. "A reversion to barbarism after a catastrophic diminution of the globe."
3. "A unification of the world order under a single Govt. possessing the monopoly of all the major weapons of war."

He does not know which of these dire possibilities is most likely but he naturally would prefer that it would take place under United States rather than under Russian, auspices.

Pakistan, a lifelong protagonist of Islamic theology what Mr. Russell says in 'Unpopular Essays' that in theology, there is only opinion, but no mathematical accuracy and precision in opinion. Pakistan, being very much deep-rooted in theology, is contemptuous of moral weaknesses in many areas of her administration vulgarly executed and nauseatingly motivated. She praises militancy as the only constitutionally correct action in the circumstances over the Kashmir question. It simmers down to a conflict in policy between the President and the Povincial govts. of Pakistan. Militancy, extremism, fanaticism, Jehad and a syndrome of all other socio-religious diseases are tributes to the charm, courage, cynical realism and capacity for public emotion of Pakistanies.

The direct controversy has always been the form of a long series of Kashmir disputes. Some are public knowledge, others are recorded in documents that are still in secret files.

Asia has always been touched off as one of the most dramatic incidents in American foreign policy. The U.S. foreign policy makers have always hammered out at the fact that it is in Asia that shooting war goes on. Americans will never be able to dicatate peace on our terms unless they maintain strength in Asia. Why? Because Asia, with its vast resources and enormous pool of manpower, is the key.

On Kashmir question, Pakistan is dark with the portentous shadow of the atomic power. It glitters with minute splinters of melancholy satire. As an Islamic nation full of fantasy in theological notions, the country is as insubstantial to measure up the yardstick of her game plan over the Kashmir question as thistle down to sink in political garbage. Through agreements and insubstantial verbosity, the country concerns wondrous supernatural events through terrorism. Muslim clerics in the present civilisation are mingled with the guests like politicians, diplomats, screen stars and literary critics ... a deplorable specimen who has taught an entire generation that venery, depravity, malevolence, turculence and assault and battery are the proper subjects for Muslim culture. Naturally, the Devil feels grateful for such assistance. Pakistan's comments in the U.N.O. on the lamentable state of Jammu and Kashmir and kindred matters such as theology, morality, psychology, literature and international relations is undeniably clever in its gossamer, typically Pakistani fashion. But now unfortunately, we have to consider how much permanent damage will be done to our neighbouring country's own standing throughout the Continent of Asia if we fail the Pakistanis in this hour of despatch need for basic democracy. Islam always preaches non-violence, peace, truth and world brotherhood. But General Musharraf, a confirmed political gambler, has always been gambling away over Islamic religion as his predecessors did. And the leaders of regional heavyweights have been backed up, fanning out the growing Sunni-Shia strife in Pakistan ... the greatest danger facing the sectarian blood-shed. Gen. Musharraf was trying to divide the Islamic world after fuelling the tension between Sunni and Shia Muslims. Such declaration of a threatening purpose and the proclamation of a gathering storm and deserved evil are maintained by recourse to every form of violence. Pakistani leaders have not yet realised that the sectarian bloodshed has engulfed Iraq battling over the once-ruling Sunni minority there. Otherwise, Pakistan's independence, national unity as an Islamic nation and equality must be handicapped. D.H. Lawrence says in 'Men like Gods' : "When men think they are like gods they are usually much less than men, being conceited fools." General Musharraf played game with Islam as balls on the Kashmir question. The lust of crude religious passion is succeeded by the rage of conquest. Sectarianism separates friendship and creates civil war as fanaticism generates violence. A return to the blood-letting communalism that will tear Pakistan apart as we see in Iraq. The Kashmir question will devour Pakistan, indeed. Islamabad is bumping and gyrating like a political gambler. It is awfully shallow thinking.

According to Surinder Singh Oberoi, in 'Kashmir' : 'Then and Now', says : "Kashmiri separatist leaders are challenging the instrument of accession which was signed by the erstwhile Maharaja of Kashmir. Hari Singh, the hereditary ruler of Kashmir, who accepted to live in the Indian dominion on 27th Oct, 1947. This challenge is supported by Pakistan. India terms the accession as final an undisputed ... It is alleged that the Islamic twist by Pakistan is attracting muslim mercenaries, while Pakistan denies the charge and says that it is their moral duty to help them diplomatically." (New Approach).

Now it is their moral duty to help them in a terrorist way by using the weapons of religious fanaticism. And life in Kashmir is a festive mood of Roman Holiday to the supporters of religious fanaticism ... one of the encouraging by-products of the defect of Pakistan's policy and sectarianism. So, a new disillusioned romanticism. Pakistan believes scientific killing has rendered a fantastic solution of Kashmir question. Every country in the world is more anxious to avoid the expansion of terrorism than Pakistan is. Because Pakistan is just one hundred percent believer in war of terrorism. She believes that the enormous sacrifices that have been brought about by the scientific methods of killing innocent men, women and children have rendered terrorism a fantastic solution for Islamic globalisation, and all other international disputes, like America's role over the Middle East, Indo-Pak relations and others. Pakistan-sponsored Madrassas have been housed with girl students hailing from poor families in the North West Frontier province and other provinces of Pakistan including denaturalised girl students of other Islamic countries. So, the Western countries must be aware of the political fallout of an attack on burqa-clad women. Taliban-style campaign in Islamabad is on the go. Because it tries to impose Shariat law in the country after receiving the support of radical clerics.

In terrorism, as it is waged now, with the enormous losses on both sides, both sides will lose. It is a form of mutual suicide. And Pakistan firmly believes that the entire effort of modern Islamic society should be concentrated on an endeavour to outlaw terrorism as a method of the solution of problems between nations. The great questions are to Pakistan now : How are you going to end it? Are you going to let it go on indefinitely, destroying the fabric of society? You certainly have a tremendous calamity on your hands right now. Pakistan, a true believer in the otherness of Islamic orthodoxies and staunch supporter of triumphalism as an Islamic country, has, like a bird ostrich, always ignored and sidetracked all fundamental issues of Kashmir questions. And like a Spanish moss, they rely to grow up on other insubstantial issues so as to make the Kashmir question worse in a crucible of war on terrorism. The spoon-fed bureaucrats of timocracy tinted with greasy Islamic thoughts come to New Delhi to make as many as different forms for even trivial complaints as not related to the Kashmir question. Such double-dyed rascality and sin-laden moral illiteracy of Pakistani leaders fumbling with the Kashmir question have spoiled the record of being an Islamic country. Shameful and disgraceful is her principle of evil. Even General Musharraf was walking alone heinously with his old-trusted friend, religious fanaticism.

Islamic fanaticism over the vale of Kashmir and other European countries is a symbol of death and decay. This symbol is all around Pakistan as she sits playing solitaire, braiding classic Islamic myths into present relations. That sense of shattered fortitude, of picking up the pieces of fragmented ideologies in a kind of stoic anger after fortitude has been shattered, animates other Jehadi groups in the Islamic garden of terrorism. The spiral of security panic over the vale of Kashmir works like a spiral of inflation. The hysterical spy-scare and the west phobia of the Islamic countries have their repercussions in the western world. Everything is chained by habit. In their indefatigable hunt for subversive elements through Muzaffarabad smuggling out terrorism into the vale of Kashmir, the editors of Pakistani newspapers have come up with a major find. Pakistani clowns wear U.S. coats. Worse still, they indulge in slapstick. Their blood, frozen with horror at such an Un-Islamic behaviour, the editors have exposed these goings-on in print and demanded that clowns be sent to school for ideological re-education. There can be clowning around on such vital matters : And it is amazing that these iniquitous practices have lasted so long. Clowns will go to school. And when they escape they will be so dull that even the editors of Pakistani newspapers will approve.

A bit of friendly advice may be offered to our Foreign Minister. Mr. Foreign Minister, your prestige on the Kashmir question is slipping. If you do not surround yourself with stronger staff, better advisers, and make decisions faster and more courageously without regard for the flirtations of the politics over the Kashmiri people; if you are not less profligate of time and strength on the ceremonial and banquet circuit of New Delhi or Islamabad, to the certain detriment of serious Kashmir question, you will soon find public opinion turned against you. We would like to see that happens on the Kashmir debate, and neither would you. An insidious cunning should be shaken off.

The symbiosis of tinpot dictatorship and Islamic fundamentalism, over the Kashmir question, getting particular benefits from the others, is the standpoint of pulpit politics in Pakistan. It presents categorically the deep-seated shadows of this symbiotic relationship. If Islamabad cultivates fundamentalism at the margins for strategic ends, sooner or later it will bleed into the rest of Pakistani society. That, indeed, has happened, Lal Masjid, a large mosque and madrassa complex in the centre of Islamabad, has raised the flag of rebellion by saying that it will no longer follow the laws of the state but instead enforce shariat law on the rest of the country. A shariat court has been set up in its precincts... "such pulpit politics, conducted by the pulsating Jehadi slogans," has pulsed through the active veins of Jehadi groups. Pakistani rulers, shaken off with fear of their voice-worn phrases of death and destruction, have been nervous of their own self-created shadow of terrorism over the vale of Kashmir and even across the Western countries. It also reflects that any interference in its activities will supposedly bring forth a horde of suicide bombers, or so the leading maulana of Lal Masjid has warned. There is an ironic symmetry here, because Lal Masjid is as the literal as well as symbolic centre of power. It's located in one of the Islamabad's poshest areas, on land partially donated by late military dictator, Zia ul-Haq, and leading luminaries of Pakistan's establishment have been known to worship here. Yet it is trying to replicate the Taliban-like conditions of Pakistan's remote north-west.

Why? This is the deficit of democracy. What is democracy? It has come to mean whatever anyone wants it to mean. In Pakistan, it means the illiterate masses fight and die for the cause of Islam. All they work in private, not in public. They do not know why it wants anyone else to be free. It is fact, Pakistan, for over sixty years, has exercised tyranny of priesthood and despotism of mullocracy by many, more rigourously, more grievously, and more severally than by one. It is the mistakable form of the doctrine of sour grapes. This fallacious theory has not yet been resisted. A good world will shy away from a beautiful one to admire from a warm and safe retreat. The captain suggests that you need what is going on in the world and then let us know if you still want to be rescued.

And the Encyclopedia of Pakistan is supposed to say that Kashmir is an integral part of Pakistan. To wage of terrorism all over the vale of Kashmir is the birth-right of Pakistan to liberate the people of Kashmir. Like the 'Great Soviet Encyclopedia', Gen. Musharraf's 'In the Line of Fire', is something appalling in the history of distortion and untruth. George Orwell's nightmare of 'double-talk' and 'double-think' is now reality ... not only for Pakistani masses, but for the Islamic thinkers and researchers.

Pakistani rulers are likely to have learnt well 'The Great Soviet Encyclopedia' so as to distort the Kashmir question to the world. What is the 'Great Soviet Encyclopedia'?

'A' is for Atom ... but in its section on the development of atomic energy. The Encyclopedia makes no mention of Einstein. It was a Russian named Lebedev, apparently, not Einstein, who conceived the famous formula which is the basis of nuclear fission. In 1940, it seems, two Russian physicists discovered 'the fact that neutrons can start a chain of reactions from the nuclear fission of uranium, and so made the atomic bomb possible.'

It was Hitler who first extolled the merits of the Big Lie. If you tell a little lie, ordinary sensible people will see through it. But if you tell a great whooper of a lie, people will say, "Look, no one would dare invent a thing like that, there must be something in it ."

Pakistani rulers, following the footsteps of Stalinism, have long known and improved on the technique of Big Lie on the Kashmir question. Churchill, as we all know, is a cannibal. Like the Russian despotism, Pakistan's despotism over the vale of Kashmir is a democracy. Pakistan's war of terrorism single-handed. However, Pakistan Govt., like the then Russian Govt. under Stalin, is elevating the lie into a system of thought. It is also sickening and frightening the Kashmiri people.

Another interesting point is that the more Pakistan will be aggressive on Kashmir question, the more Pakistan's policy on Kashmir will ruin Indian Muslims. So many reasons are there :

1. Flummoxed by the ever-increasing fluidity of opinions on the Kashmir question, Pakistan's interests and welfare do not coincide with her conception of the welfare and interests of Muslims in Pakistan.
2. This is clear from Pakistan's attitude towards Kashmir.
3. Pakistan claims Kashmir first on the ground of the majority of state's people

being Muslims, and secondly, on the ground of the state being essential to its economy and defence.

4. To achieve her object, she has been threatening to launch Jehad against Kashmir and India.
5. It is a strange commentary on political beliefs that the same Muslims of Pakistan who would like Muslim of Kashmir to join them invaded the state in Oct. 1947, killing and pleading Muslim women, all in the interest of what they described as the liberation of Muslims of the state. In her oft-proclaimed anxiety, Pakistan is evidently prepared to sacrifice the interests of millions of Muslims in India.
6. Now the question is : if Muslims in Pakistan can wage a war against Hindus in Kashmir, why should not Hindus, sooner or later, retaliate against Muslims in India?
7. Pakistan is incapable of providing room and livelihood to the millions of Muslims of India, should they migrate to Pakistan? Yet her policy and action, if not changed soon, may well produce the result which she dreads.
8. India must be aware of committing no folly.
9. Pakistan is never tired of asserting that she is determined to protect the interests of Muslims in India and Kashmir. Why does not Pakistan express the same concern for Pathans, who are fighting for Paktoonistan, and independent homeland of their own?
10. Pakistan's policy towards Kashmir in particular tends to create conditions in this country which in the long run can only bring to create conditions in this country a widespread suffering and destruction.
11. Pakistan was not created on a religious basis. If it had been, our fate as well as fate of other minorities would have been settled at that time. Nor would the division of the sub-continent for reasons of religion, have left large minorities in India or Pakistan. This merely illustrates what we have said that the concept of Pakistan was vague, obscure and never clearly defined, or its likely consequences foreseen by the Muslim League, even when some of these should have been obvious.

Supporters of the idea of Pakistan, before this sub-continent was partitioned, discouraged any attempt to define Pakistan clearly and did little to anticipate the conflicting the problems which were bound to arise as a result of the two nation theory. The concept of Pakistan therefore became an emotional slogan with little national content. It never occurred to the Muslim League or its leaders that if a minority was not prepared to live with a majority on the sub-continent how could the majority be expected to tolerate the minority? What is Pakistan? A single undivided community has been broken into three fragments, each faced with its own problems.

SIMI's wicked programme of terror-mongering has made millions of muslims in India has thoroughly disgusted, fully flummoxed by the madness of Pakistani war-lords. The viciously executed Pakistan's propaganda abroad of presenting India in the role of an aggressor has lost all its charm. The world knows now who is the mischief maker? A plain man in plain thinking runs afield as humours and conceits shall govern. An army of evil words is planted in their memory on the Kashmir question. We expect a gentle answer not from rough and stubborn hearts who are never trained in offices of tender courtesy. Pakistan does a thousand harms and shortens life of terrorism. She has painted her face with Islamic extremism and used herself like a fool. Sometimes she smiles, sometimes grows impatient, making shrill echoes from Islamabad. Such is the infection of the time over the vale of Kashmir, stepping after fanaticism and marching upon the gentle bosom of Kashmiris.

We want to know who wants to read a book. An eager man always wants to read a book and a tired man always wants a book to read. To read a book or a book is a question of privacy to a country like Pakistan. The banned militant terrorist groups like Jaish-e-Mohammad are very much eager to join the ranks of radical clerics, spearheading a campaign to impose an Islamic law in the country. Jaish-e-Mohammad was supposed to pitch up a base in the Pakistani capital for the propagation campaign and distribution of pamphlets in tribal areas in 2001. And the outfit of Jaish-e-Mohammad was linked to a number of violent attacks in Jammu and Kashmir besides the attack on the Indian Parliament on December 13, 2001. And Pakistan sponsored terrorist groups are trying to defend SIMI with the help of radical clerics of Pakistan. Even anti-national slogans of Islamic groups in Kashmir are as suffocating as nauseating to any democratic country. For example, for the first time during the 18 years of insurgency in Jammu and Kashmir, pro-Laskar-e-Taiba (Let) slogans rented the air on April 22, 2007, at a meeting a hardline faction of Hurriyat Conference Chief Syed Ali Shah Geelani. Geelani said the Kashmir issue could be resolved only by allowing the people of Kashmir to make their choice. Any agreement between India and Pakistan would not be in accordance with the wishes and aspirations of the Kashmiris. Kashmir is just like a kidney to a body of Pakistan. If it be damaged, Pakistan's lifeblood will go to a burial ground. The nimble-minded and high-spirited juniors, in the institutionalised Islamic law, have reached the age of promise, being used to practising anti-India slogans as Geelani does. Every stage of development is catered for ... the bright percussion set with drums of Jehadi slogans; and other instruments of theocratic rulers will cultivate a musical instinct of anti-India slogans, and teach accuracy and precision of Islamic laws all over the vale of Kashmir. The library unit is stocked with bright, well-printed Jehadi books. Old-fashioned desks and hard chairs have been replaced by spacious table-topped desks and chairs with padded seats. Step by step, he or she is trained and fitted for the membership of Jehadi group and for the most suitable career.

ULFA is primarily a non-Islamic organisation. According to U.S. Security think tank, Stratford, "Religion, ethnicity and ideology lose relevance within this military network, as each group has a common interest in furthering their military and financial capabilities by working together." A growing

'Islamisation' of north-eastern military movements in India is being actively promoted by Pakistan's ISI and Bangladesh's intelligence service and could constrain India to dig itself out of the militant trap Pakistan has set. ULFA's growing links with Bangladeshi Islamists and Jihadist elements in the area are increasingly coming to light. Pakistan's ISI has aksed ULFA to refuse to negotiations with the Indian Govt. These two agencies are working clandenstinely to bring all North-East-based insurgent outfits and Jihadist elements under one umbrella. This is why India is investing heavily in a neighbour like Myanmar, which is the only country in the neighbourhood that extends some cooperation in going after Indian militants. Both Pakistan's and Bangladesh's intelligence services have told the outfit not to hold the talks. It means that for India to deal with its North-East problems, it will first have to neutralise the effect of the ISI on these groups.

Now it is clear that a vengeful canker would eat both Bangladesh and Pakistan upto death. Because truth needs no colour. Their eyes look red and raw. Bangladesh has now become a marvellous neighbour to Pakistan. Owing to Islamic fanaticism, Jehadis are toying with Islamic gospel of truth, and make that truth a labyrinth of riddles. Shakespeare, in 'Love's Labour Lost', says : "Wise things seem foolish and rich things but poor."

Pakistan has kept up the terrorism hysteria with the help of Jehadi lords for a pretty long time. She knows that she has not the strength, without being-aided, to take the remaining part of Kashmir by force. And she has been working feverishly by means of her foreign propaganda to convince the world that Kashmir, the population of which is largely Muslims, really belongs to her. Some foreigners have expressed their concern in platitudinous languages. And Pakistan has repeated the fiction that the 'Hindu Maharaja' of Kashmir was the arch-devil. Why? Because he had been continuing his oppressive rule over the Kashmiris who would have rebelled but for the fact that they had been held by the Indian troops. Nehru has acknowledged his defeat at the hand of Pakistan's way of propaganda. On August 10, 1951, Nehru said : "Pakistan is such a past master in the art of telling lies that even if India wants to compete with it in this campaign, we are bound to fall. Nobody can beat Pakistan in spreading falsehoods." Strange to say, Md. Ali Jinnah and other Pakistani rulers had been for years the friends and allies of the Hindu Maharaja and had supported him through thick and thin against the struggle for freedom led by Sheikh Abdullah. Former rulers of Pakistan had been able to cover this story by a mendacious propaganda.

The liberators of Kashmir today are the rulers of the State just as the successors of the liberators of the U.S.A. are today the rulers of that country. What would the U.S. leaders think, if the enemies of the American struggle for independence claimed theselves to be the liberators of his country as the Pakistani leaders have been doing at the present moment in regard to Kashmir?

For over sixty years, the rulers of Pakistan have been able to mislead millions and millions of men, women and children so much so that even the political parties opposed to them have been forced to join in the cry of Jehad thus reducing themselves to the solution of utter helplessness. Is this, too, a small gain?

There is another record of Pakistan's achievement. The constant cry for Jehad has nullified the agreement between India and Pakistan. The Jehadi gives the finishing touch to the edifice of the Islamic state the like of which will not be found in any part of the modern world, including the Muslim countries in Asia and Africa. She has been able to throw a carpet over this catastrophe. Is this a small gain? This is a different age ... the age of vast population, of propaganda, of ballistic missiles and of politics based on a very different kind of power.

The Anglo-American friends of Pakistan, having deliberately tried to twist the facts of the Kashmir question, have come to realise that they will lose and lose heavily. From Liaquat Ali Khan down to the present rulers of Pakistan, everyone was, and is, America's stooge number one.

A battle is going on inside Pakistan. The battle between two wolves is inside the provinces of Islamic country like Pakistan. One is evil. It is anger, envy, jealousy, sorrow, regret, greed, arrogance, self-pity, guilt resentment, inferiority, lies, false pride, superiority and ego. The other is good. It is joy, peace, love, hope, serinity, humility, kindness, benevolence, empathy, generosity, truth, compassion and faith. Now the question is : Which wolf wins? The answer is the one you feed.

According to Virgil : "Happy is he who has been able to learn the causes of things." Pakistan has not yet learnt that lesson and not been able to learn the causes of her nefarious but henious activities over the vale of Kashmir but nurturing the faculty of inquiry how to gather up the gathering storm over the Kashmir question, and dispatching all sense of proportion and exploring alternative means of assessment on Indian question.

Defying all norms of eschatological belief, such inconsistently variable shambolic logic is praising the hymnody of Islamic fanaticism to Jehadis on the Kashmir question and erring on the side of Islamic globalisation.

So, the shambolic administration fully banks on the terrorist groups. Healing is a matter of time, but is sometimes also a matter, says Hippocrates. But the Portugease proverb says, "There is a remedy for everything. It is called death."

Islamic countries are concerned with the murderous clash of two faiths ... the Shia and the Sunni ... inextricably mingled with sectarian politics for their own religious-cum-ideological goals. All they stand on propaganda machine and on police tyranny over the Kashmiris. Besides having this, Pakistan is wrapped up with unusual buoyancy of religious frenzy on Kashmir, headed by Jehadi militants whose natural instincts have always turned towards prudence and procrastination. The blood courses the whole body of Islamic nation like Pakistan when the heart of the nation throbs. And the future of Pakistan, the security of the state and the inner harmony of a people still anxiously divided by an unbridled faith are all in doubt. Such romantic temperament creates a mystery in the vale of Kashmir in order to impose on Kashmiri people an artificial concord, paralysing hopelessness of those who allow themselves to be dazed by possibilities of disaster. The rejuvenation of Pakistan's traditional patriotism on the Kashmir question begins when they have discouraged in the writings of Kashmir the dynamic concept of terrorism has somehow gone wrong. These idiosyncracies of the youth, remain with them and keep them laughing inspite of an ageing body of old thoughts, passing, guiding and weathering through more than sixty years of ever-mounting anxiety. Dismay becomes despair.

The infirmity of Pakistan's politics and the dubious facade of military preparations against India, with its load of shame and bewilderment have weighed more bitterly on Islam than on most of the Muslims in Pakistan. Many of the stories on Kashmir, Pakistan has so far deliberately cooked up and spiced up with ill-digested propaganda, through press and other media, are unbearable and pathos. It is the dark side of crescent-shaped moon. If we can afford to be patient, Pakistan's hand over Kashmir may be found to contain within herself the seeds of her own destruction. It is the long canker of hypocrisy and indifference that wears down Pakistan on Kashmir question. Truly speaking, Kashmir is standing in a deceptive quiet. So, our minds teeming with memories of Kashmir, half in a trance; so strong is the question that forgotten events have chanced upon us; we go down the little winding road to where the pastures of old memories open at the foot, on either side. It is the shadow of the past. We can pull up from our rag-bag of historical learning enough information of Kashmir debate to put personalities in this regard into the Kashmir issue. We can go so far as to what Jinnah in his futile attempt had to retreat from Kashmir crisis ... from crisis in his own career and in the fortunes of the party 'Muslim League' with which his own career was inextricably connected. In courage, energy and resolution, the virtues distinguish Nehru, the man of action rather than the thinker. His outlook on Kashmir problem undoubtedly was not an exalted one. He differed only from only too many of his contemporaries and remained almost unswervingly loyal to Lord Mountbatten and his wife.

Terrorist camps in Pakistan are indeed 'a world apart' a world in thrall to the monstrous buffonery. They live on beneath the pall of an irredeemable evil; organised horror has massed upon horror into one vast bludgeon of the valley of Kashmir. Pakistan is like a Hitler's concentration camp of religious fanaticism showing the horrifying abstract of their destiny, ... a hideous hunger in their bellies, terror in their bones. Democracy has lost its values on most Pakistanis. Why? A majority of Pakistanis favour army rule. According to the survey on the choices of the people of South Asia, six out of ten Pakistanis prefer military administration. Because, the higher the education, the lower the support for the army.

Half of Pakistanis are not keen on democracy, the CSDS (the Centre for the study of Developing Societies) survey said, ostensibly reflective of the sentiment in urban areas that have been critical of the two short-lived tenures of Benazier Bhutto and Nawaz Sharif. The only democratically elected government to complete its tenure was that of Z.A. Bhutto (1972-77), when the country got its present constitution. Pakistan appears to be an exception in that people in South Asia overwhelmingly support democracy. In Pakistan, about the half respondents said that democratic or non-democratic forms of govt. made no difference to them. Why? South Asia is more eager for democratic pattern of society than South East Asia, East Asia, post-Soviet Europe and Latin America. Whereas seven out of ten persons in East Asia say that democracy is suitable or very suitable for their own country. With the exception of Pakistan, about two thirds of those who responded preferred democracy to any other form of govt. Why? The answer is very simple. If Pakistan had a purely democratic country, Kashmir question would not have appeared. The poor would have plundered away the rich, religious fanaticism would not have been there, property would have been saved and liberty would have been crowned with success. The past sixty years in Pakistan experimented with fascism embalmed by terrorism over the vale of Kashmir. Today, to Pakistan, Kashmir question means, 'Fanaticism is as good as terrorism. Mullocracy is as good as theocracy.' To Pakistan, terrorism is dynamic, but democracy is static. And the ills of Kashmir problem cannot be cured by democracy. Timid rulers of Pakistan get used to the calm of despotism to the boisterous area of liberty in Kashmir. Because, for the solution of Kashmir problem, tyranny and despotism can be more accessible to Jehadis, more rigorously, more severely than by democracy. Cervantes, in Don Quixote, says, "Revenge is not good in cold blood." Killing Kashmiri Hindu Pundits is better than money in the bank. So, what an eye does not see, the heart does not grieve.

The pattern of power politics in Pakistan has changed. Whereas in power politics, our politicians, on the Kashmir question, delighting in the nuances of power politics, have been playing a long game of bluffing and manoeuvring, for over sixty years, each move and counter-move being made with the intention of strengthening their position but also of preserving peace in Kashmir.

The first problem of political controversy on the Kashmir question is that of making the words. The bulletin and platform tell us that the Kashmir issue lies between two abstraction ... the one called secular democracy or a planned economy. Our country will remain a free country whether it will return to individualistic anarchy, the unbridled rule of the rich and mass unemployment.

Kashmir is only for those who are incapable of quiet abstraction and who love the game of party politics for its own sake who can take such language very seriously. It is a trick of shambolic words to the Kashmiris that they own the lands and they are a part of the state. It is equally a trick of words to tell him that he is as free as press lord to start a newspaper because there is no law on the statute-book which forbids them to do so. Neither language corresponds to realilty.

There are grave problems in the political life of Kashmir today. If we are not able to meet the foreign and domestic threats with which we are menaced, catastrophe awaits us, and it would indeed be a superficial frivolity which at such a time as this suggested that it does not matter how we are governed or who governs us. The leaders of one party rather than the other are more likely to carry through an effective foreign policy, or an effecitve rearmament, more likely to balance trade, to improve economy at home, or to preserve industrial peace.

The Indian tradition on Kashmir question has shown in the past an affectionate leniency both towards the sincere and convinced objector in matters of personal conscience. How far this tradition was the result, and how far one of the moving causes, of the strength and cohesion of the social fabric of Kashmir would be an ideal inquiry.

A good leadership must be there in Kashmir. Why? To educate for leadership is still a primary duty of universities, and to get such an education should be one of the chief motives which bring students to them. For the most part, our political leaders, either in parliament or in the State of Jammu and Kashmir, are merely following out in front; they do not marshal the sufferers the way they are going. Because Kashmir question is to them a milch cow. Words are used but they are in a foreign tongue but not meant to be understood. How little they know themselves. Whereas the head of the State considers himself outside the law, and imposes inhuman activities on the innocent people of Kashmir. A good leader talks little. On the Kashmir question, words are used, characters of politicians are used, nature of terrorist activities is used, situations in Kashmir are used but there is no direct contact between New Delhi and Islamabad, and between Govt policy and public understanding. It is called Romantic Agony. So much has Romanticism by now become part of our daily lives and thoughts in the vale of Kashmir. The homely features of our political leaders on the Kashmir question are etherealised into the saturnine countenances of international dictators whose secret no man can fathom.

India has already celebrated her sixty years of independence. But no solution on Kashmir issue. Sixty years old? Or 60 years young? A super power of the future? Or in the danger of falling by the wayside as the reality of the 'other' India catches up? Who will answer this question?

While British media were in no doubt that Pakistan had failed on almost all counts and had little to celebrate about on its 60th birthday. India proved trickier to categorise neatly as either a half-full or half-empty glass. Mystery plays a blustering tyrant.

The Times found itself caught up between Confucius who, it recalled, described 60 years as the 'age of wisdom' when all things could be seen clearly. But the Kashmir question has not yet been clearly visualised by our psychologically half-baked political leaders. Picasso who believed that at 60 one could start to be truly young ... "except that by then it was too late."

Now the question is : How did India measure up to these two contradictory definitions? The answer was a bit of both. The country was certainly 'determined to demonstrate that it is never too late to be young. We are all religiously or politically etherized by our political ethnocentrism.

"The nation has a dancing step, an elan that eluded independent India until well into the middle age," the newspaper noted in an editorial headed, "After Midnight" highligting India's economic growth in recent years. But India was still carrying too much baggage from the past that was likely further progress. Democracy, it said, was thriving in India but accountability was quite "another matter." The Guardian on 15th August, 2007, was even more forthright pointing out that India might be on the verge of becoming a great power "but at what cost?" (Hasan Suroor, from London, reported to the Hindu, August 16, 2007, on 'British media cheer India).

Truly Speaking, India today is a land of deadpan comedy, of fifth columnists, of hypocrites, of opportunists, of political jargonism, and of myriad fold of nefarious activities rolling down under the red carpet of democracy, secularism, and evil-digested Kashmir question. This is the land where once the cultivator and the herdsman and the hundreds of thousands of small, humble village communities whose way of life had not changed in the slow centuries since Alexander of Macedon and his warriors had poured through the passes to conquer the unknown land that had been old when Greece was young. The villagers were more tolerant and charitable than the city dwellers, for ploughing, sowing, reaping and irrigation would not wait while men sat in circles and listened to windy and grandiloquent phrase-makers who promised overnight Utopias provided that this or that class of sect, creed or colour were first destroyed or routed. They toiled hard and they were a kindly people, and the English in India listened to them and felt more relaxed and at peace than they had for many days.

The same gloomy and funereal picture as is seen today is pathetically heartaching scenario not only in Kashmir but in India also, even after 60 years of independence. And the Kashmiris have still endured the heat and hazards of hot political camouflage over the valley. Terrorism and conspiracy have swallowed up the aromatic scents of flowers and all the familiar sounds of so many Indian villagers lying about the vale of Kashmir. With a savage and concentrated fury, Islamic fanaticism has razed down the valley in a dazed nightmare. The valley feels a terrible pain in its heart, finding no room to sheer panic and horror.

The Hindu minority in Kashmir seems to have been living under the shadow of a gradually increasing terror. The closing years of 2000 were marked by a massive wave of Kashmiri Hindu Pundits from Kashmir. It is conditioned partly by deteriorating economic conditions but more by the scare raised in the Kashmiri Hindu mind by incessant talk of making Pakistan a full-blooded terrorist state. The criminal's mind is abnormal and diseased, and needs a remedy rather than annihilation. Pakistan has perfected the technique of affecting injured innocence even while harbouring evil desings. For all her acts of hostility towards India, she tries, often crudely, to shift the blame on to this country which is really the aggrieved party. Pakistan evidently believes with Goebbles that a slander, repeated a number of times, will stick. That this is unfortunately true in the perverse world of today, in which not moral values and considerations of justice but power politics and selfish game of defeatism hold away is clear from the measure of credence which Pakistan appears to enjoy among certain groups in the international arena.

By piling up provocations, she hopes to drive India to exasperations. India should be careful not to do anything that would help Pakistan's false and pernicious propaganda. To say so is by no means to suggest that we should for ever submit meekly to pin-pricks. Shocks and hostility. Preoccupied as she is with her own internal affairs, she can ignore the potentialities of the present only at grave peril to her hard-won freedom. Having accepted partition on a communal basis, India cannot afford to be blind to these tragic developments in Kashmir.

One principle reason why people in Pakistan are so often useless is that the rulers divide and shift their attention among a multiplicity of objects and pursuits.

False friends are like our shadow, keeping close to us while we walk in the sunshine, but leaving us the instant we cross into the shade. Men of great parts in Pakistan are often unfortunate in the management of public business, because they are apt to go out of the common road of terrorism in Kashmir by the quickness of their imagination. Another reason is that it is foolish to live on past experience. Why? Because it is very dangerous, if not a fatal habit to judge ourselves to be safe because of something that we felt or did sixty years ago. The decline of Islamic thoughts due to intensely perverted fiendish nature of fanaticism over the vale of Kashmir and even other countries is the decline of Islamic nations. Why? Because the two keep pace in their downward tendency. It is known to all that men always lose half of what is gained by violence. And the primary objective of India should always be : what is gained by argument on the Kashmir question is gained forever. And the alienated barons of Islamic terrorism set serfs and villians free over the valley. Ideologically, there is little to choose between Pakistan's objectivity on the Kashmir question and the heat of cold-blooded terrorism which is Pakistan's pet fantasy except that each militant flaunts a different religious banner. Patriotically, both are pointing to the dubious glories of a dim past. She has totally forgotten how to walk boldly and wisely in the light she has.

Fears and suspicion are still the dominant factors in Kashmir, paralleled in potent demagogy or tyrannical repression in the domestic lives of Kashmiri Hindu Pundits. Lip service is paid by all and sundry power to direct the affairs, and governance of mankind seems to believe those goals attainable in practice save through the exploitation of fear. This complex is like a Babylonian captivity which feeds on itself by luxury and extravagance which the bitterness of partition proved incurable by the international surgery of Islamic fanaticism ... a surgery of Armageddon. It is a dread gamble of Pakistan over the Kashmir question. History is being made very rapidly in Pakistan now. Her complacency of terrorism in Kashmir is one of the most insiduous and the worst diseases, for it can eat like a canker into the very heart of Pakistan. Count that day lost, whose low descending sun views from your hand no worthy action done. Contemporaries appreciate the man rather than the merit but posterity will regard the merit rather than the man. If religious fanaticism is the mother of terrorism, want of education is the father of them. For many centuries, sword and blood were allies in Islamic thoughts and ideologies. Now it is harmful to the masses of men in Kashmir and can be enforced on them only by terror. Because they live under the weight of old and odious views. Truly speaking, it is a frightful leap in the dark. For this reason, we call Pakistan a lover of death instinct. People in Pakistan share with fanaticism and dies with terrorism. She runs faster than death, either by economically or by politically or by religiously or by other deadly means. A single conversation across a table, on the Kashmir issue, with a good but sensible leader, is worth a month's study of books. The desire of power in excess causes any ruler to fall; the desire of escapism, sidetracking any deal or conversation, in excess causes a ruler to fall; but in a well-calculated and well-furnished conversation is no excess; neither can a ruler nor a dictator come into danger by it. Faced with a world of rapidly becoming conscious of militant jehadis babying away their exuberant religious fanaticism, the disadvantages of Shia-Sunni disparity are too obvious to allow any danger of a split amongst the Islamic nations.

So, the Kashmir solution lies, therefore, in the rejection of the totalitarian concepts of Pakistan which makes a marionette of man, and in the reorientation of Pakistan's political philosophy, on the Kashmir issue, where in man is considered as a supreme value and the degree of freedom enjoyed by the Kashmiris becomes the progress of Jammu and Kashmir. Genuine good taste consists in syaing much in few words, in choosing among our thoughts on the Kashmir issue, in having order and management in what we say, and in speaking with composure. History, through God, reverses man's transitory decisions. The early Christian martyrs suffered with fortitude their long agony under Nero in the strength of their faith ... on the place of their martyrdom the Cross now stands, and the City of Rome, scene of incredible horrors, is now a stronghold of the Church of Christ.

Most of the political hurdless have not been cleaned but the clouds of terrorism still lower menacingly on the vale of Kashmir. Any person belonging to India, philosopher or politician or any one else, talking about world peace will, before he proceeds any distance with this theme, be asked, what about Kashmir? what about India and Pakistan? The problems of yesterday are also with us today.

If any historians live to tell the tale they alone will be in a position in years hence to assess the true implications of Nehru's many momentous decisions on Kashmir. Terrorism is so tremendous and the desire for peace is so inextricably intermingled with the desire for security in Kashmir that there is a certain unreality in the moral values involved. That a destructively potential weapon of religious fanaticism loses its moral justifications today in proportion to its powers of destruction is a contention which is seen to be without validity. Truly speaking, Nehru has made a mockery of all provisions about Kashmir. Not only that he has inflamed the fires of fanatical Muslim opinion all over the valley in favour of Jehad in Kashmir. Inter-Services Intelligence (ISI) in Pakistan the most political barometer of Kashmir question for the ruling Govt. ... surrenders its sovereignty at the altar of the collective ego of the general will of Islamic jehadis on the Kashmir issue.

As the Kashmir problem was brewing up, there had been an all-round deterioration of the Congress party, leading to apathy and cynicism. There was a rivalry for selfish and emotional advantages. Solving the Kashmir problem was becoming a gallery of mockery and a ding-dong battle of mocking-bird. And the Congress organization had then become totalitarian. confidence is a plant of slow growth, especially in the Congress.

Roman holidays of terrorism, coordinated by Pakistan-sponsored stratocratic Govt. and Bonapartism, in the valley and other parts of the world, are familiar pattern. Muslim terrorists kill their own brethren. Those who are killed are obviously wolves and political hyenas. These holidays are like breezes of fanatical air to the flame of carnage; gentle ones will fan it out, but strong ones will put it out. The wolves are only amused and the hyenas ae laughing in their lairs as bleary-eyed packs of humans stalk the valley fringes, whistling for Jehadi slogans. The realisation of Truth is incomparably more than belief in Truth. Machiavelli said : "he who establishes a dictatorship and does not kill Brutus or he who founds a republic and does not kill the sons of Brutus will reign only a short time." As from Machiavelli's point of view, Benazier Butto was laid to rest next to her father's grave in Ghari Khuda Baksh, deep in Larkana in rural southern Pakistan. Pakistan, enshrouded in with political nihilism and social anachronism, is now on a volcanic rock of religious fanaticism. Pakistan may be a bundle of contradictions because her educational and religious systems are a mixture of conflicting principles and tendencies. That Pakistan has nuclear weapons is the most significant problem to the rest of the world. Today Kashmir has been thrown out of focus and rendered 'curioser and curioser'. Avarice is wider than injustice, and all fallen nations lost liberty through avarice which engendered injustice. Benazir Bhutto's assassination would be the direst one to the future of Pakistan.

Who was Benazier Bhutto? And what was her reaction to India on Kashmir issue during her tenure as Prime Minister of Pakistan? While reacting to India's national security advisor M.K. Narayan's remark that Benazir Bhutto cannot be trusted, she said : "We cannot leave the people of Kashmir at the mercy of India ... Kashmir is certainly a core issue but it is not an issue that should be allowed to derail Indo-Pak relations or dialogue ... Rajiv called me on his way to the Commonwealth (summit) to say that he could not keep his promise to withdraw from Siachen and that he would do it only after the elections (1989) ... India was in a complete mess at that time. Does anyone remember that it was I who kept my promise to Prime Minister Gandhi when we met and he appealed to me for help in tackling the Sikhs. Has India forgotten December, 1988? Have they forgotten the results of that meeting and how I helped curb the Sikh militancy? ... Does India really believe I am not a friend? I thought India always regarded me as a factor for peace, as a factor for India-Pakistan stability."

In comparison with her father's mental make-up against India on the Kashmir question, Mr. Zulfiqar Ali Bhutto's statement on the creation of Bangladesh is rather invulnerable. Accusing India of starting the 1971 Indo-Pak war, he said : "We will for a thousand years .... My dear countrymen, my dear friends, my dear students, labourers, peasants, those who fought for Pakistan. We are facing the worst crisis in our country's life, a deadly crisis. We have to pick up the pieces, but we will make a new Pakistan, a prosperous and progressive Pakistan." Mr. Bhutto lived through the inescapable, but encouraging tug-of-war between the two systems : that of power and that of principle. Whereas Islamabad is constrained by the pains and horror of "Merchant of Islamic terrorism." One does not like hot, the other does not like cold, make it tepid to make an agreement on Kashmir issue.

The first principle of Islamic politics in Kashmir is Machiavelli's : that there are no principles in it : that wielding of power over the Kashmiri Muslims must occur. The second principle is Islamic aphorism about power : that it demoralises. Our own era seems to bear out both. For Machiavelli's emergence of the new nation states ... India and Pakistan ... we can furnish the emergence of international groupings. We can offer the same secular absolutisms, still proliferating within the Islamic groups strictly obedient to their own established institutions. We can show clashes of secular religions especially on the so-called pseudo Left on the Kashmir question. Our national, international and continental groupings clash. Anarchy seems to be coming with great strides upon Kashmir.

All over the world, contaminated by our immediate past errors, we strive to bring back order, scruple and principle into societies which willy-nilly face a crowding, narrowing, common future. Everywhere leaders get more scared, more disposed to mere expedients. Everywhere the leaders in India get more sceptical. Everywhere everyone feels more emptiness at the core of his ideologies. Whence is it to come? Not from the discredited disillusioning compulsion of collectivism. So much is clear from the tide beneath the waves of Kashmir politics.

Why will not Pakistan long for democracy? The problem of democracy is therefore the problem of obedience. To whom is it given and why? In the past there were kings and Emperors, but they were disposed by colonial rule. The transition to democracy now demands that obedience should be given to an elected Govt. as altogether vague concept for the Indian peasant. The failure of obedience at the mass level is understandable, but it is the failure of loyalty in the upper ranks that has led to the downfall of democracy in the Islamic countries like Pakistan and others. Is a rigorous doctrine like Islam the only answer? Pakistan has moved closer to authoritarian rule. Every Pakistani ruler, a man of contrarities, but he was, or are, usually disguised, or so pleasantly revealed, as to give the semblance of a harmonious nature.

American blood and money are being poured into Asia in continuation of the same old story and not for safeguarding the freedom of Islamic countries. Indeed, the fact of her imperialism is the very essence for properly assessing America's policy and role in Asia. According to the Persian proverb : "One pound of learning requires ten pounds of common sense to apply it." Our middle-of the-road policy is founded mainly on the idea of a moral force ... really a euphemistic for an overall importance very largely exhibited in the last sixty years by the standstill in our whole life and finally laid bare either by the Pakistan-sponsored Machiavellian policy over the valley or by the Chinese note on Tibet. It is the irritability at the sang froid with which we are endangering ourselves and the whole world that has expressed itself through the editorial pen.

Imperialism has given birth to terrorism. By agreeing to partition. India had agreed to the principle of self-determination. If we had followed the same line the case of Tibet, we might have avoided the birth of the Tibetan problems? Because peking would have had no excuse for her military action under cover of suzerianty. It is a pity India accepted the principle of suzerainty one people over another. Suzerainty smacks of imperialism. Geographically, racially, culturally, and even historically, Tibet may be a part of China. But that should not mean that the Tibetans must live under peking.

Pakistan is lacking in the qualities of self-determination. That leads us to the conclusion that self-determination is the only correct remedy against US imperialism in Pakistan. Between two evils, choose neither, between two goods, choose both. It is Pakistan that invites US. to be a banana republic. A fool may have his coat embroidered with gold, but it is a fool's coat still.

As the Kashmir happened to step in this sub-continent, the Congress at the Centre were not popular but parlour politics on the Kashmir issue. The people cried and irritated by Congress's sins of commission and omission on this issue are ready for change. But are the groups, dissident and rebel, sufficiently infused with those Jehadi slogans which alone have induced the Kashmiris to change sides? Why ... logically and philogically ... blood, toil and unrelenting violence should be sandwiched between 'to pour oil on troubled waters of Dal Lake'. It arouses a pleasant, playful disturbance in the valley. It is a general indictment of the entire body of Kashmir University students that the indiscipline and laxity complained of is a legacy of the tumultous days of the past when defiance of law was encouraged. But what was glorified then is now frowned upon and what was patriotism then is now branded as indiscipline and disgraceful behaviour of Islamic organisations like SIMI. The education doled out in our universities particularly amongst the Muslim students of India is regimented and uninspiring. Initiative and natural aptitude are automatically stifled. So. the Kashmir question keeps going with its deadly wings of invulnerable passion of religious fanaticism. That the world is now divided between the Islamic and the Western blocs ... is a fact. It is idle to concieve of an altogether independent foreign policy to combat terrorism if we exist as a nation. Where none of the two mighty blocs considers India an ally. The irresponsible expression of opinion by some of our leaders, either on nuclear deal or on the Kashmir issue, may have enlisted India a doubtful ally. Very much suspicions happen to rev up the by-product of conspiracy on the Indo-Pak ties in the times of Benazir Bhutto, Prime Minister of Pakistan (1988-1990) and (1993-96). In an interview in 2006, she says, "When I look at the rise of religious parties, the reorganisation of the Taliban and the persistence of the militant groups, I worry for Pakistan's future." In 1988, she pulled back on Pak support to Khalistanis, but upped the ante on Jammu and Kashmir. In 1989, Jehadis launched into Jammu and Kashmir from POK starting a period of bloody insurgency. A famous video show Benazir at a meeting in POK shouting 'Azadi' and pointing towards India. In 1993, Dawood Ibrahim came from Dubai, given safe haven in Karachi and even a Pak support. In 1996, it was during her tenure, the Taliban took control of Afganistan. During 1989-90 Benazir Bhutto's government stopped supporting the separatist forces in Punjab but began to back terrorist operating in Jammu and Kashmir. The following are the excerpts from the Pakistani leader's (Benazir Bhutto) famous book, 'The Daughter of the East'. On Simla Agreement, Benazir Bhutto says :"If there is an agreement, we will say a girl has been born. If there is no agreement, we will say a girl has been born." What a dirty play of her chauvinistic character! Benazir says :"The Simla Accord returned the 5,000 square miles taken from us by India. It laid the foundation for the restoration of communication and trade between our two countries and did not prejudice the stand of Pakistan or India on the Jammu and Kashmir disputes."

While her father, Zulfiqar Ali Bhutto criticised the US for providing military aid to India during and after the Sino-Indian war of 1962. In 1963, he was appointed Pakistan's foreign minister. He blamed India for the 1971 war.

It is fact that Pakistan's Islamisation was born under the constant surveillance and spying supervision of General Zia-Ul-Haq; and General Musharraf had fertilized the well-grown up tree with sap and juice of Al Quaida and other terrorist organisations. Pakistan's policy over the valley is conducted by the militant groups today. Pakistan is the largest prison house of terrorism locked with the levers of religious fanaticism, guarded by the terrorists. So Pakistan is disgraced with inexpiable broils, and deluged with blood. The secret is out and the world knows that Pakistan is a terrorist country. According to Bacon, "He that gives advice builds with one hand; he that gives good counsel builds with both; but he that gives admonition and bad example builds with one hand and pulls down with other." In all debates on the Kashmir question, it has exposed Pakistan's antagonism. Looking beyond Pakistan, who can believe that the Pakistani people desire war? They are a peace-loving people and for that reason have never been strong outside their own territories. Have the common folk of Pakistan any voice in the politics of Kashmir which their resolute rulers are pursuing? No more than under the tyrannies of military rulers. The responsibility of the ministers who speak for the freedom loving nations and the liberation movement of Kashmiri Muslims is immense. If true to their role, they dare not miss any straw pointing to peace. The best that can be said of it is that it does not bang the door to furhter discussion on the Kashmir issue. Discussion would produce nothing but further wordy warfare. Well, why not say so in the fewest possible words? All at night are indoors joining the family circle, when all was risked and much was lost in strategical direction of Kashmir operations. No such leadership is discernible. Is anarchy then to take hold of the valley? All Pakistani rulers are ambitious, particularly on the Kashmir issue. As dogs in a wheel, or squirrels in a cage, ambitious men still climb and climb, with great labour and incessant anxiety, but never reach the top.

Tremendous happenings like partition, Kashmir problem, Hindu-Muslim disparity leading to communalism, and the long-standing agony of Pakistan-sponsored terrorism violently sweeping all over the valley following the massacre of many Kashmiri Hindu pundits together with thousands of innocent people, and the tragic march of religious fanaticism with their almost unbelievable tales of human cruelty, Bonapartism with rapaciousness and lust has mirrored upon the artist and writer. And the sixty years of independence followed up by the Kashmir issue had fantastically shrivelled up the bygone years. The narrow cultural walls of ten divide Indian from Indian due to Kashmir issue. And this tends to morbidity of outlook. Is Islamabad a good watchdog? If it hears a suspicious noise at the gateway of Kashmir at night, it has only to wake the terrorist groups and it begins to bark.

The Congress capacity and calibre on the solution of Kashmir problem are painfully evident. Why? A fair proportion of the cabinet was drawn from outside the Congress. It was the lack of ability and character in the second rank of Indian leadership to fight out the Kashmir problem. Mr. Nehru faced a crisis in character but the rot had already infected other branches and twigs of acitivity. And Mrs. Indira Gandhi had a symptom of a wide-spread absence of any seriousness of purpose and solid study of facts. Congress atmospherics are largely responsible for this lacuna. Does it not shame the leaders into camouflaging the people?

Even the policy pursued by the Sheikh Abdullah Govt. was crippling the Hindus of Jammu and Kashmir, making them economically weak and ineffective. And the provocative speeches delivered by the Pakistani politicians, occupying responsible positions, have aggravated the tempo of Kashmir problem. He only explored contrasting views.

People tend to divide themselves in the present world into two categories, those who are actively preparing for war and those who, whatever history and warfare may bring, must passively endure the discomfort and austerity to carry on the work and the life of the world. Islamabad has got a training in anti-India hymns of hate and betrayal in peace. Terrorism is more horrible than bloodshed and slavery.

Mrs. Indira Gandhi's touch on the Kashmir issue as she saw it is so keen and fresh, her wit so clinching, and her ability to grasp the Kashmir issue so all-round and balanced that to read her is a tonic, and to disagree with her an exciting danger. There is no nonsense about her decision on the liberation of Bangladesh. And Mr. A.B. Bajpayee's touch on the Kashmir issue is that he had never been bamboozled by any spacious idea. Though he does not stand any flummery, he is tolerant and genial. A sagacious man of the world has gone through the world. He seemed to have been animated by a buoyant gusto which made him relish all that he met with Gen. Musharraf at the Agra Summit. He did not expect perfection on the problem. But he was undismayed by the contrariness of Kashmir question. Mr. Bajpayee seemed capable of many ideas. Gen. Musharraf followed cleverness till he fancied he was clever. Being perfect sure of what Mr. Bajpayee wanted to say, he said it without stint, and said all of it. If he had an argument to develop, he would not let Musharraf off a single step, and rammed his conclusions with a shrewd thrust or two.

Mr. Zulfiqar Ali Bhutto had and kept, in spite of increasing bad temper and arrogance, the gift of winning people of Pakistan and of not making any more enemies than he had to. But he was a victim of his own misjudgement of the situation, of his exaggeration of the need of fighting for a thousand years. His method is nearer than that of the need of fighting for a thousand years. His method is of the therapeutic positivist ... dissolving many a controversy by a bombardment of argument directed without evidence, either disapperaed altogether or reappeared in new clothes and with a new aspect. From the beginning, the Kashmir issue has been rather haphazardly done. The result is long and thorough account of Pakistan's involvement in the career of terrorism in the valley that dedicated religious fanaticism through the vicissitudes of partition, Hindu-Muslim disparity, independence and communalism. The bewilderment today lies not in the changes but in the sense of anarchy and confusion that haunts over India.

Life of democracy in this sub-continent is a constant struggle against terrorism and religious fanaticism. Though terrorism is considered to be a Delphie Oracle. And the tinpot diplomacy of Pakistan is always shuffling away its frenzied way of talking, capitalising a horde of morons and bullies altogether aiming at the Kashmiri Hindu pundits on the Kashmir issue. Such a way of bullying is invariably a major problem for the Indo-Pak relations spiced up either by media or by a pack of moronic yahoos of Mosque diplomacy.

Pakistan's nuclear weapons are a great worry not only to Kashmir but to the worshippers of democratic countries. Why? Because Pakistan's nuclear arsenal can fall into extremist hands, in Pakistan or in Afganistan. ElBaradei told the Pan-Arab daily 'Al-Hayat' that he was "worried" and at the same time he said, "I fear that chaos ... or an extremist regime could take root in that country which has 30 to 40 warheads." On the assassination of Benazir Bhutto, he said, "I fear that war in the Gulf or in the Muslim world could have great repercussions in Pakistan, more than in Iran." Mohammad ElBaradei heads the International Atomic Energy Agency (IAEA). It is alarming not only to the Kashmir issue but to human beings, the possibility of such ferocity, of such cowardliness. Pakistan alone sinks to the slaves of extremism. The infantile cowardice has no further duty and demands an external pattern because the rulers of extremism are anarchists. This adventurous thinking is a stimulant and as dangerous as the party line of the communists. Truly speaking, Pakistan is monopolised by the one and only a new class of extremism. This fuzzy-minded totalitarianism threatens to degrade and destroy the human race. Today Islam in Pakistan is not secured by noise and shouting; and misdeeds are committed under the spell of certain magic words or phrases of Mosque diplomacy. It is coordinated by a rude and clownish people. They call a spade a spade, and are haunted by the grossest religious dictions. Everything is richly puzzling and damaging.

Leaders of both the countries on the question of Kashmir and terrorism lose their exactitude and the fine edge of thought is blunted; judgement and discrimination are befogged. Bureaucratic jargon and a go-as-you-please attitude have crept into the language, fostered by the performer's anxious dread of appearing, cultured, academic or pedantic. So the Kashmir issue remains unsolved. The remedy does not lie in appointing a commission to draw up rules, for no living language can or should be static. It is their privilege to depress or raise the ground level of Kashmir problem.

And finally, the true explication of Kashmir question ruins like the sun out of foggy mists. And most alarming of all is not so much the catalogue of senseless violence as the apparent paralysis of American opinion in trying to end the Kashmir issue. The world of the gangs reflects all the expected features of insecurity. India's manifold woes spring from a single source ... partition. And it is difficult to conceive of Pakistan as a Moses leading the Kashmir issue to the promised land. Why? Because Pakistan is a fortress of fear. 'Pakistan's Eyes' have been trained to shoot first ... and ask questions afterwards.

Kashmir solution is harder than uncertainty. Because the intolerable heat of partition as well as the memory of its horrors were seen and endured. So the dread of Kashmir issue has become worse to come. A severe attack of political fever on the Kashmir question has delayed the Kashmir solution. And tidal wave of communalism and partition has swept up the problem to a siccipian task that looks as colourful as a poppy growing on a rubbish-dump. There is noise and talk but the solution has remained unsolved. Owing to our so-called opportunist political leaders, Kashmir issue is breaking into pieces and dissolving in blood and tears and terror. Owing to their follies and foibles, terrorism has gone about the valley of Kashmir in a desperate grip. Terrorists are deeply and desperately physical. There is neither love nor tenderness. The twilight in Kashmir is closing in and unsure of her direction. Because all political animals hanging out their rapacious but blood-stained tongues are about the valley. The Dal Lake looks appallingly wide. Its bank seems to be miles away. And the terrified religious leaders forget their own danger in these alarming atmospherics. All they are oddly stupid and lightheaded. Like the noise of quacking and quarrelling birds, the ruffle of fanatical wings makes the situation worse and worse. Under the pangs of embarrassment and religious strain, Kashmir tries to relieve itself of its humiliating collapse.

Morever, the gathering storm of hypocrisy and holier-than-thou-attitude has carried all the way of apprehension and foreboding, even after sixty years of tossing discomforts. In a complete and horrified uncertainty, the Kashmir problem is common to both India and Pakistan. A fool even after sixty years of independence is always a fool indeed. Because fools never see the half-done work. More people in India know Pakistan a fool on the Kashmir question than the people of Pakistan know. The bigger the terrorism is, the harder it falls. Islamabad, emaciated in thought and ragged in political ideology and drooping with exhaustion, parcels out another set of hypocrites for agreement on the Kashmir question every after tragic retreat. They talk in whispers and mutter in undertones, controlling the nervous wreck with apparent ease. They make all attempt to disguise, and turn and go out of the conference room, leaving scraps of sentences. The result is that Kashmir remains silent, and shudders from the shambles and from the stench of fresh-spilled blood and from the pile of the newly dead. The blood dries in the searing heat. The innocent men, women and children of Kashmir have spent sixty years to be butchered in a systematically organised crime.Terrorism-baked valley of Kashmir has swallowed up all the familiar sounds of Kashmiri Hindu pundits and other aromatic smells of heavenly-bliss spirit of Kashmiri villages into a cauldron of dizzy stupidity of religious fanaticism. Muslim kids learn politics of Jehadis under the colours of Pakistan's national flag. 'The Economist', the most authoritative journal of free trade and free speech, has severely lambasted Pakistan as the world's most dangerous place. It says, "for some time Pakistan has been the main contender for the title of the most dangerous country on earth. Since the murder of Benazir Bhutto on December 27th its claim has been strengthened." "It also says" terrorists could strike in Rawalpindi, headquarters of the Pakistani army, despite having advertised threats against Miss Bhutto and despite the slaughter of some 130 people in Karachi on the day she returned from exile last October, (which) suggests no one is safe ... if, as many in Pakistan, believe, the security services were themselves complicit, that is perhaps even scarier. It would make to deal with the country's many other fissures the sectarian divide between Sunni and Shia Muslims, the ethnic tensions between Punjabis, Sindhis, Pushtuns and 'mohajir' immigrants from India, the insurgency in Baluchistan, and the spread of the 'Pakistani Taliban' out of the border tribal areas into the heartlands ... for too long, Mr. Musharraf has been allowed to pay lip-service to democratic forms, while the United States has winked at his blatant disdain for the substance." (January, 2008)

'The Economist' has picturized well the frightening but alluring gesture of Pakistan. Pakistan seems to be in a state of breathless uncertainty. And she has inherited this wry grimace from some long-forgotten rulers. The journal also says that Pakistan as a dark and frightening country has got chatter at going in many western capitals. In London, which twins with Washington in the possible delusional line that gives President Pervez Musharraf license, the characterization is seen as a huge blow to western attempts to gloss over Pakistan's obvious lack of democracy.

Feeling the strain and tension of Kashmir issue and of insecurity against the fury of western powers, General Musharraf discovers that he loves Al Quaida and the Taliban. So he does not feel embarrassed or shy or ashamed in doing so. He walks silently into the shadows, ringing in a noisy and monotonous chorus of Jehadi slogans around the valley. And Pakistan walks in an unbroken line towards the glimmerring stretches of unsung enigma.

From Liaquat Ali Khan down to Benazir Bhutto, and even from Mrs. Indira Gandhi down to Rajiv Gandhi, every murder was planned with extreme care and extraordinary imagination. There was blood everywhere. There must have been a great deal of blood upon the murdered. Kashmir issue was, more or less, behind all of these murders. These murders were not like school arithmatic. There was no set of correct answers at the back of the murderer's book. The authoritarians will, no doubt, kick back.

Benazir Bhutto's justification was that she was thinking in harmony with history. Mrs. Gandhi fell. Benazir Bhutto knew that she would fall; she knew that there was something others than happiness beyond. She was aware that democracy is necessary to Pakistan and that she formulated the ideas which men have found most serviceable when they band together to meet this recurrent crisis in Pakistan. None of her faults can diminish her remarkable foreknowledge of the material on which the mind of the Pakistani people has been forced to work. She was unlucky to the point of force. She wanted to get rid of political Hitlerism and bureaucratic romanticism running wild in Pakistan. So Pakistan knows everything about Kashmir problem but does not feel anything of her incredulous distaste. Whereas Pakistan is trying to melt the Kashmir issue into the shadows of the political and religious chaos. Not only that the issue has made an alarming gap wider and wider between two cultures ... Hindus and Muslims. If it were smaller, the two disciplines would act as a mutual stimulas. This desperate grip of 'The Gap' is that it has widened to the extent of total mutual incomprehension. No electric spark can cross.

There are several ways in which this problem of our age can be tackled. One is educational. If the problem is to be tackled from the educational side, it would seem more profitable to give a greater emphasis to the history of Hindu-Muslim unity and, in particular, to give a scientific discovery and invention their proper place along with political, military, and social developments in the normal teaching of history. Why? Because there is an easy and painless method of getting the future administrators to have some understanding of science, and the future scientific leaders to relate their work to humanity. If there is a revival of religious practice in between two countries, this also may bring the devotees of science and humanities to a common frame of mind and so to a better mutual comprehension.

Whereas Pakistan's endless schemes, slogans, vendettas, intrigues and conspiracies, intolerance and favouritism, her shifting loyalties, her incipient dictatorship ... all these now reach a pitch of such relentless heat on the Kashmir issue as to strike some contemporary observers as the first sign of madness. Her judgement is sometimes wrapped by a lofty (but not unkindly) egocentricity. Because Islamabad is always humourist. Its mouth is crinkled with disdain, head held imperiously above its panoply of medals, and you will find in the depths of its proud eyes an ever-prescient twinkle of conspiracy. There are times in the valley when the Pakistani rulers' streak of crafty and sometimes catty arrogance unpleasantly colours their letters; but in the end their humour triumphs. For all their faults, they are nearly always fun. Pakistan is a confirmed pathological liar. Why? Because she suffers from a pathological violence over the Kashmiris. Very much extreme and unreasonable is her paternalistic way of governance.

Prescriptions for peace in Kashmir and felicity of mankind generally rest on all over-optimistic appreciation of human nature, coupled with a profound contempt for practising politicians. The hidden premise is that if only politicians of Pakistan were as wise as tolerant as the Indian politicians, the decent instincts of the ordinary Kashmiri people could be relied on to ensure that there should be no more war. Because war is endemic among the human race, part of the stuff of history. Because war is itself the normal condition, and peace is a lucky exception which should inspire us with gratitude but not with exaggerated hope. In most languages, the word 'peace' has no plural. All subsequent wars will be civil wars.

The popular image of Mr. Jinnah was that of a bombastic demagogue with a flair for the gratuitous insult. And Mr. Nehru and co. was astonished and disarmed. The truth is that Mr. Jinnah was a great leader but a bad colleague, on the Kashmir issue. Whereas to strangers or mere acquaintances, Gen.Musharraf's callous high spirits must often have had the appearance of insanity. And Mr. Nehru's political life was clouded with grudges and grievances and his eventful career on the Kashmir issue was a failure.

When the people of India were struggling for independence, it was natural that all the most dynamic elements in the population should be attracted into the ranks of the organisation which was active as the spearhead independence of the struggle. The consequence after had been one party Govt., which was democratic only. Why? Because the Congress virtually contained an opposition within its ranks. The danger was already apparent. A split within the Congress might well be a healthy development. But so long as Mr. Nehru remained Prime Minister of India, it seemed to be an unlikely one; it was precisely to avoid such a split that he was under the constant pressure not to resign. In this critical phase of pathological muddling within the party seized by a helpless, foolish pang of pure jealousy, the Kashmir problem has raised its venomous hood, collecting the fallen feathers of partition. Such unavoidable tragedies have been resulted from the shambolic leadership of muddle-headed leaders muddling along the way of their political interests under the leadership of Mr. Nehru. A heart-aching chaos has started out by the followers of the prophet, gathering up those fallen feathers of partition. And at the same time the Jehadis in the valley, aided and abetted by the Pakistani invaders, have also started out the spreading of the Faith and the slaying of unbelievers. Listening to the words of militant crusaders, in presence of Mr. Nehru and Co., the preachers have started preaching a jehad and dreaming the Mohammedan dream to capture the valley in the name of liberation movement of the Kashmiri people. Is Kashmir problem much of a muchness to the partition of India? The shrieks of women, the terrified screaming of children, the crackle of flames and the howl of the mob have risen behind the shadows of the darkening days of partition. The raking shudders with much intolerable strain ceased the Congress party at the Centre. The Kashmir question has started camouflaging with intrigues. After Mr. Nehru had gone, moreover, there was still more dangerous possibility that the Congress might split not into two parties but into innumerable splinters, with a consequence of a kind that Pakistan had already seen Mr. Nehru was a man of compromise, even on the Kashmir problem. Why? Because his tendency was : to vacillate, to yield, to compromise and to seek advice. Michael Brecher, in his authoritative book, 'Nehru : A Political Biography' says on his peculiar tendency: "To Gandhi or his father he would give way, reluctantly and without conviction, again and again; on civil dis-obedience, on Swaraj, on the claim of national independence, on the truce with the Viceroy in 1931, and on both the kind of India that they wished to create and the kind of tactics by which it was to be created. It was always true, but it became more apparent when he no longer had his father or, in his father's place, Gandhi to turn to for guidance, that his instinct was to hesitate and to compromise." Looking at the man of compromise and a man of hesitating attitude, Kashmir issue was born with all its aggressiveness, unshakable nerve and a fatal logic. Mr. Nehru was a pioneer of political anachronism in Kashmir, recharging the batteries of ghost nightmares of communalism and the policy of appeasement and mucking up all promises to a catalogue of humourous astonishment endemic in this genre.

And the Kashmir problem, under his leadership, has taken its evil roots deeper and deeper. His character was, in fact, more subtle and complex than ever Mr. Nehru thought of the Kashmir question. He pursued the middle of the road between the "nonchangers" and the "pro-changers" in the 1920s and between the left and the right wings in the Congress in the 1930s. He sought to meditate between Bose and Patel on the issue of federation in 1939, and between Patel and Gandhi over partition and its consequences. Taking an advantage over such a man of compromise and of hesitating mind, Pakistani invaders invaded Kashmir in full swing and Mr. Jinnah had successfully muscled on the

Kashmir issue and had a down on New Delhi treating the issue an epicentre of all problems and scurrilous propganda, between India and Pakistan. In a whole series of disputes and controversies, Mr. Nehru tried to ease more contentious rivals towards reasonable, pragmatic solutions, which often meant no more than shelving the problem in the hope that it would be gradually forgotten.

What is more important is that the policy of the via-media which Mr. Nehru had pursued at home and abroad particularly on the Kashmir issue was proved no longer adequate. His first instinct was to give the benefit of doubt to the Kashmir question, and ultimately he had sent out the issue to the Security Council. With the help of some unlucky chances ... the deaths of Bose and Patel and perhaps even of Gandhi being cases in point ... Mr. Nehru's personal diplomacy was able to bring independent India into a unique position in the world under a genuinely democratic Govt. The middle road was proved, by the test of success, to have been the right one, and even the disaster of partition. The Kashmir issue and the blood-bath by which post-partition disaster was accompanied have begun to fade form the public memory.

Michael Brecher clarifies well the role of Mr. Nehru in the post-partition era. He says, "The 'new' Jawaharlal Nehru is less confident about the future, less exuberant and less temperamental than the 'old'. He has mellowed a great deal. His outbursts of anger and irritation are much less frequent. He is inclined to be more patient with colleagues and subordinates, and more tolerant of human feelilngs. An air of almost philosophic calm appears to have descended upon the mercurial Indian leader." Our leaders having a lasting illness of political compromise, need a sanatorium to be getting better.

As his philosophic calm appeared, the grown-up tree of Kashmir problem has already spread out its destructive limbs far and wide. He was losing his grip over the problem. He was a man who always worked by compromise and reconciliation. And he was always open to the influence of stronger personalities than his own. His qualities were sandwiched by the two vast totalitarian empires, China and the Soviet Union.

Mr. Nehru needed to be rescued from the myth of compromise. Character follows character, incident hooks on to incident at the speed of political blunders open up a world of indefinite possibilities for the solution of Kashmir problem. Broad masses require party leadership to keep them on the right path from which they will, in their ignorance, repeatedly stray, unless so guided. So, much of the history of the thoughts and actions of the masses, where these can be discerned in a totalitarian state, will necessarily be a record of deviation from an opposition to the true historical path, and there irrelevant as we see in Mr. Nehru on the Kashmir policy. Another weakness of the Olympian style of writing Congress history of post-partition era is that it becomes the history of Govt. policy, not the history of the people. As it is written, so is the Kashmir problem written with black melancholia. This problem is inevitable. Why? Images are still classified as a species of rhetorical figure. And the gap is ominous. The trouble is that there are other conflicting dreams involved.

Pakistan had dreamt of Kashmir with passion rather than clarity. And the politics of Pakistan on the Kashmir issue seems to have been motivated by considerations of self-esteem.

While the fanfares of sixty years of independence are still reverberating, this question is also relevant, but the remorseless Pakistan does not hesitate to ask it, and occasionally a suspicion arises that she still has her doubts. Seemingly Mr. Nehru is a political scientist. Therefore he ought to have been aware of Pakistan and Mr. Jinnah. Friendship : Confucius, a Chinese philosopher, says : "Never make a friendship with a person that is not better than yourself." Pakistani rulers leave us in no doubt that their illiberal handling of the Kashmir issue, at moments amounting to downright political dishonesty leading to brutal repression as a response to human exasperation, is a bad blot on their political Scutcheon and a reproach to the country which they lead. The Kashmir dilemma is not unusal, but the accent of partition is the accent of 1947. Behind the often tentalising scandalmongerism, the sketches of Pakistan, her politics and people on the Kashmir issue, it would be interesting to know what she is really like. The issue is still persistent today and the great question can no longer be avoided. We may remind of the incident when Elizabeth I was in the throes of her death-bed. "I will have no rascal to succeed me," said the dying Elizabeth I," and who should succeed me but a king? "There are too many combustible interests in the risky diplomacy of Islamabad.

It shows with exactitude how ISI spies are bewitched by the evil genius of Hitler that transforms them into the mechanical instruments of a monstrous mass-murderer, and a certain pride in their degradation. ISI remains a Nazi at heart and it is only too evident that Islamabad's nonsensical racialism is ineradicable.

Gandhi was impatient of theoretical disquisition and an immense patience and research are required of anyone attempting an orderly exposition of his thought. In a letter to Joan V.Bondurant, author of 'Conquest of Violence,' Nehru wrote : "Gandhi was never tired of talking about means and ends and of laying stress on the importance of means ... Conflicts, therefore, are seldom resolved ... the mistaken belief still pesists that violence can end a conflict or that war can bring salvation to the world." Misuses of agreements and abuses of authority have aggravated the Kashmir question with vampires of terrorism, and Pakistan's uneasy dreams and night-flying Jehadis with a laden tray of jehadi slogans.

The multitudes of obscure individuals in Kashmir in the name of Jehad flit into history of fanaticism and out again; they grow into vast hordes in the West, build the Pyramids of terrorism. They die in their thousands in the plague of fanaticism. They take on the readymade ideas and submerge themselves in their current. An aphorism of Mr. William Golding's sums up the problem succintly, and may stand here as Colophon to a discussion which has no inevitable conclusion: "what men believe is a function of what they are ; and what they are is in part what has happened to them." The question remains open.

There is not, and can never be, any final conclusion to the claims and counter-claims on Kashmir, the perennial, radical controversy between the historical methods of two countries and between their irrenconcilable doctrines. Ultimately, the controversy itself provides its own justification "The Devil hangs like a vampire on the side of history." (M.C.D. Arcy : The Sense of History : Secular and Sacred) Let this presnece of terrorism settle into Pakistan's bones. And the final conclusion of Kashmir problem should come out on a noble and commanding scale of congenial atmospherics, if Pakistan be humble in her sincerity of efforts and resolute determination to solve the crisis with a pinchbeck dignity. According to the Bhagavad Gita, only through humbleness, the great ocean of truth conquers everything of the world. The Gita says : "Be humble, be harmless,/ Have no pretension,/ Be upright, forbearing;/ Serve your teacher in true obedience,/ Keeping the mind and body clean,/ Tranquil, steadfast, master of age,/ standing apart from the things of the senses,/ Free from self;/ Aware of the weakness in mortal nature." (The Gita 13:7-8). Otherwise, Pakistan's dream of peace-making process in Kashmir can be a parable of those modern historians who suffer from the inexplicable fascination of some crude politicians. The parable is : Once upon a time there was a glass mountain with a princess at the top and knights came from far and wide to ride it up and claim her. Some get higher than others, but none reached the summit, and the glass cliffs were surrounded by bones of men and horses and their hollow armour. So, Pakistani ruler, being an indiviudal, is free to fleet away unembarrassed from party to party as he sees it, with only the thought of further advancement to trouble India and Kashmir. When the wine of hypocrisy is in, the wit is out. As the twig of fanaticism is bent, so is the tree of Pakistan's policy over Kashmir inclined. When there are no issues, other than the desire for office, party makes a poor showing. And it is shameful to take pleasure in Kashmir. Pakistan is guilty when she rejoices in her destiny over the valley in Kashmir. The images of political decadence in Pakistan have moved from a peripheral to a central position of the world politics. To make a larger claim for Kashmir is in some degree to share her own illusion. In the end, the man of power realises that he must stand alone as we see in Pakistan. The sad truth is that she can rely upon nobody but her own narrow political doctrines and religious hidebounds. Why? Because she is beset with real and imaginery illness of Kashmir issue.

Kashmir is the valley of anguish. This insufferable anguish is a difference between thinking about moving your hand and actually moving your hand ... that crucial difference is choice. This choice has not yet been alive with Pakistan. Many a famous Muslim poet relates an excruciating agony in the follow poems :

Who knows where my friend is? / Who knows where my friend is hiding?/ Who knows whether he is scared in the dark night? ... Shakeel Shan . This very exquisite poem prolongs the agony of the valley. Shahid says : We shall meet again in Srinagar,/By the gates of the villa of peace,/ our hands blossoming into fists until the soldiers return the keys and disappear./ Again we'll enter our world,/ the first that vanished in our absence from the broken city, ... Shahid.

This poem of Muzalim Jaleel must rack our nerves and at the same time lick our wounds.

The contours of Kashmir's poetry have changed. Irises, a token of grief are now the central metaphor rather than an idyllic image of the cold peaceful breeze on Dal Lake ... an emblem of Kashmir's natural beauty.

Only mentality presents a distinctive feature. Today when science and technology are transforming education and in the face of current fragmentation of Islamic knowledge, awkwardly abetted by professional priesthood culture, men have deliberately turned their backs on the traditional hope of Islamic culture in Pakistan. Under the threat of this vast impoverishment of religious culture, at a time when schoolboys are invited to spell out why they do not consider learning Islam in Madrassa. With an infectious gust for recondite knowledge, Madràssa-based education is rooted in the urban and commercial life of Pakistan. It is salutary to recall its ancient wisdom. If people had been happier, fuller lives and lived longer in good health, if science could be harnessed to enrich and not to destroy, and if war could be superseded, mankind could unite in an affirmation of life. By introducing 'Islamic terrorism' in Kashmir, the worst despotism of military rulers in Pakistan is that which endangers the creative powers of the human spirits and sterilises them at their source in the imagination. The vulgar Sultanism of Islamabad-based stratocracy can only conquer the world of racialism between Shia and Sunni. Judging from this fact, Kashmir issue has outreached.

Our the then Prime Minister, Jawaharlal Nehru, and Mohammad Ali of Pakistan were fittering away their energy and resources in meaningless quarrels. Today, leaders of both the countries speak with a loud speaker in one hand and a gun in the other.

Had these three problems ... the problems of Kashmir, the distribution of canal waters and the disposal of evacuee property ... been crossed, there might have been no reason of disputes. And both the countries should have pursued a common policy towards economic development and the consolidation of peace.

Do nothing from selfishness or conceit, but in humility count others better than yourselves. Let each of you look not only to his own interests, but also to the interests of others. Why? Because it is language that shapes the way we think, and determines what we can think about. Why? Because much violence is based on the illusion. According to the Chinese proverb : "The man who strikes first admits that his ideas have given out." Why? When the chess game is over, the Pawn and the King go back to the same box. Why? Becasue Chess represents the triumph of mind over matter. Why? Because Kashmir problem is like a game of Chess, changing with each move. Why? Because the masters look for the problems, the public applauds them, and the critics praise them. Why? To a great historian like Mark Twain, "The principles of give and take is the principle of diplomacy ... give and take ten."

Dates are milestones in the march of time. Achievements and Failures that go to make the history of a Nation light up particular dates and rescue them from the Stygian waters of empty forgetfulness. For all ages, these dates acquire a new significance.

To posterity these memorable dates for all Kashmir debates are Tireless Sentinels that act as a bridge of memory between the present and the far-away.

Kashmir issue is a dismal period in the history of India. Partition wrote the epitaph to a sordid chapter in the annals of India. True, there are dates and dates and in Time's passing show not many would leave a trailing shadow behind.

A Napoleon is easily adored and idolized — while Christ is crucified because the greatness of their accomplishments only slowly trickles down to our understanding.

These momentous events with these dates are more than a convenient measure of time — a tiny dot on the calendar.

When freedom should and, coercion begins. India, like a pendulum, swings backward and forward in between positive freedom and negative freedom. Negative freedom, we may say, is the immunity from external and alien agencies. Positive freedom, by contrast, is the exercise of, the self-subjection, to inner and personal agency. Freedom! Freedom is what is left to man when the effects of coercion have been deducted from the sum of his powers.

Pakistan is in bondage. Freedom in Pakistan on this view is a form of self-emasculation: but the emasculation is only partial, and is still self-inflicted.

Partition is like sudden infant death syndrome. Kashmir issue has resulted from this cot-bet. The great issue of the day, the great issue of all times, ... KASHMIR. True love for Kashmir is something archetypal, never attained.

Between goose-girl and the kitchen servant, Who have no wedding ring or mutual bed.

2

HISTORY BEHIND KASHMIR : Before the Storm

It is said that when there is new wine in old bottle, it is bound to burst. Can it be said, also, of new parties with old leaders? Everyday a new political party springs up with much dulcet phrases of ideologies and new slogans for a welfare society. How is it that everyday a new party comes into existence, but no new leaders born? If food crops grow so profusely as political parties grow on the Indian soil, there will have been no half-begging and half-borrowing of foodgrains. But Kashmir problem remains as before.

At the present rate of growth of political parties in India, even after sixty years of independence, the need will soon be felt for an organisation, to be called the Federation of Indian Political Parties, with a common secretariat and common collection and distribution of funds, the constituent parties retaining their individual and mutually antagonistic leadership and ideologies, backed by political gangsterism and the local police, so called, if necessary. Otherwise, there is the danger of overlapping, or leaders outnumbering followers, as is the case already with the new political parties. A clash between geriatric leaders and burgeoning leaders. Why? Because there is a good case, however, for controlling new party formations, with a view to checking political inflation. Damn your Kashmir problem. Muslim appeasement is the honest policy. Our leaders are extravagantly romantic in the case of appeasement. A parade of humours in the body.

Before independence, the Indian political world was divided between pseudo-secularists and communalists, devoid of all political ethics and philosophy. The bespoke Kashmir issue, doctored in a different way, is now an orphan boy. No one comes to be guilty of its paternity. So success of partition is a bastard because it has many fathers. Even the foxy formula over Kashmir has proved ineffective. The people of Kashmir patiently waited for some time in the hope that their lot would improve as soon as the dislocation resulting from the transfer of power and the partition of the country was brought under control. Gradually, they found that the Congress in power was unable to redeem the promises made by Congress in wilderness. And even the Kashmiris began to ask themselves : What did this accession mean? What did this freedom mean? And the rest of India began to ask themselves : Did it mean really the satisfaction of national pride? The Kashmiri Hindu pundits raised a question : Is it meaningless freedom as well as accession of Kashmir to India which we have won at the cost of blood, sweat and tears? The Congress leaders were not aware of the disease before they could apply a remedy.

Unfortunately, all top-ranking Congressmen under the Nehru Govt. didn't seem to be aware of the failure of the Congress to invest accession of Kashmir to India with a concrete meaning. They seemed to turn a deaf ear to the questions hurled at them from different quarters.

Statesmanship consists in recognising realities and in controlling seemingly uncontrollable circumstances. So, both India and Pakistan play a political adventurism on the Kashmir debate, of which no man can see the end. The people of Kashmir expect from their goals not words but deeds, not excuses but achievements.

In the Kaleidoscopic changes of political drama, memories of those who once played important roles are apt to fade away with the close of the scenes where they once figured so prominently. The ever-receding flow of time carries their memories further and further back and ultimately the people for whom they worked and suffered have but a shadowy remembrance of the personalities and achievements of these political heroes branded differently under the red-carpet of hypocrisy, follies, lies and Himalayan blunder on the smouldering and ever-increasing crisis of KASHMIR ... a seething hot-bed of blood-letting violence, murder and loot. But the argus-eyed history does not forget even a scrap of solid and sincere work on whom collective heaps of the foundations of national greatness are laid from age to age.

Kashmir ... a tale of two cities between Islamabad and New Delhi ... is the unfolding history of miscalculation. An idea can turn to dust or magic depending on the talent that rules against it. There is a great difference between knowing a thing and understanding it. In case of a country like India, whose struggle for freedom from an alien rule constitutes a thrilling chapter of national history, the scraps of such work, big and small, are scattered all about. Sometimes they are spectacular enough to immediately attract public notice; sometimes they lack that outward glamour, though on that score they are not less solid and substantial. The natural historian will, however, weigh both these categories of achievements in the balance and assign proper places to them in the edifice of the chronicle of the country.

In the political turmoil of the last sixty years, since independence, over Kashmir, the sufferings and sacrifices of these fighters who fought in the open field have naturally engrossed the attention of the people; but there were other heroes who, though they did not prefer, for whatever reason, to throw themselves into the thick of the fight, worked not less valiantly in other spheres and whose collective contribution to the final emancipation of the nation was not less important.

There are India's ancient links with Kashmir. When Huen-Sang, the Chinese pilgrim, visited India, the country, for sometime, came under the sway of the Hun tyrant, Mihirajuta, 'the terrible enemy of making', who had no pity for children, no compassion for women, no respect for the aged. After his defeat in India, he took shelter in Kashmir, but at the first opportunity, he treacherously usurped the throne of his benefactor. Evil-minded as the great tyrant was, says Kalhana, he yet tried to win religious grace by building Shiva shrines, and endowing Brahma monasteries, which only the lowliest of the twice-born, as vilely as their protector, did not disdain to accept.

In the seventh century, Kashmir paid tribute to Harsha Vardhana, King of the Indian Kingdom, Kannauj, and had to surrender to him a precious relic, a tooth of Buddha, which he coveted.

At the end of Huen-Sang's visit, Buddhism was on the decline, but the King of Kashmir was powerful enough to levy tribute from the kingdom of Taxila and other States, lying at the first of his mountain walks.

Kashmir's isolation from India, which came a little later, appears to have coincided with an era of decadence. Dissolute monarchs brought the country to the verge of ruin. Kalhan's chronicles, however, bring out an important principle of Indo-Aryan polity during that period. The Ministerial Council had the power to check the arbitrary rule of the monarch and to alter the line of succession, when the interests of the State demanded it.

Thus the Council banished Yudishthira I from his kingdom for misconduct and the historian pathetically describes the fallen king's departure. The citizen's distress and his delicately nurtured queen's plight, "when his wives, whose figures were as delicate as the young shoots of the lotus-stalks, had passed through the forest regions, ... they bend their bodies over their laps and swooned from fatigue, when the king's wives, after casting a long glance, at the distant land, from the height of the mountain boundary, threw all at once handfuls of flowers, as a fare-well offering, even the swarms of birds nestling in the mountain ravines, cried plaintively in their excitement, buried their beaks in their plumage spread out on the ground."

Similarly in the history of the new dynasty that succeeded to the vacant throne, Kalhana records that an able and ill-treated Minister, Shantimati, resisted the arbitrary conduct of the king, and, later, "consented to the prayer of the citizens to rule the country," when the throne fell vacant. Again when the Gondama dynasty was extinct, the Ministerial Council presenting the voice of the people, consecrated a prince of the Kalkota line, "with sacred water poured out from golden jars."

The traditional authority of the Ministerial Council makes one of the fundamental differences between the polity of the Indo-Aryans and that of Islam. In the latter, the sovereign ruled by Divine right, derived from his descent from the prophet or bestowed upon him by the Khalif as the Prophet's representative, or won by the Prophet's own weapon, the sword.

King Lalitaditya, who ruled about the middle of the eighth century, was the earliest to have connections with the Turks, whom he appointed to the five high offices of State, which controlled the administration of this ancient Aryan regime instituted by Ashoka's son.

A succession of weak and dissolute rulers next disgraced the glorious tradition of their line. But at the close of the century, Jayapida Vinayditya revived Sanskrit learning and attracted famous scholars and poets to this court.

Chaos followed the death of Jayapida, till Avanti Varman, who ruled from 855 to 883, restored peace and prosperity to Kashmir, causing learning "whose flow had been interrupted, to descend again upon the land." Authorities state that the extent works of the scholars who flourished at his court from an important part of the Sanskrit literature of ancient Kashmir.

In 939, another appeal was made to the traditional law of Indo-Aryan Kingship. Kamala Vardhana, the commander-in-Chief, was in a position to seize the throne by force of arms. Instead of doing so, he tried to obtain religious sanction for his claim beforehand. He called the Brahmans together, and tried to canvass their support. The Assembly's vote set aside the claim of Kamala Vardhana in favour of a Brahman candidate, Yaskara, who was accordingly consecrated king by the ancient Vedic rule of abhisekha.

Kalhana says Yaskara "made the Kirta Yuga come back again," and purified the administration so that the "officials who had plundered everything found no other occupation but to look after agriculture ... The Brahman Gurus did not drink spirits, as they sang their chants; the ascetics did not get wives, children and crops ... Astrologer, doctor, councillor, teacher, Minister, Ambassador, Judge, clerk ... none of these without learning."

In 1015, Mohammad of Ghazni, failed at attempt to penetrate into Kashmir soon after one of his raids into India. His army tried in vain to storm the fortress of Lahore. On the homeward march it was misled by guides and fell into extensive morasses and many of the troops perished.

In the year 1315, Shah Mirza, a Muhammadan adventurer, from Surat, entered the service of the Hindu Prince of Kashmir. When the latter died, Shah Mirza seized the throne, under the title of Shamsud-din-Shah, had coins minted and the Khutba read in his name. He ruled for 64 years.

Towards the end of the fourteenth century, Amir Timur paid Kashmir a visit. On his way back from India, soon after the sack of Delhi, he marched along the Siwalk Hills, captured Kangra and pillaged Jammu, slaughtering inhabitants in large numbers.

Zain-ul-Abidin ascended the throne in 1542. He recalled the Brahmans who had left the kingdom during the earlier reigns, admitted learned Hindus to his court, abolished the Jizya tax and granted religious freedom to all.

The subsequent history of the country is marred by considerable internal discussion, till it was absorbed in the Mughal empire. For a time, Mirza Haider, relative of Humayn, conquered Kashmir and ruled it as an independent kingdom till he was overthrown. In 1586, Akbar the Great, sent Raja Bhawan Das to capture the valley, at a time when it was distracted by dynastic disputes. It was not till the middle of the following year, however, that Akbar's army, assisted by the internal disorders, broke through the mountain passes of Kashmir and brought it under Mughal Sway. It remained part of the Mughal Empire till the death of Aurangazeb.

In 1819, the ambitious Sikh ruler, Ranjit Singh, balked by the English in his attempt to conquer the south, moved north and occupied Multan and Kashmir. After the first Anglo-Sikh war, the Sikhs ceded Kashmir to the English in 1846, and the latter, in this turn, sold it to Gulab Singh, Raja of Jammu, for one million sterling.

Forty years later, Lord Lansdowne, acting on certain vague, took over the Government of Kashmir from the reigning Maharaja, and entrusted it to a council under the control of the British Resident. For a time, it seemed as though the British intended to annex the territory. An alarm was promptly raised and in July 1890, Bradlaugh moved an adjournment of the House of Commons on the subject. In 1905, the British restored the Maharaja to the throne and made no further attempt to interfere in the administration of the Province.

In Nov, 1947, Kashmir leaped into the news when 300 Afridis carried fire and sword into the peaceful lake country. It was the first act of a new drama in the chequered history of this unhappy land. Till today, the curain has not been drawn on the tragedy that is being enacted in the 'Garden of Asia.'

Looking back today, one finds that three arms of the enigmatic triangle in the romance of the Indian history under the British rule was the alien ruling class, the Hindus and the Muslims, The pages of this romance, which has ended in a tragedy in the shape of India's partition, are filled with amorous whispers of the rival lovers into the ears of the wayward 'famine charmants'. It is well-known to readers that the assiduously courted female of the Indian romance, like her type in all romances, has always been inclined towards the stronger one of her two lovers. The Indian romance would have been quite commonplace, but for the relief provided by the rather unexpected behaviour of the jilted lover.

Unlike jilted lover of romances who either cuts the throat of his rival or shoots at the treacherous, fair-heart breaker, the befooled lover of the Indian romance, gifted with extraordinary spiritual self-conceit and capacity for self-deception, has always persisted in the faith of his power to change the heart of the beloved and refused to be disappointed. As a matter of fact, both his self-delusion and faith in the power of persuasion seem to be fathomless.

It was more than a dozen years before the birth of the Congress, Lord Mayo and Mr. Justice Norman of the Calcutta High Court were murdered by Muslim assassins. Hindus were surprised at the unexpected attitude of the Government towards the Moslems after these assassinations. The following lines are taken from the Amrita Bazar Patrika, dated 7th March, 1892 :

"We fear there is actually a desire on the part of the Govt. servants and members of the English press to bribe the whole Muslim community, because two of them have murdered two English officials. Even our own Lt. Governor has so far forgot himself as to recommend the creation of a separate Arabic College for the Mahommedans, stating that Mahommedans deserve some special consideration. Mr. Hunter wrote evidently to conciliate Mahommedans, that they were not well treated. Now Govt. actually goes on to flatter and favour them." It sowed the seeds of the beginnings of Muslim separatism in India.

In conformity with this statement, Som Prakash, a vernacular paper, dated 4th April, 1872, wrote :

"The Mussalmans have commenced committing mischief, and we hear that one in high authority has so far made up his mind to appear then that he has privately issued orders to his subordinate officers to give decided preference, when filing up appointments, to Mahommedans over their Hindu fellow candidates."

Under the "Wahabis and British Administration", the Amrita Bazar wrote again :" It is believed by many that Mr. Campbell (Lt. Governor of Bengal) has become very favourably inclined towards the Mahommedans only with a view to please and oblige them."

Commenting on the Moslem demand for special provision for study of Arabic and Persian for them. Som Prakash, dated 16th Dec. 1872, wrote :

"Were Govt, to listen to their demand and arrange to give them a separate and distinctive education, not only would the Govt. be striking its own foot with the axe but it would be doing incalculable injury to the Mohammedans themselves."

The paper expressed its apprehension that the eagerness of the Govt. to conciliate the Moslems would fill them with pride and make them intolerant of the legitimate rights of the other communities. The apprehension materialised soon.

In 1873, there was a big communal disturbance at Belgachia, Calcutta, in an undivided Bengal, at the time of the immersion of the image of Goddess Durga, due to Moslem demand for stopping music before mosques. This is the first time that this demand was heard of. The city police was accused of taking the side of the Moslems. In the same year, there were serious agrarian disturbances in some parts of North Bengal. The Mohammedan riots turned against Hindu Zamindars, talukdars and jotedars. Describing the conditions the Amrita Bazar Patrika wrote :

"The insult and destroy the caste of respectable men, to violate the chastity of females of gentle blood, to break into pieces the images of idols and plunder have become everything business with the insurgents."

Regarding the condition of Serajgunge, Pabna (now in Bangladesh), it is stated :

"This subdivision has become as panic-stricken now as was India at the time when it was invaded by Chenghiz Khan and Timur."

The sufferers bitterly complained the conduct of Mr. Nolan, Asst. Magistrate of Serajgung, and accused him openly of instigating hooliganism to teach the Hindu Landlords a lesson; they also complained of the inactivity of the police. Thus the estrangement with much soul-stirring hatred and bitterness between the two communities began under the red-carpet of blood and bloodshed.

The Indian National Congress was established in 1885 and in the same year also established the National Mahommedan Association. In 1886, the Congress met in Calcutta. Sir Syed Ahmed Khan came to calcutta to attend the Congress but he went away without attending Congress meetings. A non-Indian Muslim paper (Hablul Matin) distressing the growth of the Aligarh School of Politics, wrote in 1908 :

"When the National Congress was being organised in India, an unseen power was bringing about a rupture between the Hindus and Mahommedans. And this was no other than the opposition of Sir Syed Ahmed Khan, a man who originally came down to Calcutta to join the Congress, and who, some time before the Congress was held, had given out that the time had come when the various races and communities in India should form an association to consider their national and political requirements. But for reasons of his own, he did not attend the Congress and he founded the Educational Conference in the U.P. ; and from this date must be reckoned the beginnings of a split between the political views of the Hindus and Mohammedans. It was, however, most advantageous for the British Govt. in as much as it has during the last twenty five years retarded the advance of the progressing party in India and perhaps, for the next twenty five years, it will be in the way of the interests of the country. The conference of Sir Syed Ahmed has caused the breach between the Hindus and Mahommedans of India."

It was the Congress party that was mainly accountable for the in-depth disunity, hatred and collusion between the Hindus and Mahommedans. Truly speaking, people generally quarrel because they cannot argue. Pride of both the communities is tasteless, colourless and sizeless. Yet it is the hardest thing to swallow. When you teach your son, you teach your son's son.

From after the first session of the Congress, the Anglo-India began to deny representative character of the Congress. Why? Because Moslems had not joined it. From 1886, there was a marked change in the policy of the Govt. and a corresponding new emphasis in the difference of interests between the

Hindus and Muslims.

The readiness of the Govt. to show special favour to the Muslims prompted them to demand separate schools for their education and separate offices for them. 'Sandharani' dated 9th May 1886, wrote : "The policy of Divide and Govern seems to be the present favourite policy of the European Statesmen. The miserable conditions of the Mussalmans of Bengal is due to their own neligence to learn English for a long time. But why should they ask for separate schools and offices on that account?" 'Sachachar', a vernacular dated 20th Oct. 1886, complained that "by showing undue indulgence to the Mussalamans as to a pet child Govt. were causing dissatisfaction to the Hindus."

'Bharatbasi' wrote :

"*The Magistrates of the North-West provinces, may Govt. in all parts of the country try to produce discussion between Hindus and Mussalmans. Whenever there is an opportunity, they set Hindus and Mussalmans at feud with each other.*"

In conformity with the statement of 'Bharatbarsa', 'Navabhivakar', dated 25th Oct. 1886, wrote :

"*Owing to their being subject to the same Govt. good feelings were gradually being established between Hindus and Mussalmans. Both communities have to fight the all-devouring Anglo-Indians for rights; but the English Govt. has been trying to produce discussion between the two communities.*"

The paper points out that at Etwah and Delhi the Hindu procession was not allowed while the Mahommedan procession was allowed. "It was due to the desire of the officials to create jealousy in the mind of the Hindus."

One paper referring to these processions writes that the 'Times' had been attacking the Hindus. This attack was inspired by two objects, namely, satisfaction of grudge against the Hindus and the conciliation of the Muslims. The grudge against Hindus was due to their political agitation, The reason given by the paper for the desire for conciliation of the Muslims is interesting.

"Mr. Blunt has said that if the English govt. in India is subverted, it will be subverted by Mussalmans. Not only the 'Times' but also the authorities fear let Russia should establish her influence over the Mussalmans. Owing to this fear, the 'Times' supported the Mussalmans with reference to the recent riots and Govt. have ordered that Mussalmans should anyhow be appointed in the public service."

The 'Times' had reasons for conciliating the Muslims. The Sudanese war was then going on and a feeling of unrest prevailed amongst Indian Muslims. Anonymous handbills were secretly circulated in northern India calling upon Indian Moslems to rise in revolt against Govt. A contemporary paper refers to a secret association of Moslems with members in all Muslim countries.

It is interesting to note that a Hindu paper advised Govt. as follows : "The Russians are trying to enter India, England is entitled in difficulties in the

Sudan, there is ill-feeling between the political parties in England and the European powers are disappointed with England. Govt. should not lay the axe at the root of the royalty of Indian Mussalmans by showing distrust to them."

Nothing a change in the policy of the Govt., a paper called 'Dainik' dated 8th Dec. 1886 wrote : "Govt. is trying to sow dissension between Hindus and Mussalmans in Bengal, public schools are open to all classes of people and yet Mussalmans asked for special indulgence in the matter of appointments and obtained them. They claimed special indulgence in the matter of appointments and obtained them. In many other matters also Govt. is disposed to grant special favours to them..Mr. Harrison has asked for the claim of Mussalmans to special indulgence in municipal matters. The Anglo-Indian have taken the cue from him."

The paper warns Muslims :

"The merchants are not likely to show special indulgences to a conquered race for nothing. Educated Muslims should look into the motives of the sudden change in the policy of the Govt."

Referring to the Anglo-Indian anxiety to keep away Mussalmans from the Congress, a paper wrote : "'The Englishman is trying its best to dissuade Mussalmans from joining the National Congress. It says that those Musselmans who will join the Congress cannot be quite sane, and that Mussalman Khansamas and Khitmadgars will have to be hired for the Congress. If Indians had not been peaceful or law-abiding the editor of the Englishman should have been thrashed for making such a shameless statement."

The change in the attitude of the British Govt. and press manifesting itself in a desire to conciliate the Moslems which had been gradually first awakening of nationalism among educated Hindus throughout India brought about by the Illbert Bill agitation or the 'Banerjee agitation' as it was called at that time. The White Mutiny against 'Lord Ripon' Govt. in connection with the Illbert Bill and the agitation following the incarceration of Surendranath Banerjee for contempt of court in connection with Mr. Justice Norris's order to bring a 'Salagram Sila' into the High Court, which outraged Hindu sentiments, created an unprecedented tide of nationalism which swept the country and resulted in the establishment of the Indian National Congress. The organised and united stand by the educated Hindus compelled the British to look for allies to thwart the Hindu political organisation. They found an ally in the few educated Muslim leaders whose spokeman was Syed Ahmed Khan. A real split occurred between the two communities ... a split which widened and deepened as time passed. Since then the Muslim community in India had the pleasure of having at its ears two worse competing with each other in pouring forth protections of love and promises of handsome gifts. And it has fully exploited its advantageous position.

What did India insist on having a force, however small, in Kashmir? It is because nobody in this part of the Sub-Continent can possibly forget Pakistan's conduct in relation to Kashmir. The tribesmen began their plundering expedition more than the plundering three years before the partition of India. Indian troops were sent out to expel them. Pakistan came to the assistance of the marauders by sending regular troops. The question was raised in the Security Council but Pakistan had denied that it had anything to do with the invasion. The Security Council sent a Commission to make an investigation on the spot. Pakistan troops were reported to be among the invaders. Finding that truth could no longer be concealed. Pakistan admitted its complicity in the affairs and justified its intervention that the Kashmiris were being oppressed by India and that it was at the call of the people that Pakistan had sent its troops : This was another lie as blatant as the first.

One of the grounds for this military operation was recommended of the c-in-c of Pakistan that an easy victory of the Indian Army was almost certain to arouse the anger of the invading tribesmen against Pakistan for its failure to render them more direct assistance. Pakistan's motive was not merely to pacify the tribal raiders by giving them token assistance. What was the motive? The answer is very simple. The real purpose was to annex Kashmir by force. Anglo-American motive entered into the question of Pakistan's invasion of Kashmir. Why? Because Anglo-American did not want to prejudice the cause of Pakistan in any way. Why this softness for Pakistan, this condonation of her violation of international law? It is because Anglo-American felt that Pakistan would be a more dependable and subservien than India could probably be in the event of a global war.

Since independence, England and America have always ignored the fact on Kashmir. While India voluntarily offered plebiscite to the people of Kashmir, Pakistan wanted to coerce them into submission by ravaging their country. And she has still ravaged the country by introducing terrorism engineered by the hired terrorists of Afghanistan and other satellite Muslim countries. Both England and America know everything and have always turned deaf ear to India. Pakistan has demanded that the entire State should pass into its hand.

Pakistan was always afraid of the proposed Constituent Assembly. Why? Because she knew that it would confirm Sheikh Abdullah's Govt. in power and ratify the State's accession to India. She was afraid of the verdict of the Kahmiri people. Why? Because she knows they have not forgotten the terrible atrocities committed by her troops. She also knows the cry of 'Islam in Danger' would not mislead them. The feverish excitement which convulsed this sub-continent in 1946-47 is over. The people of Kashmir are now taking a realistic view of the situation. They have a Govt. which is predominantly Muslim in composition. The most important organisation in the State, as India got her independence, was Jammu and Kashmir National Conference which was predominantly Muslim in composition, and it wanted to remain in India. The people of Kashmir also know that India is a secular democratic State with all reasonable safeguards for the protection of racial and religious minorities, and the Govt. of which the leader was a Muslim and is still a Muslim. They know how India offers adequate opportunities to all sections of her citizens irrespective of their religious affiliations.

Moreover, India still has a Muslim population of many millions ... the third largest of any State in the world. Why should the western powers overlook these facts and continue to treat the Kashmir question as if it were a purely Hindu-Muslim question? Pakistan claimed that the Hindus of the then East Bengal (now Bangladesh), after partition, enjoyed perfect security and complete political liberty. What a fabricated and concocted device of blatant lies Pakistan enjoyed that time : Now the question is : If a professedly Islamic State could put forward this claim, why should it be assumed that the Muslims of Kashmir have no place in a secular, democratic State like India? Our Anglo-American friends have always proceeded on the assumption that in accordance with the presentiment of 1947 a Muslim Majority area like Kashmir should be made over to Pakistan. They forget that history is not a static. The British hypocrisy and cant are well-known to the world. Just for example. The claim of the Congress to be a friend and protector of the minorities was repudiated by the malicious and false propaganda of the Muslim League with the shrewd support of British imperialism during the fateful years 1937-47.

Today Pakistan stands completely exposed ... a reactionary, medieval State which exploits religion for sordid political purposes and sends its battalions to terrorise Muslims whom it has professed to protect for over 60 years. A widening gulf of blood and tears has been yawning between Kashmir and Pakistan. It is too late for Anglo-American shrewd diplomacy to search for a silken bridge.

The Pakistan invasion of the State of Kashmir and Jammu has, in certain respects, changed the very face of Jammu. It has created new problems for the Jammuites, some of which they share in common with Kashmiris. When Pakistan gave the green light for aggression in Kashmir in October, 1947, she had already contrived to practically close the Srinagar-Rawalpindi Road and the Jammu-Sialkot Road and Railway line. Evidently, she aimed at choking the tiny State in order to force its Ruler to join the so-called biggest Islamic State. The position had become so dangerous and delicate that when the first contigent of Indian troops was flown to Srinagar on Oct. 1947, there was no good road connecting India and with Jammu. The Srinagar-Jammu Road unless it was connected with the Indian Punjab by a metalled Road, could serve no purpose. The Kathua Road linking the Dogar with Pathankot (Indian Punjab) was there already; but it was atrocious ... a mere muddy track which passed through ravines and was quite unsuitable for wheeled traffic. Under these circumstances, when Jammu and Kashmir acceded to India and Indian troops entered the State, they (troops) had to walk, so to say, with bare feet, over broken glass along a very difficult and undependable supply line. But the Indian army took the risk and made use of this rough and rugged trace. And soon the air was filled with the rumble of coming and going of convoys, the clatter of passing trucks and the buzz of jeeps the Indian troops fanned out in different parts of Jammu and hurried to Kashmir to join their comrades who had been flown to Srinagar.

While the Indian Army managed ... of course after facing enormous difficulties ... to make use of this road, the State's normal trade with India and foreign countries came to a standstill practically. The air service linking Srinagar and Jammu with India, could not do much to remove the difficulty. The necessity of a good road connecting Jammu with India was keenly felt and the need for an organised transport service was the cry of the hour in order to save the State from economic stagnation. Sialkot and Rawalpindi which served as the clearing houses for Jammu and Kashmir's import and export trade for a century or more, were sealed areas for the State as a consequence of Pakistan's policy and programme before and after the invasion. The Governments of India and Kashmir realised the urgency of the situation and accordingly a survey for the construction of a gorge-metalled road from Pathankot (Indian Punjab) to jammu was hurriedly made. Work on the road was connected in right earnest and it was built in three months at a cost of about three crores of rupees, considering the terrain in which it was constructed, the 65 miles long road is regarded as a remarkable feat of engineering, making the spiritual, legal and constitutional bonds between Kashmir (including Jammu) and India stronger. Three big bridges on the road, 28,000 ft, 2000ft and 1000ft peak of the great engineering and transport skill involved in their construction.

People in Jammu and Kashmir heaved a sigh of relief, the Army felt enjoyed and a big problem confronting the State administration was solved. But there was another equally important problem which awaited solution in an expeditious manner. It was the question of reorganising the then disoranised and transport service in the State especially in Jammu.

Prior to the invasion of Jammu and Kashmir, the Pakistan authorities had suspended the railway traffic between Sialkot and Jammu city. The railway wagons had been taken away and the engines detained in Sialkot. This naturally affected Jammu to a large extent. Besides, the Pakistan authorities had detained most of the lorries plying on the Jammu ... Sialkot and the Srinagar-Rawalpindi Roads. The lorries so detained were kept in readiness to carry tribals and Pakistan regulars in plain clothes to attack the State. The withdrawal of the bulk of lorries and motor cars from Jammu and Kashmir's transport system, created a void in the State's transport structure and accordingly trade and commerce suffered greatly. It was a puzzling situation for the people of the States ... traders and others ... to face. The ingress and egress of people and the movement of goods to and from the State were rendered. Very difficult and uncertain and costly. It was a baffling situation for the State Govt. to face till at last it was decided to start a State-owned transport service which ran on the Srinagar ... Jammu ... Pathankot Road, Srinagar-Jammu Road and Jammu-Pathankot Road. It was the first experiment of its kind towards the nationalisation of the transport system.

A fleet of buses for carrying goods and passengers the Srinagar-Pathankot road was purchased which relieved the tedium of the long wait. A special department for transport was started which attended to the problems of transport in the State. This eased the situation to a large extent, at least for the time being. But as soon as the Govt. transport service began to function the main road connecting India with Jammu and Kashmir there was a lot of criticism and opposition from private transporters and others who complained that the State Govt. had already killed private enterprise, but also fixed very high rates which were deterimental to the State's trade and went against the interest of passenger traffic.

Who is to blame for dividing the world? Britain blamed the U.S.S.R. The latter blamed the Atlantic pact countries. We in Asia who belong neither to this group nor that do not attach much importance to the question of apportionment of blame. A war means suffering to all, the common man in particular. What is the obstacle to unity? It was the ideological imperialism of Russia that stood in the way. The Communists said it was British or Anglo-American imperialism that was responsible. What is the truth? Does truth lie mid-way? There can be no doubt that a great disturbing factor in the world, before the fall of communism in Russia, was ideological imperialism of the communists. It is no more theory or a guess. We see it before our eyes. There can be no mistake about it. The spectre of Russian communism was strutting in almost every part of the world. And this communism was as far apart from Democracy as the Devil is from God. In this communism, there was no liberty. There was regimentation of thought and complete subordination of the individual to the State. And the State here meant a group of individuals, the party bosses, who claimed to have monopolised all wisdom, all patriotism, and all that was good. Freedom of opinion, and of expression, freedom of association and all other freedoms which we associate with democracy are non-existent in a communist-controlled State like China. In countries, where the Govt. is not yet communist, when then Russia had and the present China has a fifth column, we find in the communist party the same intolerance, the same arrogance and the same desire to stifle freedom of opinion, the same cliquishness which are associated with a communist-controlled state. Communism as a philosophy may be acceptable to liberal thinkers, but the communist party exploits that philosophy to gain ascendancy for the power.

The New Millennium begins. The memories of Jalliawana Bagh and political serfdom no longer trouble us. But our trouble is far from being at end. In the dispension of the providence mankind cannot have any rest. If one kind of trouble goes, another quickly follows. India, politically free, is strewn with difficulties which are no less serious than those that troubled her on the Kashmir dispute ... a trouble-shooting cauldron of fire and fury, holding out a great many wings of hypocrisy, conspiracy, internecine warfare and untold plight of common people, leading to a plethora of innumerable death and destruction, under the red-carpet of blood-letting slogans on a solid ground of a see-sawing battle of fundamentalism. Last century was to India a passing phase of shame that we have just passed through. It was a shame that we had to import our thoughts from abroad. It was a shame that we had not shown greater regard for our country. It was a shame that the Congress rulers did not make more proper actions on Kashmir. It seems that the camel's back will break if one straw of shame is added to this burden of shame. But as everything is equally shared in a democratic state, let us divide the load of shame on a fifty-fifty basis between the leaders and the public. Justice has been defeated by prejudice. To run away from this problem is not to solve it.

Few years after independence, Kashmir was gradually springing back to life again after bitter frost and severe cold. The thaw had set in and even though heavy snow was still visible on high mountains, it had melted on the plains and lower hills. These usual signs of activity are noticeable throughout the valley. The hill and the dales, the river are fast putting on new hues approaching spiring. Here and there green grass is visible again, relieving the tedium of the long wait of winter. Soon there will be a mass of flowers on trees and plants everywhere, when war-torn Kashmir will be a comb of blossoms, inviting people from far and near to revel in fragrance, colour and beauty provided by a beautiful nature.

But while the average Kashmir is accustomed to rigorous winters followed by charming springs in the valley, Indian troops from the hot plains of India have many new and strange experience to gain in the land which they have been defending against heavy odds. Though unaccustomed to snow, they are by no means unprepared for the extra cold winter in the mountains of Kashmir. After going through the severe ordeal of shivering cold, heavy snows and binding blizzards for over 50 years, they have begun to appreciate the value of the land for which they have been fighting for. Encouraged as they feel, they are seen going about in far-off villages to understand the people inhabiting this country, for healthy contacts with them, and help them in the procurement and distribution of necessaries of life.

Some of our Indian troops, especially Madrasis and Bengalis, who had not so far experienced a winter in a mountainous country, at first believed that Kashmir had 'white earth'. And some of them actually wrote to their friends and relatives in India describing the 'discovery' they have made. Yet they have been fighting on this very 'white earth' even at the beginning of the New Millennium.

Since independence, American has knowingly or unknowingly betrayed many an Indian cause ... some of them vital ones. For over 60 years, there has been a unique cordiality of relations between India and America. It was an eminent Indian, Swami Vivekananda, who in the last century, speaking at the all-religious forum at Chicago, hailed Columbia as the 'Mother of Liberty'. True to his prophetic words, liberty of the world was saved in the two wars through America's instrumentality. In her freedom movement, India also got America's moral support. In 1917, the letter of the Home Rule leader, Dr. Subrahmanium putting forth India's demand was read in the U.S. Congress at the initiative of Lala Lajpat Rai. Thereafter came the Monford Reforms.

During the second world war, it was at President Roosevelt's instance that Churchill had to make an effort to placate India by sending Sir Stafford Cripps. It is also known what good intention behind the scene efforts were made by the then U.S. Secretary, Louis Johnson, in that episode. Then during the 1942 revolution, it was Secretary of State, Cordell Hull, who made a straight request to whitehall to settle with India, as F.M. Muts did after the failure of Second Round Table Conference. The news was suppressed in India. Be it remembered that the U.S. statesmen did all this without, in the least, being swayed by the powerful anti-India propaganda carried on by the British for years.

But after India got independence and the ancient land was divided, America, as far as India is concerned, inherited the misguiding policy of the British. In short, they took up the British mantle. In this, U.S. was unluckily misled by some Yankee correspondents. It was the 'New York Times' correspondent in Moscow, who by his despatches, induced the white-House to recognise Soviet Russia 15 years after the Bolshevik Revolution. What all these years had seen was that U.S. had stood against India in the U.N. and in various ways pulled strings in favour of Pakistan, of course, under the camouflage of equal dealing. Mrs. Vijay Lakshmi Pandit. India's ambassador in Washington, had to put in a word about Pakistan's purchase of American arms. America denied it squarely.

Disappointment comes to our lot in every step and in every turn. Why? Because our minds work in a complex manner. Our leaders want to execute all programmes even though in some cases, some of them may be conductorial to one another. This is just like a householder worshipping all deities in all form with the hope that at least one of them will deliver the boon, even though the worship of the deities may entail mutually contradictory observances.

Most of our political leaders, for over 60 years of independence, have not so far realized the full implications of independence itself. Why? This is because there has been a peaceful transfer of power. Had there been a violent rebellion and then forcible seizure of power, it would have been a tremendous shock to the entire process of our thinking and we would have probably been better prepared to realize the implications of independence. But we can but look on with a dead-fish stare at the sinister activities of our political leaders and ministers.

To distract the attention from the Kashmir dispute, the Nehru Govt. had set the example of how to commit political murder; and our present political leaders will obviously never be cowed by threats. Why? Because they were and are absolutely out of place and likely to strengthen the hands of mischief-mongers. The inadequacy of the law is sometimes put forward as an excuse by the Govt's spokesman, but the people find it very difficult to believe that a Govt. with a virtually unanimous legislature behind it cannot change the law.

There is no denying the fact that the popularity of the Congress has been on the decline since it assumed the reins of Govt. in Aug. 1947. The causes leading to its unpopularity have been due partly to its own defects and partly to circumstances beyond its control. In addition to its own inherent problems of reorganization, the Congress was confronted with certain external problems created by other rival political parties, mostly Leftists, by way of labour unrest, the full brunt of which apparently fell upon the Govt. Such uneasy situation reflected upon the organization which was indirectly responsible for the action of the Govt. Why? Because it is the organization which set up the Govt. There had been occasions when sharp difference of opinion over certain matters led to frictions between the Congress and the Govt. on the one hand, and among the members themselves within the Congress on the other. No consistency was maintained between the ideologies of the Congress and the policies of the Govt. And the progressive weakening of the organization failed to check in time to avert a catastrophe. And the Kashmir issue! The Congress at that time had been very much busy in their reciprocal destruction not to care at all what was going on in the Kashmir valley.

Since the achievement of independence, the Congress has thrown into the thin air the ideals which Gandhi had preached during his life time. For over 60 years, the Congress has been deluding the countrymen into believing something on Kashmir issue which is really far from the truth. Gandhi condemned the partition as a sin as soon as the cry for Pakistan came from the Muslim League. Yet the power-freedom on the frame-work of partition. Few years after partition, they felt that our relations with Pakistan had not been solved. And the Kashmir issue was in a complete shambles.

It is sometimes said that no single phrase has done more harm in the political history of India than : "Every case must be considered on its Merits." It is practically impossible even for an Indian to make any judgement about politics or morals which does not appeal to three distinct authorities, reason, experience and revelation. In general, Indian Statesmen are scrupulous about discharging treaty obligations. They justify this scrupulousness by arguing that experience has proved that it is socially expedient to keep promises. Over-looking the plains of the Indian and Pakistani Punjabs, the war-torn and battle-scared Jammu province of the disputed state of Jammu and Kashmir, is today passing through a period of transition. The country of valiant Rajputs, unassuming army-minded Brahmins, virile Muslims and depressed Harijans, has now been passing through a critical phase in its chequered history where the entire future of the land of Saint Jamawant (one of the warriors of Lord Rama's army after whose name Jammu is called 'hangs in the balance.')

With an area of 12,376 sq. miles, and a population above 35 lakhs (including Pakistan held areas) the Jammu province following the population of India has assumed great strategic importance. Bordering the Indian and Pakistani Punjabs, the hilly track serves as the vital physical line between India and Kashmir (including Ladakh). The area is the home of lakhs of hardy non-Muslims who unlike the Kashmiries have built up fine military traditions. The people of this area ... Hindus, Muslims and Sikhs ... are veterans in mountain and snow warfare, having proved their mettle even on the snow-bound dizzy heights of Ladakh and the icy regions of Western Tibet, situated to the north-east of

Kashmir valley.

After the conquest of India, the Mughals started converting the people to Islam. A section of Pakistani rulers still believe that as the Mughal ruled over India in the past, Pakistan leaders should also rule over India and Hindus. Their hopes got a momentum when our leaders agreed to partition and continued to tolerate their hostile acts. The slogan '*Hans ke liya hai Pakistan, lad ke lenge Hindustan*' was in the mouths of these Pakistani leaders at that time, and to make it a reality, they sent infiltrators into Kashmir.

It is a pity that many foreigners (and some Indians) do not try to understand the basic hatred Pakistan's leaders have for Hindus and Indians, when they try to convince India that once the Kashmir problem is solved, the relations between the two countries will improve. Bhutto's calling Indians 'dogs' has once again proved that these 'Mughals' do not understand the value of peace, peaceful coexistence or democracy. They understand only the language of war. It is natural to the ghost of the Mughal empire.

True, Hindus and Muslims in mediaeval India did not always live in perfect peace. Occasional conflicts are bound to occur when two communities, divided in religious, linguistic or any other ground, live side by side. But this does not make separate nations. The Hindus and Muslims of the Mughal period never considered themselves two different options. If they quarrelled with each other sometimes, they also "lived together". The two nation theory was a nineteenth century invention of British imperialists. They depicted the Muslim rule in India as oppressive in order to glorify their own rule. And Vincent Smith was no exception. Often it is said that the Muslim rulers destroyed Hindu temples. So did many a Hindu King (vide Jaswant Rao Holkar by S.N. Qanungo). The unproductive wealth hoarded by the priestly class prompted the rulers to attack temples. Often we hear that the Muslims oppressed the Hindus for centuries. It is incredible that the Hindus had become so weak as to suffer away, oppression for seven or eight centuries. Moreover, did not the Hindus on many occasions oppress that co-religionists? Who can forget the mid-eighteenth century Maratha ravages on the districts of West Bengal, largely inhibited by Hindus, when men were massacred, women ravished, and villages burnt down to ashes? It was a Muslim ruler, Nawab Alivardi, who checked the Maratha menace to a great extent and then devoted himself to rebuilding the desolated areas (vide Alivardi and his times, by Dr. K.K. Dutta) Looters and murderers have no religion, they are neither Hindu nor Muslim.

We ought to open our eyes to the realities of the present and the forebodings of the future, on the issue of Indo-Pakistan conflict, on Kashmir problems.

This issue helped dramatize the way the pigmented world, particularly the Asian nations are thinking. All the Asian and African nations have in some way or other suffered at the hands of the 'White' powers during the past three centuries. How the humiliations have burned into Asian hearts was perhaps decisively demonstrated when the iron bands of Marxist discipline were found woefully inadequate to overcome the smouldering racial memories of China and resulted in the bitter Sino-Russian split.

In this hardly civilized world, love rarely begets love but hate always begets hate, and with an appalling venegeance. The racial in justice piled upon the Afro-Asians by Europeans over the past centuries has hardened into memories of hatred. Racial atrocities continue unabated. Despite 'American' freedom, Russian 'Socialism', British 'democracy' and French 'Equality', Afro-Asians live very much in a world on inequality and injustice. For example, the whites form only a third of the world's population and yet occupy three fourths of the earth's surface.

When Lord Mountbatten announced in June, 1947, his scheme to divide India, Mr. Jinnah did not have a feeling of achievement but got frustrated over having got a truncated and moth-eaten Pakistan. From those days on, his anxiety ... and heritage ... had been to truncate India too so that the two should resemble each other.

Anti-India feelings of Islamabad never die as old as accountants never die; they just lose their balance. Anti-Hindu feelings of Pakistani rulers never die, as old anesthesiologists never die; they just run out of gas. The pathological disease of Pakistan against India on Kashmir never dies as old procrastinators never die; they just keep putting it off. The treacherous, unexplored areas of the world are not in continents or the seas; they are in the minds and hearts of men.

It is not surprising that a feeling of culture and economic exploitation had persisted in the minds of East Pakistanis (now Bangladesh) and that Urdu-Bengali riots took place soon after the formation of that country.

Achievement of a truncated Pakistan frustrated its author to such a degree that his first demand was for a corridor between East and West Pakistan. This reminded one of the demands for the Danzig corridor on the part of another similarly vain and autocratic person. The failure of this demand was natural as it lacked all rationale. He then turned his attention to Travancore where the State Dewan was dreaming of an independent Travancore having direct links with the British empire. The subsistence of this pocket would not only have hindered the getting together of South India but would also have provided a fuelling station on the sea-route from Karachi to Chittagung.

Pakistan's anxiety to thrust a dagger in the very heart of India in the form of an independent Hyderabad is well-known. In his anxiety to disintegrate India, Mr Jinnah also tried to entice the Maharaja of Patiala either into joining Pakistan or staying independent. Even tiny spots like Junagadh were not ignored in furtherance of his 'Master plan'. It was, therefore, no surprise that he was in a hurry about Kashmir too. Failure of political manoeuvre yielded place to invasion. If these designs had been succeeded, India would have been sub-divided into many islands.

Mr. Jinnah's successors, though of varied character and outlook, have inherited these designs. Anxiety to do harm to India manifested itself in sympathy with the Portuguese colonisers over Goa and active help to underground Nagas. Any stick was considered good to beat India with. The 'master plan' was to a degree accomplished by Pakistan when its rulers handed over a slice of Indian territory to China. It has proved that Pakistan does not need Kashmir for its own good, as is sometimes claimed, but merely to split India. Mr. Jinnah is the founder of Pakistan's neurotic behaviour drawing wide publicity as revolting as shocking.

This then is the underlying political problem ... basically it is the anxiety of Pakistan to truncate India. It is this problem that U.N. has undertaken to resolve.

Even when Kashmir is demanded for Pakistan by war or by peace, demand for an independent Kashmir to support as a second best. In the division of Kashmir, claim is laid to the valley only so that Jammu and Ladakh are effectively separated. It is part of the old game; Hyderabad was to divide North and South India ; the South was to be further disintegrated by Travancore; West India should have ulcers of Junagadh and Goa; and while East Bengal (now Bangaladesh) stood between West Bengal and Assam, Nagaland should be encouraged to divide the Assam Hills. The pattern in the North could only be completed by inserting an independent or dependent valley of Kashmir between Ladakh and the rest of India.

Mr. Jinnah dreamt of disintegrating India not only on the basis of religion but also as a geographical entity. Kashmir was the end of a shattered dream.

Pakistan is concerned neither to assist the Indian Muslims (that is why Muslims are pushed out to Assam and not welcomed into Pakistan) nor to liberate the Kashmiris (the miserable condition of the people of occupied Kashmir is the evidence) but to disrupt the unity of India within and to impede its growth.

Leaders of Pakistan, to hide their guilt, often shout that "India has never reconciled itself to the formation of Pakistan", whereas the reality is just the reverse. Pakistani fundamentalists from literate down to illiterate fanaticism preoccupied with Fraud's 'Darkomania' strive to cut India's limbs to resemble Pakistan's deformity.

Indian leaders should remind themselves (at least once every morning) that China has entered the nuclear club. What this is going to make to the security of India has been prophetically understood.

Asian nations are gradually converging towards India or China. Significantly, F.M. Ayub Khan, former President of Pakistan, having assumed office after a military coup, once told president Johnson of America, :"*If we (Pakistan) lose the West, may lose our economy; but if we lose China, we may lose our country*". It was a great blunder of Ayub Khan to ventilate Pakistan's weakness in her foreign policy. China's land hunger and desire for domination are insatiable. The challenge she poses could only be met by India's own nuclear deterrent ... bomb for bomb, missile for missile.

Asia is at stake. The Chinese believe that no sacrifice is too great to achieve the domination of Asia. By entering the nuclear club, India will make it clear to China that Asia will not tolerate any yellow or any red tyranny.

China is not a reliable neighbour. She believes in expansionism ... expansionism through the gun. The Congress rulers, since independence, have underestimated the gravity of the situation, with the help of anti-national Indian communists being engulfed in lies and moral depravity and also being created by a neighbour who is every minute developing her thermonuclear weaponry and growing into a more and more dangerous power. She will not hesitate to stretch her bloody paws across our frontiers again. China will never be honest in reaching any settlement or sincere in abiding by them. She will have to be challenged, gun for gun, bomb for bomb. We have had the Chinese hypocrisy in 1962. We must consider the past, the present and the future. Our former Prime Minister, Mr. Jawaharlal Nehru, believing China's dulcet phrases of '*Hindi-Chini bhai-bhai*', made another great mistake. A super-flop Prime Minister on India's foreign policy. Every man has a right in his opinion. But no man has a right to be wrong in his facts. A cage is a cage, even if its bars are gold. The buttressed tears shed over graves are for words left unsaid and deeds left undone. Was our Prime Minister's dream to live on in the hearts of people? The answer is : No. He seemed to prefer to live on in his hat, rose and European style of living. Nehru was like a weaver of tales. He shuttled words back and forth across the loom of his imagination. His words popped like corn over the heat of his indignation at the oppositionists. He forgot how to keep friends who always give candid opinion. He stopped taking advice from other people. His report was filled with omissions.

"Mr. Nehru, in the century of Hitler, Mao and Stalin, was a civilised politician ... an aristocrat who was a socialist, a democrat who exercised a kind of peaceful dictatorship. His two great passions were politics and women." (Octavio Pez, a Mexican by birth, a bureaucrat by profession, and a traveller by nature, wrote in his book 'In Light of India').

Pakistan can afford to manufacture the bomb. Why? Because it is a dictatorship. Secondly, it will not go against India's peaceful designs to make the bomb. Is it not better to be strong but restrained and peace-loving than to be weak and talk big?

The pathology of present discontent is properly diagnosed. Since partition, a large number of Congressmen, ... hangers on by birth and greedy for power in ballot boxes ... were suspicious that would be kicked out of the political arena of the Nehru and Co. The general splinter groups were very much prevalent in the party. They were least worried about Jammu and Kashmir but their greediness for power. The Nehru and Co. at the helms of the ideal political party of the country, especially during the Gandhian era, were crumbled into dust and became one vast area of intrigue for assumption of power through the ballot box. They, bothering about Kashmir dispute, were very much busy in the Tammany Hall methods adopted by the ruling wings of the Congress in the States of the country. Why? To capture and retain power in their own hands and incidentally to shut out others.

For over 50 years, the Central as well as the State Governments have deluded the people of India as a whole. The unrealistic hope generated by the Delhi pacts on several ties with Pakistan is the biggest factor. Political myopia and political reliance on half-hearted pacts and assurances for restoration of conditions suitable for normal life of people in Jammu and Kashmir have only unfolded the mysterious images of our leaders. For any popular govt., particularly a Govt. of the Congress party which cannot escape the moral responsibility for the problems Kashmir has now been under the travesty of untold agony. This lack of foresight is hardly pardonable. The miseries the people of Jammu and Kashmir have suffered on account of unplanned expenditure and the wastage of money the national exchequer has undergone on them add one more instances of the series of instances on the part of the Govt. in different spheres. Here is an amusing story.

A friend of mine, while going to a cinema, entered the hall only after Indian Information news-reel was over. Asked to explain, he replied : "I would rather see one star throughout ten reels of a picture than watch a constellation of Cabinet Ministers packed in one reel." A package of hyocrisy.

Is there no analogy between the Korean and the Kashmir incidents so far as aggression is concerned? The North Koreans were dubbed aggressors by the Security Council when they invaded South Korea. Did not Pakistan and its allies, the tribesmen, invaded Kashmir in the same manner? Whereas US-Anglo spokesmen deliberately said that there was no analogy between the Korean and the Kashmir incidents. If there is any difference, it lies in the fact that the North Korean invaders of South Korea did not commit the atrocities which the invaders of Kashmir committed on their victims.

The U.S.-Sponsored countries have always sidetracked the real issue by raising the plea that 'if the dispute was allowed to remain unsettled any longer, it would result in a catastrophe.' So, if this principle is accepted as sound no aggression by one State on another should go unregistered or unpunished. Whenever there is such an aggression it disturbs peace. So far as the question of punishing the aggressor is concerned what had been done in Korea should have been done in the case of Kashmir too. We do not forget that there were certain elements in the Korean problem which are not present in the Kashmir dispute. There was the question of communism and non-communism. Perhaps the most astonishing thing is the complete silence of the Security Council and the sponsored-spokesmen of the U.S. and Britain regarding the terrorist movement of Pakistan-sponsored mercenaries in Kashmir. For over 60 years Pakistan has not been treated as an aggressor. Will the Security Council be a fool for ever?

After independence, it was the Nehru Govt. that raised the political pettifoggery and criminology along the level of squabbles and party politics, sidetracking the Kashmir issue. It was the Nehru Govt. that polluted our minds through the crude and perverted vehicles of hatred, narrowness and personal ambition. Even before the Congress was born, long before there was anything like a wide political consciousness there were heroic struggles to make the country free. Who can forget the martyrs of the Soppy War? It was the Nehru Govt. that failed to share the sorrows of the common people, their hardships and privations. Why? Because, that time, the Congress bosses were ready to lay down themselves in the soiled bed of hypocrisy, lies, corruption and befooling the people for the sake of personal and party ambitions. Loyalty to the country was not their watch-word. Clandestine was permitted regarding the Kashmir dispute.

After partition, the Kashmir dispute was to the Congress Party a Jig-saw puzzle, and the Govt. began playing hide-and-seek game with the people who have been under a gloomy and staggering state of mind even after 60 years of independence. Who is behind this gasping, staggering and agonising situation in Kashmir? The placid waters of British occupation and cultural conquest had begun to be disturbed even before the Congress was founded on Dec. 28, 1885. The Congress began in a humble way, giving expressions to humble aspirations. The horizon has widened and further widened since then. For decades over after independence, the Congress rule had been the years not of freedom but of slavery and frustration. Their rule has already ceased to satisfy many of us. Our country has after all achieved its independence of discontent. Freedom, like wine, intoxicated the Congress rulers. They have created external enemies and internal dangers.

Those in charge of our States are totalitarian in any sense. They want subversive activities and wish to suppress opinions. They do not welcome criticism as well as opposition which degenerates into a desire for creating chaos. The Congress rulers did not throw open the shutters of their windows and live in their haunted house. So they could not hear strange noises and the ghosts will not depart still now. The Congress is still in our midst. From Gandhi down to Mrs. Indira Gandhi, failed to soothing our lacerated hearts, healing and wounds of communal frenzy, bringing courage to the terror-stricken areas of Kashmir and solace to the bereaved. Men and Women of all communities flocked to them in their distress as boats seek a safe haven during a storm. But they were flying to each others' throats, and fraternising in a feigned amity. It was the magic alchemy of the Mahatma, transmuting gold into baser metal, transforming love into hate, hardening tolerance and revenge into intolerable and unforgiveness.

The Indian Communists, in the name of socialism, have not so far lashed out and coughed out their thought-provoking vehemence against the intolerable misdoings of Pakistan-sponsored terrorist groups in Kashmir. They have remained silent. But they have so far curdled on blood by resorting to looting, arsoning, killing and terrorising the people. A large number of dissatisfied people are the targets of the so-called demoralised and ideologically paralysed communists afflicted with voice-worn slogans.

A small but earnest coterie of the Nehru cabinet fumbled out the Kashmir issue.

Mr. Nehru had shown hopeless and blundering incompetence in dealing with the problem of Hindus living in Pakistan. The Congress leaders who then occupied seats of power in Indian Union were a party to the partition of the country. That was their first sinful act ... an act in which the Father of the Nation refused to acquiesce. Having agreed to the division of the country, the Congress should have at least seen to this that sufficient protection was arranged for millions of Hindus left behind in the North-West frontier province, West Punjab, Sind and East Bengal, for at the time of transfer of power from British to Indian hands the Congress leaders wee associated with the Govt. of the country. In this also the Congress leadership failed miserably. The result was the terrible holocaust ... the horrible bloodbath in West Punjab in which millions of Hindus suffered. While West Punjab and other parts of West Pakistan were thus denuded of Hindus and multi-millionaires became street beggars overnight, the bulk of more than a crore of Hindus remained in East Bengal, and advice was tendered to the latter by the Congress high-ups here across the border to stick to their hearth and home. Then came the great killing in East Bengal (now Bangladesh). How did the Nehru Govt. meet the situation? They post-haste entered into a pact with the then premier, Liaquat Ali Khan and considered their duty done to the Hindus of East Bengal. Ousted from trade and commerce in which they occupied a position of pre-eminence, dispossessed of their land by a politically dishonest piece of legislation, with all avenues of employment in official and non-official establishments closed to them, with determined attempts made to Islamise their culture and language, with the honour of their womenfolk at stake and subject to a thousand and one pinpoints, the Hindus of East Bengal (now Bangladesh) since the birth of Pakistan had been made to feel at any step, at every hours of their life, that they were not wanted in that holy land of Islam and no opportunity had been allowed to go unveiled of to squeeze the Hindus out. But what had the Nehru Govt. done to ensure the protection of the Hindus of East Bengal? Except some vague statements about the deterioration in the economic condition of East Bengal and of the position of the minorities there.

Constitutional pundits shook their wise head and said that nothing could be done by Nehru in regard to the Hindus of East Bengal since they were foreign nationals. We do not understand this bunkum of Hindus of East Bengal being foreign nationals simply because certain political leaders who happened to hold the stage at a particular point in a nation's history, agreed among themselves to subject their mother country, to an artificial vivisection under the inspiring guidance of a Britisher, Lord Mountbatten, and then declared those nationals who happened to live at that particular point of time on the other side of the artificially drawn partition line as foreign nationals? The Hindus of East Bengal (now Bangladesh) and West Pakistan were as much Indian nationals as those living on the side of the Mountbatten Partition line and no amount of constitutional or legal casuistry can explain this away. The Nehru Govt. never told the Govt. of Pakistan that the Hindus living in East Bengal were Indian nationals and that any act of oppression committed on a Hindu there would be treated as an act of oppression committed on a Hindu there would be treated as an act of oppression on an Indian national and dealt with as such. It was a preconceived plan of Nehru and Gandhi who hatched mysteriously and hypocritically. Assuming that the partition agreement was perfectly valid, the whole basis of that agreement and naturally therefore of partition has gone in view of the failure of Pakistan to redeem the gentle man's pledge to provide protection for the minorities living under their charge. May one enquire from our present Congress leaders for whose benefit Mr. Nehru maintained such a costly parahernalia as the Indian High Commissioner's office in Pakistan. How many Indian nationals were there in Karachi and Dacca according to the definition of the term?

There is irrefutable evidence that wild rumours have been circulated by a certain section of the majority community in Bangladesh regarding the consequences of the Kashmir dispute. As a result of which, Hindus and other non-Muslims reading there have been thrown into a great shambles. Besides, the surging cacophony of Muslim fundamentalists living there has added fuel of fiery speech to fire of smouldering crises. To give reality, to that great shambles, a regular campaign of terrorism, intimidation, oppression and outrages has been unleashed covertly or overtly. The Govt. at that is either to fan the fires of hooliganism or weaken to keep it under control.

It is oft-affirmed policy of Pakistan to establish an out-and-out Islamic State from which people believing in religions other than Islam must be squeezed out, and that is why Mr. Jinnah at the very outset demanded outright exchange of population. But instead of following the necessary corollary of a partition and the lessons of history. Mr. Nehru did not agree to that. After the Punjab atrocities resulting in exchange of population on either side, we were solemnly answered by Mr. Jinnah that Hindus and the minorities of Sind would be given due protection and facilities so that they might continue to live with horror, and it was during the lifetime of Mr. Jinnah that the minorities in Sind were forced to migrate. Then came with the turn of East Bengal (now Bangladesh). The squeezing out of minorities from there began in instalments since Feb. 1950. Many of those who came to India were persuaded to go back to their ancestral homes after the Nehru-Liaquat Ali pact. We call it a foolish pact from the Indian point of view. Nehru never thought of economic aspect of this wholesale migration of the minorities. Nehru made no good lodging protests to the Pakistan. No more of this nonsense, please; what a tragedy of bungling! But what is more surprising is the fact that no congressmen in India appeared to be concerned about the miserable plight of non-Muslims in East Pakistan and Nehru's blundering about the gloomy picture of Kashmir in future. But they were evidently satisfied with the moth-eaten Nehru-Liaquat Pact. It was a Himalayan blunder of Mr. Nehru, wittingly or unwittingly, for the acceleration of Kashmir dispute what we have seen even after 60 years of independence. What a horrible blunder to a country like India! Whereas Mr. Nehru expected to accomplish the impossible feat of befooling all men for all time by sidetracking the issue. Throughout his tenure, Nehru and co. had kept the people deluding with false hope on Kashmir issue that the Hindus in Kashmir would receive their due protection whenever they needed it. Mr. Nehru became a silent spectator of the whole tragic drama in Pakistan and in Kashmir also.

"Since partition, the leaders of Pakistan have always been deluding and distracting the people of Pakistan. It is only Medomania." said Altaf Hussain, the ever-growing editor of the 'Dawn'. Mr. Altaf had converted through his editorial columns, every good and bad Muslims into an Indian agent; within less time than that he might have converted all these the biggest booby-trap on the entire Islamic world, and notwithstanding his pious head, U.S.A. was able to understand this.

Now the question is : What is M.E.D.O.? Middle East Defence Organisation. Lord Mountbatten was expected to be at the head of the proposed MED with its headquarters in Cyprus, functioning for the time being from Malta. Lady Mountbatten was everywhere, even outside MEDO burqua, to sell the idea while U.S.A. was asked to foot the bill for the sake of same air bases in Pakistan. Neutral India was being urged to watch the process with neutral benevolence.

The MEDO burqua was being tailored, however, according to plan with military, rather than political considerations in the forefront. Originally prepared by the British, the finishing touches were given by U.S.A. Islamic burqua is now being prepared, fomenting harmony of the Muslim countries by exchange of army and press missions.

Many a fanatical supporter of the League as they were in 1947 have become its bitterest opponent in the name of Islam. Even in Beijing, they offer their namaz regularly and object to eating a chicken that has not been killed in the Islamic way. They have the most luxurious beard in all Pakistan. From Liaquat Ali Khan down to the present ruling power, they have been portrayed an assortment of contrary pulls with cracks and fissures in the Central Cabinet and the provincial Govts. as disobedient to the very concept of a single, national authority. The self-avowed architects of Pakistan have so far administered the most treacherous blow to the last remaining strand of faith in the art of Islamization. They are all cursed with the corroding cancer of selfishness. Mysterious are thy ways, Allah!

The evil-blossoming of the Jehad spirit in Pakistan at the beginning of the second half of 1951 demonstrated most significantly how the ideologies followed by the two countries had affected their peoples. While in Pakistan, it became neutral for the press to continue an unbridled campaign of incitement to murder and destruction in the name of Allah, in India perhaps the most horrified people were Indian citizens of the Islamic Faith whose leaders in a statement pointed out that this incitement was totally against the teachings of the Great Prophet of Islam.

For many years, India had watched the mounting fever of Jehad in Pakistan and slowly a pattern had emerged. The Jehad cries waxed or waned according to the developments, in the United Nations, on the Kashmir issue. The campaign had waxed when Sir Owen Dixon in September, 1950 held that Pakistan aided tribal invasion of Kashmir in 1947, was a breach of international law. The Kashmir resolution in the Security Council and the appointment of Dr. Graham as the U.N. representative in March 1951 was another signal for the campaign to be stepped up. This time however behind the sound and fury of Jehad there was something more concrete ... the perpetration by Pakistan in rapid succession of major violations of the Cease-Fire Line.

On India's complaining to the Security Council about these violations, Pakistan took even a more threatening attitude. On June 28, 1951, Pakistan started moving a brigade from Peshawar to Rawalkote which is only 15 miles from Poonch in Indian territory. India, thereupon, drew the U.N. Observers' attention to the aggressive movement on July 3. Pakistan completed this move on July 7. As it was clear that this move directly threatened Poonch and Kashmir and Pakistan was following this up with other equally threatening movements. India started some certain troop movements, on July 10 as defensive precautions. Pakistan had of course been repeatedly warned that any attack on Kashmir would be considered an attack on India.

The aggressive action by Pakistan and defensive reaction by India was seized upon by the Pakistan Govt. to add fuel to the fire of fanatical frenzy which had been carefully nurtured by the Jehad propaganda. While Pakistan shouted from housetops that India was about to attack her, her real intentions were indicated by the symbol which she adopted, the old Fascist symbol of the clenched fist. The war fever was heightened by blackouts, Emergency Ordinances, arms training and recruitment of Razakars, Ansars etc. The only reaction to this in India was the Govt.'s decision to withdraw the main Indian forces to a distance of at least 20 miles from the Pakistan frontier. This was meant to emphasize the defensive character of the Indian troop concentrations and also to provide for a wide enough area between Indian and Pakistan troops against avoidable local clashes.

Judging from all this point of view, we may arise a pertinent question, whether our so-called popular leaders, at the helm of powers and of taking decisive action, know the real meaning of what is aggression or not. Man lives to learn. It did not occur to other learned authors of the U.N. Charter that the word 'aggression' should be defined. Yet the suppression of the acts of aggression is one of the fundamental purposes of the U.N. The very first article of the Charter which lays down the purposes and principles of the U.N. says in part :

"The purposes of the U.N. are to maintain international peace and security and to that end : to take effective collective measures for the prevention and removal of threats to the peace and for the suppression of the acts of aggression or the breaches of the peace."

But what is aggression? The matter was discussed in the General Assembly of the U.N.O. on Jan 31, 1952 and the Assembly agreed by a narrow majority on the desirability of defining aggression and passed the matter on to the agenda of its next regular session. This was done despite British and US objections.

This shows that the matter is not so simple as it would appear to a person of average intelligence. The controversy whether aggression should be defined at all or left undefined as in the Charter is easily understandable. The dictionary meaning of 'aggression' is : 'first act of hostility or injury; a search of the peace; an attack on public privileges.' Does it make one wiser as to what really constitutes aggression? Then, again, aggression as between individuals is something different from that between nations. The UN Charter deals with international aggression. But the UN has found it difficult to follow a consistent policy. In Korea, the communists were guilty of aggression. Why not Pakistan is guilty of aggression in Kashmir? The UN took prompt action in meeting on the aggression in Korea but it has been incubating for the last 60 years over the Kashmir issue. The UN, suffering from delusional insanity, has waffled on about the definition of 'aggression'.

But in the absence of a definition of aggression, various groups might view this act in different ways and as long as there is no definition of aggression an act of aggression might not even be recognised. Is UN pretending to be ignorant of the definition? Does it hope to gain from the trouble?

Why? There are very good reasons for the unwillingness of the powers controlling the UN to define agression. If the term is defined, the scope of discretion in the matter of intervention would be limited. This is exactly why they were unwilling that the term should be defined. Power politics has more to do in the matter of than the absence of a definition. If Pakistan had not proceeded against as an aggressor in Kashmir, is it to be supposed that there was a doubt in the minds of the powers as to whether Pakistan had really committed an aggression?

There is hardly any doubt that partition was the price of India's freedom. It was Nehru who was apt to underestimate the realities of the situation. Interim Government : A political jugglery. How Mr.C.H. Bhaba (a friend of Sardar Patel's son) was first appointed to, and then dropped from, the Ministry; how Sardar Patel vehemently opposed the suggestion that he should give up the Home Ministry; and how Mr. Liaquat Ali (who became Finance Minister) ruled so efficiently that not even a Chaprassi could be appointed in any department without his sanction. The situation within the Central Executive had so annoyed and irritated Patel that he became a believer in partition.

When Lord Mountbatten suggested that partition might offer a solution for the present difficulty, he found ready acceptance of the idea in Patel's mind. He openly said that he was prepared to let the League have a part of India, if only he could get rid of it.

Then came Mr. Nehru . Mr. Nehru was greatly impressed by Lord Mountbatten, but perhaps was the influence of Lady Mountbatten. She was not only extremely intelligent but had a most attractive and friendly temperament. She admired her husband greatly and in many cases she interpreted his thoughts to those who would not at first agree with him.

Another person was Mr. V.K. Krishna Menon who influenced Mr. Nehru and had often given him wrong advice including on Kashmir dispute. Owing to the ominous influence worked infectiously on Mr. Nehru, by Mr. Patel and Mr. Mountbatten, the petition of India became a settled fact. It was accepted to the straight and true, when on June 14, 1947, Gandhi addressed the AICC asking it to accept the working committee's resolution in favour of the division of India. So the Kashmir problem which has now been on the go has been categorically plugged in within the wheels of conspiracy. So just after the cradle song of partition, genesis of Pakistan's 'Hymns of Hate' against India has sealed her infamy. So pervertedly and awkwardly through blatant propaganda and bullets. Islamabad has framed up a vexatious prosecution on India.

In contrast with the restraint exercised by the Indian press, the press in Pakistan, both English and Urdu, has been engaged in a systematic campaign of vilification against India, a campaign to misinform and mislead world opinion as well as Muslim opinion in India.

The Pakistan Govt, since independence, have apparently done nothing, even at the drawing of New Millennium, to suppress or discountenance the publication of such articles. Obviously, the fanantics clothed in vicious implications of bigoted Islamic tenets, have swallowed up intensely and bitterly to battle against India. The press in Pakistan has spared no pains to eventful concocted stories, cooking up fanaticism and fabricating reports of atrocities on Muslims in India.

The fact that certain sections of the Pakistan press have been indulging in Byzantine complexities of a campaign of abuse and vilification against India and that such a campaign has been heading forward in violent and perplexing form of bitter relations shows that even if the Pakistani Govt. are not behind this curtain of cant politics, they cannot, at any rate, have been aware of it. For, indeed, so numerous have been the stories woven up dangerously, at the behest of the Pakistan Govt., day by day and published not only in Karachi and Islamabad but also in other Pakistan-sponsored Islamic countries in full swing. Administering a high infectious doses of Islamic fanaticism amidst the innocent and illiterate sections of people in Pakistan on Kashmir, such a baseless and fruitless propaganda can only be described as a hymn of hate and deliberate effort to poison the relations between the two countries with the profession of peace and friendship.

From Ayub Khan down to the present ruling Govt. all prime Ministers' and Military rulers' speeches contain oft-repeated references to 'enemies' who are supposed to be creating a watershed moment of difficulties and obstacles for Pakistan. They all seemed to be fatuated with the 'spies and enemy' agents who have been trying to undermine the morale of Pakistan and even the present rulers' talks of Pakistanis willing to shed the last drop of their blood in defending every inch of the soil of Pakistan no matter from which side Pakistan is attached. Besides having this, they have all ventured upon skatting on the thin ice of terrorist exhibition around the border. Sponsoring terrorism, and embracing viper in the bosom, Pakistan has started, defying all hazards and spurning the odds of hypocrisy and lies, terrorizing South-Asia.

In keeping with this sabre-rattling by Ayub Khan down to the present ruler, mendacious propaganda has been carried on among the masses through the agreements for example Calcutta agreement on April 18, 1948, the Simla pact, and others.

The most fanatic lies have been published such as that rivers of blood had been flowing near the Jama Masjid and Ballimarran in Delhi and that a general massacre of Muslims had been going on. The report appeared in the 'Mussalman' of Karachi on August 22,1948 and repeated by 'Anjam' of Karachi on Aug 25, 1948 and also editorially drawn attention to the 'Inquilab' of Lahore on Aug. 27.

Here are a few other glaring instances of the well-designed propaganda against the Indian Govt. gleaned from important Urdu paper in Western Pakistan.

Readers of the 'Zamindar' of Lahore were told on July 5, 1948 that Indian leaders had started a general massacre of Muslims on whose flesh dog were fed. So many facts are there how the Pakistani rulers have cooked up and been doctoring the facts and figures amounted to the basic principles of Kashmir.

Not only that the deceptive stand of China is inexplicable and unpardonable. In the conflict between India and Pakistan on Kashmir dispute, China wants both sides to lose. It is an awkwardly manoeuvering strategy of Machiavellian machination. Even if India and Pakistan were to come to an understanding over Kashmir, China's deceptive but exciting attention will not ever cease but will become more overt.

China's reply to Mr. R.K. Nehru early in 1962 lulled Pandit Nehru into the belief that China was on our side, over Kashmir. Pandit Nehru believed the Chinese. Peking's subsequent sophistry (which disillusioned us) would constitute a good joke and was not our vital national interest involved. Communism of deceptive and hypocrite China and her obstreperous communism are nothing but disguised imperialism. Why China is deliberately interested in intervening in Kashmir problem? The answer is very simple. Under the facade of 'brotherhood', China was, and is, even now avowedly hunting for an empire, fomenting Pakistani rulers to run a Juggernaut of terrorism all over

India, and even in Asia and Africa. But in doing so, she has faced in India a formidable opponent who has a strong friendship with both the Eastern and Western blocs. If India proceeds a consummate economic condition with such long strides as she is doing now and if China's perennial provocation she sticks to her policy of non-alignment and peace with such vigor and earnestness as to draw the respect of all countries, especially from the two super-powers, China's intentions will virtually collapse. That is why she has intervened so incredulously in Kashmir problem and made herself a third party with these sinister objectives.

1. She wants to snatch Pakistan army from the clutches of USA and forces her subsequently to subserve own aims and purposes; to achieve it she has wooed Pakistan, instigated her to launch an attack on Kashmir playing a key role of Machiavellian machinations on Indian soil as a past master in behalf of her own political hypocrisy behind her policy of peaceful co-existence. Besides having this, China has given Pakistan, as her foster-child, her unstained verbal support in the Indo-Pakistani crisis.
2. She has tried to convince the Afro-Asian countries that she champions the cause of liberty and justice while India has taken an aggressive attitude towards her peaceful neighbouring countries.
3. If she can occupy strategically important Kashmir she might pose a threat to India and could be able to jeoparadise India's defence more easily than now.

China acknowledged Kashmir's accession to India in the days of Sino-Indian friendship. Now she has forgotten all of her old habits, and is instantly backing Pakistan possessing of all her meritriciously done make-believe treatment behind India. She has loaded the dice of communism with a pack of lies amidst the 'lie factory' around the fanatical crusade of a most crude Islamisation, in this sub-continent. So the romance of her diplomatic illness has only offered a school of mockery, after sedulously fomenting Pakistan's belligerency towards India. And it is quite impossible to predict that a time will come when the Chinese Govt. will turn round to Pakistan with the disarming question, where did the Chinese Govt. accept without reservation the position that Kashmir should belong to Pakistan?

Since the Indo-Pakistan clash a few fresh developments have disturbed China profoundly; her friendship with her most dogmatic Indonesia had suffered a serious setback. China's image has been tarnished in some Afro-Asian countries. China has been severely condemned by other deteriorating communist countries fighting for their survival of ideology through violence, bloodshed, lies and propaganda ... the basic thoughts of world communism in practice.

China's deception reminds us of the well-known Irish bull concerning a member of the Irish Dail, who, when taken to task for saying that half the members of the House were fools, made amends by clarifying that half the members of the House were not fools.

It was Mr. Nehru who, in the largeness of his heart, had not ever insisted upon any legal phraseology when he first asked the China to defend their stand on Kashmir.

While we have diplomatic relations with hostile countries like China and Pakistan, it was surprising that Mr. Nehru refused to recognise Israel which in no way was unfriendly to India.

While the Thar desert was approaching Delhi by two inches every year and throwing most dust over the metropolis, could we not consider taking Israel's help in checking the desert and making the barren land of Rajasthan fertile producing grapes, dates and citrus fruits of the best quality?

When Mr. Nehru and Co. failed to shake hands with Israel, the congress leaders were fully contigent upon the Arab states. Why? Claiming to judge every issue in her foreign relations on its merits chose to walk meekly behind the Arab States, in the hope that some day in the future our Government would convert their neutral attitude over the Kashmir question to one of positive support. Our leaders have still been living in fool's paradise on the Byzantine complexities over Kashmir.

The misery of 'Azad Kashmir' may be lost sight of in the present turmoil. Legally and politically, it continues to be an integral part of the State of Jammu and Kashmir, in the Union of India. Since the cease fire of 1948, the region has been under the de facto Pakistani rule, but its legal status has not been altered; i.e., it has not become a part of Pakistan. Many times the people of Azad Kashmir have become with such appeals (for re-union) with Srinagar, but Sheikh Abdullah had always pushed them back. Sheikh Abdullah was no longer in control.

Our political leaders are not afraid of murder and will never be cowed down by threats. Why? They are absolutely out of place and likely to strengthen the hands of the mischief-mongers. The inadequacy of the law is sometimes put forward as an excuse by the Govt's spokesman, but the people find it very difficult to believe that a Govt. with a virtually unanimous legislature behind it cannot change the law.

After sixty years of deadly rivalries and manoeuvering among the various groups within the Congress, every congress election, both as the party in power and as a political organization, has always proved a final cockpit when the groups have had a chance to test their strength and the group that has emerged successfully is to throw the rivalries into the dustbin of hypocrisy. Non-Congress parties pick them up from the hide-out of the dustbins into the dustbins of lies and propaganda, locking themselves up into the custody of self-supporting political hidebounds.

Prior to dwelling upon the topic, we have to be back to the beginning. In the whole of India there was no better friend of Pakistan than Pandit Jawaharlal Nehru. After partition, he had been consistently generous to Pakistan in all political and economic disputes, between the two States. This generosity had been described as appeasement in certain quarters in his own country. His

Govt. paid Pakistan fifty crores of rupees at a time when Pakistani forces were ravaging Indian territory in Kashmir. It concluded agreements on trade and minorities, and insisted on scrupulous observance of these agreements on India's part even though Pakistan repeatedly violated her pledges. Nehru proposed a 'no-war' pact to the prime Minister of Pakistan and received the reply that it was far better to settle individual disputes instead of talking vaguely about 'no-war' pact. When he proceeded to deal with individual disputes, such as compensation for evacuee property, distribution of canal waters, recovery of abducted women, etc, he found himself knocking against a stone wall. And then Pakistan openly and plainly accused India of aggression. Nehru was a champion of communalism and autocracy; He sent the troops to Kashmir. Why? Simply because he wanted to perpetuate the Hindu Maharaja's tyranny over his Muslim subjects and to strangle economically and politically the Islamic State of Pakistan.

This is a strange denouement the aggressor accused the victim in the name of law and morality. Wherever India builds a temple of peace, Pakistan cunningly builds a house of devildom under the shadow of that temple.

Why does India allow Kashmir question to get entangled in such difficulties and paradoxes? Our leaders will have to know what one is talking about Kashmir. No amount of Jugglery can improve the nation unless the quality of its people can be improved. We are tired of numbers. We want quality. A well-informed public is the World's greatest security. Our leaders indulge in the arts of mummery, play-acting and footling wisdom which are parts of thc professional repertoire.

Who will be an ideal judge on Kashmir issue? A judge has not only to know the law but also to understand the men he has to judge and to whom the law is to be applied.

Remember : Pakistan is a weaver of tales. She, a state of theophany, shuttles words of cant and hypocrisy back and fourth across the loom of her imagination.

When Kashmir crows like a cock, the sun begins to rise.

3

JAMMU... ITS PEOPLE AND CULTURE : Kashmir's Nostrils

The mountainous and sub-mountain region in the north-east of Punjab (India), comprising the Jammu province of the Jammu and Kashmir State, Himachal Pradesh, Kangra and Bilaspore has always figured prominently in the annals of Indian chivalry and its bravery and heroism have been enshrined in many a legend and song. Its ancient history ... a romantic blend of facts, fancy and myths, goes back to the Vedic and Puranic times. But a chronological and continuous narrative of the history of its people, their life, culture, social and economic movements is on account of paucity of materials and lack of sound research. Well-nigh impossible. The people of this region came again into the foreground during the 17th and 18th century as the exponents of a new school of painting, known variously as the Pahari School of painting, the Kangra school, Badohil School of painting or the Jammu school of Painting. It is one of the most glorious phases in the history of Indian painting and the period culminates in the founding of a consolidated Dogra Rule in Jammu, Kashmir and northern frontier region of Gilight and Laddakh.

The culture, heritage and contribution of Dogras and Paharis of Jammu and Kashmir State have not so far been properly appreciated or assessed. Lionel Heath writes under the caption "Indian Art in the British Empire Exhibition" :

"The Jammu artists show a very definite Mughal influence, the method of their paintings approaches that of their predecessors and they have a character of portraiture in their heads and figures ..."

The people inhabiting the Jammu province of Jammu and Kashmir state are of the great Aryan race. The settlers in the hills and sub-mountain region, borders of the Punjab plains are known as Dogras. But those who spread to the mountains and went into regions, where snow falls are called Paharis. Slim in make, active and strong, the Dogras have intelligent faces, small features and well-shaped mouths in character, a Dogra is a simple and straight forward. He is sensitive and has got his individual sense of self-respect.

Dogras and Paharis have a community of dress, habits, culture, religion, and worship that unite them into a coherent social group. They believe in social gods and goddesses. Though they know Rama, Krishna and Sita and worship them like gods. They believe the God is the master of the evil as well as the master of the good. The greatest contribution of the Dogras is the political, cultural and social integration of the northern regions of Kashmir, Gilgit and Laddakh.

LAND OF DOGRAS - I (THE LIFELINE OF KASHMIR)

How the strategic and political importance of Jammu, the land of the Dogra Rajputs, has developed :

Jammu ... the land of the Dogra Rajputs both won and lost its political and strategic importance before and after the Anglo-Sikh conflicts in the Punjab. Today, after the partition of India, Jammu, with Pakistan as 'Menance Flank', has leapt into prominence. It has regained its strategic and political importance. How this has happened can be measured up by Jammu's geographical position and its past history in brief ... political, economic and cultural.

Overlooking the plains of the Indian and Pakistani Punjabs, the war-torn and battle-scarred Jammu province of the disputed State of Jammu and Kashmir is today passing through a period of transition. The country of the valiant Rajputs, unassumingly army-minded Brahmins, virile Muslims and depressed Harijans is getting through an invulnerable phase in its chequered history when the entire future of the land of Saint Jamawant (one of the warriors of Lord Rama's army after whose name Jammu is called) hangs in the balance.

With an area of 12,378 sq.miles and a population of more than 15 lakhs (including Pakistan-held areas), the Jammu province, following the partition of India, in 1947, has assumed great strategic importance. Bordering the Indian and Pakistani Punjabs, the hilly tract serves as the vital physical links of hardy non-Muslims, who unlike the Kashmiris, have built up fine military traditions. The people of this area ... Hindus, Muslims and Sikhs ... are veterans in mountain and snow warfare, having proved their mettle even on the snow-bound dizzy heights of Ladakh and the icy regions of Western Tibet, situated to the north-east of Kashmir valley.

Geological Divisions

The geographical divisions of the province over the sub-montane and semi-mountainous tract and the other hills. The first consists of the plains bordering the two Punjabs and the broken mass of foothills lying at the base of the great mountain ranges of the Himalayan series. The Chenab and the Jhelum flow through this division. The northern parts of this division consisting chiefly of foothills, known locally as 'Kandi', which rise to the height of about 2,000 ft. For the most part, they are stony and arid and always thirst for water. In the 'Kandi' areas, cultivation is generally meagre and scattered; the crops depend largely on timely rains. The area of the division is 2,609 sq.miles and the population above 9 lakhs.

The 'Outer Hills' division consists of the lower hills lying to the south of the Pir Panjal range of mountains. The latter separates the two main provinces of the State, Jammu and Kashmir, from each other. A large part of this area lies at an altitude of between 2,000 and 4,000 ft., but in some parts the hills become mountains and reach a height of over 15,000 ft.

The chief river is the Chenab which enters the area from the Chamb State and the great Himalayan range to the east and continues to the Riasi district and Akhnoor Tehsil of the province, finally to flow into the Pakistani Punjab near Sialkot. In the lower areas of this division, rice and wheat are mostly grown; higher maize is the chief crop and staple food. From elevations of about 5,000 to 8,000 ft., the mountain sides, where not exposed to the scorching winds of the plains, are clothed with fine pine and deodar forests, especially in Kishtwar, Rambas and Dhadvawah tehsils.

Except in the fertile valleys, cultivable land is scarce and scattered consisting of small plateaux and patches of cultivation. Rainfall is plenty, the highest in the entire State. The area of this division is 9,769 sq.miles and the population nearly 12,00,000. The two geographical divisions ... the sub-montane tract and the outer hills area ... together consitute the whole of Jammu province including the well-known Poonch district.

Predominantly Hindu Area

In Jammu province, broadly speaking, over these regions is the Dogar consisting of the districts of Udhampur, Riasi, Jammu and Kathua and the Bhimber tehsil of Mirpur district. This area is predominantly Hindu, at least so far as present conditions in the tract indicate. The people of this region are the thick-set, short-statured, sturdy Dogras. The Maharaja of the State was a Dogra Rajput, and came from this area. Generally speaking, this region is adjacent to the Indian Punjab and its people, as a whole, are culturally and linguistically connected with the people of Kangra valley, Gurudaspur, Hoshiarpur and Himachal Pradesh.

In other region in this province is that of Western parts consisting of the two tehsils of Mirpur district (Mirpur and Kotli) and Poonch Jagir (now a separate district). This tract adjoins the Jhelum and Rawalpindi districts of the Pakistani Punjab. It is mostly populated by Kashmir having cultural and linguistic ties with the adjoining districts of West Punjab.

Kashmir's Nostrils

While the valley of Kashmir ... a distinct linguistic and cultural unit in the State and the entire Indian sub-continent ... has assumed international importance on account of its natural beauty, superb climatic conditions and proximity to Gilgit and Ladakh. Very little, comparatively speaking, is known outside the State about the land of Dogras ... the hilly province of Jammu which has produced military strategists like Gulab Singh (the founder of modern Jammu and Kashmir State), and army leaders like Wazir Zarwar and Diwan Hari Chand. But, it appears, time has come when the more is known about the strategic state inside and outside the state, the better for all concerned ... the Kashmir question. For, if Kashmir has, in a sense, ceased to be an appendage of Jammu itself has emerged as a vital base on which it has been possible to build Kashmir's edifice of accession to India'. This is so because all roads connecting valley directly with India pass through Jammu province. Accordingly, Jammu is now the breath of 'Kashmir's nostrils' nay the very nose, the vital respiratory system of the 'Happy valley' of Kashmir.

British Strategy

Not only that. It will be interesting to know that 'one great object which the Governor General (1846) had in view when he made this announcement for Jammu and Kashmir territories (making over to Maharaja Gulab Singh) was to lessen the force of the Sikhs by establishing on their flank or power independent of them and inclined to the British. In 1846, the British were arranging for the Govt. of the Punjab by "its own native rulers" ... by the young Maharaja Duleep Singh and the Durbar or a Council of Ministers. But, in 1849, however, the Punjab fell into the hands of the British. This altered the situation materially, though of course the Valley of Kashmir which was later connected with India directly by the construction of the Rawalpindi-Srinagar Road, assumed great importance on account of Gilgit and had frontiers being adjacent to Afghan, Russian and Chinese territories.

For a century, despite the fact that the Ruling family of the State belonged to Jammu, the importance of Jammu from the political and strategic points of view, dwindled. For, with the annexation of the Punjab by the British after 1849, there was no force of the Sikhs left in the land of the five rivers to be checked by establishing on this flank or power independent of them and inclined to the British. Now was Kashmir valley entirely dependent on Jammu, for the road link with India. And Jammu had no international frontiers like Kashmir which could lend importance to the area.

After the lapse of 100 years, however, history repeated itself and Jammu leapt into province again. History is the torch that is meant to illuminate the past to guard us against the repetition of our mistakes of other days. The partition of India in 1947 which was, in essence, part of the imperialists' plan for 'safe frontiers' in the east and north-west of India, created on the flank of India a power (Pakistan) inclined to the British. The newly created power was also intended to serve as a 'menace flank' for those very Indians who carried on a baseless struggle against British imperialism in the country. The process would have been complete if the entire Jammu and Kashmir State had formed an integral part of the newly-created power. Whereas Pakistan, like a caterpillar, chooses the fairest leaves of its political hypocrisy to lay its eggs of systematic propaganda on, so the theocratic priesthood lays its curse on the fairest joys. And Pakistan always likes a solemn ass a president so that the theocratic rulers always go along with them. Like the buyer has need a hundred eyes, the seller (Pakistan) of but one.

Battle of Wits

As soon as it was definitely known in the Indian subcontinent that the country would be divided, the battle of wits started with regard to the accession question of Jammu and Kashmir State. Pakistan, after August 15, 1947, tried to reap out the maximum advantage from the Maharaja's indecision. In point of fact, the Ruler of the State was vaguely thinking in terms of independent Jammu and Kashmir and it would have meant playing with fire if he had joined one or the other Dominion without ascertaining the will of the people. The Maharaja's indecision was Pakistan's opportunity. The latter whipped her 'tribal might' into fighting spirit and attacked Kashmir. She arrogated to herself for the prescription on the prevailing situation over Jammu and Kashmir. But by doing so, Pakistan spoiled its case ... if she had any ... in the State. It was a crucial moment for the people of Jammu and Kashmir, for the Ruler and for the leader of the Kashmir masses, Sheikh Abdullah. Muzaffarbad was overrun, 'probing attacks' had started all along the Jammu border, adjoining Pakistan's Punjab and two Englishmen who were the employees of the State Govt., were busy trying to bring about an artificial internal revolt in Gilgit, with a view to handing over the strategic area to the newly created power in the north-west of India. Under these circumstances, the Maharaja and the people of Kashmir under Sheikh Abdullah's leadership, had to make up their mind. The Kashmir leader rushed to Delhi to seek India's aid in driving out the invaders. The very internecine feuds dawned upon the Pakistani officials. The Maharaja sent out frantic calls to India for help. But India could not send out her troops into Kashmir and Jammu unless the State acceded to India, at least provisionally. And backed up the mass leader, Sheikh Abdullah, the Maharaja at last acceded to India, and welcomed Indian troops who after fourteenth months' hard fighting saved two thirds of the State territory from falling into the hands of the 'power' which was to meant to serve as a 'menace flank' for India. From the beginning of Pakistan's history over the Kashmir problem, her determined policy is 55% theocratic rule, 10% mullocracy, 15% collusion and chicanery over anti-India hymns of hate, and 20% terrorist outfits for Islamic globalisation. Pakistan's history is fed on illusion.

A Menace Flank

The completion of the historical process was brought about by the unprovoked Pakistani attack on the State. The impetuosity of the Pakistani rulers egged on by certain foreign elements, upset the imperialists' apple-cart. The Kashmir adventure proved a bad egg. The Governor General in 1846, as a measure of political and military strategy, tried to establish on the flank of the Sikh an independent Jammu and Kashmir inclined to the British. The Partition of India in 1947 was made similar objects in view. The ambitious rulers of Pakistan, however, performed an egg-dance and in the process, that very power (inclined to the British) which was created in 1947 to server as a 'menace flank' for India, was outflanked. The progressive forces in Jammu and Kashmir as represented by Sheikh Abdullah, joined hands with the progressive forces of India headed by Jawaharlal Nehru. The historical blunder committed by Pakistan in Kashmir saved the State from meeting the same fate as the Pathan land of Khan brothers had met.

Anyway, the turmoil and tribulation caused by the Pakistani attack on the State were the travails of a new birth for Jammu as well as Kashmir. The Rawalpindi-Srinagar Road was closed and the only road connecting Kashmir valley directly with India, passed through Jammu. Jammu thus became the life-line of Kashmir. And while during the last 100 years, the borders of Jammu did not meet any foreign territory ... it was on all sides bounded by Indian territory ... today a large part of its frontiers are adjacent to foreign (Pakistan) territory. All this has increased the value and importance of Jammu for India and Kashmir. Mr. M.A. Jinnah, the founder of Pakistan and at the same time leader of the Muslim Leagure, explained away the Kashmir issue : "... politically and economically, Kashmir is the nerve centre of Pakistan." He also said : "No self-respecting nation can expose its nerve centre to the enemy's naked sword. Kashmir is an inalienable part of Pakistan ... it would fall into our lap like ripe fruit." (A.Beg, 'The Wailing Vale').

LAND OF DOGRAS II

The Pakistani invasion of the State of Jammu and Kashmir has, in certain respects, changed the very face of Jammu. It has created new problems for the Jammuites, some of which they share in common with the Kashmiris.

When Pakistan gave the green light of perpetration in Kashmir on October 27, 1947, she had already contrived to practically close the Srinagar-Rawalpindi Road and the Jammu-Sialkot Road and Railway line. Evidently, she aimed at choking the tiny state in order to force its ruler to join the so-called biggest Islamic State. The position had become so dangerous and delicate that when the first contigent of Indian troops was flown to Srinagar on October 27, there was no good road connecting India with Jammu. The Srinagar-Jammu Road, unless it was connected with the Indian Punjab by a metalled road, could have no purpose. The Kathua road linking the Dogar with Pathankot (Indian Punjab) was there already; but it was atrocious ... a mere kacha track which passed through ravines and was quite unsuitable for wheeled traffic. Under these circumstances, when Jammu and Kashmir acceded to India troops entered the

State, they (troops) had to walk, so to say, with bare feet over broken glass along a very difficult and undependable supply line. But the Indian army took the risk and made use of this rough and ragged track. And soon the air was filled with the rumble of coming and going convoys, the clatter of passing trucks and the buzz of jeeps Indian troops fanned out who had been flown to Srinagar.

Rs. 3 Crore Road in 3 Months

But the Indian army managed ... of course after facing enormous difficulties ... to make use of this road. The State's normal trade with India and foreign countries came to a standstill practically. The air service linking Srinagar and Jammu with India could not do much to remove the difficulty. The necessity of a good road connecting Jammu with India was keenly felt everywhere and the need for an organised transport was the cry of the hour in order to save the State from the economic strangulation.Sialkot and Rawalpindi which served as the clearing houses for Jammu and Kashmir's import and export trade for a century or more, were sealed areas for the State as a consequence of Pakistan's policy and programme. The Government of India and Kashmir realised the urgency of the situation and, accordingly, a survey for the construction hurriedly made. Work on the road was commenced in right earnest and it was built in three months, at a cost of about 3 crores of rupees. Given the terrain in which it was constructed, the 65 miles long road is regarded as a remarkable feat of engineering, making the spiritual, legal and constitutional bonds between Kashmir (including Jammu) and India stronger. Three big bridges on the road, 28,000 ft., 2000 ft., and 1000 ft. speak volume of the great engineering skill involved in this construction. People in Jammu and Kashmir heaved a high sigh of relief, the Army felt overjoyed and a big problem confronting the State administration was solved.

LAND OF DOGRAS III HAVOC CAUSED BY INVADERS : (REHABILITATION PROBLEM)

This topic is on the conditions developed in the Jammu Province during and after the Pakistani invasion ruthlessly exercised over her fellow-brethren.

Jammu was slowly recovering from the wounds caused on its body by the invaders from Pakistan. The blotches and blisters were gradually healing up and life was evidently returning to normal, even though the wrongs committed by the aggressors were constantly cutting at her heart like a knife.

When Pakistan gave the signals for 'Jehad' in Kashmir, armed bands entered Muzaffarbad and Baramulla districts in the Kashmir valley. The stories of the atrocities commiteed by the raiders in these areas reached Jammu. Meanwhile, armed hordes from Pakistan attacked Poonch, Kotli and Mirpur etc. and carried death and destruction in all border areas of the Province. Blood-letting tales of the massacre of Hindus, Sikhs and nationalist Muslims, began to pour in from all border areas of the State. Refugees began to arrive in Jammu city and other safer parts of the province in large numbers, relating tales of raiders' atrocities

... rape, arson and loot ... which set one's skin a quiver. Human life in those parts of the State was churned up like mud on a busy high way and trodden under foot.

A lamentable contrast was looming large. It was a trying time for the people of the State to watch the border areas set ablaze by the enemy. The sky was sprinkled with blood and the earth with froth and foam like suds of soap water. In this national calamity while Kashmiris kept their heads cool and refused to play in the hands of anti-social elements ... thanks to the leadership of Sheikh Abduallah and the organising capacity of Bakshi Ghulam Mohammad ... others lost their balance of mind. Why? Because little things please little minds. The result was a communal upheaval in Jammu in which quite a number of Muslim lives were lost and others migrated to Pakistan ... a strange contrast with condition in the same province only three months back when both Hindus and Muslims form the Punjab of pre-partition and post-partition days were received with open arms. In this 'sea of tears', when the two Punjabs, Jammu, Muzaffarbad and Gilgit were burning in the communal fires, the valley of Kashmir stuck to the Gandhian principles and appeared to be an 'Island of smiles'.

The influx of refugees from the border districts and the communal flare-up in the Dogar completely disrupted the economy of Jammu. The Civil administration came very near a virtual collapse, rendering the situation all the more confused and chaotic. Only a miracle could save the province from total annihilation, especially when the raiders were advancing on all sides and the valley of Kashmir was involved in a life and death struggle against the so-called 'Mujahidis' from Pakistan. Even the stout-hearted lost hope in the darkness that descended on Jammu from one end to the other.

Meanwhile, Indian troops started their operations against the raiders in Jammu. While fighting the enemy, the troops ... Indian as well as State forces ... tried to evacute people from danger zones and such areas as were surrounded by the enemy. Survivors of the unfortunate victims of armed aggression from Pakistan were seen trudging along the dangerous mountain roads leading to Jammu and swelling the number of those who had already reached the city. At this crucial hour, the Emergency Administration with Sheikh Abdullah, head, had been set up in the State. The Indian Army stopped the onrush of raiders in Kashmir valley, and Sheikh Abduallah, therefore, deputed Bakshi Ghulam Mohammad (The Deputy Premier in the State in 1951) to Jammu to set matters right there. It was a herculean task for the 'iron man of Kashmir' (that is how Bakshi Ghulam Mohammad was called) to reassemble the fragmented parts of the civil administration in Jammu, oil the wheels of official machinery in the enemy free areas of the Province and restore order and communal peace in the Dogar. And the tough-built and strong-willed man succeeded in his task admirably well in a few weeks' time despite the criticism in certain influential quarters in Jammu.

But the problem of refugees could not be solved in a day. The slender finances of the State and the then military situation in the Province forbade any speedy action. Cash doles or payment in kind could not solve the question satisfactorily. And the State had little money to dole out substantial help to the unfortunate people. The poor victims managed to pull on with little aid and facilities they could get from the State or private institutions etc. for some time.

Finding these conditions in Jammu had become bad no account of the tribal invasion, Muslim and non-Muslim refugees from East and West Punjab who had taken shelter in Jammu, hurried to migrate to the two Punjabs. A large number of Hindus and Sikhs, belonging to the enemy parts of the province, had crossed the border and had taken refuge in East Punjab, Delhi and Uttar Pradesh. And as the Indian troops began advancing in different sectors in Jammu, the refugees were gradually induced to return to their homes to carry on the normal business of their life. Though all of them did not return. most of them did. But in those sectors, where fighting was still going on or where the outcome of the many bloody battles waged by the troops, was not quite certain, the refugees could not be repatriated. The future of the refugees from Mirpur, Kotli, a part of Bhimber, and a large part of Poonch ... areas which were and still are, under the firm grip of the raiders ... persecuted a serious but grave problem.

Meanwhile, 40 thousand refugees from different parts of Poonch Jagir overrun by the enemy had gathered in Poonch town. They were without rations, even without vestments on their body. And as the Poonch town itself was isolated from the rest of Jammu those days due to enemy action, the problem of feeding and evacuating them presented enormous difficulties. The Indian Army, however, took the initiative. Air supplies were dropped in Poonch town to let the refugees keep their body and soul together. Arrangements were speeded up to evacuate them by air. It reminded one of the mass evacuation of refugees from West Punjab by air when non-Muslims were squeezed out of that Pakistan Province.

The upkeep and resettlement and rehabilitation of the mass refugees from Mirpur, Kotli, Bhimber and Poonch etc. presented a herculean task. The Governments of India and Kashmir felt very much worried about the situation and utlimately the former undertook to start a big refugee camp on the outskirts of Jammu to house the uprooted people who were penniless and nothing to fall back upon. Before that a large number of people had run away to the East Punjab while others who were not altogether without means settled down in business or eked out their living by taking to small arts and crafts in Jammu city and its suburbs. The return of the bullk of the refugees to their houses, in their houses and in their areas was an encouraging sign. Till 1951, 32 thousands refugees had already been left who had needed care and shelter. They had been removed to Nagrota Camp on the outsides of Jammu, where a city of tents to house the refugees had been fed and clothed and sheltered in the camp, even the medical facilities were given to the refugee boys and girls.

As time went on and cease-fire order came into force, it was thought desirable to rehabilitate the refugees one way or the other. Experience had shown that by living upon cash doles and free rations, these people, generally speaking, had lost the sense of respect, rendering them 'useless as citizens'. Besides, certain vested interests in combination with some 'communal elements' tried to exploit the uprooted, unfortunate people to meet their own ends. Accordingly, the Government of India set up a joint rehabilitation board with Major General Tara Singh Bal, G.O.C. Indian troops in Jammu as chairmen. Rs. 42,00,000 lakhs was sanctioned for the resettlement and rehabilitation of the refugees. Not only that the Pakistani cattle-lilfters started their notoriously mechanised heinous activities like lifting the cattle grazing in the field, crossing the Indian territory just after the partition.

A scheme had then been evolved according to which each refugee family was given 8 acres of irrigated or 12 acres of non-irrigated land. Reduced land revenue was changed on the evacuee property held by the refugees. A loan of Rs. 500 was given to each refugee family in addition to one month's ration and three month's cash dole. Refugees had been given free transport when rehabilitated. The people of non-liberated areas, Mirpur, Bhimber, Kotli, Poonch and Muzaffarbad had been rehabilitated in Akhnoor, Riasi, Rajouri, Rambirsinghpur, Jammu Tehsil, Sambha, Kathua, Jasawargarh and Basoli. There had been some opposition on the part of the refugees regarding the choice of the areas where they had been resettled.

By the end of December, 1950, about 16 thousands of the refugees were resettled, and it was expected that the rest of the lot would be rehabilitated very soon and the camps dispersed. And when the refugee camps were dispersed and all the inmates stood on their feet once again to resume the normal business of their life, one of the major problems confronting Jammu would be solved.

But while refugee rehabilitation work was going on at a rapid pace in the interior of Jammu, about ten thousand Hindus and Sikhs were still left in raider-held areas of a province, living in utter misery ... in hotels and caves, and gaping and waiting for an early union with their kith and kin on the Indian side. This is a problem which still needs to be tackled by the Indian and Kashmir Governments, effectively and expediently as its solution would remove the bitterness still lurking in the minds of refugees and their kinsmen in Jammu and thus pave the way for better relations in the province. Side by side, the question of rehabilitating the State's refugees lying in Yole camp and at Hosiarpur in other Indian Punjab was taken up. Why? This appeared to be necessary for more reasons than one.

This is one more thing about which the people of Jammu felt strongly and that was the slow, undetected infiltration of Pakistani elements into the Dogar. The infiltration was not only wrong, but also threatened the economy of the province with disruption.

In view of the difficult terrain and on extensive border, it could not be totally checked. There was a genuine desire on the part of some people to come back to their homes left by the earlier. Such people were welcome and could not be turned back. The local Govt. was firm in sending back those unwelcome elements who had infiltrated into the Indian side. But the question of firmness was disputable. At the end of 1950, about 25,000 Pakistanis were awaiting to take their chance in crossing to the Indian side. Strange to say, among these 25,000 people, disguised as Azad Kashmir's soliders, Pakistan's spies and other doubtful elements were suspected.

LAND OF DOGRAS (KASHMIR'S FUTURE E-L DORADO FOR PLENTY AND PROSPERITY)

Jammu ... the land of Dogras ... is surprisingly rich in potential resources of wealth ... universal, agricultural and forest. The strategically situated Jammu with its wonderfully diverse geological formations and geographical conditions, presents a more or less complete scheme of mineral products, forest wealth and agricultural resources. Political conditions permitting, a little effort is expected to make the province self-sufficient, to a large extent, in the matter of agricultural products like food grains and enable it to export a large part of its mineral wealth like its forest products.

In modern times, without power there is no escape from industrial stagnation. Jammu province, in addition to its extensive forests, is likely enough in possessing good mineral fuel in the shape of coal and in the possible occurrence of Petrol.

Coal of excellent quality occurs in the Riasi district and its continuity over a distance of 36 miles has proved, though concealed here and there under debris or under overlying rocks. The quality is reckoned to be over 100,000,000 tons, easily available within a reasonable depth. Samples from the various deposits are said to have yielded sixty to eighty two percent of fixed carbon.

The discovery of a bituminous horizon with thin veins of asphalt at various places in the province, holds out the hope that liquid fuel in the form of petroleum may be hidden in one or more suitable geological structures, such as the Nav-Budhan dome and Ramnagar 'terrace'. Others may be brought to light by future survey work in rocks of the same age and composition as those existing at Khaur (near Rawalpindi). But this is a matter about which can be no certainty until deep drilling is undertaken.

Iron whcih is the very basis of industry and whose occurrence in a country in close association with coal, determines the industrial supremacy of that country, is also found in the Riasi district of the province. This iron was once worked out at several places and the excellent suspense bridge at Ramban over the Chenab, connecting Jammu with Kashmir was built of iron smelted from the ores of chakar and Matah in Riasi during the rule of the late Maharaja Ranbir Singh (1857-85). A 15ft. thick bed of pure haematite has been located at Khandi in the Rajouri. This ore is said to contain 60 percent of iron.

Other minerals such as bauxite, Kaolin, Copper ores, lead silver ores, nickel and zinc ores as also bentonite and maganese ores are to be found in different parts of Jammu. The great diversity and extension of mineralised areas in the mountainous areas of Jammu indicate the probability of much additional mineral wealth which remains to be discovered by further exploration.

Experts believe .... and it has been proved ... that cement of good quality exists in the rich Riasi district. It is only when cheap transport is available freely in and around the mineralised tracts, that all these resources of the province can be exploited to the benefit of the people and the Govt. of the State. Till then, one has to wait and watch how things take shape on the political front ... the final solution of the bigger political problem confronting the State presently. The so-called shyness of capital need not be in a discouraging factor so far as the exploitation of these minerals is concerned... For, if and when the time comes, industrial capital would be forthcoming from inside and outside the State provided the necessary facilities are given by the Govt. of the State.

At present, Jammu is a deficit area so far as the production of foodgrains is concerned. Barring the hilly areas, where people take maize, the staple of Jammu is wheat. And it is in respect of wheat that Jammu province is a deficit area.

During the pre-partition days, the province used to import about 15 thousand tons of wheat yearly. The tribal raids which disrupted the economy, including the agricultural economy of the province, the deficit went up to 30 thousand tons a year. The deficit had again been brought down to the normal level from 1948 to 1950. The devastating floods in the province in 1950 had again raised the deficit as a large part of the flood crops was damaged or destroyed. The Govt. is quite unaware of the smuggling of foodgrains outside the State Jammu is suitable for tractor cultivation which can help in producing more foodgrains. The lands which are lying uncultivated would be brought under the plough. The digging of more irrigation canals would bring water to those areas which have been thirsting for it.

A little more effort and some sort of planning would make Jammu not only self-sufficient in foodgrains but also a surplus area.Rajouri (Riasi district) and Mendar (Poonch) could easily become the 'bread-basket' of Jammu as the areas were very fertile and there was very great scope for expansion of agriculture there. Vast tracts of rich land are lying fallow or quite unbroken in those places as in Thana, Narain, Chingas, Naushera, Pir Bedesar, Bhawani, Oila Darhal, Sandarbani etc. If and when these are properly cultivated, Jammu would not depend on imported food.

Closely connected with the agricultural policy of the State is the 'land to tiller' programme introduced in Jammu and in Kashmir by Sheikh Abdullah, credit for working out plans for whose implementations must go to the State's revenue.

Aimed at the abolition of big landed estates in the State, the 'land to tiller' is expected to set free the actual cultivators from their centuries old economic slavery and thus induce them to take more interest in the land they cultivate.

Next to agricultural exploitation of the extension and valuable forests of

Jammu, especially in Kishtwar, Bhadrawah, and Ramban, constitutes the largest industry in the province. The extraction of timber, collection of minor forest products and other activities play a very important part in the life of the rural population.

The industry has immense possibilities of development and extension in the province. Closely connected with forest industry in Jammu are Rosin Turpentine factory and the willow factory at Miran Sahib on the outskirts of the city (the erstwhile Jammu Sialkot branch line of the North-Western Railway. The former is said to be passing through a difficult time for want of chief transport and the latter is reported to be carrying on good business in the manufacture of sports goods.

4

The Story of Pak-Occupied Kashmir : Dangerous Pastimes of Sad Variety

There is a magnetism in the very names of Pakistani rulers that will ever cease to attract the interests of students of Pakistan in future. Many of their acts have not yet been prompted by wiser men than themselves. The painful transition from the dream of democracy to the reality of double whammy ... bureaucratic absolutism and rigid doctrine of theonomous state is the most important element of the interregnum. This irony is most successful in analysing the Kashmir issue. Modern Pakistan today is with all its political beastliness, theological smells, sectarian noise, religious agonies and nagging discomfort of anti-India hymns of hate. It has the authentic stench of partition ... the pain, the heat, the panic, the obscenity and the shattering boredom of religious jingoism. And the double-barreled combination of crude nationalism, pernicious doctrine of communalism and bickering provincialism causes all the confusion in the production of lies.

The two-nation theory of the Muslim League and the fratricidal feud are responsible for the partition of the ex-princely State of Jammu and Kashmir like that of the rest of the Indian sub-continent.

The Pakistani press flashed on October 4, 1947 ... almost on the morrow of the partition of India ... that a meeting held the previous day in Paris Hotel at Rawalpindi had taken the decision to form Azad Kashmir Govt. A proclamation at the meeting reads, inter alia, ... Maharaja Hari Singh's title to rule has come to an end from August 15, 1947, and he has no constitutional or moral right to rule over the people of Kashmir against their will. He is consequently deposed from Oct 4, 1947.

A provisional Govt. of Azad Kashmir was set up at Muzaffarbad. The identity of the leaders had been established. One Anwar was the first president of the Azad Kashmir Govt. He was perhaps Ghulam Nabi Gilkar, one of the prominent leaders of the Kashmir Muslim Conference. Anwar left for Srinagar immediately after the formation of the provincial Govt. with the object of arresting Maharaja Hari Singh. Anwar, however, came to grief himself in December, 1947, when he was jailed by the Govt. of Kashmir. None suspected that he was the first President of the provincial Govt. of Azad Kashmir. The Azad Kashmir Govt.was reorganised on Oct. 24, 1947. Sardar Md. Ibrahim Khan, a top-ranking Muslim Conference leader, became the president. The head quarters were shifted to Rawalpindi. The newly formed Govt. had the fullest sympathy and obtained much support of the local and non-official circles. Muslims in large numbers from the Indian side of Jammu and Kashmir crowded the borders and rallied under the banner of Azad Kashmir. The retired military personnel of Punch and Mirpur areas formed the nucleus of the Azad Kashmir Army.

The Kashmir question first came up for discussion in the Security Council early in 1948. Sardar Ibrahim and Chief Advisor M.D. Tasser sailed for America to place the case for Azad Kashmir before the Security Council. The Council refused to give them a hearing. Azad Kashmir was soon torn by internal dissensions. An undignified scramble for power began. Chaudhuri Abbas, the President of the Muslim Conference, and Sardar Md. Ibrahim entered the list as rivals. Pakistan lost no time in seizing the opportunity to establish her stranglehold over Azad Kashmir.

A large number of well-known Muslim Conference leaders were packed out of the country to Pakistan in January, 1949, after their release from the jails in Kashmir. Many of the extemes had pro-Abbas sympathisers. A convention of the Muslim Conference worker at Sialkot (March 2, 1949) decided that the Govt. of Azad Kashmir should take orders from the Muslim conference. The Convention was a packed body. Most of the participants were nominees of Chaudhuri Abbas. Abbas acted as a dictator after the above convention. He came to grief before long and 'retired' from political life for reasons of health (May 5, 1949). He named Allah Rakha Sagar as his successor. The nomination was unconstitutional. The rank and file of the Muslim Conference protested. Abbas ignored the protest. Allah Rakha dismissed Aga Saukat Ali, the General Secretary of the Muslim Conference. Some members of the Conference executive too shared the same fate. Sagar's friends and favourites were nominated to the consequent vacancies. Allah Rakha Sagar's short-sightedness created dissension among the Muslims acceded to India. Riots were reported from various places. A new Muslim Conference came into existence, under the leadership of Mir Waiz Yusuf Shah. A Minister of the Azad Kashmir Govt.

Sardar Md. Ibrahim, President of the Azad Kashmir Govt. refused to accept Allah Rakha Sagar as the President of the Muslim Conference. The Conference executive nominated by him was not recognised.

The sufferings of the masses in Azad Kashmir went on increasing in the meantime. The leaders were indifferent. Sardar Ibrahim was determined not to recognise Allah Rakha Sagar as the Muslim Conference Chief. Chaudhury Abbas now staged a come-back and assumed the Presidentship of the Muslim Conference. He convened a general meeting of the Conference at Rawalpindi on January 10, 1950 (Tuesday). More or less 70 attended. Fifty among them were supporters of Abbas. He was given the fullest authority to recognise the Muslim Conference and the Azad Kashmir Govt. Abbas replaced Ibrahim by Syed Ali Ahmed Shah as the President of the Azad Kashmir Govt. The Govt. of Pakistan supported Abbas. Abbas, it should be noted, had at first offered the Presidentship of the Azad Kashmir Govt. to Ibrahim. The offer had been respected by the latter as he was to have no voice in the appointment of his cabinet.

ANTI-ABBAS GROUP

The Muslim Conference leadership had long forfeited the confidences of the masses in Azad Kashmir and of the refugees from across the frontier. The policy of the former had embittered and alienated them. Ibrahim tried to recapture his lost power and ascendancy with their help. The anti-Abbas group under his leadership demanded an immediate reorganisation of both the Muslim Conference and the Azad Kashmir Govt. on a democratic constitutional basis. An ad hoc committee was formed with Mirza Waiz as its President. Mir Abdul Aziz was the Secretary of the committee, which started a non-violent disobedience movement in Azad Kashmir. The movement did not long remain non-violent. Stern measures by the Govt. notwithstanding, the movement engulfed the wilderness. It became more and more intense everyday. About 500 were jailed. Unable to bring the situation under control, the Azad Kashmir sought and obtained military help from Pakistan. A number of battles were fought between Pakistan army and non-violent Azad Kashmir volunteers.

The anti-Abbas faction in the Muslim Conference met in January, 1951, and elected Col Sher Mohammad Khan to the Presidentship of the Conference. Mir. Abdul Aziz was elected General Secretary. The Conference headquarters was transferred from Rawalpindi to Punch. The newly elected President and General Secretary demanded the reconstitution. An Azad Kashmir deputation next met A.M. Gurmani, Pakistan's Minister for Kashmir affairs. The deputation placed before the Hon'ble Minister all the sins of omission and commission of the Azad Kashmir Govt. and requested that matters be set right immediately. The policy of the Govt., the deputationists said, had been driving the people to despair. The Hon'ble Minister invited the deputation's suggestions for the redress of the popular grievances. Suggestions were accordingly given.

Parallel Govt. was another question on the formation of Azad Kashmir.

The pro-Ibrahim faction of the Muslim Conference decided in June, 1951 to form a parallel Azad Kashmir Govt. A committee was appointed to draw up a scheme for the said Govt. The General of Pakistan feared breach of peace and armed conflicts. Pakistan's detachments were despatched to Azad Kashmir. Ibrahim and followers were not cowed down, however. The Muslim Conference under his leadership met at Dhirkot and decided to inaugurate a parallel Azad Kashmir Govt. on August 29, 1951 (Wednesday). An agreed list of the leaders of this Govt. was drawn up. A proclamation was also drafted.

The Govt. of Pakistan next brought Abbas and Ibrahim together. The rivals met and held parleys. But the gulf between them remained as wide as ever. A representative of the Pakistan Govt. met at the pro-Ibrahim leaders at Kohala. The latter agreed to put off the inauguration of the threatened parallel Govt. for a month. Pakistan, however, could not take any decision during the extended time limit. Prime Minister Liaquat Ali Khan waited to see things for himself in Azad Kashmir. An assassin's bullet laid him low in a public meeting at Rawalpindi on his way to Azad Kashmir. His successor Nazumuddin paid a visit to Azad Kashmir with two of his cabinet colleagues. After protracted negotiations with the various factions, they recommended an all-party Govt. for Azad Kashmir. Abbas, however, did not agree. Pressed to agree, he expressed his desire to retire from political life and set his resignation to Nazimuddin.

The action of Abbas is a pointer. Had the Muslim Conference on the Azad Kashmir Govt. been really independent, Abbas would not have sent his resignation to the Pakistan premier.

The Govt. of Pakistan began to interfere directly in the internal affairs of the Azad Kashmir after the resignation of Abbas. They promised a general election of the Muslim Conference within three months. The new conference was to form its own working committee and also to recognise the Azad Kashmir Govt. On December 2, 1951 (Sunday), Mir Waiz Yusuf Shah took over the administration of Azad Kashmir under the orders of the Govt. of Pakistan, Mir Waiz was, however, the smoke screen behind which Pakistan entrenched itself securely in Azad Kashmir.

The 'Ibrahimities' hailed the eclipse of Abbas. They did not, would not, realise that the prospects of an independent, democratically ruled Azad Kashmir had been blasted for all time to come.

The Muslim Conference election in the beginning of 1952 resulted in the victory of the pro-Ibrahim factions. Ibrahim became the President of the newly elected Conference. Quereshi Mohammed Yusuf became the General Secretary. Raja Md. Haidar of Muzaffarbad was nominated President of the Azad Kashmir Govt.

The Govt. of Pakistan, however, did not recognise Raja Md. Haider and nominated an Azad Kashmir Govt. of its own choice (June 22, 1952). The president and the members of this Govt. were in fact officials of Karachi. Azad Kashmir became in reality a dependency of Pakistan. Col. Sher Ahmed Khan, the leading light of the Ibrahimits, was Karachi's nominee for the Presidentship of the Govt. of Azad Kashmir. So, Pakistan had drafted out few articles to grip up Azad Kashmir.

The Muslim Conference claims that it alone represents Azad Kashmir. Pakistan too accepts the claim apparently. But no less than those Muslim Conferences were functioning in Azad Kashmir. Ibrahim, Abbas and Mir Waiz had each a Muslim Conference under his arm-pit. Each claimed to be the president of the Muslim Conference. Each had tried his best to seize the reins of power. Pakistani had taken the fullest advantage of the situation and had made itself the 'arbiter' of the destiny of Azad Kashmir.

The 'Abbasite' Muslim Conference workers met in a Convention at Mirpur in March, 1953. The Convention announced that Abbas, who had retired from politics in 1951, would re-enter the political lists. It supported the anti-Ahmedya agitation then raging in Western Pakistan and requested the Govt. of Pakistan to declare the Ahmedya to be a non-Muslim minority. Abbas told the assembled workers that he had his own plan for the liberation of Kashmir. He did not say at the time what this plan was. He, however, took the public into confidence a few days later when he gave out in the course of a speech at Guzranwalla that the salvation of Kashmir lay in a compromise between him and Shiekh Abdullah and in an Abbas-Abdullah coalition Govt. for the whole of Kashmir. Sheikh Abdullah treated those ravings with the contempt they deserved.

Azad Kashmir leaders did not seem to be anxious for the solution of the Kashmir question. The Prime Minister of India and Pakistan met in August, 1953 and agreed to resolve the Kashmir tangle by peaceful methods. Abbas and his followers were unhappy over the agreement. They demanded instead that "all restrictions and responsibilities in connection with Kashmir should be ended and a struggle for liberation should be launched afresh". Hamidullah Khan, the Finance Minister of Azad Kashmir Govt., took a prominent part in the meeting which formulated the above demand.

The Azad Kashmir Govt. has no power of its own. It can lay down no policy, can take no initiative. Everything must be decided by Karachi (now Islamabad) in advance. Hamidullah Khan had once the 'territory' to criticize the Kashmir policy of the Pakistan premier. He was dismissed for the audacity. The dismissed minister remarked ruefully, "... an ordinary clerk in the Kashmir affairs Ministry has a greater say in problems affecting Azad Kashmir than the President of the Govt. of the territory."

Very much irretrievable are the sufferings of the common man in Azad Kashmir. The following extract from Nazir Hussein Khan, an ex-minister of the Azad Kashmir Govt., spoke for itself :" When we unfurled the banner of Azad Kashmir, people were confident that Azad Kashmir will prove a heaven on earth for the people of the State and they will be sound politically as well as economically. But what do we find today after six years' struggle : conditions are worsening day after day; there is famine everywhere, people eke out half-starved lives; hundreds have died of hunger; the avenues of employment and poverty are widespread; necessities of life have grown scarce and taxes have increased. As a consequence of economic deterioration people are forced to commit more and more crimes." Even after 60 years of independence, the funereal but sordidly accumulated appalling and harrowing faces of the whole Azad Kashmir is the same as before. No change but ebbing away day by day. The political, social and economic circumstances all over the Azad Kashmir territories have brought the Pakistani rulers into nighmares how to revive the irretractable situation so as to get free from the interference of India as its old counterpart.

Lord Morley, a moral politician, confessed that he spoke two voices in denying popular institutions for India ... one to humour the Britisher at home and the other to humour the Indians with ambiguous assurances.

In other words, politicians on the Kashmir affairs played and have to play their political gamesmanship as they think best for their party or country and what one professes while in opposition may not be practised when in power. Neither Machiavelli nor Kautilya was a personification of wickedness when they compiled the rules of State-Craft.

The honest politicians are those who have no principles. Vehemently criticized by the clergy, Walpole once said : "If I had not been a Prime Minister, I should have been Archbishop of Canterbury." All that it means is that political saintliness is incompatible with private morality and that most statesmen may not do for themselves what they do righteously for their countries.

The partition of India was the parting kick of the British just before they relinquished their hold on this country. The British by the partition of this country had made a great, though silent, contribution to the stability of Asia. This hallelujah to the British had to come as a shock and a surprise to many not only in India but in other countries as well. Now the question is : How has the creation of Pakistan contributed to this stability of Asia? Pakistan has always opined that if the Kashmir problem is not peacefully settled, it would disturb not only the peace of India and Pakistan but the peace of the world as a whole. What is peacefully settled is a questionable composition of Pakistan's futurity. The partition of India has very much disturbed a great part of it by uprooting millions from their houses on a scale unprecedented in World history. The influx of huge number of refugees in Europe and Asia following upon the second world war had greatly disturbed the peace of the world. The exodus of refugees has not only disturbed peace in the Indian sub-continent but by embittering relations between India and Pakistan has contributed to the instability rather than the stability of this continent. Since partition, every prime minister of Pakistan has been out on a tour of propaganda to enlist the sympathy and support of the West for his country in case there is a conflict between India and Pakistan. Hardly do they know that it would be difficult to convince a Westerner that a theocratic State, particularly in the present age of science, is justified by any consideration.

To the Americans, every head of the State says in effect that the Islamic State of Pakistan is the most effective bulwark against the spead of communism, and the mass upheaval that communist philosophy tends to would remain the citadel of anti-communism.

But here is a puzzle. If Islam is a sufficient guarantee against the evil of communism, what is need of the kind of economic assistance form U.S.A.? The basis of discontent in Asia is economic. In other words, Islam cannot be the only cure. There must be other cures and the economic cure will add to the efficacy of the Islamic cure.

Kashmir has suffered as Indian has owing to this over-generosity towards Pakistan. Sheikh Abdullah, than whom Mr. Nehru had hardly any greater admirer and a friend, had been frothright in saying that the result of this misconceived generosity in matters involving the fate of millions had been inter alia that a large chunk of Kashmir's territory was still in Pakistan's hands. But the Govt. of India's lack of foresight the raiders of Kashmir would have been driven out long ago and the whole of the State freed from the bandits who have still behaved worse than beasts even in their dealings with the Kashmiri Pundits and Muslims. India and also Kashmir have been terribly suffering in all directions on never reciprocated it.

When you see a good man, think of emulating him; when you see a bad man examine your own heart. We have to judge our next-door neighbour at heart, to heart and in heart, what he is. A DOG is a dog except when he is facing you. Then he is MR. Dog.

Confucius was once asked what he would do first, if it were left to him to administer a country. The Master Said, "It would certainly be to correct language. His Listeners were surprised. "Surely," they said, "This has nothing to do with the matter. Why should language be corrected?" The Master's answer was "If language is not correct, then what is said is not what is meant ; if what is said is not what is meant, then what ought to be done remains undone; if this remains undone, morals and arts will deteriorate; if morals and arts will deteriorate, justice will go astray; if justice goes astray, the people will stand about in helpless confusion. Hence there must be no arbitrariness in what is said. This matters above everything."

The hopes of the world, proclaimed in manifestos of goodwill, came to grief at the barrier of a whispered comma, and the highest expectations of mankind were frustrated by the verbal alliance with a cliche. Phrases over Kashmir issue are more germane to the matter of war or peace than the number of cannons carried by each side. The German language is the profoundest of all languages but German speech is the shallowest.

Had Hitler's speeches been accessible to the West in their unspeakable original, a war might have been spared. For this war was partly caused by Hitler's innocent translators, unavoidably missing in smooth and diplomatic French or English the diabolical resonance of the original. A compost of political jargonism and hyperbole complemented by the unwarranted languages, full of fiery words of Islamic Jehadis, have not only raped the political goodness and rectitude over international politics but dismantled the spirit of good relations between two countries on Kashmir issue. Language is the first barrier between the relationships.

Pakistan's pathological doubt on the Kashmir settlement is not in a happy state in which to dwell permanently and in consequence it is of ten by-passed or repressed. Judging from the conflagrations over Kashmir problem, it is an undeniable fact that of all the miserable, unprofitable and inglorious wars in the world is the war against unwarranted words. We need better words and better thoughts. So to win in the great moral and intellectual duel that is always going on over Kashmir and on which all progress depends. Pakistan is an absent-minded nation with a mathematical imagination. Give Pakistan the right choice of words and the right accent on the settlement of peace in Kashmir and Kashmir will move the world. Words are the dung that keeps the roses sweet.

The relationship between India and Pakistan on Kashmir problem is thus, depending on the words :

Two pairs sat down to a game of bridge in Kashmir. They were playing for big stakes and playing, as each thought, as bridge should be rightly played.

It ended in a disaster.

'One no trump' said the declarer,

'Two no trumps' said his opponent.

'Three no trumps' said the partner,

'Four no trumps' said the other opponent.

'Double' said the declarer.

'Redouble' said the opponent,

'Damn' said the major to the left,

'Re-damn' said the General to the right.

Pistol shots whizzed and there was tragedy.

Pakistan's endeavour to bolster up its claim on the territory of Jammu and Kashmir has been prettily pronounced. The Security Council's own unrealistic approach to the problem of Kashmir has encouraged Pakistan's recalcitrance. Inspite of threat of fresh aggression and false hostile propaganda, India has remained calm with the hope that time will make Pakistan see reason. Otherwise an orgy of violence and destruction will happen to sub-continent. Because the people know that at the zoo the animals will not tell them what to do and what not to do. Sometimes brute silence is more entertaining than repeated speeches.

Illusions of free Kashmir : It was Sheikh Abdullah who had talked in terms of independent Kashmir without caring to know the urges and aspirations of the people of Kashmir. Why? An independent Kashmir will be a cockpit of international intrigues and incubating infectious diseases of conspiracy and political gamesmanship for a war base under the cloak and dagger of peace-keeping mission over the valley.

Abdullah had himself once ruled out independent Kahmir. Few years later it was now for his own political end. What a downfall of Abdullah : Why? Mr. Abdullah did not know that the politicians are permitted to carry on the same old type of disgraceful campaign from year to year is as insulting to the people as would be a gang of thieves coming back to a town they had robbed, staging a parade, and inviting citizens to fall in and cheer. He was an honest burglar.

Sheikh Abdullah was described as Rip Van Winkle. The Sheikh was dreaming that it was a deserving time to say that State's accession was temporary. He had slept in bed of Pakistan till his death. It was a strange thing that Sheikh had forgotten this much that over one lakh rupees had been incurred by the State Govt. on his comforts, of which sum Rs. 53,000 had been given to Begum Abdullah only. But Sheikh Abdullah was saying that he was poverty-stricken.

Each and every premier of Pakistan, dated back to the partition of India, was, and is, losing faith in India. On our part, we have also lost faith in Pakistan. So India and Pakistan are in no-faith situation. There is no chance for an All-Faith demonstration. Faith gone, hope and charity will not be there. Only the Sugar-Coated Faith lies in between them. What is the price of experience? Do men buy wisdom for a dance of terrorism in the street? What is Pakistan? It is a land of Mississipi of hypocrisy and falsehood of anti-India feelings, with much byzantine complex of a neurotic patient of anti-India campaign. If Pakistan's solicitude for the unborn generations in this sub-continent had been genuine, it would have cried halt to the campaign of calumny against India. Politicians in a land of theocratic State like Pakistan know much too well who is responsible for the current tension which bedevils the relations between the two countries, always vulnerable with each other not by words but at heart.

An untruth becomes truth if it can be ceaselessly repeated. It is Pakistani instrasigence that is preventing an early solution. National egotism of anti-India hymns of hate is inseparable from Pakistan's ideas of national greatness. The derivatives of this egotism will always appeal to arms and terrorism where other means fail. A psychosis is the outcome of similar disturbance in the relation between this ego and terrorism across the world. The 'summit' is rather a confession of helplessness and despair on the part of peoples, who have practically no voice in determining the issues of war and peace.

We find that conditions in Pakistan-occupied Kashmir are getting worse day by day. The two parts of the State on either side of the ceasefire line (now Line of Control) present a sharp contrast. On the Pakistan side of the State, You have the grim picture of 'old Kashmir' where feudal order continues holding people in subjection, squalor and poverty. All things beautiful have lost their charm because of grinding poverty and desolation of the people. On this side there is a perfect freedom and democracy. Pakistan has turned into a land of sensational rumours and heart-breaking revelations.

Every nation has a particular habit whether you call it a virtue or a vice. The English once delighted in cricket and now in soccer while the Americans derive pleasure in watching baseball. The pre-war Germans took to 'goose step' as the Russians starving both under the Tsars and under the Stalins and the Kruscheves. The Frenchman quarrels, the Spaniard enjoys bull fighting and Pakistan enjoys corruption, mullahism and terrorism. And it has earned a world recognition for its meteoric achievement in the mechanism of political co-existence. Whereas Indians have already earned world recognition as talkers both at home and abroad. At home our pet subject for talk inside parliament and Assemblies is corruption. Corruption in India is the most infalliable symptom of constitutional liberty. Most men are servants of the corporated corruption. Corruption dominates the ballot boxes in this sub-continent, even in the Arab world.

The image of Jinnah, Feroz Khan Noon and others was interesting in the Hindu religion, against India. The reward which a true believer reaps after life for having killed an infidel in the world is specified in Suratul Waquiah LVI-39 (quoted on page 449 of Hugh's Dictionary of Islam). The omission in the Hindu religion to provide for any reward for killing a non-Hindu has been authoritatively stated as one of the reasons for the gradual overthrow of the Hindus by the Muslim invaders (Vincent Smith's 'Student History of India' page : 147). Other instances of toleration (?) in the Quoran (11-220) and XXIV-31, and on Brig's translation of Ferista (Vol.11 pg. 120). Confirmatory proof was furnished by Noon himself when he said that Muslim would prefer communist domination to Hindu domination. We have to look at the present Indian Communists (?) on the Muslims in India.

It was bad enough to refer the Kashmir question to the Security Council. It was worse to have allowed Kashmir to draft its own constitution instead of adopting the constitution draft for part A, B and C States as the case may be, in the rest of India.

On the top of it all had come to the release of Sheikh Abdullah. The release was ill-considered as it was inopportune. The release was coincided with the second and unwanted visit of Dr. Frank Graham. The Govt. and the people of India were reaping the results of the ill-timed release. The strongest thing of all is that India's top statesmen including Mr. Nehru were repeatedly declaring that free India would not tolerate, even for a moment any infraction of her integrity by any foreigner, yet as everyone knows, that burning eye-sore, Azad Kashmir, is at least many years old. Such declarations served only as mere 'brutum fulmen' and excite amusement.

After the release, Sheikh Abdullah willingly stormed in the Kashmir politics, making mosques and religious places his activities. And he began playing upon the religious sentiments, ill with temperamental sadness of his political career, of the Muslims down the valley. And he had been all out to attack his Kashmir opponents and the secular policy of India. And he had challenged the validity of Kashmir's accession to India. Why did he do so? Because he was put under arrest by the Kashmir Govt. or simply because it was beneath his dignity. The

Sheikh had no compunction to ignore the role he played in bringing about Kashmir's accession to India and the resultant succour.

In one of W.Somerset Maugham's plays, a character while advising his politician son is found observing thus : "My dear Arnold, we all hope that you have before you a distinguished political leader career, you can't learn too soon that the most useful thing about a principle is that it can always be sacrificed to expediency." So all of his principles embarrassed not only crores of Indian Muslims but the whole nation. He seemed to have jumped on the bandwagon. He became a national menace. Once the Sheikh rejected the two-nation theory in 1947 and faced the tribal attack. He aired out the slogan of unity between Hindus, Muslims and Sikhs.

Many years have gone off. Indian politics have soared up with immature politicians like Sheikh Abdullah. Neither are they politicians, nor sound in mind nor judicious in taking decisions. They are the peculiar creatures of our democracy. They are as good as imbecile and good-for-nothing. The word 'immature' has been around the Parliament. They know nothing, but it is a permanent habit to voice forth on Kashmir. A politician is immature, if he calls a spade a spade. A parliamentarian is immature, if he has a sense of dignity, backbone and spirit of independence. He is dubbed as immature, if he refuses to stray from the path of rectitude and divests himself of moral principle. He is thought to be immature, if he unselfishly dedicates himself to the serivce of his country and is reluctant to make politics the handmade of self-aggradizement. Immaturity and in-consideration amongst our political leaders are thc two great causes of the ruin of our democracy. Immaturity is made up these ingredients. The immature politicians intend that the Kashmir problems be solved immediately.

Matured politicians are more and more fromidable and awe-striking than that of immature politicians. The mature politician presents a striking contrast to the immature politician. A politician is mature who has no opinion of his own but betrays a cringing subserviency in his conduct. He talks at random but does not work. Love of power is the be-all and end-all of his cherished desires. It is inherent in his nature. Nothing is dearer where he has not sown, entrenched in power, who basks in the sunshine of official functionalism in the interest of his own party to gain an advantage over the administration. His profession is always at variance with his practice.

A stunned silence is broken up when a mature politician gets up and orders, "Bring on the people. I'll play the role of the lion." There is a pleasure in being mad that none but madman knows. Insanely matured politicians often detect the nonsense of other people. There is nobody so irritating as mature politician with less intelligence and more sense than we have. Kashmir issue runs between matured and immatured politicians.

What is the Arab world? The union of Egypt, Syria and Yeman under the banner of united Arab Republic on the one hand and the union of the two Hashemite Kingdoms of Iraq and Jordan in an Arab Federation as a counter-move on the other have once again focussed the world's attention on the oil-rich and strategic region of the Middle East, popularly known as the Arab World. To an Arab nationalist, the Arab World is more than this region. To him it means the great arc of territory from Morocco to the Persian Gulf or it covers the area from Gribraltor to the Persian Gulf, bounded by race, culture and geography. This area has more or less a common language, viz, semitic. It contains within it as many as twelve Arab States with varying degrees of cultural, political and social progress ... They are : Egypt, Libya, Tunisia, Morocco, Algeria, Saudi Arabia, Yemen, Aden, Iraq, Jordan, Lebanon, Syria.

Pakistan has reached out its geometrical complex of anti-India feelings to the matrix of this Arab World, vociferously airing out its ingrained grievances and irretrievable jealousy over India on Kashmir problem.

The rulers of Pakistan are generally equipped with the wiles of British diplomacy. And Pakistan's diplomacy is a continuaiton of propaganda against India willy-nilly. Pakistanis are just like the Irish with that big obsession of Kashmir. They can have their Kashmir next day if only they were to put their affairs in order. But their disordered affairs are due to the wiles of British diplomacy, which invented the word, Pakistan, decades before Pakistan was founded. But Kashmir was expolited by feudal elements to keep themselves in power. Even Noor Khan, one of the feudal lords of Pakistan, once swore that Kashmir, like all other indo-Pak disputes, was invented for the purpose of developing armament race between the two countries and providing a ready market of U.S. army.

'Neutrality' is an impossibility for Pakistan which is only one of the many pebbles on the seashore for outside powers to trample upon. So, Pakistan cannot stand up for her own real interests. And Pakistan's position will be reduced to an explosive absurdity, according to a well-considered plan. Pakistan is a loyal-ally of the West. A ghost-hidden hand really rules Pakistan with a plenty of dogmatic mullocracy. In such a ghostly climate, many ghostly eventful happenings are reported to have ebbed away Pakistan's intenal character of her Islamic constitution. Obviously the spiralling crisis has now reached a stage where elemental passions are being aroused over how Pakistan was born, who really was responsible for it, who ruined its rich prospects, who invited the dictatorship that looks good until the last minutes, who created 'Lie and Deny' diplomacy over Kashmir problems, under whose guidence words must have no relation to action at the outset, whether Pakistan deserves to live as one or two entities, or not at all, whether pressure can be exercised against India by the forced exodus of terrorists, whether Pakistan will be allowed to survive or put through general elections, or be allowed either by a greater crisis or by firebrands of world-devastating terrorist outfits or by naked authoritarianism which alone comes to the top. So, there never has been and never will be in that haunted atmosphere of Islamic fundamentalists, and intellectually active people. Added to the momentum of these controversies which have almost become autophysical by virtue of the self-justifying fanaticism of the participants, lies the shadow of popular unrest and crescent triangle and golden triangle sponsored by the world drug-barons of Islamic countries of the world. It may altogther destroy the very base of Pakistan's military potentially. It was General Mirza who supplied the necessary stimulus for dragging the army into political and racial rivalries and controversies. Islamic politics has taken the form of an attack on the foreign policy without questioning the fundamental principle underlying it. Pakistan's devil's advocates are worse than their enemies living within the country. Her foreign ministry sends only 'playboys' and 'nincompoops' to worsen her prestige abroad. So this stormy petrel in Pakistan's politics has a deeply intellectual role reserves for terrorist outfits all over the valley of Kashmir.

Her dependence on foreign aid is the bottleneck of her foreign policy. The then Muslim League leader Mumtaz Daulatnama, said in 1950 : "We are not coveted for anything in the world."

Truly speaking, Pakistan, being a banana republic, has got no independent foreign policy that depends mostly on the ding-dong battle of anti-India hymns of ingrained hatred through the political grapevine. She has lost freedom of choice having tied herself willingly to series of military allainces. One power bloc regards Pakistan as enemy, other shows affection but attaches no importance to her. It was Daulatnama who categorically told, "... neither United States nor United Kingdom would support Pakistan whole-heartedly either on Kashmir issue or on canal water dispute with India." Pakistan is today orphaned soul. As Pakistan was not created to get to be the stooge of any power. Whereas the United States, Britain and Pakistan have taken a great mistaken judgement in their attitude towards 'Middle East.'

Though India and Pakistan had separated and become independent, many things are common history and a hundred other things are the breeding ground for this crudest form of political estrangement. Becasue of this it is terribly distressing that we cannot make progress in developing what is natural and inevitable to our two countries. Why? The trail of estrangement was created between them by partition, the huge migrations had been gobbled up and the terrible killings had rolled down on the red carpet of death and disaster, either by communal riots or by reciprocal destructions. It is only in the political sphere that passions can be roused, sometimes with the help of religion.

There is an amusing joke all around the Kashmir valley. An artist asked the gallery owner if anyone had shown interest in his paintings of terrorism. "I have good news and bad news," he said. "The good news is that some guy enquired about your work and wondered if it would appreciate in value after you died. When I told him it would, he bought all 15 of your paintings."

"And the bad news?"

"The guy was a terrorist."

The political climate in Pakistan is oppressive to tolerate the intolerably impassioned advocacy of terrorist fanaticism very much impenetrable to world peace mission process. It reminds us of Washington in the heyday of McCarthy, when man after man in high place would deplore in terror privately and appease it publicly. Islamic McCarthyism runs wild without any let or hindrance all along the world of ours. Under the Pakistan version of McCarthyism, anyone who despises Allah with the official doctrine of Islamic fundamentalism has a good chance of being called a traitor. Like the bird Ostrich ignoring all grave problems, Pakistan's Machiavellian character using all heinously executed immoral methods to achieve success on Kashmir problem has already dugged out. Such a brittle and fragile foreign policy has hiccupped conspiracy over Kashmir problem, after dovetailing her foreign policy with subversions.

Words may have lost their meaning in the satellite age, but when frontdoor men in power ascribe the ills of their country to the intrigues of backdoor terrorism, it becomes a jungle. After all, democracy cannot be floated in Asian lands, howsoever turbulent they may appear, by ascribing all the impediments to the intrigues and bespoke subversionists. When politicians precariously perch on the pedestal of power where maladminstration remains unchecked, they cannot defeat subversion within the framework of democracy. Politicians act only as dictators.

It is a tragedy of the highest magnitude that our political leadership has such a poor vision on Kashmir problem as not to be able to see even a few yards ahead. This is said not in the spirit of negative criticism. Our Government have gorged ahead a constant blunder mistakenly and nefariously determining diplomatic relations with others, particularly with our neighbouring countries. A Government may be changed but the foreign policies should be dynamic, realistic as well as conducive to the matters. But our foreign policies on Kashmir problem have ever been on a romantic plane that has at times almost bordered on quixotic. A queer vision of political romance of our well-prejudiced political leaders has led them adrift.

We are a people of peace. We hate the wars that Hitler loves. But for our way of life, Hitler could substitute burtality, deceit, intolerance, inhumanity, the goose-step and the Gestapo. That we shall spare no effort to preserve ... peaceably if we can, forcibly if we must. Fool me once, shame on you ; fool me twice, shame on me.

In modern war strategy, infiltrators and spies are the vicious forerunners, clothed with Machiavellian character, using the border areas and our soil with a very nefarious role of political machination and subversive activities. They are the machinaries for actual aggression and prepare the ground for invading armies. That is why in modern war popular resistance in cities, villages must be collectively organised, whose chief function will be to foil the activities of these advance enemy parties which are busy for collecting information through a gravevine and passing it on to the enemy camp. The annual cycle of a get-together is well-written in Kashmir and other surroundings as a preparation for the reception of a bridegroom impersonated as a terrorist who comes to the bride's place for the celebration of the nuptial ceremony of a political hypocrisy of Pakistan. Not long ago it was Mrs. Indira Gandhi who said in America that it was a mistake not to have fought to a finish our case with Pakistan. That experience, however, belated, should effectively harden us against any more treacherous truce.

We have to repeal out our hackneyed foreign policy in the face of common danger, from China and Pakistan. Non-alignment has not paid the dividends we expected. It has spelt out much, while implementing the policies. The enemy outside, the enemy inside. Unknown enemies are more dangerous than that of the known enemies who are bed-fellows. Pakistan does not understand the voice of reason, but the voice of firmness.

Democratic politicians find it difficult publicly to explain their foreign policies. Why? The audience they address is domestic. Foreign secretaries take risks and bargains; democracies dislike risks and do not understand bargains. In pursuing their foreign policies, both parties are in the hands of events much more than political fiction allows them to admit. Where the two powers (Indian and Pakistan) around whom U.S. policy revolves do not reveal their aims, do not obey normal political rules, seem to threaten, little room is left for public dispute. Where furthermore the leaders of both countries are without distinctive doctrine, and where the people do not want doctrine, a bi-partisan foreign policy is not so much deliberately conceived as practically unavoidable. What comparsion there can be between the leaders of two fighting nations must be a comparison of competence.

Disarmament : The pens which write against disarmament are made with the same steel from which guns are made. International diplomacy on Kashmir problem has not so far done anything which Hitler disliked. Words of Pakistan on Kashmir problem must have no relation to action. Words are one thing, actions another. Good words, to Pakistan, are mask for concealment of bad deeds. Sincere diplomacy is no moe possible than dry water or wooden iron. Pakistan has her own grammar, but not her own logic. Pakistan has so far discovered the art of diplomacy to deceive the diplomats. As democracy is doomed, Pakistan is now at the crossroads of terrorism and Islamic globalisation.

Just after the disquieting episode of Pak-occupied Kashmir or Azad Kashmir, most of our political leaders, inside and outside parliament, appear as neurotic and incompetent either on Kashmir issue or on the question of Azad Kashmir. Why? Becasue they have been dominating a romantic beauty of anti-democracy punctuated by religious thunderstorms and political quarrels.

After the occupation of Azad Kashmir, Pakistan can never strike deep roots in her honest outlook or grow into Islamic community with it and with the countrymen. No healing prescription is offered for the people of Azad Kashmir to be richly rewarding. And the rulers don't have to start from the beginning and be taught how to be human. Do they know this lesson goes deeper than reason? Even after the death of Jinnah, Islamic philosophic thought on Azad Kashmir occupation has been seeking for its own original word 'stranglehold of terrorist camps'. In the course of this fermentation, Pakistan has become finally polarized between its religious trend on the one hand and its radical Islamic currents on the other. The dilemma between Islamabad and Karachi looms large on the horizon of cross-border terrorism, and has gone far beyond mere politics of Kashmir issue. For Pakistan, after Azad Kashmir, sees the vast mass of human beings as the victims of the system.

At the end of this chapter, we may summarise the characteristic of Pakistan today, either on Azad Kashmir or on Kashmir issue. Pakistan suffers from the frenzied tempo, the disintegration of education, the loss of their Islamic roots in nature and in home life, the loss of symbols, of the vocation of woman, of organic comunity life and of the degradation of matter.These are the patient's symptoms and they are all traceable to one central cause 'an improvement of Islamic spirit' which goes very deep and which seems to lead to a final eclipse of the spirit in the life of their society.

The patient is very sick and is passing through a psychological crisis which only a radical restoration of those roots in reality can resolve. Some words of Dostoevsky, Russian novelist, may be quoted which can epitomize this truth :

"The roots of our thoughts and feelings are not here but in other worlds, and if the sense of oneness with those other worlds grows weak or is destroyed in you, the heavenly growth will die in you. Then you will be indifferent to life or even grow to hate it."

And their outer ills and dislocations today derive from their loss of Islamic relation to that inner world which religion in particular has cherished in the past but has itself so often violated or misread. Today Pakistan has harnessed a high-coloured imagination to the art of making Islamic globalisation on barbarianism.

Yesterday of partition is history. And tomorrow of Pakistan is mystery. Why? Because Pakistan always looks good until the last minutes.

Today or tomorrow, Pakistan will half-jokingly complain that she has never had her own identity.

5

GENESIS OF INDO-PAK WAR : Tales of Imagination

Delusion arises from anger. The mind is bewildered by delusion. Reasoning is destroyed when the mind is bewildered. One falls down, when reasoning is destroyed. The patch of grass in front of Islamabad has already abandoned its burgeoning glory. Why? Because its ambition was to become a lawn of peace and finally turned into the dirty yellow of poor straw. That poor straw has revealed out its ghastly jaws of terrorism and sharp claws of fanaticism that had been invisible under the dust of centuries. Since independence, the people of Pakistan have ever flown into a rage and made a bad landing. According to Confucius, "when anger rises, think of the consequences." It is not what they built. It is what they knocked down. It is not the borders. It is the spaces between the borders. Pakistan believes in new lords and new laws, in every after coup d' etat. The road to Kashmir, to Pakistan, is always paved with evil-digested intentions.

Open and unlimited war between two members is a disaster that has never yet happened, to the Commonwealth, though India and Pakistan have been close to it before. It would be a denial of all that the Commonwealth stands for, and might lead to its total disruption. This threat gives every Commonwealth country a special status in seeking and the struggle in Kashmir. What is the intrinsic truth behind the Kashmir issue? A political conundrum is the collision of indefensible provocation with inexcusable retaliation. Pakistan's guilt in launching infiltrators into Indian-held Kashmir is indubitable. Whether national or international, must deal with these hard key facts. First, Kashmir has brought the two greatest nations of Southern Asia to the rage of an all-out war which could maim them for a generation, cause misery to million of their people, and open the sub-continent to communist China. Secondly, there are parts of the State to the north-west and south-east respectively which everyone but a fanatic must recognise as irreversibly Pakistani and Indian respectively. Thirdly, the real disputed area concerns the valley and Poonch, Fourthly, the people of Kashmir themselves have never yet had the chance of deciding their own future.

For the United Nations to say 'stop the fighting', though necessary, is not enough. Fighting will break out on and off unless it stops on terms which lead towards a permanent settlement. The outline of such term is implicitly in the key facts. A wide neutralised belt should be established between India and pakistan-occupied territory.

From danger springs opportunity. The danger in Kashmir is fierce, but the opportunity is correspondingly great. Truly speaking, the nations of India and Pakistan, born and nurtured in an ambience of communal hate and estrangement, will never live up with friendship until the canker of Kashmir is excised.

Great statesmen never grow with age, and they are unforgettable. The politicians grow old and forgettable. Pakistan has so far deliberately created the incident to maintain a vitriolic tension between the two countries so that the Kashmir issue, in the curcible of troubles and ever-growing trepidations, may not be allowed to sleep peacefully. It is a gloomy picture of 'Fires in Kashmir'.

'Genesis of Indo-Pak war' may be divided into two parts:

1. Fires in Kashmir (already mentioned)
2. The price of nationhood

And the consequences of two parts lead to the genesis of Indo-Pak war.

THE PRICE OF NATIONHOOD

For one person dreams of making fifty thousand rupees, another person dreams of how to spend fifty thousand rupees. We have no acts of parliament against combining to cover the price of nationhood. As the caterpillar chooses the fairest leaves to lay her eggs on, so the price of nationhood lays its curse on the fairest joys. Everything ends in a conspiracy against the public. Democracy in Pakistan is on the wane. Why? It is because Pakistan tends to stupidity and baseness that people move so slowly. How can it be possible? It is possible to convert a young Muslim into a fanatical zealot, ready to torture and destroy and to suffer mutilation and death for an obscene faith in terrorism, baseless in fact and morally monstrous. Whereas in India, people are used as a blind tool. At present, people are lost in the crowd of political gamesmanship.

Since the genesis of disputes over Kashmir, both sides ... India and Pakistan ... have been hoping for a cheap victory; neither can yet be expected to do anything that seems to imply acceptance of defeat.

Defeat for what aim? The causus belli is Kashmir, but the longer the war goes on, and the more deeply national sentiment becomes involved, the wider the issues become. As to Kashmir itself, there is head-on conflict between the Indian legitimist claim that the whole State is part of the Indian Union, and that Pakistan is an invader on her side of the ceasefire line (now it is called LOC) demarcated by the Line of Control, and Pakistan's rejection of the State's accession to India as coercive and illegal and their demand for the whole State would yield it to Pakistan. A partition might be realistic, but not only is the disputed central valley the richest and the most vital part of the State, ever since 1947 Kashmir has become to both nations a fracas of their mutual rivalry and hate, deep-rooted in the 1,000 year history of Hindu-Muslim war in India. After partition, the transfer of power in August, 1947, both the people awoke to a harsh disillusionment. Many Hindus were never reconciled to the price of dividing Mother India that had been paid for independence; many wishfully believed that Pakistan would collapse and be re-absorbed. To many Indian eyes, Kashmir stood for the reassertion of refusal to admit the two nation theory which had created Pakistan. The Muslims had also paid a bitter price for separate nationhood in the partition of the ancient Muslim governed provinces of Bengal and Punjab. For them, Kashmir has stood for the reassertion of their historic destiny as rulers of all North India.

In this political ambience, if Pakistan is the subtlest of so-called restoration dramatists for peace-keeping mission, it is also unquestionably the nastiest Pakistan, letting out her hypocrisy over Islamic globalisation.

So behind the skirmishes across the border, behind the wrangles of the last 60 years, behind the wars, lies the clash of implacable faiths, in incompatible ideals. The nature of the conflict as an attempt to divert anew the waters of history was illumined by the re-emergence for creation of a separate Sikh State, a Khalistan; for the Sikhs also have folk memories of their mastery of thc whole North-west. These deep fires had been extinguished by military armistices.

It might be tempting to conclude that the best thing would be to let violence run its course until it is sated, and until the turbulent waters of history have cut a clear new channel at the cost of as much blood as the two nations are prepared to spill. But that is a lost sight of two hideous dangers. The first is the outbreak of mass communal warfare within India and Pakistan. That it has already happened in Karachi as well as in India on the demolition of the Babri Masjid. And so many riots have already happened to a dangerous climax. It seems almost a miracle. That it could be prevented if the war goes on indefinitely is too much to hope.The second great threat is the destruction of both nations either through the waste of their substance on war or through an unfathomable depth of terrorist activities running wild with all their well-concerted plan of diabolical lusts and prejudices. Jehadis' words are weapons, and it is dangerous in speculation. What is terrorism? It means an ugly mobmadness, crucifying the truth-tellers. Preparation for terrorism is a constant stimulus to suspicion of world peace. The strain of war on economic resources and governmental capacity would be accentuated by withdrawal of foreign aid from both sides. Even more millions might die. Given the burgeoning circumstances all over the subcontinent, Pakistan as well as all other Islamic countries in Asia has commissioned the Islamic fanatics to destablilise the stability of Indian Union either by terrorism or by fanning out the Indian Muslims to run parallel with Islamabad that has also evened out this herculean task amongst all other Jehadis. And they have been all go to exercise terrorism with a plenty of go. Such glacial foreign policy of Pakistan may have parlayed the relationship between India and Pakistan into an unfathomable dissension. Pakistan's devil-may-care attitude over ephemeral pleasures, after having terrorist exhibitions over the innocent people around the world, will one day be a boomerang to the Islamic nations and they will have to pay back their own vengeance. It will happen to them sooner or latter. All these are larded with malice. And malice-forced wit turns them mad and wild.

Bangladesh is more and more damaging than that of Pakistan to Indian democracy. She likes parodying away the same breath of anti-India hymns of hate and envy as Pakistan has so far ventured out its conspiracy in its own perimeter as a ventriloquist. The smaller the understanding of the situation, the more pretentious the form of expression. Bangladesh is an illegitimate child of Pakistan whose pre-occupied parenthetic remaks over the Kashmir dispute have not only parceled out Hindu-Muslim disunity but parceled off the dissension of Shia-Sunni relationship wider and wider amongst the Arab World.

Such hypnotic inertia may have paralysed the nucleus of Lahore-Karachi relations.What more needs explanation is not why some people are criminals, but why most people are not. The ball is in the air, and when it falls, it is either in their grasp or it is not. England's King George II once received bitter complaints charging that his brilliant military leader, General James Wolfe, was insane. "Mad is he?" the king said. "Then I wish he would bite some other of my generals." Rulers of some Muslim countries are insane. They would bite other rulers as Pakistan has bitten Afghanistan. As communists bite other communists. It is universal. The escalation of the open war itself is a less danger than that of Shia-Sunni disparity and communal warfare between two rival nations. China's menace is more likely to be aimed at pinning down Indian forces in the northeast, and so balance of deployable strength on Pakistan's behalf, than at a military invasion, though the longer the war goes on, the more the sub-Continent is exposed to China's advance internally as well as externally. At this stage, this vulnerable ambience all over the sub-Continent, judging from the old score of reciprocal misunderstanding through the grapevine, indecisive and sporadic warfare, seems the most likely military prognosis. So long as Pakistan ventures upon Kashmir as their best trump-card, America and its allied forces will have to bog down Pakistan's attempt to get attuned to China's political games play-boy thinking to India. Mullocracy has turned the country into a disordered bunch of harassed and fearful excursionists, standing helplessly all around the terrorist gardens of variety, peering anxiously about to see where the next assault would come from on their persons or their purses.

From Ayub Khan down to the present ruler, all have held a mirror up to nature in the heart of history, close under the terrible shadow of power, with nothing but unstinted pride and admiration for a better crusade. Negotiation with Pakistan! At times most of us quarrel with our fate; if only our parents had been loving. But this is a loss of time, a loss of energy, a loss of happiness. It is senseless. Why? Because fate is not subject to negotiation, agreement, change or compromise. India is free to play, not to play up with an emasculated foreign policy and with an emaciated ideology. The hard part is knowing the difference between India and Pakistan on ideology. It takes some doing. Everything is herded together into a pit of damaging estrangement. And the hired-out ideology of China has made Pakistan a nation of Hypocrisy. There are really serious side effects in the making of an agreement with Pakistan on Kashmir problem to the hiccups of Indian democracy. Pakistan has so far played up many outmanoeuvring strategy, shaking hands with India either in Islamabad or in New Delhi. Pakistan's high-stakes political theatre has gone well. When two hands meet, we pass on something of ourselves. After being introduced to Mark Twain, Hellen Keller ... who was both deaf and blind ... commented, "I can feel the twinkle of his eye in his handshake." In some indefinable way, Mr. Twain had conveyed his charismatic self to Keller.

What is true behind this handshake? That has been probably true of the handshake all the way back to its earliest days. A common explanation is that when early men encountered a stranger, he held out his hand to show he had no weapon. Not so, says Brian Charles Burke, who writes a history of the handclasp. "That idea became popular in the 19th century and just took off." Instead, the Philadelphia historian believes, the handshake meant "Putting your blood behind your breath." Pakistan has not yet learnt the immanent spirit of handshake. How to outmanoeuvre the agreement on Kashmir problem is its intrinsic spirit behind the handshake with New Delhi. Truly speaking, ancient peoples distrusted the spoken word alone, and they used the handclasp to signify that their promise was backed up by the power of their heart ... that is, their blood. Thus, the handshake connoted 'trust' ... 'trust ever-lasting'.

What is handshake? It is the easiet of gestures in an amicable way an entwining of thumb and fingers as our hand glides into another's. The handshake has a rich history as a symbol of reconciliation or rapport. The Roman co-emperors Balbinus and Pupienus Maximus put the handclasp on a coin in AD 238 to signify their harmony. One rare coin showing two couples shaking hands in thought to celebrate the wedding of Marcus Aurelius and Faustina II, the daughter of Emperor Antoninus Pius, in AD 145. What is a sign of reconciliation in American history is a sign of humiliation in Pakistan. Why? Because Pakistan has no history.

There are so many styles of handshakes; the guy with the sweaty palm, the nervous hand-wringer, the Type -A personality who shakes your hand jovially, then quickly breaks off and moves on. Pakistan only knows styles of handshakes. She likes to hold out. Pakistan is used to practising her style of political handshake, particularly on Kashmir issue, in an epigrammatic manner into the cobweb of haughty disdain, throwing a spanner in the works.

Chinese Premier Chou En-lai and US Secretary of State John Foster Dulles wee at a meeting in Geneva in May 1954. Dulles despised Chou, holding him responsible for thousands of American soliders killed in the Korean war. During the meeting, Chou tried desperately to manoeuvre Dulles into a position where the two could be phographed shaking hands. Chou's failure was summed up in a New York Times Magazine article. "Mr. Dulles has pointedly refrained from shaking hands with Mr. Chou."

Eighteen years later, President Richard Nixon sent the opposite message to Chou. A famous photograph shows Nixon striding off the plane at Peking's International Airport for the triumphant opening up of China in 1972. He was smiling, and his hand was extended toward Chou. This is the camouflage of political handshake in an ambience of ambivalence towards Kashmir issue.

Another political avalanche of camouflage was between Israel and PLO Chairman. On September 13, 1993, President Bill Clinton stood between Israeli Prime Minister Yatzhak Rabin and PLO Chairman Yaasir Arafat. The two foreign foes had just signed an agreement at the White House to end a generation of violence in the Middle East. The question in everybody's mind : would Rabin shake Arafat's hand? Would it not be a political camouflage of Rabin lagging himself with the Jews?

Three thousand spectators waited in suspense on the White House Lawn. Around the globe. Rabin tipped up. Millions were riveted to their TVS. Rabin paused for a split second before extending his hand to his long time adversary. He was noticeably uncomfortable, but managed a small smile at the crowd roared its approval.

Clinton's high-stakes political theatre had gone well. A 25 year old fanatic, Yagil Amir, was outraged that the two leaders had shaken hands. That handshake turned into vengeance. On November 4, 1995, Amir assassinated Rabin. The New York Times carried the headline "With a Handshake, Rabin's fate was sealed."

Mr. Z.A. Bhutto was sealed with the same fate as happened to him after shaking hands with Mrs. Indira Gandhi on the Simla Agreement. Mrs. Benazir Bhutto, his daughter, had been in a dilemma on shaking hands with Rajib Gandhi. So many examples are there. Mr. Nehru died after having had a warming handshake with the Chinese Premier, Chou En-lai on 'Indo-Chini bhai bhai'. All these mishaps happened to them as their confidence was sold on their counterpart. And Mr. Nehru intended to snuggle up in the arms of China.

Now the question is : which one is the best State? The best State is that in which bad men are not allowed to hold office and good men are not allowed to refuse office. Given this, Cabinet Ministers of all State Governments as well as Central Government are packed with evil men. This is the besetting sin of a democratic country like India. Pakistan snuggles up to iniquitous men very much eager to have a handshake with New Delhi. Why? Because they feel a laid-back relaxation.

We fear that the Chinese might embark first on intimidatory and then on widening military action against India. China's original aggression against India paid off handsomely in 1962. Diplomacy and handshake run parallel with hypocrisy, Chinese strength and Indian weakness, accelerated favourable frontier 'settlements' with Myanmar, Afganistan and Pakistan and extended Chinese influence over Nepal and the Himalayan States of Bhutan and Sikkim. The Chinese-built highway from Kathmandu to Lhasa has been completed.

The Chinese have not ruthlessly cleared the decks in Tibet, where despite sporadic, courageous but doomed tribal unrest they have established an 'autonomous region' ... which in Peking jargons means a region without any autonomy at all, but one controlled by the Chinese communist party.

There are around 300,000 Chinese troops, well-trenched and well-equipped along the 1,800 miles border ... 20 divisions of about 14,000 men. In particular, the Chinese have a large concentration in the Chumbi valley salient thrusting South between Sikkim and Bhutan towards West Bengal. Once it was on East Pakistan. But Mrs. Gandhi had frustrated the Chinese attempts venturing upon that mission. A maximum show of selfless communist aid to Pakistan. Obviously it is in the interests of peking to provide blood transfusions for the conflict between India and Pakistan.

Chinese diplomacy was paralysed by the image Mrs. Gandhi had projected so far trying to unite all the rural areas of the world against the imperialists. A misadventure of communism. Imperialism in disguise of communism. Why? Because communism is the death of the soul. It is the organisation of total tyranny. It is Pakistan that has learnt very well from China how to avoid an argument through many trying situations on the Kashmir problem. By avoiding fruitless arguments, everybody wins. Islamabad knows that no matter what the situation is, arguments are a waste or, at best, a misuse of time. The campaign has become ugly, with each party charging the other with dirty deeds. What do you do when someone says something unfair or unkind? Do you suffer in silence, not knowing what to say? It is natural to take offence if someone is rude. Pakistan always sets an adversarial tone and will only make matters worse. On a clear, clear dark night, see a small candle flame from 45 kilometers away. You feel your senses are working normally.

'Pakistan thanks China'

'China thanks Pakistan'.

It has always been a reciprocal thanks-giving mission between Pakistan and China for long, on Kashmir issue. An irretrievable and irresistible lying-in conspiracy within the wheels of connundrum. This hand-shake looks mercilessly ridiculous to India.

Shortly before his death, Mr. Nehru had released Sheikh Abdullah from gaol ... where the veteran Kashmiri leader's pro-Pakistani leanings had landed him ... and embarked on a rather vague search for a solution of Kashmir dispute. This reopened the issue but anything tangible could be achieved he died, leaving

Lal Bahadur Shastri to handle the pronouncements.

The steps towards incorporating Kashmir were taken to satisfy the public, but they enraged Pakistan who complained that India was disturbing the constitutional status in Kashmir unilaterally. Kashmir lost the privileges of its own special flag and elected Head of State, and a new law provided that, as in the case of other States, the Indian President could take over Kashmiri's administration in an emergency. Matters were then made worse when, on May 9, 1965, Sheikh Abdullah was again arrested and confined to the South Indian resort of Ootacamund.

Mr. Z.A. Bhutto, Pakistan's youthful, handsome and passionate foreign minister, whom many suspected of being the moving spirit behind every provocative Pakistani act. In 1951, Bhutto was the accepted leader of the Pakistani undergraduates at Oxford, widely known as the brilliant, forceful party-loving figure. Mr. Ayub Khan, President of Pakistan, was a moderate compared with Mr. Bhutto.

At the dawn of 1960s, Moslem irregulars, backed by Mr. Bhutto, had infiltrated in small groups, into the Indian part of Kashmir. They were disguised as civilians and were trained and equipped to carry out sabotage. The first stage of terrorism began in full swing. Their headquarters was at Murree. The infiltrators, in many cases, provided with Indian money and gifts for the local populace, went into action. They had the routes of Haji Pir Pass.

Intellectual arrogance and the overindulgence of irony at the expense of the less gifted is a handicap to the historians in Pakistan on Indo-Pak relations. Infiltrators, branded with terrorists, are not, like Chengis Khan, a mere machine of destruction, they, as desperadoes, without worrying about dangers to others, try to being out civilization of their own. They negotiate with other Muslim countries against the western powers after weathering the colours of their organizations into different names. Weathering the storm of their mission, they can manage to co-exist with them. The leaders are deemed to be a typical Renaissance Prince. At present, an individual terrorist is lost in the crowd of fanaticism. And in a general atmosphere of politics, he is a victim of mental slavery. In 'Doctor Zhivago', Boris Pasternak says, "Gregariousness is always the refuge of mediocrities, whether they swear by Kant or Marx."

Nehru recognised POK and loved heroism. He was on the side of the resistance movements of those who in complete simplicity made the choice to fight to the death for their country or their family or their religion rather than slavery and humiliation. He was also a lover of political hegemony that was thought to be a centrifugal force to the partition of India. Jinnah ... a mere scape-goat. Even in the great days of freedom movement, men had whispered of prophesies that it would not last for ever. The vivisection of India is a symbolic rather than an historical landmark.

On Kashmir issue, Mr. Nehru managed, rather mysteriously, to confuse functionalism with value judgements, failing to see that when a doctor makes a prescription on the basis of a medical diagnosis, the thing he is not making is a value jdugement.

Whereas every ruler in Pakistan is like a Kaleidoscope: depending on how it is shaken, so the pattern changes. And for this reason, it is difficult to know the whole man, to be both fair to him and to oneself in taking a decision about this hurricane of terrorist outfits of unpredictable direction.

Press reaction in Pakistan on the Kashmir debate is only the visible part of the iceberg. The invisibility is in the discontent in the middle and upper reaches of the Government. Men are fearful of taking initiatives. Why? It may lead to their being carpeted either by the terrorists or by the ruler. This naturally carries the dangers of paralysis. Kashmir is still agony to them.

Every ruler seems to be an idealist, something of a rebel, and not ambitious, brilliant and modest in the making of peace in Kashmir, loyal to western powers but detached from, in the case of Kashmir, but soft-spoken to western dollars. He is, mostly important, a yes man to mullocracy. Most of the adminstration has been streaming under the singularly taut reins of Presidential rule behind the military coup. Style and method of operation rather than politics. Theocracy and mullocracy in Pakistan, like the eagles, were born to be free. Yet they are obliged to make a cage of laws for themselves and to stand on the perch. Why? To render vices serviceable to the cause of virtue.

There are two types of press in the world. One is a licentious press, and another is an enslaved press. The former is an evil and the latter may cause an error, to be more current than wisdom, and wrong more powerful than right. Whereas a licentious press cannot effect these things. If it gives the poison, it gives also the antidote, which an enslaved press withholds. Pakistan is in the grip of an enslaved press. Why? An enslaved press is doubly fatal. It not only takes away the true light on Kashmir issue, but it sets up a false one, that destroys Pakistan to its destruction. And India is in the throes of a licentious press ... sensational and irresponsible to the cause of democracy. Because its humbug and hypocrisy pretend to be 'impartial'. And 'venal press'! Because it likes clamouring of the situation. Lastly, the regulation of the press : It is the most difficult, dangerous and important problem. Why? Because it gives a fillip to the amelioration of the condition of mankind, moralists, and all. The press hopes that each Pakistani ruler will remain as trustful as before to USA even if he cannot work magic overnight through a proxy war on the border.

Pakistan is the most dangerous propagandist. After partition, Pakistan has zoned Kashmir issue off, zoning out all other mischievous problems arisen out within the boundaries. Pakistan is said to be a land of the Devil's Disciple. Why? Because the interchangeability of Allah and the Devil is swapped in the melodrama of Islamic Jehadis. The dilemma of the good women is faced with a totally contrived moral choice, even in Kashmir ... an integral part of India. Both elements have finally gone under in the prevailing climate of characters nauseously beguiled by Jehadis' own paradoxes. The enslaved press in Pakistan has hardly any voice of it but, at the same time, voices forth that they are struggling away for liberty. But it is much easier to say than to prove it, or prescribe a proper remedy. The history of the press in Pakistan, even P.TV., is the same as Iraq, Afganisthan, and other Islamic nations that believe in the culture of despotism. In its infancy, the press in Pakistan is timid, distrustful and dependent on hypocrisy and falsity for success in its propaganda machinery over Kashmir. A recurring volte-face is found in Islamabad on the Kashmir issue. Religious war is a great force upon the minds of fools. Every premier in Pakistan, from Liaquat Ali Khan down to the existing ruler, has been working at the highest reaches at the international level of their ever-growing political cant and trying to manage the western leaders by their coaxing words.

The raiding party of political vampires has started out singing a solo, unsafe at last. Even the foreign policy makers, lying in the inner sanctum of Islamabad, are undoubtedly struggling to restrain laughter, which will have wounded, if it has got out. Their tittering joins Mullocracy's blustering in its gallery of comic creation.

One day Jacqueline Bonvier inquired how John F. Kennedy would define himself. He said : "An idealist without illusions," and the night before they were married in September, 1953, she asked him what he considered his best and worst qualities. He thought his best quality was curiosity and his worst irritability. By irritability he meant impatience with the boring, the commonplace and the mediocre. And by curiosity, he meant a good deal more than the purely intellectual trait; he meant that hunger for experience which caused him to demand that life be concentrated , vivid and full.

The following principal characters are involved in the genesis of Indo-Pak war :

Transfer of power in 1947 plus to reconstruct the story of partition plus the origins of the Kashmir dispute = Genesis of Indo-Pak war.

It was once said of the British Empire in India that it was acquired in a fit of absence of mind. The wars which broke out in 1965 and 1971 were the result of a similar fit of absence of mind. For though trouble was anticipated from several other Indian States on achievement of independence, nobody in the 1947 negotiations seems to have spent much time worrying over Kashmir. If danger there had been foreseen, Britain's parting would not have been that time.

Wisdom after the event is easy; some of the signs of danger could perhaps have been anticipated, had there been time to analyse every contigency. But there was very little time, and the pressures conspired to push Kashmir into background.

The most remarkable thing about the transaction to the independence of British India was the speed at which it was done. *The division of one of the largest countries ... containing just over one fifth of mankind ...was achieved in little over two months.*

Two months' hectic decisions had to have this sub-continent a cauldron of permanent discontent, and a burning crucible of fanaticisim at the optimum temparature of death and destruction. Such miscalculated judgement through and through has created a Himalayan blunder we have suffered for. Everyone denied it.

In the almost indecent haste of decision-taking, loose-ends were bound to be left, and Kashmir was one of them. To some politicians, the actions of Britain's Viceroy, Lord Mountbatten, were wilfully impetuous. Lord Alexander of Hillsborough, a previous cautious negotiator, described him as "Just a young man in hurry." *But the truth was that after years of indecision and unsuccessful bargaining, the job had to be done quickly. India, in 1947, was, said Lord Ismay, "like a burning ship in midocean with fire on its deck and ammunition in its holds."*

The previous year, religious civil war had begun. In Calcutta, a Muslim call for 'direct action' had been interpreted by H.S. Suhrawardy, Chief Minister of Bengal, as a free-for all to clear the Hindus out of the city. Things imported for the purpose swooped on the city and for a couple of days killed Hindus. The Hindus hit back and at the end of the week some 30,000 people had been slaughtered. The escalation in murder had begun; the British stood impotent; the last justification for the British rule in India had been swept away. There is nothing so good for the inside of a man as the outside of a horse. Mr. Suhrawardy came in like a lion, and went out like a lamb. The reverse, however, is also true, and the saying continues.

On top of this, the administrative machine was nearing collapse. The Indians in the Civil Service were getting politically paralysed, and failed to reason out the irretrievable problems. The Interim Govt., set up by Lord Wavell (Mountbatten's predecessor) was bogging down under the growing strain of religious nationalism. As the Indian politician, Rajagopalachari said : "If power had not been handed over quickly, there would have been no power left to hand over."

Attlee, who had made up his mind about Indian independence long before becoming Prime Minister, was well aware of the urgency. The only point on which he had doubts was whether to hand over to one India or two. He still had hopes of the former.

Lord Mountbatten, Atlee's Viceroy-elect, touched down at Delhi airport on March 22, 1947. He was preceded in another aircraft by his staff, specially chosen to augment the Civil Servants at Viceroy's House. The senior of them was Lord Ismay, just retired from a distinguished Army career, (His close friendship with Churchill and his long experience of India were to be vital assets). There was Sir Eric Mieville, a city businessman and old India colleague of Ismay's, acting as principal secretary and Mountbatten's wartime press attache, Allan Campbell-Johnson.

Among the papers they carried was a letter from Attlee, defining

Mountbatten's brief. The main points were : "It is the definite object of His Majesty's Govt. to obtain a unitary Govt. for British India and the Indian States ... and you should do the utmost in your power to persuade all parties to work together to this end ... if by October 1, you consider that there is no prospect of reaching a settlement on the basis of a unitary Govt ... you should report to His Majesty's Govt. on the steps which you consider should be taken ... *you should aim at June 1, 1948 as the effective date for the transfer of power* ... you will impress upon the Indian leaders the great importance of avoiding any breach in the continuity of the Indian Army and of maintaining the organisation of defence on an all-Indian basis."

It was clear from this letter that Attlee, at this stage, was still thinking along the general lines of the Cabinet Mission of 1946 which had proposed a loose federation, with a weak Central Govt. responsible for defence, foreign affairs and communications, and three provincial groups, one large, and predominantly Hindus, and the others smaller Muslim groups.

Attlee's letter also reaffirmed a doctrine that had first been stated publicly by the Cabinet Mission : The lapsing of paramountcy. On the face of it, this was just a legalistic nicety. In fact, it is to lapsing of paramountcy that we owe the present war over Kashmir.

In addition to the eleven provinces of British India, the Raj also included the 565 States of Princely India, whose rulers had treaties with the British Crown recognising Britain as the paramount power. These rules varied widely in wealth and status from his exalted Highness the Nizam of Hyderabad, ruling an area as big as Britain and running 21 gun salutes, to the Raja of Katodial barely owning a village green and ranked no guns.

Under paramountcy, the rulers were theoretically sovereign allies of the British Crown, but they followed Viceregal foreign policy and allowed British control of main communications while retaining all the trappings if not the reality of independence. Many of them had their own armies and some had their own currencies, postal services and railways. The precise meaning of the paramountcy ... introduced after the Mutiny ... was never properly defined beyond the cryptic announcement that 'Paramountcy was paramount'. In practice, it meant that if the prince misbehaved, the Viceroy deposed him out of hand.

The announcement by Cripps that paramountcy would lapse meant that on the day the British handed over power, each princely would become indepedent again. Only if the ruler agreed to 'accede', would his State become part of the new country. As it happens, when India's independence Day eventually came all but three of the provinces had acceded to India or Pakistan. The three which were left out were Hyderabad, Junagadh and Kashmir.

Mountbatten's team, duly installed in Viceroy House, got down to work at once. There had been a strong feeling in Britain that *Attlee's decesion on June 1, 1948 as a first date for independence was too precipitous*. Ismay at first shared the view that 15 months was too little time for the job, but Mountbatten, who had insisted on a firm date when he accepted the job, felt it would work in their favour by forcing the Indian leaders into agreement.

In fact, it was barely two weeks after Mountbatten's arrival in India that Campbell-Johnson recorded his diary that Mountbatten was convinced that the date chosen for independence was too late. The first hand view of the extent to which the administration was loosing its grip had come as a shock. It took Mountbatten even less time to reach the conclusion that there was absolutely no chance of handing over to a united India. "It was apparent within hours," says Campbell-Johnson. "At the end of the first week," recalls Mieville, "his mind seemed to be made up."

The Muslim demand for Pakistan had been forcibly expressed in 1940 when 100,000 members of the All India Muslim League met in Lahore. On April 5, Mountbatten heard it for the first of many times from M.A. Jinnah. The son of recently converted Hindu merchants from Karachi, Jinnah was a brilliant lawyer. Totally westernised, he was an agnostic who knew no Arabic, sported Savile Row suits and a monocle. Since he could not speak any Indian language his political speeches ... in flawless English ... had to be interpreted. Tall, thin, eagle-faced and incorruptible, he felt that he went on saying 'No' long enough he would win.

At the end of their first meeting, Mountbatten told Campbell-Johnson : "My God, he was cold. It took me most of the interview to unfreeze him." Unfreezing the leaders was Mountbatten's first task. He did this with finesse, getting them to talk about themselves. Gandhi, who bitterly opposed the idea of partition, as the saying goes, right up to his death, found himself talking to the new Viceroy about his early life in South Africa. Gandhi's oppose to the idea of partition is an open question. A postern door makes a thief and a whore. Jinnah was made to talk about his work at London Bar. At the end of his first interview with Nehru, two days after his arrival. Mountbatten said : "I want you to regard me not as the last Viceroy winding up the British Raj but as the finest to lead the way to the new India."

Nehru replied : "Now I know what they mean when they speak of your charm being so dangerous."

Mountbatten was determined to charm. Sir Archibald Nye, then Governor of Madras, remembered the Viceroy beginning a speech in Tamil, the local language. "As you can imagine this went down very well."

Nehru and the other Congress leaders were reluctantly driven to share Mountbatten's view that partition was the only answer. But Gandhi would have none of it. On April 11, he left Delhi telling his prARyer meeting that he had 'no desire' to witness the end of the talks. He went to East Bengal (now Bangladesh) to live among the villagers who revered him. He wrote : "Mine will prove a voice in the wilderness, but I cannot remain silent as I did not want to go down as an unprotesting witness of what is taking place around me in the country ...

I have no desire to prolong my life. I wish to die in harness taking the name of God with my last breath. I only want to die a sudden death, and if I die with God's name on my lips will be a sign that I was not an impostor or a fraud, but that I was that I tried and claimed to be." It was, perhaps, a last gentle rebuke to Churchil who had called him a naked fakir.

With Gandhi out of the way, Mountbatten could concentrate upon the two men who really mattered : Nehru and Jinnah. Mountbatten had decided on partition, he also decided that speed had become all important. There are those, old Indian hands among them, who criticise Mountbatten for 'indecent haste'. But the country was split by communal dissensions and riots, and by a red carpet of slaughter and a pool of bloodshed. The two most important men in the land could scarcely be made to sit down at the same table together. Hindu and Muslim Civil Servants had already been afflicted by the ghost of partition. Every tension-making approach was to them a haunted house of apparition. And they were beginning to look at every decision in the light of how it would affect their unborn respective nations. A shadow of conspiracy was looming large.

On May 2, Mountbatten sent Ismay to London with a premliminary progress report for the Cabinet. On May 18, the Viceroy himself flew to London taking with him his plan. It normally takes six months or more to pass a Bill through parliament. Attlee promised to push the legislation through in two months.

On June 3, the final decision of how power was to be transferred from the British Raj was published. It provided for the creation of Pakistan.

In a broadcast to the people of the Sub-Continent, Mountbatten said : "For more than a hundred years 400 million of you lived together and the country had been administered as a single entity ... my great hope was that communal difference would not destroy this." There could, he went on, be no coercion to make minorities to live against their will under the rule of a majority. And the only alternative to coercion was partition. *The day, following the broadcast, ... June 4 ... he told a press conference that the date for the transfer of power would be August 15. Mountbatten counted on the impact of the time running out to intensify the pace of negotiations. In his staff room, he kept a calender pinned to the wall-map of India and inscribed with large materials marking the days to independence.*

On July 25, the Viceroy addressed a gathering of the Indian princes in Delhi. Their Highnesses were confused and worried about their future. Some were doubtful about the wisdom of acceding to either of the new States of India or Pakistan.

In full dress uniform, dazzling white encrusted with orders and medals, Mountbatten began by reminding the princes that he was the medalised prince of Battenberg. He spoke of the link between the princely States and the Indian provinces, coordination which made India an economic entity and said : "That link is now to be broken. If nothing can be put in its place only chaos can result and that states first." For Kashmir one of the three States to delay in acceding, his words were prophetic.

Partition did not only concern land and people. It was carried out through the administration. The army was divided to give India 15 infantry regiments, 12 armoured corps units, $12^{1/2}$ artillery regiments, six armoured corps units, eight and a half artillery regiments and 34 engineering units.

But land ... and just where the partition line was to be drawn through the Punjab and Bengal ... remained the greatest problem of all.

A MAN WHO HAD NEVER been to India before, who has never been there since, decided how India should be divided during seven weeks in July and August, 1947. Within two weeks of their acceptance of partition, Jinnah and Nehru were asked by Mountbatten who they would like to perform the inevitably controversial task of dividing Bengal and the Punjab. Largely at the prompting of Jinnah, Sir Cyrill Radcliffe (The Lord Radcliffe, well-known for his chairmanship of the Vassail Tribunal) was chosen chairman of the Boundary Commission. Radcliffe arrived in Delhi early in July for what was to be the loveliest job during the transfer of power. Although he was formally assisted by four Indian Judges ... two Hindus, two Muslims ... in both the Punjab and Bengal (the two States bordering on East and West Pakistan with mixed Muslim and Hindu populations), the inevitable conflicts of opinion usually left Radcliffe with the task of taking the decision alone. Radcliffe lived and worked in a large Rutyens-designed house inside the Viceroy's Estate in Delhi ... but went away from Viceroy's lodge to avoid any suggestions of connivance. He rarely went out, and never disscussed his work with anybody. When in Calcutta, ironically for a man engaged on the division of British India, he stayed in the former residence of Warren Hastings, the man he admired so much and who had put British India together.

To make the intense heat of India's hottest summer in ten years more unbearable, Radcliffe caught dysentry. Why? Because of the discovery of the C.I.D. of the alleged plot half way through Radcliffe's stay he had to put up with the constant presence of an armed guard and the patrolling of his windows and garden by armed soliders. "It meant," he says, "that I imagined an assassin behind every tree and in every car we passed on the road."

Mountbatten had decided that the boundaries must be fixed before Britain left; both Jinnah and Nehru agreed : "Nothing mattered, comparatively, more than time," they told Radcliffe.

His method was haphazard; the census relations and the maps on which he based his judgements were often as unreliable as the evidence he received. And the conclusions were finally drawn in a vaccum since he did not have time to visit the contested areas to see for himself. It was indeed a Himalayan blunder on the part of Radcliffe. This blunder, wittingly committed, has now become a siccipian task to both the countries to settle down the differences. A small of conspiracy within the wheels of connundrum. *Why did Nehru say to Radcliffe,*

"Nothing matters on the issue of boundaries?" Was our power-drunkard Nehru so hurry to be Prime Minister of India? Conspiracy was looming large in grapevine. Always treat a man as you would wish to be treated yourself. It is a more positive social prescription of societies. The principle is that a person's plight is hopeless once his reputation has been blackened. "I wouldn't dream of defending some of the decisions in detail I made at that time," Radcliffe says now, "but I don't believe different decisions would have made a material difference," Afterall, one point emerges clearly from Radcliffe's reminiscences : No mentioned Kashmir. *"I was not aware of the Kashmir thing at all," he says, "If I had been, it might have been a factor to take into account to accede had then been taken."*

Pakistan claimed that the Boundary Award was deliberately delayed to change the line in the Punjab and to give India access to Kashmir. A hotly disputed area between Amritsar and the Kashmir border, with a Muslim majority went to India. But for this award, India would never have had access by a land route to Kashmir and the dispute may never have arisen, since India's only at alternative access to Kashmir those days was unreliable by air over a high mountain range.

A Briton who was in the Indian Civil Service at the time thinks that Radcliffe awarded that area to India. Why? Because it was an essential communication link with Amritsar, which had to go to India since it was the holy city of the Sikhs, a majority of whom lived on the Indian side of the line. Radcliffe himself no longer remembers the detailed reason of his award.

A conspiracy has been put forward to explain the delay in the publication of the award, which was published on August 17 two days after the end of the British Raj. What happened to mysteriously silent two days? During those two days, Pakistan claimed, Mountbatten bribed Radcliffe to change the award. In fact, explanation is again pragmatic. Mountbatten, Campbell-Johnson states, withheld publication for two days because he knew the award would cast gloom over both India and Pakistan, and he did not wish Independence Day to become a day of mourning.

Radcliffe left for Britain on August 16, just one day after the independence. Exhausted by the job, which he considered the most important he had ever undertaken he had never returned to the Sub-Continent again : *two many millions of people had been uprooted by the award, one of them might try to murder him.*

The INDEPENDENCE DAY celebrations were as euphoric as Mountbatten had hoped. An assassination threat to Jinnah during the August 14 celebrations in Karachi slightly cooled the ardour of the Paksitani officials and this was coincidently reflected in the attitude of the crowds. In Delhi, there were no inhibitions, apart from Nehru's handling a large carefully addressed, but quite empty enveloped supposed to contain the cabinet list to *Mountbatten (who at midnight on August 15 had become India's first Governor General), the only embarrassment seemed to be the hundreds and thousands of enthusiastic Indians who threatened to crush the Mountbattens and their entourage at every official occasion. The single sour note was the fires which could be seen burning in the Punjab as Mountbatten's aircraft flew back from Karachi to Delhi : they presaged a new and even more bitter phase in the Civil war which broke out soon after the celebration.*

Sardar Patel, who controlled the adminisitration of the Congress party, which Nehru took care of policy, *had told Mountbatten that he wanted a 'full basket of apples before independence day*: there were to be no States which had not committed themselves to either India or Pakistan.

Mountbatten's speech to the Chamber of Princes on July 25, had been more effective than most dared hope. Many princes had toyed with the idea of dealing their own independence. But for Hyderabad, Junagadh and Kashmir all the Indian States were committed to either India or Pakistan. The three odd States out had one king in common. Each had an eccentric ruler.

The Muslim Nizam of Hyderabad was one of the richest and meanest men in the world. One of his innumerable concubines insisted that he celebrated the birthday of their son. The Nizam sent to the Bizaare for a floral garland worth 3s. 9d with instruction that it should be returned after use for a three shilling refund.

In November 1948, India took Hyderabad in a swift police action, and in due course the population, overwhelmingly Hindus, voted for merger with neighbouring areas.

The Nawab of Junagadh's eccentricity was an excessive love of dogs. He once held a State wedding for one of his bitches. He too was Muslim ruling a Hindu population. He actually acceded to Pakistan on August 20, 1947, after Jinnah's coaxing. Pakistan calimed ... as indeed was the legal position ... that the decision of the ruler was the one and only factor determining the validity of the instrument of accession; it overruled geography and religion. After a blockade of Junagadh by the Indian army, the Nawab fled to Pakistan, with 200 of his dogs and his two wives' jewels (but neither of the wives) and in November the Army reached in at the invitation of the Dewan.

Although there were unsuccessful attempts to persuade the Maharaja of Kashmir to make up his mind in favour of either Pakistan or India before Independence Day, neither Mountbatten nor his Staff, nor Indian politicians had foreseen any serious problems. The Indians expected Kashmir, with its population 80% Muslim, to go to Pakistan, even though the Maharaja was Hindu. Mr. Patel, the Minister, concerned with the Princely States, had announced that Kashmir was free to decide which way it wanted to go so long as it went.

Mountbatten paid a State visit in June, 1947, to the Maharaja, Sir Hari Singh, with whom he had served on the Prince of Wales's Staff during the Royal tour of India in 1921, and as they drove through Kashmir admiring the scenary, Mountbatten warmed his hot that he simply could not remain independent. The Maharaja said he would give Mountbatten a decision at their last meeting, but he then feigned illness, and continued to vacillate. Mountbatten returned to Delhi annoyed, though still unworried. The Maharaja who was still undecided, two weeks after independence, rejected Lord Ismay's representations from Mountbatten ... preferring to talk about a game of polo they had played at Chattenham in 1943. The position was already deteriorating.

The vacillations of the Maharaja of Kashmir were not his only weakness, "He was not a very laudable object," Major General James Elliot, deputy secretary of the Indian Defence Committee until independence, recollects.

He was a playboy but there were many playboy princes. It was not unusual for an Indian Prince to have less sagacity than charm; to prefer the company of attractive women to the affairs of the State and to care more for his race horses than for his starving subjects. But few Indian princes combined all these foibles, and only in the Maharajah's case did personal foibles create an international catastrophe. An ancestor of the Maharajah had bought the State for £500,000 in the 19th century. In token of their suzerainty, the British were to receive annually one horse, 12 perfect shawl goats and three pairs of Kashmiri shawl. This tribute was reduced to five shawls.

The Maharajah of Kashmir was better known in Britain as the "Mr. A" of the sensational blackmail case in London. A casual meeting with a Mrs. Robinson at an Armistic night ball led to a Paris hotel room indiscretion which cost the young prince £150,000 in an unsuccessful attempt to keep her quiet. When his true identity came out it caused vast public amusement.

The Maharajah was naturally lavish. His private aircraft was filled with solid silver. When he attended the coronation of King George VI, he took 40 polo ponies with him. Long before his death, at the age of 65, he became too fat to play.

To pay for his whims he levied unusual if not unique taxes on his already poor subjects ruthlessly. There was a window tax, copied from the 18th century England, a doorstep tax, hearth stone tax and a wife tax. The effect on the architecture of Kashmir has been drastic; there are still many small houses with a hole in the roof, instead of windows, and few houses built during the Maharaja's reign have doorsteps.

His guests remember the Maharajah of Kashmir for his lavish hospitality. The excellence of his taste. (He was a superb cook and occupied his retirement in Bombay making exquisite petit fours). The blackmail case was never discussed. As Sir Eric Mieville says : "The poor chap had paid for the folly". So, it can be argued, has Kashmir.

On October 15, The Maharajah of Kashmir complained to the British Govt. that his border had been crossed in the Punch area, and that Pakistan had stopped supplies of petrol. There was no reply. Three days later, he sent a letter of protest to Karachi. On October 20, Jinnah casually dismissed the charges.

Almost simultaneously, however, Pathan tribesmen from North-West Frontier fortified by Pakistan Army officers 'On leave' and Pakistani trucks and weapons were on the move. Kashmir had been invaded and the conflict over Kashmir begun.

Many Muslims in the Kashmir army deserted and joined the irregulars on their trail of plunder, rape and arson to the capital, Srinagar. On the evening of October 24, the Maharajah turned to the only ally available to him ... INDIA ... appealed for Military aid. The next morning the first of the series of meetings of the Indian Cabinet Defence Committee which determined the cause of conflict over the next 60 years, took place.

Under the Chairmanship of Mountbatten, who had been called to play an active role as Governor-General, the Committee decided to send V.P. Menon, the expert administrator who had put at Mountbatten's disposal his unique constitutional experience when dealing with the princes, to Kashmir. Assessment was easy.

When Menon arrived in Srinagar on one of the B.O.A.C aircrafts sent to evacuate British subjects, he found the Maharajah was advised to drive immediately to Jammu, the Hindu-populated half of his State.

Menon returned to Delhi on the morning of the 26th and advised the Cabinet Committee to send military aid; Mountbatten almost paternally warned the Indian leaders against sending troops before the Maharajah had acceded. Mountbatten also suggested that if he did not accede, it must, in the circumstances, be conditional on a plebiscite as soon as law and order were restored. None of the Ministers present, including the Prime Minister, Nehru, dissented from this fateful decision. Menon returned to Jammu to secure the accession.

The Maharaja had lost his head; he had told his ADC if Menon returned from Delhi India would help and he must be allowed to sleep, but that if Menon did not return, all was lost, and he was to be shot in his sleep. The outcome was slightly less democratic. When Menon arrived, the floor of the palace was strewn with priceless jewels, snatched during the hasty retreat from Srinagar. Menon anxiously woke the Maharaja and received a signed statement of accession at dawn on October 27.

The way was clear for Indian troops to enter Kashmir just in time. The first troop carrying air-craft touched down at Srinagar at 10.30 on the same morning. The tribes who had dawdled were engaged that afternoon by the Indian Army for the first time at Baramula, 17 miles from the airport.

Jinnah reacted swiftly and, as it turned out, impotently. He ordered Pakistani troops into Kashmir. But the Pakistani Army was commanded by a British officer, Lt General Sir Douglas Gracey. General Gracey told Jinnah that he would not commit troops without the approval of his supreme Commander, General Sir Claude Auchinleck.

Truly speaking, General Auchinleck flew to Lahore to see Jinnah. He had devoted his life to the Indian Army, and built it up into a superb fighting force. Now it was divided into two, and the two parts were getting to fight each other. Auchinleck told Jinnah that if he ordered the Pakistani Army into Kashmir, every British officer would be withdrawn. Jinnah rescinded the order. From Lahore, Auchinleck telegraphed Mountbatten, calling him out of a meeting of the Indian Govt. Defence Commttee to inform him that Jinnah invited Nehru and Mountbatten to Lahore to discuss the Kashmir problem. As Nehru fell ill, Mountbatten went alone.

His relations with Jinnah had not imporved since independence. They failed to agree on the nature of a plebscite. The talks were inconclusive.

On Kashmir's accession to India, Sheikh Abdullah, the one really popular leader in Kashmir was released from gaol and made Prime Minister. Five years later he was put back in gaol by his pro-Indian Deputy.

On November 2, Nehru made a broadcast promising, as he was to promise over and over again, that once order had been restored in Kashmir, the referendum on its further would be held, under the auspices of the United Nations or some other international body. The promise was not kept.

The Indian Army pushed the tribesmen and the Pakistani soliders back. Yet throughout all this fighting, the two British Commanders-in-Chief kept telephoning each other daily in a desperate attempt, as General Gracey explained to his opposite member in Delhi, General Boucher : "Use the old boy not to prevent the fighting from getting too rough." Both Commanders-in-Chief kept urging on their respective Governments to accept a cease-fire. On January 1, 1949, a U.N. sponsored cease-fire line was finally declared. It was crossed in August, 1965 when the fighting, interrupted for 16 years, was resumed.

The tragedy is that the whole Kashmir question could have been easily avoided. Looking back on the succession of decisions which was once taken led almost inevitably to the war between India and Pakistan. Only two of them mattered. The first was Cripps' decision that paramountcy would lapse, a decision dictated in part by British respect for treaties and by the need to get Tory support. Had paramountcy been transferred to the successors of the British Raj, Kashmir would have had no choice but to accede to Pakistan. The second decision unwittingly was Radcliff's. Had India not land access to Kashmir, things might have been different.

However, it is easy looking back, to be wiser after the event and to overlook the terrible pressures which kept all the actors of the drama so busy that not one of them thought of Kashmir. Indeed they had no reasons to it, even the much-maligned Maharajah was only trying to get what Sheikh Abdullah was still asking for : an independent Kashmir on good terms with both sides.

That this was utopian seems clear as limpid stream. India and Pakistan were not born to be friends. It is as inescapable as inexorable fact of belligerence, bellowing out their ever-growing anger to each other. Kashmir is a teleological question of bailiwick.

Kashmir is only a pretext. It is symbolic. That Pakistan knows it very well. Ayub Khan's first foreign minister once answered the hypothetical question of his country's reaction to India handing Kashmir over to Pakistan as a token of good will : "We would never forgive them for the slap in the face."

Mr. Nehru and Mountbatten were responsible for the creation of Kashmir problem. Behind the curtain were some British officials and some Congress leaders fanning out the issue into a Byzantine complex.

Never bid the Devil good morrow until you meet him. Marriage, hanging and created problem go by destiny.

These are the root causes of the genesis of Indo-Pak war.

Some say the whole Kashmir question could have been avoided if the judgement were valid. Britain's folly in 1947 would have been responsible for the creation of Kashmir controversy and, therefore, indirectly, for the present warfare between India and Pakistan. But, how without gross interfernce in the internal affairs of the two countries, could Britain have continued to exercise its responsibility for the defence and external affairs of the Princely States after August 15? It was, for this reason, that Attlee, in his letter to Mountbatten, endorsed the statement of the Cabinet Mission that paramountcy would terminate with independence. Indeed, the lapse of paramountcy was an inevitable corollary of the independence of India and Pakistan. According to Lord Listtowel, Secretary of State for India, April to August 1947, says : "On the facts as they are known today, British policy in 1947 could have done nothing to avert the Kashmir controversy, or tragic conflict that has now ensued."

Who was behind the Kashmir problem? Nehru. Why? The undertaking Nehru had given to hold a referendum to ascertain the wishes of the Kashmiris in the matter of accession was not fulfilled. The promise was not kept. The explanation of Nehru's conduct is that Pakistan failed to withdraw her troops and irregulars from Kashmir as required by the United Nations commission. Why? Strictly speaking, Nehru had the law on his side; moreover in 1950, India might have won a plebiscite as matters stood. Unfortunately, Nehru stuck to the letter of the U.N. resolution and allowed India to bring pressure on Sheikh Abdullah. Delhi's failure to realise that in Kashmir, unlike in the other Princely States, there was a popular Government capable of resisting merger led to the alienation of Sheikh Abdullah and made it unlikely that Kashmir would choose India if it were free to express its news. Somethings are news and the rest is history.

Having witnessed Jinnah's failure over the accession of Kashmir valley, Pakistan has started out her dirty game of politics upon the Kashmiris by the multifarious means of terrorist outfits. After the destruction of World Trade Centre, America's biggest business centre, terrorism is much the most contagious disease amongst all Islamic countries. *When politicians lose their principles, they play a dirty game. What is politics? Multi-choice of tricks is politics.* Metamorphosis of Islamic globalisation into the crucible of world terrorism is light and frothy, and a set of complicated formula to search out its unchartered territory for a religious bailiwick, in the topsy-turvy world. *Politicians are full of cheats. Like a fruit vendor, they give the people a counterfeit ten-rupee note*. Pakistan has now been in a state of dangerous flux of frightening gesture fringed with a new wave of adolescents ready to get to work with the elders. Both in India and Pakistan, the Criminal law regulates sanctions, and provides a legitimate satisfaction for the revenge : the criminal law stands to the passion of revenge. It is much the same relations as marriage to the sexual appetite.

What is behind Pakistan's foreign policy over Kashmir after partition? A daring antagonism of theocracy and terrorist elements. Pakistan has modified her foreign policy over Kashmir without mopping out her atavistic passion of cruelty. And she has dismembered her predominantly labyrinthine sentences in foreign policy subdivided its luxuriant chapters with great skill and relegated its countless foot-notes to a voluminous appendix of how to terrorize the world altogether. Since partition, she has unequivocally axed down all agreements and pacts over Kashmir problem in the harshest terms. She ignores the fact. In the "Education of an Army" (1815-1940), Jay Luvaas writes : when in 1855, Sir William Napier was invited to join the Army Reform Association, he refused, "If the persons composing the society are military, this proceeding is an act of grave insubordination; if they are civilians, they are incompetent persons, perniciously meddling with what they do not understand."

Every ruler in Pakistan has emerged as a cold, desperately self-aware neurotic whose hatred of India and the world is secretive. The belief that the world is a straight forward battlefield where the forces of Western Parliamentary Democracy contend with the dark powers of Islamic terrorism, totalitarian communism and the dictatorial absolutism for the soul to the underdeveloped countries is one which has not waned so rapidly in India during the past 55 years that we sometimes forget how fundamental it is to the thinking of even sophisticated and intelligent Indians.

Western Civilization dedicated to action, motivated by total beliefs, armed with a transcendently advanced technology, has destroyed the static reflective cultures of Asia and Africa, leaving nothing in this place but envy and hatred, while simultaneously itself collapsing into violence and despair. This is the Asian politics of hysteria. So there will be a continuous dull pain on Kashmir problem.

PAKISTANI POETS ON KASHMIR PROBLEMS

Indian poets are totally ignorant of the progress of poetry in Pakistan. Pakistani poetic genius has reached its peak in Punjab. After the death of Iqbal and the birth of partition, the voice of the poet had been hushed for ever. As we now see, poets grow in West Punjab as mulberries grow in the bush or as martyrs grow in Pakistan in general.

West Punjab poets have derived their main inspiration from the defeat of Pakistan's design to forcibly occupy Kashmir. To give a few extracts from their poetic works. Let readers start with Liver extract. The following extract from a poem entitled "Kashmir ... Our Liver" by Amini Hazino, Sialkot.

"Kashmir is ours
... This is our artery. We shall
not allow to be cut
Kashmir is ours and we shall have it.
Kashmir is our heart, Kashmir is our liver,
Can we see it being plundered?"

After partaking of Kashmiri 'Kalija', another 'Shair' takes us through the fiery ordeal. Haji Laq Laq of Lahore issues the following lyrical threat to India :

"O : enemy save thyself from us ... we
are five without smoke,
It is impossible for thee to face us in Kashmir
Run for life. Be off, for we are
gun-powder magazine."

This poem only fans out the would-be fanatical crusaders for jehad. The school-going children getting to be trained ideologically in Madrassa-based theocratic institutions would get fired up with zest and zeal for terrorist outfits. We know poets are born, but such poets were born with the blood-stained sword of anti-India hymns of hate. So far, however, the smoke is more visible than fire. The threat of 'jehad' has probably misfired, ending only in smoke by the U.S. dollar diplomacy.

The lyrical threat, wrapped up with non-compliance to the Islamic belief, quoted above, gradually assumes the more menacing murderous threat, as a non-conformist. Haji Laq Laq threatens :

"O plaintiff (Bharat)
We send you to the other world in no time."
And finally : "We will quench our thirst with
the blood of our enemy."

The blood thirsty poet of Lahore draws with daggers of jehad furthering away the fanaticism of Kashmiri Muslims to draw out their swords to fulfil their cherished desires. If Omar Khayyam were alive, he would have aptly said :

Ah : beloved, spill the blood that clears today of our past threats and future tears
Tomorrow ten thousand Indian (Bharati) troops may cross the border and turn our 'Jehad' into tears :

Truly speaking, ours is an imperfect world, full to the brim with imperfect people. Maulana Sahib will not be content with the conquest of Kashmir valley. Having sat in the back-benches of the Indian Legislative Assembly, before partition, he now wants to sit on the takhte taus of Delhi.

Leaving Maulana Sahib enthroned in the Indian Capital, another poet, contributing to the columns of the 'Zamindar', proceeds to conquer China. The poet sings :

"We conquered China and territories beyond China ...
The unknown voice commands us again today to purify every polluted territory ..."

Another Lahore scribe, urging Pakistanis to "March on Kashmir or to Death," says :

"Rise and tell these cowards that a lion's life for a day is better than a hundred-year life of a jackal."

That means "Ek din ka sher-e-Kashmir, baki din gidar-e-Pakistan :"

The research in the White paper lends to the further discovery that there was a 'Vana-Mahatsova' in the mid of the year 1951. A budding poet of Lahore has written the following 'Student's Prayer' :

"I am a sapling of the garden of Punjab and will prove to be a fragrant tree of the Kashmir Paradise..."

So, with such a puffed-up jingoism, the lost paradise will be repaired by this Pakistani Milton through a botanical process when the sapling will grow up into a tree and the 'shair' will become a 'Sahid'. It is an excruciating mission of Pan-Islamic thoughts Pakistan has so far cherished since independence.

However much the muslim leaders of Pakistan National Assembly like Messers. Maulana Sahib and Co., talk of Pan-Islamic Federation and Coperation over the Kashmir valley and support of the Muslim States in other parts of Asia to Pakistan, these are mere propaganda talks for the impressing upon India the might of Pakistan on account of the support Pakistan enjoys from the Muslim States of Asia. But such support does not and cannot exist in fact for the following two reasons :

1. Pan-Islamism has little or no attraction for the Muslim States of Asia other than Pakistan as these countries have no theocratic basis and as all of them feel that there should be unity among the Eastern nations not on religious but on purely political basis. This is the impression Maulana Azad formed as a result of his tour of the Middle Eastern Muslim countries.
2. From reports appearing in newspapers almost everyday regarding important Muslim States Egypt, Iran, Iraq etc, it has become quite clear that the other Muslim States of Asia are solely and mainly concerned with their freedom from the exploitation and domination of the Western imperialists.

From the second reason pointed out above, it must be concluded that the genuine Muslim States of Asia totally differ from the artificially created Muslim State of Pakistan, on a fundamental question. Most of the former States are anti-British and anti-Americans. They want to get rid of their damaging but sinister influence and connection altogether. But Pakistan is not only a creation of the British imperialists but one of their most faithful followers and supporters.

So this is the irony and tragedy of today's Pakistan, and her people are in the burden of a nation-seeking terrorism with a theocratic leadership. An ancient Indian proverb says : "Without literature, music and the arts, man is but an animal without tail and horns." We know the Old Testament tells us that the sins of the fathers get visited on the children, Pakistan must have a hand in that. Let every tub must stand on its own bottom. When British-created Pakistan was born, her trouble begins. According to Fables of Aesop (clxxxiii) : Jupiter appointed Murcury to make him a composition of Fraud and Hypocrisy, and to give Every Artificer his Does on." Since her birth, there is knavery in all trades of Pakistan.

And the pro-Anglo U.S. attitude of Pakistan and its collaboration with some British agents of the British imperialists, but one of their most faithful followers and supporters cannot but alienate the testings of most of the Muslim States in the Middle East which are anti-U.S. in their outlook. So Pakistan's boast of forming Pan-Islamic Federation against India on Kashmir need not be seriously taken.

Pakistan has so far sucked milk of hypocrisy and lies, chanting away the hymns of peaceful co-existence with India on Kashmir dispute, through the feeding bottle of a travesty of justice. Everything is as shocking as offensive to all international law. For example. Having occupied one-third of Kashmir's territory, Pakistan has been fully exploiting the State's rich forest areas and appearing as India's competitor in the Chinese market. Since independence, Pakistan has been waging a devastating outlook after extracting 'Kuth' in the richest forests in Karnah tehsil of so-called Azad Kashmir and exporting same to China the sole consumer of this valuable Kashmir forest herb. The total forest wealth in the State is two hundred and seventy five crores cubit feet of timber spread an area of 10,000 sq.miles.

A false friend is more dangerous than a sworn enemy. Why? Because one can be one's guard against the latter but not against the former who stabs in the back. India should remember, in this connection, the most epoch-making saying in Sanskrit : "To have a false friend and to live in a snake infested house means death." India's false friends ... China and Pakistan ... are on the same boat. These two are wrapped up with narrow-doctrinal frame-work of doing treacherous things against India. They might come from outside the country triggering off a trouble here and sowing the venomous seeds of dissension, after tricking away our country's political stability into unfathomable doldrums. One must not change long-established beliefs in the face of death as a tree falls, so shall it lie.

We know Hiroshima is a living replica of a pocket medical-indentification certificate to all people who have lived through the atomic bombing or entered the radiation area. If Pakistan drops an atomic bomb, what will happen to our sons' sons. The survivors seem to be affected by something deeper than hypochondria, deeper than lethargy. They will undergo a great shock any time they get ill. They will feel doomed. We do not know how long this mental suffering will continue.

Leukoemia, cancer of the blood, will rise sharply among people exposed within 3 miles of the blast centre. Mental retardation in offspring of women is noted who will be pregnant at the time of the bombing. It is called A-bomb disease. It will be the repetition of horror upon horror. The city will seek in the beds of the atomic bomb hospital. The noisy commerce of the city will be found in some piece of symbolism.

Power has gone to the departments and whenever power goes it is the job of the journalist to follow and to inform. Real power often tries to hide its hand, and to leave mock power to appear to exercise its function. There is after all good reason for journalists concerning themselves with constitutional realities and not with constitutional fictions.

There can be no doubt now where power has flown. For over the last 60 years, Parliament has become steadily weaker and weaker. Most of the parliamentarians have no requisite qualifications to be a parliamentarian either by politically or by morally or by socially or by officially. Criminals infested political parties send out their associates of Mafia-barons to the Parliament. Some of them are accused of murder charges. Little do they know about the historical on-goings of Kashmir. Parliament has become the Parliament of wheel-chaired Parliamentarians.

The Civil Service is a sober enough subject. Civil servants are aristocratic clerks, to predominate over the half-witted and half-tutored Ministers to take a decision on any important problem like Kashmir that may have a political apocalypse in the labyrinth of hypocrisy and cant. It is right to discuss the masters and wrong to discuss the servants. Kashmir problem has so far been hanging about in a criss-cross way, having no upright decision, due to the Civil Servants' half-boiled and hasty decisions. Because power has so far been exercised in secret and in clandestine way so as to hide out the people from what is going on around the gathering storm over the valley.

GENESIS OF INDO-PHOBIA (A FATAL WORD)

Phobia is an instructor of double whammy ... fear and anxiety. Indo-Phobia is the herald of all jehadi slogans. And Pakistan's Indo-phobia is gibbered over religious extremism. Pakistan's ill-humoured Indo-Phobia has so far been carefully ill-judged and unreasonably ill-tempered on Kashmir issue, and doing injustice to India. Owing to Indo-Phobia, she does not know when to stop, how to tread wearily and where to play safe. Truly speaking, Pakistan's Indo-Phobia suffers from delusional insanity.

While it is no secret that Pakistan's foreign and domestic policies are conditioned by and large by what, for want of better expression, may be called Indo-Phobia, few, if any at all, have expected the Prime Ministers and military rulers of has beens to make open confessions that Pakistan's acquisition of arms from the United States and her membership of the South-East Asia Treaty

Organisation and the Baghdad pact are to guard against 'Indian aggression'.

Yet, that is precisely what Mr. Suhrawardy asserted in the course of his statements during the first ever debate on foreign affairs in the National Assembly. Mr. Horace A. Hildreth, U.S. ambassador in Karachi, who was instrumental in no small measure in negotiating the Pakistan-U.S. Military Aid Agreement, heard from the diplomats' gallery the statement of the Pakistani premier.

Mr. Suhrawardy made no direct reference to 'communist aggression' to guard against which American military assistance was avowedly intended. On the other hand, his reference to China and Soviet Union ... which alone in the eyes of the United States are 'aggressive' ... were couched in cordial terms. About China, Mr. Suhrawardy said : "My visit to China and the subsequent visit (to Pakistan) of the Prime Minister of China, have consolidated the bonds of friendship which have existed between Pakistan and China since 1951 when we established diplomatic relations with the People's Republic of China. And about the Soviet Union, he declared : "We have been consistent in our policy of being a friend of all countries and it is our endeavour to improve our relationship with Russia." But Pakistan has always been inimical to India. Why? Because anti-India hate campaign is regarded by the lowest common dominator as true, and by the rulers as useful. Why? Because Pakistan is built upon a theological foundation.

Explaning the reasons which made Pakistan join the Western military pacts, Mr. Suhrawardy said :

1. India did not give Pakistan her share of armaments under the partition agreement of 1947.
2. Pakistan is fully conscious that there are several important parties and personages in India who had made it their plan to re-unite Pakistan and India and to undo partition.
3. After the ceasefire in Kashmir on June 1, 1949, India massed up its troops on the boundaries of Pakistan in March, 1950, 'period for an attack' ... a time when Pakistan was practically defenceless. Again in July, 1951, India considered it necessary and justifiable, in order to resolve certain disputes to mass its troops on Pakistan's borders.
4. Pakistan's resources are limited and it is spending a far greater percentage of its revenues that its national economy could support on the armed purely for defensive purposes. Pakistan found it necessary therefore, to look out for friends and allies.
5. India is a little bit frightened of her vast amount of armaments which India has embarked upon.

Mr. Suhrawardy said he was not prepared to take the risk of being defenceless against this vast armament of India. So Islamic terrorism is inevitable. And it is very clear that Pakistan has suffered from a double-dyed whammy of Indo-Phobia and phobiac delusion of fear and anxiety. It is also clear that Pakistan does not appear to be bothered about 'communist aggression and imperialism', although American apologists appeared to argue that a militarily strong Pakistan ... no matter what the country's objective might be ... would be a natural deterrent against the alleged 'communist threat'.

For, no Pakistani will believe that the country is faced with U.S. imperialism from outside; but many will fall a prey to the Indian bogey.

If war is an extension of policy then abuse is an extension of argument. When arguments exhaust themselves, people try to indulge in abuse. When abuse rises, people are servile in the face of hate-campaign pitiless in the face of weakness, implacable before blunders and indulgent before crimes. So jehad will be the guide and blessing of the future. Pakistan knows how to lie well. That is what Mr. Suhrawardy was trying to do in advancing Pakistan's case on Kashmir. In her double-delusion to defend her own case, Pakistan, since partition, has started abusing India. If she thinks that this tactic has any logic in it, then there can be no trouble at all in this sub-continent. Why? Because that man is supreme who can outshot and out-abuse another.

Since Suhrawardy, Pakistan has blown hot and cold in the same breath. On the one hand, Pakistan does not want to embark upon a war and desires to have peace with India while on the other she asked her lieutenants the Fakir of Ipi and Khan Abdul Qayum Khan and his other brand of warriors to declare a holy war on India in the name of Islamic terrorism. Pakistan's Indo-Phobia turns into mass destruction through religious extremism.

Even after sixty years of independence, more and more Pakistani army officers, plagued with Indo-Phobia and passionately psyched by anti-India hymns of hate, have psyched the extremist groups up for terrorism in India. They have been identified with extremist beliefs, as well as with links to Taliban and other related organisations which are the greater worry inside Pakistan. Pakistan today, flummoxed by Indo-phobia, has been pressing ahead with militants. Many of the terror-training camps across the border are in the vicinity of military bases, pointing to the active collusion between anti-India militant outfits and the Pakistani army. Why? Because Pakistan army often resorts to giving covering fire to militants crossing over into the valley to divert the attention of Indian soliders.

The cry of 'Jehad' has echoed through the months and years since 1947. This has been combined with abuse of India and Islamic terrorism. All these are the resultant effects of Pakistan's Indo-Phobia. Why? Because Pakistan exists among the ignorant classes, where it rules by falsehood. So, these ignorant classes have to get used to being plagued by the army. Here are a few examples :

The Times of Karachi in an editorial on New Year's Day, 1957 wrote : "We have to liberate four million souls from the deadweight of Brahmanic imperialism ... To us Kashmir is the fulfilment of our freedom; without it our independent existence is seriously threatened. It is clearly a matter of life or death for us."

The Dawn of Karachi wrote editorially on Jan. 6, 1957: "The Security Council will have barely ten days to decide upon some concrete, tangible, unequivocal and compelling step whereby that rapacious brigand of Asia, that hypocrite masquerading as an apostle of peace with his hands red with the blood of Kashmiris as well as Bharati Muslims, what double-facing, double-talking and double-dealing Brahmin Janus who shamelessly woos both Moscow and Washington in order to have the best of both the worlds ... can be prevented from accomplishing his designs."

Again on Jan. 13, 1957, The Dawn wrote under the caption "The man of Peace" : "With God's grace, the sons of Islam need not fear if the sons of other things force them to a trial of military conclusions. Indeed, the Kashmir dispute may perhaps be thus more quickly solved and the Radcliffe iniquities satisfactorily adjusted. But such a choice will not be voluntarily ours. It is upto Bharat's war-minded peace monger to keep the peace or make a war."

Since independence, Pakistan has not yet figured out the suspicious circumstances, and dishonestly cooked up a swashbuckling story of anti-India hymns of hate, sweeping India's allegation under the carpet of Jehad.

Even Chowdhry Md. Ali, former Prime Minister of Pakistan, at a public meeting in Karachi on August 14, 1956 said, "I am ready for the liberation of Kashmir," he said and added, "but I want the people to get ready ..." He said the Kashmir dispute was now going before the Security Council, but asserted that the nation would not rest there. (Report in the Times of Karachi).

Does Pakistan know it is on the sound education of the people that the security and destiny of every nation chiefly rest? Does Pakistan know human life may be likened to the flowers on yonder tree, and the wind blows down the flowers, of which some are caught by the screens and scattered on the beautifully decorated mats and cushions, while others are blown over the fence and dropped on the dung heap? So, this obstinacy of Indo-phobia is certainly a great vice; and in the changeful state of political affairs is frequently a cause of great mischief. And this brazen idol of jehad is hoary with years, upon a leering pyramid of lies and propaganda.

When Abdul Qayum Khan, former Chief Minister of N.W.F.P., said : "The day we become desperate and lose all hopes of a just solution of the problem, not only the entire Pathan population of Pakistan and the tribal areas will rise for the 'holy jehad' in Kashmir, but our brothers from across the Afgan frontier will also throw in their lot with us for the cause." Political horizon in Pakistan has stiffened. Why? Becasue Pakistan's Indo-phobia brings the tragedies and griefs of others to notice. A perfect Roman holiday. Goethe, in 'Deathbed Words', says : "Open the bedroom shutters and let in more light."

Mian Mumtaz Daulatana, former Chief Minister of West Punjab, said : "If the U.N. proves to be a band of thieves, we will have nothing to do with it. We will prove that we can liberate Kashmir with the strength of our arms." (Reported in Zamindar, Lahore, Jan 17, 1952).

Does Pakistan know the whole of the United Nations is founded upon the basic principles of international law and behaviour and that is based upon equity? Does Pakistan know British India obtained independence and India became the successor State by the Act of 1947?

Is she well aware of the fact that the Constitution Act of 1935 passed by the British parliament dealt only with what was British India? But Pakistan has now been in a hypnotic inertia of religious dualism ... a monumental chapter in a history of egotism.

Does Pakistan know the Indian peninsula comprised two gorups, the British provinces, which were ruled from London by the Secretary of State, and the other, the Indian States indirectly ruled, of which there were 562? Does Pakistan know the British Govt. in the third decade of the last century had tried to define the relations between the British Crown and these states by the doctrine of paramountcy? Does she know when India became independent, the British Govt. proposed under the doctrine of paramountcy that the Crown withdrew from effective control of British India? So, whatever remains thus in the British Govt. remains in the Govt. of India by virtue of its succession. But Pakistan today is infatuated with wild lust and boundless ambition, using the utmost care to support anti-india hymns of hate all over Pakistan. *What is independence? Independence rests upon function, upon territory, upon the capacity to exercise sovereign rights and upon the recognition of the world. So, Kashmir was never a part of Pakistan and has not acceded to Pakistan.* Pakistan has entered into our territory either by cross-border terrorism or by religious extremism, or by fiery words or blows, or with both. It is a hereditary State of Indo-Phobia. A man must not formalise on everything. He who does so is a fool; and *a grave fool is, perhaps, more injurious than a light fool.* With perseverence key many doors can be unlocked. In the ultimate sense, Pakistani rulers do not count. Why? Because they are merely like the crackling of thorns under the pot. What phantoms they are and what phantoms they pursue.

Pakistan's Indo-Phobia begins, when she has declared again and again that both SEATO and the Baghdad pact have brought them the political support of the western powers in their dispute with India on Kashmir issue and also added military strength with which to back their claims in Kashmir.

This indo-Phobia holds out a veiled threat of 'jehad' in Kashmir, and categorically says that people in Kashmir can act like those of Cyprus who were fighting for freedom from British rules with bomb.

You (Pakistan) often tell us that those who are not with you are against you. You believe in military and in partisanship. Can't you see that some of the worst features of Stalinism have their roots in your conception of militant outlook? Stalin did not agree with those who differed from him. He shot them. Do you know military interference in public administration is a cartload of explosives?

You (Pakistan) tell us that pessimism is out of place in militant outlook and that so is doubt or despair. Does it not mean that your creeds are against your constitution Inflamed with jealousy and inflated sense of egotism?

You (Pakisatn) go on having long-winded debates on Kashmir. Your drama is typical of your character. Have you ever asked yourself why should a character be typical? Was Hamlet typical of Elizabethan society? Are there no Hamlets among you? The problem of the typical is always a political problem. Why has there to be such a hue and cry over the Kashmir drama? A lyrical tragedy.

Have you (Pakistan) ever explained to us how the so-called dictatorship of the majority have to resort to police terror to a much greater extend than the minority dictatorships? But you have found clever alibis for the State's failure to wither away.

You (Pakistan) say that one man rule is over and that all Kashmir issues will be deomocratically debated and decided within the party now. Do you know more than sixty percent of the people are outside the party? How do you assume that the majority of those outside are always in accord with the majority inside when even the pros and cons of Kashmir debate are not explained to them? How do you propose to secure their participation in Kashmir debate?

You (Pakistan) tell us that all moral ideas on Kashmir issue arise out of social process. You say every ethical or ideological superstructure of an Islamic nation has a social issue. Would you please tell us what their social base is? Or are we to believe that these particular superstructures have no social base in your Indo-Phobia or in Islamic terrorism, that these monstrous trees grow upside down with their roots up in the air? Why? In every compartment of your society, you are fed on double-dyed illusions and endowed with three rare qualities of dissimulation, equivocation and mental reservation. You are quite deluded by mental mathematical calculation.

Endless frustration amongst the Kashmiri people means endless experiments of our leaders on Kashmir issue. Hero is the making of anguish as also of despair. Once they build up tensions in the valley, they can't help relieving them. How do they know that bodies choked with tenderness of our leader's soothing words will not writhe in cold hatred ten nights later? A midsummer madness. Who says the little vamp has no brains? They watch these experiments.The mystery of their hearts still eludes us on the Kashmir issue. The more self-conscious they are, the more painful the complications. Kashmir issue is a terrific burden on Indian people. There are many questions which remain to be asked. We wish they could be asked in private. Who will answer them?

Owing to Indo-phobia, Pakistan has regularly impelled her hero-worshippers of terrorism and militant crusaders of Islamic jehad to tell the story of an Islamic nation in a fog of political dualism. But Albert Camus, in 'The Fall', once told us that 'the world of the novel is a rectification of the world we live in'. Now the question is : where is the rectification of the world where everything springs from egotism and selfishness? How shall we redeem this world which according to you, cannot be redeemed?

What is Pakistan's crime? She is a bit of an egoist. So are all of them. We watch you peel layer after layer the story of your political dualism on Kashmir issue like an oninon. But when all the layers have been peeled off, all you see is nothingness within it. The peeling process is Islamic terrorism. Who wrote : "I laughed besides of coffin." Pakistan could never make out whether she had put on a mask or gone out of her mind. Why should Pakistan allow Indo-phobia and hate campaign so corrode her mind as to make her write that 'there are always reasons for murdering a man', and that 'on the contrary, it is impossible to justify his living? The world knows she does not mind it. Why? Because Pakistan is as vulnerable as any of other fascists. Does Pakistan know mere tabacco smoke will not cover up the devastation of the bombs which she has exploded in our minds?

There lies the Pakistan's tragedy. But there are escapes and escapes. Suicide ... politically, religiously and socially ... is only one of the escapes. There is no reason to pull her hair or beat her breast. Why do you want to take the mask of every face? Don't you know that some characters do better with a mask than without one? A wishful falsehood told by Pakistan on Indo-Phobia is a cripple, not able to stand by itself without another to support it. It is easy to tell a lie, but hard to tell only one lie.

A double-whammy of Indo-phobia and Islamic terrorism is as dangerous as the definition of revolution enunciated by Mao-Tse-Tung. Why? "A revolution," he once warned, "is not a dinner party, nor a literary composition, nor painting, nor embriodery. It cannot be done so deliberately, so gentlemanly, and so gently, kindly, politely, plainly and modestly."

In 'the Plague', you, Albert Camus, made Torrou say to Dr. Rieus : "Each one of us has the plague within him; no one, on one on earth is free from it. We should keep endless watch on ourselves lest in a careless manner we breathe in somebody's face and fasten the infection on him."

Even India's foreign policy either on Kashmir issue or on cross-border terrorism has become fossilized. Why? Because our policy of compromise is growing old. Because "compromise" brings you nothing but misfortune, so long as a horde of knaves shall rule over India. Who will battle crime, selfishness and cowardice with the name of prudence? They are ten times as deceitful as slippery, ten times as pharisaical as perfidious on 'compromise'. What they feel, believe and say is always hypocritical either on Kashmir issue or on 'compromise'. That is all.

"The superior man will watch over himself when he is alone. He examines his heart that there may be nothing wrong there, and that he may have no cause of dissatisfaction with himself," says Confucius.

The Pakistani press, since independence, crudely intoxicated with anti-India hate campaign, has fallen on New Delhi like a pack of wolves and successfully made it out to the world as an epicentre of all problems in Kashmir, with a penchant to burst into tears at the slightest or no provocation. 'Compromise' is still going on. Even after partition, they were only interested in getting at Mr. Nehru, who as the spearhead of Asian anti-colonialism, was their public enemy No. 1. Many a strong man of the Congress had eaten the dust. But 'compromise' is still going on.

Today Pakistan needs a society which can hear about Kashmir issue. No twists and turns of dialectics can explain away the tragic fact that after sixty years of political dualism, Pakistan society still cannot bear to hear the truth about Kashmir. Why? Because Pakistan is drunken with the laughing gas of the abyss. It is not difficult to decipher or detect the general pattern of Pakistan's international strategy on Kashmir. India, of course, is pinpointed as the villain of the piece.

India is well aware of the fact that Pakistan is passing through the three varieties of subversion. The first category smacks of ill-famed McCarthyism, changing the country's govt. The second category brings about internal disruption by methods not sanctioned by democracy. The third category is subversion at the instance of foreign powers anxious to bring about the downfall of Pakistan. Within these categories, Pakistani leaders squabble and intrigue against each other, and the country's economy goes to the dogs, building up a high wall of hatred and malice between their people and the people of India. But 'compromise' is still going on.

'Compromise'! The omniously-woven symbiotic relationship between Islamic nation and Islamic Jehad ... each getting particular benefits from the other ... represents a symptomatic disease of Pakistan's foreign policy on anti-India hate campaign.

In a world full of torment and trouble, Pakistan has pursued these three categories unflinchingly and engaged themselves in the mighty task of building a new Islamic terrorism and a great adventure of Indo-phobia. And there would be unfortunate repercussions that the Muslim minority in India will have to be exposed to bitter hatred and violence from the Hindus.

6

JINNAH AND KASHMIR-I : From Lies of Tongue and Pen

People have become so touchy that it is now impossible for a comedian to laugh at any one but himself. Politics in India, like a comedian, is a cunning device of the devil through the channels of falsehood. A murderous rush of infiltrators is a pure manifestation of mass hysteria and wasteful dissipation of energy. It is a time-old jealousy between the people of India and Pakistan. What is partition? Partition means the noisy riders of great causes. Partition between India and Pakistan means the parasites on evil ideas not for great causes. After the partition of India, Mr. Nehru called in a party of pressmen in Delhi and cautioned them against partition's immediate popular reaction to call India Hinudstan vis-a-vis Pakistan. Why? India must remain India and continue to be so called considering Pakistan a seceding area. In the Constituent Assembly, thanks to the over-zealous nationalism of some members. Bharat was adopted as an alternative name to India. How avidly the opportunity was seized by Pakistan, the Govt. have since adopted the uniform practice of calling India Bharat. East Bengal was considered a ceded area and Bengal should continue to be called Bengal, even in her present attentuated form instead of West Bengal which is an obnoxious title denoting disintegration of this State as an entity.

Though Pakistan is, to all intents and purposes, a monolithical Islamic State, the cry of self-styled jehadi slogans for Muslims has provided the basis of Pakistan and the slogan of India's supposed design to destroy her has supplied the parties or rather the jehadi group in power with a handy device for maintaining a semblance of unity. But political rivalry within the parties, flummoxed by theological dualism and ethical dualism, the discontent of the suffering masses, from time to time, breaks through the cover of the so-called Islamic unity and reveals the game of power politics in Pakistan and even in Kashmir to spearhead the movement. Politics were once the results of group squabbles within the parties. This confusion centres around the failure of Pakistan Govt.'s Kashmir policy. Miss Fatima Jinnah's broadcast on the Quaid-e-Azam's death anniversary day in 1951 has made the situation in Kashmir worse and worse, diverting public attention from all internal fissures. Miss Jinnah said : "It was the last wish of the Quaid-e-Azam to see Kashmir a part of Pakistan." She delivered the broadcast on 21st Sept. 1951. So the general tenor of the jehadis was more vigorous and direct in their policy in Kashmir, whatever that may mean.

We have closely followed the developments in the Kashmir situation right from the beginning. We have read the statements and communiques issued by the Pakistani authorities on the matter, including the press communique issued on Oct. 30, 1947 by the Govt. of Pakistan from Lahore and a speech of Mr. Jinnah, Governor-General of Pakistan, on the same day and at the same place with a stream of profanities. Curiously enough, Jinnah's Lahore speech made no mention at all about Kashmir, for reasons best known to Jinnah himself. Was it mere an accident or a case of studied omission? Besides indulging in a glorification of Pakistan and an impassioned exhortation to his people, we cannot see why Jinnah made the speech at all and what precisely he wanted to impress on his audience. "We have been," he said, "the victimes of a deeply laid and well-planned conspiracy executed with utter disregard of the elementary principles of honesty, chivalry and honour. We thank providence for giving us courage and faith to fight these forces of evil."

Partition, Jinnah, and Kashmir lie in an equilateral triangle, restraining intercourse of thought. Historical change is undermining our peace-keeping role in other ways. Standards of education, administration and technology have advanced in many of the emerging countries.Tacit assumptions of racial superiority, which once gave strength to our leadership, have vanished. Asians, Africans and Arabs understandably prefer to see the peace kept by people from their own region and race, preferably with the blessing of the United Nations.

Memories and myths of the days of colonialism and anti colonialism, essential props of many of the new societies, add to our difficulties. Clear distinctions are not always drawn between today's peace-keeper and yesterday's colonial ruler. Defence planners ignore these political and psychological facts at their peril. The resistances which are growing year by year to Western peace-keeping create specific and serious military problems. Today the situation is very different. Indigenous forces are becoming much stronger and outside aid much more accessible. As the balance against India evens up, deterence is lost and 'peace-keeping' loses its meaning.

Such a horrible situation of indigenous forces of Pakistan and other Muslim countries is getting to a conclusion of full horror. What a butchery escalated in Indonesia in Holy war! It began just over 12 months ago on the night of sept. 1964, when President Sukarno, 20 years dictator, was first dislodged from his pinnacle. It continued with a series of massacres in which more people were killed in five months than in the five years of Vietnam War. In the first three weeks of October, 1965, most of the deaths were caused by armed action on both sides. By the end of the month, a few army entered the field : the fanatical Muslims who claimed it as their religious duty to cleanse Muslim Indonesia of atheism. Such religious duty as we have seen all around the Kashmir valley is playing up with dangerous gamesmanship. Pakistan-based religious extremists, intoxicated by Miss Fatima Jinnah's fiery speech and encouraged by the most appalling massacres in Indonesia, have started out the spiritually escalated butchery inside and outside Pakistan, establishing their own particular brand of obscurantism, in the name of Islamic globalisation. What an inherent character of Holy War! Death by bullet and by blasting bombs is far too good for the infidels. Devout Muslims regard Kashmiri Hindu Pundits as infidels. Does Pakistan know only 7 (seven) words ended Sukarno : 'Get to the bottom of the coup'? Does Pakistan know this holocaust in the name of holy war went almost unnoticed? Were not Jinnah's Muslim League and Co. responsible for the present Islamic terrorism in and outside, in the name of Kashmir issue? After Jinnah, some leaders wanted to be transformed into enormously heroic figures. Today Islamic theocratic dogma looms large all along the border of Kashmir. The crusaders go along to their local teachers of Islam, and seek their ruling. The teachers promise to think about it and let them know their answer. There is a nationwide terrorism. Indian leaders should be careful of your tongue. Because tongue is a savage beast, leave it freely, it will wound you.

Just after partition, a contigent of Afridis, soliders of the Pakistani Army who were on leave and 'desperadoes' fully armed with modern weapons entered the vale of Kashmir on Oct 23, 1947 from Manshera ... Ramkot side in about 100 trucks, resorting to arson, murder and loot of non-Muslims. Pakistan has started out their game-plan of the same Hitlerian policy in Kashmir as they had done in the Frontier province long before its incorporation to Pakistan. The first weapon of their policy is propaganda through the press and on the radio. The object of the propaganda was : To coerce the State to accede to Pakistan. That was the propaganda policy of Hitler and his Nazis.

When Abdul Quayum Khan, Prime Minister of North-West Frontier Province, stated before August 15, that if Kashmir had not joined either Dominion there would be no objection." The official policy of the Pakistan Govt. so far, "said a Pakistani Govt. official at Karachi on Oct. 16, 1947, "has been to give the Rulers full discretion to declare themselves independent or to join either Dominion." Yet the same premier of N.W.F.P. said on Oct 23, 1947: "It would be wrong to say that the Muslims of Pakistan were not interested in the future political set up in Jammu and Kashmir. The overwhelming majority of the population is Muslim and they were in the clearest terms and stated that they wish to join Pakistan." That the Muslims of Pakistan are interested in Kashmir is evident from the statement of the Governor-General of Pakistan himself. Jinnah's tone and content were the same as those of the Pakistan Govt's statement of Oct 20, 1947. Jinnah was reluctantly forced to the conclusion that the unfounded allegations and accusations were only a smoke screen to cover the real aim of your Govt.'s policy. What is the real aim? "The real aim of your Govt.'s policy," according to the Quaide-e-Azam, "is to seek an opportunity to join the Indian Domnion as a coup d'etat lay securing the intervention and assistance of that Dominion. This policy is naturally creating deep resentment and grave apprehension among your subjects 85 percent of whom are Muslims." Now the question is : Was it a business of the Pakistani Govt., or its Governor-General, the Quaide-e-Azam Jinnah, to interface with the policy of a State which to all intents and purposes had as much independence as Pakistan itself? In its statement of Oct 20, 1947, the Pakistan Govt. stated : "If this policy is not changed and the preparations and active measures that you are now taking in implementing this policy are not stopped, the greatest consequences will follow for which you alone will be responsible." What did the Quaida-e-Azam say to this? Was it not extremely offensive? Was it not a threat pure and simple to the Kashmir Govt.? Why this threat? Because the Kashmir Govt. proposed to follow a policy of strict neutrality, towards the Dominions of India and Pakistan and remain on friendly terms with both of them. Strange to say, On 23rd Oct, 1947 on the day of invading Kashmir, Khan Abdul Quayum Khan said : "We have to observe strict neutrality and scrupulously to follow a policy of non interference in the affairs of any state ... We have strict orders to our officers to prevent any attempt at infiltration of men or arms from the N.W.F.P. into territories ruled by the Maharaja of Kashmir." What a sample of strict neutrality! What a fine example of non-interference and strict orders! Was it not one forcibly reminded of the Hitlerian method employed in the rape of Czechoslovakia?

How did they enter the territories ruled by the Maharaja of Kashmir? It was much graver than was thought it first. Pakistan invaded Kashmir with two columns of invaders ... one coming from Rawalpindi and the other from Abbottabad met near Domel and crossed Kohala bridge across the Jhelum into Kashmir territory, burned Muzaffarabad and surrounded Uri. They had advanced about 55 miles into the State and were about 70 miles from Srinagar. The world is under the impression that since the British were left India, Indians cannot maintain peace in their country.

Today the two-nation theory has been exposed in all its ghastliness. Nearly about half of the Muslim population of the sub-continent has been left in India. If the two-nation theory were right, what is the political position of the Muslims in India and in Kashmir today? Are they not foreigners? Is not the word 'secularism' coined only for the ballot boxes? But Mr. Jinnah has left them to their fate. His advice to them on the occasion of the opening of the Constituent

Assembly was to render unqualified loyalty to the Govt. Under which he had left them. The refugees in both the Punjabs have left behind them all they possessed and most of them have been ruined. Does the tragedy prove the two-nation theory? Does it not prove on the contrary that it is the introduction of the two-nation theory by continuous injustice of the communal poision that has made brother strangers, nay even enemies? The vast majority of the Quaide-e-Azam's co-religionists were not so fortunate even if they had any inclination to leave their hearths and homes for the purpose of settling in Pakistan. No Hindu ever believed in the two-nation theory.

Jinnah felt that he could no longer claim allegiance from at least half of the Muslim population of the whole sub-continent. He found himself reduced to the position of surrendering half of his kingdom. His first Id message in 1947 repeated the word 'Enemies' several times. It speaks of "our new born State bleeding from wounds inflicted by her enemies." He invoked the examples of prophet Ibrahim "who sacrificed the object he loved most," and called upon the Muslims not only in Pakistan but in the Indian Dominion to emulate his example. Now the question is : what further sacrifice did Mr. Jinnah expect of his co-religionists in India and Pakistan? Truly speaking, Mr. Jinnah's only object was to keep up the spirit of hatred and ill-will which had won for him, that time. And the consequences of his statement, after sixty years of independence, has now kept the passions of the ignorant multitude in Pakistan and even in Kashmir to wage a war of fanaticism. And it was Mr. Jinnah for his inflammatory statement, the shadows of the extremists have been looming large over the vale of Kashmir. Infuriated with outrageous passion for jehad and buoyed with sophisticated barbarism down to the fields of Afghanistan, they have so far exhibited an atavistic behaviour. There is no doubt that times have changed. We are in the early stages of a great popular reaction against the hysteria and the demagoguery, the lawlessness and the cruel injustices which we call rightly the era of McCarthy's sin.

Having failed in his mission of Kashmir, Mr. Jinnah was afraid of the disillustionment which overcame Hitler in his last days. Mr. Jinnah had, in the true Hitlerian fashion, hurled abuses at his 'enemies' so that his blind followers and devil advocates today may continue to follow him unto further distraction and ruin over the vale of Kashmir, through the jehadi slogans. The peaceful celebrations of 'Id' after independence have the answer, in the observance of 'Id' and 'Puja' both in East and West Bengal.

What we see today an invincible lordism over terrorism in the vale of Kashmir is the legacy of Jinnah's untoward religious romanticism. Lewis Carroll in his immortal 'Alice's Adventure in Wonderland' writes about a whitting asking a snail to join him in a Lobster Quadrille : "Will you, won't you, will you, won't you, will you join the dance?" The world seems to be asking Pervez Musharraf a similarly pertinent question. Will he, won't he, will he, won't he stop cross-border terrorism in Kashmir? The general's latest response to that query was also quite similar to that of Carroll's snail. While he admits the possibility of

Islamic militants crossing the border into Kashmir, he states that there is 'Nothing happening on the Line of Control' and that the world cannot expect Pakistan to 'Block the borders to stop the actions of rogue militants. Truly speaking, Musharraf 'would not, could not, would not, could not, would not join the dance. It is Musharraf's Lobster Quadrille.

This Lobster Quadrille that Pakistan has initiated on the Kashmir question under the stewardship of Mr. Jinnah has still been going on in full swing. The Quaide-e-Azam told his audience that "there is no power on earth that can undo Pakistan." 'Do not for a moment 'imagine', "he continued," that your enemies can never succeed in their designs." He assured his audience that "Final victory will be ours." One wonders why he thought of 'enemies', 'conspirators' and 'forces of evil' and hopes of achieve 'victory' in the long run. Moderation was never the forte of Mr. Jinnah while he was agitating vehemently for Pakistan. He did not seem to have acquired that virtue even after becoming the head of a State. Is 'frank consultation' possible with persons of one-track mind and whose invariable tendency was, and is, never to weigh dispassionately both sides to a question but to put the other man in the wrong?

Britain's departure from India has been followed by a long series of sanguinary convulsions over the vale of Kashmir. It was Mr. Jinnah who had fastened blood guilt on his followers who have got beyond the greatest heart-searchings in the breasts of all who for over sixty years have been tearing down peace in Kashmir under which millions of Indians have lived. Who is responsible for the slaughter in India? Pakistani rulers do not have a heart to search for it. Why? The Churchills in Britain created the Jinnahs in India and it was the joint conspiracy of the Churchills and the Jinnahs that was responsible for the terrific carnage in India. A Soviet commentator in Moscow said on October, 1947 : "The seeds of national and religious strife were planted deliberately in the British politicians' plan." These imperialists Churchills in Britain introduced 'divide-and-rule' which remained the sheet-anchor of British policy in India and even in Kashmir, for generations. Mr. Jinnah has only grown up the venomous seeds with sap and juice of religious fanaticism over the vale of Kashmir. Can Mr. Jinnah's followers deny it? If they are honest and fair, they cannot.

But what about the little Churchills in India, we mean the British Governors, the British personnel of the I.C.S. and the reactionary British businessmen in the country, who were in cahoots with our top-seeded Congress leaders? The big Churchills pulled the strings from England : the little Churchills the so-called 'men on the spot', slowly but quietly set the two communities against each other and thereby prepared the ground for a general slaughter. Is it not a fact that many of the British members of the I.C.S. had opted for service in Pakistan? Both Mr. Jinnah and Mr. Nehru knew it very well. And the British Governors of both the countries were functioning as such. Have people forgotten all about the mischievous activities of Sir George Cunningham in the Frontier province and those of Sir Francis Mudie in Sind? Sir George had retired and left India. Francis, he was recalled and reappointed Governor of the very province where he was alleged to have done a lot of mischief by way of helping Mr. Jinnah and his Muslim Leaguers on Kashmir question. Was this a more accidental appointment or was it done with a definite motive? Sir Francis was in Sind but under the new Pakistan dispension he was the satrap of West Punjab as Mr. Jinnah and Mr. Nehru the satraps of the British personnel of the I.C.S. as well as the British Governors. Was this accidental or deliberate? So the events in Kashmir are sufficiently revealing.

The Frontier tribesmen traversed 250 miles of territory in the Frontier province and in West Punjab to make an incursion into Kashmir. Did the British Governors of the Frontier Province and West Punjab lift their little fingers to stop this wanton and unwarranted aggression in Kashmir? Were not these little Churchills the agents of the big Churchills? Had not these big and little Churchilles, in secret collusion with their creations, the Jinnahs, been responsible for the slaughter in India? And remember Mr. Churchill said this was "the first of a long series of sanguinary convulsions." Did he imply that more and more sanguinary convulsions were still to follow? So, Mr. Jinnah and his Muslim Leaguers with the help of the big Churchills had laid the foundation stone of colossal conspiracy of gun-running and arms-smugglings over the vale of Kashmir. Today Pakistan has been battling on against India on the Kashmir question.

Shouting loudly and raucously over Islamic gloablisation, Pakistan has now become a private Limited Company of terrorist organisations under the supervision of theocratic rulers and eschatological discourse. The raiders of Pakistan are such a private army. If they succeed in venture, Pakistan will have taken the fruits thereof. If they fail, Pakistan disclaims responsibility for what they have done. This is what is called 'heads I win, tails you lose' tactics with which Pakistan has made us familiar, with her pefunctory and rough-down phrases of love and peace.

Dr. Ambedkar condemned Mr. Jinnah for his retrograde policy. "The Muslims," he said, "wanted the support of the scheduled castes but they never gave their support to the scheduled castes. Mr. Jinnah was all the time playing a double game. He was very insistent that the Scheduled Castes were a separate entity when it suited him but when it did not suit him, he insisted with equal emphasis that they were Hindus." He also said, "The Scheduled Castes in Hindustan are being tyrannised by the caste Hindus in all parts of the country. While in Pakistan, they are subjected to forcible religious conversion, in Hindustan they are subjected to forcible political conversion." (Thoughts on Pakistan : Dr. B.R. Ambedkar). Why? Because Mr. Jinnah intended to have increased the strength of the Muslim population. Whatever it is, Dr. Ambedkar's main thesis is that Pakistan is a hell for Harijans. In Pakistan, Harijans had been converted to Islam by force or by violence. His dis-illusionment was as significant as the great Muslim leader of Kashmir, Sheikh Abdullah, who said, "Kashmir's fate is interlinked with India. We have joined India neither to satisfy

Mr. Nehru nor Mr. Jinnah nor the Govt. of India, but to save ourselves from poverty and destruction ... Neither the Hindus nor the Muslims of Kashmir can be deceived by the cry of 'religion in danger'. "Pakistan will be reasonable, when she will know that the opposite party is strong. Let us remember the word of advice Cromwell gave to his soldiers : "Have your faith in God, but keep your powder dry." Is this Pakistan the Quaide-e-Azam fought for so many years? What had Mr. Jinnah done for the Muslims in Pakistan in the past? And what could he do for them in future? These are the questions which they are naturally asking themselves. Mr. Jinnah had only bullied the innocent Muslims of Pakistan into swallowing up the poison of dual theology of religious fanaticism and religious dogmatism over the Kashmir question. So many question have been hewed up till now. His philosophy is to carry on the same old type of disgraceful campaign over the Kashmir question year in and year out, and is insulting to the people of India as would be a gang of terrorists coming back to Kashmir they had robbed staging a parade of religious fanaticism and inviting all frenzied Muslims to fall in and cheer. Poision is in everything.

That poison has still been working in the body politic of India. It is the two-nation theory. That theory is responsible for the partition of India and the partition has been responsible for the untold misery of countless human beings. Has that poison ceased to work? It has not. In Kashmir, it has been working virulently. In the rest of India, the outward symptoms have abated somewhat but the poison has not yet been eliminated. Even after sixty years of independence, Pakistan is to keep up the working of the poison as long as possible. Instead of flowing from one source, it will now flow from two.

Kashmir has continued to suffer most. Nobody is in a better position to asses the extent of their sufferings than the Kashmiris themselves. Speaking at Srinagar, Sheikh Abdullah gave an idea as to how the two-nation theory had worked in Kashmir. "The two-nation theory has spread poison throughout the land. Having failed to convert the Kashmiris by arguments to the ideology of the Quaide-e-Azam, they tried to conquer us by physical force and so planned the attack on Kashmir."

The pink revolution ended on August 15th, 1947 but the yellow revolution was on. The British India was painted pink on the map, while the Native States received the yellow hue. Sardar Patel may go down in history as another Wellesley. The yellow revolution! Because all the Indian States had acceded to the Indian Union.

There is no doubt that fifth columnists, even after sixty years of independence, have been very much active in Kashmir as in almost every other place in India. These traitors have probably joined hands with the infiltrators and militant groups invariably. Sheikh Abdullah as well as Nehru and Co. knew that it was to be under the rule of Quayum-Cunningham combine. Kashmir is now a democratic state, and every loyal citizen of Kashmir, he be a Hindu or

Muslim, must shed his last drop of blood for the defence of his own Govt. and his own country.

The Maharaja of Kashmir : His short-sightedness had been proved by yet another disastrous result. Fifth columnists had been able to disintegrate his army and there had been disertions. Sheikh Abdullah had to reorganise the army and strengthen the civil adminstration which might be on the verge of collapse. So Jinnah's conspiracy ended in a fiasco and his preconceivedly cooked-up plan frittered away. And the declaration of war by the Prime Minister of N.W.F.P. was not a civil war, not even revolt, that had been taking place in Kashmir. But for a few fifth columnists the bulk of people were loyal to the Govt. and their country. Success here means restoration of confidence not only in Kashmir but in the rest of India. Jinnah's failure means the opening of the flood-gates of anarchy and stratocracy for Pakistan. Today the gravity of crisis has bulged out in Pakistan and it can be easily discerned.

Pakistan was an error but it need not be an irremediable error. Yesterday it was accepted grudgingly and by many with distrust. Already there was much foolish talk of Muslim state and a Hindu state. A constant friction of racialism and perpetual worry of tinpot dictatorship in Pakistan will lead from social enmity to economic enmity and finally to total war ... the eclipse of all freedom and ... perhaps all life. Why? Because the terrorist groups forming a pall of political nightmares all over Pakistan have started out recruiting and arming their own jehadi groups.

Jinnah was banking on the proverbial shortness of public memory of his failure in Kashmir. But the sores Jinnah had created are too deep and painful to be healed up and forgotten at least during the present generation in Pakistan on Kashmir question. His followers are also helpful in restoring confidence. So, today's Kashmir problem is a legacy of Jinnah's Himalayan blunder, bumping down on the red-carpet of terrorism and religious fanaticism, and burbling on and on about her preposterous demand over Kashmir. He had gambled away the Muslim audience in Lahore in support of two-nation theory due to his sudden change of front, when he faced with loss of power, over the vale of Kashmir, irrespective of religious persuasion in nationality, language, culture and blood and economic interests, and again hymns of hatred are facts fresh in the minds of the people.

What was the emergency that had compelled him to promulgate an ordinance to enable the formation of a National Guard in Pakistan? Was it a failure of his mission of Kashmir for invassion? Was it beacuse of the situation in kashmir? But Jinnah had disclaimed all responsibility for the invasion. Kashmir is not in Pakistan, neither has it acceded to Pakistan. Did Mr. Jinnah consider that Kashmir had already been annexed to Pakistan? It was only on that supposition that he might find justification in promulgating ordinance in question. The ordinance extended to all territories of Pakistan. Unfortunately, the ordinance rested on the assumption that Pakistan was at war or was about to be at war with India.

The National Guard was no innovation. It was to be subject to the Indian Army Act as adopted in Pakistan. True to the tactics of Hitler, Jinnah made a legal garb to illegal things after these illegal things had been sufficiently long in existence to be an accomplished fact. They had indulged in illegal activities, chasing down the vale of Kashmir. They had been fairly known as regular organisation of Jinnah's Muslim League. He invested this illegal army with a legal position. This is exactly what Hitler did.

We need not speculate as to what was in Jinnah's mind on Kashmir. It was only the other day that he issued a stirring call, almost a war cry, to his followers in these words : "Do not for a moment imagine that your enemies can ever succeed in their designs but at the same time do not make light of the situation facing you ... All I require of you now is that everyone of us whom his message reaches must vow to himself and be prepared to sacrifice his all, if necessary in building up Paksitan." Is he not supposed to be the founding father of today's Kashmir question and Islamic fanaticism over the vale of Kashmir? Is he supposed to be a statesman? Is he not considered to be a fanatical crusader and not responsible for the decadence of Islamic culture in Pakistan? What was the nature of the 'sacrifice' he had in his mind when he sounded this bugle call?

Take the declaration by Khwaja Nazumuddin, the East Bengal premier, from Karachi where he had gone for a confabulation with Jinnah that his Govt. would consider all talk of a re-union of East and West Bengal as high treason. Was it without significance? Was there no significance to the closed door meeting that Mr. Suhrawardy was going to hold out his house in the immediate future closely following upon his trip to Karachi? Was it without significance that the Nizam had been buying arms in England even by selling his crown jewels? It was Jinnah who had watered the poison of Kashmir problem with conspiracy and stratagem. According to the News Chronicle, Mr. Jinnah had issued orders on the 28th Oct. 1947, to move Pakistani troops to Kashmir but was prevented from doing it on the threat of Field Marshall Auchinleck that all the British officers in both the Armies (India and Pakistan) would resign immediately as they would not like to take part in an open war between India and Pakistan. A single feather shows which way the wind blows.

Partition of India was as physically and geographically a monstrocity as the partition of Palestine. Confronting Pakistan with an acid test of our sincerity of purpose, Kashmir like Palestine might prove to be the fuse setting off a conflagration vaster and more horrible than the world has yet witnessed. Both the problems would destroy the confidence in the history, fairness and sense of justice of the combined nations of the world. Like Kashmir, Partition of Palestine was to Pakistan and to all Muslim Leaguers headed by Mr. Jinnah more than half of the country the Arabs of Palestine would be converted into minority so that jews could set up a politically dominant state. Partition of India has been achieved by agreement. But the partition of Palestine was created by immigration financed from abroad.

Did Mr. Jinnah think that they were so foolish as to wash their hands full with disorders and upheavals? Who among them would desire that hundreds of thousands of their Muslim brethren should lose their homes, their property, many of their lives, and be driven out of the land where they and their ancestors had lived for centuries to flee into the wilderness in mortal terror of theocratic rulers and terrorist outfits? Mr. Jinnah and his Muslim Leaguers neither desired nor intended nor expected that horrible future for millions of human beings. They have now faced their calamities with undiminished courage. Today, Pakistan, due to unpardonable blunder of Mr. Jinnah, has bent all her powers to stop war on terrorism and geared her entire administration to the task of overcoming the worst obstacles. Terrorism is a shooting star that shines for a moment.

Mr. Jinnah knew that an attitude of hostility to India and non-Muslim minorities in Kashmir, whether disguised or screened by sweet words or pious platitudes, would lead Pakistan to disaster. Mr. Jinnah also knew that there must be no loose talk or senseless repetition of shibboleths which got on the nerves of all decent men and women. It was Mr. Jinnah who first introduced a double-edged weapon against which Pakistan must warn all concerned, when Kashmir was simmering with a distressingly disquieting communal situation.

The value of Mr. Jinnah's assurances on Kashmir question was writ large on thousands of murders, abduction, forced marriages, burnt houses, maimed children and the treatment of Kashmir Hindu pundits in utter distress but still being subjected to most harassing and humiliating experiences. Mr. Jinnah's so-called assurances of a fair deal which were being offered to non-Muslims in Pakistan were disgraceful. Mr. Jinnah, having failed in his mission of Kashmir, inflammed passions, The wholesale pilfering of fleeing refugees, men and women in tattered clothes, who had found refuge in India, persons deprieved of all their wordly possessions, children from whom the last bottle of sweets were snatched away and stripped to the last ornament on their person and standing with just the bare clothes on their body shows he understands nothing better than force.

Pakistan, it is true, has no dearth of fighting races. The so-called martial classes have been drawn mainly from the Punjab province of Pakistan. But modern warfare needs brain as well as brawn. It is all the better if the officers who constitute the brain of the force are imbued with an ideology which like Fascism is fanatically jingoist. The intial success of the German offensive during the last great war was in no small measure due to the fanatical devotion of the German Army to the Fuehrer and the cult to which he gave the final shape. Who among the Quaide-e-Azam's followers were better fitted to inculcate among his forces the cult, Pakistan has still been symbolising, than the youthful products of the Muslim universities of Pakistan? Pakistan on the Kashmir question is in the culminating stage of the evolutionary process of the doctrine of separation which the Quaide-e-Azam and his devil advocates had enunciated and the succeeding generations of teachers and students nursed and nurtured.

The seeds of communal distrust and half-belief Mr. Jinnah had planted well in the vale of Kashmir have today scented a fallacy and blossomed forth into a mighty hatred, genocide and overwhelming holocaust. Not only that Mr. Jinnah had fanned out the Jehadis but succeedingly misled the youth to the decadence of a true nation.

Pakistan had introduced 'The Jinnah Fund', which in its monstrocity surpassed even the infamous Jizia Tax. Small businessmen, professionals and others had been compelled on pain of arrest, attachment of properties etc. to contribute. Holders of gun licence, motor licence and others had been made to pay huge amounts. 'The Jinnah Fund' had seriously caused a good deal of discontent among the Hindu citizens of Eastern Pakistan (now Bangladesh). Were the methods allegedly to have been adopted by certain over-zealous Muslim District officers the best ways of making Pakistan prosperous? Mr. Jinnah only knew it.

Was there no connection between the withdrawal of troops from Waziristan? Had there been no understanding between Mr. Jinnah and tribesmen? Mr. Gandhi had long been reticent on what was happening in Kashmir. But it was at his instance that the tremendous gesture of goodwill was made in the financial agreement between India and Pakistan which, frankly speaking, came to the Indian public as a profound surprise. Having regard to the well-known facts about the Kashmir invasion how could the Govt. of India agree to shoulder Pakistan's debt? How could Sardar Patel persuade himself to make an advance of Rs. 55 crores of rupees to Pakistan knowing that the leaders of Pakistan would exploit this generous concession for their own ends? Such an agreement could be possible between the States whose relationship is the friendliest possible. The gesture of Mr. Gandhi had fallen flat on the Quaide-e-Azam.

Has the gesture been allured by the iota of the policy of Mr. Jinnah in regard to Kashmir? The raiders were being reinforced even then. Arms and ammunition had continued to be supplied. Mr Gandhi in his post-prayer speech on 25th Dec. 1947 referred to the propaganda that was being done through the columns of the 'Zaminder', an urdu daily of Lahore. In that paper Muslims had been openly invited for the recruitment and to join the jehad against Kashmir. Had Jinnah put any restraint on that paper? Nothing of the kind. Morever, Pakistan under the leadership of Jinnah had been putting her fresh ounce of strength in men, women, money and material on the invasion of Kashmir. Money is the sinews of war. Rs. 55 crores was added to the strength of the sinews. What a Himalayan blunder was committed!

The solidarity of Jinnah that was being sought comprised Muslims of both the Indian Union and Pakistan. That such solidarity of the Quaide-e-Azam was likely to be a highly potential danger to India's security was no idle fear, nor was the misgiving baseless that it might develop into an underground practising gallery for the pursuit of the ends of the two-nation theory. Memory of the Nazi cult in Germany, which created a solidarity of the German nation in other countries of the world, invested that word with disturbing significance.

How long was the Muslim League of Jinnah going to keep up its silly pretension that it was the Muslim community? This bid for power on the part of a number of fallen stars who had to shoulder the main burden of responsibility for misleading, misguiding and exploiting millions of Indian Muslims, in the name of religion. And this process is still going on and rubbing away with ever-growing lies and hypocrisy. So long as Muslim solidarity means allegiance to the Governor-General, Jinnah, whom feudal foundation was the theory that the Muslims belong to a separate nation. The top-most leaders of Pakistan, headed by Jinnah, who belonged to the Western limb of that state, were preaching that hateful theory.

Under the pretensions of Jinnah and other Muslim Leaguers, the Muslim refugees came to Kashmir and Hyderabad from the adjoining provinces belonging to another category. They were not refugees in the proper sense of the term, for they were not victims of riot and terror. They left their peaceful homes at the instigation of Muslim Leaguers of Jinnah who allured them by promises in order to increase the Muslim population in Kashmir and Hyderabad. These misguided sufferers were not sent back to their ancestral homes. Like Jinnah's Muslim Leaguers, that the tribes of Churchill are not yet extinct in liticians over the Kashmir issues. Like the American press, the British have deliberately refused to see the facts and tried to feed the British public, with distorted half-truths, as Jinnah did on the Kashmir issue, and irritating falsehoods. In an article, in the October issue of 'Cavalcade', 1948, a Major General Fuller gave his views on the 'Turmoil in India'. According to this, "India is progressively becoming one of the major danger zones of the world." Why? Because India is politically divided and internally disrupted. The Maharaja of Kashmir was stampeded to accede to the Indian Union by a Muslim revolt in his State and this was followed by an undeclared war between India and Pakistan. Aided and abetted by such mischievous propaganda, Jinnah initiated an unabashed trade of religious fanaticism in lies and hypocrisy over the vale of Kashmir. Intellectually, knavery seems to be the striking feature of Pakistani rulers on Kashmir question; and emotionally, Pakistan is no better than any other country in ethical dualism. All of her political ventures gravitate towards the common centre in Kashmir. Even after sixty years of independence, Pakistan has miraculously got through the vale of Kashmir directly from barbarism to terrorism without the usual interval of civilisation. A plethora of good theological thoughts for food and drink makes the Jehadis look and feel happy. Tender girls pine away lonely under the tyranny of snobs; and the gallant generous lads, blooming with hearty youth swell into bloated old bachelorhood. And the kidnapped women wither into shrunken decay and perish solitarily when snobbishness of Pakistani rulers has cut off the common claim to happiness of the people. Women dare not love for fear of religious snobbishness.

The young men of Aligarh Muslim University who formed the spearhead of the crusade for a homeland for Muslims. Who was behind them? Only the architect of Pakistan knows. It was intriguing in diverse ways. Coming after the noteworthy statement of Prof. Habib of the Muslim University in Oct. 1947, makes confusion worse confounded. He told the press : "The unity of Islam in this land is broken for ever, and within a generation or less the Mussalmans of India and Pakistan will be as distinct as the Persians and Turks. The process of separation has already begun and is going on at a rapid speed." These are indeed brave words deserving approval and support they are sincerely implemented. The creation of that chasm had ultimately divided the faithful in the two dominions. Who is responsible for that chasm? It was Jinnah who was likely to tamper with the loyalty of Muslim students and professors and hinder effectively the growth of healthy nationalism in the country. In the mental conflict that must in that event ensue which claims ... the claim of nationality or the claim of religious and communal affiliation ... will supervene? In this welter of confusion, all that they (SIMI) can do is to cry like dying Goethe, "Light, more light."

On Kashmir question, Jinnah had always been suffering from illusion. Why? His faith in invasion and religious fanaticism and profanity is based on illusion that can't be shared. The shock tactics employed by Jinnah on the Kashmir to compel this State to accede to Pakistan have perhaps been started with regard to Kashmir aw well. But if Pakistan has come to entertain the idea that lies can be made to appear as gospel turth by unscrupulous propaganda, disillusionment will not be long in coming and that with a vengeance. Jinnah did not forget that fascist methods with all their initial glamour of success ultimately lead to disaster.

From the beginning of the birth of Pakistan, she has been afflicted with compromise, under the horrors of a spirit of quietism, caution, agreement, collusion, threatening and political chicanery. Abracadabras of the conjuror lift up his voice in the echoes of old hopes, with his blighting thought in his soul. Such a piece of play-acting will make the desperate retrospect of his last hours. A monstrous falsehood and consummate fabrication over the Kashmir question have invited the terrorists to read the invisible message of Jinnah in every blackboard in a class room and in every school book. The country has become a vast factory for the manufacture of furture terrorists. It can only be achieved by the loss of so much blood ... like a bastard on the doorstep of his father.

And all the terror-mongers were invited in the midst of their preoccupations to this organised trading in human misery in Kashmir. Composed entirely of sectarian-vested interests, Kashmir has been the rallying-point of all reactionary forces. Added to the silence of the Pakistani Govts. concerned, all the Pakistani premiers, appearing almost simultaneously, have, in all likelihood, created for the unsophisticated public a thick veil of mist clouding for the time being their judgement so far as the Kashmir question is concerned. The nearness of Indo-Pak border in view of the developments of military strategy and the ever-extending fingers of theological propaganda in the vale of Kashmir have given a definite anti-India swing to post-Independent India.

On the other side, Congress' normal evolution, surprising as it may seem, in the light of the origins, is as a party of the Right. Its backbone in the upper ruling brackets is Brahmin and big business ... both naturally conservative elements. Even in the days when the British still ruled India, Nehru puzzled and worried the socialist wing of Congress but he could say that after the British were driven out of the country, all India's troubles would be solved; but when he himself had to deal with the Kashmir question, it was naturally another matter. He seemed to have thought that the policy he had fashioned in the vale of Kashmir, and which has fashioned us still now ... the foreign policies he made, the cells that grew, the honeycomb that was created ... was self-destructive in its nature. And Mr. Jinnah and his Muslim Leaguers had fully taken an advantage over it. Today Pakistan thinks the true discovery of their own mission on Kashmir question is still before them. What they talk about their birthright over Kashmir is high and holy. It is not the daughter but the Mother of Order. And Kashmir has now become many years of race experience. Is the death of democracy in Pakistan likely to be an assassination from ambush? Or is it a slow extinction from apathy and under-nourishment? Who is responsible for that? Mr. Jinnah or other Muslim Leaguers? All are silent.

To all the political players, Nehru wished the best of luck and to the foreign guests a pleasant and enjoyable stay. Party system under Congress which is still unhealthy, corrupted, totally vitiated, having no backbone to face any problem over Kashmir. Is not Congress a party afflicted with spinal-polio?

It would be a great question what foreign policy India should adopt in the event of certain things happening in Kashmir. The foreign policy is not to be static. It will not get along a fixed groove. Foreign policy on Kashmir question will be very much dynamic. It changes in accordance with changes in world conditions and world politics. The Second World War, we must say, greatly helped the Indian people in this respect. It taught them geography, history, international diplomacy, including strategy, geo-politics and what not. We would not be far wrong if we say that it is practically since the outbreak of the world war that Indians have begun to take increasing interest in the affairs of foreign countries. Foreign policy should not be self-deceptive or hypocritically deceiving that Pakistan has executed over the Kashmir question. Her foreign policy depends upon Banana Republic, upon drug trafficking, upon patronage. It was Quaide-e-Azam Jinnah who had practically used camouflages, his plans and purposes to gain power in Kashmir under the guise of 'super-patriotism' for the liberation movement of Kashmiri Muslims. He was not stupid nor naive. He was successful in rolling down the red carpet of worst anarchy and confusion, civil discord and bloodshed through 'super-terrorism' for 'Super-Islamisation'. Distortion of constitutional rights makes Pakistan today ridiculous. Mr. Jinnah never hesitated to steal or to falsify the Kashmir question.

A middle way solution is being freely mooted. This verges on the partition of the State with Kashmir going to Pakistan and Jammu coming to India. There is an alternative suggestion in view of the prevailing Hindu-Muslim unity in

Kashmir valley. The alternative suggestion is that only the Poonch-Muzaffarabad area should be given to Pakistan. But the best solution is that the valley should be a free zone and there must be, like U.N.O., United Nations of Asia.

The Kashmir problem will not end either with the driving out of the infiltrators or terrorists. We will have to resolve the proverbial triangle in the form of India, Pakistan and tribal area before we could write a finish to the Kashmir drama.

What has the unseen hand of a cruel fate made a terrorist? There is no trust, no confidence, and no spirit of neighbourliness. There is suspicion and mistrust all around. This legacy of suspicion, with much deeper sin and bottomless conceit, Jinnah has successfully planted in Pakistan about Kashmir, has lived by foul-devouring. Such sickness of fanaticism and life-poisoning political pestilence are worse than civil home-bred strife. Such bewitching wanton talks, blotting India with blame, are as flimsy as caterpillars do the tender leaves. Foul words and frowns, with blindfold fury, are conquerors. Whether India is one nation may be a debatable issue. That is composed of two nations ... Hindus and Muslims ... is an absurd and fantastic doctrine which is being tested in the crucible of undreamt of happenings in Kashmir. In this country we have grown and developed in our own way. Different national patterns with linguistic and cultural claims have been evolved through long centuries of effort, experiment and trial. Pakistan cannot divide India between an exclusively Muslim region and an exclusively non-Muslim region. Muslims and non-Muslims have been brought up together by centuries of cultural contact and they are so intermixed that it is difficult to create a purely Muslim state in Kashmir as against a non-Muslim state Jammu.

Whereas Pakistani rulers have transformed Pakistan into a theocratic state with a stratocratic Govt. knowing sufficiently the dangerous and disastrous consequences of the policy over the Kashmir question. But Mr. Jinnah and his Muslim Leaguers associated themselves unhesitatingly with the sentiments. Just after sixty years of independence, that theocratic state with tinpot dictatorship has become a counsel of despair and defeatism. It is a philosphy of reaction and counter-revolution which is a challenge to democracy. It is no use enunciating the principles of human behaviour in surroundings, which have been darkened by mass killing, arson and loot. It is no use telling them that Peshwar has now become a Baghdad, Paktoonistan a Kabul and Sind a Jerusalem. Does Pakistan know the butchery in Indonesia, at first, was confined to East and Central Java, but by December, 1964, the infection had spread to Bali, Makassar, Sumatra and the Celebes? Does Pakistan know in five months between 300,000 and 500,000 people were killed? Does Pakistan know rivers in Solo, Sumatra and Medium were choked with log-jams of human corpses? No one should underestimate the pains and sufferings of Pakistan today. When politicians loss their principles, they play a dirty game. Pakistan was better to be born democratic than to be born fanatic.

Unfortunately, Pakistan has created a three-headed monster ... militant crusaders. ISI and the army ... by grafting the severed head of unfortunate Islamic terrorism on the neck of democracy. The three-headed hound ... a horrific account of the tragedy of Islamic nation and a repulsive and blood-curdling character of Pakistan on Kashmir issue ... is guarding Islamabad. The infernal ingenuity of Pakistan has already surpassed all demons and filled the world with many-headed monsters of Pan-Islamic terrorism, devouring all of our country's substance and making nights hideous with their howls. A Frankenstein monster too may realise the dream of Mary Shelley, even as the Nautilus has fulfilled the fantasies of Jules Verne and Spaceships and Sputniks lend colour to the imaginative excesses of the Arabian nights.

The virtue of Miss Fatima Jinnah's speech has been worm-eaten by the insects of Muslim League whom Mr. Jinnah had kept under his feet. So the ups and downs of Kashmir politics and the vicissitudes of political trade on Kashmir issue will be a great shame to our so-called pseudo-forgetting the wet eyes of widows and broken old mothers. Some slaves, some free. Political leaders, through defective political institutions, enjoy this process of grotesque self-deception. They shout hoarse and common man ventures to open his mouth. And New Delhi invents cheap lies, putting the blame upon the nation that is attacked. And our foreign secretaries refuse to examine any refutations in the wilderness of falsehood. We should adjudicate between conflicting arguments of liars and truth-tellers. The prince of darkness is a gentleman in politics, either in Parliament or in Assembly, as we are told he is. And Kashmir Liberation Movement was born and brought up in the jungle heritage of force, fraud and violence. And Kashmir solution is covered with communal fungus, the foliage diseased. Our leaders fear their own weaknesses. Distrust feeds on itself. Hysteria of any kind is deplorable. And when it begins to interfere with routine examinations, it becomes positively dangerous.

When Pakistan was grown-up, she continued to behave with a capricious egotism, on Kashmir issue, that seemed to have no guiding principle. As a result, Pakistan has now plunged herself into a reckless course of expenditure on terrorism and in doing so, hung a millstone of debt round her neck from which Pakistan will never be able to escape. The most intriguing feature of the period of Pakistan's policy over Kashmir is her unexpected loyalty to hypocrisy, lies and propaganda.

Bertrand Russell, a great philosopher, in his book 'New Hopes For A Changing World', is quite clear that nothing short of unification will save us from another and perhaps final catastrophe.

"The fight between the Hindus and Muslims was not religious but economic. We were unable to fight the British single-handed. We wanted some help. Muslim Leaguers and Muslim Leaders refused to help us, no other was left to us except to join hands with the Congress. We in the Frontier Province are Muslims, and we have had no quarrel with the Hindus. Whatever we said in the Congress was accepted ... Mahatma Gandhi was prepared to give more to the Mulsims than their due rights : If Jinnah was prepared to give up his opposition to the Congress, I was prepared to stand surety for the rights of Muslims in whatever way the Muslims wanted."

This categorical statement was given when Khan Abdul Gaffar Khan was being tried in respect of three speeches made by him in Peshwar and Mardan districts during the period between March 24 and June 5, 1956, in the West Pakistan High Court. He further said : "Sardar Nishtar wanted to consult Jinnah and tried to persuade him, but he could not prevail upon him, and the conference failed." He also added: "In the Simla Conference, when serious differences arose on the fundamental issue, I called so Sardar Abdur Rab Nishtar and told him to persuade Jinnah who finally refused."

Now the question is : why he refused to join the Muslim League when asked by Jinnah? Because the majority of the League leaders were Khans and Nawabs and had never served the nation. They were subservient to the laws of the British.

So Pakistan, on Kashmir issue, confuses and befools democracy with benevolent autocracy. Civil liberties are not a happy phrase, but a historic concept for which millions have fought and have died. Individuals enjoying the benefits of a complex Islamic society have everything their own way; but neither has a mjaoirty the right to deny freedom of action to individual minorities, so long as it does not cut across the freedom of their neighbours.

Since the birth of Pakistan, Islamic diehards in Pakistan have now riven with ideological and personal feuds. They have lost ground and strengthened the hands of the militant Islamic groups in Kashmir. So every agreement on Kashmir issue has not supplied the antidote to the war psychosis sweeping over this sub-continent. Whereas the class-ridden society in India is taking to the outlandish forms of attire, trying to mix the indigenous and foreign fashions in an attempt to combine utility of Indian sartorial rabble. What a gallows humour to India!

THE MAKING OF PAKISTAN

The situation in Kashmir has the makings of religious disaster as well as political apocalypse. The nature and extent of the disaster and apocalypse will be flummoxed by the degree to which a Kashmiri's life and the life of Kashmir society have had that. The ultimate test and triumph of Jehadi's creativity would come through the denial of any Islamic value or meaning in the world of Islamic globalisation, through the discovery of an image of terrorism powerful enough to deny their nothingness.

It is useless to ask what this powerful image of Islamic militancy represents in Kashmir, or what the superman is supposed to. It is the image simply of their nothingness. The image of a Muslim is aware of affirming this situation in Kashmir, the aesthetic savouring his nihilism. The creative pleasure of Roman holiday lies in the making of the image of anti-India hymns of hate, in the imaginative exploration of liberating the Kashmiris from the clutches of democracy. Paradoxically, the old magic of Jehadi slogans continues to work. It is an Islamic country like Pakistan that has shown that pure poetry of terrorism can be made out of disillusion and despair, out of degradation and derangement of the senses, and delusion and every kind of fantasy. This is the fatal discovery of modern Islamic aesthetics. Ideally, Pakistan believes that all the products of a strong Islamic culture should possess a unity of style, and it is to test the authencity of this style of hypocrisy over the valley that a terrorist goes round sounding things with his famous hammer of religious fanaticism. Pakistan's language of political cant on the making of Pakistan is notoriously metaphorical and rhetorical, and its meaning can scarely be paraphrased in any other style.

Autobiographical writings by leading statesmen are eagerly awaited but usually disappointing, except to their uncritical admirers. Ayub Khan's autobiography "Friends Not Masters' ... a political autobiography" is no exception. The image of the plain-spoken solider, Ayub Khan, who by some strange alchemy, transformed himself into a political saviour, needs some modification. There is an element of megalomania in Ayub's make-up. From the birth pangs of Pakistan to the present, all the rulers who brought their country to the brink of ruin were corrupt, quarrelsome and unprincipled politicians particularly on the Kashmir issue. Gen. Musharraf is not an exception. They are all born to the manner. Mr. Z.A. Bhutto launched out the development of Pakistan's highly idiosyncratic version of 'neutralism'. We are obviously intended to believe that post 1958 Pakistan is the exclusive creation of Ayub himself, in alliance with the 'masses' whom he had mobilised, almost single-handed, for the performance of nation-building tasks. While there is some element of truth in this boast, it is no more than a fraction of the whole truth.

Pakistan has so far not succeeded in creating a scrupulous and passionate regard for peace in Kashmir with which all her technological and scientific progress is a dreadful menace ... a sword hanging over her head. Even today the safeguarding of peace and the future of mankind in Kashmir are considered to be less important than the service of narrow, national or religious interests. Pakistan fails to eliminate the class of priests who stand between man and God. She has sharper claws than any other Islamic country. So, Kashmir issue has always been clouded with the makings of political and religious prostitutions, because of the activities of a gang of fanatic and hostile jehadis and their agents who are known to have a plan to frustrate the democratic order. The most successful fund-raiser of the jehadis is naturally attached to I.S.I. Democracy ceases to function when things are so adjusted or mismanaged. The jehadis of Kashmir are symptoms of a dangerous malaise for Jehadis alone who cannot be held responsible. Islamabad is guilty of a variety of provocative acts along the border, but the scale and ferocity with which I.S.I. has launched its series of massive retaliation can be classified as cross-border terrorism. The dragon of linguism has to be killed once for all if we are to have the substance and not the shadow of democracy. As virtue is necessary in a republic, and honour in a monarchy, fear is what is required in a despotism. As for virtue, it is not at all necessary and honour would be dangerous there. Shakespeare, in 'Titus Andronicus' says : "Vengeance is in my heart, death in my hand, blood and revenge are hammering in my head." Pakistan should learn it carefully. Otherwise, Pakistan will be, like a cancelled note, torn in two ; and it never can be shown against one. Why? Because Pakistan believes in monotheism ... religion of terrorism. Man is an animal that makes bargains ; no other animals do this ... one dog does not change a bone with another.

A big disaster is not always a vice. It is true that Pakistani newspapers, like men, are tainted with original sin over the Kashmir question ... that vice has a fascination for them. But except in the case of a perverse few who may be obsessed with vice, they suffer from a split personality. With all their vice, Indian newspapers are fond of reporting speeches of public men and four-fifths of their speeches are moral exhortations to the people. Our political orators talk an unconsciously long time for their speech. Whereas our newspapers bellow forth over their hearers' weary heads.

Mr. Z.A. Bhutto was capable of contributing the crudest form of political exploitation amongst the Kashmiri Muslims; partly because he had lent themselves to this ambitious manner of thinking. The disastrous parallelism between Lahore and Karachi, between a creative inspiration of the democratic mind and a catastrophic abuse of life in Pakistan, between democratic aestheticism and fanatical barbarism on the Kashmiri Hindu pundits is the tragic concluding discovery of Pakistan's mission over Kashmir. Only the irony is true, indeed tragic.

The dissemination of Islamic ideas through books, irrespective of language or creed may sound a more high-falutin ... even pompous ... phrase than the medium is the message. The message is in Kashmir, writ large, for those who wish to register it. Who is a writer? A writer is more than a reporter. He is a mediatory agent between the thinking in this country and the doing overseas.

Ayub Khan evidently believed that he had the touch that could heat the breach between the two wings, that the 1962 contribution is uniquely adapted to the political temper and capacity of the Pakistani people, and that a modernised Islam provides all that is needed by way of a unifying ideology.

Chowdhury Md. Ali, in 'The Emergence of Pakistan', tells the story of this extraordinary and deplorable operation. Md. Ali had a case to make out for the Muslim League, against Congress; for Md. Ali Jinnah, against Lord Mountbatten (next to Sardar Patel, his favourite bete noire).

Society in Pakistan everywhere is in conspiracy against the manhood of every one of its members. Everywhere, everyone. The virtues and vices of this shamanistic approach are patent. Kashmir issue concerns the relation between the use of regimented humanity for vast technological projects and the concomitant development of despotism over the vale of Kashmir. Pakistan plunges with gusto into the tangled matter of the origin of Kashmir problem and into the question of political violence and regligious fanaticism in Kashmir.

The ciritical moment in Kashmir is Pakistan's discovery of her own many-faceted mind, and her fascination with what she finds there. She has to learn to be human. Never does she think dialectically and with a genuine insight into the tragic paradox of the miracle of Islamic identity. She never forgets where the difficult question lies. Even after 60 years of independence, liberty in Pakistan is everywhere in peril : and Islamic globalisation is ganged up with Jehadis at the corridor of Kashmir. And the year 1947 was to Kashmir is fateful one. The so called Azad Kashmir ... once an arsenal for American gunpowder ... has now become an arsenal for Islamic militants trained for terrorism in India.

Human nature will hardly ever change. Human behaviour is, however, something that reflects an individual's cultural background. Misbehaviour of our leaders with the people is generally indicative of ill-breeding and all those who are responsible for must share the blame.

What the world is experiencing today is more than disllusionment. There is a new canker of cynicism in men's minds. They see freedom violated in the name of reason, equality done away with in the name of social justice and peace menaced in the name of Islamic terrorism. It is not surprising that at such a time the Pakistani rulers should ask if the ideals of equality, freedom, fellowship and peace in Kashmir are at all practicable. The question is not whether there is a middle road between the doctrinaire and the empiricist way.

The coat-and-tie mentality of Nehru and his henchmen are grown out of this weakness of an earlier age. They congratulated themselves on the superiority. They should have asked themselves whether they were not less pedantic simply because they had less learning on the Kashmir issue. This mentality flourished equally under the communal shirts of the roughest home-spun. Their education, language, recreation, income, way of living conspired to separate them from the people of Kashmir. It is also true that officials did not learn to give up their bureaucratic approach to Kashmir problems. Such an approach was the inevitable result of a bureaucratic machinery which grew more ponderous and more complicated everyday. The Nehru and Co. was responsible for these problems in Kashmir. When responsibility was distributed over half a dozen tiers of bureaucrats in every office of bureaucracy in Kashmir, no one felt really responsible. The old British ways of thinking is over. So long as officials continue to enjoy all the old privileges, the Kashmir will remain unsolved. After all, the coat-and-tie mentality has taken a sixty years to grow. A readiness to change from old to new laws enfeebles the power of the law.

Kashmir issue is full of wrong answers. Why? Because we ask the wrong questions. We jump from answer to answer, from solution to solution, from conclusion. A mind that is fragmentary thinks in parts.

The Muslims in India are Indians as well as Muslims; and that is what they must try and keep in the forefront of their minds. There is no room here, and certainly no wisdom, for separateness on their part. They are part of the nation, and must completly identify themselves with it. If the Muslims themselves try to remain separate; they may ultimately be forced to be separated; and the blame in that case would be no one's but their own. These wise words should dissolve their anachronistic league in this country as an anarchist devoid of all laws and governments. Pakistan is an Islamic country that is admittedly considered to be anchorgae of world terrorism. Why? Today their consciousness with sensation without thought; and it affects the whole body of Muslim community with loss of consciousness. This wishful thinking is nearest to the direction of the prevailing winds of Pakistan.

The present history of Pakistan shows that all Islamic countries have been the result of concentration of absolute power in the hands of a few cunning people around a king or oligarchy. Islamic empires like all other empires invariably disintegrate with the coming of liberalisation after consolidation or with the advent of a democratic system of govt. through secret ballot. The Egyptian and the Babylonian empires were powerful with people subjugated and without pollitical rights. So were the Asyrian, the Persian, the Greek and the Roman empires. They alll crumpled through liberalisation and consequent corruption.

Every military rule in Pakistan came into being because of the continued concentration of power in the hands of the dictatorship. Thus it will be seen that Islamic terrorism under Islamic imperialism comes into being and remains in power through the exercise of monopolistic power by an oligarchy and crumbles through internal weakness. Even the history of Pakistan, since independence, has been deceiving the world Muslims through the beguiling Islamic theology and story of all life ... a story of betrayed innocence and blighted love, of anguished loneliness and remorse.

Jehadi's crying : There is about the personal cry a sense of ecstasy, as of an artist consumating his vision alone, with none to praise him.

Pakistan will once watch the surface of the valley in an agony of suspense and see at last a dark shadow, clear over the valley. Without moving, she will begin to sing, in low, clear, liquid notes like the rain. It will be one of the tunes she had loved ever since she could one note from another.

The tortuous path of jehadis has been strewn with obstacles and barriers born of their ignorance, their aspirations and longings, their history and misguided struggles and their inexplicable fate. Their persistent striving for liberation movement in Kashmir, accompanied by Himalayan blunder and short-sightedness, will inevitably, though slowly and imperceptibly, yield only a dreamland of religious nigthmares. The genealogical tree of Pakistan-sponsored jehad is predestined to be at the crossroads of religious fanaticism branching out political hide-bounds and narrow religious doctrines, and doomed to pay the price to both oscillating between conflict and cooperation.

This is their fate for over sixty years; and their salvation seems to lie, as it is half-jokingly remarked, only if someone can by some miracle transfer Pakistan to some other place. Major historical conflicts in between India and Pakistan, on Kashmir issue, have swept across the border, leaving behind a trail of blood and devastation, destroying the entity of Kashmir valley, and raising impenetrable barriers for what seems as interminable period.

Truly speaking, we are living in a culture of Byzantine complex, shrouded in with religious dogmas deliberately meant to hide the truth and political powers camouflaged by fiendishly nurtured slogans. Religious extremists often reject the authority of secular governments and view legal systems that are not based on their religious beliefs as illegitimate. They often view modernisation effort as corrupting influences on traditional culture. Over the past 25 years terrorists have committed extremely violent acts for alleged political or religious reasons. Political ideology ranges from the far left to the far right. For example, the far left can consist of groups such as Marxists and Leninsts who propose a revolution of workers led by a revolutionary elite. On the far right, we find dictatorships that typically believe in a merging of state and business leadership.

We must learn to walk before we can run.

The quadruplicity of Quadruple Alliance between Libya, Pakistan, China, and Iran makes the situation of this sub-continent worse and worse. Words and sentences are no more ornamentation on a nation's structure. As they lose their exactitude the fine edge of thought is blunted; judgement and discrimination are befogged. The remedy does not lie in appointing a commission, either on Kashmir issue or Middle East crisis, to draw up rules, for no living language can or should be static. Neither can it, like a faulty road, be closed down for repairs. Stumps and shoots of righteousness always remain scattered over the mind. What a Socratic Irony!

7

Pakistan Before And After Jinnah-II : Tradition and Originality

Leaders fall into two categories. There are those who appear in public manage somehow to be garlanded, make loud noises from the brain, and when elections are near, go about giving affectionate pats on the heads of little children whose parents are on the voting register. The other kind of leader is the one that appears in print manages to get read, makes emphatic statements in the hope that emphasis would be mistaken for knowledge and, when the day is done, ends up as a wrapper for fish and chips.

In India, most of our leaders are recruited from among the ignorant and the reckless masses of people. They are just indulging in a mild leg-pull of that learned and highly responsible section of the population. The best leaders are still those that are either born or written. So, leadership crisis makes the Kashmir question worse. New Delhi may be accused of 'paralysis of indecision'. The cant, claptrap and hypocrisies of our politicians on Kashmir issue particularly and Islamic extremism in India echo diurnally. They soil their hands and damn their souls with the muck of politics. And they turn their backs altogether upon the madding crowd's ignoble strifes. For, although the pen is mightier than the sword, their tongue is mightier than either. That is why the world has always been ruled by politicians. Hitler in one of his apoplectic verbal explosions bragged that all great things have always been achieved by the spoken and the written word. Our political leaders! Partition in India came like a thief in the night, instead of thundering along majestically.

Pakistan before Jinnah's death : Karachi saw very little of the Qaid-e-Azam, Mr. Jinnah during 1948. Owing to failing health, he used to be more and more at Ziarrat or Quetta. Both have a salubrious climate. Zirrat is famous for its beauty.

Mr. Jinnah had never experience of adminstration. We doubt if he was at all efficient as an office-man, quick at disposal of letters, papers and files. It is quite doubtful that many of persons who wrote to him received replies from him. Many of the letters remained unanswered. Even an important secretary of the Govt. of Pakistan was in despair. Mr. Jinnah appeared to have had a desire of concentrating all power in himself. He certainly did not want anything to happen in Pakistan without his knowledge and consent.

Pakistan has been called the geographer's nighmare, a quaint 'biped' of a nation. Why? Because of the immense physical distance that divides the two wings. What is the difference between Pakistan and Bangladesh? Pakistan, an Islamic nation with its rambling camel carts and sleek American cars as well as Indian cars, its jazzy night clubs and sprawling slums and mosques beseiged by jehadis and terrorists and protagonists of anti-India hate slogans is more akin to the Middle East of oil rich Sheikhs with no responsibility towards the people. And Bangladesh with its poor but politically immatured peasantry is in tune with turbulent South-East Asia. If they feel strongly, why follow the herd.

In West Pakistan, there is almost pristine feudalism in large pockets. One does not even hear of any talk about the abolition of zamindar. In Bangladesh, feudalism is readymade relic of the past. In West Pakistan, a feudal oligarchy backed by political parvenus is in complete ascendancy; even the mullahs and theologians are composed of zamindars and big landlords, while an overwhelming majority of the members in Bangladesh are representatives of the middle class peasantry or landless labour.

The first anniversary of the establishment of Pakistan fell in August. Though Pakistan and India must be regarded, historically speaking, to have emerged as free and sovereign states simultaneously at the stroke of midnight between August 14 and 15, 1947. Mr. Jinnah always regarded his own State to have come into existence a day earlier; and Pakistan celebrates the anniversary of its birth on Aug. 14, while we do it on Aug. 15.

Do you know Mr. Jinnah was not in Karachi, on Aug 14, 1948. Why? On the first anniversary of the establishment of Pakistan? Do you know Nawabzada Liaquat Ali Khan, in Jinnah's absence, took the salute at the parade that morning? Why? Contigents of the Pakistani army and navy took part in the march-past. Aeroplanes showered greetings from above.

Do you know when the show was over, and the then Indian diplomat, Sri Prakash, was about to leave, some members of the crowd laid violent hands on the Indian flag on the bonnet of his car? Heads of diplomatic missions must have their flags on their vehicles, despite the danger this may entail, when they move about in the country of their assignment. It is sorry to say that our national flag was eye-sore to many in Pakistan at that time. Was it a genesis of Indo-Pak conflict on Kashmir issue? Conspiracy has started out the travails of political trials, troubles and tribulations, exhibiting blind, prejudiced and unreasoning allegiance to the crescent.

The September 11, 1948 was the day of Jinnah's death. Sri Prakash, the then India's diplomat in Pakistan was in Karachi at a cocktail party given by the French Ambassador at the palace Hotel that evening. Also present there were Prime Minister Nawabzada Liaquat Ali Khan, Foreign Minister, Zafarullah Khan and other ministers and secretaries. Naturally, guests were asking them about the Quaid-e-Azam health. The Prime Minister, the Foreign Minister, the Foreign Secretary all assured Sri Prakash that the Governor-General was much better and was resting at Quetta. It must have been about half-past seven in the evening when the party broke up.

In those days, the Hindus who were still left in Karachi used to be in constant fright. The Sindhis had perhaps all left, but many Gujrati, Kutchchi and other merchants were still there. Parsees had reconciled themselves to the change and had become Pakistanis.

Well-to-do-Hindus, who made their fortunes in commerce and industry, were reluctant to leave. But they too had to move, leaving their fortune behind them. The High Commissioner had the unpleasant experience of persons rushing to him at midnight, asking him for permits to enable them to go to India. They would say that warrants had been issued for their arrest the following morning, and unless they were able to escape by air about three in the morning, they would be in danger.

Sri Prakash therefore kept these permits near his bed at nights so that he could sign them whenever required without his having to call for any assistants. He did his work in a very informal manner.

The death of Mr. Jinnah is shrouded in mystery. All the facts are not known and will never be known. The only person who could perhaps tell them was his sister, Miss Fatima Jinnah.

It is quite clear that Mr. Jinnah did arrive in the Governor General's special plane from Quetta at Mauripur, the military airport at Karachi, sometime in the afternoon of Sept 11. Miss Fatima was with him. It was said that no doctors or nurses came with the party. This, if correct, was truly strange. Who else came, no one knew. Usually whenever Mr. Jinnah came, the diplomatic corps was also informed, and they all went to the airport to receive him. Ministers, high Govt. officers and a fair number of members of the public were always present at the airport to welcome him.

After partition, conspiracy was whispering all around. Conspiracy and Pakistan, since partition, have always been running faster and faster. The members of the diplomatic corps all stood in a line, and were properly introduced. His arrival was always public. This time nobody was informed of his arrival. At Mauripur, he was perhaps put in some sort of an ambulance which was in a far from good condition. It broke down as it was proceeding to Govt. House.

The Head of the local Red Cross Society at that time was Jamshed Mehta ... the well-known and highly respected citizen of Karachi. He told our the then High Commissioner, Sri Prakash, in Pakistan, that he received a message that evening that some one was very seriously ill. He was not informed that it was Mr. Jinnah for whom a Red Cross Van was wanted, otherswise he would have surely gone himself.

He sent a van on which Mr. Jinnah was brought to Govt. House. This was about half past five. He was reported to have died about half past seven. No one was informed of this at the time. Mr. Liaquat Ali Khan later told Sri Prakash that as the Qaid-e-Azam was a very simple man and disliked fuss, no one was told of his late journey to Karachi.

Many people thought that he had died at Quetta and that his body was brought to Karachi by his sister for the last rites ... Anyway, it is clear that the Prime Minister and others were not told about his death till about midnight. Why were they not informed of his death for nearly five hours? It was reported that Mr. Liaquat Ali Khan was actually going to bed when the news came and he hurried to Govt. House. He and other dignitaries were in conference from midnight till four in the morning regarding the succession. Many in Karachi felt that Miss Jinnah herself had the greatest claim to succeed her brother. The powers ... that be, however, decided on Khwaja Nazimuddin.

His last days were undoubtedly not happy. He was a lonely man. He had few friends, for he would give equality with himself to no one.

As a lawyer and jurist, he undoubtedly felt insufferably sad at what had happened after the partition. He was too proud to say so. He had evidently hoped for a peaceful division of the country. He had perhaps never dreamed that it would uproot millions of men, women and children from their homes, and that so much murder and violences would follow in its wake.

What would have happened to Pakistan, had he been alive today?

Today Pakistan is sitting on a powder-keg. Islam, hijacked by obscurantists, fanatic extremists, has fanned out the psychotic young Muslims voicing forth facist obscenities outside the Pakistani Embassy, and at the same time enjoying the fruits of Western freedom of expression. What Jinnah would have witnessed, had he been alive today? Is this the nomenclature of hard-earned freedom? Ziauddin Sardar, in 'The Guardian, London' says : "Muslims are proud that Islam is the fastest growing religion in the West. Evangelical Muslims, from Saudi Arabia to Pakistan happily spread their constricted interpretation of Islam. But Christian missionaries in Muslim countries are another matter ... So, all good and concerned Muslims are implicated in the unchecked rise of fanaticism in Muslim societies. We have given free reign to fascism within our midst, and failed to denounce fanatics who distort the sacred concepts of our faith. We have been silent as they proclaim themselves as martyrs, mangling beyond recognition the sacred meaning of what it is to be a Muslim." (The Guardian, London, September 24, 2001). Mr. Sardar has vociferously lashed out the fanatic extremists who are involved in the planning, financing, training, recruiting support or harbouring those who commit act of Indiscriminate violence against persons or the apparatus or infrastructure of States like India is guilty of terror and criminals of justice in the valley of Kashmir also.

Had Jinnah been alive today, he could not have been, we hope, ruthlessly. silenced. He could have suffered from a travesty of mental anguish as his country is on the brinkmanship of religious nightmares. Why? Because Pakistan recalls the bygone and romantic age of Jehad. There are many delightful variations on this theme. Gen. Musharraf is the very modern version of the clown with the broken heart who in our age of half-tones reappears as a very respectable clown with a slightly cracked heart. Mr. Z.A. Bhutto was a most engaging personality. He had more warmth than brilliance and he was more exciting than enduring on Kashmir issue. We quote Mark Twain, explaining why certain ancient and once popular humourists and clowns have perished : "Because they are merely humourists. Humourists of the 'mere' sort cannot survive. Humour is only a fragrance, a decoration. Often it is merely an odd trick of speech and spelling".

Whereas Nehru was himself clumsy and helpless on Kashmir issue. He involved his characters in uproariously ridiculous and extremly unlikely situations, nor was his humour of the circumlocutory and polysyllabic kind. Gandhi was the cultured sightseer, understanding and forgiving all the follies of world, never surprised, never taken aback, always slightly amused, chuckling with a twinkle in his eyes, but never roaring with laughter. Nehru's leading theme on Kashmir question ...at least a heart-felt sigh ... was the slow disappearance of the individual, his utter defeat by, and unconditional surrender to, religious regimentation and Islamic jehad. He himself could not escape his fate. A few of his comments are as refreshing as entertaining, but the majority seem stale, laboured and sometimes unnecessarily aggressive, waving the banner of 'secularism'.

If the leaders at the centre anticipated and designed this result in Kashmir, there is nothing more to be said except that their tactics have paid off. But they are evidently perturbed by the result. Much of the damage has already been done to maintain the status quo.

To see us as others see us is a gift possessed by few of us and least of all perhaps by our External Affairs Ministry. For years, our international relations were in terms of abstract principles which our diplomatic representatives tried to apply best they could to the situations facing them. The Chinese invasion, Indo-Pak wars and Islamic extremism in Kashmir and other places have not yet created a greater awareness of the need to assess more carefully the reactions to our policies in neighbouring countries. Winston Churchill in 'The Second World War', says : "The veils of the future are lighted one by one and mortals must act from day to day ... There comes a time in a man's life, when he stand back and consider what he has built, written or begotten and whether it was worth doing." (Vol. VI, Triumph and Tragedy)

Jinnah's lack of intensive self-study on Kashmir issue is perhaps a laudable fault. After his death, each and every ruler was, and is, a political adventurer, unscrupulous, anarchic, brash, immensely courageous and very independent. Even Mr. Jinnah was simply rather puzzling on Kashmir issue, because he did not have that single unifying quality of goodness and rectitude on Kashmir issue. After sixty years of independence, we can add to our knowledge. But we cannot substract from it.

Why? This is true in the sense that intellectual number cannot be destroyed. It takes up room. The only way to get rid of it is by the human expedient of forgetting what we have learnt from our neighbouring countries like China and Pakistan. It is perhaps the most effective method. Progress and regress on Kashmir issue precisely depend on how much of some of the human knowledge periodically breaks surface causing great disturbance of cross-border terrorism.

The suppression of our early insights on Kashmir question is not entirely due to our cussedness, however. The hedgehogs have totally supplanted the foxes and with this the capacity for the single decision has run out. Many people think this is not a bad thing. Why? Because schemes and systems free intolerances and hatred.

Appropriately, the modish philosophy of our period is existentialism which accepts the dilemmas of the human condition, offers no solution or consolations. It is the direct descendant of epicureanism and like it offers only a tactical expalantion of a temporary period. Afflicted with anti-India hate slogans, schools and sects in Pakistan have erupted furiously and cooked-up gummings and bickerings with one another. So the criterion of Islamic extremism has had a big part in diverting man from contemplating the wood to monkeying with trees.

After Jinnah's death, Pakistan's propaganda campaign is more ominous than the arming of the so-called Jehadi groups in occupied Kashmir. Pakistan seems to be driven forward by some blind fury which is neither deterred from falsehood by the risk of exposure nor held back from wooing new friends by the fear of straining old and well-tried friendships. Do you know Mr. Z.A. Bhutto, during a stop-over at Beirut in 1963, on his way back from Washington, said that the apathy of the Arabs on the Kashmir issue was in painful contrast to Pakistan's support for all Arab causes?

Zafrullah Khan, the then foreign minister of Pakistan, depressed at the following partition repeated the same as he had told in 1937. "Jinnah is a fool".

"Pakistan, if formed, will harm Muslims more than Hindus." When he was asked what he thought of partition in 1947, he said: "I think the same today." Had he been alive today, even after sixty years of independence, he would have to say : "I think the same today."

If any diplomat arrived in Pakistan (Aug. 1947) he realised that perhaps the most powerful and influential person there was Mr. Altaf Hussain, Editor of the English daily, Dawn. The daily, which poured forth poison against India from day to day, seemed to exercise great influence in the shaping of Pakistan's policy both domestic and foreign. Regarding Kashmir, it was vitriolic. One of its cartoons had depicted the Maharaja Hari Singh, his Dewen, Mr. Mehr Chand Mahajan, later Chief Justice of India, and Sheikh Abdullah, all hanging with their necks broken, showing what fate was awaiting them when Kashmir was forcibly grabbed by Pakistan.

Due to Nehru's pronouncement on Kashmir issue, Kashmir problem was getting worse and worse. His pronouncements were often too finely balanced, sometimes to a point where the first part almost cancelled out the second. Such continuous improvisation also led sometimes to vagueness and generalisation. Among reporters this style has come to be described as 'Nehruism'. There is no doubt that the situation in Kashmir is a dangerous one, dangerous in the sense that small things lead to great things. A little war might lead to a big war. This is a typical 'Nehruism'. He often failed to provide readymade 'leads' or 'headlines' on Kashmir issue, and his loud-thinking manner of speaking on Pakistan was reporter's despair, as his putting down his statements on paper, it was most difficult to pinpoint what exactly he said or meant. In a similar situation, Mr. Jinnah would have snarled : "Irrelevant nonsense."

In contrast, President Truman, when confronted with an awkward question or a question to which he did not know the answer, used to snap out : "No comment." But not so far our Prime Minister, Mr. Nehru. After partition, actions spoke louder than words. Many a true word is spoken in jest.

Whereas Mrs. Indira Gandhi's words on Kashmir issue were so personal and so determined, so disinterested and so brave, that it compelled admiration even from those who did not think and feel as she did. But in making herself a centre of controversy, in stating a particular and startling view of Kashmir question or political organisation, she made it possible for her supporters as well as for her opponents to forget, or to take for granted the very considerable Prime Minister that she was. There is a saying : "Anyone can live without rules;" it would be nearer to say that no one can live without them.

Mrs. Gandhi had studied Pakistan well. After the death of Jinnah, Pakistani rulers were engaged in manufacturing a religion of Islamic extremism, not in devising a political programme. They supposed that the past was all much of a muchness, and they deduced laws from wildly distant periods with any suggestion that time changes all things. The result is : there are many conflicting and incompatible schools of Islamic education, while psychiatric body is rent by fierce intestine feuds on matters of theory and practice. There is no psychological medicine against Islamic extremism today. Bertrand Russell, in 'Nightmares of Eminent Persons', says : "Every dominant passion generates a dominant fear, the fear of its non-fulfilment. Every dominant fear generates a nightmares, sometimes in the form of an explicit and conscious fanaticism, sometimes in a paralysing timidity, sometimes in an unconscious or sub-conscious terror which finds expression only in dreams." Pakistan suffers from this disease of dominant passion generating a dominant fear of Kashmir ... an integral part of India. Does Pakistan know 'dreams go by opposites.?'

After Jinnah, Pakistani rulers today are dastardly daredevil and recklessly wicked, dreaming a dream of Islamic globalisation. Stricken with fear of pharisaical self-righteousness, flummoxed by winds and tides of religious dualism, laden with free flow of U.S. dollar diplomacy, and burdened with self-cooked up religious fanaticism, Pakistan is in danger of thinking too much about her sense of humour on Kashmir issue. This humour has always been with them since Jinnah's death. This is the reality show of Pakistan laughter.

Those who plead for deletion of the name of Sind from the national anthem suffer from a hypnotic inertia of mental depression. They do not appear to be aware that Sind is very much in the life, language and literature of India even if it is not geographically its part today. Since Sindhis and their culture ... which forms a significant cross-section of the composite Indian culture ... are subsisting and pulsating with life in this country, it would be against the emotional integration of the people of our country to omit the name of Sind from the national anthem. Those who plead for it will only inspire the Pakistan-sponsored terrorist groups. An importunate persistence.

After Jinnah Pakistan is a political slave to Western powers. He, who has no opinion of his own, but depends upon the opinion and taste of others, is a slave. Communists believe in slave culture. The true history of Kashmir issue has been distorted to please the common people of Pakistan and Kashmiri Muslims.

From time to time, Pakistani rulers have been accused of 'conditionalism' on Kashmir issue. Pakistan's own analogy is made with verbal barrages. Because the rulers are at their wit's end, they don't know how to repair the rupture. Othello-like, they are perplexed in the extreme. They have the mighty sword of religious fanaticism. After Jinnah, they are defiant in defeat, but magnanimous in hypocrisy on Kashmir issue. The political storm has already bypassed the ideals of Islam. Wider cultural exchanges are no substitute for a political settlement. Cultural exchange is all high-falutin talk. It does not explain our quarrels with Pakistan. In a genuine friendship one should know how to listen to the other. A fain smile appears on Pakistan's lips.

Freud himself has told us how the love of ideals in an individual is always self-love or narcissism, or portion of the libido going to ourselves not as we are but as we would like to be. We all know that dreams have a meaning, that early childhood is decisive in forming a man's character. From the very cradle song of partition, Pakistan has suffered from reminiscences, that even fictitious situations often influence them profoundly, that the myths of Islamic extremism express and conceal the sufferings of mankind and that men are both more immoral and more moral than they imagine. The growth of Islamic civilisation can only be achieved by a repression of the aggressive impulses. Whenever the militants try to control their aggression, it will turn against the self.

After Jinnah, what we see today in Kashmir is commercialising politics. It is no longer a struggle for power but a scramble for power. What nationalism does preclude is the practice of religion as a political creed. For that there is another name : communalism. Secular India has no place for such bigotry; nor irionically enough for Sheikh Abdullah and his co. had religion in its broadest sense. Because Sheikh Abdullah's long-suppressed communalism was erupting in a manner which was rapidly descending from the merely vicious to the ridiculous. His speech on Jan. 31, 1958 at the Hazaratbal mosque in Srinagar was an example of monumental absurdity. It only instigated the liberation movement of Kashmiri Muslims. A delusion-related complex.

After partition, communalism and communist culture are twin brothers on the question of Kashmir issue with the utmost scepticism. You are free to light your lamps but you shall keep them behind barred doors and black curtains, lest their lurid light should enlighten and cheer an innocent public. Such apparently is the curious creed of communist culture ... full of pretensions. A crassitude of slave-making ant. A communist is a licensed terrorist.

Kashmir ... the Playground of Asia ... has become a major problem. The material for such a history is vast and varied. Ruins and architectural monuments of the ancient and mediaeval periods, literary works in Sanskrit, Persian and Urdu, accounts of foreign travellers, ethnographical and linguistic data still await proper investigation at the hands of experts. A vast amount of travel and political literature has grown round the problem since the British connection with the province. A general description of the beautiful country and of the wretched condition of its people may be followed by a detailed political narrative of the Hindu dynasties, of the Muslim Sultanates, and of the Mughal, Pathan and Sikh rulers in succession.

It is known very well that a narrative of war and diplomacy of political winds and tides of hypocrisy, and even court intrigue do not make for the history of a people, which in the right sense, must describe how the people organised their communal strife, how their genius expressed itself in their social institutions, literature, art, architecture, music etc.

The Muslim Sultanates of Kashmir were tyrants immersed in their own pleasureness. The benign rule of the Mughals from 1586 A.D. to 1750 A.D. proved beneficial to the people, while the Pathan rule that followed was a nightmare to the people and brought the country to a level of degradation from which it has not yet recovered. The Sikh rule that followed was little better. The Dogra rulers created a new problem by introducing the Rajput element in the army and administration.

In the earlier period (500-1000 A.D.), Kashmir made remarkable progress in philosophy, religion, astronomy, medicine and literature.

Khan Abdul Gaffar Khan, known as Frontier Gandhi, said in Sept 8, 1956 : "I told Jinnah that Hindus had left property valued at crores of rupees which the Muslim Leaguers had looted. This property belonged to Pakistan, but the

Leaguers would not surrender a single penny to the State. I invited Jinnah to show me a single important leader who was not involved in this issue could have been settled long ago."

Now the question arises : Was Mr. Jinnah a share-holder of that looted away property left by Hindus? Is not Nawaj Shariff, former Prime Minister of Pakistan, a co-partner of that looted-away property? Maybe the Muslim Leaguers have wallowed in that property stolen away.

In United India, all the Maharattas and the Pathans were regarded by the British as two important and dangerous martial forces and to weaken them the British had divided them into parts. In India, all the Maharattas have now been united. There is no reason why Pakistan claiming to be an Islamic Republic should not be prepared to see Pathans in one province. Why? Because doubt is the vestibule which all must pass before they can enter the mosque of wisdom.

In this garrulous age, words pile upon words. Our much vaunted-Islamic civilisation continues to build on the verbiage. And Pakistan will lose herself in a maze of words in the valley of Kashmir.

An incorrigible garrulity is the main exercise of our parliamentarians. Our parliament cries for speech, and yet more speech. And the Kashmir issue has arrived at the age of conference, debate and negotiation. Silence has been banished from the valley as well as from the parliament. One lesson of history is that delay does not conquer ... it only accumulates troubles and gives a longer rope to trouble-makers. Fabianism is the refuge of the faint-hearted ; as a political doctrine it has proved a snare and delusion.

Khan Abdul Gaffar Khan did not believe that Muslim leaders were sincere when they claimed that they demanded the formation of Pakistan in the territory of the Muslim masses. Why? Because the Muslim League leaders had never served the people nor made any sacrifice for Islam or for the common people. Another reason is that the Muslim League leaders wanted Pakistan for their ownselves and had succeeded in their objective.

Dealing in detail with the bloodshed and misery that was inflicted on innocent humanity in the wake of partition of the sub-continent, the Red Shirt leader, Khan Abdul Gaffar Khan, disclosed that after partition was established, Sir George Cunningham, the then Governor of the NWFP, sent word to him and suggested that Khudai Khidmatgars should join hands with the Muslim League in forming a coalition Govt. in the province.

He believed that the Muslim League wanted power for the sake of ruling the people. Geogre's attempt failed.

Our leaders are castigated for their weakness of leadership on Kashmir issue. A serious survey has not been undertaken to examine the changing attitudes and cultural assimilation of Kashmiri refugees. So it brings to light the disquieting feature that many refugee families are disintegrating under the strains and stresses of Pakistan-sponsored infiltrators. Two unfortunate effects of this increasing disintegration are specially notable. Social vice is mounting as women in Kashmir find life more and more difficult to sustain on virtue; and children, forced to become bread-earners at a tender age, ill-treat their parents. These factors are fatal to family life, and can bring disaster to the community if they are not controlled and remedied before the position worsens much farther.

What the animals and birds think of us humans, and how they would describe us, if they could. Their remarks echo the sentiment of Victor Hugo, who was fond of saying that the more he saw of human beings, the more he loved dogs. Inspite of our civilisation and culture, men are in many ways wilder and more dangerous than any of the so-called wild animals. Bernard Shaw thought similarly. The alleged courage of the lion-tamer, he once said, had never impressed him, for when he was with the lion in its cage, he was at least safe from other men.

If there is levity in these remarks of Hugo and Shaw, there is also an essential core of the truth; and indeed, human beings are less than consistent when, in moments of anger or bitterness, they liken one another to animals in a manner which is intended to reflect credit neither on themseleves nor on animals. For singly, we are accustomed to attribute some of the highest virtues to our feathered or four-footed friends. What man could be better than the one who combined in himself the courage of the lion, the wisdom of the owl, the strength of the bull, the loyalty of the dog, the diligence of the ant, and the memory of the elephants?

What would not our ambitious politicians give to acquire the cunning of the fox? How utterly hopeless is the future of a politician unblessed with the thick skin of the rhino? What musician does not dream of singing like the nightingale? Where would a bureaucrat be without his gift for burying, like the ostrich, his head in the sands of the valley?

But we are content to ignore these virtues of the birds and the animals, and continue to deride them when we might with advantage be following their example in one field or the other. That is bad enough; but how much worse it is that, even when we do follow the example of an animal, we first take care to make sure that the example is a bad one? We emulate the pig for its greed, the mule for its obstinacy, the rabbit for its fecundity and the snake in the grass for its treachery. We take no account, on the otherhand, of the horse-sense of the steed who knows better than to bet on the human race. When we decide to drink like a fish, we foolishly overlook the fact what the fish drinks is water. The human being will never change his blind-spots.

Man is an animal that makes bargains; no other animal does this ... one dog does not change a bone with another. Terrorists are religiously passionate. Why? The passionate are like men standing on their heads; they see all things the wrong way. Pakistan's approach on Kashmir solution is not endearing. The colonial system in religiously-torn Pakistan is necessarily autocratic. Why? Because it is Govt. without the democratic consent of the governed.

A long-standing honeymoon of Pakistan-sponsored Islamic terrorism has snowballed the Kashmir issue to the wilderness of frustration, peace and negotiations. This unhappy outcome is a successful case of surrogacy. The agreement for surrogacy, betwen Islamabad and Jehadi militants, is made on a secret resolution signed by the surrogate father 'Islamic fanaticism', attending ISI, the Army and mother leaders of religious gansterism. Why? Because Pakistan's identity would be protected on Kashmir issue. A morbid tale of perfect Roman Holiday in Kashmir. This agreement for surrogacy is in games that many Jehadis and militant crusaders play havoc and discover their paradise of Islamic extemism in and around Kashmir.

Pakistan, with her Joan of Arc complex and Napoleonic notions of the greatness of Pakistan, has only made Kashmir issue worse and worse. Paksitan-sponsored Islamic terrorism in Kashmir and in other cities of India is nourished with a feeding-bottle of militant extremists like a vassal's fidelity to his feudal lord. And the politically-perverted rulers eulogise the anti-Islamic songs of militant jehadis.

The bane of civilisation is the power of catch-phrases. Kashmir issue is the business of teaching militants to learn the technique of research on terrorism and thinking which is so essential a part of the present Islamic culture of anti-India hate slogans over which they stand guard. These symptoms of socio-religious anaemia goes undetected for years. An excessive production of religious haemoglobin and unhealthy red blood cells of anti-India slogans make a sick nation sicker.

Disturbed by intimidations, plagued by doubt, confused by narrow-doctrinal religious dogmas, consciousness is split. Without the sense of sin and guilt, without the fear of death and terror of the pit, can they assuage their crassitude? These bogies hardly bother them. The terrible fact about Pakistan today is the country's inexhaustible unhappiness, its religious deformity and political ill-health, its enthusiastic but unbrageous character, its unbounded but ever-frustrated ambition, its inevitably disappointed ideals, its passionate hate of provincial towns of Baluchistan and Pakhoonistan, its estrangement from its austere but very well-meaning parents, with a moment's respite, are combined to make Pakistan's anti-India hymns of hate worse and worse on Kashmir issue. Everything falls short of its ardent imagination : there lies its tragedy. The dictator pursues his aims with a concentration which would have been admirable, had it not been inhuman. Pakistan loathes war and declares her a pacifist; that she sees the world as a theophany; that she reveals statements about conscience ; she loves argument and seems anxious to remould every Islamic institution in India; that she has reform in the blood, and like many reformers seems to lack the god-given facility to laugh heartily and happily at herself. Thus Pakistan interrupts the episode of Kashmir issue with interludes and explanations which suspend the character of Pakistan.

Kashmir is beauty, it is poetry, it is a great orchestra. The game of questions and answers on it is just a game. Pakistan answers but answers playfully.

Pakistan's seriousness on Kashmir issue is part of her ignorance; her seriousness is a shadow of her ego. Exceptional talker has become a museum piece. And yet it is from good talk that good judgements get much of their virtue. Jammu and Kashmir is a sensitive State. Let us keep in mind that the Kashmiris want effective governance to be put in place effectively against the agenda of the separatists in a blood-soaked valley. Democracy in Kashmir sometimes entails agonising twists and turns. Political brinkmanship is also an accepted part of this gamesmanship, as are ego clashes and expressions of personal ambition. The taste of democracy's victory in Kashmir turns sour, with negative consequences. Gender injustice is perpetrated in the garb of Islamic tradition and culture.

Kashmir dwells in an age of disillusionment. Because the terrorists hijack Islam by misquoting the Koran.

A.Q. Khan, the notorious self-confused nuclear-proliferator, is a nuclear spy who was able to obtain the centrifugal technology and the list of contractors from Dutch facilities and transfer them to Pakistan.

At present Pakistan's work is the material of Hitlerism rather than Mussolini. It might be a fine portrait of Pakistan today ... that dirty, proud, disfigured beauty, with her ancient lineage of violence and terrorism, her passion for Islam and anti-India hate slogans, her irritating mannerisms, and her obstinate individuality, so precious to a Pakistani growing year by more uniform.

To combat this morbid inconsistency of Pakistan on Kashmir issue, Mrs. Indira Gandhi never failed to arouse emotions varying from animosity to veneration, and perhaps the reason is that her own reactions on Kashmiris were always suffused with emotion. She was the woman of feeling and distrusted the expression of Pakistan's feeling on Kashmir liberation movement, the woman of moods to be impatient of moodiness of others, the woman of strong and positive principles and was herself such a mass of contradictions that she was profoundly charitable to the weaknesses and feelings of Kashmiri Hindu pundits.

Mrs. Gandhi gained for herself, partly by her natural gifts and partly by her hard work, a commanding place in the hearts and minds of her contemporaries and of posterity. She found every Pakistani ruler a talkative man, but like many other talkative rulers, she was very reticent. But Pakistan, at heart, is a romantic, a fanatical champion of the irrational instinct and essentially of Jehadi instinct. And yet their unreal personages sometimes say real things ... so real that we can accept the blatant circus tricks of Pakistan on Kashmir.

Religion in Pakistan! In Pakistan, a religion divorced from spirituality, is shackled by imposed rules of Islamic terrorism and instead of developing religious awareness, frustrates it. Can an Islamic structure in Pakistan build on worship without morality be able to afford proper protection to the people? Will Pakistan tumble in the absence of morality? Will Islam be safe on this earth? Morality is assessed by personal purity, not by oppression, arrogance and frenzy in the behaviour of a religion-based nation like Pakistan. Shall we call Pakistan an Islamic nation where the spirit of religion does not reflect?

Is the connection between Abdul Qadeer Khan, a nuclear spy, and the CIA a mystery? Is not Khan a nuclear black marketeer in Pakistan? Could it provide a civilian govt. or a military ruler with leverage, strengthening its smuggling ring when it comes to Rawalpindi?

Does Pakistan know the human mind is like a double-edged sword where its potentialities, if mishandled, can cause so much of havoc in the form of diseases? People who look through keyholes are apt to get the idea that most things ae keyhole shaped. Scriptures are full of answers.

What matters is, therefore, not merely that the disease should be got rid of, but that it should also be understood in relation to the patient : for all disease has a meaning. Hush! Hush! Pakistan is lying in bed of acute religious allergy to her grumbling.

Some of our Hitler-like political leaders are buffoon, drunkard, debauchee, their temper uncontrollable, their cruelty leading them to Nero-esque enormities, and also tireless workers, men of Spartan habits, generous to their enemies, quick to recognise ... such are they, virtue and vice being constant bedfellows in that tangle of complexities. Two traits only seem absent in them: idleness and boredom.

8

Kashmir After Jinnah-III : Hither and Thither

In a world of wickedness and sin, plague and grief, joy and sorrow, corruption and roguery as well as guilt and criminality in every form, political tricksters and jehadis come across everywhere in Kashmir.

The facile tendency of Congressmen after Jinnah on Kashmir issue was 'yes men'. Even after sixty years of independence, they have not yet developed the habit of serious thinking. Opinion is like a pendulum and obeys the same law. If it goes past the centre of gravity on one side, it must go alike and finds the true point at which it can remain at rest.

The Kashmir problem is a simple one. The question is whether India can afford to allow a part of its territory to be occupied by someone else. It is a challenge to India's unity. *Those who have now occupied a part of Kashmir and called it 'Azad Kashmir' .... though there was no 'Azad' whatsoever .... have no business to be there.* They had come to plunder and loot Kashmir. Pakistan is now flexing its religious muscles.

Fanatic Mullahs, after Jinnah, in a spirit of abounding love for all Islam, warn the incorrigible western powers that unless they abandon their 'aggression', Islamic terrorism will combine their forces to crush imperialism and establish world all over. It is a timely threat and a brave promise which will hearten fanatics and disconcert Islamabad ... the Devil's disciples of Islamic terrorism. Cursed are the trouble-shooters of Babeldom for they shall inherit the devildom of anarchy. After Jinnah, Pakistan was reborn with a loud bang, whose echoes reverberate down the corridors of Time. Islamabad, on Kashmir issue, with a constant rattling of ISI and periodic rumblings of Jehadis demands peace of their pattern. Did not Cicero declaim long ago that the most unjust peace is better than the justest war?

The situation in Kashmir is, no doubt, complicated; but it teaches a lesson .... that military alliances create far more problems than they can ever solve; They may help in crushing one head of a terrorist group; but ten other heads sprout.

The words 'Hindu-Muslim Unity' have a strange, old-fashioned ring about them these days, but who possesses unpartitioned memories will have little difficulty in recalling the days when Sardar Abdur Rab Nishtar was a staunch supporter of the fashionable drive for inter-communal rapproachment. Once a prominent member of the Khilafat Movement and a staunch Red Shirt, he was arrested during the Congress Civil Disobedience Movement in 1930 and sentenced to nine month's rigorous imprisonment.

But human beings undergo strange metamorphoses when their ambitions are thwarted. Nishtar took shelter under Jinnah's wing, became one of his trusted followers and a pillar of the Muslim League. With a meandering change of Karachi politics, he completed his transformation and became President of the Muslim League by 1956, and started out fulminating publicly against India as 'Pakistan's one enemy'.

So, the anti-India slogans, as virulent as vitriolic, were born and brought up in Pakistan in the cradle of 'Hindu-Muslim disunity' under the careful supervision of Jinnah's Muslim League. When a child is a year old, it has no memory. Even after sixty years of independence, Pakistan is still in a short of memory. But like all spurious additions and subtractions, Pakistan hardly even succeeds in Kashmir question. And there is still a fighting chance for honourable cheating with our Indian Muslims. Sanity, objectivity and good sense have suffered a reverse with Jinnah's death. Several futile attempts were made and nothing clicked. Irrationality-held truths may be more harmful than reasoned errors. Pakistan's political wizardry and religious witchcraft come and change like a pendulum.

After Jinnah, institutionalised religion has driven out religion as spirituality. Today their leaders constitute fanaticism the most attractive face of Islam. They do so because of genealogy, not religiousness. Pakistan is disturbed not by politics but by ingrained religious fanaticism. Fools and bairns should never see half-done work.

We are amused by 'Gulliver's Travels' and disconcerted by its savage indictment of the follies and conceits of mankind. We know that 'Hamlet' is more than the story of a neurotic young man; that is also a drama of human existence. As we read 'The Magic Mountain', we see that the sanatorium is not merely the place for those who suffer from tuberculosis. As we read Pakistan's history after partition, we see that the sanatorium is a deserving place for Islamic rulers of Pakistan. Why? Because life itself in Pakistan is a never-ending trial.

Pakistan has already lost her nerves on Kashmir issue and cried : "For God's sake call the militants and open it. I have too many enemies." What an enemy .... Pakistan has got shuddered, remembering what Oscar Wilde once said : "*A man can't be too careful in the choice of his enemies.*"

It is the price of Islamic terrorism that these poor, helpless creatures called Ministers are being made to pay these days. Despite the mighty paraphernalia that surrenders them they seem, in the final analysis, as helpless as the ruled. As Colton has put it, "The worst thing can be said of the most powerful is that they can take your life; but the same thing can be said of the most weak."

The poet Coleridge exclaimed : "O God, how glorious it is to live! "But the thinker Renan asked : "O God, when will it be worthwhile to live?" In nature, we echo the poet; in politics the thinker.

Not to be austere in politics, Pakistan leads a disquiet life with ISI and militarism.

Furthermore, the Christians have been as jealous of Arabism as the Muslims; in fact, among the founders of modern Arab nationalism there are many Maronites, some of whom gladly went to the Turkish Scaffold before the First World War for espousing the Arab cause. In the early days of the struggle, Beirut, with its Christian majority, was the centre of Arab intellectual and cultural activities. The several Christian colleges and institutions founded to spread the Western way of life became instead hotbeds of Arab revivalism and cultural renaissance. Two of the internationally best Arab thinkers, Khalil Gibran and Ilia Abu-Madi, who have influenced a whole new generation in the Arab world, are both not only Lebanese but also Christians. Why not Pakistan?

The dispute between India and Pakistan is a long-standing issue. It started on the 22nd of October, 1947, when Pakistan invaded Kashmir. Kashmir had not then acceded to India but within three days it did and although, quite correctly, Mr. Nehru had refused the request of the late Maharaja Hari Singh to provide arm assistance to him until he had constitutionally acceded to India, on accession our army marched in and turned the tide of battle. Now it was a Himalayan blunder for Mr. Nehru to lodge a complaint of aggression, at the United Nations, committed by Pakistan in our territory of Kashmir. And it was Pakistan that continued to deny that its army was in any way involved in the fighting in Kashmir until the United Nation's Commission found to the contrary stating that with their discovery 'the situation had changed'.

Now the question is : What is dispute? According to Aristotle, "How many disputes could have been deflated into a single paragraph if the disputants had dared to define their terms." So the affirmative pursuit of one's conviction about the ultimate mystery of the Kashmir dispute is placed beyond the reach. Why? *Pakistan has raised the question of Kashmir issue with certainties : and she will end in doubts. Whereas India is content to begin with doubts; and she will end in certainties*. 'Kashmir is an integral part of India' is an incentive to truth and patient inquiry leads the way. Pakistan's geriatric slogan on Kashmir is the only one that should have the privillege of lying, either at home or abroad. Pakistan may be allowed to lie to befool the countrymen for their own political interests to capture power, either by military coup or by Machiavellian policy after rigging away the ballot boxes.

The hatred in which Pakistan was born still haunts her and constitutes the spring-board of her bitterly inhibited psychology against India. Paksitan is a State without any history or tradition to sustain her religion, the king-pin of present-day Pakistan can sustain and stabilise aspirations to a certain extent only, and not beyond that. At present, Pakistan is run by two powerful pillars .... Mullahism of Pakistan's Islamic priesthood and dollar dipilomacy of Washington so as to suppress India over the Kashmir problem. Acts of terrorism have resemblance to the prescription of Islamic Jehad. They are purely and simply acts of war. They have the value of military demonstrations, and serve the mark the separation of classes. Everything is predestined and preoccupied with narrow-doctrinal framework of terrorism and anti-India hymns of hate and suspicion. Indoctrinated by the old bogey of India's super-power mission, the military dictators of Pakistan springing up with hypochondriac disease are used to getting about China how to hammer out India on the borders.

Pakistan has not been shied off what a mischievous deed she has mistakenly intended all over the world after the beaten track of terrorism. To write a love letter we must begin without knowing what we intend to say, and without knowing what we have written. Terrorism is a love letter of Islamic globalisation to all Muslims to get united. Children of Muslim countries who have grown up in the Space Age understand things, out of their continuous experience, that adults have to learn. They are standing on the earth looking at the moon, whereas fanatical crusaders are standing on the moon looking at the earth. As they are growing up, one gets farther and farther away from them. If we are to have beauty and poetry, we must be intolerant of vulgarity and religious fanaticism. If we are to have learning, we must be intolerant of ignorance. If we are to have excellence in anything, we must be intolerant of non-excellence. But Pakistan has not yet learnt of anything else. A doctor of anti-terrorism germs has got to examine her chest.

Political gummings and bickerings, across the provinces of Pakistan, have brought out political cant and gyroscopic hypocrisy in the name of mock democracy. It is considered to be a parliament of political vultures of Islamic Jehadis hovering over the Kashmir problem to make it more and more a sissipian task to control. India, together with other western countries, has got to foil away the world's master king-pin of terrorism with a cracking combination of ingenuity and technology. Because it is a fact which Pakistan has sought to realise by forging a myth to which all her anti-India designs and aspirations are skillfully hitched.

The myth is forged and fostered round a supposed sense of danger coming from 'neo-colonial India'. Pakistan's highly perfected propaganda machinery as communists by dubious means and ways has painted India as a Frankenstein, casting ominously covetous eyes on Pakistan.

Tomorrow about Kashmir! We don't know a thing about those tomorrows which we vainly try to insure ourselves. Tomorrow is the carrot, Man is the donkey. In time's calender, tomorrow is the Cinderella, 'yesterday' the favoured one. 'Yesterday' receives the homage, the poetry, the tears, idle tears. Tomorrow is the enemy. Yesterday was the Sunlit, tomorrow is the rainy day.

Never before in human history has 'tomorrow' been such a spectre as it is today. The prospect of being blown to bits is not a pleasant one. Yesterday wept when it saw the relics of Hiroshima many years after the event. Yet Hiroshima may have been a picture compared to the next bomb, that someone sometime is bound to drop somewhere, unless deterred by circumstances or the collective conscience of the world.

From Plato to Bertrand Russell, man has always dreamt of a nobler destiny. These dreams are symbolised by tomorrow.

The greatest impression amongst the people of India is that India has deliberately precipitated the crises to divert the attention from the ever-growing problems arisen inside the country and to combat the separatist trends after conjuring up the alarming threat of external aggression. Another aim, it is suspected, is to secure larger arms either from USA, or Russia or Israel by persuading them that Pakistan's friendship with China will tend to encourage further aggression against India. It is Pakistan that has gambled away .... covertly or overtly by the ISI .... the border areas. Pakistan's aggression and concentration of troops all along the Indo-Pak border draws attention to the problems connected with our border extending to 650 miles with Pakistan in Rajasthan.

The border which runs through the districts of Jaisalmer, Barma, Ganguaga and Bikaner is well-demarcated. The problems of defence here are almost similar to those encountered in Ladakh, and NEFA. Although they differ in character, the complexities of the problems are no less acute. The inaccessibility due to vast expanse of desert, lack of drinking water and poor means of communications and transport poses serious difficulty.

Strange to say, during the 1954-55 and 1960 over the anti-Bengali drive, some of the Pakistani-sponsored ex-leaguers took a very significant part. Such a garden variety of fifth columnists-cum-gangbusters has dovetailed the evil-hands of the then President Ayub Khan. Gaining an advantage over this politically-manoeuvred scorching gamesmanship, these insiduous infiltrators with Pakistan had managed to create border trouble without provocation. When the Nehru Govt. was preoccupied with defence and multifarious troubles and trepedations, these overnight patriots could not control their irretrievable passion to create another disruption in the country and to embarrass the Govt. Their bid was well-tuned from their point of view. Now the question is : Who was responsible for the disruption in Assam? The answer is : the then Congress rulers in the State and the Centre. Whereas the Congress rulers played up with silly games of miscalculated political blunders, in Assam. Assam has had now an indissoluble political bickerings and social gummings all over the State. Mr. Nehru as good as peppered our foreign policy with secularism! Assam has now been in a never-ending quagmire of political bankruptcy. Most of the shadows of this life are caused by our standing in our own sunshine. On Kashmir problems, Mr. Nehru had failed to measure up the shadows of our foreign policy in the sunshine of his diplomatic achievement, inside and outside the country. How you start is important, but it is how you finish that counts. In the race for success, speed is less important than stamina. The sticker outlasts the sprinter. Cronyism, to the Nehru Govt., was the first track decision. The predecessors of our present Congress leaders were responsible through and through for the making of Kashmir problem. Some people run away from grief, go on world cruises or move to another town. The memories, unbidden, spring into their minds, scattered over the years. But they do not escape. There is something to be said for facing them deliberately and straightway. Pakistan, like a weaver of tales, shuttles words back and forth across the loom of its imagination, while making an entente on Kashmir problem. China's words, on the political geometry of Kashmir problem, come out slowly and carefully, like railway carriages easing around a bad curve in the tracks.

In connection with the eviction and deportation of Pakistani Muslims from Assam .... there were some well-known Muslim leaguers of Pre-independence Days who had made a bid to merge a part of the Goalpara district with Pakistan. After 1950 trouble, these leaguers managed to infiltrate a large number of Pakistani Muslims through the loopholes of Nehru-Liaquat Ali pact and mobilised these illegal infiltrators on the border .... specially in the 'Char' areas as also in the stronghold pockets to achieve their ulterior motives.

Thereafter, with difference at different times and circumstances, they became patriots overnight by changing their political colour following the footsteps of the then Congress leaders who were basically corrupted, invidious and nefarious in the crucible of brain-twisting political riddle. So, it was very much easier to them to gain seats in the State Legislature and in the Parliament. Later they advised their followers to accept membership and Assamese as mother tongue.

These overnight patriots worked to a schedule and hatched a conspiratorial political gangland around Assam. Our leaders failed to have a smell of well-organised conspiracy like a black Muslim in America. The reported threat of resignation en bloc by the overnight Congress Muslims from Assam Legislature added to the communal frenzy but strengthened the hands of the Pak-rulers in their 'Late-India' campaign. It was on the issue of deportation of Pak-nationals. It is evident that this threatened resignation was something very much deep-rooted and bespoke a sinister move like a black widow with an unhappy augury.

So, many problems, labouring under unmanageable difficulties, confronting the country today, either by terrorist outfits or by the well-calculated communal riots in the scorching cauldron of another riot, are the legacy and lapses of the past Congress rulers in the States as well as at the Centre. Who is to blame for such a bizarre situation smouldering away in a colossal crucible of bloodshed and violence meshed up with a cesspool of crude political mongerism? The words men fight and die for are the coins of politics. In a country like India, good words are a mask for concealment of bad deeds. On Kashmir problem, Pakistan has learnt well how to and where to utter good words. The fidelity of the Muslims in Assam to Pakistan's charlatanism is unquestionable in practice.

Head-hunting diplomacy of Pakistan! Pakistan has always employed terrorist groups, of the age group from 12 to 50, for head-hunting in Kashmir. Before the partition of India, every jehadist producing a chopped off head received from the Govt. of Islamic Republic of Pakistan the magnificant reward of Rs 25 only. The victim need not a Hindu or Sikh. Why?

Because Pakistan wanted to constitute an overwhelming majority of the population of Kashmir. It claimed to be their liberator from political bondage. Believers in terrorist activities mean that no discordant voice jars upon the harmony of belief in Islamic globalisation. Jehadism marries old opinions to new facts of terrorism.

Head-hungting might be a pleasant sport for a particular species of humanity but the latest place of the Pakistani crusade in Kashmir is inspired by a mere love of sport. If it is a madness, there is a method behind it. If it is a horrible intrusion of barbarism into civilization, it is inspired by a well-calculated political purpose. That purpose is to engineer a potential anti-India front in Kashmir with a view to making the Kashmir valley a catalyst of lively issue in international politics. Sheikh Abdullah's crusades in foreign lands had won few converts to the Pakistani plea for 'liberation' of Kashmir. The Sheikh's detention had left Kashmir indifferent and quiet. The Pakistani cause was irretrievably lost. But the Ayub Khan's regime after partition knew no defeat. He sought to resume the sinking boat.

In every theatre of political romanticism, Pakistan is diligently pursuing the same policy of provocation and aggression with same end in view. i.e. to drag India into the Serbonian bog of international diplomacy.

On the question of boundary, the official Gazette of Sind, published in 1907 by the then British Govt. has defined the boundaries as follows :

"Bounded on the east by the native states of Marwar, Jaisalmer and Bhawalpur, on the north by a small corner of the Punjab and by the level and sandy portion of the territories of the Khan of Kalat known as Kachhi, on the west by the mountainous part of the same territories, the boundary line running along the ridge of the Khirihari Range and the Habb river and on the south by the Arabian sea and the Rann of Kutch."

In 1910, the British Commissioner of Sind states as follows : "There is a mass of evidence that since 1837 the boundary between Sind and Kutch has been recognised and shown on all maps which have been prepared from that date to the present day to be a straight line due south from the trijunction of the Badia Taluka of Hyderabad district, Jatitaluka of Karachi district and the Rann of Kutch."

Under the Indian Independence Act, which the British Parliament passed in 1947, Sind became part of Pakistan, as a result of accession, as provided for by the British Act of Parliament.

Pakistan has described the Rann of Kutch as a landlocked sea or inland lake. This is incorrect. As early as 1906, the then British Govt of India decided that it was more correct to define the Rann of Kutch as a marsh rather than as a lake.

So the Rann of Kutch wholly belongs to India. Now the question of boundary has ever been aggravated, covertly or overtly, by one of our neighbouring countries, China. A clue to the aggressive character of China's policy was provided by President Ayub Khan. China's relations, he said, with many countries were strained. Why? Because China wanted a place in the sun, commensurate with her size and strength and was being denied it. It might be admitted that communist China's exclusion from the United Nations was a denial of her political importance in the States system of the world. India, under the leadership of Mr. Nehru, had consistently supported her claim for admission. Nehru's Himalayan blunder supporting China's inclusion into United Nations has buffeted out India's old-cherished claim over Kashmir. China, in return, knows it well how to make India dwarfed in this sub-continent. One man's folly is poison to another one to swallow up. China knows when to wind the watch in time. China is a past master in the art of artifices and of being an arrant knave. Whereas Pakistan is a past master in the art of making a fuss over a trifling matter. And India is a past master for whiling away the time for shilly-shallying as the opportunity comes in. Our country is in the know of her shilly-shallying character on any important question.

China's bid for 'a place in the sun' reminds us of a similar cry in Germany in the years preceding the two world wars.

Washington maintained discreet silence when Pakistani troops tried to cut off Srinagat-Leh road with the obvious motive of mobilizing the defence of Ladakh against China but American protests became loud enough to be published in the press when India took counter-measures in Kargil. It is a good example on the part of U.S. Govt. about its generously brazen-faced patronage of Pakistan. America is a consummate opportunist of the deepest dye. And Pakistan is a tub-thumper.

Pakistan was created on the sole understanding that once Mr. Jinnah's demand for the establishment of a State on the basis of religion, had been conceded. India would be let alone to develop along secular liberal line. This hope was dashed to the ground on the day the tribals from the north-western province assisted and led by Pakistan's army regulars, invaded 'peaceful Kashmir'. Why did they do so? Because the forces that created Pakistan were not satisfied with only what they had got; this extra-territorial and crude political ambition in a disquiet and harrowing ambience has not abated after the creation of Pakistan. Kashmir may, in Mr. Bhutto's language, be 'the bigger issue' ; but behind all these bigger and smaller issues, Kashmir might be the biggest issue to the sectarian and ambitious-minded forces pitching up many terrorist camps along the border.

After the basic elections, Mr. Ayub Khan had not established his entente with China with reinforced clan but had also established and intensified his hushed-up designs against India with renewed enthusiasm. The successors of Mr. Ayub Khan had followed the same track of evasively outmanoeuvred Machiavellian trickery over the Kashmir valley. What were the results of Mr. Ayub Khan's shrewd diplomacy? The results are :

1. The signing of so-called boundary agreement with China at Rawalpindi that can best be described as a huge fraud posing a stupendous threat to India's security and
2. The naked aggression committed over India in successive way has flagrantly violated.

Truly speaking, India's foreign policy has not ever been dynamic in comparison to international diplomacy.

Limitless is human folly in politics. When T.S. Eliot was asked about the future of our civilisation, he said, "Internecine fighting .... people killing one another in the streets." Civilization seemed to him a crumbling edifice destined to fall to pieces and perish in the flames of war. This despair of life cannot be the end of things.

India had no foreign policy of her own. Indeed for centuries, India had led no independent foreign policy. During the British period, India's international relations were rigidly controlled from Whitehall. British relations with peripherial states such as Afghanistan, Nepal and Tibet were conducted through the Foreign and Political Department of the Govt. of India, but every communication from the Govt. of India to Dalai Lama or to the Govt of Afghanistan or to Nepal or even to the Khan of Kalat, had to be approved, to the last comma, by the India office in London. Towards the end of British rule, India began to enjoy a certain amount of autonomy in internal matters, but in the international field she had no voice of her own.

What is foreign office? A foreign office is essentially a custodian of precedents. Independent India has no precedents to fall back upon. She had, therefore, to devise foreign policy ab initio. In a way, this was a mileage, for India started on her international journey without any inherited animosities or even prejudices. Truly, she could say that she had no enemies. Pakistan, it is true, was born out of the artificially inflated enmity between a matrix of politically mixed Muslims and Hindus, but once Pakistan conceded it was their hope that both States would settle down.

Nehru's foreign policies? Nehru's policy of non-alignments! How ironical those words sound today? No one can say that India has no enemies. Is this the net results of Nehru's highly sounded vaunted policy of non-alignments? Was his policy insufficiently realistic? In most civilised countries, there have, broadly speaking, been two main schools of political science, namely, a realistic school and an idealistic school. In China, there was the school of Mo Tzu who believed in universal love, side by side with the school of Yang Chu who believed in brute force. It is said to think that the present rulers of China have taken the road of Yang Chu, spurning the teachings of Mo Tzu, Mencius, and Confucious. In India, too, there was the realistic school, represented by Ashoka, whose edicts exhorting man to follow the way of non-violence and righteousness from the most enduring peace manifestoes ever issued in the world. Nehru, though, oriented to the West, grew up politically under the shadow of Mahatma Gandhi and was drawn to the ideals of Ashoka who, in turn, derived them from Gautama Buddha. Hence his insistence that wrong means will not justify right ends and his faith that right action will produce right results. Nehru knew how ghastly and interminable is the sufferings caused by the enmity between neighbouring States from one generation to another. Kautilya has defined an enemy as that State which is on the border of one's State. If Nehru had followed, he would have begun by treating China as an enemy, but he did not want to do so and thus to bequeath to future generations the kind of enmity which has existed between France and Germany for centuries, caused many a war, including two World Wars, and poisoned the history of Europe, as Nehru had intensifically poisoned the relations between India and Pakistan on Kashmir issue, on non-alignments and on the question of secularism. The political instability in and around the Kashmir valley is the Achilles' heel of India's foreign policy makers. When a Prime Minister was in the wrong, are the people bound to follow him then too? It is not one's duty to do wrong. Nehru was not a statesman at all but a politician. Nothing else more. Why? There is a difference between a politician and a statesman. A politician thinks of the next election, whereas a statesman thinks of the next generation. Pakistan's primary responsibility is not to transform the world by the crudest form of Islamic globalisation, but to transform itself. Terrorism, to the Islamic code of ethics, is the mother-in-law whose visits never ends. The idea of annihilating all that is made to a green thought in a green shade may seem eccentric today. The shades and shadows over Kashmir remain permanent symbols of sad and transient things. The two words necessarily mean the same thing. Shadows are what the shade creates, but in fancy, very much more. Life in Kashmir is but a shadow of conspiracy within the wheels of well-shaded connundrum.

Shadow was Shakespeare's favourite word. Why? Possibly because it declared his own notion of the unreality of the actor's profession. Thesus in 'A Midsummer Nights Dream' rebukes the Athenian rustics "mockery of the murmers'. The best in this kind are but shadows." So, every terrorist battle cry is of collaboration. It is ironical again that a clay-footed idealism is being permitted to try to buy peace in Kashmir. Islamic extremism is a chosen rapporteur of Pakistan on Kashmir issue.

Inspite of all periodic professions of goodwill between two countries, our relations with Pakistan are hardly cordial. Why? This is because the cesspool of age-old animosity in which Pakistan was born still haunts it and constitutes the spring-board of its bitterly inhibited psychology against India. Even the people were, or will be, born under the ever-increasing travesty of anti-India hymns of hate and propaganda running wild under the damaging but traumatic influence of Islamic terrorism. Pakistan is a State without any history or tradition to sustain its religion that is made the king-pin of present day Pakistan, abound with Islamic jehadis that can sustain and stabilise aspirations to a certain extent only, and not beyond that. It is a fact that Pakistan has ever sought to realise by forging a myth to which anti-India designs and aspirations are skillfully hitched.

Pakistan's highly-perfected propaganda has painted India as a Frankenstein casting ominously covetous eyes on Pakistan. Pakistan must do so, for, it has failed on so many accounts to make the people better and there is nothing to sustain its basic democracy except this myth of supposed danger from India. For ungodliness' sake, Pakistan must hit and humiliate India as frequently as possible and that it has been doing abashedly in unmitigated vigour since the very day of partition.

In fact, Pakistan, in alliance with China, is playing the same obnoxious game against India as was played by Mussolini, Hitler's ally, against France in 1940. The aspirations of both China and Pakistan are of identical nature how to outmanoeuvre India's military strategy over the Kashmir politics. Judging from the present political scenario, it would not be wrong to say that Pakistan is virtually a Chinese satellite as much as Albania in Europe. Without any fear of contradiction, the threat to India's security is two-pronged because of the present 'Unholy' alliance between China and Pakistan.

At the time of partition, the overall armed potentiality between us and Pakistan was in the ratio of three of two. Now with U.S. arms aid, the ratio of armed potentiality between the two countries is just on a par. A nation's foreign policy should be primarily related to the Nation's interests. This must be admitted that Pakistan has formulated her foreign policy according to the compulsions of her national needs, without indulging in meaningless platitudes that yield nothing. In the context of international relations today, most nations are non-aligned and yet they are aligned. From Eisenhoweuer down to the present ruler in America, everyone assured and has assured us that American arms will never be used against India. U.S. foreign policy is itself properly a double-distilled lie, the materia prima of the devil, from which Pakistan has so far learnt well all falsehoods, imbecilities and abominations body themselves. Through all these opinions Pakistani rulers are enabled to spread and rivet among the people by reducing their minds to a state of sordid ignorance and staring timidity, and by infusing into them a religious horror of letters and knowledge that Pakistan has learnt to make her people the only susbsistence to live on. There is no room in the country for any Muslim to be hyphenated-Americanism. Pakistan's hypocritically deceiving dependence upon the dollar bags, upon bribery, and upon the patronage of White House is considered to be the Islamic heritage. Such solecism in Pakistan's politics, imperium inperio, is leading directly to the worst anti-India hymns of hate, civil disorer and bloodshed in Karachi. All wise laws are excluded from such intolerable subversions. Let Pakistan hasten to retrace her steps and to find out the road which alone leads to peace and safety from the irretrievably collusive alliance with U.S. and China.

China, desperate with land-grabbing ideological policy, is fast preparing herself to fall on her prey, Inida : atomic explosions by her are a sharp pointer to this crude fact. That day is not far when China will expose herself to the world as the Asian counterpart of the German dictator whose pride, ambition and land-hunger shepherded destruction and annihiltion all over Europe, nay the world. This is the world of nuclear giants and ethical infants. Few nations, like China, commit the same crime with a very different result.

The problem of Hindu-Muslim disharmony is neither religious nor constitutional. It is a pure, and simple political issue, it needs no reiteration that the politik of Pakistani leaders to tamper with the loyalty of Indian Muslims on the one hand and persecution of minorities in Pakistan on the other hand is in no small measure responsible for creating communal tensions on both sides of the Indo-Pakistan border.

The Anglo-American politics towards India, dated back to partition, has ever been very much alarming and perfidious. They have played the old British game of power politics, gambling away the politics on South-East Asia on the part of so-called Kashmir problem. This power politics is the old concepts of balance, counter-alliance etc. the object of which has ever been to prevent the rise of any great power in Europe or elsewhere, and thus maintain their old supremacy unimpaired. In Asia, their concern to prevent such a rise is all the greater as the vast and teeming population of coloured people of this Continent poses a menacing problem to the white races of the globe, especially the Anglo-Saxon peoples, who, enjoy and appropriate much too large a share of God's earth compared to their numbers.

And with this clear-cut idea, India was partitioned and Pakistan was created by the British, when they found they could no further maintain their hold on this sub-continent. And henceforward, in pursuance of the same policy, they, with the U.S.A. as their natural ally, have been bolstering up Pakistan and aiming her to the teeth as a counterpoise to India, even in the cauldron of trials, troubles and tredpedations over Kashmir problem. So, we can easily expect that they would do everything to augment Pakistan's prestige, power and morale at the cost of India, for only that way can Pakistan play effectively the role of a counterpoise to India.

The fact is that the USA distrusts us in the heart of her hearts. Why? Because it is on account of our non-aligned policy. That has registered her explanation to stand on Pakistan and also her ready help to Pakistan not only in building Pongaldam in Jammu territory but also erecting a military air-field at Gilgit, conveniently forgetting that Pakistan has been occupying all these areas illegal.

The ordinary man doubts nothing and suspects nothing. Pakistan is a country of continual dissolution, speaks the prologue of her comedy, provoked and instigated by her distemper to search her beautiful house for her cursader's love. Since Independence, she has suffered the pangs of intolerable fright to be detected with a jealous rotten bell-wether and with stinking clothes of anti-

India propaganda fretted in her own grease of hypocrisy. Better shame than murder. Democracy in Pakistan sleeps as sound as careless infancy and hardly thinks of her upardonable mistaken behaviour towards India. Terrorism and Islamic globalisation, like a rich embroidery, have locked in hand in hand. Everything is the flesh of a corrupted administration. The sudden surprise of nuclear powers has driven Pakistan to the grossness of foppery. If Pakistan had been married to terrorism just after the partition, she would not have had Kashmir. Forced marriage brings upon the couple a thousand irreligious cursed hours, and that we have seen at present all around the sub-continent of Asia.

Pakistan has always been sick after the house beautiful in the country, after grabbing away Pak-occupied Kashmir (POK) or Azad Kashmir. In Pakistan, it categorically means the citadel of Madrassas ..... a lying-in house of terrorists bathing in the sunshine of crude fanaticism of Islamic crusade. 'The house beautiful' varies from society to society. It expresses the natural human longing for a secluded and sheltered spot, insultated from the worries and tensions of this world. What is it? This is a dream world where music and moonlight and feeling are one. Entaglement is our common lot. But the dream of the 'House Beautiful' in Pakistan is a craving for a release of terrorists and jehadis from daily demands and urgencies, from responsibilities and tempting distractions. This fugitive impulse is a powerful factor in the life of modern Pakistan.

The Great Good Place is of a pleasant well-lit writing room in good air and a comfortable bedroom to sleep in, both free from distracting noises and indeed all unexpected disturbances.

Kashmir is genius loci .... the sanctum sanctorum of Indian Geography. The tears of mankind swell the waters and wet the valley of Kashmir. The spirit of place, like the wind among the willows, is a coy thing and a sensitive plant.

The undisputed facts about Kashmir are :

1. Kashmir acquired independence along with the establishment of Independent India and Independent Pakistan. Kashmir was given the full right to remain independent, or to opt with India or Pakistan, at the full discretion of its ruler (who incidently was a Hindu).
2. Pakistan wanted to annex Kashmir, irrespective of the desire of its people or Ruler. So it invaded Kashmir with tribal people, and afterwards with its own army. It resulted in slaughter of innocent Hindus and Muslims, and ravishment of their women.
3. The Ruler of Kashmir asked for military help from India aganist that unprovoked and brutal aggression calculatedly hatched and conspired by the then well-branded anti-India slogans and hymns of hate. On India's refusal to help unless acceded to India, the Ruler opted for India, and so Kashmir became an integral part of India, both legally and constitutionally.

   The infiltrators were merely the vanguard of the Pakistani jehadis. They repeated the performance of the tribal raiders who started the invasion of Kashmir in 1947.

4. Therefore, India complied with Kashmir's request sent military aid, which drove away Pakistan from three-fifths of Kashmir. Now, a Himalayan blunder was committed. Mistakenly, India complained to the United Nations against Pakistan's aggression and a cease-fire was declared. As a result, Pakistan has been in unlawful occupation of two-fifths of Kashmir for over a half-century, without any legal or moral justification, whatsoever.
5. Afterwards Pakistan requested U.N.O for a plebiscite of the Kashmir about its accession to India or Pakistan. Although it was legally necessary. India promised plebiscite to the Kashmiris (not to Pakistan) on condition that Pakistan would withdraw its military forces from the occupied territory of Kashmir. Pakistan has not yet fulfilled that condition and has been in forcible military occupation of that portion even today.

The Vivisection of India, an unvarnished truth, was a Himalayan blunder. Indian leaders realized that they had already blundered into a great booby-trap as Mr. Jinnah had played up with a camouflage with them. He had camouflaged with communal cards. It was a trump card to him. Khan Abdul Gaffar Khan, during his visit to Kabul as a leader of a cultural delegation sponsored by the Govt. of India to participate in the Afganistan independence Week Celebrations, told that the Congress should never have accepted the partition of the country. It was a great mistake and India should atone for it. When he talked of India atoning for the sin of accepting partition, the Khan recalled a conversation he had with Mahatma Gandhi immediately after the Congress accepted the partition plan. "You have thrown us to the wolves." In reply, Gandhiji said, "If Pakistan does not treat the Pathan people honourably, we will fight on this issue." Then the Khan said." I want to remind India of this promise of Gandhiji." And he further said that Persian and Pushtoo were the official languages of Pakistan. Why did he say so? He said, "Possibly because Pushtoo is derived from Sanskrit, facilities for the study of Sanskrit are being expanded in the Kabul University."

India has now been atoning for the sin of accepting Partition. Kashmir is the bright example. It is the syndrome of all other resultant factors. It is partition that has totalled up the present Kashmir problem very much damaging and foreboding to the harrowing circumstances over this subcontinent.

The Kashmir problem is what it is today an intractable, irritating thorn in our flesh, largely on account of our split-mind, split-speech and split-action on any problem facing us generally. And what about Pakistan? Pakistan behaves as if its paternal property had been snatched away. By incessant heart-beating, loud-crying and hopping mad in and out of season, Pakistan has managed to convince the world opinion, which is not so much interested in the intrinsic justice of a cause as in preserving peace, that poor Pakistan, having no history, is the aggrieved party, pretending to be the pitiable under-dog but all the time biting us in the calves has been perfected as a fine art by Pakistan. Its propaganda carried on with a vigour is unknown to our publicity machinery.

We say accession of Kashmir is final, sovereignty is not negotiable, and aggression must vacate aggression, but we give the appearance of being in two minds by our halting, Hamletian attitudes and pronouncements. Our attitude of indifference to this pre-occupied territory betrays us before the eyes of the world. Why cannot we be vociferous about our legal portion of Kashmir as Pakistan is about its alleged moral property? Why? Do we appear lukewarm, half-hearted and apologetic, when Pakistan is assertive and aggressive?

The mounting tension between India and Pakistan is attributed by many observers to the persistent efforts of the Chinese to maintain a cross-word puzzle and instability throughout Asia. From Ayub Khan down to the present rulers, all were, and are, the genuine satellites of China's machivellian chemistry; and all become a convert to the Chinese stratagem. Since 1950s, Pakistani rulers have always been playing up with unwarrantable practices of conspiracy. Pakistan has been guilty of violating agreements after agreements solemnly entered into with India. Take the partition agreement itself, the main basis and foundation of which was that the minorities on each side would remain in their homes as full citizens. Particular hate and anger leap without warning. Crooked hearts impressively return us to the familiar ambience. The Madrassa-oriented educational institutions ..... a lying-in room of terrorism in Pakistan .... are a true drawing-out to idolise a sense of awakening maturity.

The keystone of Pakistan's foreign policy, both old and new, is belligerent attitude to India. When in the early fifties, Pakistan joined the U.S. sponsored SEATO and CENTO. Why? It was with the purpose of strengthening its position, both militarily and politically, against India and not fighting international communism. Is it true? Yes, it was proved to demonstration when Pakistan switched over its potato-hot allegiance to peking immediately after the Chinese aggression on India in 1962. Pakistan finds itself in a position to enter into hard bargainings with the White House using China as the lever. And this political finesse is still getting on and on. That alliance with China has now been transformed into a joint programme of action, both political and diplomatic, against India. Who is the common enemy and against whom both have committed aggression? Pakistan now feeds on arrogance and its peace-treads on is better than it gives, and it is more vindictive than peace. Tonight we are all friends, tomorrow terrorism that Pakistan regards it as its adopted son will meet to death. Why? Because, with too much blood and too little brain, these two run mad. Because Islamic globalisation is one of the rotten diseases of the world today. Because the former and the latter are landed with malice. Pakistan's juggling trick over the Kashmir debate is secretly open. Why? Because of its raw-eyes, dirt-rotten social livers, wheezling economic lungs, political sciaticas and incurable religious bone-ache. Confucius says, "People, who fly into a rage, always make a bad landing." It is an undenianle fact, when anger rises, think of the consequences.

Dated back to partition, Pakistan has always used itself, to carve out its stratagem adroitly or genteelly, hacking half an hour across a bone, bespattering the company with sauce of political cant and overturning the glasses of cherished hopes in its neighbour's pockets. To be genteel with knife is to display finesse and efficiency. Why? Pakistan is always fearing decline of status, and deservedly so.

The Pakistan T.V., alias P.Tv, is like a catamaran built in the dark with twin hulls pointing in opposite directions. It is the most sensitive schizophrenic media. It wants prestige. It wants very much to be admired. It wants to be looked up to as an embodiment of the national conscience, on behalf of Muslim fundamentalists and jehadis to sing out a hymn of anti-India slogans. But leadershp is lonely. This split-mind factor makes the P.Tv behave in a neurotic way. But they have a big audience to be more neurotic after the hymns of anti-India campaign, getting into a huddle with jehadis.

The P.Tv says that they are not panic movers. But what are they? They are a very fair imitation of panic. They are growing up in a world of political criss-cross. Their schedules look like a precipitate return to childhood, a deliberate regression from adulthood. The eye that sees all things else does not see itself.

Whereas Indian political leaders are little worried about Kashmir. Why? They are used to fiddling away with corruptible practices and murder, shouldering on the musclemen in politics. How to befool the people, during the electioneering campaign, are their usual practices. It is the go of the day. Little do they know what political malnutrition means. Malnutrition in our socio-political body can mean politics with swollen thoughts and deeds, peeling the skin off the political system.

The failure of the Indo-Pak talks, on the Kashmir question, from the Nehru-Liaquat Ali Khan down to the present, signifies the forebodings of disaster lurking around the corners of this sub-continent. The services of the Grand Mufti of Jerusalem and of lesser 'divines' from other Muslim countries like Iran are being sedulously harnessed to the campaign of calumny and hatred which is now recognised to be the principle ingredient of the cold war of Pakistan against India. Islamic Jehadi groups in Pakistan are emanated from the ruins of emaciated democracy and from the dull chill and slumber of politics. The confusion of today's Islamic world regarding Pakistan on Kashmir question has become the confusion of every Muslim. In the running down of moral standards, in poverty and misery, and in the lust for wealth, power and terrorism, the perversion of human relations is the shadow and the yardstick of Pakistan's marginalised claim over Kashmir. They are striving for the resurrection of Islamic culture and of themselves through the cesspool of blood in the vale of Kashmir. Pakistan's funereal loyalty to Jehadi groups is overwhelming. Now the question is : What is loyalty? Bertrand Russell, the world's foremost thinker, raises a question : Is loyalty a virtue or a vice? He says, "'Loyalty' may be defined as willingness to make personal sacrifices for the good of a group of which one is a member. Men can and do feel loyalty to many different kinds of groups, of which family, nation, race, class, party, creed, are the most important. The first three are biological, the last three mental. Buddha, Christ and the Stoics taught that we ought to feel loyalty to all mankind, but so far their teaching has had little effect." (The Sunday News of India, April 9, 1950).

And the super-national loyalty of Pakistani rulers and their satraps, sidetracking all democratic ideologies and pristine glory of Islamic thoughts, are now saturated with the traditional Islamic prejudice of blood-letting violence over the Kashmiri Hindu pundits, steeped in with the greatest numbers of terrorists, and imbued with unrestrained merrymaking for all Muslims in Kashmir .... a scene of wild revelry and a satyric drama with a chorus of anti-India hymns of hate. It is romantically a funereal display of wild loyalty to a horde of terrorists to the manner born. It is also called a comedy of wild manners. Is loyalty always a virtue? Bertrand Russell answers in a very distinctive manner, "I should emphatically say No. It is common to think that all bad conduct springs from selfiishness, and to infer that only conduct which has an unselfish motive must be good. But if by 'good' we mean 'likely to promote human welfare', then much unselfish conduct must count as 'bad'. Everything depends upon the cause to which sacrifice is made." (Ibid)

But it is distinctively clear that the loyalty of Islamic terrorists to Islam has an instinctive basis. It has manifold discontents branching into several openings of deadly instincts. It exists in savage tribes. Russell says :

"Among savages the herd is small, and every member of it is known to every other; the basis of friendliness in this case is familiarity. Although, in a large modern nation, this basis is not so directly present. Members of the same nation, on the average, have more in common than members of different nations ..... languages, ways of behaving, habits in eating and drinking, and so on. But, above all, they have the same enemies. Foreigners may always be a source of danger, and if this happens compatriots like to find themselves on the same idea. Connected with the sense of danger is love of home. A hen will risk death by crossing a road in front of a car, because she feels safe at home." So, the Pakistan-sponsored terrorist organisations in Kashmir have risked death by crossing a road of world peace in front of western powers. He finally says, "This makes all compatriots loveable in times of danger."

Pakistan has already lost her marbles. Because she is streaked with alternating layers of democracy and religious fanaticism coupled with stratocracy. She is getting stealhily across the way of her destiny and marching upon the self-cooked-up disputed land of Kashmir. Young girls, trained up in terrorist organisation camps, join up with the young mobsters who go out to maim and rob for money in all provinces of Pakistan. The Pakistan is a cat O' nine tails.

The outcome of every Indo-Pak talks ends in a trifle apologetic about its content. Optimists appear pleased that it is negatively good. There can be no real solution to the Indo-Paksitan problem unless, nomenclature apart, our neighbour behaves as a secular state. Whereas the people of this sub-continent are now living in a mortal danger, preoccupied with unfathomable narrow-doctrinal framework of hatred, suspicion and fear replaced by vitriolic hidebounds of present Islamic thoguhts. The term 'Islamic terrorism' is an unfortunate relic of imperialism. The innocent children are blindly guided by falsehood and flummoxed by voicing forth their venomous words against India on the Kashmir issue. They increase the cares of life, but they mitigate the remembrance of death. Past is full of bitter lessons.

Is it an experiment of trustfulness? Does its virtue lie in the intrinsic worth of Islam? Does this Islamic country believe in the modern conception of a mad democratic state? The clumsy machinery of Pakistani law has not proved an effective weapon against what is in fact a treasonable plot to keep Pakistan helpless and disarmed. Such a policy of driftness is likely to prove worse than the disease lies behind the Kashmir question. Strong in the arm and weak in the head. Hard cases make bad laws. The more there are laws in Pakistan to fight out terrorism, the more thieves, bandits, jehadis and Islamic militant groups are born. Islamabad does not know fire is a good servant, but a bad master. The insiduous and far-reaching influence of Islamic terrorism which is largely responsible for terrorist success in Asia has become so dominating a factor in the international affairs of today that it can no longer be confined to the restricted framework of merely social and economic reform. Political implications of terrorism are the vital concern for those who believe that terrorism amounts to an extension of Islamic globalisation. Crusades, in whatever name they are conducted, are certainly barbaric affairs, and, if the pacifist is in error in thinking that he can easily convert others to his way of thinking without force, the crusader is equally in error in thinking that he can easily convert others to his way of thinking by force showing up the medley of hypocrisy and cant. Islamic and communist crusaders suffer from an extreme mental disorder marked by egocentric and anti-national activities. Both are ideologically ill and politically abnormal full of psychological jargon. Both have been too arrogant in their assertion of their own rights and too ready to interfere in the same of a mock humanity in the affairs of others.

This predominantly metaphorical language of Kashmir liberation movement for expressing its feelings has been the besetting sin of the militant extremists .... weary Pakistan of the past sixty years. China like Pakistan suffers from too much arrogance and too much self-confidence. Dr. Butterfield in 'Christianity, Diplomacy and War', says, "....when the chances of an attack on the free world are far greater than the chances of an attack by it, it may well prove that such a warning against yesterday's danger is more of a threat than an assistance of peace." The supreme Christian interests is peace, and it is, of course, also right that the great objection to pacifism is terrorism.

Who buys jehadi books? Who reads them? Who writes them? Second thoughts are seldom either heard or seen. When the devil looks in at the window to the heart of Kashmir, by presenting occasions of tensions to the eye, and when he comes in at the door to its heart, either in lascivious discourse, or satirical and libellous defamations of other men, the devil is put to his circuit to seek whom he may devour and how he may corrupt the administration by his council. Pakistan is a double-edged sword of cunning and treachery playing with disgusting depravity ..... a devotion to Islamic jehad constituting a way to salvation in Islam. Jehadism is injuriously influenced by political witchcraft, bewitching someone for something.

Few dividing lines in history are more sharply marked than the clevage of 1947 ...... the great divide between those who lived and thought before the deluge and those who began to live and think after it, between what, before the final tragedy of 1947, were known as the 'pre-partition' and 'post-partition' generations. Does Pakistan believe in human reason as the force which can transfer this sub-continent to carry on the torch of progress through the ages to come? Does Pakistan believe in rational discussion between men of good will and the spread of education which will be the solvent of human problems, and enable this solvent to be applied even more efficaciously in the future than in the past? But the Pakistan-sponsored terrorists abandon the defence of peace in Kashmir and march to mutual slaughter at the bidding of their respective theonomy-based Govts.

The outbreak of Kashmir issue came as a sudden and shattering blow. To many of the most sensitive minds of the age it seemed the negation and the collapse of everything in which they had believed, or in which it was worth-believing ; and when the partition ended it seemed to almost everyone in this sub-continent that the one thing was needful to blot out the memory of this fearful outburst of carnage and hate, to ensure that it should never recur, and to resume .... with the added assurance of security .... the rudely interrupted course of human progress throughout the valley of Kashmir. Today, the structure of Pakistan society helps to determine the character both of communal psychology and communal institutions.

Pakistan's mental inheritance on Kashmir issue is unfortunate, the fact that leads Pakistan into a religious wilderness encumbers her penetrating and illuminating work with an absurd dialect, an economic scholasticism and dogmas divorced from reality. Pakistan has already left all connexion with reality for a cloud-cuckoo-land of pseudo Islamic nation. Pakistan became to the eyes of many symbols the scapegoat of the tragic episode of 1947. It is as silly to blame the key as to blame the door.

The great illiterate majority of Pakistan are the helpless objects of destiny, unaware of their past, blind to the future. Military rule looks like a gigantic hoax, a tragic and frightening piece of bluff. A succession of candid memoirs has pictured Pakistan herself as a mountebank on a colossal scale, a colossus stuffed with clouts. Islamic fascism is a tyranny tempered by anarchy. Wounded pride and sensitiveness to considerations of prestige have long been predominant motives in Pakistan foreign policy. The extravagant notions, the splinter groups, the quarrels, treacheries among the persecuted minority make a tragic tale. You cannot shift an old tree without it dying. If you gently touch the valley of Kashmir it will sting you for your pain. What Pakistan says today, the rest of India will never say tomorrow. Time will tell.

Many turbulent years have passed since Jinnah died. But Pakistan is pregnant with two damaging forces : one is pushing down, the other is pulling up, projecting insecurity : religious werewolves, incubi, political withces, mental patients and many other innocent victims. This insecurity is a fear. After Jinnah's death, what Pakistan wants beyond everything else is security of their country. Nevertheless, Pakistan seems unconscious that her theological fathers present puzzling indications of a hidden spiritual drama. Why? Because Pakistan is the prey of an obsessional infatuation for her religious extremism in India and terrorism which will prevent her from being a good Islamic nation to any Muslim in any circumstances.

After Jinnah, this morbid passion for her people is a homicidal maniac. Religious dandyism strikes Pakistan as a huge joke. Kashmir politics for Pakistan is the most exciting theonomous doctrine and the most romantic thing. Pakistani rulers have to read George Orwell. Born in 1903 in India, Orwell won a world-wide reputation in 1941 when 'Ancient Farm' a fairy tale written amusingly yet sadly, with its satire of totalitarian tyranny. Why? Because Pakistan has lost her most sincerity on the Kashmir question. Pakistan is a grim fantasy, in which the premonition of totalitarian wrath of terrorism and religious extremism has developed into a sense of almost fatalistic horror.

The post-war and post-partition breakdown in the economic structure of Kashmir brought administrators face to face with abnormal conditions in Kashmir, instead of mature deliberations and concentration on the economic aspect of the valley on the part of those in power, a tendency of hitching their waggons to the star of popularity by expensive plans, commissions and conferences, aiming at all-round social, cultural and moral reformation of the Hindu-Muslim disunity. Religious toleration is a dead letter in Pakistan.

After Jinnah, Pakistan has neurotically suffered from Midsummer madness, on Kashmir issue, trying out to get a mileage in the midst of political wrangle. The history of negotiations and agreements on Kashmir issue with Pakistan is littered as well as strewn with vagaries of breaches by Pakistan of her plighted word. A measure of caution is indicated in making an approach to this problem. India will be well-advised to shift the emphasis from the recent past and the present to the future. The problem lies deeper still. The horrors of Kashmir are but one manifestation, however tragic, of a deep-seated malady.

The danger of Kashmir problem lies not so much in the spread of religious extremism as in the spirit which seeks Islamic domination under the sanctimonious garb of an ideology. The persistant endeavour of the Islamic fanatics to flatten out all Islamic diversities into an uniformity, and to act as if they were the sole repositories of truth, crushes the liberty of western civilisation and reduces them to a mere cog in the Islamic structure of the world.

Pakistan is the sower of poisonous seed in Kashmir. The sower of this seed is assuredly the author of the whole harvest of mischief in Kashmir. Merit is never so conspicuous as when coupled with an obscure origin, just as the moon never appears so lustrous as when it emerges from a cloud. The mind of Islamabad and the body of Islamic fanaticism on Kashmir issue are more than married, for they are most intimately united; for when the 'one suffers, the other sympathises'. India's pathetic reliance on Pakistan's promises argues a complacency which is dangerous in the extreme. Fooling away the Nehru Govt, Pakistan had squeezed out the minority community from Sind and Baluchistan. Nehru confessed that. So Pakistan's studied policy is potentially dangerous. Did Nehru know there was something among men more capable of shaking despotic power than lightning, whirlwind, or earthquake ; that was the threatened indignation of the whole civilised world? If national sentiment is anti-India and particularly anti-Hindu that is a national outcome of Paksitan's recent historical background, but when such sentiment is shared and provoked by responsible Pakistani leaders at a time when the national interest on Kashmir issue demands the cooperation of U.S. dollar diplomacy. This attitude has ultimately caused unlimited injury to Pakistan. Assuming the power from their Islamic text books, Pakistani rulers deprived of the realism and statesmanship have committed all the follies resulting from their policies on emotion and theory rather than on the facts of Kashmir situation. So, Kashmiris have suffered cruelty for too many years.

After Jinnah, religion plays a vital role in the upliftment of a country. It cements the bonds of brotherhood and makes the nation strong. For instance, modern Israel has emerged strong out of chaos because of the bonds of a common brotherhood. Friendship with Pakistan! Confucius, Chinese philosopher, says : "There are three friendship which are advantageous ; friendship with the upright, with the sincere, and with the man of much observation."

After Jinnah, great importance is attached to the absence in Islam of a deep sense of sin and to the consequent lack of a need for reconciliation of God and man wherein, says Eric W.Bethmann in 'Bridge to Islam', : "lies the deepest gulf which separates chirstianity from Islam." The fact is that religious societies have been always less tolerant of heretics than of straight forward unbelievers.

The world is covered with ruins old and new, and choice must have been difficult, but the omissions are themselves an added pleasure; some words or phrases on Kashmir issue stir the recollection of another ruin not in the index. Words describe ruins best of all, and travellers are verbose, writting at length not only about what they see but also about their adventures and emotions about Pakistan's religious romanticism on Kashmir issue. Once the ruination in Kashmir has started, once the roof is down and the jungle in, owls in the houses and shrubs on top of the cornice, then preservation should cease. The pleasure of architecture is over and it is time for the pleasure of ruins. Pakistan today remembers that pleasure of ruins in Kashmir as a hero in the battlefield of Kashmir. It may well be that its services to Islamic culture will earn Pakistan an even better title to greatness. Nevertheless, the words and agreements on Kashmir issue have instinctly been confined to the grandeur desolations and to the destroyed houses of Kashmiri Hindu pundits ; for the particular tragedy, the houses wiped out or the street reduced to rubble, Pakistan has made a new word, 'bomb-damage'. There are many jehadis who are ready to enjoy the same melancholia.

Oddly enough, the travellers' words and pencils on Kashmir issue produce the clearest coloured pictures for us one after another, like a magic-lantern show of a cigar-box labels.

Mr. Jinnah imagined that by signing 'Two-Nation Theory', he would neutralise Kashmir. Yet his confidence in his psychological perception was unshakable, and he persisted in his view of British intentions. Finally, he was persuaded that Downing Street was bluffing. Mr. Jinnah had convinced even the most hopeful of the folly of trusting Britain. Hitler lost the war with England. Why? Because he made war on Russia before he had beaten the English.

Mr. Jinnah, after partition, was at the heart of Kashmir affairs, and although an onlooker saw a lot of the game. His uncommon objectivity, shrewd sense, clear memory and straight-forward style combined with the dramatic character of many of the Kashmir events in which he was involved to make Kashmir issue steadily absorbing and often exciting to his followers. The tales of Pakistani rulers' political dualism and religious thuggery on Kashmir issue at their most magical and dramatic form are meant to be funny. Though their sense of humour is always theirs, they have a gift for laughter in the most serious situations. The loud gale of their laughter blows down the valley. Does Pakistan know words have meanings and values which depend upon society and not upon the individual? Terrorism may stretch those meanings or may narrow them, but it is a tight-rope Pakistan is walking on and one false step is death to art. A critical befall Pakistan. Adolescent day-dreaming and self-dramatisation forbid Kashmiri Muslims to enjoy liberation movement where Pakistan's idiosyncracy crosses the border of peace-process into self-parody.

Wang Fu-Chin was once called Peking's Bond Street. But that street has been renamed 'The Great Revolution Street'. If you look at you; you laugh they laugh back, you speak English, they all answer back in Chinese. China is a monster detector.

Defeat in Kashmir policy shows Pakistan stumbling into tragedy through the abandonment of the hope of democracy in favour of militarization of theonomous leaders and of the religious unions of extremists as a permanent aim of policy.

Mr. Jinnah remained obstinately blind to the extraordinary power and acumenship of the men who were to hold the destinies of the party Muslim League and of Pakistan in his hand. As a politician .... using the term to mark a distinction on the one hand from the administrator and on the other from the political thinker and man of ideas .... Mr. Jinnah never seemd to have displayed this self-confidence on Kashmir issue. In practice, he too often fumbled, changed his ground, dismayed his supporters by yielding where everyone had looked to him to stand firm, was obstinate when obstinacy had become useless. Minds in Asia are in a ferment. The westerners should study the European impact on the East and they try to imagine how the Asians feel today. Does freedom mean freedom to make mistakes even freedom to govern badly? Too often the West is inclined to forget the present state of tension between India and Pakistan on Kashmir issue. We must lay great emphasis on the spiritual response to the problems of East and West. It is the pressure of fear which is at the root of much of the Indo-Pak tension as well as the international tension. And the Christian anwer is, they think, the renunciation of rearmament and the canalization of energy and finance into peaceful development. If sympathy and understanding are translated from the spiritual to the physical force there is no reason why East and West should not move towards one world. So, Kashmir issue still remains unsolved. Gollancz in 'Minds in Movement' says : "Tragedy is always news."

Do you know the relation between G.D. Birla, the great Indian industrialist, the very embodiment of big business, and Gandhi, the champion of social justice, often puzzled the British? Do you know Mr. Birla was not a Congressman? Do you know Mr. Birla had a furious quarrel with Lord Linlithgow for failing to distinguish between constant support of Gandhi's social campaigns and contributions to the political funds of the Congress Party? The father-son relationship between the ascetic and the multi-millionaire! By explaining Gandhi to the British and the British to Gandhi, Mr. Birla exercised over the course of events and even on Kashmir issue or any other important problems. Yet, for all Gandhi's spiritual stature, what a different person he was to work with and work for. Kashmir issue still remains a double negative. It still remains a double-stop producing two or more tone simultaneously. Every agreement appears to be earnest and meaningful but in fact is a mixture of sense and nonsense, deceiving through concealment and misrepresentation of truth. It still remains a double entendre.

Islamic terrorism is a religious drug, whereby Pakistan suffers from an analeptic intelligence. Pakistan is in an advanced stage of terror-lust which neither practical difficulties nor the prosaic realities of life have been able to cure. Pakistan's imagination of Islamic jehad enables her to extract adventure and fun from the most unlikely material. To satisfy her craving, jehadis and militant extremists risk death, diseases, discomfort and shooting.

We feel that the West can only be strengthened if it first understands the nationalist aspirations of an Asia long depressed in its living standards and humiliated by alien domination. India wants America to support the new democracies painfully struggling to build up stable societies. Pakistan should be asked to choose sides .... either for democracy or for Islamic extremism. If

Pakistan is not for democracy, Pakistan must be against the West. There is a major structural weakness in Pakistan. The West has to face up to Islam and resist Islamic doctrine, which is imperialistic and menacing, and imposes not only conversion but the absolute slavery of the soul, also.

T.D. Weldon's 'The Vocabulary of Politics' is a good example to analyse Pakistan's favourite political phrases on Kashmir and terrorism, which are almost emptied of meaning. By itself, he maintains, the word 'freedom' means nothing. Thus there is a romantic conception of freedom in Pakistan.

With the legacy of imperialism making them specially suspect of western democracies is at a distinctive disadvantage in competing with terrorism for the favours of Asia. What is known as the 'cold war' is an international crisis of cross-border terrorism from which no one can be a fool. The Islamic world of Pakistan can fashion its policies only in the light of Islamic globalisation. Those have shown an unrelenting hostility and an increasing threat to the way of their militant gesture.

Pakistan, magisterially dignified and overbearingly assured of her frenzied behaviour towards Kashmiri Hindu pundits, is associated with a horde of idealised jehadi leaders circumscribing the terrorist barons of Pakistan. Now the coloured light of crescent moon has encircled the luminous body of terrorist groups putting everything on the line and making believe that they are lovers of Islam. They have trust in the advisability of world terrorism. Islamic terrorism after Jinnah! It is a peculiar combination of unstimulating Islamic thoughts pleasing the crudest form of intellect or moral sense. Is it supposed to be health-giving elixir of religion to other Islamic nations? The syndromes of growing uneasiness, after Jinnah, in Pakistan can no longer be concealed. The administration has been gradually forfeited. It is a symptomatic outburst revealing the existence of a live volcano within. America can no longer ignore that volcano. If it tries to bury it under mounting waves of repression by means of U.S. dollar diplomacy, can Pakistan agree to slacken her hold on terrorists? Without education, a nation is like a bed-ridden spinal-polio patient. It is the middle class that has always been considered the back-bone of society. It is principally from the class that the great leaders of India and Pakistan have come. A large section of Karachi-based middle class people is responsible for the independence of Pakistan. After Jinnah, they have now been branded as 'second-citizen' of Pakistan. The rich and the aristocratic few of two countries had more or less identified themselves with foreign rule and its agents. Has this class lost its usefulness? In Pakistan, they have been used as jehadis. Even religiously-institutionalised Madrassas branched out all over Pakistan have caught a large section of middle class youth into the matrix of their anti-India hymns of hate. What a damaging odyssey of Pakistan-sponsored terrorism in the name of peaceful settlement in Kashmir!

When you are a 'Have not', you have all the virtues and when you are a 'Have', you have all the vices. But every 'Have-not' wants to have it, if he can have his way; whereas the middle class youth in India are busy in plucking up their energy for political movements either by licensed guns or by unlicensed rebellious movements.

Sixty two years of independence have, objectively speaking, aggravated the miseries of the men in the street of Jammu and Kashmir. The only change is the subjective satisfaction of political freedom from foreign rule. Nearly two centuries of colonial exploitation, the people of Jammu and Kashmir have been repeatedly told, require time to be repaired and temporary sacrifice is necessary in ultimate national interest. National interest on Kashmir is being built up with terrorism and fanatical crusade and with the sacrifice of individuals, as revealed through a series of administrative scandals and of hush-hush conspiracy between the two rival countries. If half-fed, semi-naked men and women patiently bearing up with their sufferings find that tons of money are being wasted on 'experiments' over Kashmir and a handful of men are fattening on the misery of the economically and politically hard-pressed massess; resentment and furstration cannot but be the normal reaction. And the talk of national interests turns into an empty slogan in their ears and the people of Kashmir are in no mood to suffer for the whims and caprice of a few politicians and the interest of some big business magnets.

And Kashmir has been readily solidified by crude Islamic ideology. A deep-frozen darkness of fanaticism looms large over Pakistan, yielding to jehadi slogans. Given that the ginger groups of terrorist organisations have been enchanted by the delusive beauty of modern Islamic movement in Kashmir. Even the youths, furnished with the fascinating beauty of jehadi hymns of slaying infidels, have encompassed the sensitive areas of Kashmir, fully acknowledged by the ginger groups of terrorist camps. Such evil-trodden path has not only outwitted India on Kashmir question but enchanted the western powers, radiating the heat of crude Islamic fanaticism. Why? Because Pakistan-sponsored militants, after Jinnah, can't make any compromise on their goal .... to wrest Kashmir from India. Because they also want to establish 'Islamic Jamuriat (democracy)' in Kashmir. The militants are in the age group of 22-30 years. They always seek the advice of ISI as to whether to continue fight here or comeback and go to Kashmir. Why? Owing to fulfil the dreams of Jinnah, they owe their allegiance to ISI and Pakistan military junta to wrest Kashmir forcefully. Why? Kashmir being predominantly Muslim should have been with Pakistan. They would not rest in peace till they recapture it. Pakistan Govt. is working shoulder to shoulder with them. There are around hundred offices in Pakistan which collect funds through religious organisations and individuals in the name of jehad in Kashmir. A nightmare of Jinnah's Roman Holiday in Kashmir cracking the whip has never been the best way of convincing people about a cause or belief. In this atmosphere of ultra-puritanism, enjoying of terrorism is a sin. Their lives are constricted by barbaric laws. Like Gulf War Syndrome, terrorists suffer from a fatal neuro-illnss. Truly speaking, the hazards of the modern day battlefield are more than bullet wounds and sabre cuts. The clock will not turn back.

After Jinnah, all societies in Pakistan tend to be littered with bits of deadwood ..... norms and practices that have long outlived their time and purpose .... and still continue to exist. They continue to be around disguised 'age-old' rules or traditions. They will have to be forcibly shoved into the dustbin of history before they start wearing the sanctimonious look of a hoary past. Is it not the resultant effect of Pakistan's quixotic claim over Kashmir?

Nor was it adequately understood that long before the twin tower went down in New York, the real victims of the terror networks for years were ordinary Muslims in predominantly Islamic societies, such as West Asia and Pakistan. In Afganistan, the worst hit were women and children. Even in a long-standing war between Iran and Iraq, thousands and thousands of women and children were victimised. So pervasive has become the murderous influence of the propaganda machine of today's mediaevalists that it is easy to whip up the frenzied idea that the world is ganging up against Islam.

Pakistan-sponsored terrorism in Kashmir after Jinnah : A mindless mayhem. Will Jinnah's Pakistan .... a religious nightmare .... be the United States in the war on terrorism? The Imams of India's Muslilm community remain silent. Do they know the Muslim poor become particularly susceptible to this influence? Do they know the whipping up is being done by the propaganda of Islamic militants, masquerading as religious or welfare bodies dedicated to education, healthcare or waqf matters? The blatant lies have suddenly exploded. The streets have gone quiet in Islamic lands. Do they know Peshwar and Quetta are no longer being rocked by revolt? They are trying to cash in on carefully manufactured popular paranoia among the poor Muslims either in Kashmir or in Pakistan. But all said and done, the historical retreat of the spurious jehadi sentiment must await the day when democrats speak up across the Muslim world.

The tragedy of Pakistan is that it has put a quixotic gameplan on Kashmir but does not know why. The tragedy of Pakistan is that Pakistan's already fragile economy has been hit by the war across the border. Pakistan's exports are down by 25 to 30 percent since sept. 11. Why? Because shipping companies cannot or will not pay the hefty war insurance premiums for ocean liners. It is too a relevant fact that one of the consequences of Pakistan's isolationism is the development of Islamic terrorism and ethereal liberalism on anti-India hymns of hate. The philosophy of terrorists is totally differentiated from the main population of world Islamic community either by racial origin or by cultural background.

Those who complain most are most to be complained of. The punishment suffered by the wise who refuse to take part in the Govt. is to live under the Govt. of bad men. Pakistan, that is good for making excuses on Kashmir question, is seldom good for anything else. These are called bad habits of a nation. Why? Because bad habits are as infectious by example as the plague itself by contact. Every ruler in Pakistan, since Jinnah's death, has risen to the height of momentous occasion. He or she has either indulged in any polemic or in oratorial fireworks or confined to a statement of blatant wooing and of fact which carried little conviction.

What two world wars proved have tragically and conclusively proved that in nine cases out of ten war is as certain a disaster to victim as to vanquished. From which it ought to follow that no sane men would go to war. In an age of democracy, the public is everything, and it is essential that the public be educated. Man's anarchic impulses will only yield to force. "Can the leopard change its spots?" Bertrand Russell has answered, "I believe he can, but if it not, terrible calamities might befall him."

Nationalism is regarded as something of a mystery. It is not a natural phenomenon. So far as modern times are concerned, it was "perhaps invented by Joan of Arc" says Bertrand Russell in 'New Hopes For A Changing World'. Yet its psychological power is tremendous; even Govt. propaganda is helpless to control it and it must be the chief force making for the examination of the human race. The world has already witnessed the conflicts of the past between different ways of life .... the nomads against the pastoralists, the seafarers against the landsmen, the industrialists against the farmers, the conflicts between races, creeds and ideologies.

What is terrible about ideological fanaticism of Pakistan in Kashmir and other parts of the world is that it masquerades as rationalism. These fanatics should be ready to die for their country and for some exalted ideal one can understand, but that they should die for a proposition, that they should surrender themselves body and soul to what purports to be the fruit of cold logic and dispassionate analysis baffles the imagination. For this at least cannot easily be traced back to the blind working of Islamic evolution of terrorism over the vale of Kashmir or the habits embedded deeply patiently acquired through the generations.

Today, after Jinnah's death, Islamic culture of Pakistan, on Kashmir question, appears to have arisen more from boredom and the want of something to do than for any loftier reason. That is the worst of the tendency Pakistan has done so far on Kashmir issue to reduce all the phenomenon of life to the Islamic movements of so many terrorist organisations obeying such and such mechanical or theological laws.

This is Pakistan after Jinnah. Being full of greed, hatred and ignorance, pride, conceit, dishonesty, deception and all other afflictions, Pakistan's theonomy based double-dyed Islamic rulers have therefore done harm each other, plunging each other, being enemies and malefactors to each other.

Superhuman tact of communalism, crudely wielded with infectious enthusiasm, has made India and Pakistan a confirmed and unrepentent communalist, and grown up with the ultimate triumph of obscurantism and illusion. The record of Karachi and other Indian States has confronted these hopes with intractable political realities over the Kashmir debate.

Traumatized by the travails of Islamic terrorism and thick-skinned by world criticism, Pakistan has totally forgotten the intrinsic values of YESTERDAY, TODAY, AND TOMORROW. From all the verities and realities of her existence, Pakistan today stands on the brinkmanship of nightmares. The great poet Kalidas says : "The bliss of growth, the glory of action, the splendour of beauty for yesterday is but a dream, and tomorrow is only a vision; but today well-lived makes every yesterday a dream of happiness, and every tomorrow a vision of hope". After Jinnah, the mob in Kashmir intimidates voters. Election in Kashmir is notoriously swayed by mob rule, largely based on Pakistan-sponsored terrorist groups outside the town. Little stratagems are not only harmful but also employed by all parties and most candidates. Power-drunkard politicians abetted by a score of demoralised but moronic police regret nothing. Why? Because they are arrogant. And the future generation will regret nothing. Why? Because they are inexperienced. The fanatics talk other down.

But a seasoned solider like Ayub Khan, Musharraf and others had always contemplated a quixotic coup without a reasonable hope of success and a sizeable following. Like Hitler's historic Munich beerhall 'Putsch', the coup d'etat plot in Pakistan was hatched at a cocktail party in Rawalpindi. Pakistan has adopted some phrase-making perfections with piquant expressions as 'linguistic imperialism' and 'linguistic jingoism' that ultimately lead to linguistic genocide as we have witnessed in the case of 'Liberation of Bangladesh'.

Islamistan or an all-comprehensive Islamic bloc is an idea which suffers from inherent contradictions. The only link subsisting between the various Muslim races of the world is the bond of religion. Beyond that, their national interests are bound to be divergent and, in certain cases, conflicting. To conceal the truth is an artificial garb.

People like Kashmir because of the graceful of the hilly landscape, its greenery, its rich fruits and deft people. Kashmir is a poverty-stricken state. Glory of Kashmir has got to be safe when it is deserved; it is not so with popularity; one lasts like a mosaic; the other is effaced like a crayon drawing. How little do politics affect the people, the moral life of a nation. One single good book influences the people a vast deal more. Growing misery in the valley accounts for part of the popular coldness. It is a crisis of leadership. Kashmir has always been distracted from the leadership. Fools should never see half-done work. Hope for Kashmir solution is a good breakfast but a bad supper.

Freedom found Congress in power at the centre and in all the States including Kashmir; but even after sixty years of independence, Kashmir is frustrated and almost prostrated while the party has rushed headlong down an abyss of decadence until today it has almost reached its bottom. At the rest of the Kashmir problem lies the absence of a bold leadership. Like the Communist party, the Congress has a phalanx of pseudo-intellectuals in its ranks. The party in Kashmir has been reduced to shambles, and confusion and demoralisation reign supreme in its ranks. All this is a funereal but dreary picture symptomatic of the intellectual and spiritual level of the people. Our defence preparations in Kashmir up to date are a pretentous facade. Even today the fear of terrorism is real and supreme in Kashmir. Inevitably, dictatorial control over the valley cannot be relaxed until that risky task is achieved.

Nehru's supporters or applauders were doing his injustice on the Kashmiri people by creating the impression that the talk differences reagrding high principle and high policy was largely camouflage or a decorative facade. The lure of power can work mischief enough at the Congress base. So it can do so on a national scale if it moves its focus to the apex of the Congress pyramid. On the Kashmir question, the Congress undeniably suffers from the malady. There is a Chinese proverb : "What time is it? High time."

Now the Pakistan propaganda machine is working overtime, if there is a drift towards communalism in Indian politics today. Pakistan's contribution to it is indeed very large. And the windows of terrorism lie in Islamabad, and experiments in Kashmir.

What is the duty of a statesman? A statesman should follow a public opinion as a coach-man follows his horses having firm hold on the reins and guiding them. In India, it is farce. Who is misleading when? Yet acting in an irresponsible manner and shambolic thoughts, all political parties in Kashmir have decided to use pre-calculated violence as a pawn on the political chess-board. He that aspires to be the head of a party will find it more difficult to please his friends than to perplex his foes. The ballot-box goes to spring a surprise and belie all forecasts. If you tell the crocodiles of the Nile, they remind you of the politicians in India. They open their mouths so wide. Here in India tears roll down their cheeks.

While going down the rat-hole of political conspiracy in Kashmir, our so-called political leaders in the valley begin to get rather sleepy and go on saying to themselves in a dreamy sort of way, 'Do cats eat bats?' and 'sometimes, 'Do bats eat cats?'. For, you see, as they could not answer either question, it didn't much matter which way they put it. And it matters even less what questions have so far been discussed by our cabinet minister's meeting on Kashmir question either in Islamabad or in New Delhi. Why? Because they fail to reason out the answers that have been found for them by our foreign experts. When they do, they do not act to apply the remedies. So, the crisis-ridden Kashmir question is sick of the garrulous mockery. To be angry about trifles in the valley is mean and childish; to rage and be furious is brutish; and to maintain perpetual wrath is akin to the practice and temper of the devils; but to prevent and suppress rising resentment is wise and glorious. To Pakistan, New Delhi is a devil on the Kashmir question. The Devil is not so black as he is painted.

Pakistan's glib talk over the precious possession, the Nuclear Bomb, reminds one of a little school boy with a lollipop in his pocket asking himself, "Shall I eat it or keep it?" Garrulous ministers and politicians have loudly discussed, with the naive of the little school boy, why Pakistan should not use it against India. One man's terrorist is another man's revolutionary. And the magnetic forces of meledramatic alliance between Islamic clerics and Islamic fundamentalists making a well-organised magnetic field with many Islamic organisations lying about the valley of Kashmir are a seething melting pot of ethnocentrism and religious chauvinism in Pakistan. Such manoeuvring ways of hypocrisy run parallel with racialism and imperialism, terrorism and fascism, individualism and fanaticism, isolationism and collectivism which are the making of Pakistan today. Democracy is still a mighty creative force with moral and material strength to overcome its totalitarian challengers. You cannot teach a boy to do right unless he is free to do wrong. New Delhi had become a political Mecca of the East. And there has been an unending stream of visitors and international conferences on the Kashmir question from the day Pandit Nehru spotlighted that Kashmir is not a manna from heaven.

After the Second World War, the world had been studiously receptive to alarms and excursions at any and every point of the simmering periphery of the cold war in Kashmir. Even Tibet was being pushed into battle as though it were a latent but developing issue of the East-West ideological tug-of-war. This is as patent a confusion of issues as American intervention in Kashmir. If the inhibitions and prejudices in the minds of some of the leading members of two rival countries .... India and Pakistan .... are discarded and proposals for the solution of Kashmir question are based on the fundamental realities of the situation, a solution is still within reach. If the wishes of the people of the valley are ascertained on the issue of accession, nine-tenths of the problem are solved. Such delays are due to mismanagement.

Having periodically been likened by politicians and religious chauvinists to scorpions, vultures and other unsavoury critters, Pakistani rulers have been cock-a-hoop at India's proposal over the Kashmir issue. So terrorism in Kashmir is like a headless fowl pecking at an anatomical impossibilty.

Do dreams of Pakistan have any significance? Dreams of Pakistan may sometimes show up repressed fears. In fact, much of Pakistan's propaganda against US's aggressive intentions in Asia can carry little conviction with people who are themselves neither free nor self-governing suppression of civil and political liberties in Pakistan and spasmodic outbursts of terror and violence in Pakistan lead credence and weight to the view that the military rule is bent on perpetrating its hold by means of manoeuvring ways of political cant and pyrrhonism. But the bonds of history, geography and economy in Pakistan are not made and unmade at a tyrant's will and the demand for abolishing these last vestiges of stratocratic rule and exploitation has grown more vocal and insistent after Pakistan's independence. Only bedlam has emerged from a regime of occasional eccentricity and abnormal attitudes of individualism. So it would be difficult for Pakistan to terminate an anachronism and iniquitous arrangement with the jehadi groups. Throughout the valley of Kashmir laws are silent and used as spiders' webs where Pakistan-sponsored terrorist groups entangle the youth Kashmiri Muslims. It is believed that the acceptance of the theological dogma in the valley may widen the existing gulf between India and Pakistan. The worst that can happen to you is a half-cure due to your own lack of discipline. Past experience to India will act as a danger on any undue optimism.

On the Kashmir question, Asia is now a seething hotbed of political camouflage. The Arab World is a stabilishing factor in world polity but America's interest in Israel has alienated the Arabs. It would be a great blow to the prestige of the Arab League. If the Arab is divided, it will increase the number of danger-spots of war potential. It is as base-minded as the coward who shuns the enemy from the fear of an attack.

To turn to the proposition of an atomic war launched against India, military experts in Pakistan think that for a vast country like India, several atom bombs might not be decisive. In atomic warfare, the more industrially advanced countries of the west with crowded industrial cities and large urban populations are extremely vulnerable as compared with Islamic countries where cities and ports are less important and standards of living and the people more inured to hardship. The 2400 km. porous border with Afganistan is invulnerable to the military ruler of Pakistan. There are hundreds and thousands of international soldiers in Afganistan helping the Govt. train its own security forces and fight a Taliban led insurgency, that banned girls from getting an education during their 1996 to 2001 rule. At that time the Taliban did not ban English learning centres. But today the Taliban extremists following an ideology opposed to the West have axed down the men for teaching English. They try to fencing the border with deadly mines. The uprising in Swat and the mass in Pakistan's tribal areas are considered to be death traps to the ruler. Why? Because Afganistan is a conundrum in a riddle to Pakistan. In this strait-jacketed situation, if Islamabad accepts U.S. and international security assistance forces to flush out the terrorist activities of Al Quaida and Taliban militants in Kashmir and other parts of the world, the world will have to witness another IRAQ in this sub-continent.

Democracy is arrested in Pakistan. Neils Bohr, a Nobel laureate, says : "The best weapon of a dictatorship is secrecy." Kashmir after the death of Jinnah! Some of the incidental hypotheses of theoretical construction of Islamic theology on jehad over Kashmir are questionable. They are simply militant and virulent. In a psychoanalytical study, such symptoms of the psycho-pathology of everyday anti-Hindu and anti-India slogans will not have been overlooked. After Jinnah, Pakistan's role in Kashmir is a complete and irrational philosophy based on a manichean conception of the world. These half-hidden mechanisms induce the Muslim world to cling to that entirely negative, absurd and tragic faith.

After Jinnah, Pakistan shrewdly points out that very often those who consider themselves to be open-minded, tolerant, and who dislike Islamic law in Pakistan of the blatant type, are also anti-Islamic. Why : Because they do not want to accept Pakistan's view on Kashmir whatever a terrorist does in India will not be suspect merely because he does not belong to an ostracised community.

After Jinnah, the Islamic culture of religious fanaticism is felt to be threatened from within by syncretism and from without by political events. Even Pakistani rulers, double-dyed in double-whammy, cannot wait patiently for Kashmir fruit to ripen but must always keep shaking the tree of fanaticism until the forbidden fruit falls, green and uneatable. So it was during the whole reign of Gen. Ayub Khan, the same hankering for swift success, the same hasty greed; and Z.A. Bhutto followed by Zia-Ul-Huq, Liaquat Ali Khan and others were wrecked by the desire for rapid rearmament .... the price they bought a sudden kiss of death. Why? Because they tried to manage Kashmir with a stop-watch. Because those so-called pseudo-idealists without a sense of reality or the short-sighted realists like Gen. Musharraf claimed momentary success. Today Pakistan is the power-centre of world terrorism, cherishing a dangerous illusions like albatross.

After Jinnah, blind over-estimation of their own power and under-estimation of others' reservs of strength, Pakistan has already cost the Muslims two catastrophes ... 1965 and Bangladesh (segregated from Pakistan). They would not survive a third. A bad neighbour and hanging go by destiny.

Mr. Nehru's only unpardonable fault was to believe China, and India lost the war in 1962. He should have learnt China perfectly. Nobody knows who was an old rogue, a schismatic knave and a hypocritical villain behind the Kashmir issue. Even all of our leaders today have turned up their eyes, clapsed their hands and begun to sing through their noses. Mr. Nehru, by the tone of burlesque heroics in which he presented the Kashmir episode, seems to be making light of it, and even conniving at it ... Truly speaking, he was a hack politician for the Kashmir theatre of tragedy. After his death, Kashmir has always been threatened with consumption and dogged by religious illness, and has become a tale of controversy and persecution. The Gandhi cult was born after Gandhi's death, while the Nehru cult has died with Nehru. Our leaders, for over sixty years, have been afflicted with intangible political jargonism making the Kashmir issue more and more problematic. Do they know 'words' are the realities, formulas are solutions to the concrete problems, problems seldom stated concretely? Do they know wars are begun in one spirit and one aim and ended in another breed by the duration and character of the contest, which means that, in turn, the 'settlement' settles little and may well breed another war? Who will teach them? They only pretend us. After Jinnah's death, theonomy-based Pakistani rulers, who are far more influential, at any rate negatively, than their brethren in India, are, in the medieval sense, 'realistics'. Problems of Kashmir are both concrete and complex. Intellectual elegance in posing them and solving them is probably a trap. Long distance wisdom is folly and the belief in one key to open all doors is greater folly still. Mrs. Gandhi examined both the causes of Kashmir's present difficulties and dangers and the panaceas were offered. For him the great political and economic fact of life in Kashmir is the impact of war, the fact that each war grows out of its predecessor is more wasteful, more demoralising and more pointless. Today,

Kashmir is preoccupied with the melancholy tale of horrors by which Pakistan has been parading up and down the valley showing off their well-advertised paradigm of Islamic extremism and militant jehad in parallel with Kashmir Liberation Movement. For Pakistan is fermented by the spread of Islamic culture and religion described in military terms.

Following the footsteps of Jinnah, our so-called pseudo-Islamic rulers, sitting at the helm of moth-eaten ideology, have not yet owned up to committing a blunder over Kashmir accession to India. Why? Because this double-dyed delusion has been occasioned by Pakistan's anti-India slogans which have still shepherded the rulers towards terrorism in India. Jealousy is cruel as the grave.

Now we observe Dr. Arnold Toynbee. His vast learning, his unflagging industry, the graces of his literary style, his moderation and urbanity, all these must command our admiration and respect. Dr. Toynbee says in 'A Study of History' : "..... that all men upto date have been vain quarrelsome, perhaps not continuously, but certainly at some point in their lives. This angers the spirits. Sooner or later, they kill us, either by sending bears or by allowing the evil thoughts to ferment inside us until they boil up in fits and fears, by which we are no less certainly destroyed. Evil and selfish thoughts are the cause of death, there can be doubt about it." Pakistani rulers should learn this lesson of Dr. Toynbee.

Optimists look first into the future, pessimists into the past. Their basic disagreement is in their view of the present. Things are bad, and they need to search the truth about themselves and their society. The only place we can find it is in our history. Yet, pausing on the threshold of the inquiry, they must first ask whether there is any point that is getting to know their history.

Philosophy .... either it be Hindu philosophy or Islamic philosophy or Christian philosophy or anything else .... can be practical and helpful as well as cultural. They fail to find real satisfaction in life because they have no philosophy to live by. The individual should be offered a never-before-available opportunity to find a philosophy that promises a happier, fuller, well-adjusted life free from today's conscious and subconscious tensions, worries, anxieties and fears. The bluffer's hand can only be played to win against an opponent who holds his trumps with a certain negligence and unwasteful ease. As Pak-occupied Kashmir is a serendipitous discovery to Pakistan playing a bluffer's hand.

Is Pakistan a falling State? Will Pakistan be the second Iraq? Why Not? In 1948, M.A. Jinnah died, leaving a leadership vaccum. There is no darkness, but Pakistan.

In 1951, Elected P.M. Liaquat Ali Khan assassinated.

In 1958, Ayub Khan imposes martial law, sends P.M. Iskander Mirza into exile.

In 1969, Yahya Khan takes over

In 1971, the country vivisected; the idea of Pakistan as a homeland for South Asian Muslims seems to lie in ruins.

In 1977, Rioting as Z.A. Bhutto's PPP is accused of poll rigging ; Gen. zia takes over.

In 1979, Zia hangs Bhutto, begins Islamization process.

In 1999, Nawaz Sharif overthrown, enter Musharraf.

In 2001, Post 9/11, Musharraf joins the West's war on terror.

In 2007, Benazir assassinated by suspected Taliban militants during polls; militants launch multiple attacks on Pakistan.

So, yesterday, today and tomomow in Pakistan are overlapping each other under the organised forces of theocratic ghosts and supernatural theodicy from the unstinting support of jehadis. The project of herding the Mussalmans into a single bloc cannot but arouse suspicion and misgiving among other nations. Even and then Soviet papers were full of tirade against the World Muslim Conference. Once the object of every meeting was interpreted to measure out the USA's interference and to take an umbrage on India's Kashmir policy. The formation of an Islamic bloc, particularly on Kashmir issue, is bound to antagonise non-Islamic nations and turn friends into enemies. Such political syncretism compounded with all the crudest form of beliefs and practices would not only hamper the growth of our indwelling spirit of peace in Kashmir but let the world through an indoctrinated passion of war-mongering sophism. Sectarian bigotry and fanaticism are much of a muchness.

Today, Pakistan stands as a carpet-beggar before the world, asking for nuclear weapons from somewhere, uranium from somewhere, dollars from U.S. and for something else from somewhere etc. The budget is out and out cheerless, colourless and spineless. And a bigger imagination has come forward to catapult the anti-India propaganda to stardom. It is no use blaming the activities of particular groups or sections for the troubles of Kashmir. The main tragedy of Pakistan is to put the terrorists on their back, to institutionalise terrorism, through much the worst terrorist activities.

Pakistan's foreign policy oscillates irregularly in different seasons and in different agreements on Kashmir issue, leaving the hive of fanatical workshop of militant crusaders to establish a colony of terrorism at different points about the borders. Just after the defeat of Nazism, the general question was, would it revive, and if so, when? A distinguished historian may calculate a time scale. But it can be said that terrorism is being replaced by Nazism, in new form, in new wave length, in new faces, in new ideology and in a new style of Islamic thoughts. Pakistan greedily gobbles it up. It has absorbed the same racial clap-trap, the same fatuous mythology, even the same mindless jargon of what it seems to call vociferously 'an era of human greatness unsurpassed in the annals of mankind. Why have these two movements .... terrorism and Islamic globalisation .... stirred the stagnant waters of our democratic political life today? Partly, because those waters are too stagnant. We like a ripple. And of course, it is the silly era. Boredom with democracy, nostalgia for old-style greatness, and racial and religious prejudice .... these three subjects are the common syndrome, out of which these two rootless different movements are constructed with incrustation of malice, vice, violence and faithlessness. It leads to a general degeneration of politics. It is the only way whereby a small, violent party can advance itself. In any case, there are often other violent parties which use the same tactics and welcome the opportunity. So both can grow together.

Since the glorious days of Jinnah, Pakistan has taught its countrymen one great lesson as Hitler did. For a violent movement, defenceless enemy is not enough. Violence feeds on real violence, not mere rhetoric, Islamic nationalism and racialism like Germans are authentic Islamic movements with a long history. All resentments are merged and sharpened by the great depression. And Pakistan is not a mere political conjurer like Hitler. Pakistan has a positive policy which has engaged the interest of all Islamic thoughts for Jehad as and when it happens to come. And, everything else, there is an Indian bogey. And, Pakistan is considered to be a ventrioloquist's doll.

Why Kashmir problem? The only obvious answer is : the decadence of politics and moral aberration of political leaders having a pedestrian outlook. How to capture power at the centre is only a primary objective, deceiving the public opinion and putting the worst of the candidates on the pedestal. The parades of political parties demanding ever stiffer discipline yet less and less able to give effective expression to public opinion are obvious. So many people are good at talking only because they are not good at holding their tongues. So Kashmir has now become a Roman Holiday of Islamic predation and savage over the innocent people aspiring for palmy days. Kashmir issue is like a stock market. One of the funny things about the stock market is that everytime one person buys, another sells, and both think that they are astute. Both Islamabad and New Delhi appear to be a buyer and seller using the valley as a stock market. Islamabad is a seller of anti-India hymns of hate and political stratagem. New Delhi tries to shake hands with a Slovenian proverb : Speak the truth, leave immediately after. So the Kashmir drama in the sickroom deepens and the ebb and flow of the crisis is imaginatively reflected in the world of political pretensions. The comedy of debased politics. A timeless tale of political apocalypse. Parliament is a house of entertainments and political diversions. Few fifth columnists come and go regularly raising up the collars and try to lambast the ruling Govt. on the abnormalities around the valley. But Kashmir problem is getting bigger and bigger. Parliamentarians in Parliament go and sleep like a weeping tree. Talking about terrorism and Kashmir problem is not their headache, and beyond the party ideology.

The voice of Nehru was rich, the eyes kind but wary. From the crack of dawn, after partition, Pakistan has always been ready to negotiate a settlement. What is reasonable to India and to the world is unreasonable to Pakistan. What is honourable to India and to the sub-continent is too dishonourable to Pakistan. So Kashmir question remains unsolved. The heart of darkness remains.

It is a play-acting of Midsummr Madness full of plastic smiles.

9

Pakistan Today on Kashmir-IV : Moments of Obsession

When we exist, there is no death, and when there is death we do not exist. Today, Kashmir issue meets in the midst of two nations brought on the verge of moral, political and material ruin. Pakistan is a cunning twister of words and ideas, spoiling her own national identity, going crooked, and selling out her credibility to the world. Between truth and falsehood, Kashmir issue is a thing of no consequence to the vulgar. Partition with its guilt and hypocrisy lies behind us like a museum. ..... a caricature of the men of crotchets, vagaries and isms. Kashmir issue is distracting all forms and functions of international law. The Slave Trade has made fortunes for the terrorist organisations as well as for Islamabad on recruitment policy. The recruitment policy has its refinements. Pakistan is apparently not aware that slavery was a normal social feature in Africa and other countries up to the beginning of the nineteenth century; that on the West Coast trade in slaves was a jealously guarded African monopoly; and that overseas traders who bought the slaves were obliged to carry out all negotiations through African slave traders.

The trade had its refinements. A king of Dahomey in the eighteenth made a huge fortune by having all males destined for slavery castrated so as to make them acceptable to Mahomedan buyers. Though operative mortality was high, the greatly enhanced price paid by Arab slave dealers amply compensated for it. The terrorists will have been ruined if the adolescents are not recruited from the backwaters of Islamic countries. It is, and has been, so unfavourable that it has been lead Pakistan into a troublous situation for too many times since the viivisection of India. A shoemaker's son always goes barefoot.

The First World War was fought for supremacy among great powers, and ended in destruction of four empires, 'self-determination' of little nationalities .... and the birth of a new communist ideology. The Second World War was fought for the protection of freedom and sovereign rights among peoples, and ended in their submission to the rivalry of giant powers, the spread of communism and world revolution.

Afterwards, there is a newborn world in Asia, and in the heart of Asia a new messenger of peace .... India. It would be fitting if the last hope of the dead should be fulfilled by the newborn, and if India could bring forth amidst the ruins of the past new things to come.

A few days before dying a leader of the Second World War, President Roosevelt wrote this last message :

"The work, my friends, is peace .... more than the end of this war ..... on end to the beginning of all wars. Yes, an end forever to the impractical, unrealistic settlement of differences between governments by mass killing of peoples".

Now the question is : What is the intrinsic truth behind this message? This message was both a confession of sin for all governments and appeal for their repentance. It was the last will of the dying President to a dying world .... his last will for peace. Pakistan has not yet learnt this message of a dying President.

And now more than ever peace is menaced by the same fundamental cause of war and terrorism couched in fanatical crusade of Islamic countries : governments ready to sacrifice their people to the Moloch of their creeds and greeds. Things to come are always so very different from what the nationalists in every country believe and decide. Those only who belong no longer to a people, a race or a religion but to mankind can see clearly the pattern of the future, and rejoice in it. Those only who are closer to the whole than to any of its parts, one with the world-souls and realise that all powers ignorantly, unwittingly serve the aims of a greater unknown power.

Wars are made by blind forces for national interests, ambitions, prestige .... and result in selfish purposes finally defeating each other. Through ruins and revolutions, nations destroy mutually all things not acceptable to the future. They thus fulfil the war the very aims they could have better served and secured in progress and peace. For in peace or war, the final victory is to the supreme spirit of man.

Now the question is : What would be the Third World War? The answer is : The next war would be a last one between the crumbling old order and the raising new one preparing through greater disasters and darker chaos the dawn of a new world order made of both more freedom and more unity. For these are the two opposite and complementary principles between which national and inter-national pendulums ever oscillate.

These great possibilities could be realised without the madness and horrors of war. Pakistan and Islamic terrorists should immediately take a lesson from it. Otherwise .....

there are three possible bad solutions to the problem of Kashmir which either decided through war entente or arbitration would remain a cause of permanent friction, or bitterness and menace of new conflicts. These three solutions are : exclusive possession by India, by Pakistan or partition of Kashmir between them.

And there is one solution .... only one .... which instead of creating a deeper chasm between the two several parts of the ancient common motherland would be a new link .... a bridge ..... between them, a first step towards their future re-union.

Such a solution is to be looked for at a higher level than that of national exclusive interest ..... the higher level of a larger inter-continental solidarity, inter-Asian unity.

This solution consists in freezing Kashmir from the hold of one Asian country to make the centre and meeting place .... that it is already, geographically of all Asian countries. Mahommedan States of the West and Buddhist of the South around the three great pillar republics of India, China and Russia.

If divided, Kashmir would become another Korea. If occupied by one of its neighbours, an Asian Trieste. But one and free, the Kashmir valley, with its three compliments the Indian Jammu in the South, the Budhist Laddak in the East, and the Muslim Gilight in the North will be what Switzerland is in Europe, made also of the three stocks, French, German, Italian, blended into a harmonious, unbreakable whole. Now the question is : How can this be fulfilled without war? 'Kashmir's' future must not be decided on A Religious Basis, but purely on political and economic grounds.

Since partition, the most power-drunkard political opportunists in Pakistan have not only harped on Islamic unity but declared in ambiguous words that Kashmir is a part and parcel of Pakistan. Such nightmarish thoughts have not ever been accepted by the Muslims of India. So their representatives have always been excluded from the World Muslim Conference conducted by Pakistan on Kashmir issue. An act of aggression against any Muslim country shall be considered an act of aggression.

Do you know origins of nuclear programme lie in humiliation of 1971 war with India? India's first nuclear test in 1974 was the trigger for its weapons quest. Why? Because it was the loss of East Pakistan (now Bangladesh) in a bloody war with India that probably triggered a political decision in January 1972 (just one month later) to begin a secret nuclear weapons programme. But a US Congressional Research Service (CRS) says Pakistan's nuclear energy programme dates back to 1950s.

Pakistan has long argued, and falsely represented to the international community that it was forced to take the nuclear weapons path because it was provoked by India's first nuclear test in 1974. But Z.A. Bhutto's famous call to nuclear arms in 1972 pre-dated India's test. The deep national humiliation of the 1971 war with India led to the dream of a single Muslim State for all of

South Asia's Muslim population. The military dictator, Yahya Khan, presided over soldiers in Dacca. Do you know the most enviously motivated power-drunkard politician, Z.A. Bhutto, convened the country's top 50 scientists secretly in january 1972 and challenged them to build a bomb? He famously said that Pakistan would sacrifice everything and 'eat grass' to get a nuclear deterrent. The 1974 Indian nuclear explosion only intensified the quest.

One day Mr. Bhutto received an unsolicited letter from a Pakistani who had studied in Louvain Belgium, the most notorious Abdul Qadeer Khan, offering to help by stealing sensitive centrifuge technology from his new employers at a nuclear facility in the Netherlands. Over the next years .... with the assistance of Pakistan's ISI Directorate .... Mr. Khan would steal the key technology to help Pakistan produce fissionable material to make a bomb.

Political defeatism in the interest of orthodox liars crystalises and solidifies into a terrorist country. The whole system vulgarises Pakistan's anti-India slogans and brutalises the fanatics. So long will Pakistan cry for peace, peace in Kashmir, there will be no peace. It is a thrilling pang, when cherished dreams are shattered. The discordant voice jars upon the Islamic believers.

Kashmir is a centrifugal force where from a hundred other problems have emananted, stretching away and away to the jungles and valleys of Kashmir. The filth and squalor and cruelty and the heat of terrorism that everywhere underlay, the enchanted beauty and the bewitching glamour of Kashmir have not yet lessened our inviting and haunting passion for the land. Serious issues discussed with passion and gaiety and relevant to Kashmir in general make human listen; conversely, if what is argued about is some bitten old national bone, some obsessional national neurosis with little or no relation to the people of Kashmir in general, there will be a corresponding decline of interest. And one is certainly influenced by the worn-out terminology used. The Kashmir dialogue of Pakistan where the national, historical, racial neurosis are discussed with a constant, inexhaustible, clinical passion, is often incomprehensible to an outsider. The fever of excitement and the laden weight of disappointed hope both revive regularly. Truly speaking, Pakistan's political and social kidneys are stunned by watery cataracts of theology. Such a profound and radical reaction of Pakistan against the whole tradition of the past sixty years .... Kashmir is an integral part of India .... a reaction has been labelled the 'Retreat from Reason'. It must contain within it the seeds of an obscurantism at least as dangerous as anything it sets out to replace terrorism. The secular historians erect an impassable barrier between those who hold them and those who do not. The insuperable difficulty does not prevent ingenious scholars from performing miracles. The result is a curiously prolonged quarrel on the Kashmir issue a language which nobody understands but himself. On the surface, the main role of the secular historians is a critically destructive one, analogous to that of a political opposition. So an apocalyptic theory is put on the Kashmir issue.

Whereas theological historians of both India and Pakistan, on the Kashmir issue, have displayed an understandable but disastrous weakness for trying to convince the ungodly by borrowing their own weapons of argument. This ill-advised attempt of Pakistan to marry absolutism with terrorist method has done more than anything else to discredit the whole movement.

Why religion? The answer is very simple. When the heavens no longer declare the glory of God but have become an external silence of infinite space, when the world is no longer seen as a field of divine purpose but appears to obey blindly the laws of a mechanistic science, men are still apt to retain the values which they have inherited from religion. God is both absent and present in the world. Therein lies tragedy, in a conflict between values and facts in which facts are bound to conquer.

Kashmir is a talisman to Pakistan. She has had the hot idle days of agony and sweltering sleepless nights of pathological fear, particularly on the Kashmir issue. At present, she is intrepidly daring and recklessly bold in how to be contemptuous of Islamic law, religion, culture and political decorum. So the Kashmir problem is the go of the day. Because Pakistan is a global pain. She has not yet taken any mileage or any opportunity over any sort of agreement and has lost many opportunities for making a peaceful solution on the Kashmir question. Even she has worn frozen smile on her face during the nightmarish hours of setting the stage for countless individual tragedies. Demosthenes, an ancient Greek statesman says : "Small opportunities are often the beginning of great enterprises." In the case of Pakistan, this truth is infinite. And the lost opportunities lead Pakistan into difficulties. Her satanic verses of jehadi slogans have wriggled out every possibility on Kashmir solution, hatcheting a diplomatic illness with malice aforethought. This wickedness is either deliberately or designedly or advisedly done, and the fact which is a creature of her old habits. It is like an occupational disease. According to Tulsidas in 'Shri Ramcharitmanas' : "The rises of the wicked is a source of calamity to the world .... the wicked, like the hemp, have their skin flayed off and perish in agony to be able to torture others. They do harm to others even though they have no purpose of their own to serve. Having destroyed their neighbour's property, they perish themselves, like the hail that melts away to nothing after ruining the crops .... and there is no sin as heinous as speaking ill of others." Today, Pakistan is nobody's friend. How do we expect peace in Kashmir? Pakistan is a nation of Banana Republic. She puts her trust in US dollars. She is like an orphan child in world politics. Because no one comes to claim to be its partner. She likes playing a Roman Holiday in Kashmir with burtality, violence and extinction of her moral sense that no longer worry the world. She looks a gift horse in the mouth of US dollar.

The most shattering effect of all the insane cruelty of jehadis over the valley is the complete loss of human dignity, not knowing when one is well off. They become wild beasts and, of course, this is always one of the declared aims of the whole process. They cannot harm us, only kill us. The pattern for brutality is the same for millions, the pattern of suffering and dying is exclusive and individual for each of the victims. While such hypocritical and irreconcilable hostilities are getting on outside Kashmir, Pakistan teaches the growing young students fighting for Kashmir. It is an Islamic brand of love for terrorism. The trouble is not merely that the generals and politicians would not tell the answers if they know them, but that they do not know the answers themselves.

For one grows up in Pakistan, emotionally and intellectually, as it were a jungle rather than in a national cleaning .... in a jungle of conflicting, half-understood ideas and theories, which choke one, obscuring one's free views of the world, congesting one's relations with others, dulling one's curiosity with determinate answers to those questions about life and about the ongoings happening around the world which can never be answered to which it is curiosity itself. In this jungle, one is at the mercy equally of dogma and of fiendish nature of fanaticism. For, from the point of view of a man making his life, Pakistan's philosphy on the Kashmir question is purely negative. It offers him tools to make a cleaning in the jungle, but no seeds for a garden. With all thé beliefs cleaned away, and none chosen for oneself, one is left like the best generation, to be moved this way and that by any idea or mood or passion, however cruel or hollow, so long as it is intense and exciting; or else one remains with one's own traditional beliefs and way of life.

Democracy in Pakistan society is vanished with freedom of speech. Both can never be permanently restored. The service of God at the Mosque does not mean the preservation of new blindness and insensitivity.

Today the Taliban, Al Quaida and other foreign militants use the restive tribal region like mountainous Swath in Peshwar. They use the territory as a base to fuel an instability in Pakistan and neighbouring Afganishtan and to plot terrorist attacks in India and abroad. The region is rife with corruption, and even Pakistan's own Government has limited reach there. The risk of leaving it isolated and undeveloped will be crucial to Islamabad. This is the region where almost no women can read. American military aid to Pakistan annually does not make its way to frontline Pakistani units. The United States is a country of materialism and conformity. The US was a nation born in rebellion and reborn out of a civil war. What has happened since then? Is it true that the America of today has become grossly more materialist and conformist than any other nation?

The Muslims cannot interpret their experience without some theories or theologians in their own way, to choose their own theories, unless they can hack through that their culture surrounded them as they grew up, and see the world once in its particularity. Most Afgan women still wear the burqa, which was mandatory under the 1996-2001 Taliban Govt., and cannot be searched by men at security checkposts. The Taliban have stepped up their attacks in recent years, notably their use of suicide bombings. Such attacks involve women in burqa. Equally, the Muslims in Pakistan cannot live without Islam, but they cannot be free to choose their own ..... whether it be religious one or a terrorist or a fanatic or a militant .... unless they see that no single religion is necessary that there is no way in which all Muslims, simply as rational, must view the world. Whence religion arises, religious worship is the cause why Pakistan rises to religion of terrorism, so contempt for religion brings ruin on them. Why? Because it is easy for Pakistan to keep the terrorist groups religious. So, many evils have flowed in Kashmir in the name of liberation movement. Terrorists maintain slavery of Islamabad. And Pakistan speaks with disdain of those who have not the honour of sharing it. The psycho-neurotic leaders of moronic civilisation are clothed with mob delusions and pious slogans, and the traditions of high-toned demagogues on India regarding Kashmir seek death to acquire immortality. How do we expect peace in Kashmir where most terrible misdeeds have been committed under the spell of certain magic words or phrases, and where snobbishness has cut off the common claim to happiness and affection with which Nature endowed us? How do we expect peace in the valley where honest kindly hearts dry up and die, and blooming hearty youth wither into shrunken decay? There is a corresponding fashion of placing jehad second and emotional comfort first. Truly speaking, Pakistan is a traitor to herself and to her countrymen. Every totalitarian Govt. is prepared to face the consequences of its own misdeeds. So Pakistan will always risk the dictatorship. You are exactly where you are meant to be. What political calamities have produced! Islamic culture in Pakistan is on the brinkmanship of dilemma. It is in Pakistan where mullocracy inspires bloody passion, and fanaticism does so. The traces of neuroses are unmistakable.

Mr. Z.A. Bhutto, after returning from the Simla Agreement, voiced forth a vociferous but shambolic statement in Lahore. With a clarion-call, he declared : "On the vital question of Kashmir we have made no compromise." And the issue was growing hotter and hotter. So the border dispute was getting embittered for his frenzied outlook, and vitriolic outburst of his anti-India hymns of hate and vengeance. He was mothered by a Rajput Hindu woman who had converted herself to Islamic thoughts and philosophy. Her grand-daughter, Benazir Bhutto, was a prime mover on the sponsorship of terrorism and religious fanaticism in the valley of Kashmir. She was also harping on the same string as her father did so after the Simla Agreement. She also categorically phrased out her voice-worn villifying words on television chanting : "Har gali mein bache kehte hain azadi azadi azadi." She believes in freedom for Kashmir. How do we expect peace in Kashmir while the so-called political firebrands lying in mobilisation and implementaion of the instinct of religious fanaticism? It will be dangerous if they infuse it throughout all levels of their culture and nourish it in their young. How do we expect the truth through the channels of falsehoods from those whose business is to culminate, pervert and deceive the issue? The intelligence of our people will be destroyed. The Greeks said : "All things are to be examined and called into question. There are no limits set on thought." Spiritual tyranny over the Kashmiri people is as equal as intellectual vassalage. Pakistan is the best hated and most tricky deceitful nation in the present anxiety-ridden world of obessional neurosis where political marriage to an Islamic country like Pakistan is an evil, but a necessary evil. How do we expect peace in the valley where every lash of religious fanaticism inflicted is a tongue of double-dyed villainy? Much-touted idealism of Mr. Nehru, an ever-growing influence of Lord Mountbatten over Mr. Nehru, and a well-timed advice of the then Deputy Prime Minister, Sardar Vallabhai Patel to drive out the invaders from the valley with the help of Indian Army had made the whole Kashmir episode a cross-word puzzle not knowing which way to turn. So puzzling is the question now that our political leaders, destitute of all moral catharsis, are considered to be the respectable political prostitutes to millions and millions of people. Why? Because they are decadent product of an absurdly unhealthy moronic world, whereas their presence, in any field of Kashmir question, inside and outside the parliament, bears the mark of a man of great imagination. Their habit of saying everything is more of a man of imagination. Their habit of saying everything is more of a bore than an incantation; but speech and speech has a smouldering beauty, a defiled splendour.

As a speaker, a politician's verbal expression is not good at all. The most untidy and inarticulate speakers are schoolmasters. The most volatile speakers are auctioneers and estate agents. And the best and most witty are medical men. But Indian politicians are the cheapest of all speakers to befool the public either by bearing hard-bitten malice or by showing step-motherly treatment or by bewitching devilry. They swear like a trooper, heap abuse and pour vitriol at the Indian public but their tongue-lashing reproach remains silent on the Kashmir question and even on terrorism. They have their heart in the right place. A perfect rogue.

Political asylum is not a right of the individual but a privilege to be bestowed or denied by a State. The former Pakistani premiers, Nawaj Shariff and Benazir Bhutto were political refugees seeking asylum. Two are the victims of Kashmir question. In Pakistan, it is a prized tradition and principle, not always applied with an equal generosity but never to be lost. Folly is joy to him that is destitute of wisdom. But a man of understanding walks uprightly. Against this background of political impermanence, the National Assembly of Pakistan has to face an extricable confusion worse confounded, economically bound by the closer ties to China ..... a land of merchandised communism. Pakistan should study, no less intently, the political side; they should ask why the Simla Pact is failing, and whether the chance of negotiation has gone off. The cruellest and most irresponsible maker of gibes against the arbitrary incompetence of bureaucracy has outreached the Kashmir problem. A tragic deadlock.

Pakistan has given a vortex of serious thought to her attitude of acquiescene through a pathological fear and paralysis of the mind which leaves Kashmir issue to one man to do all the thinking and the working out of the problems. She has great hopes of overcoming the fermentation of fanaticism and hiccuped irrationalism which have bedeviled her relationship in this sub-continent. The fears that obsess them at home do not reflect proportionate faith in the collective judgement either on Kashmir issue or on logistical terrorism. A frightened people cannot build on a future founded on the courage of one man. And we look all of us very much like frightened people. Pakistan is not a well-thought-of nation.

Generalisations about the culture and civilisation of peoples are always a hazardous enterprise but it is true that the people of Asia have generally set greater store by spiritual values than by values of power and wealth. They respect the religious teacher and the philosopher more than they respect the soldier and even where the soldier is idolised not for his territorial conquests but for using his sword in the cause of righteousness. Asia has a vital contribution to make the establishment of real and permanent peace in the world. So, the world should listen more and more to the views of Asian statesmen and thinkers. Pakistan, Iran and North Korea have built effective deterrents in the form of stockpiles of nuclear and thermo-nuclear weapons and big armies against the threatening gesture of Western powers. If all Islamic nations proceed on this assumption, there can be no end to the feverish pursuit of power. Their work has been publicly appreciated; and that has encouraged the Islamic rulers to perform their duties with greater enthusiasm, zeal and vigour than before. Why? Nervousness creates a scare. The endless tales of murder and massacre trickle in the valley from the outside India.

Like all other predecessors, Gen. Musharraf is the most dynamic, the most romantic and the most colourful political hypocrite having a hyphenated hyperbole and make-belief statement, in this sub-continent. Very hard to appraise him. Because his country is a riddle, wrapped up with a mystery of religious conundrum, inside and outside. He has got aristocratic connections with the Punjab province that has helped him to be enigmatic. He has blue blood in his veins like his predecessors, because he has got a striking personality to befool the western powers through dollar diplomacy, marvellous power of expression of telling lies, infinite courage to bolster up the fanatical crusaders of the valley and supreme self-confidence on China .... a dangerous political instigator in between Shia and Sunni. He may have reached the summit of his ambition. He seems to be the principle architect of present blood-letting sectarianism and racialism in Pakistan. Gen. Musharraf has never understood the psychology of the working class of Pak-occupied Kashmir and Kashmir, and has, therefore, never acquitted himself well in dealing with it. Paksitan has consistently stood for the old institutions of Islamic jehad and the old social order of fanaticism in Kashmir. Experiments in Kashmir mean diabolical not only to Islamabad but to the people of Islamic world. No ruler like him in Pakistan has written or spoken so bitterly against India on Kashmir. Pakistan still holds old lines .... the balance of power, regional alliance divisions of the spheres of influence. Gen Musharraf is the first leading tin-pot dictator who warns other Islamic countries and terrorists of the Western powers. But Pakistan has her weaknesses. With the instinct of a confirmed dissimulator, Pakistan loves to dramatise situations over the Kashmir valley, in which there is always a villain and a hare, with herself cast in the leading role. Her egoism is colossal. But she has mellowed with age of inconclusive logic-chopping. Why? Because she takes impish delight in crossing swords with her adversaries in Kashmir.

Pakistan's political strategy over the valley may be a form of compensation for suffering from authority or poverty, from thwarted ambition or personal maladjustment. That ultimately leads to the hands of gangsters or clowns or cranks to remake the world by her messianic urge. In this critical stage of political criss-cross, Kashmir stands in between the rock of Islamic prejudice and the whirlpool of religious romance. And the Kashmiri people have passed perilously close to the whirlpool.

Friends of democracy have abandoned Pakistan, some in anger or disgust and others in despair. Those who have abondoned Pakistan in anger or disgust are mostly literary or fashionable persons whose vanity has been offended by her stiff-necked swelling pride and mistrustfulness. They have seen more faults in her than she has, and their attacks on her are vicious and graceless. The others, who have abandoned her in despair, believe that the worst of all accusations against Pakistan are false; they give her credit for two sin-laden virtues which Pakistan undoubtedly possesses, on the Kashmir question, a courage of telling blatant lies and sincerity of propaganda. It is her reward for years of patient loyalty to Mullocracy, and her sole claim to theocratic rulers. Pakistani rulers certainly know, better than most of America's friends, how to manage the White House. Their seriousness and earnestness are hardly open to doubt, with the object of teaching their compatriots a better, deeper and more sympathetic understanding of their neighbours across the POK, and the tribal areas along the Pak-Afghan border.

The Pakistan's blackface is a good example of how people can be obscured by their own cooked-up problems. Is the Stone Age to be segregated from the Atomic Age with implacable regard for its lowly status or are Pakistan to be clothed, fed and rescued from its garbage, dump, or preserved in its primitive environment as rare animals are treated in game reserves? Pakistan keeps swimming in a Mississippi of terrorism in a sharp lash of fanatical waves. How far is she the victim of her own delusions? We have to accord Pakistan a little to permanent remembrance as one of the most accomplished, ingenious and interesting imposters, speaking in superlatives as an unspeakable villain of bloody-bones, in the history of Kashmir question. Her character and her place in the society have undergone a complete change, in some respects a total reversal, since the days of partition.

Critics are never tired of discussing the nature of tragedy, but when comedy is concerned, the best of them is also true of comedy. Pakistan, on the Kashmir issue, is confronted with an irascibly stupid nation or an evasively eloquent advocate of dictatorship, is often, in fact, herself a master of inellectual tragedy. She dramatises, better than anybody else, the flurry, the dismay, the indignation that are produced in any well-regulated society by the party of pure intelligence. But Pakistan is not happy herself about tragedy of her romance in the valley of Kashmir. The shadows of militancy seem a canopy of political fatalism over the valley, adding slaughter to the words of traitors and showing their teeth like apes and fawning like hounds. A terrorism-spinning Islamic country in terror market.

Besides having this, Europeans are alarmed at the prospect of greater interaction with the Muslim world. A majority of people in the US, Israel and the Muslim world feel more interaction. There is a possible clash of civilisations. Only a minority believes that the West and the Muslim world are in conflict. According to the Gallup Poll on Muslim-Western relations, it reflects an alarmingly low level of optimism regarding dialogue between Islam and the West. Why this conflict? The perceptions of this growing conflict are mostly prevalent in the US, Israel and the Palestinian Territories, partly because of violene in Iraq five years after the US-led invasion and because of the Israeli-Palestinian conflict. While two thirds of people in Muslim countries believe Muslims respect the West, almost the same number feels the West does not respect them. Another important reason behind this conflict are cartoons. Incidents like cartoons depicting the Prophet Muhammad in European newspapers have deepened distrust. These cartoons obviously hurt the Muslim world. But the levels of distrust vary from country to country. Even the Kashmiri Muslims have boiled with indignation, breathing fire and fury at the same time. Such provation may bridle up the high words of animosity amongst them.

France with Europe's largest Muslim minority, has banned headscarves and other religious garb from state schools. Italy has a decade old law against covering the face in public as an anti-terrorism measure. A new centrist coalition Dutuch Government of Christian Democrats, Labour and the Christian Union is set to impose a ban on the burqa in schools and government offices. It is a retreat from the previous cabinet's plan for a general ban. Why? Because the wearing of headscarves in schools and at work is a sensitive topic across the European Union.

Romance of fanaticism is being bristled up in Pakistan and even in Kashmir, when tens of thousands of palestinians have poured into Egypt from the Gaza Strip demolishing about 200 metres of the snow-rusting, 20ft. high metal border wall erected by Israel in 2004. It is called the Rafah Wall that has punched a new hole in Israeli efforts to keep pressure on the Gaza Strip in the face of an international outcry over shortages in the territory Palestinians call a giant jail. People are hungry for freedom, for food, for everything. This incident has unprecedentedly astounded the Islamic world. And they have poured out their vials of wrath and heart-burning rancour over the West.

It is very much appreciative that the Army Chief, General Ashfaq Parvez Kiyani has given a directive to serving officers to abstain from taking part in political activities in Pakistan. Pakistan Ex-Servicemen Society had asked Gen. Musharraf to resign in the interest of the nation. Why? Because he did not represent the unity and the symbol of the federation as President. Why? Because he was responsible for the current crisis in Pakistan and in this sub-continent. The great Buddha says, "Let a man avoid evil deeds as a man who loves life avoids poison." This is the metaphysics of the present Pakistan. Why? Because Pakistan has commanded jehadis and hired militants to initiate such things but she should never take any serious interest in them. The feeling that there is something in the very nature of political tragedy subversive either of proper respect for Kashmir issue or of a really high ideal of kashmiri people has died hard. According to Tulsidas' 'Ramcharitmanas', Uttarakanda, "The tender-hearted, like the birch tree, submit to distress .... even allow their bark to be torn off .... for the good of their neighbours."

And the rising intolerance of Hindu extremist groups and Muslim Fundamentalists in India, irrespective of religious, caste, ideological and sectarian issues, are always ready to race up an orchestrated battle plan of violence with hot-blooded and ungovernable impetuosity and potent threat either against Christians or agianst any derogating picture or art. Political parties are the main share-holders of these uproarious and anarchistic way of thinking. And the Muslim fundamentalists in Kashmir obviously may have to be furious under the shadows of unbidden mistrust. The Gita says : "For he has no tranquility, there is no concentration." Truly speaking, since independence, India has not ever produced any magnificently worth-while leader to lead the country, in a political, religious and social shambles of rabble-rousers' gangsterism. Are they considered to be the guardian angels of Indianisation? Is it a methodology of extremist groups? Extremism is nothing but a religious morphia in this sub-continent. How do we expect peace in Kashmir? For whom and to whom? If the climate changes on global level, why cannot people?

Kashmiri people, in support of liberation movement in Kashmir, Pakistan feels, are willing to devote a great deal of attention to the theory of Islamic romance of terrorism over the valley, because they feel that they will be rewarded, in the end, by grasping large truths. They are unwilling to think hard about tragedy, because they fear that such thought will only, in the end, spoil a joke for them laying bare its machinery. For Freud, wit is a kind of pyschic economy, a paradoxical condensation of aggressive or improper feelings, that affords us emotional relief. Musharraf's power and influence in the nuclear-armed country, that is key to the US campaign against Al Quaida and its strategy in neighbouring Afganistan, are bound to be diminished. The question is by how much. Musharraf, who took power in a 1999 coup, was sworn-in as civilian president of Pakistan. Civilian! A point of order.

The ultimate cause of sickness is thought to be anger, anger in men's hearts. The legitimate anger of a man's neighbour may cause him to fall ill of a fever of being a power-drunkard politician. Fanaticism is like a witchcraft that is used by an individual for selfish and immoral purposes. Kashmir issue rubs in beyond doubt that the majority of Pakistani journalists and writers suffer from professional rhetoricians, sedulously aped their poetic betters, are garrulous, gullible and addicted to excruciatingly funny stories on Kashmir question. Skimming the cream tends to make for indigestion. This at once distorts their overall picture of Kashmir issue. They are actively encouraged to forage for themselves among minor eccentrics, deadbeat pamphleteers, or the lunatic fringe of pseudo-religion. The characters in the plays of Kashmir drama are all suggested either by the military officers or by I.S.I. to whom all the rulers are well-known and the most important of them is the composite portrait of Al Quaida and the Taliban .... Islamabad engages in a struggle which is sometimes triumphant to the rulers and sometimes disastrous : one on the battlefield, the other is in the literary jungle of blatant lies. Both of them are on the field of anti-India hymns of hate. Through terrorism, they have invented nothing in Kashmir, but altered everything. The process is no doubt a Rabelaisian nature of political tragedy. All they were born to be wild. All they are politically amphibious and socially and ideologically amorphous amidst propaganda.

Terrorism, with its ridiculous name and still more ridiculous virtues, its monstrous acquiescens and still more monstrous dignity, in and around Kashmir, appears to have little to do with Islamic aestheticism. Plenty of people at all times are able to produce cogent reasons why a political drama that has exhausted its original inspiration should be acted as a surrogate mother by some other kind of religious drama of fanaticism in the valley of Kashmir. The actors play with plenty of illusions, too much talk and too little action. Even a score of political opportunists in the valley gets used to varying their skin colour from ideologies to ideologies, like an American chameleon, and they are often kept as a pet to pseudo-secularism. They are mostly damaging and prejudicial to the Kashmir solution. Romance of Kashmir drama catches the ear of a new play-going generation not by fulfilling its original purpose. The seeds of this Rabelaisian character can be seen in Indo-Pak future relationship. As Pakistan's political views on Kashmir question began to form, she became increasingly supporter of the institution of autocracy. And Islamabad is thus more autocratically inclined than the autocrat. India has been given warning of the danger of a future war on the Kashmir issue. It would be unleashed not by Islamabad but by the warlike passions of the crude jehadis. To Pakistan, war-like terrorism is a part of the divine order. Without war or terrorism, Pakistan would sink into a morass of fanaticism. Eternal peace in Kashmir, to Pakistan, is a dream; and not a beautiful one. Why? Pakistan is always haunted by the spectre of an anti-India coalition. A perfect believer in Caesarism.

Do you know a Pakistani village where women never cast vote? Sixty years have already gone even after the creation of Pakistan. It is Mohripur village, 70kms. from Multan city. A small village, having 7,000 registered women voters, in its Punjab province, is still upholding the wishes of its ancestors and not letting women vote. None of whom has ever voted since 1947. Why? They are following the decision of their ancestors who had imposed a ban on women exercising their right of vote. Interestingly, the literacy rate in Mohripur is much higher than that in neighbouring villages. Mohripur's population of over 30,000 comprises Aulakh-Jatt, Sahu, Kamboh and Sargana 'biridaris' or castes. Biridaris still honour the order and they are still complying with it. Where women are dishonored, public opinion and democracy are also to be on the streets and lulled by the rhythmic creaking of the chains of religious fanaticism. Women in Pakistan only like to count their own troubles, but they do not count their joys. The mostly well-known Indian proverb is : "Only when the last three has died and the last leaf been poisoned ..... will we realise we cannot eat money?" Many political whim-whams hibernate under the fallen leaves of jehadi slogans in a convival atmosphere of terrorism in the valley. Pakistan should learn and cultivate an ethical attitude in a congenial atmosphere of competence in social activity and political responsibility. The great epic 'Mahabharata' says : "One who is friend of all and is engrossed in doing good to all always with mind, speech and deed, he alone knows dharma .... no others." She must exert herself to her utmost. Otherwise, Pakistan will remain paralyzed by infighting and will have to make llittle headway in passing laws as vital to reconciling the country's sects and ethnic groups. It is an irresistible challenge to Pakistan immediately. Songs of love and murder run side by side in Kashmir. Glorifying the shadow, the world of drug-dealers and hit-men, composing ballads known as narcocorridos, making potential targets in reprisal attacks from rival gangs, linking to the culture of violence and of narcotics-trafficking, going hand in hand with the surge in violence between drug-gangs, and recounting tales of unrequitted love of terrorists, famous bandits or their modern equivalent drug-lords are in an orchestrated revelry of organised criminals and terrorists in Pakistan and in the valley of Kashmir also.

The sad truth is that in the prevailing climate of mutual suspicion and distrust, both the countries seem to fear an agreement more than they do a continued deadlock. They prefer the devil they know ... and they know that the deadlock means stalemate and a state of armed truce to which they have grown accustomed and which they feel constitutes possibly the least imperfect assurance in an imperfect world of anarchists against the repetition of the kind of treachery and violence by the rabble-rousing aggressors. So peace in Kashmir cannot live permanently under a nervous strain and sooner or later somone by some mad act attempts to break such a statement. And Pakistan will agree with India on the advisability of sticking to the existing plans. Pakistan utlises Kashmir as a temple of hypocrisy, a hive of malignant growths of religious virus, a place of merry-making religious honeymoon, and a happy home of Islamic terrorism where they have the pleasure, where they have no complaints, where they have much to be thankful for Islamabad, and where they have nothing to grumble. And New Delhi sits on the wall of sadder and wiser, having had its lesson of 'nothing left to worry about'. What the nice name : What the word means .... Terrorism. Ferocious. Its ferocity, behind a hoarsely whispering voice 'Long live Islam', makes the world uncomfortable. Pretence is one thing, and another, passion. This will never reach a single true equation. Why? Because fools and rhetoricians hold the stage of Kashmir drama. Because all judgements are moral if they are intentionally delivered and introspectively recognised. Ghosts may enjoy the last enchantment of partition. But if the whole human being is our point of departure and the ordinary language of ordinary men the matter of our enquiry, we shall be concerned not only with the logic but with morality of morals and it will be a pertinent question for the solution of Kashmir problem. We have neither forgotten nor outgrown the definition of moral good propounded by Gandhi-Nehru co. sixty years ago. Who distinguishes between rules that are right and rules that are wrong in the valley? Pakistan's art of peace is gunnery, not edification. Pakistan remains concerned with ethical statement, nor moral judgement and with the logic of anyone's preferences, not with the intentions to reason out the problem. Intentions appear in every first person singular indicative, denying possibilities in the present. The situations are really grave and importunate. We fail to weather the temptuous storm of violence over the Kashmiri Hindu Pundits, trying to weasel out all treaties or agreements if the worst comes to the worst. Islamic terrorism in the valley is like a suspension bridge between Islamabad and I.S.I. .... totally indifferent to suss out the destiny of Pakistan.

India's foreign policy is indeed as incomprehensible as her Kashmir policy. Whereas public opinion on Kashmir policy in Pakistan is being stifled with dictatorial high-handedness. The growth of many political parties in India has been going on since 1939. All India National Congress officially didn't attach much importance to them, although ostensibly the Congress leaders cried themselves hoarse on behalf of the former. It requires not extraordinary talents to lie and deceive. Every hope is slipping away.

Faith may move mountains but contradiction is the power that moves all things. It excites and impels though not necessarily in a forward direction. The existence of an element of universal contradiction is the essence of mutability, in the affairs of men; it brings change. Whereas the Islamic terrorism in the valley and the vulgarity of religious extremism feed upon the inner contradictions of Islamic society. And uncertainty is sown in the minds of Kashmir people on the Kashmir question. All business does not proceed on certainties. Pakistan's policy over Kashmir is considered to be a worship of humbugs. A cat may look at a king in the country of the blind. The gates of mercy are forever shut against them. It reminds us of a Japanese proverb; "When you buy a vase cheap, look for the flaw; when a man offers favours, look for the motive." Hobnobbing with Pakistan is as slippery as treacherous. If will be a gross mistake.

Climate is not influenced by politics. A well-educated and united population, however small or large, is likely to be more effective than an ill-educated and disunited one. Pakistan wishes to encourage the practice of group singing which has suffered from other distractions. In her propagandist zeal, she sometimes exaggerates the domestic religious passion and sentiment that is a better indication of Pakistan's passionate life a strange, mysterious and frightening religiosity, than jehadi concert going and listening to masterpieces of unlawful religious delight.

The whole of human life in Kashmir is seen in the imaginery of personal salvation through faith. With a kind of passionate religious blindness, they refuse to notice anything else. It is useless for Islamabad to argue with India about logistics of terrorism in and around Kashmir. Given the fact of her paradoxical honeymoon with militants, both the Islamic and the Christian world find a parallel with the terrible doubts and struggles of solitude. Pakistan is subjected to prolonged brain-washing by the Chinese. She is basically ruled by the fundamentalists. And her outlook and her well-calculated misleading and ambiguous weasel words remind us of her old traditional habits of talkathon .... full of malicious gossips. Her allegiance to the policy of a straitjacketed narrow-doctrinal foreign policy over the valley is a perpetual crisis on the road to her salvation on Kashmir policy. Because Pakistan belongs to a group of invulnerable militants who retain in their religion the dramatic tone of puritanism. They are acutely aware of the struggle between Kashmir and fundamentalism. Two wrongs don't make a right. Our leaders have always pigeonholed the Kashmir drama.

The youth in Pakistan painfully swings back and forth between fundamentalism and scientific and technological development. Undecided about his future, he is watched with suspicion because juvenile deliquent has brought his whole age group into disrepute. They feel helpless and saddened by lawlessness, and at the same time aggravated by their own self-pity and stubborn pride of their religion.

Democracy in India is a spiral staircase to all our piggish politicians. All pigs are messy. Pigs eat like pigs and go slurp, slurp. Who ever heard of a pig not liking mud? They like mud. They love it. All pigs like mud. It is part of the joy being piggish. It may be a story of an endearing piglet who lives up to his name. Most of our politicians are living politically naked and wild with religious foxes, sharing not very competently, their life, without language, with only the most rudimentary of their basic instincts. They dedicate this political gamesmanship to the liars and deceivers in the parliament; to those who daily deal out treachery in and around Kashmir; to those who handle their professions as instruments of debasement; to those who, for a salary cheque and less, successfully betray their public; and those who will do it for no inducement at all. They may go down as a time of considerable talent in writing. The tone of their commitment on the Kashmir issue is unmistakable. They discover in themselves a capacity for moving the crowd by oratory and are elected either to the parliament or the State Assembly or to any other committee ...... piggish to the core of their instincts. How do we expect peace in Kashmir? What a sort of romantic nihilism throughout the valley! Omar Khayyam says : "How time is slipping underneath our feet! Unborn, Tomorrow and dead Yesterday, Why fret about them if Today be sweet". There appears a mysterious chemistry of infidelity with faithful and faithful with infidelity, throughout the valley, blundering into a sickening and disgusting phase.

The slithering path of Islamic glory in the valley often leads to the grave, and the encomiums, which Pakistan-sponsored militant groups have earned from their compatriots for their gallantry, discipline and unflinching devotion to their own terrorist organisations, have had their price not merely in the glorious deeds of extremism over the Kashmiri Hindu Pundits but also in the maimed and the disabled who now find many avenues of gainful employment closed, the whole systematic operation in and around Kashmir reminds us of the book, 'The Theory and Practice of Hell', written by Eugen Kogon who focuses his attention on the German Concentration Camps and the system behind them. It may so deeply shock even upright men and women that they will be tempted to put it aside. When a child can be brought to tears, not from fear of punishment, but from repentence for this offence, he needs no chastisement.

Jinnah's production of Kashmir drama, released after partition, is powerfully predominated by his versatile role in partition theatre. Pakistan has directed it, and Jinnah also starred in the title role. He has hacked the original to bits and amended, and deleted at his own sweet will, and pleasure the original with transpositions of text and interpolations of performances. His descendents have tried to join, after blurying out the truth, the dismembered limbs by introducing a sermonizing political hypocrisy as a connecting link. Today, Jinnah's Kashmir drama is a turbulent drama of confusion, disagreement and violence, full of spooky claptrap, but its central figure invests it with the classic tragedy of an Islamic nation. It is deluded into wrong doing, getting bogged down in religious bankruptcy and messing up every ideology. The central characters rant and have far too much in the big scenes of U.N.O. to their liking. Furthermore bewilderment is provided by the cacophony of diverse accents during the peace-making process in the valley. The brave leaders are being bluffed out by their confused ambitions into murder. It has all the glossy, glassy glamour of a fabulously expensive production of Islamic terrorism, conducted by Paksitan-sponsored U.S. dollar diplomacy.

The gem cannot be polished without friction, nor men perfected without trials. Today, Pakistan's role on the Kashmir question is ironical and degrading. Her tendency to war has a habit of brutalishing the Muslims as a whole. It takes off the thin veneer which separates the theocracy from the democratic process. Education commences at the mother's knees, and every word spoken in the hearing of little children tends towards the formation of character. Let parents of Pakistan always bear this in mind.

Theocratic rulers in Pakistan, called by some the Goebbles of Pakistan, are the brain behind the voice of Pakistan which hourly pours out political diatribes with military officials and religious dialectics with I.S.I. for the education of Pakistani people. It is proud to be a major event in the Kashmir politics of Pakistan. It is Pakistan that is betrayed by her own well-cooked up terrorist groups. "The knot of the heart is loosened, All doubts are cut off; And one's deeds cease when He is seen; both the higher and the lower." (Mundaka Upanishad 2.2.8)

Kashmir issue provided by psychological research for what are called veridilal hallucinations, and the hypotheses Pakistan puts forward to account for her occurrence. Veridilal hallucinations suffer from those produced by drugs, disease, and the projection of day dreams in eidetic imagery, in that Pakistan can be shown to have exasperated with some actual event in Kashmir. Power can be attractive for many reasons other than profit; one of them is for its own sake. It is like an old surgeon dying by dissecting himself. Pakistan's claims over Kashmir is worse than dissecting .... tearing, and with circumstances of horrors and political gamblings about the treatment of crude chauvinism into which another horrors will enter. This profound and painful mistake is to have far-reachings, rueful consequences. Gen. Musharraf is an individual with the individual's inevitable bias. Love has gone wrong in the valley, ruled by a hideous but frightening ogre, haunted throghout by a childhood fantasy of Evil, and exorcised by half-reciprocated affection. The ending seems contrived and perfunctory. Underneath their reactions to sudden shock have thrown light on the whole moral dilemma of human relations, and attempted suicide in hopeless spite against recapturing the sensuous atmosphere of surroundings in the valley. Islamic terrorism is not a debunking legend. It is the malaise of the soul of mankind. And terrorism is an unnatural growth due to a misuse of historicism and a misinterpretation of Islamic theology .... a continual crossing and re-crossing of old habits. The tendency to religious diffusion and political separation has been counteracted by intermarriage.

Looking through the political spectrum of present day terrorist outfits in India, particularly in the valley, Islamic fundamentalism in India has now become a political Frankenstein of fraternal twin .... Islamic radicalisation of Al Quaida and the Taliban born from the same mother, Pakistan .... to Pakistan herself having been worn out to a frazzle. She fails to brave it out because she crosses a dangerous bridge when she comes to it. Because she is offensively bumptious, delivering her self-assertive boasful statement on Kashmir solution. She is definitely unrepentant under censure. According to Turkish proverb; "A fool dreams of wealth; a wise man, of happiness." Darkness in Pakistan falls like a sorrow. And life in Pakistan is a great charitable hospital of religious fanaticism and the people are the patients in it where the chief joy is luxuriated in wildly eccentric conversation. Any political illness is as dangerous as extremely painful. Woven about the flimsy framework of ideology, every plot of terrorism in the valley is a great deal of army force. That ideology is grotesquely manoeuvred over 'the dirty tricks' agency .... a state within a state. This political grossness of Pakistan fully depends on three 'A' s .... America, Allah and Army. All three 'A' s are very much collaborative to Pakistan's political destiny.

Our era is one of masses; yet they are either tyrannized by totalitarians or pseudo-secularists or un- or mis-managed by the sham modesty of our democratic leaders; shoved from behind by communal despots or misled by provincial leaders, suffering from political neurosis. Since Attic days these masses have not changed their spots, even now in the valley today. They have greater powers and authority, but it is doubtful whether they have greater knowledge how to rule themselves. A few leaders in a few restricted areas of our outworn phrases of 'secular society' have found it easy to lead and manage the impoverished masses ..... a political time-bomb even to the Kashmir solution. It is far from easy now, in our fluxlike era of quick technical changes and immense powers, to lead them for all purposes, either to fight out religious fanaticism or to lead religious extremism, carryings-on. The heat of this political consternation gets the whole Kashmir question a social shock and political anxiety. It is easier to force than to lead freely, to compel than to persuade. The perfect political business is what has made society modern and enjoyable for the masses, not economics, not politicians. The serious criticism of all the negative positions adopted by many rulers in Kashmir is that they almost inevitably tend to look at their problem from the outside.They consider abstract images. They tend to examine what they see as the operation of inescapable outfits of terrorism, the obeying of inherited instincts, the escape from dour reality into day dreams. It is more hallmark than that any other problem in the valley.

The former prime minister, Benazir Bhutto, in her last book, 'Benazir Bhutto ... Reconciliation, Islam, Democracy and the West' wrote that extremists had made inroads into the very structure of Pakistan government, making the country a 'tinderbox'. Describing the country a 'tinderbox', Benazir Bhutto, wrote, in the 328 page book, that the nation faces the threat of 'Talibanisation and Balkanisation'. "Pakistan today is the most dangerous place in the world. Pakistan faces the threat of both Talibanisation and Balkanisation, which are gaining in strength." Describing the role of ISI, she wrote that the ISI tried to wreck the 'budding relationship' between Rajiv Gandhi and Benazir Bhutto the then young prime ministers of India and Pakistan, who were willing to think out of the box to break the stalemate in ties. The slain Pakistani leader said "The Pakistan people's Party continued to get reports of widespread rigging preparations. These included bulk transfers and postings of the judicial officers who have custody of ballot papers."

Why Kashmir? The masses everywhere show they want to benefit materially by businessman's translation of inventions into productive realities. They like better products than those of the State. They accept business. What the people of Kashmir do not see, and what few have dared to tell them, is that to realise their wants they must obey ..... not the bosses of terrorism, who are, as they ever were, human, but the exigencies of the machine, the factory, the business organisation, the process, the scientific discovery's own principles. Our shambolic political intellectuals and dons, on the Kashmir question, are divided into those who can outclown the clowns in the modern arts of mass communication, and those who despise such arts because they cannot; thus into clerks who betray because they cannot. So many aspects of common man's life in Kashmir is moulded, straitjacketed, or stream-rollered by our political leaders. The magnitude of political managers and business dons can be gauged from the present criss-cross situation in Kashmir. And the magnitude of this misdiagnosis can be gauged from the disarray inside their disintegration and the equal disarray inside their hypocrisy. And the combined result is the increasing tension in the valley. It has always been a murder in the valley, hiding a multitude of sins and mumbling away nervously. It bodes ill for all of us. The rough tongue twists in their lips. It is an unvarnished truth that the miserable, despised and forgotten are regularly inflicted by our politically naked leaders with much howling and naked savagery in and around Kashmir. This is the progeny of political prostitution .... an expression of stupidity and cowardice. Who will show you the secret gateway of Kashmir solution when the tottering edifice of prejudices gets away with murder and weaves garlands round the butcher's sword, and when the Kashmiri Hindu pundits have yielded to Hitlerism and to the handful of noisy traitors? How do we expect peace in Kashmir when our leaders producing horror in a beholder seize the opportunity to change things for the better? Kashmir question is not a web woven with innocent hands. One thing is lacking : good will and understanding. How do we expect peace in Kashmir?

Our criminal-sponsored political leaders, unrestricted by law and dictated by the unchallenging force of power, are the share-holders of all problems in India, and even in Kashmir. And the Indian masses, like the masses of an iceberg, are not in the obvious, visible top, they lie below. And our well-paid parliamentarians whose work becomes briefer and less onerous, but also more productive because the fixed capital would then be allowed to work to the full. They don't bear most of the capital for human work. Like fedual barons, they have played into courses calculated to advance neither their cause nor their understanding by the masses. Teamwork becomes more curcial for the Kashmir question. If management fails to get teamwork, it fails altogether on the Kashmir question. Why should not the bosses of our foreign policy work out productive solution profitable to all, when all fail to? It is the nature of their job. If they cannot deal with other wild cats by effective leadership, teamwork will have to. The intoxication of power has seduced our leadership. Fair becomes foul, and foul becomes fair. Like a perfumed paris, they will turn and fly. How do we expect peace in Kashmir? Who drinks out of American glasses? Who eats from American plates? Who wears American coats or gowns? Who sleeps in American blankets of U.S. dollar diplomacy? Kashmir issue! Fight against the absurd. Our wisdom is in our inexperienced leadership. Sixty years have already gone, but the issue remains the same as it was before. And the issue will serve as a cloak for the pseudo-patriots of foreign or native land.

We know Pakistan is married to a go-getting and bullying religious fanaticism. She erupts in religious boils, she specialises in political Machiavellism using immoral methods to achieve Islamic predominance in Kashmir to get success. Kashmir has now become a magic carpet of infiltrators for carrying out terrorism. She is thrown out of School of democracy. Both Pakistan and crude religiosity are taken up with parent-child relationship, electric with day-to-day frustrations, misunderstandings, bossiness, rebellion and the desire to explode in the very face of Kashmir issue, the face has turned to the world.

The first necessary for Kashmir development is the right politician. And that no amount of aid can transform Asia and even the Kashmir development until the local leaders are of the right quality. It needs a skilled and well-trained bureaucracy. "India's bureaucrats and politicians are not supposed by those of any other undeveloped country." (Maurice Zinkin : Development For Free Asia). In practice, 'Asia' means South Asia. Asia is exposed to be a meaningless entity. The sacredness of cows or the undesirability of untouchables would seem just as alien and incredible to the rational America as to a Chinese or to a Russian or a Frenchman. It will be China and India who will be looking at Europe as a unit and unity comparable to themselves. And political and religious boulders can come crashing through the economic arguments in Kashmir. Prestige and many other unassilable psychological factors will remain.

In making political judgements on the Kashmir issue, we should not depend solely on Paksitan's own private stock of wisdom but should compare its contents with the wisdom of her forefathers. Sometimes beneath the surface a valuable consensus may be found and this on purely mathematical grounds may claim some authority. We shall learn more of what we are by studying the process of our becoming, and it is what we are that indicates not only what we can become but also what we are intended to become. Since Kashmir question is the arena in which by the operation of nemesis, the judgements of God are administrered. The Kashmir question is just like a courtroom. Why? To swear to tell the truth in a courtroom and then have some lawyers constantly object. Since partition, Pakistan has always been on the disastrous plank of 'Future Tense' occasioned by the myriad fold of politically fractured democracy, caricatured by some ambition-drunkard politicians inflicted with paranoid delusions of suspicion and fear .... border confrontation, nuclear policy, cross-border terrorism and smouldering crisis of infernal racialism between Shia and Sunni. Aldous Huxley says : "Those great motivators of malice and stupidity : proselytising zeal on behalf of religious or political idols." Truly speaking, Pakistan's politics over Kashmir is like a pantomime dame playing with music of jehadi slogans, with dancing of religious fanaticism, and with electric banterings ... a paradigm of Pakistan's evil gesture over the valley.

If the military intelligent agencies are not involved in national politics, and the political establishment, Pakistan will obviously taste the ideals of democracy. And the military officers taking up senior posts in the civil service, universities and ministry should be removed. Because civil officials have long complained about them and their nefarious but sinister influences over the cabinet. There is another darker side of Pakistan. It never finds space in any western media .... it goes almost underground. The elite in Islamabad speak English, dress well, drive a car and care a hoot about politics. It is very insulting for them to stand in line with the ordinary people to cast their votes. They feel disgusted to stand in the scorching heat of the afternoon sun. Why? Beacuse the elite in the country live here, but their hearts and souls are in London and

New York, not for Pakistan at all. They are all born and brought up in the cradle song of intellectual dandyism. All are well-educated people with white-collar jobs; they all live in huge mansions. And on the other are those who are born and brought up in panicky and poverty-stricken atmosphere. They have been inflicted with the extremities of political shambles. This distinction is very clear on the day of election. While young men in crisp white pathan suits are eagerly waiting to cast their votes, the English speaking elite are observing a national holiday. On the day of election, almost all languages of the world ..... from French to Korea to Persian ... can be heard in the corridors of the Pakistan's Govt.offices and the hotel lobbies. Social issues like poverty, inflation and gender bias are the main theme of Pakistan today. Fantastic as have been the practical results of these political abnormalities and social morbidities, Pakistan still lives on Kashmir issue and anti-India hymns of hate.

Failure in Kashmir solution is as enigmatic as formidable argument against policy. A failure may be merely apparent, a disaster may be an inevitable part of the process by which Kashmir question is seeking to drive us to a knowledge of where its peace lies. When the morality and utility are in conflict, Pakistan's interpretation of one of them must be at fault, and the function of political thinking on the Kashmir debate is to discover where the fault lies. If both our reasons and feelings are thus directed, the Kashmir issue will not lead us in contrary directions. But Pakistan's philosophy of Kashmir politics is built on religion, and on the tension between the ideals of international order and the facts of international politics. Pakistan is to detach herself as best from one's own particular situation, to learn to laugh and weep with her countrymen to act and at the same time to suffer, and to interpret with the mind the inclinations of the heart. It is Pakistan that always prefers extremely annoying disease of despotism to the plague of socio-political anarchy. In a recently held election to dethrone Gen. Musharraf, some candidates were seen to have arrived with men with long hair, flowing beards, automatic guns and rocket-propelled grenades in North Waziristan, a safe haven of Al Quaida and the Taliban militants. The voters could not believe their eyes. The candidates were roaming about with Taliban fighters. But fear turned into curiosity, when they saw security forces doing nothing to stop the men. To everybody's amusement, the armed men were not Taliban but their look-alikes, hired by some candidates to protect themselves from the militants. What a nursury of Islamic fundamentalism in Pakistan! When violence is tormenting people and inflation is making their lives rough and tumble, slogans of religion-based political parties lead the country into a dreamland of nightmares abound with hypnotic inertia. How do we expect peace in Kashmir when the war against Al Quaida and Taliban and the safety of Pakistan's nuclear assets are in doldrums?

The people in Kashmir live in a muffled age, in which they bear witness to their loyalties, their faiths or their principles either apologetically or in double negatives. A Kashmiri says that he goes on voting for one great party or another because it has always been his habit to do so; driven into a corner, he confesses that he would not exactly say that he is not a pro-Pakistani or not a Pro-Indian. He is combined with, and to a mask, a deep-seated puritan guilt and disgust. How do we expect peace in Kashmir?

Fear is unfortunately still the most potent stimulus to international action and a visible danger inspires a livelier reaction than a theoretical argument. Infiltrators' entryism into the valley makes a feeling of discontented or resentful longing aroused by fanatics' better fortune in Kashmir. The lower classes of any country are always far more socially conservative, far more tenacious of old customs, habits and prejudices, than the intellectuals and the fashionables of the upper classes; and most of their women are still afraid of thinking and feeling for themselves, still very ready to take a male lead. In such women's eyes, vulgarity may go deeper than crudity of bad manners as we see both in India and Pakistan. We should not forgive wrongs darker than death or night.

Pakistan goes deep into the emotional and spiritual lives of her characters, combining themes in a most skillful manner, sometimes slovenly or sometimes redeemed by masterly construction of hidden plot over the Kashmir valley. And the young men are driven forward through a series of ludicrous and disastrous adventures by what seems a largely motivated fury and disgust, where common sense and other civilising forces in other Islamic societies break down. This terrifying society has become a society almost utterly uncertain.

The caterpillar is transformed into a butterfly and the tadpole into a frog. And the innocent youth of Pakistan is being transformed to a terrorist to do violence to the religious view of a universal consciousness, and flummoxed by fears of large-scale violence, political subterfuge, spiralling inflation and the army based stratocratic govt., combined with electric terrorism in and around Kashmir so as to make a choas in the democratic process of India. The new military supremo, Ashfaq Kiyani, a taciturn, chain-smoking military General, is widely respected in western circle and is seen as a safe bet to pursue Pakistan's difficult campaign against Al Quaida and Taliban militants. Truly speaking, the people of Pakistan have already left their destiny to the hands of feudal lords who control the constituencies, singing out in unison a chorus on seeking cross-border terrorism and denouncing peaceful resolution of the Kashmir problem and all major issues with India. Pakistan's former dictator, Zia-Ul-Haq vowed to 'bleed India with a thousand cuts,' How do we expect peace in Kashmir under the shadow of terrorism and Saudi Arabia outfits preaching Islamic fundamentalism?

Islamic theology is the science of the divine lie, and idealistic philosophy of Pakistan on Kashmir solution is the science of any half lie. Why? Because she believes in masquerade. Because she begets enmity, discarding both victory and defeat with the uninvited bogeyman, Iran, to revive the decades old Kashmir conflict. So peace in Kashmir will remain a pipe dream. It is the same response as Shakespeare's 'Romeo and Juliet', seeking to shed a brilliant light of peace in the valley where militants want to keep the valley in darkness and shadow. Pakistan is of different opinions at different hours, as the caterpillar chooses the fairest leaves to lay her eggs on, so does Pakistan choose the fairest place to lay her double standards on the fairest joys, to germinate and grow up future terrorists. It will corrupt Islamic institutions and finally destroy their liberties.

The religious view of a universal consciousness finds a unity beneath Pakistan's double-nature and is based on a study of the facts of growth and development in living militant activities in Kashmir and particularly of the self-regulating, goal-seeking qualilty of Pakistan's policy on Kashmir, so miraculously manifest in their activities. At the same time, she neglects a number of key problems in Kashmir. The multi-dimensional effect of her character possesses a touch of her intellectual arrogance, inspite of her several emotional entanglements, and seems to hold her apart from the other characters as well as from the people of Kashmir. It shows clearly but cruelly much of her enchantment lying in her torment and when finally she is exorcized of her own demon, fanatical terrorism. Evil appears only transiently and is rapidly exorcized. And the advocates of liberation movement in Kashmir are not concerned with their characters as human beings rather than pawns in any political game on the Kashmir question. Pakistan's national power is declining, perhaps their public standards are declining too. They fail to understand, partly because of this misleading sense of propinquity, partly because of a residual sense of superiority, and partly, too, because of a rather airy assumption that India would eat away the marrow of Pakistan's integrity over Kashmir either by hypocrisy or by reciprocally hidden reconciliation through agreements or bilateral talks. This feverish pride and mad arrogance are more symptoms of a sinister infirmity which has devoured the social Islamic community. Who sometimes doubts in regard to everything, sometimes believes a little, sometimes believes nothing. Intolerably conceited, she is in any sense a charlatan, in this or in any other matter. She is her own first victim on Kashmir issue. It is an unvarnished truth that both India and Pakistan are on the same boat of corruption. Both of them were born and brought up in the palace of currruption. Alexander Pope, an English poet, says, "At length, corruption, like a general flood, shall deluge all." Corruption is an epiphenomenon of Kashmir issue.

We may see how and why certain features in the modern theological temper in Pakistan have cropped up. The current theology develops out of earlier stages, not merely revolting against error. Islamic religion marks for tolerance, courage and belief in the intelligibility of nature. Monotheism arises from speculation, not natural emotion. It makes men intolerant, grovelling, and subject to intellectual puzzles. So Pakistan's view of religion is onesided but her blows are shrewd. In modern theology, her challenge is a point of departure. In fact, the Pakistanis are not happier, nor more enlightened, nor more creative than all other peoples of Europe. It is difficult for outsiders to learn them, to persuade them and to live in peace with them. All these major mysteries have been accompanied by a number of murders and an evil sprinkling of more orthodox crime and racketeering, in which both Islamabad and its sponsored-terrorist groups have been closely involved.

Like many weekly selfish people, Mr. Nehru had diddled himself. There is nothing nice about his policy on Kashmir issue. He was a psychopathic bully and pathetically lonely man. All is said about the poverty, fear and suspicion in Kashmir is no doubt perfectly true. But none of our political characters is more than a paste-board figures. War is really juvenile activity ; for Pakistan's children, brutalized and undisciplined, take a sinister pleasure in Kashmir drama. All the bestial instincts of infiltrators come out in these children, who form their own guerrilla groups, murder and execute one another in the saddistic manner, playing a street drama, in their own areas. These children seem to be the precursors of the cruel and discontented youth which is to be found not only in Kashmir but all over the world today.

Both Nehru and Gandhi, on the partition of India, seemed to have no political wits and to leave their first class brains inside their brief-cases of hypocrisy. Their attempts at friendly discussions proved unavailing, our astonishments have changed to vexation and impatience. Both offered eager greetings to their colleagues before the interest for leadership on the issue of partition. Both had been cocooned by the plots, counterplots and combination in layers of politeness. Their very physique and voice and their fine-grained personality were those of a king-maker; their love of intrigue, their capacity for power and leadership, their pragmatism, all combined to advance them as a prince of Congress party. Some of other leaders seem more earthly, less ethereal than formerly.

On the Kashmir question, Nehru shows himself modesty and with self-advertisement, as a profoundly human man whose life has been dedicated to his conception of Kashmir progress through Govt., is, paradoxially enough, an anti-intellectual .... if by inellectual we mean one who separates ideas from their application.

A rich balance of good intentions is the common diet of the day. We are much too self-conscious. Both the urbanity of our older writers on partition and the anger of our younger ones spring ultimately from the same self-consciousness, a self-conciousness which itself reflects a lack of self-knowledge. The ragging, based on small failures, must increasingly be balanced by a mutual respect founded on a large merits.

The theme of Kashmir drama is more complex and bigger than any other Pakistani has previously attempted, the comedy is wry and the climate is dark. The real agony of an impossible relationship starts magnificently and remorselessly disintegrates. The melancholy of clowns is a notorious fact. Pakistan turns back on herself, like some wounded beast, in a blind fury of self-destruction. She provides a melancholy casebook of many of the deep-seated ills afflicting Pakistan's society. She deals Kashmir issue mostly with childish emotions, with shapes and colours of mullocracy, with distinguished personalities, and with troublesome and perplexing adventures. The most gifted people like Nehru and Jinnah are often victims of a lack of balance which expresses itself in visionary fancies and romanticising. They should have looked with an honest freshness of thought at the world of our times. Like cockroach, both lived in their own deserts where there was dirt.

The behaviour-patterns of their hypocrisy on the Kashmir question really are unpredictable. Jinnah's anti-India hymns of hate have passed on into the sphere of the abnormal, and this principle is evident in the phenomenon of insecurity. And his delusion over the valley is preserved in logic-tight compartments secure from the disturbing influence of hard facts.

When a tyrant dies in his bed, suspicion always begins to circulate that he has been poisoned by frightened men who feared to become the victim of his vindictiveness or by eager heirs in a hurry to divide the heritage.

The fortunes of the Second World War brought large areas of Eastern and Central Europe under Russian political, economic and military influence of tutelage. As the philosophy of terrorism envisages ceaseless struggle until the whole Islamic world is converted to Islamic globalisation. Pakistan is the last invincible bastion of world terrorism. Pakistan and her politically vitriolic vampires are responsible for the post-partition crisis in Kashmir, by the excitation of jingoistically electric nationalism in all their various twisted and spurious expressions. The only way to derive pleasure from displeasure is to make displeasure a pleasure. What is the sum and substance of co-existence in the economic sphere of Kashmir? It is not to make the rich richer and the poor poorer. Let them .... the rich and the poor .... stay where they are, the former flourishing and the latter famishing in their respective spheres of continued co-existence without complaint. The new Moghuls of New Delhi are more monarchial than the Great Moghuls of old Delhi.

That Kashmir is the linch-pin of all the disputes embittering the relations between India and Pakistan is made no secret of by the latter. If a solution of this principal issue by mutual discussions can be found, other-optimism, specially when frustration may lead to more bitterness and further worsening of the situation. The disputes are pretty large in number. They are, again, varied in nature and have so far defied all attempts a settlement by negotiations, either direct or through intermediaries. The hard reality is that once politics is allowed to get the better of the normal sense of justice, it becomes almost impossible to get rid of the miasma and see things in clear light. Because Kashmir issue has always been governed or determined by the stochastic distribution of probabilities.

The political parties on the Kashmir issue are the most glaring examples of this heart-sundering. Being the biggest and oldest amongst all other parties, the congress party should have surpassed its rivals on this issue. It has, therefore, changed from a platform voicing the supreme interests of the nation to a market place where might is right. After the British departure, the words of the Acts of the constitution make no distinction between the political leaders and the poor or the ruler and the ruled. Today the complaint of the congressmen is that he has to answer for all omissions and commissions of the Govt., on Kashmir issue... Effective leadership never complains nor falters. Nehru had all the opportunities of building the Kashmir policy on the basis of a clear ideology and also of turning the administration in accordance with that ideology. The congress has shown a distinct partiality towards the poorest, the lowliest and the lost, or only satisfy itself by catering to the whims and caprices of the exploiters and their hangers-on who pretended to speak in the poorest, the lowliest and the lost. This is the Kashmir question which the congress rulers have to answer. They can evade their reply only at their peril. It should have tackled one fundamental problem on Kashmir and given it all priority. But it played with too many issues at one.

What is congress? It is a tear, fallen from the suffering and agonised heart of humanity in bondage. Congress today : A dead man tells no tale nor tenders evidence before the post-mortem partition. The same old Congress with deteriorating health vigour, partly on account of age and partly on account of the change in the circumstances is still plodding on. Nehru was congress and congress was Nehru. No leader has been spared by history, if he has left the organisation in a helpless position.

But, exuberance, engendered by military strength and modern accoutrements of nuclear varieties, delights to fish in troubled waters of Kashmir. The I.S.I. (Inter-Services Intelligence) with the approval of Islamabad takes hazardous step which cannot but seriously jeopardise peace in Kashmir. Mutual charges and recriminations go on interminably. There is still time for calm thinking and a detached perspective, so that an armageddon can be averted and humanity should be saved from the deadliest effect of a possible atomic warfare. If interventionists keep aloof from what is a domestic concern of Pakistan, peace in Kashmir can hardly be disturbed. Partition is theory. Kashmir is condition.

Who is conisdered to be a leader of our country? In India, every leader considers himself outside the law, and imposes inhuman acts on the people. He is a good leader who talks little; he is a good leader when people barely know he exists. Whereas our leaders begin with lies, with lies and die with a pack of lies which surround them. They are not ashamed to tell big lies on Kashmir issue. Only one man in a thousand is a leader of men, the other 999 follow women. They are consciously and intentionally bad. How do we expect peace in Kashmir? The are like a changeable silk. We can easily see there are two colours, but we cannot easily discover where the one ends, or where the other begins. They try to befool and mislead the people on Kashmir issue. While others become gangsters or millionaires, clown or cranks, driven by a messianic urge to make peace in Kashmir. Do you know 'Darra Adam Khel' .... known for its weapons bazaar and illegal arms factories .... has recently become a stronghold of the banned Sunni Muslim extremist group Lashkar-e-Jhangvi, in Peshwar, which is said to have links to Al Quaida? And the suicide bombers are the residents of Darra Adam Khel. Key religious leaders and influential tribal chiefs have decided to raise a tribal army after dealing with Taliban militants. How do we expect peace in Kashmir where hypocrites and religious cranks, govt. officials and educationists, romantically religious lovers and scholars are seen as a destroyer of democracy and a preserver of Islamic terrorism in the valley, least of all an idealistic visionary? How do we expect peace in Kashmir where Pakistan, within a short compass, has been able to reveal the lurking visionary behind the lynx-eyed critic? Kashmir is a thorny question. The men with the air of men with many preoccupations are usually the men with the least to do. Pakistan-sponsored terrorism in Kashmir is a psychological affair, and when the process starts on the mental horizon, its manifestation on the physical level is impossible to prevent. But the change need not come through violence and blood-shed. All the best stories in the world are but one story in reality .... the story of an escape. It is the only thing which interests us all at all times .... how to escape.

Judging from this political decadence in the valley, both India and Pakistan are facing one another across the yawning psychological gulfs of suspicion prejudicial to each other, hiding away everything by promiscuously invented religious thoughts and projecting terrorism into the valley. Pakistan's psychologically abnormal behaviour aggravated by religious delusions and resulted in loss of contact with external activity is like a perennial crop. It grows vigorously in the public domain. And nobody can say what is in the womb of future.

Dr. S. Radhakrishnan, a great philosopher and former president of India, remarked in a speech delivered at U.N.E.S.C.O.'s fifth general session at Florence, on the future of our world, focussing his attention on arms race of belligerent nations. "The psychological and physical preparation for a third World War is going on. It will break out not by deliberate intent, but if the fates are unkind, by an incident or accident. Democratic liberties are curtailed, social welfare programmes are being postponed. While more than half the population of the world in Asia and Africa lives under normal subsistence level, the other part is spending its time, wealth and energy in building armies, navies and air forces which will avert nothing, which will solve nothing. While there are millions who are hungry, millions who have no home, millions who have no hope, our governments are engaged in war preparations. Whatever may be the military results of another war, which is likely to be atomic, biological and ideas throughout the world. Nobody will stand to gain from it. Whoever may be the nominal victors, neither democracy nor communism would survive in the present forms."

After the war, U.K. and U.S.A. found that Russia and Russian ideology was a menace to them like Pakistan possessed on Kashmir with her vagrant policies of Islamic terrorism. One of the serious errors of America is placing its military power influence behind some of the most vicious elements in Asia. The key to Asia is now India, and if India goes with China then all Asia will be lost in dire consequences and we will have to be pierced with sharp arrows of terrorism.

The use of respectable political doctrines as weapons of party controversy is always a dangerous practice, and this is particularly so when the doctrines are complex and inexact. Thumping the table in parliament is not easy to find out peace in Kashmir. Kashmir situation may be stimulated by the looming and unhappy possibilities of the Indo-Pak partnership. The sower of the seed is assuredly the author of the whole harvest of mischief. Why? The despot lives night and day like one condemned to death by the whole of mankind for his wickedness. Pakistan is known to be a puppet on a chain of three 'A' s .... Army, Allah and America. And this ignominously coordinated chain has translated Pakistan into a big giant of terrorism to lead the juggernaut of Islamic globalisation all over the world .... a confluence of theology, I.S.I. and extremism. Every election is held in Pakistan on their choiceable man to lead the people of Pakistan. The owner should be an ornament to the house, and not the house to the owner. The mind of theology and the body of despotism are more than married, for they are most intimately united; for when the one suffers, the other sympathises.

Pakistan does not know name is a fence and within it you (Pakistan) are nameless on Kahmir question. Why? Because she spies her authoritarianism under her muffler of terrorism. According to Sri Ramkrishna Paramhansa, one of the mighty minds of the world, "Flies sit at times on the sweetmeats kept exposed for sale in the shop of a confectioner; but no sooner does a sweeper pass by with a basketful of filth than the flies leave the sweetmeats and sit upon the filth basket. But the honey bee always drinks honey from the flowers. The worldly men are like flies. At times they get a momentary taste of divine sweetmeats, but their tendency for filth soon brings them back to the dunghill of the world. The good man on the otherhand, is always absorbed in the beatific contemplation of divine beauty." (Ramakrishna Kathaamrita). Pakistan leaves the sweetmeats of peace in Kashmir and sits upon the filth basket of Islamic terrorism in the valley.

The terrorist who plays terrorism safe, who sticks to his rut and his illusions and thinks that his life embodies all decent moral values is a moral anarchist. At a time when they have begun to take a rather silly pride in their national as well as religious eccentricities the Pakistani army ranks among the richest minds of eccentricity that they have got. For any ruler like Gen. Musharraf in Pakistan is as unruly as independent thinker, tireless in setting down his thoughts on paper, and relentless in pushing them through. Always unusual in personal appearance and behaviour, often contemptuous of seniority, he drives and disciplines himself beyond all normal limits, and expects subordinates and superiors alike to keep pace with him.

The Islamic terrorism has passed through the first phase in which enthusiasm for their creed has been bolstered up by a stout self-righteousness and readiness to believe the worst of the capitalist enemy. Though these attitudes still survive and are shored up by the force of electric propaganda, by the ignorance of the outside world and by the surviving assumption among many of the older generation that America seeks the destruction of Islamic terrorism.

Yet there is among the younger generation a far less doctrinaire attitude. The conventional wisdom is being undermined by a curiosity and America being the big outsider; it is America about which the young are most curious. Curiosity is outrunning theoretical prejudice. Because some Islamic countries are looking more and more like the United States.

In 1949, Mr. Nehru states these as objectives of his foreign policy : "the pursuit of peace, not through alignment with any major power or group of powers, but through an independent approach ... the liberation of subject peoples; the maintenance of freedom, both national and individual; the elimination of racial discrimination ... want, disease and ignorance." (The diplomacy of India, Ross N. Berkes and Mohinder S.Bedi).

The book shows the policy in action over twelve years of United Nations debates in which India has demonstrated a monolithic preoccuppation with nurturing the environment of negotiations. India's cardinal rule has been to refrain from all words and actions which might increase tension between the Great Powers, and she believes not in peace through security but security through peace. She is equally opposed to S.E.A.T.O. and the Warsaw Pact and as a result of American military aid to Pakistan the preservation in the Afro-Asian world of the last great area of the uncommitted has become a major challenge which has tried to meet with Bandung and the Panch Shil.

What terrorism is to the West, colonisation is to India. Yet although in 1947, Maharaja Hari Singh quoted the adage "good Govt. is no substitute for self-government." Since then India has seemed to become less intransigent on the issue.

The chief criticism of India's policy has been that it seems to apply a double-standard. This dual diplomacy has still hung over the valley. The superiority of top people and top nations to emerge from this bog of superstition, poverty and fecklessness due, most likely, to permanent congenital inferiority and their refusal to accept the verdict of natural reason is a symptom of mental derangement.

The embarrassing puzzle is that under the dispassionate and sceptical scrutiny, the hapless fundamentalists seek to clear themselves, only to find that they are hopelessly enmeshed in circumstantial evidence of religious romance. Religious passion and crime are plotted with mathematical precision and is extremely easy to read.

The image of Kashmir episode is a recurring one in Pakistan's strategy, and it is often associated with profound mental disturbances; the image reflected in itself may be associated with ignorant classes, the image reflected in itself may be associated in turn with the achievement of a degree of terrorism. We find the image of that mirror of nostalgia for dead beauty, looking in and seeing no reflection of oneself, seeing someone else instead of oneself, suddenly realising one's own degradation and ennui. In the lunatic world of lies, pain and solitude, some form of cooperation is the only alternative to suicide. So the whole Kashmir issue is preoccupied with devious and surreptitious way of a Byzantine power struggle. Today foolery governs the whole Kashmir.

The so-called note-doubling trick is a notoriously old trick in India. Progressively, what used to be a doubling trick over the Kashmir question has now become, not a trebling nor even a quadrupling trick, a multiplying trick. Pakistan's Machiavellian trickery over the valley is the job of a master trickster. It is more than the Arabian Nights Phantasy. The proverb says : As you make your bed, you must lie in it.

Irritating denunciations and provocative threats are not the way to do it. Kashmir is a question which would presumably pooh-pooh the idea of a conference with a precondition of this nature from the opposite camp. Asia herself will decide her destiny without any unwanted military assistance or political advice from people masquerading as saviours of democracy and peace. One-third of our country is ill-housed, ill-clad and ill-nourished.

It is time that USA should realise that the peoples of Asia consider that country as much an intruder into their affairs as they look upon the terrorist expansionists or communist imperialists. Let the Islamic expansionists confine their anti-democratic crusade to their own homes. The China armoured-doves have been candid enough to declare openly the purpose as well as the way of retaining for themseleves these countries. But, curiously enough, the protagonists of peace do not hesitate to demand from others what it itself would spurn at disdainful.

Experience is the name which everyone gives to his mistakes. The ten percent Hindus can no longer enjoy monopoly in trade and commerce after the liberation of Bangladesh. And the confirmed satraps of Dacca have worked hard to create hatred between Hindus and non-Hindus. The Dacca rulers shut their eyes and refuse to take any notice of sabotage.

In politics, there is no effect without cause. Passion and prejudice hardly allow any politician sometimes to see the cause before they are borne down by the effect. The Pakistani rulers, blinded by militant extremism and suspicion of imaginary enemies, have failed to perceive the sleeping volcano of popular anger on whose precipice they steadily climb by steps of continued misrule. They have now been compelled to reap the whirlwind growing out of the wind they had been sowing sedulously in Kashmir since the creation of Pakistan. The lesson that forces down the throat of those myopic politicians is an oft-repeated historical fact and is a fresh warning to purblind leaders and parties everywhere. Victims of anti-India slogans create mass hysteria in Pakistan. Pakistan and her friends are sitting on a live volcano. Why? With the arrival of Islamic terrorism, they will sit on their own-made nuclear bomb, both being equally explosive .... a mixture of fear and fatalism. Even spiritualism is not unaffected by nuclearism. It represents an attempt to fly off at a tangent. Our Indian leaders, the tender mothers of political adventurers, must be rejuvenated.

Is Washington going to strengthen India with a view to enabling her to play the role of a neutral in a future global war? Foreign policy is closely interlinked with domestic policy, particularly in Pakistan. Society is a circle in which everyone who is anyone knows, everyone who is anyone else. Has Pakistan totally forgotton the five pillars of Islam, inflicting a war of terrorism over the valley?

The five duties incumbent on every Muslim :

1. Shahadah or profession of faith
2. Salah or ritual prayer five times each day
3. Sawm or fasting during Ramadan
4. Zakat or charity given to the needy
5. Haji or pilgrimage to Mecca.

They need right view, right intention, right speech, right action, right livelihood, right effort, right mindfulness and right concentration to make peace in Kashmir. You should not make wrongful use of the name of Islam, the Great.

The scriptures of all the great religions of the world are devoted to the basic themes of "Light", "Love" and "Life". Today, life is a perpetual crisis on the road to salvation. We are acutely aware of the struggle between good and evil. When the first night of portion came upon us, we supposed that the day would never return. When the sun of partition sank the following day, we in our ignorance believed that it had gone for ever.

10

JAMMU & KASHMIR : Yesterday, Today And Tomorrow (I-VI)

INTERESTS OF FOREIGN POWERS IN THE STATE:–

Kashmir : The tiny frontier State, in the north-west of India which has passed through many vicissitudes for centuries past, continues to be an anxious part of the globe. Since October, 1947, when Pakistan invaded the State with the help of tribesmen from the north-west frontier province, Kashmir's importance in the global strategy of ambitious world powers has become increasingly clear. The political importance of the region lies in its geographical position and the composition of its population. And if the disputed State is a big question mark on the political map of the world, one need not go very far to know the facts of the situation.

Bounded on the north-east by China (including Tibet), on the north of Russia, on the north-west by Afganistan and on the west by Pakistan, the State of Jammu and Kashmir consists of an area of 84,258 sq. miles (222,236 sq.kms.) in the heart of Asia where the frontiers of five countries (including India) coverage. This explains the strategic value of the land which the Anglo-Americans are well-aware of and which neither Russia nor the people's Republic of China can altogether loss sight of. Accordingly, if in the present context of the international situation the Anglo-Americans have evinced keen interest in the Kashmir question and tried to use methods which could give them an advantageous position in the area, it helps one to understand the causes behind the failure of the U.S. dominated Security Council to deal with the old dispute between India and Pakistan in a straight forward and equitable manner. And keeping in view the fact that in the first phase of other existence, Pakistan was greatly influenced by the British and was later sucked by the U.S.A. to her sphere of influence, it becomes evident that if the newly-formed Islamic State could summon courage to attack Kashmir, with the blessings of those powers that wanted to spread their tentackles in the strategically situated state. The American administration made its intention clear in 1954 when it decided to arm Pakistan. Against whom was the arms aid to Pakistan meant. Evidently neither against Afganistan nor against Iran, but obviously against Russia. And Mr. Mohammad Ali let the cat out of the bag when he said that the arms aid from U.S.A would enable Pakistan to deal firmly with India on the Kashmir issue; count that day lost, whose low descending sun views from your hand, no worthy action done. Pakistan has started vibrating with feverish passions of anti-India slogans and oscillating between quivering jealousy and grossly immoral conduct of propaganda. It is as disgusting as shameful to any country of the world.

British Interference

Since 1846, when according to the Treaty of Amritasar, Jammu and Kashmir (including Ladakh) was made over by the British to Maharaja Gulab Singh in 'independent possession', the history of the troubled State is a story of how those who signed the treaty with the first Dogra Ruler of the State, tried to interface in the affairs of the frontier region in order to have a firm grip over it. In 1846, the British were arranging for the Govt. of Punjab by its 'own native rulers' .... by the young Maharaja Duleep Singh and a Council of Ministers .... and the main object which the then Governor-General had in view while handing Jammu and Kashmir over to Gulab Singh "was to lessen the force of the Sikhs by establishing on their flank a power inclined to the British." Presumably, at that time the British were not fully aware of the strategic value of Kashmir, but as time passed on, and as the Punjab was annexed by them in 1849, they (British) realised that the situation had materially changed and thus began to interfere in the affairs of Maharaja Gulab Singh. Gradually, pressure on Gulab Singh began to increase. In 1851, a seasonal British officer 'to look after the interests of European visitors to the valley' was thrust upon the State. In 1885, the British Govt. was successful in appointing a regular political Resident in Kashmir much against the wishes of the State ruler.

But as time went on, the British went a step further in order to annex the entire State, including Gilgit and Ladakh, and rule over it directly. Accordingly, secret plots were laid to depose Maharaja Pratap Singh. This was done in 1889. The exposure made the British very cautious and prevented them from annexing Kashmir. But they did not abandon their plans. Only eight years later, they succeeded in posting a separate political Agent in Gilgit to look after 'British interests' in that area.

In the political uprising of 1931 which was led by Sheikh Abdullah, the British saw signs of their success. They sympathised with the movement to the extent that 'it remained communal in outlook.' As if a political Resident was not enough, an Englishman was thrust upon the State as its Prime Minister. Soon, however, negotiations started on the question of transferring Gilight to the British, and on August 1, 1935, the frontier was transferred to the British Govt. in India on sixty years' lease. Immediately after the transfer, the British withdrew their open support to the Kashmir movement, but they tried all means, albeit unsuccessfully, keeping it within the narrow limits of communalism.

The ill-fated Afghan War of 1877 had made the British understand fully the strategic importance of Kashmir and its Gilgit frontier. Accordingly, they took certain steps "to control the State in order to safeguard the interests of their empire in India, against any aggression from Afganistan or Russia."

Safe Frontiers :–

It would be puerile that the British who ruled over India for such a long time could be totally unaware of the policy that the leaders of the National Congress would follow in international affairs when the country became free. The history of the last sixty years has already indicated that the division of India was cool, calculated move, married up with sinister conspiracy and stratagem, on the part of the British and their allies who, inter alia, aimed at creating 'safe frontiers' in the sub-continent .... frontiers which they could use and convert into bases if and when the time came. Evidently, they could not be obvious of the fact that after she attained freedom, India would not allow even a budge of an inch of her territory to be used against her neighbours. At least, they were not clear on the role that India would play in international affairs. Under these circumstances, one could not understand the anxiety on the part of Anglo-Americans to keep Jammu and Kashmir (including its frontiers of Gilgit and Ladakh) within their own sphere of influence either by facilitating its accession to Pakistan or by allowing it to remain independent which meant her virtual dependence on them (Anglo-Americans). So long as the Maharaja vaguely thought in terms of an 'independent Kashmir', there was practically no trouble but when, in October, 1947, Mr. Mehar Chand Mahajan who later became the Chief Justice of India was appointed Prime Minister of the State, Pakistan attacked Kashmir. That Pakistan which had not till then consolidated its position, mustered courage to invade Kashmir, indicating that there was a 'secret hand' behind the attack. The role that two Englishmen played in October and November, 1947, to start an uprising in Gilgit, cannot be taken as an isolated event. It was not out of fun that they managed to imprison the Maharaja's representative in the region (The Governor of Gilgit) asked Gilgit scouts to rebel and facilitated the entry of Pakistan's regular troops in the area. The partition of India had not altered the Geography of Gilgit. Russia continued to be its neighbour and the Chinese communists were advancing towards Sinkiang with which Gilgit is connected by a land route.

If the geographical position of Kashmir has attracted the attention of interested foreign powers since 1846, the composition of the State's population has not escaped their notice. The Rulers of kashmir from 1846 to 1952 were all Hindus, but the bulk of the population was Muslim. When the British began to interfere in the affairs of Kashmir, they did so in the name of the State's Muslim subjects. When they lent support to the movement of Sheikh Abdullah in 1931, they did so for the sake of the 'oppressed Muslims of Kashmir'. Again, when in 1939 the Muslim Conference was converted into National Conference, they opposed Sheikh Abdullah out of sympathy for Kashmiri Muslims. When in 1947, Pakistan attacked Kashmir, she did so to defend the Muslims of Kashmir. When Sheikh Abduallah himself fell into the trap laid down for him by interested foreign elements, he pleaded for an independent Kashmir with a view to safeguard the interests of Kashmiri Muslims : Poor Kashmir Muslims : They had always played a political dice with devilishly nurtured British hypocrisy, breaking up hope and despair, at the hands of Sheikh Abdullah, into different colours.

For decades together, they have been silent spectators of how interested people and interested foreign powers have, from time to time, exploited their presence in the State to serve their own ends. In 1846, they still remember, the British sold them and their Muslim brethren to Maharaja Gulab Singh and gave away Kashmir in independent possession to him. Soon after, the then Governor General tried to have a direct hold over the State because it was no longer required to serve as a menace flank against the Sikh State of the Punjab but could serve as a base against Afganistan and Russia. In 1889, in furtherance of its policy and programme in the north-west of India, they tried to depose the then ruler of Kashmir in order to annex the State. Though they failed in their attempt they succeeded in snatching away Gilgit ultimately. An attempt was made in October 1947, to overrun the State when the newly born State of Pakistan (inclined to the British) launched an armed attack against Jammu and Kashmir. It was a strange spectacle of Muslims killing not only Hindus and Sikhs but also Muslims. The situation left to alternative for the Maharaja and the National Conference but to seek military assistance from India. The State acceded to India. Indian troops marched into Kashmir and Pakistan which the British and their allies had created to serve another things as a menace flank for India, was outflanked. The imperialists' apple cart was upset though the enemy was not dislodged from Gilgit, and some other parts of the State. Stunned by the march of events, the Kashmiri Muslims asked : "Has time taken its revenge from those who played with his interests in order to serve their own ends?" The answer to this question has not been provided yet. Because partition is the witching hour at midnight.

Today Pakistan, flummoxed by British diplomacy and, at the same time, outwitted by U.S. dollar diplomacy, has parcelled out Pan-Islamic terrorism over the valley. Tomorrow, she is supposed to be sitting on a volcanic rock of self-propelled nuclearism. It will be a gruesome and uncanny play. A harrowing play of wild language .... worthy or unworthy .... will be on the same pedestrian.

JAMMU & KASHMIR (YESTERDAY, TODAY AND TOMORROW):II (FACTS OF GEOGRAPHY CANNOT BE IGNORED)

When Prime Minister took the Kashmir issue to the Security Council in December, 1947, fighting was still going on in the State. Obviously, he took the step in order to avoid a full-scale war with Pakistan and inspite of the fact that Indian troops were advancing on all fronts in Jammu and Kashmir; he welcomed a ceasefire on January 1, 1949. The Govt. of India believed in the Council's sense of justice and fairplay, but to the utter disappointment of Nehru and the people of India and Kashmir, no equitable solution of the tangle was evolved. Led by U.K. and the U.S.A., the world body avoided naming the aggressor in Kashmir though at a later stage and in a different country .... in Korea .... it lost no time to adopt this course. The result is obvious : the Kashmir case has been hanging fire for the last 60 years with nothing to relieve the tedium of the long wait. The State stands practically divided a present with two thirds of the territory and three-fourth of the population in Indian hands and one third of the territory and one fourth of the population under Pakistan's occupation. Even the census of 1951 could not be taken in the State and thirty lakh people on the Indian side were separated from ten lakh people living across the cease fire line. The two armies were facing each other on the soil of Kashmir and there was a cease fire.

Whatever circumstantial evidence is available there, it points to the conclusion that the Security Council failed to name the aggressor in Kashmir because interested world powers did not want Pakistan to withdraw her troops from those parts of the State which were under her occupation. For example, how could those powers like the idea of Pakistan retreating from Gilgit if she was named as an aggressor in Kashmir? The issue was side-tracked with the result. There is a mocking silence in Kashmir.

World Powers Interest! The world situation today has lent importance to the Kashmir issue. The future of the State has now become an international question. It is not simply because the case is before the Security Council but also because certain world powers are also interested in the Kashmir question being decided in a particular way. It is an open secret that the U.S.A. in collaboration with her allies wants to throw a ring around Russia, China, North Korea and Cuba. That explains why the western-sponsored SEATO has been set up and why a series of defence pacts are being concluded among Middle East countries, including Afganistan, Iran, Iraq, Saudi Arabia, and even Pakistan. What are the damaging effects of U.S.A. in Asia? Cheap distempers very soon crack or fade. Better be safe than sorry. India is the best bargainer to attain that purpose. According to western military strategists, Pakistan is one of the main factors in any Middle East Defence Organisations, and, therefore, she would be able to play an effective but significant role as a Banana Republic over the Middle East countries. Pakistan would be the scape-goat to western powers to fulfil their cherished desires over the Arab world through the gateway of Kashmir.

When Kashmir was attacked or when India referred the matter to the Security Council, Pakistan had not defined her attitude towards the two power blocs, though there were some indications of what she might do in the future with her acceptance of arms aid from America, the context of the Kashmir question, Nehru pointed out, had changed. In the first place, Pakistan has turned her back on Asia and joined the western bloc openly. And she has committed a great blunder. Nor she pays back for her old mistake. As a free Asian country, India has to see if any concession given to Pakistan in Kashmir does not go against the interests of Asia in general. Secondly, as the policy of India is to extend the area of peace and keep the present international tension as far away from her borders as possible, she cannot afford to be unmindful to her interest in Kashmir, especially when in the face of American military aid to Pakistan, the unfortunate State with its international frontiers can be turned into another Korea with obvious consequences for South-East Asia. Thirdly, since in the interest of her own defence, India has to be watchful about developing Central Asia, she cannot wash her hands from Kashmir which is the only route connecting her (India) directly with Central Asia. Before Pakistan joined the western bloc, it might have been possible for India to enter into a workable management and safeguarding Indian's interests in Central Asia, but in view of the latest developments, such an arrangement would neither be feasible nor expedient. In the fourth place, Pakistan's acceptance of the American military aid cannot but be a danger and a threat to India. Accordingly, Jammu and Kashmir may prove to be necessary for the defence of India. And lastly, the offer of a plebiscite was made by India in a given set of circumstances. Those circumstances have materially changed with the American Govt's decision to arm Pakistan. And the State Constituent Assembly in Kashmir has confirmed Kashmir accession to India and people feel their nerves cracking under the strain caused by the last sixty year's uncertainty. The vale of Kashmir has been scared out of its wits.

The Wrong Angle : A tendency has been noticed in some quarters in India to think of Kashmir in terms of the money that New Delhi spends in the State. Of course, if the Indian tax-prayer wants to ensure that the money spent on Kashmir is properly utilised, he is justified in his demand, but to believe that Kashmir's importance to India lies in the amount of money the latter has 'sunk' in the State, would mean closing one's eyes to the realities of the situation. Competent observers view the Kashmir question from a different angle and not merely from the 'bread and butter' point of view. They assert that the decision of a Muslim majority area to remain with India proves and, at the same time, strengthens the secular character of Indian polity so necessary if India has to become a strong stable democracy. Kashmir can, therefore, play its role in exercising a healthy check on the vagaries of communal groups in the country. Again, as keen observers emphasize, the defence of India should be one of the main considerations with the Indian tax-prayer while taking stock of the Kashmir situation. But for money and the need of it, there would not be half the friendship in the world. It is powerful for good, if divinely used. Give it plenty of air and it is sweet as the haw-thorn; shut it up and it cankers and breeds worms. An Indian tax-prayer cannot ignore the fact that if Kashmir is allowed to remain independent or it joins Pakistan through some contrivance, the defence of India would be vitally affected. This is so because Jammu and Kashmir which is directly connected with India will be turned into a cockpit of international intrigue once her connections with India are severed. Left to herself, the State has not the resources to resist foreign intrigues and naturally, therefore, she would fall a victim to the machinations of interested foreign powers to the detriment of India's safety and security.

India's Stake : From the partition of has beens, the Congress rulers at the Centre have been used to pooh-poohing the Kashmir issue, wittingly or unwittingly, at the cost of human lives. That India has been staying in Jammu and Kashmir for the last sixty years has crores of rupees and has sacrificed hundreds and thousands of Jawans in the State, her withdrawal from the area is fraught with grave consequences. How can one prevent a civil commotion in the country from the Punjab to Chennai and from West Bengal to Saurastra if the Govt of India leaves the State to its fate and quits the region? Will not the disturbances spread to Pakistan also and thus involve the entire Indian sub-continent in a civil war? Incidently, will the creation of such conditions help western democracies to check the spread of communalism in South-East Asia for which they seem to be so anxious at present? After all, the Kashmir question is not so easy as some people seem to believe. India has a stake in Kashmir. The holding of a plebiscite was a secondary consideration though that too was not without its risks. For, when it is finally decided to hold a plebiscite, Pakistan resorted to a religious propaganda to win Muslim votes. Thus an apocalypse of communal fires, raising a monstrous hood of religious fanaticism, has fanned out throughout the valley; and the whole mechanism has started out as a matchstick to the tinder-box in the sub-continent. Ultimately, Kashmir has gone down the gutter and the State has gone to shambles. We are never deceived; we deceive ourselves.

When everything is said and done, there is the other side of shield also. If Kashmir does not want to become a willing tool of foreign powers and thus sacrifice her own interests for the sake of others, she cannot join a country which does not steer clear of power bloc politics. The states's frontiers touch the border of five countries and she is, therefore, placed in a very difficult position. For the sake of her own existence, she cannot but remain with that country which is neutral so far as power bloc politics is concerned. Any other course, it is becoming increasingly clear day by day, would mean inviting death and destruction for herself. Kashmir cannot ignore the facts of geography excepting at her own peril. China is her immediate neighbour and if under the present circumstances, the USA succeeds in getting bases in Kashmir as a result of the State deciding to join Pakistan at any time, it is Kashmir and its people, who will suffer in this atomic age. China has already declared Sinkiang to be a 'closed territory' which shows that it is quite aware of the aims and objectives of her adversaries so far as Kashmir is concerned and, therefore, she does not want to take any chance. This should be enough to serve as a warning to those in Kashmir who may have a leaning towards Pakistan. If America is provided a way to fight China on the soil of the State Kashmir and not Washington, will go to rack and ruin. That is the lesson of history and that is Kashmir's geography.

Today, diplomacy has an amazing reservoir of wiles and guiles, on the question of Kashmir. When one's vision is blinded by prejudice or religious passion, however high his position may be in the public life of the country to which he belongs, he sometimes acts in a strange way bewildering the common people of the world. The voice of Pakistan echoes the agonised voice of the extremists. The Indo-Pak struggle .... a 'touch-and-go' affair ... is almost sure to touch off another international war on the Korean model if the West's united action plan is actually sought to be put through in desperation. It is idle to try to hide the fact that the solidarity of Islamic countries has been achieved by the abject surrender of Iraq and Pakistan to the wishes of the real director in corporative peace-making business in Asia. The puppet regime of Gen. Musharraf was being boosted and supported merely because he was expected to be helpful in beating away the extremist groups. The pathos of the whole thing depresses and saddens. Kashmir issue has always been India's burden as the rich to the poor.

Our Independence Day broadcast to the nation often falls on the borders. There are threatening and heavy clouds of terrorism on the borders of our country. Curiosity is naturally transferred to Pakistan to know how they celebrate their own Independence Day. Display of clenched fists in posters curiosity.

Tomorrow, it will be a celluloid clenched fist along with display of jehadis, fanatical crusaders, and Madrassa-based terrorist groups ... a gesture of political histrionics. A false friend is more dangerous than a sworn enemy. Why? Because one can be one's guard against the latter but not against the former who stabs in the back. India should remember in this connection the very valuable old saying in Sanskrit : "To have a false friend and to live in a snake-infested house means death." One of the best foreign friends of Pakistan is China who is helping Pakistan in her war preparations against India, also professes to be a friend of India. China is more and more invulnerable than that of Pakistan, in all respect. Why? Because there lies hyporcrisy and sham modesty behind China's diplomacy with India. Communism is totally farce. No bird soars too high, if it soars with its wings. Pakistan should be aware of China.

Tomorrow, throughout the long and unhappy history of the Kashmir dispute, India will at no stage show any disinclination to hold negotiations or meet in conferences for a peaceful settlement. Even though Kashmiri people themselves unequivocally declared their final and irrevocable accession to India, and they resent any more talks on the political future of Kashmir.

Roars of applause are nice too, but there is a historical evidence for the belief that you get, in the end, better service out of a sound piece of denunciation and insult by some properly accredited reviler.

JAMMU & KASHMIR (YESTERDAY, TODAY AND TOMORROW):III

Sheikh Abduallah Brought About His Own Fall :–

Modern Jammu and Kashmir came into being as an 'independent' State in 1846 when its founder, Maharaja Gulab Singh, showed leanings towards the British. The State could not, however, maintain its independent existence even for two years, and had to yield gradually before the British expansionist policy. After the lapse of 100 years, when the British finally decided to withdraw from India, Maharaja Gulab Singh's great grandson, Maharaja Hari Singh, also began to think vaguely in terms of independence. The result of his indecision was the Pakistani invasion of Kashmir in 1947 which eventually cost him even the rulership of the State. Maharaja Hari Singh could not maintain that position even for two months. Later, when Sheikh Abduallah changed his convictions and began to recline more and more on foreign elements, he also fell from power to pass his days as a 'princely prisoner', in the Maharaja's palace at Udhampur or in a stately house at Kud. If Kashmir is a volcanic area geologically and vulnerable geographically, politically it seems to be both. No wonder, therefore, if many fire slumbers below its cool surface!

The history of Kashmir is replete with instances where a ruler now and then tried to carve out an independent position for the State but failed and brought untold misery for the people. The topography and environments of the region are such as induce high flyers to become political adventurers, but the geographical position of the area and the composition of its population set their plans at naught ultimately. The latest example is of Sheikh Abduallah who, if he would not have lost his bearings, might have attained a better position in India than he could ever dream of in an 'independent Kashmir'. He became a prisoner of the circumstances which were mostly of his creation. A chain of actions and reactions followed which brought about a mental chemistry in him. Instead of controlling the factors which produced unhealthy effects, he lost control over himself which ultimately brought about his downfall.

Hopes Belied : When Sheikh Abduallah came to power, people looked forward to 'better times and richer rewards for their labours'. There was enthusiasm among the masses 'to participate in the task of nation's reconstruction'. They expected that a socialist society as promised in the National Conference Programme of 'New Kashmir', would be set up in the State to enable them to improve their lot. Since Sheikh Abduallah and the National Conference had been swept into power, the common man in Kashmir hoped for better things to come. Gradually, however, he began to realise that he was hoping against hope and that even though a popular regime had been established in the State, his worries were not over.

As soon as he became head of the administration, the former premier handled the Govt. machinery in such a way that it began to creak. The secretariat was reorganised and either raw and inexperienced men or political favourites were appointed to responsible posts. More often than not, experienced and efficient officers were tossed from post to pillar and in many cases, to translate a persian saying 'the work of carpenters was entrusted to masons'. Side by Side, a policy of appeasing communal elements was started and with that end in view a large number of new but superfluous posts were created to provide jobs for them. Whether he did so with or without the advice of his colleagues is not known, but since he was both the leader of the Govt. and the leader of the country, the responsibility was ultimately his.

Since the birth of partition, Kashmir has been severely infected with an incurable disease of maladministration and malpractices in all corners of officialdom, defying all forms of healthy outlook and sincerity of purposes. From its embryonic stage, Kashmir has been sick of corruption, political camouflage, high sounding promises and communal feelings. Kashmir, under the birth pangs of partition, has always been the Cinderella of New Delhi, and has drifted away in a circuitious way of political hypocrisy.

While handling the administrative machinery, Sheikh Abduallah forgot that it was a very delicate affair which needed enough of skill and experience. In his enthusiasm for reforming it, he actually deformed it with the result that he created difficulties for himself and for his Govt. An agitator can't necessarily be a good administrator and that is what the ex-premier proved by his plans and policies. He conveniently forgot that the State's administrating machinery had been evolved through the efforts of able and experienced Prime Ministers like Raja Hari Kisen Kaul, Mr. N. Gopalaswamy Ayenger, Col. K.N. Haksar, and Mr. B. N. Rau. As men of considerable mental dimensions, they had ploughed the sands; they had left the administrative machinery sound as a roach. During the first popular regime, however, nepotism and jobbery, complete disregard of the sincerity and experience of all types of Govt. officials, indiscriminate recruitment to Govt. services and constant interference from the top in the work if responsible Govt. officers brought down the general administrative efficiency to such an extent that if a man-in-street had to describe an uncommon experience .... not to speak of gross irregularity or lack of efficiency ... he would derisively call it 'Awami (peoples') Raj'.

Credit Side : As in the administrative field so in other spheres of his activity, the ex-premier's impetuosity, blazing indiscretion and absence of an analytical mind landed him in a morass. Credit must be given to him and to the National Conference for introducing land reforms in the State at a time when nobody in Pakistan and very people in India had thought of making the experiment. But the reforms in Jammu and Kashmir were introduced in a huff. The Land Reforms Committee of which policy-maker, Mirza Afzal Beg, was the Chairman, had not concluded its deliberations, nor had the committee submitted its reports and recommendations to the Govt. Secondly, ... presumably or account of political exigencies ... he thought of abolishing the big landed estates and transferring lands to the tillers. The question had not been examined in all its details and no regular plan had been prepared when one fine morning he announced the reforms from the National Conference platform. The law had not been prepared and the assent of the Head of the State, which was necessary before the reforms of such a far-reaching character could be announced, had not been obtained. Though the announcement was regularised later on, the breathless hurry, in which a time-old system was abolished without even proper obsequies, left everyone wondering. The result was that the reform was not implemented properly. Avenues of greater corruption were opened out and the gift was bereft of the benefit.

Truly speaking, Sheikh Abduallah got against the clock. So the administration turned the clock back. And he failed to disentangle Kashmiri people from the cloistered world of multifarious problems. Even the administrative activities were secret and mysterious, sometimes in a way that the people of Kashmir thought that what he undertook was unnecessary and ridiculous. Whenever law ends, corruption begins. And there was a wide gap of communing with the people. A biased politician can see a question only from one side. And a wise politician can see a question from all sides as we cannot see in Kashmir today.

The ceiling of the holding was put arbitrarily no matter if the land was irrigated or dry. Some tillers got less while others got more land. There was thousand of others who did not have anything. Some of the landlords who had been feasting with princes could be seen feasting paupers the next day. Village economy was completely dislocated by the complete elimination of credit facilities for the needy agriculturists. The liquidation of the indebtedness and the centuries old system of money lending were undertaken, but no effort was made to provide alternative means of credit. The cooperative movement was monopolised by a few individuals to further their own interests and while in the spheres of industrial development, employment, health, and education, the Govt. followed policies which were totally inadequate for the growing needs of the people. Public resources were in certain cases spent on costly schemes which yielded scarcely any benefits for the common men.

Reforms Satisfied None :–

The agrarian reforms had satisfied neither the dispossessed land lords nor the tillers. Why? Because of their defective implementation. What was given to the peasant with one hand was snatched away from him by another through the iniquitous system of food procurement. Foodgrains used to be collected from the peasants through the Govt. cooperative and private agencies. These did not only extort all sorts of bribes from the peasants during the collection operations, but even made him purchase paddy on cash payment from the blackmarket to be handed over to the Govt. procurer at a lower rate. The Wazir Committee which made a detailed study of the question wrote in its report :

"Persons who could not produce from their lands enough to eat even from three months a year were subject to the levy of 'Muzawaja' or food procurement. No consideration was given to levying enough food for families according to their strength or the size of their holdings."

The producer was fleeced in the name of the consumer, who never had his requirements fulfilled and consequently sacked by the hoarder-grain dealer in turn. The procurement policy which caused widespread resentment was a source of profit to officials, of great loss to the State and of misery and demoralisation to the people.

Again, so far as other essential commodities like salt, sugar, cloth, tea and kerosene were concerned, price control was necessary in the beginning, but the system gradually developed into a State trading. Huge profits were charged from the consumer and all sections of the people felt that the Govt. played a shylock.

"All these acts of omission and commission" to quote Bakshi Ghulam Mohammad and his lieutenants, "inevitably created large-scale discontent in various parts of the State." Kashmir wails, Ladakh's laments and Jammu's jingle and jobation provided an opportunity to reactionary elements both outside and inside the State to exploit the situation with a view to precipitating a crisis. Bakshi Ghulam Mohammad explained the position by saying : "The Govt. instead of making a sober appraisal of the situation, vacillated and reacted, with acrimony and bitterness. This tendency reached the climax when some of the leaders of the National Conference holding cabinet positions began to talk in terms of communalism with equal virulence and touched off a series of crisis in our political life. In actual fact, this course of action was dominated by the desire to escape from the responsibility for its failure to remedy the economic distress of the people. It was, therefore, natural that in order to escape public odium, desperate and dangerous remedies had to be devised."

What was the desperate and dangerous remedy devised by Sheikh Abduallah? Nothing but neutralisation of the Kashmir valley .... to make it independent ... an idea which had been nursed by the ex-premier since 1949 and nourished by his policy-maker, Mirza Afzal Beg.

Sheikh Abduallah's Dismissal :–

As time went on, disputes arose within the Govt. and within the National Conference .... the Party was in power. Towards the end of May 1953, Mr. Nehru visited Kashmir and advised Sheikh Abdullah and his colleagues to compose their differences. Nothing happened and the Prime Minister of India left the State disgusted to proceed to Europe. Later Maulana Azad paid a visit to the valley and tried his best to bring about harmony among the leaders of the National Conference, but failed in his mission. Meanwhile, it became clear that the ex-premiers were opposed by three out of his four cabinet colleagues. Most of the members of the National Conference Working Committee were also opposed to him. The two groups began to speak against each other openly in order to enlist support for their respective stands. Mr. G.M. Sadiq, President of the State Consembly, fired the first shot when he publicly denounced Sheikh Abdullah's idea of independence and called it 'Childish'. Mirza Afzal Beg, wherever he went, spoke against non-Muslim and tried to rouse the communal passions of Muslims. Both he and Sheikh Abdullah cast the blame for economic ailment of Kashmir on the Govt. of India. They could not see the remedies as they did not analyse the causes : they drifted away. A combustible situation was created. Nehru invited the ex-premier to come to Delhi, but the latter refused to come. Why he refused to go to have a discussion with Nehru? Finally on August 8, 1953, the Sardar-i-Riyasat, Yuvaraj Karan Singh, asked Sheikh Abdullah to hold an emergent cabinet meeting at his (Yuvraj's) residence so that they could jointly explore the possibilities of securing a stable, unified and efficient administration for the country. The ex-premier evaded the issue and left for Gulmarg. Feeling convinced that the unity, prosperity and stability were gravely jeopardised, the Sardar-i-Riyasat dismissed the cabinet and invited the Deputy leader of the National Conference Party, Bakshi Ghulam Mohammad, to form a new Govt. which the latter did.

Today, the communalism and political gummings and bickerings created by the partition of the country, and the confusion and conflict followed it kept the Govts. apart and it is probably difficult on political and diplomatic grounds. Can a Govt. in Pakistan survive without the bogey of Kashmir? The glamour of the Chinese to the Indian eyes will be worn out as the glamour of the Westerners is worn out. Jawaharlal Nehru is the first Asian protagonist and practitioner of the compromising creed of peaceful co-existence. Because the alternative to co-existence is no-existence.

General Musharraf is a successful dictator and deviationist who does not appear to be anxious to carry his quarrel with U.S.A. to the grave. The Western power bloc has ruled out co-existence talks as nonsense. Whither goes Nehru?

Tomorrow, it does not require a prophet to tell us that Pakistan is now in the last stage of the process of liquidation. Not even the powerful country in Asia can fight successfully for an indefinite period against the inexorable forces of history. Unfortunately, she has irritated the Indian Muslims by her insistence on antiquated rights over the valley. She has injured the feelings of her own subjects by a policy of blind repression and terrorism. Peace is indivisible. But comparatively speaking, earth, on which peace is sought to be brought, is divided. Pakistan : Is this name not sufficient to make people's blood curdle and flesh creep? Can a Muslim be proud of a tree whose roots might be in America but its leaves and branches are in Pakistan? This abominable conspiracy must be foiled by the Asian themselves.

Tomorrow, man will be fully dominated by multiplicity of fears, we will live in a world of morbid fear, suspicion and hatred. It would not be possible to create a better world and healthier atmosphere in Kashmir in which our political will makes the best use of their opportunities and potentialities. Terrorism is a common heritage of Pakistan.

JAMMU & KASHMIR (YESTERDAY, TODAY AND TOMORROW) : IV

New Chapter Opened In Relationship With India :–

The deposition of Sheikh Abdullah and the coming into power of Bakshi Ghulam Mohammad showed that there would be no more vacillation and no more of pragmatism to rationalise myths. The buoyant Mr. Bakshi and the suave Mr. Sadiq rose to the occasion which enabled the National Conference to ride out the storm.

It did not take long for the new regime to formulate its policy and programme to tackle the problems of the State. Conscious of the fact that mass support for them would depend on how expeditiously and effectively relief was provided for the people and the leaders took speedy decisions and introduced a number of economic reforms. In the first place the new Govt. made a bold admission that the State was deficit in foodgrains and accordingly decided to import large quantities of rice and wheat from India. This enabled the Govt. to abolish the compulsory procurement of foodgrains from peasants.

Thus a vexatious systems of procuring foodgrains to feed the cities and towns of the State was done away with and lakhs of peasants at once felt relieved of a great burden which was the cause of much corruption and nepotism, Sheikh Abdullah and his colleagues had ploughed in all over the valley and even among the Govt. officials, in a cauldron of ever-increasing communal faction. The price of paddy in the valley of Kashmir offered for sale by the peasant was raised from Rs. 9 to Rs. 10 a khirwar (82 seers). Another rupee was paid to him to meet the charge of transport. The peasant was free to sell or not to sell his surplus to the Govt. All the restrictions on the purchase or sell of foodgrains and their movement from one place to another within the valley were similarly removed. About 12,00,000 maunds of rice, paddy and wheat were imported from India and supplied at reduced rates to the consumers in the cities of Srinagar and Jammu and outside. The sale rate of Jammu rice was reduced from Rs.25 to Rs.8 and of Atta from Rs.25 to Rs.20 per maund. To provide relief to the villagers in deficit areas, 70 relief centres were opened in Jammu and Kashmir (including Ladakh) where rice, Atta and Maize were distributed among the people at reduced rates. So, Sheikh Abdullah and his vicious circles were the besetting sin of all growing problems in the valley just after partition. And crudely-infested maladministration was the bottleneck to the development of Jammu and Kashmir altogether.

Vicious Circle Broken :–

The Abduallah regime never gave much importance to the fact that Jammu and Kashmir did not grow enough food to feed the State's increasing population. The result of such an attitude was that the powers be depended on the State's own food resources which brought about famine conditions everywhere. Foodgrains were procured from the peasants on a compulsory basis to feed the towns and cities and other deficit parts of the State.

It was Sheikh Abdullah who, behind the curtain, hampered the free exchange of views at future conferences on Kashmir issue. His attempt was both unfair and indiscreet, for he and his co. violated the very sanctity of confidence and privacy. He should have been advised to direct his attention to his own flaws instead of merely challenging well-grounded criticisms.

The farmers complained that after paying 'Muzwaja' not enough was left with them to eat for the whole year. The urban population cried that food rations allowed to them did not suffice for their purposes and that they had to depend on the black market. A vicious circle had been created and then Govt. could provide no relief to the people. On several occasions when people held demonstrations and demanded food, Sheikh Abdullah, acting upon the advice of his lieutenant, Mr. Afzal Beg, told the semi-starved people of Kashmir : "Eat potatoes. If you can't do that, then it is better to live on a half loaf of bread than to mortgage your freedom to anybody or any country". Freedom for empty stomachs! The common man felt distinguished and asked in bewilderment : If Kashmir has joined India of its own accord and if an autonomous position has been guaranteed to the State by the Indian Constitution, where does the question of mortgaging our freedom arise? The poor creature did not know that as early as April, 1949, the ex-premier had dreamt of 'independence for Kashmir valley.' When a statement to that effect was given by him to a correspondent of the Daily Mail, London, Sheikh Abdullah was evidently referring to 'freedom' in that context, though the average Kashmiri could not read that meaning in the former Prime Minister's early speeches and statements.

The problem of improving public health in Jammu and Kashmir is stupendous requiring immense resources in men and material. The biggest achievement of the Bakshi Govt. had been the implementation of the Delhi agreement. The slogan of 'independent Kashmir' raised by Sheikh Abdullah and some of his colleagues in order to divert public attention from the disastrous consequences of their administrative and economic politics was at the same time meant to shelve the decisions of july, 1932, arrived at between the Union Govt. and Kashmir State notwithstanding the fact verified by the Indian Parliament and the State Consembly. The new regime implemented the agreement in full and terminated the widespread political uncertainty occasioned by the volte face of the previous leadership. The agreement defines the scope and quantum of the State's accession to India. This decision was subsequently *incorporated in the Indian Constitution in the form of Presidential order of 1954*. The autonomy of the State has been preserved and fundamental rights and citizenship rights have been given to the people of Jammu and Kashmir who will have the right to move the Supreme Court for enforcement of these rights. Among other things, appeals can lie to the Supreme Court from any judgement, final order or sentence passed as a result of the criminal proceedings of the State High Court.

Thus a new change was opened in the history of Kashmir's relationship with India.

Today Pakistan's relationship with U.S.A. is the same as the relationship between the giant and dwarf. In 1954, Pakistan has signed away her freedom, integration, dignity and national spirit to the U.S.A. What is more, she has agreed to act as the latter's agent in tying up the Middle East Muslim countries to the America's chariot-wheel. She has agreed, moreover, that her trade would be controlled by the U.S.A. Furthermore, she would allow a larger number of Americans to settle in various parts of the country and to grant them diplomatic privileges and immunities. In actual operation of the military aid pact, Pakistan would be guided by American policy. It is too tragic for words. Pakistan has ever been in support of this suicidal action over the valley of Kashmir. The majority of Pakistan's population has condemned the pact. It was only the Muslim League of Jinnah who had arranged this pact with the U.S.A. in total disregard of the opinion of the people of Pakistan.

Long before the U.S.A. thought of sucking Pakistan into her orbit she had endeavoured to rope in India. All sorts of temptations were held out .... from military aid to free gift of food.

It was August 1947 before we knew where we were. And with it has dawned on us a change in our whole mental outlook. Many feel a strength that appears automatically to have descended on them. In many ways we feel lost but in many others we feel we can rise to the occasion and prove our worth in shaping a country's destiny. Our first reaction, however, has ever been one of the callousness to those who ruled us and who, as many believe, 'bleed us white' in that process. On Kashmir question, this callousness is, of course, not visible, fortunately, in our foreign relations. We cannot ignore to take cognisance of the attitude of the mind of the average educated citizen, the erstwhile 'WOG' ... Westernised Oriental Gentleman : He was callous in 1947; he still was, in his attitude to the land which he once dreamed of visiting, come wind, come weather.

Signs of antagonisn between village folk and townsmen have still been in the valley as it was before. During the regime of Bakshi Ghulam Mohammad, people in urban areas were satisfied that they got enough to eat and the rural population also was happy because compulsory procurement of foodgrains was a thing of the past.

Anyway, Nehru's statements on the Kashmir issue were longwinded and marked by a characteristic nebulous quality. He sounded pedantic and verbose. He projected the mental confusion and mystic hallucinations of which he was a chronic victim of 1962's Chinese aggression. Mr. Nehru, the Indian Caesar, was the making of Kashmir problem as he took pleasure in bragging about his superiority of mind. Nehru's Eastern logic is unacceptable to the world. Even Mohammad Ali Jinnah suffered from certain hallucinations and worked himself into a hysterical fit. Zia-Ul-Huq, former dictator of Pakistan, exhibited his ignorance and lack of understanding on the Kashmir issue. Pakistan is a surviving dictator of extremism in Islamic world and is servile to the United States of America on whose military strength and dollars she banks. For, she tries to be insolent to India on the Kashmir question. Today Pakistan has unleashed a barbaric terror of saddistic torture on the Kashmiri Hindu pundits with organised beatings up of civilians suspected of being nationalists and sympathisers of Kashmiri Hindu pundits. The scenes of infamous inquisition in Europe are enacted. Pakistan has fabricated a tissue of lies and a myth of heroism out of his inglorious retreat and megalomaniac act of cowardice. Like men, like State.

Democracy in India, particularly in the valley, ruins itself by excess of democracy. Unfortunately, our democracy becomes disastrous as the people of Jammu and Kashmir are not properly equipped by education to select the best rulers and the wisest courses. Terrorism, trampling meritocracy, is a rough sea for the ship of democracy to ride. Every wind of baseless political oratory, in and outside Parliament, not only stirs up the waters of Dal Lake but deflects the course of the river Yamuna. This upshot is definitely autocracy. Why? The crowd loves flattery. Why? Our wiliest and most unscrupulous flatterers, getting used to be pretentious manners, call themselves the protectors of Kashmiris. Why? Parliament is confined to a plutocratic oligarchy that is hungry for honey. How do we expect peace in Kashmir?

Tomorrow, in Pakistan, racialism will be a legalised robbery to the rulers. Enslaving their mental and spiritual growth through the new wave of religious extremism would vitiate the Kashmir solution and add poison to the racial policy of permanent inferiority of Indian Muslims.

Relations between different countries are of vital importance in the world today. Without harmonious relationship peace but economic development is not possible. Such relations are determined by a country's conception of its own interests and its immediate and distant objectives. Until the last beginning of the last century, what mattered most was relationship between different countries of Europe many of which had far-flung empires and with sources of raw materials and market abroad.

And the Kashmir problem is a bitter derivative of Indo-Pak relationship as a socio-political compound of another .... a delusion-covered barren period of deserted look. The moments and split-parts are coming in endless procession, out of the depth of what goes by the name of future and losing themselves in unending series of what is known as the past.

JAMMU & KASHMIR (YESTERDAY, TODAY AND TOMORROW) : V

Ladakh And Jammu Get More Attention in New Setup :–

The Kashmir problem is the direct result of partition. It has become complicated not only by the geographical divisions and strategic importance of the State, but also by the diversity of religiously professed and languages spoken by its people. If the areas on the Pakistan side of the cease-fire line (now Loc) are not taken into account, the present Ladakh is predominantly Buddhist area, Jammu a predominantly Hindu area and Kashmir valley a predominantly Muslim area. On the whole, Muslim population in the state preponderates.

During his time as premier, Sheikh Abdullah created doubts in minds of Ladhakis by practically neglecting their homeland. The leader of Ladakh, Kushok Bakula, who was also the head of the National Conference Organisation in the region, repeatedly requested the Kashmiri authorities to pay some attention to the problems of that area. No serious attention was, however, paid to what the Head Lama said. On the contrary, he was threatened with arrest and was even insulted. Feeling desperate, the Ladakh leader demanded the merger of his homeland with India and warned that if nothing was done to improve the lot of his people, he would consider other means to achieve his purpose. Instead of trying to understand the problems of Ladakh, the ex-premier of the people of his way of thinking tried to use such methods to pull down the Head Lama as smacked of communism. This naturally created a strong psychological impact among the Buddhist of Ladakh who are known for their non-communal outlook. Kushak Bakula's popularity went on increasing day by day and Sheikh Abdullah practically lost whatever ground the National Conference had gained for him in the area. Feelings of antagonism were created between Ladakh and Kashmir which threatened to disintegrate the State.

Under Kushok Bakula's leadership, Ladakh had become conscious of its rights in the new set-up things in the State. The people of the region had become quite aware of the strategic importance of their homeland, especially since 1949 when a communist regime was set up in the Chinese Turkistan. Later, when Tibet came under the communist fold, Ladakh with its border touching both Sinkiang and Western Tibet for about 750 miles, emerged as a focal point in the north-west of India. But Sheikh Abduallah's attitude remained unchanged, unyielding and even challenging. A parting of ways, in consonance with the ex-premier's scheme of 'independent Kashmir valley' was imminent just before Bakshi Ghulam Mohammad assumed the reins of the Govt.

The new premier had felt the pulse of Ladakh and accordingly he invited the Head Lama for talks with him. A free and frank discussion followed when Kushok Bakula flew to Srinagar from Leh. Plans were evolved for the educational expansion of the region. Not only that premier Bakshi Ghulam Mohammad extended an invitation to the Head Lama to join his cabinet as a Deputy Minister for Ladakh affairs which the latter accepted. This step created a fund of goodwill and restored mutual confidence. The Ladakhi no longer felt that he was treated as an orphan and he began to take interest in the problem of his homeland, but also in the State as a whole. The Ladakh's association with the administration had paid rich political dividends to Bakshi Ghulam Mohammad.

Ladakh's problems are food, fuel, communications and modern education. In this connection, work on two irrigation canals ... one in Kargil and the other in Leh ... had been commenced. The Kharbatung canal estimated to cost Rs. 12 Lakhs, irrigated 1,000 acres when completed. Some 'khuls' were being repaired while others were being remodelled so that they would supply water to the field regularly.

Two demonstration-cum-production farms .... one in Leh and the other in Kargil ... have been started where different varieties of paddy, wheat and barley as also vegetables are grown and experimented upon. Forest officers had prepared schemes for the afforestation of the entire region which were expected to be given effect to shortly. Nurseries had been started for the supply of sapplings and seedlings of all types. Seven state gardens had been walled for.

A jeep road from Leh to Khalsa was constructed. This roads improves the means of communication in the interiror of Ladakh.

Under the community project scheme, six new primary schools had been opened before 1955 in Leh and the same number in Kargil tehsil. In the same year, three primary schools in Leh and three in Kargil had been upgraded and converted into Central Schools. At present, more primary schools have been opened in Leh and Kargil. Education has been upgraded even in Central Schools and other educational institutions.

Realising that the cessation of Central Asian trade via Leh had seriously affected the economy of Ladakh and caused much employment in the region, the new regime in Kashmir advanced an interest free loan of Rs. 5 lakhs to a syndicate which had been formed under the patronage of Kushok Bakula.

Just after 7 years of partition, about 300 Tibetan goats were purchased and distributed free among villagers for improving the breed of sheep, in Ladakh so that better wool is produced in the area.

Whatever basis thus might have been for the Praja Parishad movement in Jammu, it cannot be denied that the agitation was responsible for the metamorphosis of Sheikh Abdullah that ultimately resulted in the crisis of August, 1935. No doubt, the ex-premier did not pay sufficient attention to the problems of the land of Dogras, but the way in which the Parishad tried to ventilate the grievances produced its reaction in the Kashmir valley and created further complications. Though there was no common programme and no political alliance between Kushok Bakula and the Parishad. Ladakh's cry for merger with India made an echo in the 'Crobriform' political life of Jammu. Instead of trying to know, if anything was wrong with the policies and programme of his Govt., Sheikh Abdullah began to feel that the valley of Kashmir was placed as an 'earthen pipkin between two iron pots (Ladakh and Jammu)'. Instead of toying to control the situation by applying proper remedies, he played escapologist and hastened a crisis in the State.

The situtation in Jammu had reached a flashing point during the former premier's rule. When Pakistan formed new Govt. he lost no time to create a proper psychological atmosphere in the province by assuring the Dogras of a fair deal. The Praja Parishad had already withdrawn its movement and the new premier began to attend to the problems of the people.

The first problem which the Govt. tackled was the question of the resettlement of refugees. The problem of the rehabilitation of the displaced persons on land was two fold : firstly there were refugees who had been put in one camp or the other and secondly there were those who had not joined any camp. In the case of those who had joined any camp, some allotment of land had been made, but it was inadquate and in the case of those who had not joined any camp, no allotment had been made. The Govt. described to allot to persons of both the categories according to the prescribed scale and took steps to implement that decision. As a result of this policy, 6227 non-camp displaced persons and 1,478 camp refugees had given land since 1953. In addition to this, the number of camp refugees whose deficiency in land had been made up by additional allotment 2,473. The total land alloted to the refugees for rehabilitation upto 1956 was about 20,000 acres. The non-camp displaced persons were allowed rehabilitation fascilities other than the allotment of land such as loans for building hutments, purchase of bullocks and agricultural implements. Substantial concessions were allowed to refugee widows, orphans and invalids in respect of rent payable by them for the houses of evacuees in their occupation. Fascilities regarding education and medical aid in areas inhabited by displaced persons were given and orders were issued for the immediate payment of deposits and other dues by the Panchayat and P.W.D. and Jammu and Kashmir Bank. Refugee colonies were ordered to be set up in Jammu, Udhampur, Rajouri and Nowshera for urban rehabilitation. The construction of such a colony at Roulki was making steady progress while plans for setting up other colonies were given final touches.

Another problem which the Govt. tackled was the question of ex-servicemen, mostly confined to Jammu. A board known as the Jammu and Kashmir State Soliders' Sailors' and Airmen's Board, was set up under the chairmanship of Yuvaraj Karan Singh to promote, among other things, measures for the welfare of ex-servicemen and the families of serving soliders. The Board had since taken up the question of rehabilitation of ex-servicemen and organisations had been set up in all tehsils which look to the requirements of ex-servicemen and their families.

A fund had been started by the Board to grant relief to the ex-servicemen in the shape of monthly pensions or otherwise for bonafide and legitimate purposes.

Today, Pakistani poilticians practise the same abusive but a double-faced code of conduct as before .... for believers and non-believers. What they say in Islamabad, they deny in New Delhi, and what they agree to at New Delhi is denied on reaching Islamabad. Strange to say, Indo-Pak history on the Kashmir issue is replete with dishonored agreements. Why? Because Indians are non-believers.

Today, Pakistan has applied the same accusation of prejudice and pressure as before regarding fair elections in Kashmir as if they were paragons of justice and fair play. They have hardly held a single election in their country in which official pressure, police force manipulations and other unfair means are not used. Let them hold a sample of fair elections in occupied Kashmir under the aegis of U.N. observers. They will have 'fatwas' condemning people who do not vote for them as 'Kafirs' and traitors and use all sort of foul tactics and pressure to get 100 percent yes votes. Since their conception of fair elections reeks with foulness, they measure others with the same yardstick. Like communists they insist on having everything on their own terms rather than negotiated terms. Similarly, the only authority they appreciate is brute force either by terrorism or by religious extremism or by Machiavellian way of thinking. Both communists and Pakistani leaders run parallel with each other. What they say in the party offices, they deny in public gatherings. 'Say' and 'Deny' are two pillars of communist and Pakistan ideologies. Most of our political leaders are used to having loose-talks as the Indian housewives. Their husbands fall prey to their loose-talkings as the parties to their leaders. Like the housewives, our political leaders' first sentence : rather balanced; second sentence, rather disbalanced; third sentence, rather tottering and wavering; fourth sentence, distracting and denigrating; fifth sentence, loose-talks start out profusely. Prostitutes are less harmful than our leaders.

Indian and Pakistani leaders seem to believe in their own political nomenclature of 'say' and 'deny'. Under these circumstances, there is no hope of a political solution of the Kashmir dispute in the foreseeable future.

Today, Pakistan's strong attitude has always inimically resorted to old tactics. On all crucial matters on Kashmir issue, she has generally adopted an evasive attitude. Her leaders say different things at different times. Even when she enters into agreements with India, giving all sorts of assurances, she has no intention of carrying them out. At first she tries to evade ratification of agreements and if some ratified she treats them as mere scraps of paper. For instance, during Mohammad Ali's visit to Delhi, an agreement was negotiated and signed between Mr. Iskandar Mirza and Mr. G.B. Pant on the question of preventing border incidents. That agreement was acclaimed to be great achievement by Mr. Mohammad Ali himself. Mr. Iskandar Mirza also declared during his stay at Delhi that agreement would definitely be ratified and implemented without any delay. But inspite of the repeated reminders by India, it had not been ratified by Pakistan. A similar treatment has been accorded by Pakistan on so many agreements like the Simla agreement and so on. And the oft-repeated reminders by India have gone into oblivion. How do we expect peace in Kashmir? Really bad singer usually resents candid criticism.

Tomorrow, like other old agreements, any future agreement between India and Pakistan on Kashmir issue will be deliberately misinterpreted and distorted. And the press propaganda will still be inspired by the authorities to befog and becloud the main issue. No amount of propaganda will, however, help Pakistan in the face of the clear verdict of the world. Like Mohammad Ali, all other future premiers of Pakistan, incubated upon impudent hypocrisy and administered by inexperienced or malexperienced dupes and their power wielded by cowards and weaklings of I.S.I. will roll down a cruelly dogmatised religious extremism over the valley. Why? Because India is an enemy of the existing order. Why? Because it will be the insurrections of ignorance, conducted in the name of unrealizable ideals. Forefathers started out an Islamic revolution that still goes on in the valley of Kashmir, bellowing the empty phrases of soapbox demagogue.

JAMMU & KASHMIR (YESTERDAY, TODAY AND TOMORROW) : VI

The people's standard of living has not improved, regional concord has not been restored, communalism has raised its vitriolic hood, terrorism has flourished, violence and a cesspool of blood have set up on a solid ground of Pakistan-sponsored Islamic terrorism. Everything brings destruction and dissolution wherever it goes. The lawless power in all ages has sacrificed to its wild lust and boundless ambition the blood of the best men that ever lived. After sixty years of independence, Pakistan has plunged into the strife for power. Indian poiltics are nothing but corruption. Fallacious editors and time-honoured frauds have enriched the Kashmir problem. In consequence, Kashmir squirms beneath the feet of monstrous extremism in impotent fury or sullen hate. Who is responsible at the same crossroads : the police, or military or folly? Any kind of peace-making process is dissolved into dust and ashes or evaporated into air.

No doubt, Jammu and Kashmir has turned over a new leaf, but it would be a gross exaggeration to say that all the problems of the people have been solved and every element of maladministration, inefficiency and corruption has been eliminated. It must be admitted that certain steps were taken up by the Govt. to tone up the administration and check corruption.

Sixty years have already passed under the travesty of holier-than-thou attitude and shifty manners. It is a herculean task to reform the administration and run it on sound lines : the power that must be prepared to plough over the entire weedy field without showing any mercy or weakness for any individual or a group of individuals belonging to any community or religion. The ethics and efficiency of the administration cannot improve satisfactorily unless disloyal elements ... those lion-hearted limpets are sternly dealt with and nepotism and jobbery were completely stopped. True, a Recuritment Committee had then been appointed to select candidates for Govt. jobs, but without the setting up of a regular Public Service Commission, not much can be expected so far as the proper selection of the candidates is concerned. Special provision could be made for safeguarding the interests of those communities and regions whose representation in service is not adequate. But if a Muslim or a Hindu, a Jammuite or a Kashmiri had to be recruited, the Govt. could have taken the best available Muslim, the best available Hindu, the best available Jammuite or the best available Kashmiri in accordance with the policy and needs of the adminsitration. Any other course .... arbitrary selection or favouritism .... was sure to cause dissatisfaction and demoralise the Service in general. So long as a proper system of recruitment to Services and grant to promotions was not evolved and strictly adhered to, mere warnings to Govt. servants were unavailable.

Loss of Initiation

It has been observed for sometime past that, generally speaking, officers of the Govt, had lost much of their initiative. It may be the legacy of the past, but in the interests of efficient administration, the situation has to be remedied. One way of dealing with it was to devise proper methods of work so that different officers were encouraged to exercise their powers and discharge their functions in a systematic way. There were spoon-feeding Ministers and their secretaries assumed the powers of office working under them. There was interference from high quarters as low as officer faithfully followed a clearly-laid-down policy of the Govt. This did not make the task of ministers light and they could not attend to more important business. An officer was found deliquent or disloyal.

It became impossible for an officer to function properly when angry oaths buzzed about him like hornets and threatening shouts from political workers and others rent the air. The prestige of the Govt. also suffered. A democracy was allowed to degenerate into mobocracy. No doubt, Bakshi Ghulam Mohammad had been successful to a large extent in checking interference of these workers in the day-to-day administration of the State. He encouraged Govt. officers to act quickly, firmly and with a sense of responsibility under normal as well as abnormal conditions.

Corruption Checked

Credit was given to the new regime for taking some important steps to check corruption among Govt. servants. The setting up of an Anti-Corruption Tribunal and the framing of an Anti-Corruption Law welcomed moves. The abolition of 'Muzwaja' customs duty and commodity control had reduced the chances of corruption among Govt. employees. This was, however, a negative approach to solve the problem simply because a Govt. could not abolish all its departments in order to eradicate corruption. The most effective way of checking corruption among Govt. servants is to remove the causes of corruption. In this connection the revision was made in the pay scales of Govt. employees. It was a step in a right direction. If appropriate laws had also been framed to reduce substantially the financial commitments of people in the discharge of their social obligations, better results would be expected to follow. Persistent efforts are always needed to be made to raise the ethical standards of people and emphasis must be laid on smple living among Govt. employees. The Ministers and their deputies could set an example by leading austere lives.

It would seem desirable to evolve a proper system of distributing forest, irrigation and PWD contracts. The chances of corruption were more in these than in other departments, especially when crores of rupees were spent on developmental activities in the State. So far as the execution of various plans entrusted to those departments was concerned. If an officer was found to be living beyond his means, time was lost to enquire into his conduct. *It was the scenario of yesterday's Kashmir.*

Percentage of Colleges

It is generally admitted that education has made great progress in the State since 1953. The abolition of tution fees in all Govt. schools and colleges has provided facilities to people to read and write. The opening of more schools and colleges is considered to be a reform of far-reaching consequences. Since food is cheap, people in rural areas have not yet exercised great caution and care in the selection of teachers. Indiscriminate recruitment of teachers for schools and colleges was, and is, not allowed if there is the slightest doubt about the political leanings of any candidate, he will not be appointed. According to the order, the percentage of Muslim and non-Muslim students in the Kashmir province had been fixed at 70 and 30 and vice versa in Jammu province. There had been public crtiticism of the order and the communities affected by it felt very bitter about it. Critics point out that the orders went against the very fundamentals of the constitution and the ideals for which the State stands.

The anti-India propaganda of a section of foreign missionaries created so many complications. It is unnecessary to recall those unpleasant episodes at the present stage. But foreign missionaries who are really anxious to carry on evangelical work in India are naturally expected not to do or say anything which wounds the susceptibilities of the Indian people or defames their culture and tradition as Pakistan has been exercising anti-India hymns of hate for over sixty years in Kashmir. There can hardly be any compromise on this point. Why? Because a country like India with one of the most ancient and richest civilisations in the world can hardly be expected to tolerate the activities of foreign missionaries and parochial Indian Muslims who have no respect for the people's cultural heritage.

The foreign missionaries and SIMI (Students of Islamic Movement in India) and their associates must not allow themselves to get entangled in political issues, sitting behind the curtain of Kashmir issue. In some strategic corners of the country, particularly in the North-east frontier, some foreign missionaries have not only participated in political activities but encouraged the tribal people of these areas to start movements against the Govt. of India, as SIMI does in India. From political and military points of view, it is the primary duty of the Govt. of India to suppress with an iron hand all persons and organisations connected with subversive activities, in the matrix of political camouflage all along the border. *A reactionary is a person who sits in his arm-chair on sunday never thinking that tomorrow is Monday but only that yesterday was Saturday*

Regional Concord

"The rights and privileges that we secure for the State as a whole have to be shared in equal measure by the people of its different parts." Bakshi Ghulam Mohammad promised when he assumed power on Aug. 9, 1953. In this task the Prime Minister seemed to succeed to a large extent. The demands of each one of the constituent units gauge, services, education, lands etc. were being met adequately with the result that there was more regional concord than that it was ever found during the last seven or eight years. But the situation demanded more effort to be made in the direction through official and non-official agencies. It was desirable to organise cultural missions in Kashmir to visit Jammu and Ladakh and vice-versa. In summer months, student parties from Jammu toured Kashmir valley and Ladakh and met people in two regions. Similarly, student parties from Ladakh and Kashmir valley visited Jammu in winter months, toured different areas in the land of Dogras, met people and created goodwill. Organisation of art exhibitions created a healthy atmosphere throughout the State. Today Jehadi slogans overflow the borders and bring wild lust and boundless ambition wherever they go.

In this connection, the Kashmiri pundit played a prominent role. On account of his social and cultural ties with Kashmiri Muslims, he could very well interpret Kashmir, Jammu and in view of his religious ties with Jammu Hindus, he could interpret Jammu to Kashmir in an effective manner. In these circumstances, a Kashmiri Hindu pundit was competent. He was facing a serious economic and social crisis and if Yuvaraj Singh found Kashmiri pundit youngmen even in far-away Madras and Travancore-Cochin, apparently they were not there on a sight-seeing tour.

The people of Jammu had a special responsibility to discharge the task of shepherding the people of entire State into India's tent. They could have helped in strengthening the ties between Kashmir and India by their approach to political problems from a broader point of view. They had been well-aware of the fact that the type of autonomy allowed to the State was a concession made by the Govt. of India in view of the peculiar circumstances prevailing in Jammu and Kashmir. If the people had tried to reverse that position, they would naturally create doubts in the minds of State Muslims, and thus create a sort of aversion among them. So they had to guard against that danger and helped Bakshi Ghulam Mohammad and his colleagues by adopting a correct attitude regarding political and other matters. The voice of Jammu in the State administration has got to carry weight and people in that province need not entertain any undue fears on account.

Jammu's Gain

The accession of the State to India has brought rich gains to the people of Jammu. Today the land of Dogras stands as the clearing house for the import and export trade of Ladakh and Kashmir. The importance that Islamabad had gained in pre-partition days on account of Kashmir trade, has now been assumed by Jammu. This has benefited Jammu and is sure to increase the prosperity of the area with the passage of time. Why? Because Jammu is the life-line of Kashmir : all roads connecting the valley with India pass through Jammu. Under these circumstances, when Jammu has definitely gained by its association with Kashmir and India, the people of that Province, must not grudge any political concessions given to Kashmiris, most of whom are Muslims.

If any one in Jammu still thinks in terms of separation from Kashmir valley, he does so probably because he cannot look beyond his nose. Firstly, one can't be sure that if Kashmir goes to Pakistan or decides its future, in any other way, Jammu will necessarily go to India. From the international point of view the future of the entire State and not merely of Kashmir valley and Ladakh is under dispute. Secondly, if Jammu will throw away its association with Kashmir, it cannot remain as a separate entity. It will be merged with some adjoining States of India. The land of Dogras will lose many of its material advantages with the obvious consequence for the people of the region.

Today, goondaism in the valley is an abnormal social feature. The growing disease inside and outside Kashmir has also nothing startling about it. Rowdyism in the valley is not a normal social phenomenon. The mendacious propaganda of Islamabad against India proves the best breeding ground of Islamic chauvinism and serves a cold war strategy in the valley. Pakistan must get out of their narrow shells of religious doctrine and give up their crudely fermentated terrorist passion and think in terms of Pakistan as an Islamic country.

Today, it is an axiomatic truth that the accession of Kashmir to India is final and irrevocable. The agreement could not be implemented earlier because the past leadership of Kashmir swerved from the right path and adopted a course which could only bring disaster to Kashmir. If they had not changed the leadership, the history of Kashmir today would have been quite different.

Danger arises when a man feels secure in his position. Destruction threatens when a man seeks to preserve his worldly estate. Confusion develops when a man has put everything in order. Therefore, the superior does not forget danger in his security, nor ruin when he is well-established, nor confusion when his affairs are in order. In this way he gains personal safety and is able to protect the empire. According to the Uttaradhyayana Sutra : "Step carefully in your walk, supposing everything to be a snare. Bestow care on your life till you win the stake." (4.6–7)

The Pakistan Prime Minister has every right to pass any remarks on the Kashmir issue. But if Pakistan tries to repeat the 1947 history, they will have to repent in the long run. Kashmir has not become a cockpit of international intrigues and politics. Certain interested parties wanted to disrupt Kashmir's unity with India. But they were greatly disappointed as their plans and machinations did not succeed. When a man is tempted to do a tempting thing, he can find a hundred ingenious reasons for going for his liking.

The people of Kashmir had made tremendous sacrifices in the past. Many lost their lives in their struggle against the autocratic rule. But these sacrifices were not made just to hand over the territory to the foreigners and allow them to establish their bases or carry on their intrigues there.

The August 9 revolution in Kashmir was undoubtedly a great day in the history of Kashmir. Why? Because it saved the State from a disaster. The first thing they did after the revolution was to implement the Delhi Agreement in toto. The people of Kashmir are very poor that is primarily due to continued slavery. We have to improve their economic conditions. Why? Because a strong Kashmir will be a great asset to India.

Rice is the staple food of the Kashmiris. It has immense potentialities for development. The zamindari and jagirdari systems which were the relics of the past have been completely abolished. The land is given to the real tillers of the soil. This is a great step towards ameliorating the lot of the peasantry. The Kashmiris are a brave and virile people. They have faced unprecedented difficulties and hardships in the past, and they are today marching ahead with firm determination and courage keeping in the forefront the principles and ideals of Indianisation against the unprecedented character of Pakistan-sponsored terrorism and jehadi slogans.

In the world as it is, with millions of people still being taught and trained to fight out terrorism and with millions of others dependent for their livelihood on war industries in this sub-continent, real people must be a distant ideal in Asia. The Adi Grantha says : "Those who see Truth and speak Truth, Their bodies and minds become Truthful. Truth is their evidence, Truth is their instruction, Truth is the praise of the Truthful. Those who have forgotten Truth cry in the agony and weep while departing." (Adi Grantha, Sri Raga 3.69).

Pakistan has got a lurking suspicion that the Security Council would not be able to make a gift of Kashmir to Pakistan in defiance of the wishes of the Kashmiri people. If we fail to settle the issue in the Security Council, the responsibility would be that of the Indian Govt. Why New Delhi should be responsible for the Security Council's failure to settle a sixty-year old issue is known, of course, to our Pakistani friends only. And the mounting crisis in Azad Kashmir is no longer a secret and continues to be a headache to Islamabad.

Today Pakistani leaders, impregnated with anti-India hymns of hate and indignation, are desperately in search of scapegoats. The dislocation in West Punjab's economy, caused really by partition and maladministration, is attributed to India's attempt to secure her legitimate share of canal waters. Truly speaking, an unworthy claim can never accomodate itself in a high position. Pakistan, from the very embryonic stage of partition, has suffered from constitutional indigestion or from rickety religious dogma. If the whole of Pakistan becomes a single political unit on Kashmir issue, it is likely to be dominated by West Punjab, which is numerically stronger than other provinces and richer in wealth as well as in talent. That possibility has already alarmed Sind and N.W.F.P. Apart from political difficulties in a labyrinth of dark, narrow, dirty and blind-alley of religious fundamentalism and racial passion, and the question of Kashmir issue, which practical statesmanship cannot ignore, insuperable administrative difficulties have arisen in connection with the unitary Govt. of a vast area having no geographical or linguistic homogeneity. An indissoluble basis for political-cum-religious-cum-administrative unity is a medieval myth which cannot survive the shock of complications in Pakistan. A man who does not read good books has no advantage over the man who can't read them. India and Pakistan are twins but step-sisters who, since their simultaneous caesarian birth (vide Partition), have not been on speaking terms. Every hero becomes a bore at last, after asserting an untenable proposition by sheer weight of his personality,

Today the voice of Kashmir itself is the decisive factor in determining its fate and that voice has unreservedly declared, through the Indian constitution, its unity with India, the matter should be finally closed. But they seem to be yet hesitating with the result that the people concerned have been kept in the midst of uncertainties. It is an issue between the people of Kashmir and the Govt. of India and Pakistan is being provided with the opportunity for mischief-making over it now and then. It is an issue between the people of Kashmir and the Govt of india and Pakistan has nothing to do with it. Why terrorism has been impregnated with the heat of a deep and long-laid plan in which many of Pakistani rulers are scandalously involved? Certainly history is a Muse, but with too much paint Pakistan may easily look like a political prostitute. Terrorism is one of history's worst holocausts. When a terrorist kills his overlord in the valley, the shadow of the crescent moon is skillfully thrown on to the sackcloth. And this play is actually produced by Islamabad itself. Yet, by the manoeuvrings of the United Nations, the aggressor has raised its aggression in course of the last sixty years to the position of a legitimate disputant and all sorts of complications .... foreign intrigues and jchadi militant groups ..... have followed as an inevitable consequence. Pakistan and her sneakish supporters are in no mood to accept the decision of the people of Kashmir about their fate that should be wise in all actions. Why? Wise men avoid the troubles and distresses that affect so many others by taking counsel with those who may know more before they commit themselves finally. A jehadi slogan is simply a bundle of tunes. While in I.S.I. tunes, they are an end in themselves. In jehadi slogans, Islamic tunes and also words are only the means to an end, namely, to give a set of ideas their poorest and ugliest. As in chemistry, hydrogen and oxygen have to lose their individual existence in order to produce water, so also in jehadi slogans, words and tunes have to sacrifice their separate entities and an entirely new entity of Islamic terrorism is born with all of its vitriolic passion and menacing look out of their happy blending. They are inextricably mixed into one, you destroy the whole. Never tell people (Pakistanis) how you are; they don't want to know. Why? Because they know something of everything is apt to turn into something and nothing. If wrinkles must be written on their brows, let them not be written upon the heart.

If soliders in Indo-Pak border can now rest, diplomats and politicians cannot. They are too busy to get away from the path of corruptible practices. The law of gravity is doubted when it is mcuh easier to pick up a girl than to drop her. The evils of Hindu society itself should be first eradicated. Social injustice and inequality are the only fundamental reason why the people of

India have deserted Hinduism. They have been sinned against rather than actually sinning. The rigours of caste system are one the many deep sores from which our Kashmir society today miserably suffers. The system has already outlived its existence. The noted Pharaohs of Egypt failed to keep up their dynastic purity even by practising much-abhorred marriage within clan policy. But that was in age passing long before history was born. What astounds is how in this modern world of science and technology, a horde of religious fundamentalists can be so much superstitious and conservative as to uphold such a downright heinous practice that is terrorism. The hardest job in the world is finding one for one who does not want one. Even the bogey of provincialism has raised a distinct disservice in terms of Kashmir issue.

Due to insurgency of terrorism for over decades, the Srinagar based cultural identity ... the valley's 41 monuments of historical importance .... is now in a pitiful state. Terrorism is the only reason behind this well-calculated insurgency for the tottering condition of this enormous heritage value. Sooner or later, everything will get into a clutter of stones. Who is responsible for the pitiful state of 13th-century temples at Naranag in the constituency of Ganderbal district? Who is accountable to the pitiful remains of the Jhelum valley civilisation at Kutbal in Anantnag district and the tottering remains of a 5000. year old civilisation discovered in 1963 at Burzahama near Srinagar? And the Archaeological Survey of India is entirely slothful and unresponsive to protect the national heritage sites under the Ancient Monuments and Preservation Act. This slithery administration, living in a dreamland of political nightmares, is gradually but steadily drifting towards a status symbol of our Govt. It is not by ignorance, and still less by downright falsehood, that any virtue worthy of the name can be produced. Compromise and appeasement will in the end mean India being subjugated. Shaking hands either with the Kashmiri leaders or with pseudo-communists are alike and have pained and embarrassed India. It goes to confirm the suspicion that there is topsyturvydom everywhere. Shaking hands have always been a time-honoured custom between India and Pakistan on Kashmir question. He that is down can fall no lower.

Fear psychology of Islamic terrorism seems to envelop the whole world; as a result mutual hatred and suspicion, intolerance of others' ideology and social customs follow all of which contribute greatly to this delicate situation in the valley. Peace is sought to be preserved by warlike measures. Peace in Kashmir is preserved by threats.

Today, a terrorist! he is ready to risk his own life for blood. Like a weasel, terrorists sever the valley, constantly rising up, stretching high their long-neck of vigilance to look around. Like weasels, a terrorists's lust for blood is a frenzy, whether he is hungry or not, and the cry of any sort of little children is music to his ears. A terrorist does not know his limitation. He seems to possess an abiding belief that all things in the non-Islamic world are his rightful prey. In his hunting, he, too, takes desperate chances. The normal instinct of fear is only a minor nerve sensation compared to the shock caused by the sight of a terrorist. A terrorist evidently possesses sharp eyes and sensitive ears, his sense of smell is even greater. So he follows the scent trail of his prey, which often leads into dark and obscure places where sight and hearing would be useless. Pakistani diplomats and Islamic militants fight side by side for a common cause and take shelter under the same flag. To be happy now is a tremendous sin amidst the surrounding unhappiness. Pakistan is living in a peculiar world of nightmares. There are tensions and conflicts. And the valley is full of violence, jealousy, suspicion and animosity ... the worst possible atmosphere in the world today. God is a great comedian. And the laughter of terrorism breaks into thousand pieces that appear to be insane, foolish, misled and blind. Pakistan is in a great melting-pot of self-destruction.

Kashmir is as a clash between the cherished heritage of the majority and the hopes of the minority as a clash between the Jewish identity and the Israeli Arabs. Arabs are one of the central challengers for Israel's future ... one intractably bound to the search for an overall settlement between Jews and Arabs. Jews fear ultimately losing the demographic battle to Arabs, both in Israel and in the large territory it controls. It is as ruthless as devastating to the present world.

When Pakistan chooses to open her lips she should be taken more seriously than some western statesmen who are almost daily shouting slogans and suggesting remedies for Kashmir's ills. Some friends of America are far more anxious to preserve their colonial heritage intact than many Americans. Throughout Asia, the general feeling is that the blind and barren diplomacy of Pakistan is largely responsible for delaying the restoration of peace in the valley of Kashmir. The creation of 'discord' and 'division' is a time-honoured weapon in the hands of powerful States. *The U.S. plan will thus divide Asia into opposite groups. Why? Because it will facilitate American domination over Indo-Pakistan, Indo-China and South-East Asia. The security of South-East Asia is an Asian problem.*

It is in general more profitable to reckon up our defects than to boast of our attainments. Even the most amateur adolescent politicians would dismiss the words of Pakistan as being at best at hyperbolical expression of tender sentiment, at worst a rhetorical affectation. A good statesmanship should be needed to weed out the problems arisen in the Kashmir issue. Why? Because the principles of the political art to fight out the problems, the ways in which our politicians may commend themseleves and the methods they can most efficiently use in fulfilling their offices in Kashmir society, have not been changed fundamentally since the days of partition. This political hypocrisy and religious romanticism are arranged by discussion so as to rule the valley by pleasing. For peace in Kashmir, the statesman cannot dispense with the science of pleasing, and his usefulness and honesty are injured when convention requires him to pretend that he can. To make peace in Kashmir, a statesman must see that his suppliants are seated near the door so that they may be disposed of with the least possible embarrassment; but a statesman also disciplines himself with as much rigour as a priest against the corrupting and enervating effects of social and political anger, and remember always that his power is gounded in humility. But Pakistan manages to square her religious views, in the most ingenious way of religious extremism, with a staunch advocacy of anthropology and sociology as ancillary techniques in historical method. Pakistan is blind to all fresh terrorist outfits in Kashmir. Her ideas get within a narrow groove; the world changes, but that ominous circle goes as usual. But international law is a feeble reed to lean upon in an age of blind conflict. Victory has thousand fathers. Defeat is an orphan. Where the ruler confines himself to eliciting the more or less voluntary cooperation of a minority of thugs and then uses them to paralyse the rest of the society, the result is normally described as authoritarian government. It is directed towards the enlarging the area of consent. So it is only a false conception of liberation movement in Kashmir.

The overall picture of Pakistan on the Kashmir question is of an unclean, uncomfortable and moronic, where roots go down very deep. Why? Because the need for nobility excludes any kind of permanent bonds. At the centre there is emptiness and indifference. Their secret is routine. They have everything routinised. What makes the climax in Kashmir so dramatic is the spectacle of Pakistan's going round and round in an ever-narrowing circle as Gen. Musharraf with his pack of political hangers-on and religious fundamentalists close in on him. The victim's death does not put an end to the chase. The psychological circle of religious fanaticism is formed all around the valley by the people with their stupid remarks fully endorsed by Islamabad. Both Pakistan and ISI were born and brought up in the school of religious communities but leaders grew up hedonists. Both have begun to predominate the fanatics of blood sacrifice on the question of Kashmir issue. What their blood feels and believes and says is true.

We know Pakistan through her bad temper, her contradictions over the issue, her perpetual shooting off at a tangent, her occasional sick misery in agreement, her palpable enjoyment of hunting grounds in the valley and personal oddities, her gregariousness. Effect, isolated from cause, has become an end in itself and is united by their triviality. Getting a preferential mileage of U.S. dollar, Pakistan is on the edge of precipice.

Whenever human beings in the valley of Kashmir stand in a social relationship to one another, they begin to talk in terms of morality, in terms of mutual obligation to the interests of Kashmir. Men are at least as bitterly divided by Kashmir disputes about its historical and social facts as they are by conflicting ethical assumptions of Islam. Belittling the importance of circumstance is a typical vice of rationalists and one of the most prominent features of contemporary Islamic terrorism. Great harm has come, both in the form of their despair and in the form of their arrogance. A religious fanatic who is a teacher gives it a fresh impact as he follows its ramifications over much of the contemporary scene. The contemporary Islamic teaching has already damaged the idea of God as love.

11

INSIDE PAKISTAN TODAY : Malicious Prank of Noisy Extroverts (I-IV)

Aristotle had once described his pupil, Alexander the Great, as many in one : man of action, romantic dreamer, believer in magic and so on.

Like Alexander, the Islamic rulers of Pakistan too have become many in one : men of anti-India hate slogans, romantic dreamers of Islamic globalisation, rulers of being christened with religious fanaticism at birth, believers in orthodox Islamic rule of endless catacombs of religious mindset. Whatever Alexander did, he was inspired by the thought of adding fresh glory to the name of Mecedon. Whatever the Islamic rulers of Pakistan might do, there is a simple aim that directs their jehadi activities in India and helps Pakistan industrialising terrorism to their teeming millions in the name of Islam. Pakistan was born to live in theonomy and double-dyed delusion.

When a man is brute, he is the most sensual and loathsome of all brutes. What is the difference between the two leaderships of India and Pakistan? One looks to the future while the other is still sulking about the past. Why? The Paksitani leaders are no longer deeply rooted in the people's conscience. Their opinions are false. Why? Because though certain religious manifestations may have reached the disappearing stage, others survive and some are even at the stage of formation. They don't mind lying.

Day-light looting and cold blooded murder in the valley of Kashmir confirm one belief that the communists and terrorists have no faith in democratic principles and no intention of treating the opposition justly. Both of them take the law into their hands. Kashmir issue was born with evil and planned products of political obsolescence.

What is Pakistan today? When nine hundred and ninety-nine of her friends think Pakistan is wrong on Kashmir issue where Pakistan's psychological depravity is itself the very acme of vulgarity and where some Islamic organisations breed like vermin. The condition of their servitude is inherent in terrorism. Pakistan cannot be easily discovered if you allow her to remain silent and look wise, but if you let her speak, the secret is out and the world will get to know that Pakistan is a terrorist country, where violence is certainly a substantial enough interest for fettered religious sentiments. She thinks too as a slave and as a coward, to the legacy of lies and damned lies.

The idea of dictatorship in Pakistan appears to have found favour with many divinely guided Islamic theologians and governed by a distinctive body of theocentrism because of its ostensible promise to solve Kashmir issue. Whereas a military dictator in Pakistan has always liquidated all opposition, prohibited free criticism of his actions and thereby destroyed all the means of knowing the people's wishes.

But as a votary of Kashmir solution, is it not the sacred duty of Pakistan to condemn in unequivocal, the barbaric manifestation of violence and outrage and total disregard of the rule of law in Kashmir in the name of Islamic theonomy? It is neither a popular uprising of the people of Pakistan against a despotically theocentric rule nor a revolutionary insurrection against an unpopular tin-pot dictatorship in Pakistan. It is a revolt by some mentally distracted youth of Kashmir Liberation Movement against the authority of New Delhi to whom they are bound by an oath of allegiance. Is it a movement or a mutiny? Is it a movement of spreading out dissension and calumny among the Indian Muslims? Hell is now held in more honour than Islam. They trust not one another. They flatter and mislead the multitude. Are the spies and informers the principal instruments of liberation movement? Do they invite tormenting stings behind them? It is a malignant disease under the Hippocratic oath.

Pakistan nationalism has a right to grow and no one would support an anchronistic and despotic rule based on the mystical insight of Islamic terrorism. But the crucial question is whether with the end of military rule and religious fanaticism, conditions in Pakistan would really improve and whether genuine democratic process would be established, ending all vestiges of dictatorship and totalitarianism.

The present structural unrest having been licensed by a State authority heated by contact with anti-India hate slogans is not artificially stimulated. In the midst of awful and desolate shadows, we stretch out our hands in vain, and strain our eyes upon dark and dismal vacuity. Pakistan is a political pawn-broker. It is depressing that Pakistan has not yet learnt the lessons of history, and particularly those of the years immediately prior to 1939. During that period the West permitted Hitler to storm bastion after bastion until the inevitable clash came when the alternative left is a general war. The same theory of political gamesmanship is implemented in the case of Pakistan. In a world faced with Islamic policy of imposing its rule all over mankind and also with the spread of dictatorship in the Middle East, it is desirable that steps be taken to call a halt before the situation reahces when the only alternative is a general war between Islamic world and Christian world. The Americans, always the champions of democracy and given to non-intervention, have incurred the wrath of the whole Islamic world. The Americans know it, and pay it back as the situation gets worse and worse. The Third World War will begin. The growing terrorism cannot be caged and tamed for the purpose of perpetuating the grip of America. Pakistan's position in the world is like an unmarried widow. She gets used to make the best of a bad job.

Many a Pakistani ruler was a stooge in the hands of U.S. imperialists who, in order to establish their empires in this sub-continent, used to banish, dethrone or enthrone them arbitarily as they did in Afganistan. This has been a familiar method of stripping them of their ruling power, converting them into puppet potentates and openly mulcting the people of their natural resources. To be weak is to invite intervention. Bombers loaded with bombs cannot take off from air-field authorities. And the air-fields are all in the territory of U.S. Puppets whose life would not be worth a month's purchase without U.S. financial and military aid. Will Pakistan have dreamed of intervention in Kashmir if the army revolts against the civil authorities?

Who is Pakistan's family physician in this grave situation? Don't you know his name? Dr. Islamic Theology used to be her family physician but now-a-days mother (ISI) goes to a terrorism-specialist, father (The Army) to a jehadi specialist, her brother (Mullocracy) is in the care of a religious fanaticism and the U.S. is taking treatment of 'Drone' from the White House.

Will there be a war? Who is responsible for avoiding war? The West, despite its armed intervention in South-East and West-Asia has disclaimed any intention to start one. India has proclaimed its mission of peace in Kashmir and elsewhere. But Pakistan has talked less passionately than during the Bangladesh war. The fact is that the world comes so near war that no one wants to risk it.

But war does not always break out because someone wants it ; very often situations develop so unexpectedly that it becomes inevitable. The conflict between India and Pakistan on Kashmir issue is pregnant with such situations.

Since the death of Z.A. Bhutto, Pakistan militarism has made a quantum jump from the bayonet age to the thermonuclear age. Zia-Ul-Haq and his lieutenants had to strike against Z.A. Bhutto and his corrupted officials; the regime they overthrew was rotten to the core. It had a secret service but it was in the hands of inefficient and indolent men, who were more interested in women, wine and religious fanaticism. Gen Musharraf and his close associates on the other hand were up and against the shrewdest and wiliest politicians of Pakistan. Jinnah was a pastmaster in the art of political manoeuvrs and intrigues.

He ruled as a dictator but he was neither corrupt nor pleasure-loving. His secret service was the best in West Asia.

The rulers of Pakistan continue to sit pretty and are afraid to face their own people; they are, however, not tired of talking of a democratic and popular movement of the Kashmiri people. This reminds us of the story of Lycurgus who, according to Plutarch, on being asked by a legislator why, despite being so zealous of the equal rights of men in other respects; he did not make his Govt. democratic rather than oligarchical, replied : "Go you and try a democracy in your house." Pakistan should learn it.

In a sharp reaction to the post-mortem of democracy and elections, Khan Abdul Qayyum Khan, after partition, was emerging more and more as the stormy petrel of Pakistan politics. He had dubbed the move a conspiracy and talked of the Baghdad drama being enacted in Karachi and warned the rulers : "Your doomsday is not far off." Who will solve the Kashmir issue?

After the death of Jinnah, Pakistan has lost all her friends. And after the violent slogans of Islamic crusade in Kashmir, not only has Pakistan committed herself to secret military pacts of doubtful utility but she has lost the sympathy of most of the Muslim brethren on Kashmir issue. As years rolled on, her spirit gets more fiery and rebellious. Her men plan and wait to strike the blow. She shakes not only Kashmir but all the capitals, big and small of the whole world.

After partition, when Pakistan was a nascent child, her ambition was to be democratic country. Pakistan is in luck. Because it is not every nascent nation that can realise the dreams of her youth. There is merit without elevation, but there is no elevation without some merit. He who accounts all things easy will have many difficulties.

Do you compare the Lebanon episode with India's action in Kashmir? By no stretch of the imagination could any part of our action in Kashmir be compared with the landing of U.S. and U.K. forces in West Asian countries. India was never a foreign country in relation to the State of Kashmir. The Govt. of India was, and is, the legal heir of the British Indian Govt.; and though some legal pundits may contend that with the departure of the Britishers from India the paramountcy over the Indian States lapsed, the relations and responsibilities of the Govt. of India vis-a-vis the Indian States, until altered or repudiated, continued to be similar to those of the British Indian Govt. before the transfer of power, and the Indian Govt. was, therefore, in the same way as its predecessor, responsible, in its capacity as heir of the British Indian Govt. ; to see that the State of Kashmir and its people were duly protected against any aggression or raids by foreign elements.

A yet more important question in this regard is : for whose benefit or aid did the Govt. of India go to Kashmir? Granting that the Ruler's authority in the State, as alleged by Rothwell, an American diplomat, did not enjoy any popular support. Did the Govt. of India go there to aid or perpetuate the autocratic regime, or to protect the State and its people against foreign raids? Events that have happened since amply bear out the intention. Though, formally, aid for the Govt. of India might have been sought by the Ruler, had not that the support of the people been there. Has Mr. Rothwell even the slightest evidence to suggest that the landing of the U.S. and U.K. forces in the West Asian countries has any such support? If not, under what civilised law or moral concept does he support the U.S. and U.K. action which has the sole object of perpetuating the unpopular Govts. of these countries by the display, if not use, by force? The foolish man seeks happiness in the distance; the wise grow it under his feet.

The legally constituted Govt. of Kashmir of that day acceded to India and then India sent an army to protect its own territory. If Lebanon had acceded to the U.S., the latter would have had a perfect right to send its marines into its own territory. The same would have been true of British troops if Jordan had acceded to U.K.

Pakistan has no locus standi in Jammu and Kashmir which is Indian territory. Neither the United Nations Commission nor the Security Council had any time questioned the legality of Jammu and Kashmir's accession or the lawful presence of Indian troops in Jammu and Kashmir. On the other hand, the basic resolutions of the Security Council and the United Nations Commission required India to keep sufficient troops in Kashmir for its security, including observance of law and order. What is the problem? The problem has been created and bedeviled by Pakistan's aggression which continues to this day, and without the ending of which it is futile to look for a lasting solution in Kashmir. The entire Kashmir business is based on a fundamental lie ... the lie Pakistan has told in denying that she invaded Kashmir. The Pakistani leaders must do some heart-searching on Kashmir issue.

What is Pakistan's charge against India? That the rulers have a nostalgia for the old order in which the tradition of the past will not be broken down and faith will not be declined. That they have still some pity left in them for the 'waiters with their dirty love affairs', old men drooling at the mouth and serving maid with humid souls. That Pakistan thinks poorly of new deals and welfare State. But India will not have Pakistan make this valley of theirs into a soft-boiled egg. Their eyes fix hypnotically on anti-India hate slogans and not at all on what they are doing.

Until 1947 Pakistan was a part of India and was as fit or unfit for parliamentary democracy as the rest of India. It had the same contitutional background, the same governmental set-up and the same political outlook; British rule prevailed everywhere and the struggle against it was carried on uniformly in both parts of the sub-continent.

After partition, the pattern of things in the two regions, no doubt changed, India democratised and popularised its administration while Pakistan became a cess-pool of power politics. In the result, a military dictatorship has come to the fore and Pakistan which the Qaid-e-Azam carved out as a refuge for the

Muslims of the sub-continent has become the private property of the Mirzas, the Ayubs, the Khans, the Bhuttos and others of whom the creator had not perhaps heard. The tragedy is too for tears. It makes partition appear ridiculous in retrospect and the whole struggle for Pakistan meaningless. For India it is not only a question of heart-searching in regard to the past but also a grim warning for the future.

The Armed Forces and the Civil Services which conspired to bring about the change in Pakistan were, until Pakistan, part and parcel of the Indian Armed Forces and the Indian Civil Service. As for the vastness of our country, let us not forget that East Pakistan (now Bangladesh) was more than twelve hundred miles away from West Pakistan, and the distance proved no problem to the Ayubs.

But some of our political leaders are so fond of exploiting situations and encouraging popular discontent. Will they learn from the Pakistani lesson or will they also dig their own graves like their counterparts across the border?

Today the tunnel-visioned Pakistan has become a propaganda-mongerism and terror-stricken country; and there is even talk of political assassination on the same line as that which resulted in the death of Gen. Zia-ul-Haq. Pakistan politicians are in disgrace these days like communists in several parts of Asia and it is the militarists who are having the glamour of power. The people are fed with the politicians. Their very names cause hatred. Their political leaders become connected with the ideas of treachery, cruelty, fraud and tyranny either on Kashmir issue or in any other political scam. Because treachery is the plague of Pakistan and the idol of the rulers. And the armed forces are going to stage a 'Baghdad' in Islamabad.

Pakistan, even after sixty years of independence, is still a theonomous State and semi-fedual in her religion-based politics. So Kashmir issue remians unsolved.

What was the attitude of Miss Fatima Jinnah ... popularly known as Mother-i-Millat or 'Mother of the Nation' .... to the imposition of martial law in Pakistan? Like her brother, she rarely spoke; but when she did, she hit hard. Stern, hot-tempered and iron-willed, Miss Fatima Jinnah was a terror to the Muslim Leaguers before partition. She said : "Like a magician somebody is playing tricks before our eyes. No sooner is cabinet formed than new intrigues and tactics are applied to dissolve it and soon another cabinet is installed in office .... Is this a constructive way of governing the country? There are millions and millions of our people who hardly get one meal a day .... Is this civilisation? Is this the aim of Pakistan? We have been made silent spectators of this farce ..." Today Miss Fatima Jinnah's view is categorically true and crystal clear. Pakistan's economy today is in a desperate state and civil disorder is ripe. Democracy without education is hypocrisy without limitation. If she had decided to come in the open, Pakistan's politics on Kashmir issue would have taken another turn.

So,the integrity of Pakistan has ever been seriously threatened by palace intrigues, by farming up a ruthless intrigues of traitors and by the political adventurers of selfishness, for power and unpatriotic conduct. And the rulers today remain a silent spectator of wanton-religious activities designed to destroy the country. The Koran is sacred to the fundamentalists. But more sacred than the Koran is Islamic terrorism and internecine provincialism to the extremists. From the babeldom of religious tongues, more complex than primitive savagery and Kashmir issue, but less sophisticated than advanced civilisation, come sounds of hearty-laughter of traitors and loud, crying of peace-loving people. This awesomely thundering slogans making more and more youths, all over Pakistan, muddle-headed and criminally insane are a type of barbarous intellectual condition that is only uplifting mournful and high-brow stuff to be put over the air for the benefit of stuffed shirts.

Religious extremism : An extreme chauvinism and a chauvinistic song of Islam by a belligerent Islamic movement with quick evasive turns and shifts. Talibanism is as dangerous in religious or philosophical manichaenism as metaphoric in manic-depressive Pakistan. What is Talibanism? Women even normally have highly ridiculous ideas about what they are entitled to do with their husbands' lives. Talibanism has advised the girl to marry only those young men who have a desire to change the Islamic society. Talibanism wants every marriage to be a sort of revolutionary cell in a vast design to shake society. Women are being asked not to give away their hearts in marriage but to invest them in Islamic revolution. This changes the whole concept of marriage. If women forbid : Men will no longer talk of marrying and settling down in life; but will begin to think of wedlock with somethings of the feelings of a coummunist like terrorist organisation. From being the very foundation of a stable society, marriage will become a subversive conspiracy against the existing order. Gone will be the days when ardent young men poured sweet nothings into the ears of blushing maidens; now reform hungry Muslim women (Fidayeen) will be for the sound of stirring slogans in and around Kashmir.

Our leaders, on Kashmir issue, must be silent before they can listen to what Pakistan says. Our foreign policy makers must listen before they can learn. New Delhi must learn before the rulers can prepare. The people must prepare before they can serve. A nation must serve before it can lead. Whereas the political and ideological threat of religious banner is a collateral damage either to Pakistan's role on Kashmir issue or to India, from all geostrategic challenge.

The leaders of Jammu and Kashmir must handle criticism and the scathing remark of extemists without losing their cool. They must realise that they are at a historic juncture. People have ignored boycott calls from separatist groups and diktats from militants with the hope that a representative government is best placed to tackle civic issues and other matters of governance. But the rulers, dissociated from ethics and philosophy, in the asembly, makes a chimerical and dreamy mockery of their trust in parliamentary democracy. Do they know it amounts to betrayal of the hopes of a people who have lived through unimaginable violence of Islamic terrorism for long time? Is it the preference among mainstream parties for histrionics at the cost of statecraft and Kashmir's political culture? Theatrics and exaggeration have been an integral part of political activity in the State since militancy broke out in the late 1980s. But measured political articulation may have become impossible in a vicious climate of terror-crazed self-distrust. If they mess up their mandate by indulging in silly spats and mindless allegations, the situation will be destructive and unsuitable for governance. For whose interests are they creating such a mess-up in the assembly? Responsible are commanders who have served Pakistan's strategic objectives in Kashmir. If they do not make an honest job in the assembly, Pakistan can easily establish the centrality of terrorist commanders to the plot in the valley. We should recall what President Reagan once said : "Trust but verily. There is no other way unless we go to war."

Pakistan has always turned a blind eye to the metamorphosis of terror outfits into another group. Playing hypocrisy and political cant on Kashmir issue is one kind of joy, winning is another kind. India should identify joy exclusively with winning. The function of the seed is the same for everyone.

Why does Pakistan pretend on Kashmir issue? A pretending self creates false images in Pakistan and, ultimately instead of boosting confidence, ends up lowering their self-esteem. Feeling good involves being authentic.

Pakistan today : In Pakistan, where the civilian government does not control the military, jehadi elements permeate both the military and the ISI and the generals still cling to disastrous tenets of strategic depth, the fallout is likely to be worse. Some generals are giving the terrorist groups breathing space still believing them an asset to be controlled even if it means compromising the integrity of the Pakistani State. The Taliban is running a quasi-state stretching from east of Kabul to the west of Pakistan with Al-Quaida elements finding safe haven in its territory. If the terrorist groups access to Pakistan's nuclear assets, it will be a game-changer for the world. The extremist elements in Pakistan have posed a direct threat to the U.S. Threats have been made against India and there are indications of an eastward expansion by the jehadi group like Taliban into Islamabad where corruption and terrorism thrive in secret places. According to Samuel Johnson, "Where secrecy of mystery begins, vice or roguery is not far off." In Pakistan the definition of God is not mathematically correct because it is restricted only to militant groups. Why? Because Islamic scholars in India have said that the militant jehadis have imposed a grossly misinterpreted version of Islam, maligning the faith that stands for liberty, equality and justice. Scholars are aghast at the imposition of jazia on Sikhs in Swat. Some religious groups are against the forced implementation of Shariat.

The people of Pakistan remain silent. There is a Jewish proverb : "A mother understands what a child does not say."

What threatens Pakistan's existence today? The rhetoric has always been compromising, the measures outlined to ensure that Islamabad does not deliver on its promises, concrete and actionable. It is a beginning towards the tangle of religious extremism, terrorism and governance that collapses and threatens Pakistan's existence. Washington's message has been clear and consistent. It is terrorism, not India, that is the enemy. In this context,, an agreement to open the Wagah-Khyber trade route between Pakistan and Afganistan has important implications. Beyond opening up Afghan and Central Asian markets to India, it has the potential to establish economic linkages that could underwrite a softening of relations in years to come.

What we have seen today in Pakistan are the outer garments of anti-India slogans. To solve Kashmir problem! Those who praise their own doctrines and disparage the doctrines of others do not solve any problem. All the doctrines are right in their own respective spheres .... but if they encroach upon the province of other doctrines and try to refute their views, they are wrong. A man who holds the view is right or that a particular view is wrong. Thereupon, the Kashmir dispute is not at an end.

Indian Muslim fundamentalists cling to blind opinions imbibed in their infancy, which interweave themselves with their existence in India, the consequent prejudice that wraps their mind, that prevents their expansion with our national integrity, that renders the slave of fiction, appears to doom them to continual error. For every blast in India, terrorists, with the help of ISI, link up with India's fundamentalist elements like Indian Mujahideen (IM) in Hyderabad and other cities. Most of India-based Muslim fundamentalists are recruited by Pakistan's Inter-Services Intelligence (ISI) and sent them to terror camps in Pakistan, for indoctrination and training in subversive activities either in Kashmir or in other parts of India.

It is nature that tells man to be sociable, to love his fellow creatures. In 'The System of Nature', Paul Henry Thiry D'Holbach says : "Nature tells man to consult reason is corrupted, that it is only a treacherous guide, given by deceitful God to lead his creatures astray. Nature tells man to enlighten himself, to search after truth, to instruct himself in his duties : religion enjoins him to examine nothing, to remain in ignorance, to fear truth."

Nature will return Pakistan's goodness in mysterious ways. A farmer, in Scotland by the name of Fleming, heard a voice calling for help. He immediately ran towards the call for help, and there he saw a boy neck-deep in quick-sand. Fleming struggled and pulled the boy out of the quick-sand; he affectionately patted him and told him to go home. Then, he returned to his farming job again.

Next day, a well-dressed gentleman visited the farmer and thanked him for saving the life of his son. He wished to reward the farmer. Fleming declined, saying he had done only his duty. Looking at a little boy, the gentleman asked Fleming if that was his son and was told : "This boy, one day will make you proud."

Then on, the gentleman took full responsibility for the upbringing and education of that boy. He grew up to become a world-renowned scientist. He was Alexander Fleming. He benefited humanity by his invention of penicilin. A few months after this invention, the son of that gentleman was hit by a severe attack of pneumonia : you know how his life was saved for the second time? With Penicilin. He was Winston Churchill.

So, it is true that what goes around, comes around. Nature does not retain anything. It returns everything with interest.

Pakistan should learn from nature. Mr. D' Holbach says again : "It says to him be useful to thyself, and do nothing for others." It impacts the collective conciousness and in turn it also impacts the people of Pakistan around on Kashmir issue. If you are mechanical, you are not free. Forget ideology. Because it does not work either in Indian politics or in Pakistan politics, or in Kashmir politics.

Both Islamic fundamentalism and decadent communism are a miscalculated adventure of misalliance. Both believe in mischievous gossip as harmful to social development as detrimental to individualism. Pakistan's misalliance with China makes this sub-continent worse and worse. Both live together in a symbiosis of two dissimilar organisms of violence and terror. Both are distrustful to the world and suspicious of strangers. They never stray beyond the narrow schedules of the decaying slogans and their guides intoning the patter they had used a thousand times before. Their products are, at their best, like the stammer who took a much-advertised course for curing the impediment in his speech.

This is the nomenclature of Pakistan today. To talk nonsense on Kashmir issue in a tone of profound sincerity is the peculiar gift by which the monomaniacs, having first persuaded themselves, continue to influence their neighbours. Both slid back into comparative political oblivion, hanging over too much doctrinaire talk. Their miserably mistaken ideologies are today a forbidden fruit. A beautiful eye makes silence eloquent, a kind eye makes contradiction assent, an enraged eye makes beauty (forbidden fruit) a deformity.

Pakistan today : Barking and bitten are both considered highly skilled jobs, and the practitioners of the one are not allowed to encroach on the terrritory of the other. Barking dogs don't bite : and those who bite are strong silent creatures whose presence never even suspect till they have slunk on you from behind. Democracy as a watchdog will warn you with a bark when (and if) danger of communism and terrorism approaches. Because both are accused of the common crime of violence and murder, and believe in hypocritical pretence of the common crime of violence and murder, and belive in ostentatious pretence and despotism either on Kashmir issue or any other issue related to terrorism.

If India is to survive as a nation or even as an independent politcial entity, Indidans should learn to be first Indians and then anything else. Double thinking and double-preaching should be given up.

Kashmir issue shows two faces .... private face and public face. Private faces in public faces. A pitiful hotch-potch (of ideals) in Kashmir is avoiding real issues, expressing a tender solicitude for every vested interests, bowing down to many a declared enemy of freedom, but showing great truculence and courage in facing the advanced and fighting elements in the leaders' ranks. This is bound to lead only to confusion but to demoralisation during periods of reaction, and to the emergence of the demagogue and the reactionary on the Kashmir issue. Pakistan is considered from today on as a perfect protagonist of Islamic terrorism, and at the same time thinks it is too small a matter for them to worry about.

Provocation of military dictatorship in Pakistan was fairly and squarely provided by Gen. Ayub Khan's blunt reference to 'war' as being inevitable in this thinking about Pakistan. Is India not linked in friendship with dictatorships? Have we accorded ready recognition to military dictatorships elsewhere? And is Pakistan the only country where dictatorship flourishes on and off?

What is wrong with military dictatorship anyway? The cases of Iraq, Argentina and others are particularly notable. Is 'naked dictatorship' worse than simulated democracy? Is the rule of a political junta any better than the rule of a military junta? Can we honestly say that the Rule of Law gives way to the Rule of necessity only in military dictatorships? A military dictatorship may be a desperate remedy, but desperate ills call for desperate remedies.

One by one ...... almost in rapid succession ... the newly freed countries of Asia and Africa were being taken over by their respective army commanders; in the sunshine of their freedom, might was emerging as right.

The pattern was set by Col. Nasser in Egypt in 1952; and then a military rule in Thailand, Iraq, Lebanon, Burma (now Myanmar), Pakistan and then the Sudan.

All democratic nations seemed to join Mr. Nehru in his condemnation of military dictatorship, but his naivete while cementing on military dictatorship of Gen. Ayub Khan in Pakistan (naked dictatorship), was typical of one who went on sapping with a chain of devils and then suddenly realised that they were breathing down his neck. To say that "nowhere in the wide world today is there such naked dictatorship as in Pakistan" was to give history a queer twist.

Col. Nasser and Brigadier Kasim are just two examples. Nasser had in a short period shown what military dictatorships could do. His regime was fomenting upheavals in every Arab country which refused to toe his line. Egyptian attacks on established authority in Jordan continued unabated. And yet Col. Nasser had been an object of Mr. Nehru's admiration. A strange bed-fellow indeed! Nehru didn't know when to be silent.

Did Mr. Nehru think that Gen. Ayub would go one better than Col. Nasser? The resolutions in Egypt, Iran and Pakistan have been inspired by similar motives. They all offered bread in an escape from feudalism. Was Ayub's naked dictatorship' an object of scaremongering to Mr. Nehru on Kashmir issue? The only reason why the coup in Pakistan seems to us to be particularly irksome is that country's proximity to ours. Otherwise, if there is any politician of world stature who has given moral support to military dictators in the past few decades, he is Mr. Nehru. In the mid of 1958, India recognised the Kasim regime in Iraq with indecent haste, even before the blood of the murdered King Faisal had died, and hailed it as a development for the good of the Iraqis. But all these dictators and their regimes have so far been at a comfortable distance from our shores. Mr. Nehru seemed to have realised the great folly and futility of giving support to these military dictators. A true leader defends his countrymen.

What is Pakistan's position today? According to the Spanish proverb, "Four persons are wanted to make a good salad : a spendthrift for oil, a miser for vinegar, a counsellor for salt, and a madman to stir all up." Pakistan today is in a hell of a rage of religious fanaticism and we now know why. All her sympathies are with the monster who has been dumped on an ash-can as dirty and as dangerous as the old one. The idea seems to be that if you shower Pakistan with enough cultural, emotional and spiritual rubbish, she will sit quite happily a great soft, cosy mountain of religious fanaticism and never notice the stink. If you hurl it Pakistan from your cinemas and T.V. sets, and magazines and newspapers and then dodge away quickly, holding your nose, and hoping desperately that one day, Pakistan may bury herself in it and disappear. Who will solve the Kashmir question?

Pakistan today! Pakistan's cynicism on Kashmir issue is no more than a cover for her shame. But her failure is more shameful than the successs of being an Islamic nation. The angry rulers of Islamabad do not seem to know why they are angry about Kashmir issue. They snarl and sneer at little success and little failures on bilateral talks on Kashmir problem. And Jinnah's failure on Kashmir was no more shameful than the success which came to him at the end. When a hack producer vulgarises a play of his to make it into provincial hit, a flop or a hit is all the same. Today Pakistan's role on Kashmir is an organised evasion creating fin de siecle climate all around Kashmir, and tricking away Simla Agreement by adroit manoeuvring. The job they have done so far is hysterical. Like a Turkish Kazi or a Chinese mandarin of the old obsolete order, Pakistan rules the nation with benighted laws. This apocalyptic scene has an resultant effect of Pakistan today.

The monomania of jehadi campaign filling the Kashmir valley with its radiance of Islamic fanaticism, covering the sphere of this sub-continent with the lustre of a syncretistic religious dualism, and spreading out the effulgence of anti-India hate slogans is an inimical to the progress of peace-making process in Kashmir. To compartmentalise each activity is to make Pakistan weak by time and fate. Islam, to the rulers, is in their brain, not in heart. If there is no will to solve the problem, the setting up of an ostentatious display of Islamic terrorism for the purpose is not going to be much helpful.

Apart from the Kashmir episode, the anti-India feelings in Pakistan stem from, first, the natural jealousy of Islamic organisation and power in Pakistan and, secondly, the widespread belief that India has been playing either too big or too small a role in Kashmir. Propaganda for jehad contravenes not only the Indo-Pak agreements but also violates the Security Council's resolutions of Jan. 17, 1948 and Section 5 of part I of the UNCIP resolution of Aug. 13, 1948. It will only marginalise Pakistan's claim over Kashmir.

On the question of banning the burqa, the crucial differences between secularism as it is understood in France and many other democracies of Western Europe and North America and the version that is practised in India become apparent here. The danger of the former is that a secularism creating too rigid a barrier between religion and public life can be perverted, at times, into a form of extremism itself. It creates an uneasy tension with other core tenets of decomcracies; individual liberty and freedom of expression. The Indian version, on the other hand, despite its cynical manipulation by various political groupings, gains from its malleability, based as it is on the principle of inclusion rather than separation. It has proved repeatedly that the rights of the individual and the perogatives of the state can overlap in this regard without cancelling each other.

In some ways, it is an extension of the Middle Path Philosophy that is at the heart of Buddhism. It steers clear of the extremes of a theocracy and a state where keeping religion out of the public sphere can take precedence over its citizens' liberties. One-time French Resistance fighter Andre Malraux once said : "A life is worth nothing, but nothing is worth a life." History suggests otherwise. Hundreds of youngsters in Pakistan and India-based Islamic institutions schooled in the arts of violence and religious fanaticism have a chance to get their lives back. Veneration of Pakistan's military valour may grow from the tendency of human communities to see the world in terms of 'US' and 'Them'. Nazi youth, the backnone of Hitler's movement, were soldiers par excellence in terms of skills and motivation. But their goals were perverted. In more recent times, Iraq showed that waging war even against a brutal dictator does not always subscribe to logic.

Men in general valorise masculinity and aggression what Pakistan today does in Kashmir. Women are perhaps better able to grasp that there is nothing to kill or die for. So it may be the time to corporate mother's intuition on what to reach their children into official curricula. In a world where sexual crime is rampant, the burqa denotes comfort, security, and allows a woman her dignity, A burqa is an article of faith, a pillar of support.

Our deepest fear is that Pakistan is most powerful in its theonomy. Pakistan is more powerful than Islamic theology. Everything is filled with darkness that comes within the country. Islam today is enmeshed in name and form and its changeful play. It is a paradox. To resolve this paradox, there must be clarity within. Then Kashmir problem will remain solved.

Not only that Pakistan seems to see Indian foreign policy goals in Afganistan as a way of attaining a hegemonic position in the region and emerging as a global power. Besides having this psychological fear, Pakistan thinks that India is trying to make Afganistan dependent on Indian support and, at the same time, a launching pad for its influence in Central Asia. It is a self-styled nightmare of Pakistan. Why? Pakistan still knows that the bad memories of Taliban rule, the Kandahar hijacking and support to Indian separatists on Kashmir issue are still fresh and alive in their memories. The brave Afgans had a bloody nose to the colonial British, not once but three, when they tried to invade their country in the 19th century.

Islam has all the ingredients to make a creative perception. But Islam in Pakistan feels victimised. You might think that what is easy is beautiful. You need to work out new combinations. Difficulty has such a joy. Discovery has such a joy. Seeking out has such a joy. You have choices and that is your freedom. You are born free, and are not condemned to be not free. But he who is filled with religious fanaticism is filled with terrorism and syncretism.

Strange to say, in the tribal areas of Pakistan, Quaida and Taliban forces have drawn for protection on Pashtun tribes. Why? Because they have deep-seated familial and tribal ties. Dozens of fighters with terrorist organisations are moving to Somalia and Yemen from their principal haven in Pakistan's tribal areas. The steady trickle of fighters from Pakistan has worsened the chaos in Somalia where an Islamic militant group has attracted hundreds of foreign jihadis in its quest to topple the Government in Mogadishu.

The danger today is surely not that we shall too readily plunge into a war of righteousness but that through pusillanimity we shall seize almost any execuse for having no foreign policy at all. It is our duty to tell the truth. It is indeed our duty to correct the puerilities of a patriotic legend, to explain to the countrymen how there was a great deal more to be said for our enemies than the legend allowed, how we ourselves were guilty of more fault than we commonly admitted. It is not unnecessarily the easy generalisation. Every sin of the British or the untold sinful activities in India should be brought unsparingly to light. Every allowance has been made for the exaggerations of Pakistani propaganda, the Pakistani rulers for their absolutism undoubtedly do flourish as a totalitarian country.

Even our political leaders, particularly on Kashmir issue, have jumbled the last sixty years together in moods of irony or contempt, juxtaposed the present and the past, the lofty and the trival. Today, Pakistan's eventful episodes on Kashmir issue from an essential part of her embarrassing experience which will be superceded as a thesaurus of her vast activities of hypocrisy and cant, until the psycho-analytical school throws light on Pakistan. What are tentative speculations about diagnosis, prognosis and therapy have now become part of the Chinese structure upon which communist psychology is building.

Our leaders on Kashmir issue! Mr. Nehru had none of the qualities of the practical politician. He became an easy target for the enemy, a liability rather than asset to his friends ; and the end came in bitterness, prejudice and frustration which eclipsed his immense service to the party in the past. Mrs. Indira Gandhi was, in any ordinary sense of the word, a politician. She was also a thinker. She had an unbounded verve and versatility in the acquisition of knowledge. Where she skimmed everything, she plunged deep. Mrs. Gandhi was always herself.

In 1962, Mr. Nehru found himself in a situation where he could not have effaced himself from a position of influence in Kashmir affairs, even had he so wished, but where equally he had no direct authority and no responsibility. Super-human tact would have been required to navigate these treacherous waters without shipwreck, and this Nehru did not possess.

Mrs. Gandhi never laid herself time to find a permanent resting-place for her ideas. In this respect, Mrs. Gandhi had many of the qualities of perpetual youth ... always curious, always seeking, always enthusiastic over some of new discovery that might provide just the key which she had been wanting to the problems of Kashmir.

All our tomorrows will lit fools to dusty death. Having in shallow roots, Pakistan is able to accept the conditions of her servitude to banana republic. The harvest has been her row of militant organisations. Shuffling and shaking those coloured disks, Pakistan could experience all the pleasures of illusion. Today the most striking of post-partition experiences on Kashmir issue is marked by the defeat of democracy, understanding mistrust of the people, only qualified by fear. Pakistan has now become a prisoner of the two-edged sword of craft and oppression serviceable to the cause of Islamic terrorism, blunting the senses and chilling the affections .... the base alloy of hypocrisy.

INSIDE PAKISTAN TODAY - II (ON KASHMIR) (RESURGENT OF ASIA AND KASHMIR)

The resurgent of Asia, says Arnold Toynbee, is the most significant event of the present century and is more explosive than the atom bomb. During the last ten years (1948-58) over 600 million people nearly 29 countries of the world have emerged from their dependent status. Many of these countries have achieved national freedom through the enlightened policies of the ruling powers and some have done so after a period of violent resistance. In countries in Asia has grown.

The movement in Asia for independence, equality and development is a positive endeavour form growing cooperation among Asian countries and for partnership with the west on a free and equal basis.

Nationalism which has been the primary impulse of Asian nations has taken diverse forms. It was European dominance over Asia which generated in course of time a spirit of resistance against foreign rule and developed a feeling of nationalism in different countries of Asia. Initially, national movements were inspired and stimulated by western ideas and national revolutions. Agitations for self-government became dynamic mass movements. Leaders like Gandhi, Sun yat Sen, Mustafa Kamal and Nehas Pasha became pioneers of a resurgent Asia.

Today, when we look around this continent, we find that nationalism is no longer wedded to democracy. From the Suez to Pakistan-cooked up Kashmir issue, democracy faces a hypocritical sorrow and a tale of political intrigue. It would be presumptuous for anyone to judge these developments in other countries. Asian countries with entirely different backgrounds and conditions. They have to evolve their own patterns of democracy. For example, Pakistan has translated democracy into Islamic nation which has ultimately metamorphosed into militant Islamic jihadism. Because their history, their traditions and culture, their economic conditions and ways of living are very different from those of the western world. Their economy is based primarily on drug-trafficking from the Karachi port. 70% of Pakistan's national income comes from this port. A handful of feudal lords and barons know the interests of drug-traffickers better than the people themselves. But the whole question in Pakistan today is what is 'best governed' and who is to judge this 'beastliness'. We are all in favours of govt. by the best people but the difficulty is that it is the 'best people' who would like to decide that they are the 'best' : And, after having considered themselves the 'best', they tend to equate their own power with public good and to maintain themselves in office through coercion and force.

What are the lessons we can learn from happenings in the world during the last few decades if democracy is to survive? The First World War was ostensibly waged to make the world safe for democracy, but we have now to make democracy for the world. In the Second World War, four freedoms were stated as the objectives of those who fought fascism.

Leaders in a democracy have to lead by persuasion and example. And leaders in a military rule have to lead by intimidation and repression. With the resurgence of Asia, Pakistan, since independence, has not ever produced any statesman who thinks of the next generation. When Islamic leadership is weak and effete or corrupted and selfish, the public loses confidence in such leadership and faith in the system as governs them. Because there are always opportunities to take advantage of such conditions.

People in Pakistan yearn for 'benevolent dictatorship' but no dictatorship or despotism can be really benevolent. Why? First, because anyone with irrepressible power and authority will always have the temptation to use it for his own ends and for maintaining his power; and secondly, because such dictatorship with the help of fanatical fundamentalists invariably leads to intrigues and corruption at the top and moral debasement all round. So, Kashmir question remains unsolved.

The stupid makes a disturbance; the fool laments; the honest man, when he is cheated, retires and says not a word. The impact of dictatorial govt. cannot be popular, liberal or progressive. Dictatorship in Pakistan might be able to deal Kashmir issue superficially with some hardships and difficulties but it can't solve deep-seated social maladies. So, dictatorial regime, either in Pakistan or in any other countries, leads to intolerance and fanaticism and cannot improve the quality of a people.

In India, we are all aware of the machinery of the wire-pullers, the party 'boss' the pressure groups and lobbyists. To make a mockery of it is merely to quarrel with human life in and around Kashmir. Heroic methods and short-cuts are likely to have results often precisely the opposite of what is intended. When once democratic method in Kashmir is abandoned, there is no knowing what forces may be generated. If Pakistan can destroy the case for democracy in twenty minutes, she can destroy the Kashmir agreements for solution for any other system of govt. in five. So, on Kashmir issue, a conspiracy is hatched in secrecy and executed in darkness. Do you know the Islamisation of Pakistan's military began in earnest under former president General Zia-ul-Haq? Walt Whitman seems to know of today's dual diplomacy. In his poem, he says : "I think I could turn and live with animals, they are so placid and self-contained, /I stand and look at them long and long./ They do not sweat and whine about their condition,/They do not lie awake in the dark and weep for their sins,/ They do not sick me discussing their duty to God." What a thought-provoking analysis on a brutish nature of a brute! As an Islamic country, Pakistan is afflicted with the disturbance of mental equilibrium, which results in nervous disorders, caused by continuous states of excitement or excessive stimulation of the fanatic senses.

Pakistan today in Kashmir : Major Pakistan-sponsored terror attacks in J & K.

	Year	Security Forces Killed	Terrorists Killed	Civilians Killed	Total
N	1999	355	1082	873	2310
D	2000	397	1520	847	2764
A	2001	536	2020	996	3552
	2003	314	1494	795	2603
U	2004	281	976	707	1964
P	2005	189	917	557	1663
A					
	2006	151	593	389	1133
	2007	82	358	131	571

If one goes merely by statistics, the 2004-08 period of the UPA Govt. does not appear worse compared to the NDA regime (1999-2003). When terrorists struck Mumbai in Nov. 2008 was when Govt. took some positive security measures after some dithering. The setting-up of the National Investigation Agency and making the existing anti-terror law tougher are likely to change the scenario if Govt. continues with police modernisation scheme and strengthens the intelligence set-up and paramilitary forces of NSG, CRPF, CISE, ITBP, BSF and SSB. The NDA had enacted POTA to deal with terrorism, but its misuse where even children were booked under this law. For example, Jharkand. The UPA repealed the act. Mumbai 26/11 forced the Govt. to see merit in POTA. And the Multi-purpose National Identity Card (MNIC) scheme is the other measure initiated by NDA which the current regime found worthy of continuation when it came to power. Everything has so far been enacted in law to counter Pakistan-sponsored terrorism in India.

Statistics of Major Islamic terror attacks outside J & K and North-East.

	Year	Security Forces Killed	Terrorists Killed	Civilians Killed	Total
N	2000	9	5	8	22
D	2002	5	2	32	39
A	2003	2	0	62	64
U	2004	0	0	0	0
	2005	0	6	63	69
P	2006	0	1	261	262
	2007	0	0	141	141
A	2008	27	9	328	364

Source : SATP

Terrorists left no part of the country untouched, having made roads into the south by attacking Bangalore and Hyderabad twice. Ayodhya, Delhi, Baranasi, Lucknow, Faizabad, Rampur, Ahmedabad, Surat and Mumbai ... the list is Pan-India. The Govt. responded with piecemeal measures. Schemes city policing, desert policing, coastal security and police modernisation .... remained confined to a few mettings till 26/11 happened.

MNIC includes an individual's biometrics and fingerprints. Govt. has also pushed the plan to provide every citizen a Unique Identity Number. Centre should procure modern weapons and increase their strength from the existing 7.5 lakh to 10 lakh by 2010. That is the only way they can fight terrorism, naxalism, Maoism and insurgency in north-east and pseudo-communists believing in terrorism.

The US in its role as Pakistan's chief benefactor and partner by compulsion must rethink of US supplied Harpoon anti-ship missile for use against land targets. Enhanced non-military aid is well and good; a Pakistani Govt. too weak to provide governance and infrastructure will create a socio-political space for radicalism in the country that will benefit no one. But in the aftermath of 9/11, expedience has been allowed to take over too often. Billions of dollars have flowed into Islamabad with no credible benchmarks in place. Verifications of mechanism have been lacking with US personnel in Pakistan having no access to Pakistani military records for purposes of oversight. The lack of transparency has been such, infact, that at times there has been little clarity even in the US Congress about the exact nature and quantum of aid being pumped into Pakistan either in the name of development of the country or in the name of Islamic terrorism in India or in the name of nuclear proliferations. This is the apocalyptic situation in Pakistan today.

The result has been predictable. Both civilian and military aid have been diverted to boost military capabilities effectively detrimental against India on

Kashmir issue rather than bolstering anti-insurgency operations. An upsetting of the status quo in the subcontinent and diversion of the Pakistani resources to its eastern border will set back Washington's efforts in Afganistan by years and perhaps condemn them to failure. With 400 million dollar for military aid and 1.5 billion dollar for civilian aid to Islamabad pending, it cannot afford not to. What is elusive and deceptive of Pakistan attitude on Kashmir issue resolves itself into crystal clearness. Well-timed silence of US officials is the most commanding expression.

What is 'lend-lease' programme? During the Second World War, It was US that supplied the U.K. China, France and even Soviet Union with 'war materials' between 1941 and 1945. Do you know the U.K. repaid the last of its debts on this score only by 2006? 'Lend-Lease' programme means using Pakistan territory for war against China. This US 'lend-lease programme' will have to lead Pakistan into a dreamland of nightmares using scurvy trick to a boiling inferno.

Why? Because Pakistan has always been governed either by the de facto govt. or by martial law or by theonomous rulers guided by the protagonists of anti-India hate slogans or by Kashmir based Islamic organisations. Who is a part of the constitution? Do they have some lessons to learn from events in Kashmir? President Iskander Ali Mirza once declared that his regime would be a revolutionary regime. Did it derive from a constitution or from an act of revolution? They talk about the free world including dictatorship. It is very confusing and bewildering. Why not US 'lend-lease programme' for Pakistan? China has now been in a dilemma, using Pakistan as 'US stooge' for future war. Who will solve the Kashmir issue? Even people talk vaguely of democracy and, sometimes, people who have no democracy, talk loudest about it. Pakistan started with democratic institutions has gradually transformed itself into a govt. of anti-India hate slogans on Kashmir issue. So Pakistan is different. Why? Pakistan is not politically, ideologically and organisationally a continuing entity. It is based largely on communal reasons and on negative politics.

Hush! Pakistan is lying asleep in a painful bed of US dollar diplomacy. Pakistan, U.S. Trojan horse in Asia, loves to attract pain and sustain pain. A hurt body looks at the world through pain. A hurt body will try its best to sustain pain. It is a matter of survival. No dichotomous key for identification of diseases.

Moreover, the bestial depravity of ISI, the ferocity of jihadis' feral impulses and the brutish stupidity of low intelligent leaders throughout the valley and other Indian States are not the offshoot of any criminal intent in the ordinary sense but due to a superstitious belief that Kashmiri Hindu pundits are a wicked witch responsible for the Kashmir problem. Crimes of this character prompted not by selfish or sordid motives but purely superstitious fears of India are unfortunately not as infrequent as one would wish, and they pose a rather perplexing problem unpredictable and unforeseeable, not knowing which way to turn.

The terror of imaginery evils engendered by superstitious belief in Islamic terrorism will always outweigh the fear of legal penalties. Islamic superstition operates as an agent of atrocious crime in a dual manner. At one end there exists, in benighted areas, malignant sorcerers of anti-India hate slogans and militant friends who indulge in murderous magic wand of Islamic globalisation involving bloodshed and terror quite apocryphal to Islam and world peace. On the other hand, Islamic superstition often impels the murder of helpless men, women and children believed to be the authors of Kafirs. This latter class is inevitable for eradicating the deadly evil from the valley. This is the bondage of superstitious terrors. The evils in Pakistan should awaken us to the dangers of frittering away our energies in petty quarrels. Years of such living make the people of Pakistan automatically conformist and blindly complaint. The most obedient to the anti-India hate slogans is Islamabad's favourite political weapon the worst way wormwood.

Pakistan sponsored liberation movement in Kashmir! Everything is empty inside ... empty and threadbare. Everyone is in fact no more than a carricature. They act and talk as carricatures. Their existence is one great cliche that they carry about with them like a snail in his little house and they live in it and die in it. A perfect moron who is always staring at the mirror of fluffing up their eyes or stroking themselves dreamily is bored all the time. The basic fact about Kashmir issue is not that it is a tragedy but that it is a bore. The feuding and bickering inside Pakistan still looms larger and larger. Pakistan's so-called 'loving and devoted' future Indian Muslims is really in love with India and her democracy and that a life long marriage is only a thing of the past.

Today, Pakistani rulers, sitting at the helm of Islamabad, have been forced to placate a growing legion of ambitious feudal lords and theonomous Islamic culture at home and abroad. So manoeuvring for power, corruption and subsequent economic instability have increased in the last sixty years. The question being asked here is : 'For how long?'

Not only that Pakistan's pretended relations with Islam procure her numerous followers among the jehadis. Islamabad's preaching becomes everyday more and more violent against the Kashmiri Hindus, and at length it advocates the extermination of that accursed race, which would cause the ruin of Islamic movement in Kashmir if not properly destroyed. A conspiracy has been organised by these self-styled sacred persons.

The constitution which was brought into being on March 23, 1956 after so many tribulations is unworkable. It is so full of dangerous compromises that Pakistan will soon disintegrate internally if the inherent malaise is not removed. It is seriously threatened by the ruthlessness of traitors and political adventurers.

Islamic Stalinism in Kashmir and in other parts of India has been restored all but in name, and the example of the Ayub Khan's regime is as good example as any of the limitations within which a totalitarian system is compelled to function. The post-Ayub crisis has confirmed among other things that a dictatorship can't liberalise itself without committing suicide which is why both Zia-ul-Haq and Gen. Musharraf have beaten a hurried retreat from Islamic de-Stalinisation. Why? Because a totalitarian system must necessarily remain totalitarian if it is to be true to itself; to pretend otherwise is to invite the kind of basic challenge wherwith Pakistan has faced in Afganistan and to which it responds with all the instincts of survival in full play.

There are five layers in Pakistan's Islamic body. The body suffers from swelling fever of religious fanaticism, the body suffers from a gathering storm of political consternation, the body suffers from a contagious disease of trans-national Islamic jehadism, the body suffers from a romanticism of feverish temperament on Kashmir issue, and finally the body is nourished with a feeding-bottle of militant crusaders like a vassal's fidelity to his feudal lord. These five layers, altogether, make Pakistan a feather-bed of Islamic terrorism, fashioning Islamabad into a lump of clay. Islamabad believes in proverbial saying : 'Fast bind fast find'.

The following is Thomas Paine's gibe about Edmund Burke's oratory in a house of commons debate on the subject of the French Revolution : "Up like a Rocket, down like a stick". Pakistan's ambition over Kashmir and pride on Islamic terrorism goes up like a rocket, and will go down like a stick as the country will die, loaded with religious fanaticism. Even Robin Hood could brave all weathers but a thaw wind. A thaw wind is 'a cold piercing wind'. Does Pakistan know Kashmir accession to India is not made with rose-water? On either side harm must be done before good can accrue. Terrorism is as tasty as secret resolution, as the communists or terrorists generally do. Both were born and brought up in the house of this evil nature.

Demagogues can distort the issues of Kashmir policy, and well-organised parties, pseudo-secularists and communists loaded with antic slogans and voice-worn phrases of euphemism can even get the votes of ignorant citizens by representing the Kashmir issues to them. It is no accident that the first action of every dictatorial regime ... military, fascist or communist ... is to muzzle the press of the country so that public cannot know anything apart from what the regime wants it to know. The Indian press has every reason to be proud of its past. Even in the worst period of British rule it was never cowed down.

As the advent of Ayub Khan, Gen. Zia-ul-Haq, and Gen. Musharraf got to supreme power in Pakistan, with their Joan of Arc complex and Napoleonic notions of the greatness of Pakistan, a critic immediately asks the tourist for his opinion on Pakistan today. He must say : "It is very refreshing. Very refreshing. I feel like a new man when I wake up."

Some birds are beautiful because birds of the opposite sex prefer the beautiful to the ugly, and that mind is sufficiently similar in birds and Pakistani rulers who eulogise the anti-Islamic songs of militant jehadis. For all practical reasons, the long-drawn-out debate over Kashmir ... a dead dogma ... is quite marginalised today. Pakistan's foreign policy on Kashmir issue is an immoral doctrine and ideologically shambolic and funny. Why? The answer is that the brutal and fiendish forms of a theonomous country like Pakistan has always been in a dilemma. Since independence, every ruler, even the military dictator, and all other jehadi groups have been connected to the same ultimate unreality and lead people towards a common goal ... terrorism in Kashmir. Affirming the existence of ultimate unreality, they assume that terrorism in India can be only one, regardless of the various beliefs in agreements, pacts, deal and compromise on Kashmir issue. It is an absolute empitness of their self-styled assumption. Pakistan has learnt a good lesson from Afganistan's long history of civil war. And it is encouraging for Pakistan to redirect euphemistic slogans of Islamic jehad in Kashmir through gunfire and bomb blasts. In this criss-cross situation, Pakistan needs a fairy godmother. Democracy, like Rome, can't be built in a day, but it is the only long-term vaccine that can deliver Pakistan from a long-standing shackles of political instability and religious fanaticism. Taking care of one's own children is on the whole a more efficient form of the struggle for life than feeding the children of others. Pakistan thinks more of Islamic terrorism than that of Islam. Sixty years have already passed. Another decade, another agreement, another deadline, for what seems like the zillionth time. An ape is an ape, even if it has gold insignia. It is a true picture of inside Pakistan today.

A want of single-mindedness is fatal to a just decision on Kashmir solution. The State bureaucrats very scrupulous to every detail and meticulous in taking decision have sought to encase the consciences of their rulers in a panoply that no conviction can pierce through. Pakistan racialists and their fellow-travellers defend Islamic concept with all the fanaticism at their disposal. China's pseudo-communist ideology is ringing India with its military bases. In the language of chess players, they often declare they want to check us ... that is, to place India in a tight spot. But China should be remembered that if one side wants to check, the otherside, in turn, cannot only check but checkmate. Even Pakistan, with the help of China, has successfully extended the activities of Islamic nation to the manifold branches of Islamic terrorism in India so as to weaken India in all respects. Pakistan's new movement on Kashmir issue has varied between 'awe' and 'anxiety'. Without incentives, it is quite impossible to bring millions of people to anti-India hate slogans. Pakistan likes to go through the Inferno of the fires and the purgatory like Dante. Islamabad has one eye on the present, the other is always busy in scanning the past.

Peace is pro-family, pro-economy and pro-turtle. Do you want peace? Scipio Africanus, the Roman, who defeated Hannibal, put it this way : "If you want peace, prepare for war." India should think of the matter very meticulously, not vacuously and stupidly.

The Kashmir issue has emerged both India and Pakistan in larger affairs, cared not to understand one another. Partition challenged Pakistan into military lines, cutting off from the vortex of world politics. After partition, a new upsurge of nationalism has jerked the traditional political structure. Will furious gales of political convulsions and religious typhoons be artificially provoked to uproot and annihilate everything? A terrorist moves as if he had no bones.

INSIDE PAKISTAN TODAY : III (ON KASHMIR) (LONG MONOLOGUE OF HUNGRY DESPAIR)

It is a wise child that knows its own father. Pakistan today! More people know their own country than Tom fool knows his country like Pakistan. Why? Because the self-esteemed movement is based on simple-minded shibboleths such as 'love yourself' rather than 'know yourself'. This is Pakistan today. There are so many reasons for 'love yourself'. One of the reasons is the emergence of independent Asian States.

Independent Asian States emerged from the clutches of colonialism are not invariably hostile to their former colonial masters. History has a bad habit of running according to pattern, though not always to schedule. Today, there is so much restlessness, frustration and burning desire of some politically lustful leaders seasoned with a chorus of satyrs to make the most of opportunities even in the valley of Kashmir. Its tragedy has been its weak, vague and vacillating leadership characterised by unrestrained merry-making for all terrorist activities in the valley. Soaked thoroughly with much-vaunted prejudice, imbued with misjudged Islamic fanaticism, and often mixed with other ingredients of unwanted political dogmas over the valley, there has been no public life for the last sixty years in Kashmir.

Islamic fanatics in Kashmir : A fatal infections to the Islamic world. Ruled along Islamic lives, Saudi Arabia has exercised a conservative influence over Middle Eastern politics, although the position of the ruling house of Saud was severely threatened by the brief seizure of the Great Mosque in Mecca by Islamic fantics in 1979. In 1987, violence in Mecca during an Iranian political demonstration in which over 400 people were killed and many others injured led to strained relations with Iran. Such Islamic fanaticism is placed not only in the orbit of Kashmir but all around the Islamic countries also.

Islamic fanaticism is a religious fabric of various theologian-made fibres, with a glossy surface of Islamic terrorism on one side produced by a twill weave with the weft-threads almost hidden, and on the other side embroidered by jehadi slogans to expose folly or vice or mislead a Muslim youth, making insecure or destroying insidiously by removing the foundations of true Islamic philosophy. If anything has antagonised the non-Islamic world towards the Islamic world, it is the unscrupulous conduct of Pakistan, in Kashmir. To Muslims all over the world, Saudi Arabia is the holiest place on earth; here is Mecca, the birth place of the prophet, with her none but Muslims may go; and also Medina, where the last remains of the prophet were laid to rest. All the age-old romantic notions about the Arabia were fed on the legends and stories connected with the heart of the Arab land : the romantic world of the Arabian Nights; fearless, long-robed tribesmen always on the move on horseback along the burning sands of endless deserts. For the history of Arabia is as old as creation.

Is Pakistan a happy nation? Not at all. Why? Because happiness depends to some extent upon external conditions, but chiefly upon mental attitudes. In the midst of economic and social crises of varying gravity, a state of jehadi slogans has still existed in Pakistan for over sixty years. It was not a foreign war, but a war in which treachery and deportation, hunger and terror, death, whether in the form of slow brutality or an inevitable threat over the valley of Kashmir, the operations of a corrupt police force of Kashmir, military occupation and ignominies of every kind, have become familiar : a war in which Kashmiri Hindu pundits were sacrificed to a minority view of mankind and in which many Islamic rulers of Pakistan were able to find the occasion of achieving a prosperity.

Kashmir issue appears a gigantic failure, 'a broken Kashmir'. Pakistan seems to be set in opposition to humanity; existence reveals herself in all her tragic fragility, her total nakedness, and she has revealed herself as foolish, absurd and solitary; Pakistan no longer appeared as a spectacle, or as a catalogue of facts of which a reasoned inventory can be made, but rather as something at the heart of which it is impossible to find refuge; her existence is attacked in the root of her being.

What has to be saved is not Pakistan only, but the people of Pakistan themselves. The echo of Nietzche's prophetic phrase, 'God is dead', can still be heard. Pakistan seems to be responsible for the death of Islam and wandering in the maze of world terrorism which therefore has no meaning. Pakistan cannot but compare herself at times to that hero of the absurd, Sisyphus, in terms of whom Albert Camus has summed him up.

Is not Pakistan responsible for the death of god by waging war of Islamic terrorism in Kashmir? If it is impossible to speak of the sanctity of vice, of the purity of evil, it is because, if sin is born of knowledge, some sort of knowledge may be born of sin. The demon may perhaps be transformed into an angel and a welcoming light appears at the further end of darkness. Did not Pakistan choose to be born? Did she not choose her own nationality and her identity of anti-India hate slogans? Pakistan has to be responsible for her existence. Will a mansion without a strong foundation endure? Mental conflicts result from the rejection of the internal. Pakistan has not yet distinguished between nectar and poison, and edible and inedible.

Since partition, Pakistan has followed the footsteps of the Stuart regimes. Why? Throughout the Stuart reigns, judges had been dismissed if they withstood the king ... too often they had been his servile creatures. Most of the provincial judges, keeping pace with some Indian judges, have indulged in the travesty of truth. It turns into servility when the thin demarcation line is crossed, wittingly or unwittingly. They are considered to be demi-gods during the intervegnum period.

Was Mr. Nehru the lotus eater from Kashmir? The foreign and domestic policies of Nehru are brought under bitter criticism. His administrative miscalculations were exposed to the people, inconsistencies were pilloried, practice was contrasted with professions. The result? The result was a formidable attack on the entire system of his foreign policy and of his govt. of which he was the pivot. Too much talk ... too little action, and that of the wrong kind. This is the burden of the accusation. No statesman in this position of Nehru can fail to make serious mistakes. Why? Because of the importance and variety of the questions with which he was called upon to deal. And it was his personal misfortune that, since the death of Sardar Patel, there was no man in the Congress as well as in India who could even approach him in national reputation. His monopoly of power was little short of a national disaster. In search of political adventures, India and the political firebrands have always exhibited military skill, prowess and generosity. Nehru's hold over the country, the people and Kashmir could not have survived the dangerous days that followed partition. He failed to save the land from the disruptive forces of sectarianism of Pakistan's ever-growing malevolence, political dualism combined with double-dyed theonomous mania and irreconcilable animosity, and of Chinese aggression in 1962.

His lack of farsightedness, administrative capacity, and his poor judgement in picking men for key positions were defects which at the moment outweighed his past claims upon the gratitude of his countrymen. He tried to do miracles over the Kashmir problem immediately. What a blunder! Opportunity and merit have their incentives and rewards. Ideas might be more explosive than bombs. Hand-shaking diplomacy and compromise still go on. Who will solve the Kashmir issue?

Gaining an advantage over Nehru's political short-sightedness, hand-shaking diplomacy and compromise on any issue year after year, Pakistan played a Machiavellian dice with mental and verbal dexterity to spice up the Kashmir issue shambolically.To Pakistan, the accession of Kashmir to India was the result of conspiracy.

India denies Pakistan's allegations. The accession of Kashmir to India was not the result of a conspiracy. To Pakistan, it was quite conspiracy. Why? Because, Sheikh Abdullah, the Prime Minister of Kashmir, was a tool. The following facts are ture.

1. The Indian Army had been flown to Srinagar on the very day Lord Mountbatten accepted the accession, viz. Oct. 27, 1947.
2. The first request from Kashmir for accession and military aid came on Oct. 24, 1947.
3. By the 26th the raiders had already caused considerable damage and the fate of Kashmir hung in the balance.
4. India decided to send troops on the afternoon of Oct. 26 and these were despatched by air on the 27th.
5. Pakistan's allegation was that Sheikh Abdullah had entreated the Maharaja of Kashmir in a letter from prison to accede to India. This allegation is quite misleading and apocryphal.

6. India ruled out that allegation and said Sheikh Abdullah was released from prison on Sept. 29, 1947.
7. According to the press of that time : what happened was that while the Kashmir Govt. and Sheikh Abdullah were considering the question of accession, the invasion was planned for the purpose of compelling them by force to accede to Pakistan once and for all and without reference to the people of Kashmir.
8. The Nationalist Muslim leader was asked to form an interim Govt. by the Maharaja during the crisis immediately following the invasion of the State by the tribal raiders from Pakistan. Why? Because Sheikh was able to command the confidence of the citizens to the people of Kashmir.

   All these facts mentioned above are well-known in India and Kashmir. It is only lake success that fantastic theories are put forward for the consumption of the members far away both in time and space from the relevant events.
9. Under the Truce Agreement contained in the resolution of Aug. 13, 1948 the Govt. of Pakistan had agreed to withdraw its troops from Kashmir.

   Pakistan is a pious fraud, defying all resolutions.
10. As per Pakistan, Pakistan Army entered Kashmir in self-defence. This double-dealing diplomacy and treacherous movement has made Pakistan an evil- painted Islamic nation quite empty and pharisaical in diplomatic illness.
11. Under article 51 of the Charter, the right of self-defence begins only when there is an armed attack against a member.
12. Kashmir is a unit of the Indian Federation and has to be governed accordingly.
13. Turning to the views of Pakistan, the occupation of Kashmir by India was a threat to the existence of Pakistan, since India thereby aimed not only to encircle Pakistan strategically, but also to have its economy at its mercy by control over the rivers which were the life-blood of Pakistan. If as the result of a plebiscite Kashmir goes to Pakistan, the question does not arise. The question can only arise if Kashmir decides to remain in India.
14. It is not a threat of aggression if there is a constant preaching of jehad or holy war and the systematic incitement of feelings of religious frenzy and hatred.
15. Is it not aggression to give all help and succour to the invader?

When a sub-continent which has grown up as a single economic and political entity for centuries, as India had, is suddenly split into two separate States, a host of complex problems is bound to arise.

When Burma was a part of India, it was separated in 1936, but experts started from, it is believed, 1931 and worked at the problems that were likely to arise from the operation and only after solutions had been found for most, if not all of them, was the separation effected.

In the case of Pakistan, the partition was effected in a few weeks necessarily, a plethora of complex questions remained unsolved. And then, owing to the outbreaks of communal feeling and other causes, the atmosphere was vitiated. Not only did the partition create new problems but the atmosphere of peacecful and successful solution was destroyed. If there are unsolved disputes between India and Pakistan, the reason is to be found largely in the circumstances of the partition. So Kashmir problem is the troubled sound of partition.

And it is quite misconceived but preoccupied and mysterious judgement of Pakistan that the accession of Kashmir to India was the result of a conspiracy. Now the question is : What had happened before Oct. 24 which would show whether there was or was not a conspiracy? Another ill-conceived judgement of Pakistan was that Sheikh Abdullah was released from gaol on Sept. 29. He went straight to Delhi and remained there throughout the period intervening between his release and the Maharaja's letter on Oct. 26, 1947 intimating to Lord Mountbatten Sheikh Abdullah with the administration of the State.

The fact is : Sheikh Abdullah, after his release in Oct. 1947, had pleaded for time to consider which dominion the State should accede to. In reply, Pakistan voiced forth again, 'with whom was the pleading?' 'With the authorities of Delhi?' And 'Why?' And Pakistan replied that they were putting pressure that Kashmir should accede to Pakistan. What a good explanation! This is the nomenclature of Pakistan today. Pakistan knows at heart that Kashmir is an integral part of India. Why terrorism? Living in a world of frustration and a fissiparous situation of political doldrums and religious fundamentalism, has repeatedly raised a series of allegations. Sheikh Abdullah was not a personna non grata with the Prime Minister of India but not with the Maharaja. India had been blamed for not doing her part under the Security Council resolution of Aug. 13, 1948.

World trouble centres in Kashmir. Until it is settled, the atmosphere would not only continue to be extremely explosive, but the maintenance of peace between two countries in Asia and even of international peace would be put in jeopardy. Pakistan's holier-than-thou-attitude has to run wild, because her walking with resolution is not enough.

Pakistan today : If the world talks ill of Pakistan's hypocrisy over the Kashmir debate, Pakistan's heart shall harbour no ill-will against them. Why? Because Pakistan has ever been inbred with incrustation of sophism on Islamic globalisation. If jehad is the step-mother of terrorism, Islamic globalisation is the parentage of Pakistan and theocratic society. Does Pakistan know in every part of Kashmir, there were well-known Rishis whose abodes have become the places of worship, both for Hindus and Muslims?

According to the Bhagwad Gita : "From anger delusion arises, and from delusion, bewilderment of memory. When memory is bewildered, intelligence is lost, and when intelligence is lost, one falls down into irrational fool." Truly speaking, anger is a brief madness.

Kashmir seems to be destined by its topographical and ethnographical peculiarities to remain a contentious issue between two powerful neighbours. It suffered like the rest of Asia under many invasions. The Firsts World War had been fought .... for reasons which, it need hardly be said, had nothing to do with Asia in general. For over a half century, Kashmir has been made the controversial territory a chessboard of international politics. In foreign policy, non-alignment is less of a holy cow than it is used to be.

Nuclear deal with US! Pakistan has been scared out of her wits. If the deal is stymied at this stage due to domestic opposition, India's international credibility will be at stake. The world will doubt India's ability to deliver on its words, and New Delhi will find it difficult to engage world capitals on any issue. Even Beijing, who the Left thinks will be provoked if the deal goes through, will refuse to take New Delhi seriously. This nuclear deal is not just a question of nuclear trade. All sorts of high-tech areas are potentially dual-use ... from IT to defence, to space, to biotech. The deal would lift restrictions on supply of dual-use technology terms to India from other nations.

Our so-called Left parties on deal! It is selfishness if they consider themselves as a separate entity and work with the sole intention of amassing wealth, power, titles and such other benefits for themselves. This entity will disappear today or tomorrow.

Is there any sort of fallacy that Pakistan is potentially the most dangerous country in the world today? Is there a sham virtue of left-wing intellectuals who have exercised little influence on the Kashmir debate? Emotional and prodigiously fluent over the problems, they have lacked something of both substance and depth and have only explored the perilous gaps or still more perilous ambiguities of their formulation of theory. The truth is that in immaturity, the so-called left-wing intellectuals have paid the penalty of their dazzling precocity in thoughts and deeds. On Kashmir issue, they have played an actor on the stage but rather as a presence behind the scenes. They have failed to prune out the far-reaching practical influence of the Kashmir problem around this sub-continent. Their presence behind the scene is an incentive to Islamabad.

Why Kashmir? Even Nehru, during the Congress rule, was also inclined to cast his net much wider. From this desire sprang most of his ill-judged actions, his often naive interventions in all important matters, his magisterial pronouncements as Prime Minister of India, the letter which unloaded on Kashmir debate. It was all done with the most patient insincerity, but he certainly exaggerated. He had next to nothing of the poltician's sense of the possible, and indeed it might be said that he had no real instinct for politics in Kashmir at all. He failed at all times to perceive the springs of Pakistan's policy over Kashmir.

It was Mrs. Indira Gandhi who only showed courage and acuteness in the eventful role of Kashmir with a difference. She had arrived at the crucial examination of a materialistic view of the character of the State, Kashmir, with a belief. Whreas Nehru had neither leisure nor the capacity to undertake the work of scholarship and research on Kashmir debate which upto a point continued to tempt him. A still greater number of people has recognised Mrs. Gandhi's exceptional abilities on India's foreign policy and her devotion to the work she had made her own.

And the liberation of Bangladesh from the irretrievable clutches of Pakistan, has been one of the achievements of the fluid and mobile Indian parliamentary system. This has been possible not only because of the persistent factors in India's international position but also because certain personalities like Atal Bihari Bajpai, have for long periods controlled the foreign policies of India over the sub-continent. Mr Bajpai has moulded India's foreign policy without interruption. This modest and self-effacing man clung to his principles with such persistence in Asiatic countries and pursued his aims with such energy, precision, and success that he has become more than any other single man.

Mrs. Gandhi's aim was to undermine the schemes of Pakistan in Kashmir to enhance the India's prestige and strength in Europe, and to cement a peace-making process in the valley. What was new was the pertinacity and skill with which she had grasped every opportunity to achieve these ends. Foreign policy is like cobwebs which a spider (shrewd foreign policy makers) may spin in the attic of some old house, intricate, delicate and even beautiful, but which at any moment the housemaid's broom with brutal common sense may sweep away. And all that fulsome adulation must be highly offensive to any country's foreign policy.

Politics is an autonomous science. And the State has no special relation. The special interest of the Mosque in Islamic countries arises from the monopoly of learning. In societies with a wholly Islamic thoughts and creeds, it is logical and proper that the control of education should still be vested in Islamic hands. The moral foundations of democracy and other western countries are pathetically indistinct but they cannot be described as fully and distinctively Christian. Throughout the western world political sovereignty is always subject to tacit reservations; it operates in the framework created by the older framework of fundamental law.

At times, religious controversialists, particularly both in India and Pakistan, appear to treat political sovereignty as the equivalent of a claim to moral absolutism. Both countries, on the question of Kashmir debate, have constantly raped the essence of political sovereignty. The temporal sword of justice can be equated with the prison and the hangman; the spiritual sword with anathema. But the result on examination proves dubious. A military ruler in Pakistan can be held to impose on the jehadis the duty of rebellion. The military ruler is in fact in possession of political authority. The spiritual quality of his sanction does not fundamentally distinguish him from a temporal ruler. The temporal ruler is not his own prison-warder and hangman. His armies obey him. This is the gloomy picture of Pakistan today.

Why? Because they recognise an obligation of loyalty as terrorists to the dissemination of Islamic thoughts all over the world. The mosque will be his master. It is more difficult to draw a line of demarcation which rests on the difference between the content of the Shia and the Sunni belonging to mosques, Pakistan's theocratic rulers, preoccupied with religious dualism of theonomy and mosque culture, judge the matters of the Kashmir debate, and the extent of their collusion with Islamabad is determined largely by the confidence with which they judge them.

Today Pakistan traces out the progress of hypocrisy over the Kashmir valley from wolfish bachelor to sad widower. The true actor is the true chameleon. The covetous man will exercise a spiritual covetousness, and the amorous man will turn to God, with all the loving approaches and applications of his earlier passions. Pakistan is an enemy of truth. What suffering it caused is keeping people in chains and torturing others. A jehadi is like an owl who falls upon its prey from a hidden perch in a hollow tree. And that's how Pakistan lives, her sins cover up.

Pakistan today : Pakistan believes in theonomous and messianic society of Islam. But Islamic globalisation believes in Islamic messianism. A theocratic nation rambles from one thing to another, from the fantastic encylopaedia of indoctrinated crude nationalism to the horrors of mass-murdering adventure. One has been at the core of one's religion. The crudest form of such misadventurism, in Pakistan on Kashmir issue, advocated by other fellow creatures, is common to young and old, to stout and strong, and to meek and bold. The most antagonistically perverted racialism between a Shia and a Sunni is a class antagonism as well as the antagonism of men belonging to different psychological types. It helps to create the bustle over the Kashmir valley. Their heroes generally are notorious rogues. These rogues are produced in the factory of ISI-governed Theocracy and Mullocracy. This factory is a convalscent home of terrorism. The windows of this factory reflect the funereal faces of the jehadis but a monster it remains, and as you turn your eyes, you murmur to yourself ... who?

Who will solve the Kashmir issue? Nuclear-armed Pakistan and India routinely carry out missile tests despite a peace process they launched in early 2004 and both have agreed to inform each other of such tests in advance. Living in hypocrisy is an art, a skill, a technique. India should be a self-realised nation. And Pakistan should change her character from Islamic terrorism, to preferential attachment.

Terrorists turn children from poor families, for committing acts of terrorism, into suicide bombers to kill innocent citizens, in the name of Islam. If suicide bombers are headed to Islamabad, Lahore or Karachi to wreak vengeance for Pak-US understanding, the army can try to redirect them to J & K. If civil strife in Pakistan grows worse, India might well be lapped on the periphery by its waves. India must remain prepared for the darker possibilities.

Pakistan has not yet forgotten the tragedy of partition and Kashmir accession to India. Pakistan should know loss and gain, praise and insults, life and death, all of them go together. Everything has its limits. Pakistan's normally vocal foreign policy remains silent on Kashmir accession to India.

Pakistan has always been in mystery on Kashmir issue. Mysteries never open up for those who go on questioning. And her mysterious mind is overwhelmed with negativities propagating anxiety, worries and depression. Even Iran's nuclear cooperation with Pakistan is adversary, and also a mystery.

After a long innings of political prevarication and denial on Kashmir issue, Pakistan-based terrorism is wreaking terror and mayhem on Pakistani soil. Terrorism is a powerful talisman to Pakistan on Kashmir issue. And the rulers are tantamount to rubbing salt into the wounds of the nation. Why? Because dictatorship has already pushed Pakistan towards political and constitutional anarchy. Pakistan has received 80 billion dollar since 2002, but no project has yet been executed for development in the country. The Army has a chief and the ISI also has Director-Generals. So if any conspiracy is hatched against India on Kashmir issue, they have the right to speak. So, why is Pakistan pleading the case of the two institutions? Since the birth of Pakistan, every ruler, even every dictator, has pitched the Army against the people, which led to confrontation between the military and the people. And the ISI has been used to gain political objectives.

The army does little to take on the forces of theocracy, while milking for aid that goes primarily towards building the military's anti-Indian capabilities. Even Af-Pak is more dangerous than North Korea. Everything is in a sorry mess.

Who will teach Pakistan? Pakistan does not bow down to those who have reached omniscience in the flesh and does not learn the road to everlasting life in the liberated state. Pakistan does not bow down to those who have attained perfect knowledge of how to attain peace in mind and heart. Pakistan does not bow down to those who have experienced self-realisation of their souls through self-control and self-sacrifice on any disputed issue between India and Pakistan. Pakistan does not bow down to those who understand the importance of spirituality. So, the world has not ever produced any ideal teacher to teach Pakistan.

It is the big negative energy. There is a wise saying : "What angers you, controls you." The darkest red colour of her anger over Kashmir's accession to India is the worst fear of Pakistan. Fundamentally, Pakistan is an Islamic nation of three 'A' s ... The Army, Allah, and America. Islamic dictatorship is never tired of praising political eunuchs as all other dictators do. Even Hitler and Lenin the two dictators, played chess across the board some 100 years ago in the house of a Jewish family in Vienna. Hitler was then a jobbing artist while Lenin was in exile, and the house where they played chess belonged to a prominent jewish family which fled in the run-up to the World War II, giving the etching and board to their housekeeper. The image is said to have been created by Hitler's art teacher, Emma Lowenstramm in Vienna in 1909. The image according to the Daily Telegraph, London, is titled : "A Chess Game : Lenin with Hitler ... Vienna in 1909". Communism and Facism live together. Hey presto!

When the etching was made, Hitler was 20 and Lenin was twice his age and the house was where politics went to discuss things in that city. "Lenin at the time was moving around Europe in exile. His movements are hazy and it is known that he did play chess and later he certainly wore wigs as a disguise. It is also known that Lenin was German agent and the house was where people went to exchange political views. The chess set is clearly the same chess set as that in the etching. It is a box chess set that folds out and pieces are identifiable, particularly the kings and bishops." Richard West-wood-Brookes, great-great-grandson of Emma Lowenstramm, of Mullock's auction house, said this, while selling the items. Where is communism, there is facism coming by back-door like a thief and a prostitute.

So, Pakistan wears wigs as a disguise of being a pacifist on Kashmir solution, and has so far played chess with China either in Islamabad or in Beijing. This is Pakistan today. Nothing is more dangerous to Islamic terrorism than the anarchism of the masses, and the utopias and illusions of their leaders on Kashmir accession to India. Why? Because Pakistan has not yet traced out the issue systematically, relentlessly and triumphantly, the successive defeats of these illusions. Even Pakistan intelligentsia has not yet emerged from the penumbra of the crazy anti-India hate slogans and despair. The switch over to shambolically digested unprincipled power politics has started from the era of Gen Ayub Khan.

In the name of Islam, there are terrible acts of incendiarism and murder at which the votaries of Islamic organisations of Kashmir liberation movement laugh helplessly. Pakistan history today and Islamic philosophy tomorrow are veiled in esoteric mysteries impenetrable to western man. The low quality of the instruction and the bullying pedantry of the teachers often bitterly offend the more pupils. Their unsatisfied religious longings have left a vaccum, soon filled by jehadi ideas. The estrangement of educated men and women from the whole established order of Islam continues, and the mental climate has grown even more favourable to anti-India hymns of hate on Kashmir issue. Defeat in successive wars or public revolt has shaken the Islamic infrastructure — a bewildering assortment of knock-down-and-drag-out arguments on Kashmir.

Kashmir issue is a tale of impious adventures of a secret benevolence and fraternal order of pious hopes.

12

Pakistan's Sinister Game-plan On Kashmir (I-XII): A Campaign to A Dream Within A Dream

Books are masters who instruct us without rods of ferrules, without words or anger, without bread or money. If you approach them, they are not asleep; if you seek them they do not hide; if you blunder, they do not scold; if you are ignorant, they do not laugh at you. Neither has Pakistan any books nor masters who instruct them without rods of ferrules. If you instruct them, all are asleep. Rather they laugh at you. Better to lose a thousand now than several thousand every year. Why? Because hypocrisy is the best, nobody can steal it or carry it away. It cannot perish.

Pakistan's Indo-phobia is a house-hold word to every Pakistani. While it is no secret that Pakistan's foreign and domestic policies are conditioned by and large by what, for want of a better expression, may be called 'Indo-phobia', for few, if any at all, had expected the Prime Ministers of Pakistan, to make an open confession that Pakistan's acquisition of arms from the United States, of nuclear weapons, of terrorist outfits sponsored by themselves in India, are to guard against 'Indian aggression'. They think that they are in danger of being swallowed up by a more insidious and destructive type of tutelage than old-fashioned colonialism. They feel it their duty not only to save themselves from this but also to offer their sympathy and moral support to all the countries struggling for emancipation from whichever type of tutelage.

Why Pakistan joined the western military pacts? Pakistan has explained it away in the following way :

1. India did not give Pakistan her share of armaments under the partition agreement of 1947.
2. Pakistan is fully conscious that there are several important parties and personages in India who had made it their plan to reunite India and Pakistan and to undo partition.
3. After the ceasefire in Kashmir on January 1, 1949, India massed its troops on the boundaries of Pakistan in March, 1950, poised for an attack ... a time when Pakistan was practically defenceless. Again in July, 1951, India considered it necessary and justifiable, in order to resolve certain disputes, to mass its troops on Pakistan's borders.
4. Pakistan's resources are limited and it is spending a far greater percentage of its revenues than its national economy could support on the armed forces purely for defensive purposes. Pakistan found its necessary, therefore, to look out for friends and allies.
5. India is purchasing war planes and modern technological aircrafts and paying for them out of its own resources. Not all the wealth of Pakistan which comes into the hands of their Govt. can afford these, and therefore, they have to turn to others. For what? Only to defend themselves.
6. Pakistan is a little bit frightened of this vast armament which India has embarked upon.

So Pakistan was not prepared to take the risk of being defenceless against this vast armament of India, although they would like to hope that the protestations of the Prime Ministers of India are exactly what they mean.

So, it is very clear that the purpose of Pakistan in acquiring arms from the United States ... and, consequently, the objective of the United States in arming Pakistan .... is to defend the country against Indian aggression. Pakistan does not appear to be bothered about 'China and imperialism', although American apologists appear to argue that a militarily strong Pakistan ... no matter what the country's objective may be ... will be a natural deterrent against the alleged communist threat. Ridicule disguised as praise.

Preventives of India are better than licking the dust of U.S. dollars. Why? It is cheaper and easier of application, and surer in result of world terrorism. Pakistan is always prejudiced about India-phobia. She goes with a biased mind and parochial doctrine to listen to what she is convinced is pure rubbish. The religious bosses, with that heartless formalism for which Pakistan's officialdom has always been able, are pursuing the young people's minds towards protesting against the whole system of political and bureaucratic absolutism of democracy. Who is to blame? They shout demagogically about the liberation movement of Kashmiri people, while in fact these phrases mean to them only terrorism to lead a light of Islam.

Why is it that Britain has chosen to allow her relations with India to be seriously strained over Kashmir and the United States has nipped in the bud whatever positive results have so far been achieved? In India, there is a tendency to interpret the British support for Pakistan on Kashmir as an act of revenge on India, a bid of cut-down Nehru to size or to chill Nehru by isolation. While this explanation is justified, it gives only one side of the picture, and, that too, a small side.

The British are hard-boiled politicians; in the course of their long eventful history, they have digested many setbacks, swallowed many insults. If vital British interests in the wide area vaguely defined as the Middle East were not in serious jeopardy, and if Pakistan were not to Britain like a straw to a drowning man, no British Govt. would have risked its good relation with India over such a limited and indeed unreal issue as Kashmir.

And if the United States were not convinced of Britain's desperate position, it would not have lent her this support that has lost America a world of goodwill and friendship.

Pakistan's positions in Kashmir equate with Israel's present position in palestine. With Anglo-US connivance, both are reaping a harvest of aggression. There is a sinister consistency in their Middle East policy.

If Israel is stubbornly refusing to pull out of two strategically important strip of Gaza, so is Pakistan introducing warlike elements into an area that links Russia, China and India and undoubtedly one of the world's most strategic spots.

The cold war between India and Pakistan has again entered an ultra-glacial period.

Pakistan which has had more than ten Prime Ministers in sixty years, where chronic political instability and hard-boiled Islamic ideology have led to serious economic problems, has nevertheless to be maintained as a dependable ally. Its people are seething with discontent by this expression and its eastern wing has emotionally broken away from the internal and external policies followed by the successive Govts. Kashmir alone can provide the people of Pakistan an emotionally unifying cause; Kashmir alone can keep a Govt. in power for some reasonable time.

Hence, on Kashmir, the United States Govt. has to support Pakistan, at whatever immediate or long-term cost. To the American mind, ... there is none in Pakistan ... if the present Govt. set-up fails, who can keep the country firmly in the western alliance. There may, of course, be a military regime, such as Iran and Iraq. But such a regime would find it difficult to keep the two wings together.

One day after the declaration of assisting and strengthening the security of four Muslim States under the Baghdad Pact, the New York Times, in an editorial gave an inkling of the official American attitude to the Kashmir issue. The New York Times completely ignored the question of Pakistan's aggression and said : "There is neither need nor point in going back to the dispute as to who was an aggressor, or where or when. What is at issue is simply whether the Kashmiris will be allowed to decide their own political future in a free election. Pakistan is quite willing to put this to the test. The United Nations has authorised it. It is hardly responsible to expect either the Pakistanis or the world organisation to accept as a fait accompli a complete by passing of this agreement and this machinery." It is called the Socratic irony.

Today political atmosphere in this sub-continent on Kashmir issue has been totally changed. The most naked display of might cannot defeat the human spirit especially when sustained by faith in God, not by religious fanaticism. Just as elephants are needed to catch elephants, so does the United States need Pakistan to capture Pakistan's hypocrisy on home-grown terrorism. Why? Because Pakistan is only the guiding star of world terrorism. The winner is still a rat. And usually a very large one. Frustration, depression, and stress are on the physio-psychological front of Pakistan that has already mortgaged their hard-earned freedom at the feet of terrorists and fanatical crusaders. They are worth no more than a glass of water and a loaf of bread. Kautilya, in the Arthashastra, says : "Obstruction, misuse of Govt. property and false accounting by Govt. servants lead to a reduction of wealth." Terrorism may well be at the gates of Islamabad.

STORY BEHIND KASHMIR : II (A SOCRATIC IRONY)

It would be wise for the democratic lamb not to be overtrustful of the totalitarian wolf. Having gone up like a rocket, Pakistan will come down like a stick. There will be sudden disillusionment which will be reflected in the abrupt end of the middle. Because they are trouble-shooters.

India's position on Kashmir rests on two fundamental propositions : The legality of the State's accession to this country on Oct 27, 1947, which was full and complete, and fact of Pakistan's aggression.

A third factor of vital importance in any consideration of this market lies in the violation and non-fulfilment respectively by Pakistan of Part I (cease-fire order) and part II (Truce Agreements) of the U.N.C.P.I. Resolution of August 13, 1948, thus rendering Part III (proposals preliminary to ascertaining the will of the people) infructuous.

The U.N.C.P.I. Resolution of Aug. 13, 1948, and January 5, 1949, are the only international commitments accepted by India in respect of Kashmir. These two resolutions were also accepted by Pakistan and have been endorsed by the Security Council.

Part I of the August 13, 1948, resolution proved for a cease-fire. If further stiuplated : (B) India and Pakistan agree to refrain from taking any measures that might augment the military potential of the forces under the control in the State of Jammu and Kashmir; and (E) India and Pakistan agree to appeal to their respective peoples to assist in creating and maintaining an atmosphere favourable to the promotion of further negotiations.

Pakistan has violated the clause (B) in the following instances ;

1. The 'Azad' Kashmir forces which had been built up with 32 battalions at the time of ceasefire of January 1, 1949, have since been expanded to oversize high-trained and equipped battalions constituting a powerful

fighting force of terrorist camps. In 1956-57, it was exclusive of the Gilight scouts.

2. In 1956-57, a reserve of about 45,000 trained men had been established in 'Azad' Kashmir.
3. Many hundreds of guerillas had been trained and thrown back into the 'Azad' Kashmir population.
4. A Brigade Headquarters had been established at Muzzafarabad and military bases established at Chakoti, Mirpur, Palandri, Bimbar, Kotli and Bagh, all within Azad Kashmir.
5. Since 1954, about 900 miles of all weather roads and bridges have been constructed linking these bases with a string of Pakistan's Cantonments at Abbottabad, Rawalpindi, Murree, Jhelum, Kharriar and Sialkot all of which are between only four and 31 miles from Kashmir border.
6. The striking power of the Pakistani Army itself has been vastly augmented by U.S. arms aid which includes tactical atomic weapons and sabre-jet fighters.
7. The air-fields at Gilgit and China have been enlarged and improved.
8. New air-fields have been built at Skardu, Bhimbar, and Do Patta in 'Azad' Kashmir. The Skardu air-field takes Dakotas.
9. Apart from Pakistani troop concentration on the Indian border, tribesmen are once again being massed for action. *Ex. Major General Akbar Khan, the Gen. Tariq who organised the 1947 invasion, had again been placed in organisational command.*

Clause (E) of the part I of August 13, 1948, Resolution has from the start been observed by Pakistan more in the breach than in the observance. A continuous hate-campaign against India had been in progress, oftentimes with official support.

The cry of 'Jehad' has echoed through the months and years since 1947. This has been combined with abuse of India and other leaders. Here are a few examples :

The Times of Karachi, in an editorial, on New Year's Day, 1957, wrote :

"We have to liberate four million souls from the dead weight of Brahmanic imperialism ... To us, Kashmir is the fulfilment of our freedom; without it, our independent existence is seriously threatened. It is clearly a matter of life or death for us."

'The Dawn' of Karachi wrote editorially on Jan. 6, 1957:

"The Security will have barely ten days to decide upon some concrete, tangible, unequivocal and compelling step whereby that rapacious brigand of Asia, that hypocrite masquerading as an apostle of peace with his hands red with the blood of Kashmiris as well as Bharati Muslims, that double-facing, double-talking and double-dealing Brahmin Janus who shamelessly woos both Moscow and Washington in order to have the best of both the worlds ... can be prevented from accomplishing his designs."

Again on January 13, 1957, 'The Dawn' wrote under the caption 'The Man of Peace' :

"With God's grace, the sons of Islam need not fear if the sons of other things force them to a trial of military conclusions. Indeed, the Kashmir dispute may perhaps be thus more quickly solved and the Radcliff iniquities satisfactorily adjusted. But such a choice will not be voluntarily ours. It is up to a Bharat's war-minded peace-monger to keep the peace or make a war."

Choudhary Md. Ali, former Prime Minister of Pakistan, at a public meeting in Karachi, on Aug. 14, 1956 : "... I am ready for the liberation of Kashmir," he said, and added, "but I want the people to get ready ..." He said the Kashmir dispute was now going before the Security Council, but asserted that the nation would not rest there. (Report in the Times of Karachi).

Malik Jehangir Khan, Tribal Representative in the Pakistan Constituent Assembly : "... I have consulted the tribal Maliks and people and according to their advice, I am sponsoring a proposal at the All Parties Conference that the Kashmir dispute cannot be settled without a war and consequently the tribesman be permitted to go in for 'jehad'. (Report to 'Shabaz', Peshwar, Nov. 7, 1955)

Main Mumtaz Daulatana, Chief Minister of West Punjab : "If the United States proves to be a band of thieves, we will have nothing to do with it. We will prove that we can liberate Kashmir with the strength of our arms." (Reported in 'Zamindar' Lahore, January 17, 1952).

Khan Abdul Qaiyuum Khan, Chief Minister of N.W.F.P. "The day we become desperate and loss all hopes of a just solution of the problem, not only the entire Pathan population of Pakistan and the tribal areas will rise up for the holy 'Jehad' in Kashmir, but our brothers from across the Afghan frontier will also throw in their lot with us for the future cause." (1951).

Part III of the August 13, 1948, Resolution laid the framework for a truce agreement. Taken with the assurances given by the U.N.C.I.P. it provided for the total withdrawal of Pakistani forces and tribesmen from Kashmir and the disbandment and disarming of the 'Azad' Kashmir forces. Pending a final solution, the 'Azad' area was not to be consolidated while the administration of the northern areas was to revert to the Govt. of Jammu and Kashmir and its defence to India.

Here again, there have been violations by Pakistan. India accepted the Resolution on Aug. 20, 1948, but it took Pakistan five months from August to December 1948, to signify acceptance. This period was utilised to invade and occupy the northern areas in violation of the Resolution. Subsequently, the Truce agreement was never signed. It was frustrated by Pakistan. Meanwhile, the Pakistan Army has not withdrawn and the 'azad' forces, far from being disbanded, have been augmented.

At the same time, the entire 'Azad' Kashmir area has been incorporated into Pakistan.

Article 203 of the Pakistan Constitution provides that "When the people of the State of J & K decided to accede to Pakistan, the relationship between Pakistan and Sind State shall be determind in accordance with wishes of the people of the State". But this applies to that portion of Kashmir which is now with India. The incorporation of 'azad' Kashmir had been effected under Article I, Clause II, sub-section (C) of the Pakistani Constitution which lists the territories of the Republic. This refers to territories which are under the administration of the Federation but are not included in either province (of west or the then East Pakistan).

By this provision, all the residuary areas come directly under the Central Govt. at Karachi, the then capital of Pakistan. This applies to Gilight, Baltistan, Hunza and all the other areas of 'Azad' kashmir. Chitral, a feudatory of Pakistan as described by the Constitution of that country. All this is a gross violation of the August 13, 1948 resolution which recognised the sovereignty of the Govt. of Kashmir over the entire territory of the State and affirmed that there should be no change in sovereignty.

So, any agreement with Pakistan leads to destruction. Why? Because the gate is narrow and the way is not broad. Do not give what is holy to dogs, and do not throw your pearls before swine, or they will trample them under their feet, and turn and tear you to pieces. Don't worry about tomorrow; for tomorrow will care for itself. Each day has enough trouble of its own.

ACCESSION, AGGRESSION AND PLEBISCITE : III (A SHADOW THEATRE)

The two factors of Kashmir accession to India and the fact of Pakistan's aggression against the State are basic to any proper understanding of the problem.

The Independence Act passed by the British Parliament provided in article 6 (1) that "an Indian State shall be deemed to have acceded to the Dominion if the Governor-General has signified his acceptance of an Instrument of Accession executed by the Ruler thereof ..."

On October 26, 1947, the Maharaja of Kashmir offered accession to India. Sheikh Abdullah, leader of the National Conference, who had just been released from prison, also simultaneously appealed to the Govt. of India to accept accession. The Instrument of Accession was accepted by the Governor General, Lord Mountbatten, the following day. Both the offer and the acceptance of accession were unconditional and on the same basis as the accession of all the other princely States.

In a covering letter, the Governor-General did, however, state : "... it is any Govt's wish that as soon as law and order have been restored in Kashmir and its soil cleared of the invader, the question of the State's accession should be settled by a reference to the people."

The accession of Kashmir to India was legal and complete on October 27, 1947. Kashmir is an integral part of India and is listed as one of the Constituent Units of the Union of India, in the First Schedule to the Indian

Constitution. Pakistan on June 11, 1949, protested to the U.N.C.I.P. against the decision taken by the Constituent Assembly of India to reserve for seats for the representatives of Kashmir. The Commission, however, reported : "In the Commission's view, it is difficult to oppose this measure of the Indian Govt. on purely legal grounds."

The legality of the State's accession to India has never been challenged except by Pakistan. On the contrary, the legality of accession underlies the U.N.C.I.P. resolutions of 1948 and 1949. The Commission affirmed the sovereignty of J & K Govt. and the integrity of the State. It also affirmed India's right to be in Kashmir and its responsibility for the security of the State. And it expressly stated that Pakistan must withdraw from Kashmir and could claim no part in any plebiscite.

Is there any lot of internal debate within the Islamic community about the legality of Kashmir's accession to India? It is a larger question, much larger than the question of terrorism. You hypocrite, first take the log out of your own eye, and then you will see clearly to take the speck out of your brother's eye. Why are you worried about the legality of Kashmir's accession to India?

If, however, hypothetically, the people of Kashmir did not want to remain in the Indian Union, it would be for Parliament to legislate for its separation from the rest of the country. Kashmir by itself cannot unilaterally secede.

With Pakistan obstructing a plebiscite or any progress to a settlement, the people of Kashmir held free elections in the summer of 1951 and elected a constituent Assembly which again freely endorsed accession to India.

It is instructive, too, to recall the statement made by Sheikh Abdullah in his inaugural address to the Kashmir Constituent Assmebly on Nov. 5, 1951. He said : "... Our movement (National Conference) grew and thrived side by side with the Indian National Congress ... Throughout the struggles that the people of Kashmir waged against autocracy. We should never forget that the Muslim League leadership had completely disassociated itself from them and that during the upsurge of 1946 their local party organs had assisted the administration to suppress the movement."

"...we were (thus) still struggling against autocracy and for freedom when the State was suddenly invaded from the side of Pakistan (even while a National Conference representative was talking things over in Lahore with the Pakistani authorities)... when the raiders were fast approaching Srinagar ... the representatives of the National Conference ... flew to Delhi to seek help from the Govt. of India ... showed readiness to accept (accession) ... since the people's representatives themselves sought an alliance...."

"In the final analysis ... it is the kinship of ideals which determines the strength of ties between two States ... The Indian Consitution has set before the country the goal of secular democracy... Any unnatural cleavage between religious groups is the legacy of imperialism and no modern State can afford to encourage artificial divisions if it is to achieve progress and prosperity ...

The National Movement in our State naturally gravitates towards these principles of secular democracy..."

Sheikh Abdullah discussed the pros and cons of accession to India and accession to Pakistan. He replied the latter :

He added : "Certain tendencies have been asserting themselves in India which may in the future convert it into a religious state wherein the interests of Muslims will be jeopardised. This would happen if a communal organisation had a dominant hand in the Govt., and Congress ideals of the equality of all communities were made to give way to religious intolerance. The continued accession of Kashmir to India should, however, help in defeating this tendency. From my experience of the last four years, it is my considered judgement that the presence of Kashmir in the Union of India has been a major factor in stabilising relations between the Hindus and Muslims of India."

"Some argue, as a supposedly natural corollary to this, that on our acceding to Pakistan our annihilation or survival depends. Facts have disproved this. Right thinking men would point out that Pakistan is not an organic unity of all the Muslims in this sub-continent. It has on the contrary, caused the dispersion of the Indian Muslims for whose benefit it was claimed to have been created. There are two Pakistans at least a thosand miles apart from each other. The total population of western Pakistan, which is contiguous to our State, is hardly 25 million, while the total number of Muslims resident in India is as many as 40 million. As one Muslim is as good as another, the Kashmiri Muslims if they are worried by such consideration should choose the forty millions living in India."

So much for accession. What of aggression?

Pakistan signed a Standstill Agreement with Kashmir on August 16, 1947. On August 31, Major-General Scott, Chief of Staff of Jammu and Kashmir forces, submitted his first report of border raids from Pakistan. During the next three weeks, the tempo of armed raids and tribal infiltration increased. An economic blockade was imposed by Pakistan by suspending the Sialkot-Jammu railway service and withholding entry of essential supplies such as petrol, foodgrains, salt and cloth.

A good name is like an precious ointment, it fills all around about, and will not be easily away, for the odours of ointments are more durable than those of flowers. Pakistan's history on Kashmir issue has been always a struggle involving pretensions of what they are not and in the process they do not feel good. Now the question is : Why do they pretend? A pretending-self creates false image in them and, ultimately, instead of boosting confidence, ends up lowering their self-esteem throughout the world as an Islamic nation. Why? Because self-esteem will improve if the pretending self is dropped.

Pakistan should be mindful of today and tomorrow. She has not yet learnt from history. It is said that, one of the reasons, Hitler lost the war, was because he did not learn from history. He attacked Russia in winter. Had he learnt from history, he would have known that Napoleaon had lost many of his men by attacking Russia in winter. Whereas Pakistan creates her own path of destruction attacking India with an incantation of political exorcism.

On October 15, the Kashmir Govt. cabled the British Prime Minister about the invasion of Poonch and the economic blockade of the State. A weak later, the main invasion began. Baramula was sacked.

India complained to the Security Council on January 1, 1948, under section 35, Chapter VI of the Charter (relating to pacific Settlement of disputes). The complaint was one of aggression : "The Govt. of India requests the Security Council to call upon Pakistan to put an end immediately to giving of such assistance (to the raiders) which is act of aggression against India."

In the Security Council, Pakistan emphatically denied the charge of aggression or rendering of assistance to or control over the tribesmen. About 19,000 raiders were reported inside Kashmir. They moved in lorries and carried substantial arms and were offered by regular Pakistani Army officers. *And the descendents of the so-called raiders have now lived in the valley of Kashmir and been branded as the protagonists of Kashmir liberation movement sponsored by Pakistan. They are blessed with Pakistan's compassion. The consequences of their actions are quite indifferent to their claim. They have no control over the results.*

On March 17, 1949, the Chief Minister of NWFP, Abdul Quayyum Khan, in his budget speech, advocated a special grant for the tribesmen in these words : "The House will recall with pride the fact that in our greatest hour of danger the Masuds responded to our call by rushing to the rescue of the oppressed Muslims of Jammu and Kashmir State."

The U.N.C.I.P in the resolution of August 13, 1948 ... which was accepted by Pakistan ... stated : "As the presence of troops of Pakistan in the territory of the State of Jammu and Kashmir constitutes a material change in the situation since it was represented by the Govt. of Pakistan before the Security council, the Govt. of Pakistan agrees to withdraw its troops from the State."

Two years later, the U.N. Mediator, Sir Owen Dixon, found, "... when the frontier of the State of Jammu and Kashmir was crossed on, I believe, Oct. 20, 1947, by hostile elements, it was contrary to international law, and that when, in May 1948, of the U.N.C.I.P. Pakistan formally admitted the presence of its troops in Kashmir since May (although the evidence is that other Pakistani army was actively engaged much earlier). Mr. Zafrulla Khan said Pakistan had moved into Kashmir to protect Pakistan from possible aggression by Indian forces, to prevent the influx of refugees into Pakistan and to prevent a fait accompli in Kashmir by India. The Pakistan High Command stated its objectives as no more than holding the Naushera-Poonch-Uri line."

Their sense organs trick the brain into believing the separate existence of different leaders on the same track. Their energy vibrates at different frequencies, resulting in plethora of political designs and dualism. These sense organs are designed to further refurbish this illusion of double-standard on Kashmir issue. According to Guru Granth Sahib, "Faith does not stick to those who are true, but filth attaches itself to those who love duality. This filth cannot be washed off, even by bathing at the 68 sacred shrines of pilgrimage." Why? Because Islamabad is a place in the world where the terrorists and jihadis descend and facilitate the crossing over Islamic thoughts in the multiplicity and diversity of Islamic terrorism ... a nightmarish experience of the great koran. They have showcased the tired and weather-beaten voices of the past. They don't know where to look and how to look. Because they incarnate syncretistic religious dogma in political institutions.

Yet Pakistani, employed the period between the U.N.C.I.P. Resolution of Aug 13, 1948, and the cease-fire on January 1, 1949, to extend its aggression. During these months it invaded and occupied the vast northern areas.

Finally the plebiscite, India offered to consult the will of the people of Kashmir as an alternative to war. It was a unilateral contract with the people of Kashmir and the U.N. But the condition was that this would and indeed could only be done after the aggression had been vacated and peaceful conditions restored. A plebiscite was accepted as a means of ascertaining the will of the people. It was exclusive ; and the U.N.C.I.P. itself later agreed that other methods to this end should be explored if a plebiscite was found impracticable for any reason.

The U.N.C.I.P. Resolution of Aug, 13, 1948, made a plebiscite the end process of a cease-fire (which has been violated by Pakistan) and a truce-agreement commencing with the total withdrawal of Pakistan (which has not been signed or fulfilled by Pakistan). Old sins cast long shadows. And the moral of Pakistan's present situation on Kashmir issue is : If ignorance is bliss, why aren't the people of Pakistan happy? Evil doers are evil dreaders.

Here, too, conditions were attached and assurances given. There were that the plebiscite proposed would not be binding on India if Pakistan did not implement parts I and II of the August 13, 1948 Resolution and that we lose the peace of years where we hunt after the rapture of moments. Pakistan will lay her whole fortune at jihadis' feet. It is not a very big fortune. Why? She knows but she will look awfully big beside her little feet.

Pakistan and the 'Azad' should have no part in a plebiscite. Further, acceptance by India of a proposal for a plebiscite was not to prejudice its rights in Kashmir. That is, the sovereignty of the State of Kashmir and the legality of its accession were not to be called in question.

Finally, this is what was stated in the aide-memorie of discussions between Nehru and the U.N.C.I.P. on Dec 23, 1948; "India is a secular state; the United Nations also is a secular organisation. Pakistan aims at being a theocratic state. An appeal to religious fanaticism could not be regarded as legitimate political activity. Dr. Lozano (the U.N.C.I.P. reprsentative) agreed that any political activity which might tend to disturb law and order could not be regarded as legitimate. The same test would apply to freedom of press and speech."

This, again, is a condition that Pakistan has consistently violated with continuing talk of 'two nations' and cries of 'jehad'.

This was the position regarding a plebiscite. The view expressed in the London Tribune, weekly journal of Mr. Aneurin Bevar, in an article that appeared two days ago, is pertinent : "Socialist should be beware of the cry of 'let the people decide' coming those who never let the people decide anything. 'We should consider whether in or Pakistan has the better title to use the language of democracy."

A plebiscite had not been held. But the moral commitment made by India to the people of Kashmir to consult them has been fulfilled.

Pakistan has not learnt the lesson of 'from the errors of others a wise man corrects his own'. Pakistan's jehadi attitude is more important than facts for the right attitude. Why? Because her emotion is low. Thought is nothing but a movement of the mental word. And the previous memories of fears have snowballed her mental attitude. What terrorists say today, the rest of Pakistan says tomorrow. He who lives by terrorism dies by terrorism. The road to terrorism lies by doubt. So, the Kashmir question still remains unsolved.

Disputes Over Canal Waters

Not only that the canal waters dispute between India and Pakistan has still assured special urgency. Why? Like the Kashmir case, this dispute is an offshoot of partition, and, from Pakistan's point of view, linked with its claim for Kashmir itself. Because the rivers which flow through west Pakistan have their sources in Kashmir, Pakistan's claim for a larger share of the waters of these rivers than India is prepared to give, becomes inter-connected with Kashmir issue. And both these problems have dragged on for over sixty years.

However, to advance a claim for territory which does not belong to a country on the basis that the rivers which flow through that country have their origins in that territory, amounts to assuming a ridiculous position. For instance, the river which flows through the East Pakistan (now Bangladesh) has their sources in India. And this fact, certainly cannot be advanced to make a claim on Indian territory. Again, the river Indus has its source in Tibet, and the river Kabul in Afganistan. And both of them flow through West Pakistan. Obviously no claim by Pakistan either on Tibet or Afganistan can be advanced or sustained.

When the subcontinent was partitioned in 1947, an artificial boundary line fell across the Indus and its Eastern tributaries ... the Jhelum, Chenab, Ravi and Sutlej. The Beas remained wholly in India. Thus these five rivers, whose extensive basin has been the cradle of many civilisations, including one of the earliest, Mohenjodoro, now flow from India into West Pakistan. Today for Pakistan, tomorrow for India.

One of the great rivers of the world, the Indus, which gives India its name, is 1,800 miles long and in some places, nine places, nine miles wide. By itself it carries as much water as the Nile and four times as much as the annual flow of the colorado river in the United States and Mexico.

Next to the Indus, in terms of water supply, rank the three rivers nearest to it ... the Kabul, Jhelum and Chenab, each carrying about one and a half times the annual flow of the Colorado. The remaining three tributaries, the Ravi, Beas, and Sutlej are comparatively small and carry about one fifth of the flow of the enitre system.

The area at present irrigated in the plains of the Indus basin comprises some 26 million acres. This irrigated area is by far the largest on anyone river system in the world, in fact, larger than the total irrigated area in any country outside the Indian sub-continent. Some of the canals in the Indus basin carry more water than the Thames in flood. These man-made water-ways are as intricate as the streets and traffic arrangements in a big American city ... only the water-ways of the Indus basin are very much bigger.

Nearly 50 million people, more than the entire population of Italy, depend for their livelihood upon this complicated canal system. Nevertheless the waters, which now flow into the Arabian Sea without being put to any purpose, have an equally large potential. The waters thus going waste can, if properly harnessed, turn another 26 million acres of desert and arid land into smiling fields growing wheat, rice and cotton. Most of the irrigated area went to Pakistan as a result of partition; 21 million acres of irrigated area went to Pakistan and only 5 million acres remained in India. One of the reasons why, during the British regime, the land law forming part of Pakistan was developed was that it constituted Crown land. Why? Because it was more profitable for the British regime, both economically and politically, to irrigate its own crown land and sell them in return for money and political support than develop land which was a private ownership. The latter was mostly in the region now falling within the geographical limits of India.

It was natural for West Pakistan to expect that all the waters of the Indus river system should be available for use in West Pakistan. It was equally natural for India to expect a share of these waters. Why? Because the rivers have their sources in India and flow partly through India.

Fortunately, there is enough water in the river system of the region to meet the requirements of all.

The basic position of the two countries was stated in an agreement signed soon after the dispute arose, on May, 1948: "The East and West Punjab Governments are anxious that this question should be settled in a spirit of goodwill and friendship. Without prejudice to its legal rights of the matter the East Punjab Govt. has assured the West Punjab Govt. that it has no intention suddenly to with-hold later from the West Punjab without giving it time to tap alternative sources. The West Punjab Govt. on its part recognises the natural anxiety of the East Punjab Govt. to discharge the obligation to develop areas where water is scarce and which were underdeveloped in relation to parts of West Punjab". And the sound of Kashmir dispute is not audible to Pakistan beyond certain decibles, even the canal water dispute. The Yiddish proverb says : "If things are not as you wish, wish them as they are". Pleasure disappoints, possibility never.

KASHMIR QUESTION ..... A CONTRAST : IV (HOPES AND FEARS)

There are three classes of people in the world. The first learn from their own experience ... these are wise; the second learn from the experience of others ... these are happy : The third neither learn from their own experience nor the experience of others ... these are fools. Pakistan belongs to the third. Neither do they learn from the Indo-Pak wars nor from the 1971 war. Political cheers mix with sarcastic laughter. There are two ways of living; a man may be casual and simply exist, or constructive deliberately try to do something with his life. The constructive idea implies constructiveness not only about one's own life, but about that of society, and the future possibilities of humanity. Does Pakistan belong to these ways of living?

Pakistan's sermons on subversion have a sinister ring. It very much suggests that the old technique of giving the dog a bad name before hanging it. Pakistan and Indian political leaders after winning over the elections, wipe their brows and rub their hands on their dirty trousers as admierers rush up to them and slap their backs and shake their hands. The losers suffer the indignity of being ignored. Terrorism and pseudo-terrorism still go on as it was before. No one bothers about it. After the blasts, it is not the winning that matters, but the spirit of the fun and joy, the cackle of the laughter, the glow of gaiety and the light-heartedness that it spreads, whether you are anxious to survive or not. It is all part of the fun of mockery of Indian democracy. And our demoralised but self-centred political leaders always speak to us what is beyond them, and beyond the grasp of their minds.

The State of Jammu and Kashmir has an area of 82,258 sq. miles and a population (1951) of 4.41 million. Of this Pakistan occupies an area of about 42,000 sq.miles with a population of a little over a million.

In addition, Pakistan has incorporated Chitral, a dependency of Kashmir, which has an area of 4,000 sq.miles and a population of 107,000.

Thus over half the territory of Kashmir and a quarter of its population are under Pakistan. These are territories acquired by invasion or as in the case of Chitral by two wholly illegal 'accession'.

What has been the record of Pakistan in 'Azad Kashmir'? The latter enjoys no independent or autonomous existence and was ruled by the Ministry of Kashmir. The so-called 'Azad Govt.' was only a front. It is now responsible to one and represents only itself. Nobody has ever dared to hold elections in this area. This is perhaps not surprising as no election had been held to the Pakistan National Assembly since independence either. This, however, had not prevented Pakistan from demanding a plebiscite in Kashmir despite its own non-fulfilment of the agreed pre-conditions, and from seeking to oppose the holding of general elections on the Indian side of the cease-fire line.

Such has been the political intrigue in the 'Azad' area that there had been six changes of Govt. in first nine years. This only just surpassed the record of Govts. made and unmade in Karachi itself.

This is the consequence of worst-regulated administration. 'Azad Kashmir' is to Pakistan is like 'when a witless man marries a foolish woman'.

In Oct. 1948, the 'Azad' Govt. was headed by Md. Ibrahim Chowdhry Ghulam Abbas was the 'supreme Head'. In May, 1950, Col. Ali Nawab Shah became President. He was followed the following year by Mir Waz Yusuf. In July, 1952, this gentleman gave way to Col. Sher Ahmed who survived nearly four years before being replaced once more by Mir Waz Yusuf. But this return was short lived as Sardar Md. Abdul Qayyum Khan took over as President a few months later, towards the end of the year. The members of other ministerial charges had been legion.

In what was probably one of his early public pronouncements, Mr. Qaayum Khan said : "Pakistan will remain insecure if Kashmir does not accede to Pakistan. We are fighting for the glory of Islam which can only be achieved by making Pakistan immune from all external dangers." ('Dawn' of Dec. 1956).

This statement like most others made in the name of 'Azad' Kashmir makes no reference to the will of the people or their interests. The argument always is that Kashmir must be part of Pakistan for the benefit of Pakistan. Truly speaking, all the political leaders, from Jinnah down to the present fledged anti-India campaign keep pace with the ideological twists and turns with which international jehadi groups have been convulsed ever since the partition of India.

This disinterest of the welfare of Kashmir is evident in the abject political and economic conditions of the people, conditions of political servitude and economic distresses that are so bad that over 3,00,000 refugees had risked their lives to slip across the cease-fire line to India.

The followings are extracts from a memorandum sent in 1955 to the members of Pakistan Constitutional Assembly by All-Jammu and Kashmir Muslim Conference, which was the political party supposed to be in power in 'Azad' Kashmir.

"For the last few years the people of Azad Kashmir in general and those of Poonch in particular have been subjected to great torture and terrorisation ... At least a dozen houses were blasted with a dynamite ... and random firing by mortar guns took place resulting in many deaths ... Simultaneously, Punjab Constabulary was imported ... The Azad Kashmir Police and Punjab Constabulary practically plundered the villages in Pulandri area, Malot and Harveli Tehsil ... about 400 persons are still under detention in the concentration camp at Pulandri."

The memorandum refers to a Civil Disobedience movement and to sub-human conditions in concentration camps in all three districts ... at Bagh-Bari, Pulandri and Sarswat. It goes on : "Mohammad Siddique, a new arrival from

Karachi who was arrested at Muzaffarbad, was tortured and forced to say that he had been sent by India-held Kashmir Govt. for espionage. He referred to say so and was tortured all the more .... Face of Ghazi Feroz Ali, secretary of the Pulandri Muslim Conference was blackened ... could anybody dream of anything shameful like this in the biggest Islamic country of the world ... women arrested and subjected to unbecoming and insulting treatment ..."

Mr. Nehru was the man who preached co-existence abroad which crushing at home. He had refused independence to the Sikhs and to Kashmir .... Then Mr. Nehru was receiving credit for counselling restraint towards Goa. But who started the crisis? Mr. Nehru himself. He inflamed feelings against the Portuguese. Then he feared that bloodshed over their tiny settlement exposed his pretensions. And, of course, just as Nehru attacked the Portuguese, so did he slander the British.

Nehru was as wrong-doer as Jinnah on the Kashmir issue. Why? The wrong-doer is in no mood to put things right. According to the Manchester Guardian, on August 25, 1955, "... after Chauri Chaura incident, when some trapped policemen were murdered, Mahatma Gandhi repented and said that he had made a Himalayan blunder, and suggested at least by implication, that Nehru as a Gandhian, should do the same."

Nehru was sometimes criticised for not denouncing colonialism and racialism in sufficiently strong language. He could not freely express himself on issues which other powers considered as their domestic concerns, Nehru's foreign policy was too timid in dealing with Kashmir and Canal Waters disputes, vitally affecting the country. The diplomacy of peace is more infinitely difficult than that of an orchestrated battle plan of terrorism. And Pakistan is doing the cause of justice and peace in Kashmir by aiding and abetting the existence of religious extremism in Kashmir and perpetration of colonialism and racialism. The anti-Indian tone of the Pakistani leaders is a part of these tactics.

A reactionary is a person who sits in his arm-chair on Sunday, never thinking that tomorrow is Monday but only that yesterday was Saturday.

Muslims and Congress : (Illusions Lost At Sea)

During the early days of Congress, when Mahatma Gandhi assured its leadership, vast sections of Muslims joined the organisation and cooperated with other fellow Congressmen in the struggle for independence of India. Later on, however, a great majority of them under the leadership of M.A. Jinnah broke away from the Congress and started the Pakistan movement under the Muslim League. Ultimately, the country was divided and the Pakistan dream was fulfilled. One obvious result of this has been that the Muslims in India are finding it difficult to adjust themselves to the idea of a common nationalism, and are naturally suspected of having a pro-Pakistani bias. So the Kashmir issue has raised its hydra-headed monsterism with fire and brimstone. Actuated by inordinately and unreasonably done enthusiastic zeal, Nehru had fanned out the Kashmir issue.

Why Kashmir? It must be remembered that the conception of nationalism is inherently different to the conception of Muslim brotherhood, which is the basis of Islam. Till the end of the First World War, so long as the Turkish Empire was there, Islam and most of the Islamic countries did not countenance the theory of nationalism. So, Kashmir issue was born with poisonous sap and juice. It was only after the Arab countries had seceded from the Turkish Empire, and other European near-East countries had become independent, that Kamal Ata-Turk, for the first time threw overboard the concept of Khilafat, and established the Republic of Turkey confining it only to the people of Turkish nationality. Unfortunately, however, the Muslims of India, being at that time along with the rest of the country under a foreign yoke, were unable to learn this lesson of history and did not fully grasp the implications of nationalism. The fantastic idea of a 'Muslim nation' propounded by the Quaid-e-Azam was gullibly accepted by the bulk of the Muslims of India. Even after sixty years of independence, the people of Pakistan are still adhering to the outworn concept of Islamic brotherhood and talking of having an Islamic State as their goal. Obviously, if the Muslims of India still cling to this concept and are still unable to imbibe the true spirit of nationalism, they may never be able to form a useful part of a homogenous Indian nation. Why not Kashmir? Such conception totally based on unity of religion is an anachronism in the modern Pakistan. So, Kashmir issue springs out with all its religion based mass-murdering agency. This kind of rise the Pakistani press has adopted so far against India is not surprising. For many of these newspapers take their cue from the Pakistani Govt. which has seldom been friendly but which has recorded periods of increased or decreased hostility to India. Normally Pakistan whose people have almost as bitter an experience of colonialism as Indians should have been expected to support the struggle of Paktoonistan against their Pakistani overlords.

The Indian Muslims, therefore, have two-fold task before them and it is up to them and them alone to decide what steps should be taken to overcome these problems, not by terrorism nor by fanaticism. In the first place, they have got to live down and, by their conduct, wipe out the pernicious propaganda, which was carried on by the Muslim League for about ten years before India attainted its independence. It is only by their conduct over a sufficiently long period of time, that they can prove that they believe in the ideology of secularism and democracy which has been accepted by the people of independent India. In the second place, they have got to accept the concept of nationlism. Both these tasks require a revolution in the settled ideas and conceptions of the entire population of this great country. The task is of great magnitude and pseudo-Indian communists are bound to adversely affect the progress of the country and its reputation among the comity of nations. Communalism, among Muslims, is bound to be interpreted as disloyalty to India and allegiance to Pakistan. And communalism, among non-Muslims, can never be interpreted as being seditious or disloyal to the country. The Congress has always fanned out communal feelings with a view to taking an advantage over thier political interests. The only other group of Pakistan, fighting for political powers in the country, are operating in the country in the garb of communalism to their best efforts.

Pakistan is a great propagandist as the pseudo-communists of India. Their ideologies are misguided and led to believe that their religion and culture are in danger. Such parties appeal to the sentiment and fanaticism of the people in their own respective areas. Both are slave to their own slogans. They know their limited value. There is an English saying : "Sticks and stones can break my bones but words can never harm me."

Kashmir is preponderantly an agricultural state. More than 80 percent of its population depends on land for its livelihood. The ownership rights of all land in the State rested in the ruler. A deep realisation of the need to eliminate all chances of exploitation of man by man in this and other forms and to check out a long term development plan gave birth to what Pakistan appears to have resiled from the basic positions as evidenced by the statement of Prime Minister M.S. Suhrawardy. He said : "If India wants more water for the Ambala division or to water its deserts, it cannot draw on the waters which used to flow into Pakistan, it cannot deprive Pakistan of its just rights, if it (India) wants water for itself, then the obvious course is that it should make its headworks, it should make its dams, it should make storage in its own soil at its own expense and from that increased supply make storage in its own soil at its own expense and from that increased supply use water for itself. Many blunders have been committed in the past by some of our leaders. But they cannot by their blunders take away the right of Pakistan." This would mean that Pakistan wants even the headworks which fall within Indian territory to be made over to Pakistan.

The World Bank has, however, suggested a compromise plan which is not acceptable to Pakistan. The proposal, briefly, is that the waters of the form Western rivers, Indus, Kabul, Jhelum and Chenab, be reserved exclusively for Pakistan, and the waters of the three Eastern rivers, the Ravi, Beas and Sutlej for India.

It remains to be seen what further steps Pakistan will take in order to restore this dispute with Kashmir issue. Obivously, it claims that India can draw at best only 30 percent of the waters of the three Eastern rivers cannot be, and has not been sustained by the World Bank.

But this cannot be the end of the story. The longer they rule in the name of the president, the more they will discredit themselves in the eyes of the people of West Pakistan. They may have saved themselves for the time being, but how are they going to save their Govt.-sponsored Islamic terrorism and salvage its democratic credentials? If they hope to achieve political stability by subverting normal democratic procedures they will soon be disillusioned. The impositor of the President's Rule can only deepen, not allay, the prevailing political unrest.

History cannot be erased because of an act of partition. Pakistan is very optimistic about the future of Kashmir. But she is quite uncertain whether her optimism is justified. Pakistan does not believe that it will have to tread the road to ruin to the end.

Priorities are the other way around in Pakistan where an entrenched hierarchy far removed from the masses seems busily engaged in making the rich richer, and the poor poorer. Such contrasts are not unknown in India. But in Pakistan, they are more sharply posed, and the sense of poverty and depression somehow seems more intense even than one encounters at home. God alone knows where is 'Don't ask where terrorism lies?' Pakistan is quite happy wherever she may be. A hen tomorrow is better than an egg today.

Is Pakistan going to sweep the country of terrorism? Why not start with the National Assembly? Pakistan has all the invidiousness of self-praise, and all the ill-desert of falsehood. It will damage the cause of Islam about life under the terror, when the people are morally chocked, remaining blind to the harsh relations of today and yesterday. Why this craven fear of facts, of free-debate or reason? Will it undermine Islamic society? No twists and turns of Islamic dialects can explain away the tragic fact after sixty years of political dualism and religious hypocrisy over Kashmir and Canal waters dispute. Pakistan cannot bear to hear the truth about Kashmir and Canal Waters dispute. There are times when silence, too, is a lie for the very raison d'etre. But neither the long silences nor the loud cries of jehadi horror settle the Kashmir issue. Why not admit that the cap-touching, the silence, is the result of fear? Why pretend? No one is deceived. It is not as easy as you think. What is known as the 'New Kashmir Plan"? This charter of the rights, privileges and obligations, which the people of Jammu and Kashmir gave unto themselves, several years before the transfer of power to them, and in which they consitently from time to time reaffirmed their faith enumerates in very clear terms certain basic principles for the solution, among other things, of the land problem and of the consequent agricultural development in the State. So, Kashmir question has always been in a critical phase of multilateral problems. The Congress lost a word unguarded from its tongue on Kashmir issue. There is a Maltese saying : "Better one word too few than one word too many."

The present rulers of India and their political hangers-on will have us believe that the best way to destroy evil is to allow it to destroy good and that somehow or other evil will perish or good is relentless in making more and more sacrifices. But facts of history tell a different tale. Did Duryodhana relent inspite of uttermost appeasment on the part of Pandavas and Krishna? Was not Buddha's gospel of unalloyed non-violence and consequent weakening of martial spirit in India responsible for preparing the ground for foreign conquest? Perhaps Bernard Shaw was right in saying that "The only lesson that we learn from history is : We learn no lesson from history." During the riots, non-violence is considered to be a useless weapon otherwise the death toll will have been much higher. When the adversary of terrorism in a savagedom of cruelty is in association with rapid movements and quite untutored in canons of morality, then the nearest approach to non-violence is cutting short its violent activities. There is no sense in allowing foreign invaders or terrorists to kill our own people on our own soil.

The Govt. should clear the soil of Kashmir of the remnants of Islamic terrorism with the help of the armed forces. Why? Because Pakistan has already raised the relative value of violence and non-violence. The battle against crime can be won on the playing fields. The heartless and unjustifiable firing on unarmed people of Kashmir has once again brought to the fore-front the nature of evil superstitiously believed to be able to cause material harm. There is a Portuguese proverb : "God writes straight with crooked lines."

Nehru was blamed for the bloodshed perpetrated in the valley. Nehru was in one respect like King Henry II. Henry asked if no one would rid him of "this turbulent priest", meaning Thomas Backet. Some one did. They murdered Backet in Canterbury Cathedral, and Henry did penance for the dead. Nehru did penance by apolising for the Bombay riots. And he should have done penance for his political romance over the valley. Nehru was as much responsible for the blood affair in Kashmir as was Henry for the unintended assassination of Backet. If Nehru did not adopt his smug, priddish 'holier-than-thou' attitude to the rest of the world, one could bear with him better. But he even said about Kashmir in 1950 that "my patience is becoming exhausted. It makes you shiver. It makes you sick." Nehru may profess to follow Gandhi's great and gentle message. There is a Yiddish saying : "Words should be weighed not counted". Those who live in a high-rise building are at first extremely careful of their words particularly on Kashmir issue. Why? Because they would fill every room of the valley with grief, no matter what word was said either in the Parliament or outside the Parliament. When you make a mistake, don't look back at it long. Take the reason of the thing into your mind, and then look forward. Mistakes are lessons of wisdom. The past cannot be changed. The future is yet in your power.

The year 1947 that was rung in with so much joy and hope is rung out today with almost total bleakness in retrospect. The merry bells welcoming the arrival of new hope drowned the doleful knell announcing the departure of the old enemy. Ane we, the people of India, the eternal dupe of tomorrow, eagerly look forward to the fresh-born year of political chicanery and religious hypocrisy for a worse and uglier order of things than in the year just now dead. This is what we have been doing through the worn-out ages of despair and blunders all over the Kashmir valley but the ideal, we strive after, remains as distant as ever through numberless years of has beens, has emerged from and merged into a myriad fold of religious passions and bickerings. A clever but misleading talk begins.

Even after 60 years of independence, Pakistan- sponsored hymns of hate have been alive today and waiting for someone to pick it up. And in the terrorism-gifted state of Pakistan, there are carriers for everybody ... political brigands, religious adventurers, non-entities. The speeches delivered by top-ranking politicians of Pakistan are dangerous babies of jehadi slogans and resourceful carriers of that terrorism-gifted State. The main theme of these Philippies is the vilification ... deliberately and confusedly planned ... of the Prime Ministers of India.

The Demosthenes who started that oratorial campaign was Md. Ali Jinnah. A British politician once remarked on the basis of wide political experience that consistency was the hobgoblin of little minds. Once ...long ago ... Sheikh Abdullah was a Congressman, just like his more fortunate and more successful Kashmiri comrade. But the Congress is too hot a place for great minds like Sheikh Abdullah. So Sheikh Abdullah joined National Conference, and so did Khan Abdul Quaiyum Khan in the Muslim League of Pakistan. The result was that he was the Quaid-e-Azam's choice for one of the posts reserved for the Muslim League in the Interim Govt. of 1946-47 by its clever patron, Lord Wavell. After the establishment of Pakistan, both Khan Abdul Quaiyum Khan and Sheikh Abdullah naturally became the most dazzling luminaries of Pakistan and Kashmir respectively. It was hardly a secret to the fanatics of Sheikh Abdullah in the markets of Kashmir that Sheikh Abdullah was very anxious to dethrone the mild and soft premier Bakshi Ghulam Mohammad. Preoccupied with vacillating mind and volatile nature, Sheikh Abdullah wanted a liberation movement at the cost of war with India. This is a well-cooked-up conspiracy of liberation movement in Kashmir.

Mr. Jinnah was well-convinced that Mr. Nehru was a 'great bluff'. He knew that India was weak and Pakistan was strong. On that basis, Pakistan declares we shall succeed in the war with India. Why? Because we are in the right. Now the point is that right or wrong has no place in the calculations of a particular class of politicians in the terrorism-gifted State of Pakistan. Ambition is the last refuge of failure. The authoritative interpreter of Pakistan's foreign policy really believes that the problem of Kashmir can, and should, be solved by war. If that remains the basic point of Pakistan's policy, how are we to explain that Indian-Pakistan disputes have been rejected by India? It can only lead to overall ruin for the peoples of India and Pakistan.

A British writer on 'The Transfer of Power in India, correctly assesses the origin and influence of communalism in India when he writes that religious, historical and economic factors did not impair harmony in social relations between Hindus and Muslims and that, in fact, a kind of Hindu-Muslim socio-religious synthesis was being evolved when all prospect of it was destroyed by a process of political preference starting with separate electorates and weightage and ending in the two-nation theory and partition.

The Indian National Congress was, in this period, forced into the mould of communalism and vested with the aspect of a Hindu body by making it politically profitable for the Muslims to seek their fortunes from outside it and impossible for those who prized national freedom above the temptations of personal gain to seek with any prospect of winning it, the suffrage of their co-religionists. The surprise was that the Congress had not any Muslim adherents at all. Who was responsible for the creation of Kashmir issue in India?

The gatherings of Muslim forces outside the Congress as an exclusive factor impeding the struggle for political freedom, produced a reaction in the Hindu community in the form of exclusive political bodies and militant proselytising religious sects. Even the Congress was not free from it. The Congress has handled out the Muslim community for its own interest and suffered unnecessarily for imperfect handling of imperfect men.

Political freedom was a by-product. Why? It was because we failed to understand Hindu-Muslim unity. We only generated passions in the vortex of power politics that ultimately compassed the destruction of Indo-Pak unity. Following this way we are pressing sectional demands with the support of religious sanctions ignoring the fundamental differences between India and Pakistan. All linguistic agitation carried on associated with each originates in this fallacy. So, Kashmir issue still remains unsolved.

That fact that our Pakistani friends look upon Kashmir as a mere lucrative possession is clear from Pakistan's statement. Why? Because Pakistan's prosperity and political weightage seems to depend on Kashmir if the people of Kashmir do not propose to oblige Pakistan by contributing to her prosperity. What does Pakistan propose to do?

Why Kashmir issue? The problems of poverty and ignorance are common to Hindus and Muslims alike in Kashmir. It would be impossible to tackle them in a sectarian and communal way. If any section of the people in Kashmir lags behind at this time, it will continue to live in backwaters. From this point of view, the indifference of Muslims to the problems of national reconstruction would be ultimately harmful to their own interests. Getting good politicians is easy, but getting them to play together is hard. Religion cannot be allowed to be dominated by politicians. Why? Because politics has no heart ... religion is pure heart. Politics is like a stone, dead, but stone can destroy the flower and the flower has no defence. So politics is aggressive. Whereas religion is the physician who can heal wounds and cure the sickness of humanity. And Pakistan has managed to create enough destructive power to destroy all life through religious fanaticism. In ancient India, the king would go to religious people for advice. Kings used to touch the feet of those who had realised themselves. Why? Because their blessing can transform them. Pakistani politicians should take lessons from the Koran. And the ego of Indian politicians wants nobody to be higher than them.

In the face of organised banditry from the terrorist groups, the burgeoning fundamental forces have to eat away the Islamic infrastructure in Pakistan with a mixture of Islamabad's legalese and dilatoriness.

The Indian Muslims should not consider Urdu as the monopoly of Muslims. Why? That attitude has got to create prejudices and will be a great disservice to the language itself. Urdu is the common heritage of Hindus and Muslims alike and its growth and preservation can be ensured through their joint efforts.

The Muslims in India should realise that freedom and peace in Kashmir as well as in other states are on the basis of communal unity. After all, sentiments cannot be as sacrosanct as freedom and peace of the valley.

The liberation movement through terrorism and religious fanaticism that has been constantly disturbing the peace of mind of Indian Muslims is the lip sympathy that is paid to them by the ruling class of Pakistan. These sympathies are born out of dishonest motives and are being used by them for self-aggrandizement. This policy has brought a good deal of misfortune to Indian Muslims.

The Muslims in India are faced with certain problems which have come in the wake of partition. These relate to rehabilitation of refugees, the fortune of Urdu and maintenance of religious institutions and opportunities for employment. But the echoes of religious fanaticism are reverberating in men's minds throughout the world. This murderous product of man's inventive genius is portents of world destruction. One world power uses it to frighten the other.

Among cultured people, the honour of the plighted world is always respected. We have lost this sense of honour. *Between 1920 and the outbreak of World War II in 1939, 4568 treaties of peace were signed. In the eleven months which preceded the outbreak of World War II, no less than 211 treaties of peace were signed. They were all broken.* What does this show? How do we expect peace in Kashmir? How do we expect Pakistan will not break away the Indo-Pak agreements signed so far on the Kashmir issue?

Let us pursue this harrowing tale of man's lust for violence further. Twice within a generation man has taken away the life of man, resulting in a heavy toll, the effects of which still persist.

In World War I, 97,00,000 men were killed. In World War II, 54,800,000 died or were found missing and presumed dead; that is, eight times more than in World War I. The total human loss in these two World Wars, therefore, cause roughly 64,500,000. 56,100,000 men were wounded; in addition, the fate of two millions is unknown. And for everyman who died or lost, a mother, a widow or a sister was left heart-broken and in many cases a child became destitute.

Could human wickedness go further?

The Islamic culture, which is slowly spreading over the world, glorifies both violence and vulgarity by every means. The cult of violence is not peculiar to totalitarian states. It has its followers in other lands also. Nor is the cult of terrorism an isolated phenomenon. The great Quran, 47.14, says : "Is he who relies on a clear proof from his Lord like those for whom the evil that they do seems pleasing while they follow their own lusts?"

Our political leaders are hardly disciplined in words and deeds. Why? They don't incite the good impulse in their souls to fight against the evil impulse against terrorism. Even the Indian Muslim leaders should practise Sufism. Why? Because Sufism is among the easiest and the most unique path to achieve ultimate flowering. It is not a religion but the way ... It is the art and science of correct living through a systematic understanding and following of austerities. Do they feel insecurity in India? Why? You are ready to sail your boat without a map to navigate the unknown. At the centre, you are an Indian, then Muslim. It is an axiomatic truth.

Where is democracy in the valley of Kashmir? Some people smile and some say democracy is in England and America. Democracy in Kashmir and in other parts of India is half-naked. And in Pakistan, it is coup d' etat in the name of democracy. Why? Pakistan has set up a record in 'art of lying'. A country-wide competition in lying is organised, perhaps in recent history, by the Pakistani patrons of liars. The wide interest of this delectable art aroused in the country is evidenced by the number of competitors, participating in it and of judges, leading their expert services in deciding the qualities of the competiting liars. It is the path of their nationalism on Kashmir issue. Pakistan, in the freshness of religious extremism, has earned for herself the distinction of holding almost a national competition in lying on the Kashmir issue, as she has acquired remarkably bizarre reputations in other fields of agreements, treaties, peace-loving process and so on. Lying is the bastard child of faith and reason. Why? Because Pakistan begets a suspicion against all relations with India on Kashmir issue. Because the incredulous are the most credulous. These instinctive appetites are well-established in the path of Islamic terrorism.

Every poeple is said to have a genius which impresses its stamp on the behaviour of men, women and children constituting that nation, Pakistan, barely sixty two years old as an Islamic country, has not yet been able to discover her genius. She is out and out saturated with the spirit of lying on cross-border terrorism to such an extent as to justify the assertion that she had found her 'genius' lying. Pakistan has already left the legacy of an honest name and duty done. She has been false to others, so long as a horde of knaves shall rule the country.

Not being veteran and hard-boiled liars, they are not in a position to appreciate the merit of 'Liar number one' in Pakistan. Gen Ayub Khan had been adjudged the best liar in Pakistan on Kashmir issue. Mr.Z.A. Bhutto, who may be declared the second best, has made contributions in lying, which may be called 'white lies' against 'black lies'. These two champion liars of Pakistan, bringing the tragedies and grief of others, have deservedly secured national recognition by their skill in an art that is as old as civilisation itself. For lying, like many other of its sister arts, is a gift of what is commonly known as civilisation. With the progress of Hindu-Muslim disparity, after partition, the primitive crudities of lying have refined, by stages, so much so that now it has become almost as fine an art as any of those that satisfy our aesthetic sense.

Constant practice of our leaders in telling lies on Kashmir issue immeasurably improves the capacity for dissimulation and sharpens the intellect of our leaders' intellectual dishonesty. A blunt and idotic politician can never be a good liar. Skill in lying goes, generally speaking, in direct proposition to the keenness of the mind. Pakistan's constant practice of lying ... the honeycomb that is created ... is deathless, undiscovered, and immortal, and must live so long as Kashmir issue remains unsolved. It becomes thicker and more impermeable. A replica of leaden rule of leaden rulers.

The military pact between the U.S. and Pakistan is the pathetic attitude of complacency. Pakistan has entered into this military alliance with a view to coerce India into accepting its unjust claim to Kashmir. Pakistan is a nation of upstart dictators. When an upstart dictator succeeds, the ballot is useless. And when the Govt. rules everybody anonymously, the rule has become the modern form of despotism as communists exercise.

If America had crossed the Pacific, tending support to Asia's independence movements, America's prestige would not be high. If America is to win the friendship of the peoples of Asia and enjoy their confidence, America must stand first to her allies and must remember that the present day struggle for the balance of political power in the world can be won only by ideas. If it be thus, Kashmir question will remain solved.

It is an undeniable fact that America as the most powerful world power is interested in the ideology of Asia. Most of the countries in Asia at the present moment represent the most troubled theatre in the world. Indian diplomacy should be careful of its priority over the Kashmir issue. Why? A diplomat is a person who is appointed to avert the situation that would never occur if there were no diplomats. And Pakistan : Really bad singer usually resents candid criticism.

In this political juncture, Indian diplomacy should whip up Pakistan's anti India campaign. The Pakistani public has always been on the way of their campaign of lies, calumny and sentiment aimed at depicting India and the Indian Govt. as aggressive imperialist walking in the footsteps of Hitler. If this fantastic and disreputable campaign really reflects the views of any substantial part of the Pakistani public, Pakistan's continued membership of the commonwealth will be incompatible with her sense of respect. Pakistan has got used to playing the old dirty game of power politics over the valley. The paper 'Dawn' has always been engaged in periodic sniping at India and casting reflections on our political integrity. It is a complete anachronism. We do not count a man's years until he does nothing else to count.

History slowly smothers truth, but hastily struggles to revive it a terrible penance of pain. New Islamic civilisation which thousands and thousands of terrorists, hundreds and thousands of fundamentalists and a zillion of jehadis beget regularly has something wrong with it. This civilisation is proud of producing so many extremists. The very foundations of Pakistan's nationhood rest on the principle of jehadi slogans which are the historic and unique legacy of Islam. You can't teach old dogs tricks. If you are nobody and nothing, do something, even if it is anything.

In Pakistan, suspicion and diplomacy go together. Politics and religious fanaticism dine together. Terrorism and fundamentalism shake hands. And last of all, people, in general, yawn together waiting for another Indo-Pak war. Peace has suffered a crushing defeat. *Without American direct military intervention, there will be no absolute chance for India to recover her Pak-occupied Kashmir*. It is fact. New Delhi knows that the bulk of the people of Kashmir are eager for complete independence and it is only certain puppets who have been pretending to speak for the people without authority.

Pakistan is a new Fuehrer of world terrorism. She does not talk in terms of political parties ... she talks about Islamic terrorist groups. Yesterday, it was Hitler. Tomorrow it will be somebody else like Pakistan. He is always a terrorist, not a leader. Patriotism is profitable in Pakistan as in our political leaders. Laughter among the pseudo-political ideologies is a prohibitive luxury, tears being so cheap and overflowing.

War is not a solution of Kashmir issue. Why? This is the proper time to look back at the sanguinary pictures of the last Great wars and limited wars in Korea, Iraq, Indo-Pak, Vietnam and Indo-China and take lessons from the horror, death, damage, destruction and devastation ... all these concomitant evils of war ... and to visualise the consequences which the third recrudescene of world war will entail. Mr. Bertrand Russell, the celebratd British Philosopher, believes that "an impartial investigation into the probable consequences of a third world war would prove exclusively the impossibility of success of either side," and such a proof will help to avert the calamity ahead. The power-intoxicated nations like Pakistan-sponsored terrorism should try to understand that war or preparations for war is politically stupid, economically futile and morally derogatory.

From decade to decade, man has been spending enormous sums for destructive purposes. In 1913, expenditure on world armaments was 2,531 million dollars; in 1925, it was 3,522 million dollars, and in 1934, it was 4,900 million dollars. If take the five leading powers ... Britain, USA, France, Italy and Japan ... the official expenditure on armaments in 1912-13 was 1,243 million dollars and in 1931, it was 2,209 million dollars, an increase of 78 percent. (F.A.E. Crew ...' Must Man Wage War?' (p-71).

The World War I and World War II cost mankind in money £ 35,448 million and £ 2,23,342 million respectively. (A. Enock, 'This War Business', 1951) Between 1900 and 1948, twenty four countries of Europe, Asia and America spent 321,316 million pound sterling on war measures and 3,13,759 million pound sterling on all other measures. (Ibid).

The World War I cost mankind 39.7 million dead and crippled, and the toll of human life taken by the World War II amounted to 27,995,971 military and 13,252,997 civilian casualities. (Ibid).

Will Pakistan get to mortgage her Islamic nation to America and its allies? *Kashmir question is not an issue. It is nothing but a symbolic one to Pakistan.* Will Pakistan's cultural identity be lost if they are not given regional autonomy?

Are the framers of the Pakistan Constitution deliberately weakening the forces of nationalism by dividing the people on religious lines and dealing impatiently with those who should be treated with civilisation and tact because of their fears, real or imaginary? Pakistan's amateur theatricals are the all-pervading disharmony among the religious sects. Does Pakistan find harmony in disharmony? As a lovely flower of exquisite colour but lacking fragrance, so are the fair words of Pakistani rulers who act not upto them.

Terrorists (Chamber of Horrors) : Before hiring personal servant, careful man usually checks his belongings. Does Pakistan find any master who can bridge and guide towards her own inner master? Does Pakistan know the masters appear from time to time to take lessons of her faith? Does Pakistan know why her people are undisciplined and unhappy over the turmoil in Kashmir? Does Pakistan know the brave and the wise who intend to overcome their foes, must first of all strive to subdue the internal enemies of their own heart and mind? Take responsibility for the most difficult problem. First choose 'who might be your boss?' A shattering experience to Pakistan.

Pakistan believes in militancy and partisanship. Can't you see that some of the worst features of Stalinism have their roots in the conception of militancy? Stalin didn't argue with those who differed from him. Was Lenin always fair to his opponents? Rosa Luxemburg, for instance. Was Marx justified in branding Bakunin as a spy?

Every Govt. in Pakistan, believing in Stalinism in the last analysis, is a class dictatorship. The Islamic intellect like the communist intellect has forzen under Islamic iron rule; its thawing certainly has released unknown forces, unforseeable elements like terrorists. An all-round stultification of life faces the new rulers of Pakistan. Most of the coummunist leaders who had come to power after the war had been purged or executed by Stalin. In the same way as most of the rulers in Pakistan, after partition, were replaced by a group of hand-picked puppets who enjoyed power at Pakistan's theologians' pleasure, under them, democracy has choked. So, democracy is no longer inspiring the masses, but is rather the object of popular hatred and contempt. Even the functionaries of ISI are used in most militant jehadi groups and produce terrorism by killing innocent men, women and children. Such inter-personal relationship makes democracy crippled. So, they are with their own hands digging the grave of democracy, and, with the old man Jinnah gone, they wanted to save the system and to ensure its further progress. How do we expect Kashmir solution?

Epicureanism is human nature drunk, cynicism is human nature mad and stoicism in our foreign policy is human nature in despair. They have kept isolated from outside contacts except Kashmir and Pakistan. Today the pubilicity of the Govt. should be to convert people abroad rather at home. When you make a mistake, don't look back at it long. Take the reason of the thing into your mind, and then look forward. Mistakes are lessons of wisdom. The past cannot be changed. The future is yet in your power. Is our Kashmir policy going in the direction of peace or of a nuclear blow-up? Is it going to secure happiness for all or total despair?

Unfortunately, India extends this idealistic approach of compromise even to those world problems which do not concern us much. Our policy is a curious mixture of Ashokan principles and Quixotic methods. In this connection, what a Corinthian leader said to Sparta at the time of the Peloponnesian War is worth nothing: "You will see that the likeliest way of securing peace is .... only to use one's power in the cause of justice, but to make it perfectly plain that one is resolved not to tolerate aggression. On the contrary, your idea of proper behaviour is, firstly, to avoid harming others and then to avoid being harmed yourself, even if it is a matter of defending your own interests. Even if you had on your frontiers a power holding the same principles as you do, it is hard to see how such a policy could have been a success. But at the same time ... your whole way of life is out of date as compared with theirs."

What is wrong with our policy either on Kashmir issue or on terrorism is that it is too right, over-right, and it is in this that it is wrong.

MISTAKES ON KASHMIR ISSUE : V (A NEW TWIST TO OLD TALES)

Pride is the master sin of the devil and devil is the father of lies. There is a false gravity that is a very ill symptom; and as rivers which run very slowly have always most mud at the bottom, so a solid stiffness in the constant course of a man's life is a sign of a thick bed of mud at the bottom of his brain.

There was a thick bed of mistakes at the bottom of India's foreign policy. *It was a mistake in the first place for the Govt. of India to take the Kashmir issue to the Security Council under articles of 34 and 35 of the Chapter 6 of the Charter which is entitled "Pacific Settlement of Disputes". A more appropriate head for involving the Security Council's intervention would have been Chapter 7 (seven) which is specially concerned with "Acts of Aggression". By involving Chapter 6 (six) India enabled the Council to traverse a field which included changes by Pakistan of genocide against India instead of pin-pointing the issue of Pakistan's aggression against Kashmir.* Nehru was responsible for the Kashmir problem. The prudence of the best heads is often defeated by the tenderness of the best of hearts. So, the socio-political atmosphere in the valley has still been vitiated by the misunderstanding of the past and it is easy for trouble-makers to foster distrust between the two communities.

It was the second mistake for the Govt. of India to needlessly place herself at a tactical disadvantage by later adopting the term 'Plebiscite' which did not occur in the earlier communications. The first document emanating from Delhi after the Maharaja of Kashmir's accession was Lord Mountbatten's letter of Oct. 27, 1947 accepting the accession. "It is my Govt.'s wish," wrote the Governor-General, "that as soon as law and order have been restored in Kashmir and her soil cleared of the invaders the question of the State's accession should be settled by a reference to the people." Similarly, Nehru in a statement made to the Constituent Assembly shortly after Kashmir's accession while reiterating that "the decision must be made by the people of that State" did not specify the machinery to be employed as that of a plebiscite. "We decided, "he declared, "to accept this accession and to send troops by air, but we made a condition that the accession would have to be considered by the people of Kashmir later when peace and order were established." The point is that evasion, like equivocation, comes generally from a cowardly or a deceiving spirit, or from both; afraid to speak out its sentiments, or from guile concealing them.

It was the third mistake that the Maharaja's accession was endorsed by Sheikh Abdullah and the National Conference in Oct 1947. In Feb. 1954, the Constituent Assembly of Kashmir ratified the decision. In Nov. 1956, this decision which was constitutionally and legally complete was given the formal sanction of the people of Jammu and Kashmir as reflected through their democratically elected Constituent Assembly it was "considered by the people of Kashmir". The later intrusion of the term 'Plebiscite', although conditional, has enabled India's critics to fasten on the plebiscite while forgetting the conditions.

The point is that pride is the master of premeditative intent and anxiety is the father of depression. India's claim to Kashmir rests on firm, fair and solid grounds.

The fourth mistake was tactical one. In our anxiety to reach a settlement, we have undoubtedly made certain tactical mistakes which our critics have quite naturally attempted to turn to their advantage. We have, for instance, in the protracted process of negotiation allowed ourselves to be persuaded to side-step certain preliminary hurdles, which action has later quite unjustifiably been interpreted as acceptance by us of these preliminary points. New Delhi has learned its lesson, and today India will not budge until the root of the matter ... who was the aggressor? ... is settled. From that decision, all things flow for once Pakistan was named the aggressor which she was.

Now the point is : It is a very easy thing to devise good laws : the difficulty is to make them effective. So, terrorism in India afloats. The great mistake is that of looking upon men as virtuous, or thinking that they can be made so by laws; and consequently, the greatest art of a politician is to render vices serviceable to the cause of virtue. Short is the course of every lawless pleasure.

If Pakistan seeks for greatness on Kashmir issue, let her forget greatness and ask for truth on Kashmir issue, and she will find both.

It is known to all that the birth of Pakistan, with active British help and goodwill, is a landmark of Pakistan history the importance of which is impossible to exaggerate. It represents not only the religious evolution of a long dependent people to independence and nationhood, but also the first really fateful crack in the colonial chain which coils around the body of Islamic theology. The crack has now spread and widened. The flame of religious fanaticism has been lit in a far-off corner of Pakistan in the gloom and enduring light of Islamic terrorism where everyone is master of his fate. Its guidance and help from the planners. It was the first mistake for Pakistan to reason out the truth behind Kashmir issue.

The second mistake is that Pakistan has all the invidiousness of self-praise, and all the ill-desert of falsehood on Kashmir issue. It will damage the cause of Islam about life under the terror when the people are morally choked, remaining blind to the harsh realities of today and yesterday. Why this craven fear of facts, of free-debate, or reason? Will it undermine Islamic society? No twists and turns of Islamic dialects can explain away the tragic fact after 60 years of political dualism and religious hypocrisy over Kashmir. Pakistan can't bear to hear the truth about Kashmir. There are times when silence, too, is a lie for the very raison d'etre. But neither the long silences nor the loud cries of jehadi horror settle the Kashmir issue. Why not make a clear breast of your old crimes on Kashmir? Why not admit that the cap-touching, the silence, was the result of fear? Why pretend? No one is deceived.

The third mistake for Pakistan on Kashmir issue is that to explain away the cause of terrorism in India is not as easy as you think. The wrong sort of question can still cost a hell of a lot of trouble. Pakistan has not spoken about her sincerity on Kashmir issue since 1947. God alone knows Don't ask where terrorism lies Pakistan is quite happy where she may be. A hen tomorrow is better than an egg today.

So many mistakes have so far been committed by Pakistan. One of the serious mistakes is that during the days when former Gen. Musharraf was riding triumphant over broken and tarnished reputations that this pernicious disorder in Pakistan politics would disappear as suddenly as it had originally flatted that is the peculiar tragedy of Gen. Musharraf. What I am and what my country Pakistan is, are as secret as maidenhead.

Another grave mistake is : the term 'peace offensive' although outworn has never been more appropriate than in the latest phrase of Pakistan's political hiccups. It can well be that Pakistan has been studying the text books of terrorism on which militant Generals are reared. Why? Because Pakistan was grown up to don this batteledress and make polite conversation in genteel drawing rooms of civil society and to eat fashionably cooked-up food of Islamic terrorism at elegant tables decorated by ISI. This is exactly what Pakistan has been trying to do ... unsuccessfully and with a slowly-growing frustration.

Does Pakistan know without a thread, there is no garland? But Pakistan never wears a garland for its thread of Islamic terrorism. She has to have some stuff of her self-made delusion. God has sent Pakistan into the world to develop every kind of virtue or strength among the Muslims. Only terrorism makes Pakistan feel like a better nation. Everything that needs to happen, will happen. And what kind of garland Pakistan makes out of this thread of Islamic terrorism is left to each master of Islamic theology or baron of terrorist groups. Pakistan, isolated from the world and branded as a sponsored country of Islamic terrorism, reveals her loneliness, her vanity of being a great Islamic country, and her sense of depression. The more Pakistan is romantic in terrorism, the worse.

Security Vs. Freedom (Go On or Get Out)

The great debate of the past days posed communism over against the different version of the free society represented by Britian and U.S.A. Today the stakes on Islamic terrorism involved are so great that the tension results in nervous extremism and loss of sense of security. The search for security through jealousy-guarded secrecy has only led to more insecurity and further curtailment of the liberty of the privacy. Words of freedom are as full of peace as security.

Is there any distinction between privacy and secrecy? Privacy is the voluntary withholding of information reinforced by a willing indifference. And secrecy is the compulsory withholding of knowledge, reinforced by the prospect of sanctions for disclosure. The Pakistan's pattern of the equilibrium between privacy, publicity and secrecy, either on Kashmir issue or terrorism, is very interesting. Pakistan's pattern is the bulwark of privacy. And India's pattern is of 'luxuriating of secrecy afflicts Pakistan much more than it afflicts India. India's suspicion of secrecy is traced to its deeper sources in the political, social and cultural history of the Indian people; hyper-patriotism, xenophobia, populism, Islamic jingoism and anti-India hate culture throughout Pakistan are always with her tradition of aristocratic amateurism and deep-seated privacy. A grain of sand leads to the fall of a mountain when the movement has come for the mountain to fall. The Christian believes in a hereafter ; the Marxist believes in a rehabilitation hereafter; and the Islam believes in hereafters.

The feeling that the safety of the nation depends on jealousy-guarded nuclear weapons leads to a demand for absolute secrecy in the matter of scientific research. Now the question is : Has this led to tremendous disturbance and degradation of well-advertised Islamic social life without any compensation in the way of real security in Paksitan? Does not the destruction of the autonomy of science at the hands of Islamic terrorists involve the eventual destruction of science and Islam? Pakistan has arrived at such a high pitch of secrecy on anti-India culture that all institutions of lies and hypocrisy, which act in any way to obstruct or thwart the development of Islamic culture, and compress the people towards into vast uniform masses of religious fanaticism, are now far more hurtful than in earlier ages of the world. Secrecy brings destruction and desolation wherever it goes. India should achieve a proper equilibrium between privacy, publicity and secrecy and get rid of dangerous extremism of Pakistan-sponsored terrorism. It is, therefore, of vital importance to science, security and democracy.

Secrecy is an integral part of Pakistan on Kashmir issue. The world sees that the uprising of Islamic fanaticism and militant jehadis is either organised or controlled by fascists or reactionaries. Even after 60 years, the incessant mistakes of the Pakistani leaders, the brutality of the State security police, the widespread bureaucracy and the mismanagement, the bungling, the arbitrary methods and blatant lies have led Pakistan to total collapse. It is the upsurge of the whole Islamic community in which rank and file terrorists and jehadis take part, against a stratocratic Govt. backed up by a tinpot dictatorship. There are Gestapo-like torture chambers, all over Pakistan, including POK, with whips and gallows and instruments for crushing the people's limbs as they do in Kashmir over the Kashmiri Hindu pundits. By means of secrecy, Kashmir issue is an issue of compromise. Why? Because nothing is gained, everything is lost by subordinating principle to expediency. It is the weak Govt. that urges compromise. Any compromise on Kashmir issue makes a good umbrella, but a poor roof. Words can add no bitterness to it. We lift up our voice in the echoes of old hopes. Effects of compromise accumulate from generation to generation and work evils far greater and less remediable. The Indian politics is, at bottom, a struggle not of men but of corruptible practices. Behind that word 'PEACE' in Kashmir, demons lurk. Words like 'agreements' and 'treaties' and 'pact' on Kashmir issue are a mask for concealment of bad deeds. And sincere diplomacy! It is no more than dry water. Today's diplomacy is a crass propaganda and grossness of mind.

Even the disquieting growth of the evil of casteism and communalism are the most unwanted effects of compromise running wild to all corners of our Indian society. Even the valley of Kashmir has been severely afflicted with much-vaunted incurable disease. And this frightening gesture appears not to have pained and disappointed our rulers at the Centre more than any other development. Why? Because rank indiscipline and corruption within the ranks of the Congress, for over 50 years, have polluted the Indian society and obviously dismantled the Kashmir solution. Are all the political parties. branded with dulcet phrases of secular forces, backing their Kashmir policy, flummoxed by security and freedom? Is its face not seared by lines of worry? Is the unholy matrimonial home of casteism and communalism the precious life-blood to our morally denigrated political leaders to finesse a deal of compromise? Is there any artificial aristocracy founded on wealth, without virtue or talents, amongst our leaders? Is not this artificial aristocracy a mischievous ingredient in our country? Who will solve the Kashmir question where these Fuehrer-personalities enrich the whole combination of conspirators, whose business it is to dupe and to govern the nation, playing an unofficial ordinance to plunder and murder, in presence of the legal solmnities of a bench of lawyers, whether it be purchased by the treasurers of a nation or by the aristocratical tyrannies or by the badly educated government? So Kashmir question still remains unsolved. And compromise is an evil substitute. Compromise between India and Pakistan on Kashmir issue smiles less and less these days.

It is difficult to tell where regional autonomy ends and where national sovereignty begins. Take currency which the Centre would control, where do the borders of currency end those of trade and commerce begin? The whole thing generates a chain reaction on the Kashmir solution.

After partition, the Hindu vote for the Congress was only equal to the average, while the Sikh, Christian and Muslim votes in that order were well above the average. The minority were thus more pro-Congress than the majority community. What seemed to pull down the Congress was considered to be non-Hindus in the classification of religion. The Congress party had a consistent support among all the three age groups : The young (21-35), the middle age (35-50) and the old (above 50). The enthusiasm of the Muslim voters for the Congress is not as high as on this occasion as it was before 1977. *The lower the Muslim votes, the worse the condition of Kashmir issue*. While the Congress seems to have done no better among Hindus than its average, the party that belongs to the saffron colour, and its acolytes, branded with Hindu fundamentalists, seem to have a larger hold on the Hindu vote. A growing bitterness with all its feverish excitement, between two estranged communities, living within the same social infrastructure, is getting wider and wider. And the Kashmir issue remains perturbed. The Congress is quite responsible for growing tension.

It is extremely hard to distinguish the true limit between political licentiousness and social liberty. Like a changeable silk, we can easily see there are two colours, but we cannot easily discover where the one ends, or where the other begins. It is the most dangerous of errors.

The Muslim vote has always been a matter of special significance. Why? Because the presumption is often made that it stands solidly behind the Congress, though this has not been certainly in Uttarpradesh in the prestige contest. This uncertainty has still been going on even after 60 years of independence. The sun of popularity over the Congress sets in a blaze of golden glory. Today the Congress is as wrong as wrong can be in all spheres of activities in and around Kashmir. Moreover, Nehru's successors, who were more on a level with each other and each of whom aimed at occupying the first place, adopted methods of demagogy which resulted in their losing control over the Kashmir issue. Frustration amidst growing generation in Kashmir is the fashionable malady from which an intellectual suffers today. Indian politics too is not wholly devoid of romance. Do our political leaders, abhorrent to our civil society, know and hear the hissing of communal forces, the hiccups of religious fanaticism down the cross-border terrorism, the intrigues of internal dissentions and the machinations of militant jehadis from the border state? They have only produced in the millions of our people an adequate sense of rebellion, of horrors, of disgust. Is it not humiliating to human beings, the possibility of such ferocity, of such cowardness? How long will the people be patient to the point of martyrdom before all the violences of bold despotism over the people? *Is it the pain of 'security Vs. freedom'? So Kashmir is imperilled by noisy traitors and by would-be dictators who within our country, have already yielded to Hitlerism. Who will solve the Kashmir issue? Secrecy or privacy? That is the fate of the people who unhappily commanded.*

Police continue to hover round the slaughter house and the police cordons off the prohibitted area. This is the go of the day in Kashmir. It is fact. Anger is a brief madness.

INDIAN OCEAN AND TERRORISM : VI (IGNORE THE AFFECTIVE REALITY)

The history of India should be studied, not as a record of a series of political defeats, but as a story of ultimate triumphs over invasions. The long-term effect is more important historically than the short-term one. Although the Greeks, the Scythians, and the Huns founded kingdoms in India, all of them were ultimately defeated by the Hindus and Hindu suzerainty was re-established. Why India was conquered? While Egypt and Syria were conquered by the Muslims within 6 years, Persia in 10 years, Africa and Spain in one year, Turkey in 8 years, it took them more than 300 years to conquer India. Even the British in their turn had to relinquish their sovereignty due to the vigorous political agitation.

The Islamic bloc is designed to embrace all the Muslim countries of the world even though some may be separated from others by thousands of miles of land and water. Another sea-route is the Indian Ocean. This route is a perpetual danger to India.

After 450 years, a storm is again gathering over the Indian Ocean, bringing to the forefront the question of India's security and independence. In 1947, Britain withdrew from the Indian sub-continent, but not free the Indian Ocean. Its waves are still ruled by the British Navy. Now this supremecy is questioned not by a rival naval power but a stronger force or resurgent nationlism stretching from Aden (Sudan) to Singapore.

Every State has a right to preserve public peace and order, and therefore has a right to prohibit the propagation of opinions, which have a dangerous tendency. But Indian public opinion is not assured that New Delhi attaches to the Indian Ocean the importance it deserves, taking a lesson from India's past history.

Historically, all Indian Govts. seated in Delhi tended to ignore the sea; the conception of a Hindu Empire was limited to the land from the Himalayas to the Ocean and not beyond. Kautilya's definition 'Chakravartin', the King Emperor, does not mention the sea. Even the Mughal emperors had no naval power. Only the Hindu rulers of peninsular India ... more particularly the rulers of Calicut Malabar and Andhra ... realised the importance of the Indian Ocean; their military was based on the navy and they were able to put up a big fight against the portugueses, the Dutch, the French and the British.

K.M. Panikkar, the only Indian who appears to have given serious thought to the problem of the Indian Ocean, says in one of his books that the "Future of India will undoubtedly be decided on the sea. It is indissolubly connected with developments in the Indian Ocean." Panikkar thinks that India, which in any case cannot expect to have in the near future navy strong enough to protect the Indian Ocean, should seek British partnership in a machinery designed for this purpose.

"An independent India," he says, "cannot by herself undertake (the defence of the sea). Even if she were in a position to do so, which she obviously is not, Great Britain's own interests in the Indian Ocean are such that nothing short of a major defeat will force her to withdraw from that area. Therefore, no less in Indian than in British interests, the defence of the Indian Ocean msut be a joint effort of India and Britain."

In peace, Indian mercantile interests will not clash with Britain's and in war the two countries will fight together on the same side, defending the Indian Ocean against a common foe ... Pakistan or China.

Do our foreign policy-makers hear the rattling of Islamic dice of terrorism that it does not sound to them like the funeral bell of the whole family? Must they be disappointed with the lesser things before they can comprehend the full value of the greater? When there is much pretension of Pakistan and China, much has been borrowed. India should be aware of Pakistan's suspicious look over the Indian Ocean, breaking our resistance without fighting. The Indian Ocean is porous to the infiltrators and terrorists. Because the enemy is old as Time, and evil as hell, and that Pakistan has been in Kashmir from the beginning. George Orwell says in 'Animal Farm' : "All animals are equal but some animals are more equal than others."

Why? Because India has been invaded by land and from the sea. Because all the foreign invaders who came by land routes in the north-west either withdrew after some years or were absorbed into Indian life. Some of them became Indian rulers, founded Indian Empires. But the Europeans who came by sea converted India into a colony of their far-flung empires. The Persians, the Macedonians, the Greeks, the Mongols, the Tartars ... all those who came by land routes added something to India's life and culture; the Europeans who came by sea reduced India to slavery. All increases of slavery represents in all places, at all times, under all circumstances. So this is the importance of Indian Ocean to India's defence from the common enemy like Pakistan and China. In Pakistan where fantasy of religious fanaticism and Islamic jehad are metamorphosed into a work of terrorist culture. China where the ignorance of communism cannot seal the mind and imagination in a locked cell is more secured.

Another significant importance is : The Himalayas have given India's natural protection; the Indian Ocean has exposed her to perpetual danger. For a hundred years India's land power fought the British, but the foreign might, based on a powerful navy, was ultimately successful in bringing the entire sub-continent under imperial domination. What was clear to the Zamarin of Calicut in the 15th and 16th centuries was never clear to the Moghuls, and even to the Maharatis.

The Indian Ocean washes three shores of the Indian peninsula; the entire east coast of Africa, the south coast of Arabia, the south shores of Iran and Baluchistan, the western shores of Myanmar, the Malayan peninsula and Sumatra.

The vital feature which differentiates the Indian Ocean from the pacific and the Atlantic ... is the sub-continent of India which juts far into the sea for a thosand miles to its tapering end at Cape Camorin (now Kanya Kumarika).

It is the geographical position of India that changes the character of the Indian Ocean. The Bay of Bengal also gives it a unique character possessed by no other ocean.

Not only has India an open coastline of two thousand miles, but the bulk of the foreign trade flows across the Indian Ocean. She has no nearby island, except Daman and Diu, to afford her advance cover. The Andamans are 800 miles away; the far-off Laccadives and Maldives have no suitable harbour; Colombo, Rangoon, Singapore, and Mauritius, none of these can give India advance cover unless they are friendly hands. So, there can obviously be no safety for India unless the Indian Ocean is an effectively protected area. Because both China and Pakistan are knocking at the door of Indian borders. Because both the countries believe in a more horrible and pernicious tyranny than that which should restrain intercourse of thought. Because both believe in a mental and spiritual poison. Because both are deluded and then disillusioned, cynicism and confusion follow. Time has decomposed both Pakistan and China.

Criticism is something, one can avoid by saying nothing, doing nothing, and being nothing.

PAKISTAN'S POLITICAL RIDDLE ON KASHMIR : VII (AN ENDEMIC VICE)

Diogenes was the founder of cynic. His main principles were that happiness is attained by satisfying only one's basic natural needs (and in the cheapest and easiest way) practising self-sufficiently and that what is natural cannot be dishonourable or indecent and should be done in public. He became a legendary figure, and among the many stories told of him is that he took a lantern in daylight, saying that he was seeking an honest man. Pakistan, a Diogenes of world today, has still been strolling about the dark places of her country with her lantern of anti-India campaign to seek out an honest terrorist. What a political depression around the orifice of religious volcano!

There are three classes of intellects : one which comprehends by itself; another which appreciates what others comprehend; and a third which neither comprehends by itself nor by the showing of others; the first is the most excellent, the second is good, the third is useless. This richly satisfying comment of Machiavelli seems to perturb Pakistan's amorphously dictated policy on Kashmir and her political carricature on Islamic terrorism. It is totally useless. If Pakistan is a 'map maker's nightmare' ... to borrow a phrase from C.L. Sulzberger ... it is the constitution maker's headache. Some of Pakistan's present constitutional difficulties are due to the fact that the country consists of two halves separated by more than 1,000 miles of Indian territory. And each half is vastly different from the other. These difficulties were highlighted by the President of Pakistan, Major General Iskandar Mirza, on the first birth anniversary of the Islamic Republic, when he said, "I comment to your consideration a careful study of the American system of administration with the necessary modifications to suit our own conditions."

The fact that Pakistan consists of just two provinces has a direct impact on the Central Govt. A political crisis in one province brings about a crisis at the Centre. If West Pakistan had not been integrated into one unit but had remained as three different provinces ... Punjab, Sind and North-West Frontier ... a political storm in anyone then would not have affected the centre so directly as to disturb its equilibrium. If India were to consist of only two provinces, North and South India, political storm in either or both would immediately affect the centre.

Therefore, in integrating West Pakistan into one unit and balancing it against East Pakistan (now Bangladesh) with party as the basis, the makers of Pakistan consitution unwittingly subjected the centre to the vagaries of Provincial politics to a larger extent than would have been the case otherwise. This, indeed, is the principle difficulty in working the constitution in Pakistan; the shifting politics in the provinces has brought about difficulties at the Centre. Therefore, the advantages of one unit and party ... advantages from the point of view of West Pakistan ... have been lost at the altar of political instability and the dependence of the centre on provincial politics. Why Bangladesh was born? Why Pakistan is a sanctum sanctorum of Islamic terrorism and vitriolic hotbed of provincialism and communalism?

In the face of the snowballing insurgency of terrorism, Pakistan is now waiting for apocalyptic timetables, changing toward increasing economic and political instability and even ultimate failure. Pakistan is deeply attached to religious fanaticism, that considers terrorism to be eternal, struggles hard to obtain Islamic globalisation. Whatever happens to Iraq will happen to Pakistan. Why? The answer is simple. A country that seeks security and refuge in America and its allies become a cypher to itself. Because it depends upon them to save her. Since partition, she has never tried to stand on her own feet. She has forgotten that her salvation lies in her own soul, in her perception and in her character. Pakistan that visualises a haven in Islam is suffering from a big illusion. So this illusion constitutes in-security in Pakistan. In this context Mahavira said : "He who mistakes insecurity for security and security for insecurity goes astray .... He who seeks refuge where there is none is destroyed ... Seek refuge in yourself."

Truly speaking, Pakistan has been racked with maladies of anti-India slogans and beset with problems of sectarianism, factionalism, communalism, provincialism and, above everything else, religious fanaticism. Who will protect Pakistan? And who will solve the Kashmir issue? The sands are running out.

With 56 percent of the population and its linguistic, cultural and economic oneness, the then East Pakistan (now Bangladesh) not only commanded 56 percent of the seats in a unitary legislature, but exercised a far greater influence over the heterogeneous representatives from the Western half. To put it crudely, the then East Pakistan (now Bangladesh) divided and ruled West Pakistan .... a prospect from which all West Pakistanis recoiled with horror.

Why does Pakistan like every student loathe question papers particularly on Kashmir debate? How does Pakistan account for the fact that even after burning gallons of midnight oil Pakistan like the poor student finds herself in the grip of cold fear of self-created terrorism, as she faces the Kashmir question paper with a vacant expression on her face and scratches her head in despair? The usual form of Kashmir is rude and impolite. But her tone is superior and pedagogic, and here in lies the cardinal defect of modern Kashmir question.

What are the characteristics of a syllogism? When the question is shot at Pakistan, so to say, Pakistan, like the timid candidate, goes all to pieces. Her wool-gathering head begins to gather more wool.

If Pakistan is still awake, would she mind finding out in the fallacy in the following syllogism : Great men are careless about their dress, so Pakistan is careless about dressing up her Islamic constitution. Therefore, Pakistan is a great nation! Logic is defined in your Madrassa-based Islamic education as the science of reasoning. And if you don't recollect this answer, please don't get disspirited. Because you are a bold-faced liar. A dyed-in-the-wool bureaucrat, however efficient he may be in his routine work, can hardly cope with these new responsibilities which demand a high degree of initiative, zest and the ability to mobilise the jehadis for constructive work.

The American system, if adopted in Pakistan, will lead to the stability of the executive branch of the Govt., but may bring about administrative chaos especially if the legislature is unable to command a two-third majority ... a situation preferable to instability of the executive is, therefore, the lesser evil. But in order to introduce it, a major overhaul of the constitution of the Islamic Republic of Pakistan will be necessary.

Mr. Nehru was a haughty man. It is hard for a haughty man ever to forgive one that has caught him in a fault on Kashmir issue, and who he knows has reason to complain of him; his resentment never subsides till he has regained the advantage he has lost, and found means to make the other do him equal wrong.

The eminent historian, Dr. Arnold Toynbee, on Jan 7, 1957, in Madras, compared the American impact on eastern civilisation to the spread of the Roman influence towards the close of the third century. Why? He said, "Americans have no positive political ambitions in other parts of the world but only limited economic ambitions .... the Romans engulfed the Macedonian influence in the Western end of the world in almost the same way as the Americans are now spreading. The Romans had initially encouraged the liberation movement against Macedonian rulers, although later they directly ruled certain regions, until replaced by the Spanish-Portuguese influence in the fifteenth century after Christ."

Dr. Toynbee said that the impact of the modern west on the east fell into three distinct categories. They were :

The Portuguese Spanish, who forcefully propagated their religion and converted subject people to Christianity, attempted to maintain their hold through religion. He further said that the Dutch-French-British, who deliberately refrained from propagating their religion brought with them technology which was still gathering momentum, although on the economic and political planes they were receding.

But by this comment, it has been established that all great religions of the world are gradually losing their hold on mankind. This may be partly due to the incompatibility of religious tenets with modern science although a major reason was the moral shock caused by successful jehads in the last 300 years. But mankind always depends for growth and for solutions to personal problems.

He could not say whether traditional religions like Islam would reform themselves of unconvincing superstitions to reclaim their hold on mankind or whether they would be supplanted by new religions. There is no historical parallel which can answer this question.

Judging from this point of view, it can be said that the idea of peaceful coexistence between India and Pakistan on Kashmir issue with different social systems hardly begins to penetrate more and more profoundly into the minds of the people. All peace-loving peoples of the world must be constantly watchful and ready for a consistent and prolonged struggle against the intrigues of the Pakistan-sponsored aggressive but militant fanatical forces. The conspiracies of terrorist organistaions in Kashmir would suffer a cruel defeat.

There is a great vacuum in Asia. Pakistan helped by others to grow strong is unfortunate and relying on the military way of doing this. This has worsened the Kashmir issue. A vacuum has already been created in India after the departure of the British.

What is the impression of Pakistan today to the world? A people's strength derives greatly from its govt. where the Govt. is unstable and suspended in a vacuum which separates it from the people, the country as a whole acquires a cost of instability and unreality, a certain curious restlessness which makes for restiveness and, within the country, generates an atmosphere of mutual irritation as between the rulers and the ruled. This is the overwhelming impression Pakistan leaves on any visitor. Pakistan lives with her superiors as she does with an inferno of the fires of terrorism; not too near, lest she burn; not far off, lest she freeze.

The test is to ascertain the cohesive force which unites a country and which binds together the people and the Govt. It can be the will to lift one's country by the bootstraps, to work unitedly for better days and happier living. It can be other things. In Pakistan, one has the odd feelilng that the only cementing force is an appeal to extraneous, largely emotional impulses, to fear and hate of a neighbour, to a cry of religion in danger, often concentrated on a political issue such as Kashmir. India is the big bad wolf... which is Pakistan's misfortune. But Pakistan is certainly no lamb.

To an Indian, the sight of old and dear friends in Pakistan induces a sense of melancholy and frustration characterised by an orgiastic emotion and ecstatic singing of jehadi slogans. The joy of meeting old friends is tinged by a feeling of differentness and separateness in which neither has had any direct share and which seems so utterly purposeless and wasteful. The divorced from the people has generated a fear-and-hate complex which, the powers that be ensured, is directed towards them.

The solution of the Kashmir problem will, by no means, signify the end of things. *For the basic problem, so far as Pakistan's rulers are concerned, is not Kashmir. The basic problem is India.* The fundamental strategy of Pakistani rulers is guided by the calculation that popular attention can be diverted from political and economic problems at home and sustained there only by a bogey abroad. And that bogey is India. Pakistan has not yet learnt the proverb : "The smallest good thing is better than the grandest intention." Terrorists have a free run. And Pakistan has already surrendered large tracts of territory to the Taliban's writ in a dubious deal to buy peace. Even the Taliban's barbaric writ has consumed the rest of Pakistan's society. So Pakistan now faces a political, security and economic nightmare. Does Pakistan know Islam makes people honest and committed and this is necessary to create a crime-free-society?

Tomorrow the Kashmir problem might be solved. No one believes it. Pakistan has so far missed the opportunity of Indo-Pak friendship. There are other convenient sticks to beat India with the threat that we intend genocide in relation to the large non-Hindu minorities in India ; the allegation that the whole of the punjab should promptly have belonged to Pakistan; the accusation that the division of Pakistan's two wings by 1,100 miles of Indian territory was monstrous and artificial, and that a corridor on the polish model is the answer.

So long as Pakistan has an unstable Govt., the possibility of such irredentist methods cannot be ruled out. It is, therefore, vitally in their own interests .... to put it at the lowest ... that one neighbour should be strong, viable and subtle. The people of Pakistan have been brought up on the doctrine of anti-India propaganda which begets a deep-dyed dogma that India threatens their existence.

Every war supposes a discipline, every revolution a dictatorship, every political move a certain amount of lying, and every Islamic terrorism is certainly a religious mystification. And even every political hypocrisy leads to a psychological disturbances and domestic unhappiness. The worst traits in Pakistan. Mr. Z.A. Bhutto's devotion to political hypocrisy on Kashmir issue was as dangerous as hero-worship. Why? Because in the Pakistani bureaucratic excesses and authoritarian regimentation in the name of Islam are associated not with an entire system of crude Islamic rule but with a single personality, no such convenient identification has been possible in Islamic Republic like Pakistan suffering from variety of ills that are recognisably Islamic.

Hardline clerics have played a key role in enforcing Islamic law in Pakistan's restive north-western Swat valley, decrying democracy. Why? Because there is no room for democracy in Islam and it contravenes the Quran. Because democracy is an unislamic system. Why? Because the hardline clerics have accused Pakistan's rulers of appeasing the West by thrusting the system of 'Kafirs' or infidels on the people of the country. A Sanguinary temper.

Why Talibanism in Pakistan? Is Pakistan considered today a pariah state? Talibans have seen a wide vacuum ... a collapse of governance, exploiting the anger and despair of disenfranchised elements to enlist them. This confluence of radicalism, terrorism and poverty has given the Taliban a greater mileage of influence and dynamic spirit that has allowed them to begin probing Pakistan's core province, Punjab. Taliban elements are present in every part of the country, finding this vaccum. The work for the Taliban is to solve the religious calculus of Islam in Pakistan and mathematical equations of Pakistan's politics on Kashmir issue. We are also obscured behind a fog of political rhetoric.

Pakistan's policies are generally controlled by the military-intelligence complex. It was Gen. Musharraf who had kept the Taliban pot boiling. The evildoer continues to harbour evil inside. Pakistan's constant meditation on Kashmir issue is sorely limited by time and space. All of her thoughts becomes shabby and the contradictions therein can never be resolved. It is easier to polish the manners than to reform the heart, to disguise a fault than to conquer it. He who can venture to appear as he is, must be what he ough to be ... a difficult and arduous task, which often requires the sacrifice of many a darling inclination and the sacrifice of many a painful effort. In a violent and destructive whirling wind of political gamesmanship, our leaders, as a professional, like fence-sitting diplomancy.

Through a small aperture of bad governance, Pakistan becomes victims of self-created terrorism. Mind is a bundle of thoughts. More than heart attacks, Pakistan suffers from thought attacks. Time will melt into timelessness. What is timelessness? Pakistan lives in two worlds ... a world of the mind, which is in time and a world beyond the mind that is timelessness. Is it the duty of the youth of Islam to join the caravan of martyrs until the sufficient is complete and the march to aid the high and omnipotent continues? Is there a huge difference between hypocritical ulama (Islamic scholars) and the path of these noble young men?

Do you know Indian Security Services helped the Soviet Intelligence Agency KGB in foiling an assassination attempt on Mikhail Gorbachev plotted by 'Afghan terrorists' during his visit to New Delhi? Do you know a terror group was sent into India across the Pakistani border with the aim to scuttle the visit of the Soviet leader? Maj Gen (Retd), Victor Aleinikov, Chief of the bodyguards of the then KGB, said in an interview to popular daily 'Moskovsky Komsomolets (MK). Due to the 'Afghan syndrome' and presence of about one million Afghan refugees in the country, it was quite a complex situation in India.

Disarmament in the literal sense is a political unreality that has been confused with the actual problem of Kashmir with which the Disarmament agreement is concerned ... that of reducing the danger of armed attack as well as cross-border terrorism. Thus defined the task is less glamourous and more prosaic but it gains immeasurably in a kind of realism that is an insurance against excessive idealism. It estimates 'paper promises' at their paper worth firmly denies the feasibility of abolishing nuclear weapons and rejects any so-called formula by which the military power of India and Pakistan can supposedly be measured. The most hackneyed phrase 'peaceful co-existence' is a danger to Kashmir peace, but it is less dangerous than uncritical acceptance of jehadi slogans that are as attractive to militants as they are meaningless.

Pakistan's special virtues ... hidden by an obscurity of political vision ... are those of insincerity and political dualism in which there is no room for wishful thinking. Why? Because Pakistan has taken dancing lessons of hypocrisy but cannot follow the rhythm. With a propaganda facade and with dishonesty as silly as it is cynical, Pakistan is still talking about Kashmir solution. Terrorism is not a mistake. Fake trials are not errors. Political perversions of anything are not malpractices. This, of course, is the language of the moral bankruptcy of Pakistan. Winston Churchill says, "Always remember, a cat looks down on a man, a dog looks up to a man, but a pig will look man right in the eye and see his equal." Pakistan needs a cultural change.

INDIAN MUSLIMS AND KASHMIR : IX (AIRS AND GRACES)

Many men spend their lives in gazing at their own shadows, and so dwindle away into shadows thereof. The upholders and lovers of democracy using backroom methods want to destroy the main fibre of national integration and dominate over the Kashmir issue for their personal purposes. Pakistan's allegation is a white lie, a figment of Pakistan's imagination and contrary to facts. This is a period of political uncertainty in Kashmir, of constant infiltration of physical discomforts ... ranging from the inconspicuous to the derpressing. The strange perversity seems to be everywhere in the valley. A small mistake of judgement on Kashmir issue can destroy and bring misery to countless individuals. This is a dangerous state of affairs. In a true democracy, the individual must experience responsibility and have the power of taking decisions in all vital matters that concern a Kashmir Hindu pundit. Actually a handful of people, that is not more than five or six, has all the initiative and power in their hands; the rest are just yes-men. Who will solve the Kashmir question? And the vast electorate, the real masters are blissfully ignorant and indifferent to what the Govts. are doing. All they are back-room politicians.

Today, the Govt. sitting at the helm of J & K State is all powerful over the individual. Particularly, the Kashmiri Hindu pundits have become insignificant and powerless. It is only an error of judgement to make a mistake.

There are two kinds of charlatans. The power of the first is that he advertises ... and cures. The power of the second is that though he is not learned enough to cure he is too learned to advertise. But there is a third kind. In this country, we often know the cure and advertise it even when we have no intention to take the cure ourselves. Secrecy behind the Kashmir solution : A secret is too little for one, enough for two, and too much for three.

Prior to dwelling upon the topic, 'Indian Muslims and Kashmir', it is interesting to note down the fact that the hiatus between the Congress and the masses of Kashmir, which had formed the backbone of the Congress movement during the struggle phase, was widening. At the same time, the many measures of social and economic reform adopted by the Congress Govts. had been so half-hearted that they had failed to win the allegiance of the middle class inside and outside Kashmir. This increasing loss of contact between the Congress leadership headed by the Nehru and the Gandhi dynasty and the Kashmiri people was tending to exaggerate this estrangement, while the advent of the new class of opportunist bandwagon Congresswallas and the consequent growth of corruption and the loosening of the ideological roots have converted that estrangement between India and Pakistan into a positive mistrust of the organisation.

Before independence, the Congress slightly and deservedly claimed to the voice of the nation. Today that claim has worn thin. And yet by sheer force of habit, the Congress continues to take the Kashmiri people for granted and then gets into hot water, when it discovers its action does not reflect the people's will.

Ridicule may be the evidence of wit or bitterness and may gratify a little mind, or an ungenerous temper, but it is no test of reason or truth. People who don't trust the Govt. cannot be swindled.

Only reason will show the way of Kashmir solution. Why? Only reason solves each problem on the way. It is only reason that would unlock the barren womb of Kashmir problem. It is reason that would enrich the people of Kashmir. It is reason that would ensure the freedom of thought, the freedom of trade; by destroying the false, misguided causes of war, it would lead to peace in Kashmir; and finally it would liberate human nature from the yoke of religious fanaticism, from the limitations of Pakistan's ignorance, and from the cramp of poverty. Pakistan was born to be the lord of Islamic terrorism, conquered and ensalved by it. The child who sees its mother kiss the hand of a useless begging friar insensibly adopts a religion of idleness.

Those fanatics who try to abandon the civil society of Kashmir join automatically the great class of useless folk who live by their tongue ... whose words sail high above the realities of the present world. To the end, their house was ripped open and their fields ploughed by bombs.

The forty million Muslims of India rejected the irrational Two-Nation Theory, at the time of the partition of the country; but rejection of the theory, by them, is of little account if they do nothing to counter the activities of the leaders of Pakistan who are desperately trying to make more mischievous use of the theory than even in the days of Mr. Jinnah.

Pakistan's claims on Kashmir, the efforts of its Govt. to get foreign sympathy and the whole logic of Mr. Feroz Khan Noon's legalism before the Security Council all stemmed from the Two-Nation Theory. Pakistan has already passed sixty years of independence. Terrorism dawns in Pakistan. Every windstorm of terrorism pulls her out of her likes and dislikes. And she accepts all that comes with both arms open. This is crucifixion. Wherever she goes, she creates her own storms. The waves and commotions of religious fanaticism are much bigger than the geographical areas of Pakistan. One storm comes and subsides, another comes and subsides and it goes on all over Pakistan. She is thrown off balance. Her politically immatured mind cannot yet grasp the simple truth in all its nakedness ... 'Kashmir is an intgeral part of India'.

The challenge that Kashmir poses to the Muslims of India is to proclaim with a united call ... so that all the world may hear and understand ... that Indian Muslims have decided that Kashmir is no longer anyone else's business but India's own and that they will not permit the unity of their country, achieved through the accession of Kashmir, to be disturbed by any foreign Govt. or international propagandists.

Kashmiris indeed are realising with greater force everyday that in the ultimate analysis their own economic, cultural and economic progress depends on firm and permanent association with this great country. Such a development is intolerable to the present leaders of Pakistan. Therefore, inspite of the greater clarity of the Govt. of India's expressed views and inspite of the achievements of the democratic Govt. of Kashmir, danger of cross-border terrorism daily increases, finding no alternate way in comparison to their own ill-conceived plan on Kashmir issue and allowing the infiltrators a free hand for the greater part of India.

The accession of Kashmir, it is true, was achieved formally by the signature of its ruler; but what Pakistan and the world outside have to be made to realise is that the reality of this accession resides in the unity of the people of Kashmir and the people of India, particularly the Muslims, and their indestructible loyalty to the concept of a democratic and secular India in which every faith is equal in the eyes of law.

This urgency lays very serious task on the Muslims of India to bestir themselves and to assert that as citizens of India, who have a special responsibility in regard to Kashmir, they will not permit anyone to question the validity of the present sovereignty of India in Kashmir because that sovereignty expresses more than anything else the Indian Muslim's right of self-determination.

Indian Muslims don't look at the deeper layers of Pakistan's fanatical approach. If they do so, they will find themselves empty and shallow and experience a sense of loneliness. If they think they belong to minority group, they will experience a sense of loneliness which seems to be utterly boring. They should know whether the Kashmir problem really exists or not. They should overcome this illusion. Then all fear and insecurities will drop off.

Do our Indian Muslims know why Nixon was defeated by Kennedy. A real democracy will choose the wise people. Nixon did not listen to the millions of people on television. Because television has changed almost the whole political phenomenon. We want you to be in Parliament. Why will Islamic terrorism be an election issue?

Today, in conversation, many Muslims in India are personally friendly but intellectually aggressive. Are they all looking for the wrong fellow? The brave and wise man, who intends to overcome his foes, must first of all strive to subdue the internal enemies of his own heart and mind, and the members of his own body. Every Asian nation is today wide awake. The Muslim leaders of India will have to get forward how to suppress the babbling of Pakistan's propagandists who strive to confuse the world with slogans of sub-continental Muslim communalism.

Do they know Buddhism reached before Asoka's time? Do they know Surendra, the Pre-Asokan Buddhist ruler of Kashmir, remains a shadowy figure even in Kalhan's account? With the despatch of Madhyanta by Asoka to propagate the faith in Kashmir, we are perhaps on somewhat surer ground, and we have it on Hieun Tsang's authority that about 500 Buddhist monks had settled down in the valley of Kashmir in Asoka's time. With Kanishka, Kashmir gains an importance in the Buddhist world, and though opinions differ on the venue of the Buddhist Council called by the Kushana emperor, there is reason to believe that the celebrated Buddhist philosopher, Nagarjuna, lived in the valley for sometime during Kanishka's reign. After time Kashmir was for some time on the main centres of Buddhist learning. It was from here that the faith spread to China ... and it was here that the renowed savent, Kumarajiva, who later went to China, studied. It was still a seat of Buddhist learning in the days of Hieun Tsang who stayed in the valley for two years.

Pakistan's drum-beating hate propaganda has taken a firm root within Pakistan itself and on behalf of Pakistan in the reactionary section of the foreign press. Partition has only sharpened Kashmir's challenge to Indian Muslims who should squarely lay the weight of a great national task on their shoulders sweeping away all jehadi organisations like SIMI within India. Even a hundred years of life is too little. Sleep takes away half of it and the other half of it is expanded in childhood, disease, misery and old age. Only mature minds grasp the simple truth in all its nakedness. Indian Muslims should keep running away from small things which may lead to more feverishness. The secret is in your action.

There has been an increase in the number of very critical and blistering sarcasms on Indian Muslims not for their allegiance to the militant crusaders of Kashmir. They know a great number of foreign fighters has travelled to Pakistan's tribal areas to join with militants there. They know the flow may reflect a change that is making Pakistan, not Iraq, the preferred destination for some Sunni extremists, from West Asia, North Africa and Central Asia, who are seeking to take up arms against the west. Indian Muslims also know even many of the fighters are making their way to the tribal areas of the Uzbeks, North Africans and Arabs from Persian Gulf states, having been encouraged by some jihadi websites, to go to Pakistan and Afganistan to win over Pakistan. Even the sanctuaries in Pakistan have always been more and more blisteringly uncomfortable with a very blizzard of fanatical winds than before. They are much aware of every aspect of a politically blinkered situation in Pakistan. They are likely to remain in blissful ignorance of Pakistan's cracked situation. Even the porous border has allowed insurgent militant groups for a greater liberation movement across the border, and for a greater freedom of supply, to allow leadership to sustain stronger sanctuaries, and to provide fighters across that border.

Islamic terrorism may be compared to Heathcliff, the tempestuous anti-hero of Emily Bronte's 'Wuthering Heights' (1847) is depicted as a moody, vengeful and romantic figure. He is also ruthless and vindictive. He ended his life a broken and tormented man haunted by a ghost. Even Pakistan, haunted by a ghost of self-created Islamic terrorism on Kashmir issue, has turned to domestic abuse like possibly committed murder and dug up the remains of her dead lovers of Islam. This mind-shattering political scenario has chilled the Indian Muslims to the bone. Indian Muslims need to feel the undercurrent of jihadi militants behind name and form. What has not, however, been adequately realised by Indians of different persuasions, but chiefly Muslim Indians, is the vital bearing that Kashmir's future has on the prosperity, security and independence of the nation as a whole, and therefore, on the Muslim section within it. Kashmir's inviolable accession to India is a factor that can permanently strengthen the concept of secular democracy more than any other factor, in our country. Hypocrisy is the necessary burden of villainy; affection, a part of the chosen trappings of folly. The deliberate breaking of agreements is a serious offence on Kashmir issue. It is doubly unethical because Pakistan, as an offender, not only commits a breach of confidence with India and with Indian Muslims but tries to score an unfair advantage of terrorism over India.

Never bid the Devil good morrow until you meet him.

The-not-so-gentle art of sophism calls for a more skillful expositor than Pakistani rulers. Goebbels is evidently the model. But Goebbels had the finesse of a quick mind and agile tongue. But Pakistani rulers — from Jinnah to the present rulers — flounder from one sophism to another. Pakistan is devoid of serious interest on Kashmir solution. And partition appeared to be moving but this proved a false start. All extremes are error. The reverse of error is not truth but error still. Terrorism is getting into communal movement with dangerous potentialities. We are all affected by the good opinions, others entertain of us, and are not easily induced to lose it.

Dated back to the birth of Pakistan, every military ruler in Pakistan had always been treading the footsteps of the President of Indonesia, Dr. Sockarno. He had dreamt of pan-Indonesia to include Papua and the Philippines as well; but the Phillipines was already independent. Politically, Sockarno's answer to

Malaysia was 'Maphilindo', a proposed confederation of Malay, the Phillipines and Indonesia which, if it ever got off the ground, would give Sockarno his empire, since Indonesia's 100 millions would soon dominate the 11 million Malaysians and 30 million Filipinos. But Maphilindo was clearly emotional in Sockarno's mind. On the abandonment of Malaysia as a project, and there, too, he had been frustrated.

American military aid to Pakistan inspite of Indo-Pak collusion seems to be significant and indicative of another political explosion of the Indonesian type in Pakistan. According to U.S. officials, Pakistan's collusion with China will eventually end as soon as the problems between India and Pakistan would be settled. The Chinese military help to Pakistan should be no bar to American resumption of aid to that country.

The continued Sino-Pak collusions, military supplies to Pakistan and the arrival of Chinese nationals in Paksitan in large numbers and their reported matrimonial relations with Pakistan may have alerted the Americans of an impending political crisis in Pakistan. The Americans understandably intend to continue strengthening Pakistan. Why? Because the right wing people and personnel can rise up to tackle any apprehended Chinese plan for subversion.

This seems to be major concern for the Pentagon. The Americans consider it more urgent to save Pakistan from any Chinese-aimed disaster than to take steps to counter any joint Sino-Pak adventure which India fears impending along its border. The threat to Indian diplomacy from Sino-Pak collusion is far less possible than the threat to Pakistan itself from danger and her bed-fellow—China. Indian Muslims have got to know the real enemy of Pakistan. China has come along Pakistan's traditional sentiment against India. So the Americans need India to settle up the disputes with Pakistan to invalidate the major reason of Pakistan's collusion with India because Pakistan was not born to be friends.

On the question of Kashmir issue, the difference between the countries lies in two factors. In the words of Jalaluddin Rumi, it can be said, "The satiated man and the hungry one do not see the same thing when they look upon a loaf of bread."

Intrigues and stinking corruption amongst the political leaders and bureaucrats have brought the people of Kashmir to the verge of desperation and disillusionment, and led the common man to listen to the voice of destructive thinking and doing. The arm-chair protagonists of religious dogma suffer from persecution complex. Why? Because the process of history has been away of its own to avenge the wrong done to a people by the monopolists of pseudo-patriotism. Even our India's communists have never fulfilled an avowed objective on Kashmir issue. Why? They are using democracy in order to destroy democracy. It is this danger that New Delhi cannot or will not see. The danger to democracy is enhanced by the fact that India's pseudo communists can legitimately claim to have been returned by democratic methods. They are past masters to disintegrate civil society by their hyperbolic statements on haves and have-nots.

We all need to clean our mental cobwebs. The paramount need of Indian politics today, particularly on Kashmir issue, is not to put a premium on political equivocation, at the cost of moral principles. India's communists are not apt to utter a single word on Kashmir issue. Do our Indian Muslims know India's communist regime may rejoice the hearts of crypto-democrats living within the atmosphere of democracy? They are, like women, partial to noisy confusion of voices. It is unwittingly transferred to the unconscious mind. This is known as repression, when the mind relegates to the unconscious painful memories. Psychological logist Sigmund Freud divided the human mind into three specific regions, the conscious, subconscious and unconscious. The unconscious patterns of India's communists are thus reflected through various a social behaviour that manifests through feelings of vanity, anger, greed, treachery, jealousy and indifference. Indian politics is governed by criminals as animals by nature.

Judging from this point of view, it would seem to be Houseman's "Demise of an Imperceptive Youth" : "The Grizzly Bear is huge and wild./ He has devoured the infant child./ The infant child is not aware/ it has been eaten by the Bear." The nomenclature of India's communists on Kashmir issue is an unholy combination of indifferent care and careful negliance, restful for the restless, restive for the uneasy. This truth takes many shapes, sometimes the lines are straight and fixed, sometimes they consist of dancing curves. Do they understand the importance of punctuation on Indian politics? What a great tragedy of a peter pan!

Indian Muslims should be aware of Pakistan's hypocrisy on Kashmir issue. What is hypocrisy? Hypocrisy is the necessary burden of villainy. In conversation, Pakistan is personally friendly but intellectually aggressive. Over mugs of foaming beer, Pakistani rulers discuss Kashmir issue with theologians. We have a solution for every difficulty, and a difficulty for every solution. Islamic theology has for long been regarded the brains of Islamic rule in Pakistan. So, Pakistan is regarded as theologically brilliant and therefore religiously arrogant.

New Delhi should have toned down the Gujrat riot episode. Because it can serve as a turning point in Kashmir controversy. A word of kindness is seldom spoken in vain, while witty sayings are as easily lost as the pearls slipping from the broken string. If the sufficient representatives of patriotic Muslims, from all parts of India, including Kashmir, are taken, it can once and for all put an end to the use of the Two-Nation Theory by Pakistan on Kashmir controversy.

The followings are the very serious and significant tasks laying on the Muslims of India :

1. To bestir themselves and assert that as citizens of India who have a special responsibility in regard to Kashmir.
2. They will not permit anyone to question the validity of the present sovereignty of India in Kashmir.

3. The challenge that Kashmir poses to the Muslims of India is to proclaim with a united will ... so that all the world may hear and understand ... that Indian Muslims have decided that Kashmir is no longer anyone else's business but India's own and that they will not permit the unity of their country, achieved through accession of Kashmir, to be disturbed by any foreign Govt. or band of international propagandists.
4. Their challenge should be their indestructible loyalty to the concept of a democratic and secular India.
5. They should lead themselves in favour of democracy to deter the short-sighted leaders of Pakistan from resorting to the adventures of terrorism.
6. The Muslims of India rejected the irrational Two-nation theory at the time of partition, but rejection of the theory, by them, is of little account if they do nothing to counter the activities of terrorism and of the Pakistani leaders' narcissistic attitude who are trying desperately to make more mischievous use of the theory than even in the days of Mr. Jinnah.
7. They should abide by the rules and regulations and the verdict of the judiciary on Kashmir issue.
8. They will not retain any undemocratic group within the country on Kashmir issue with the aid of an external hate-object.
9. They should cooperate to improve the conditions of all classes of Kashmiris as co-sharers for the benefits of Kashmir. Because Kashmiris are realising with greater force everday that in the ultimate analysis their own economic, cultural, and religious progress depends on firm and permanent association with this great country. The more they try to drive out the Kashmiri Hindu pundits from the valley, the worse the fate of Kashmir will be.
10. They should remember in conversation use some, but not too much ceremony; it teaches others to be courteous, too. Demeanours are commonly paid back in their own coin.
11. They should remember separatist tendencies will never develop beyond the point of directly endangering national unity. Emotion turning back on itself and not leading on to thought or action, is the element of madness. Because the fatal makes placid air of cosy ignorance of disaster.
12. They should remember time well-employed is satan's deadliest foe; it leaves no opening for the lurking friend.
13. Don't glorify violence. 'The way of terrorism' from either side of Kashmir separatists and Pakistan has become a weapon in the tepid war, which is often joined by cultural attaches, reinforced by cultural missions, propaganda services, alliances and councils. Culture is brandished like a tomahawk.
14. They should remember pretences go a great way with men that take fair words and magisterial looks for current payment.
15. They should remember all passions are good or bad, according to their objects; where the object is absolutely good, there the greatest passion is

too little; where absolutely evil, there the least passion is too much; where indifferent, there a little is enough.

If the Indian Muslims should follow the above-mentioned 15 point programme, the Kashmir issue will remain solved.

Besides having these points, India's Muslims must be aware of an army of pseudo-secularists who have always been marked by their annoying and infuriating attitude. Pseudo-secularism is a fatal disease with fits of social sleepiness and political drowsiness not only to India's Muslims but to democracy also. They are restricted in their views on Kashmir issue, intolerant of Hindu-Muslim unity, prejudiced against social movement and illiberal of social chaos.

India's Muslims should be aware of psedu-secularism. Why? Because pseudo-secularism is a waste of time unless our India's Muslims can remember what the psudo-secularists have used it to impress people with the depth of their shallow knowledge and the breadth of their culture. Leave them alone and they will come home, bringing their tails behind them. They creep like snails in our society. A man's character is the reality of himself. His reputation is the opinion others have formed of him. Character is in him; reputation is from other people — that is the substance, this is the shadow. Nobody notices the inverted commas of their movements. They speak in a special tone of voice, in inverted commas. They are as provocative and embarrassing as hardly defensible perpetuating the gathering storm of anomally amidst our society.

In the peculiar state of Kashmir politics, it is imperative to the nth degree that the Parliamentary wing and the organisational wing should be under the control of the same leader. India's communist parties continue to display a strange tenderness for their susceptibilities and feelings. Communists! They wallowed in obeisance before a live Stalin one day and denigraded a dead Stalin on the next day. They derided the Marxist line one week and beat their breast in humble repentance the next. They don't mind keeping an animal with one eye black and the other white. They may prove a dangerous stab in the back of the oppressed and defenceless Kashmiri Muslims who must toe line dutifully under the watchful eyes of their taskmasters.

India is no fool on the question of Kashmir issue. We know that it cannot be that the sun revolves round the earth one day and the earth revolves round the sun the next day. If we make it the test of truth we will end by often be both true and false at the same time. The idea of Kashmir question which walks best on Kashmir-accession to India is also the truest. India is in a world of values which transcend experience. Perhaps Pakistan realises the mistake towards the end. So, Pakistan will have been wise to give the highest priority to the liquidation of Islamic terrorism in and around Kashmir, and to seek, if possible, to make that the liquidation peaceful and voluntary. Terrorists are embarrassingly young at heart and never alert to the possibilities of romantic adventure. Those who are without faith in Islam are Islamic terrorists. In the Bhagavad Gita (17.3, 17, 28) it is said, "Without faith, whatever offering or gift is made of work done or penance performed, it is reckoned 'not-being' both now and hereafter." Islamic terrorism ensures both the internal and external flourishing of the furies of personal interest of a sick man, soul and body sick, and the propagandists' worst friends. Truly speaking, Islamic terrorism over Kashmir and in other parts of India are the falsehood of extremes. And Pakistan's political clothes are worn out. Because she does not see the matter as she does. She makes the barren tree of Islamic theology fruitful by tying fruits of anti-India hate-slogans on its of rubbish and a thing of consequence to the vulgar.

Do India's Muslims know no nation has been so misrepresented, abused and feared as Pakistan? For over sixty years, Pakistan has been the synonym for horror and evil. It is mainly her repulsive looks that have given Pakistan her ill-deserved reputation for ferocity. She can change colour like chameleon and squirt hate propaganda to baulk her foes. India is as age-old enemy of Pakistan as the moray eel of the octopus. Like the octopus, Pakistan has got many gangrenous and death-bringing arms of militant groups with innumerable suckers attached. Like the octopus, she has got a rasping tongue of hate-India slogans.

The significance of yesterday, today and tomorrow makes no difference to Pakistan. On precious life, the great poet, Kalidas, says in an epigrammatic way, "... For yesterday is but a dream, /And Tomorrow is only a vision; / But Today well-lived makes every yesterday a Dream of Happiness,/ And every Tomorrow a vision of Hope./ Look well therefore to this Day ; / Such is the Salutation of the Dawn." It has an epoch-making effect on today's Pakistan. Terrorism is not an epilogue to a happy, prosperous and peace-loving nation.

The devastating dance of Pakistan doctrine on Kashmir issue is that it may have the effect of keeping the Kashmir Hindu pundits at the helm of Kashmir Liberation Movement and of even converting them into a mass party. Failure to win over honest Hindu pundits will mean pushing them into the devouring embrace of terrorism. There is moral apathy and spiritual vaccum in their lives. Pakistan's internal doctrine insists that rulers may exercise only such authority when exercised in a manner contrary to Islamic law and towards ends inimical to Islamic rights, may and should be withdrawn and relegated to other rulers under conditions better calculated to preserve the rights. But it is evident that civilisation has no future unless they can devise a more sensible method of settling differences and resolving conflicts between India and Pakistan than by destroying one another. Do India's Muslims believe in holocaust of terrorism? Do they believe in a potentially hazardous adventurism of fanatical crusade or the hereafter? Everything runs in a winter of despair and a series of political hiccups. And Pakistan has emerged as one of the most difficult foreign policy challengers.

Do they know China has equipped Pakistan militarily for decades? Do they know Saudi Arabia is a major source of funds for Pakistan? Both have wielded critical influence over Pakistan. Both are Pakistan's long-time allies. Will those allies help Pakistan counter the militant threat in future? China has a strong economic presence in Pakistan. Some estimate peg the number of

Chinese engineers and technicians in Pakistan at 10,000 and, for Beijing, there is a potential problem on its hands with the Ulghur population in its Xinjiang region. Why? Because some of them have trained in Pakistani terror camps and returned to create unrest in China. Both Beijing and Riyadh must help shore up Pakistan and her economy against the grave threat posed by extremists in Pakistan. Because both share amiable equations with Pakistan's political class and military establishment.

The Islamic religion in Pakistan is facing its hardest times, its economy is in a state of collapse; the Pakistani rupee is fast shrinking; the trade centre of Pakistan is almost in revolt. The Army is split into two camps, one under the leadership of the traditional elements, and the other under the deadly elements of hate-India movement.

Some tears belong to us because we are unfortunate; others because we are human; many because we are mortal. But most are caused by our being unwise. It is these last, only, that of necessity produce more. Without discipline true freedom cannot survive. Too much faith in such a philosophy can be dangerous to democracy. Most of the time Pakistan's Kashmir issue lays immersed in this haze of sweet sadness. Pakistan tries to cry out but then everyone is laughing. So you too laugh. If conscience makes them neither cowards, nor wilful and capricious beings, and if there is the development of moral sense, there is hardly such risk of anarchy.

PAKISTAN'S POLITICAL MANOEUVRE IN KASHMIR : X

Many do with opportunities as children do at the seashore; they fill their little hands with sand, and then let the grains fall through, one by one, till all are gone. The epidemic of communalism, which has been raging in India for the last sixty years, shows no signs of abating.

This is one truth ... this is the truth of the people struggling for 'Kashmir which contradicts it may be a subject of depiction but cannot be a subject of approval. One social truth and many private truths. In suppressing the truth, Pakistan mistakes her conscience, corrupts her thoughts and deeds and becomes a nation to falsehood.

The bubbles are gone. It is the same drink but more flat. It is the same words but they mean much less now. Anti-India hate-slogans. It was a slogan of steel once. They said it was stainless. But it has rusted. Is there rust in their brain? What is the truth?

They say there is nothing wrong with the slogan. There is nothing wrong for that matter with those who speak to us of the evil of violence in Kashmir. But there is something wrong somewhere. They sense, the moment they see the same men talking to angry crowds not with words but with bullets. Do they mean what they say? It is what the Islamic fundamentalists say they must do. They must discern in the womb of the present the embryo of the future. Do they see the shadow that falls between Islam and its practice is not merely a bourgeois vice? Those who claim to discern the future hesitate to look even at the present. They have deserted under fire. What else could they do once they learnt that they had been drafted under false pretexts? Do they know Islamic terrorism is a strange, outlandish and barbarous language or dialect influenced by political envy and religious hostility? Those who have stone hearts will not laugh at this religious joke.

Are unity and the democratic right of freedom of discussion incompatible? The tendency to hush criticism in the name of unity is a common fallacy. It is a misconceived patriotism completely out of tune with the democratic concept. The anxiety to preserve and consolidate any political institution, particularly on Kashmir issue, tends the leadership to be impatient with the many voices of democracy. That, in turn, leads to imperviousness. The psychological gap between New Delhi and Kashmir on the question of leadership gets wider. Since independence, Congressmen have been facing the naked reality of Pakistan's double-whammy — a combination of deceiving usually through concealment or misrepresentation of truth and a puerilism of a mixture of sense and nonsense. In a democracy, when the dogs bark, the caravan must halt. Elections in Pakistan take place against a hysterical background of suspected subversion, which engenders an atmosphere of such insecurity and fear that few except the boldest are willing to challenge the fundamentals of their fanaticism. This disgraceful affair shows up all the evil designs of Islamic rule. In a sublimely cynical disregard of every decency, the task of leading the Govt. case at the actual trial has been deputed to a notorious fascist who proudly backs in every election.

An idea which serves no social purpose, however remote, is no idea. The idea which works best is also the truest. What is true today may turn to be false tomorrow. There are only degrees of truth. The first test of truth is its social acceptance; the second its social application. India's Muslims examine the truth behind Kashmir issue by mathematical logic or by experiments in their mental laboratory. Do they know Pakistan was born under a travesty of artificial conditions of cultured viruses of religious fanaticism? Pakistan must have a cultural anthropology dealing with human culture with respect to Islamic social structure, language, law, religion, art and technology.

The world is full of idiots. In fact, according to all idiots, everyone else is an idiot. If Pakistan does, she will find herself in the idiot class. Some idiot classes are dwindling everyday. The problem is of world importance. Because idiots have no civilising mission. Their only purpose is to protect idiots. Who are idiots? Idiots are men who professedly deal in concealment, darkness and mystery, and who fatten upon human ignorance. Idiotic passion! It is the mark of a psychic disease, then satanic pride is on the throne. Pakistan will have never been a commentator of peace in Kashmir. Why? Because it is of her idiotic passion.

The central fact of the Kashmir dispute is the Pakistani aggression of 1947 and the continued occupation by Pakistan of a large part of the State territory. The massive military aid received by Pakistan, far from righting that wrong, has only added to its iniquity. A new history of Islamic terrorism, classed with Pakistan's vitriolic passion for sense of guilt more frightful than ignorance in action, raises the wider question of religious impact on its expression. We fear Pakistan is treading on dangerous ground. It is no proof of a man's understanding to be able to confirm. Whatever he pleases, but to be able to discern that what is true is true, and that is false is false. This is the mark and character of intelligence.

Pakistan, a fanciful nation, missed the bus in Kashmir in 1947, making a pillaging and destructive raid by a constant attack. Why? Because of clumsy and reckless activities. Yet Pakistan seems to be repeating those very malicious tactics in Kashmir through a double-whammy of cross-border terrorism and infiltration. *Had the rulers of Pakistan not been arrogant and impatient and sent tribal raiders to conquer Kashmir by force, there would be a fair chance of the Kashmiri people opting for Pakistan.*

Over-confidence and miscalculation had led them to that super-blunder. If there were any wavering minds in Kashmir on the accession issue, they were made up against Pakistan when the wild tribesmen with the cry of jehad on their lips plundered and looted the houses of brother Muslims and carried away their women and treasure. The people and their leaders gritted their teeth, swore they would never permit their fair land to fall in Pakistan's hands and decided to defend it against the invaders even with bare hands if necessary. And they offered to accede to the Indian Union and appealed to the latter for military aid to defend themselves. Pakistanis are still running that tactical stupidity and political ignorance. Those who cannot experience peace also fail to realise bliss. Her peace can only rest on the foundation of anti-India hate slogans. It is the music of Islamic terrorism. She runs after theology and dollar-diplomacy. Her peace is of a product of machine guns. Her peace resides within jehad. Her peace has always been ritualised with double-barreled diplomacy.

The most notorious Head of Nazi SS, Heinrich Himmler, categorically and systematically sided with terrorism. He says : "The best political weapon is the weapon of terror." Islamic terrorists seem to be influenced by Himmler. In this age, people cannot be bullied into any course of action. They have to be converted through civilised techniques and good deeds and not by predatory methods of arson, loot and plunder. The tactics of the middle ages, where a chieftain from Central Asia swooped down on the Indian plains and conquered territory by sheer terror and horror as today's communists do, are out of place in the present age. Yet Pakistan seems to be now resorting to those very discredited tactics in Kashmir today. What a practical joke of Pakistan backed separatist hardliners' participation in Jammu and Kashmir elections.

Devils are always trying to misguide and to protect miscreants. Pakistan has already surrendered her problems to jehadi groups. Religious alcoholism is a running plague in Pakistan having suffered from political depression on Kashmir issue for over sixty years. Paksitan is a terror-based nation that is careful and meticulous in terrorism in one stage and totally ignorant of Kashmir peace in another stage. The age of a tree is counted by the annual rings on it as Pakistan by the rings of jehadi groups. The 'cloak-and-dagger' methods of sabotage and terrorism through bomb explosions in public places adopted by Pakistani agents in India can serve only one purpose ... intensifying the hatred and uniting the people. If the idle and romantic-minded Generals believe that these terrorist tactics will induce the Kashmiris to love Pakistan, they are welcome to hug the illusion.

If the trumpet gives an uncertain sound, who shall prepare himself for the battle? Islamic terrorists and bureaucrats are basically puppets of Islamic theology. Such puppets, such bureaucrats, such hearts as are ready to growl, keep silent hate or love on order are not typical ... that their creators have sinned against the truth. They will have to learn to do more than dig up the more suitable words from the sacred texts. They will have to find answers to new questions of terrorism.

It was Mr. Nehru who accused certain interested foreign powers of seeing Kashmir only as a paper problem divorced completely from realities and basic facts which led to the whole trouble. Because a lot of unnecessary matters has obscured the real issue. Besides the historical and legal relations that Kashmir has been with India for centuries, bonds have now developed because both face external dangers together. When purification happens, higher vibrations flow in.

In most countries, political revolution had followed economic revolution, but in India, the order was reversed and this unleashed many new faces. Good intentions will no more make a truth, than a good mark will make a good shot. Pakistan, an eponymous nation of Islamic terrorism, has left a lasting impression for her epochal stupidity in the sub-continent. The 'Dawn' of Pakistan, in its editorial, on March 5, 2009, says : "Living in a state of denial is fast becoming a Pakistan's sepciality." Her denial is as virulent and devastating as infectious epidemic disease. Why? Because Pakistan's political personalism on Kashmir issue is too deadly pestilential to be trustful to India. Because she is perversely pertinacious to her Islamic doctrinaire, stubbornly unyielding to her anti-India slogans and tenaciously adhering to her old tactics of Islamic jehad. Even after an act of terrorism that chilled the nation, no one seems willing to accept responsibility. Pakistan's media is frustrated at their Govt's. inability to face the reality. Lashing out at the administrative refusal to accept Pakistan as a terror-base, the 'News' said, in its editorial, on 5th March, 2009, "There is now no doubt at all that Pakistan is unsafe .... Turning our attention to this would be a far more useful exercise than pointing fingers towards neighbours or pretending that Pakistan is not a terrorist haven." But Pakistani rulers get used to more grievous compromise.

Her denial is not to project Pakistan as global epicentre of terrorism. According to 'Atharva Veda', "No one can push a boulder away while standing on it; you cannot be free from anxiety while all the entrances through which it sneaks in are open." Truly speaking, Pakistan's destructive thinking on Kashmir issue is concerned with the problems of her livid life with her political existence.

On the reality of Kashmir issue, Pakistan's working up religious sentiments are malicious and uncalled for. Because she conceives a more horrible and pernicious tyranny than that which should restrain intercourse of thought. The great philosopher, Schopenhauer, says : "Every truth passes through three stages before it is opposed, in the third, it is regarded as self-evident." So self-evident is the reality of Kashmir's accession to India. It is only the truth within each moment of Kashmir issue, without end and without bottom.

Like prehistoric nuclear family, Pakistan-sponsored terrorist groups come from different areas, talking face to face, with arms and hands interlinked to defend themselves from blows. Like prehistoric tribes, they attach importance to the family unit of ISI.

In Islam, Allah is the Compassionate One. Among the 99 names of Allah that are commonly invoked the names Al-Rahman and Al-Rahim suggest tenderness, forgiveness, mercifulness and benevolence. Is Islamic terrorism the courage to die decently and to live manfully in the name of Allah? For every age is fed on illusions when Pakistan is alone in the free world of their rights.

We have not yet found out any special study of Buddhism and Muslim mysticism and are not familiar with the writings of many Indian thinkers. We need to learn the factors and traditions of various Asian religions and find out their influence on higher and lower education.

The question is : who follows the policy of war and still pretends to talk of peace? Pakistan harps on Muslim mysticism, halting of Kashmir solution. Nuclear tests and the production of such weapons are ever increasing. Such a danger exists only in their sick imagination. Pakistan invaded Kashmir, the Soviet Union invaded Hungary and the Chinese invaded North Korea flourishing appropriate invitations to justify their aggression. There are puppets enough everywhere only too willing to invite big power to intervention for purposes that have nothing to do with peace and stability. One objective of the international organisation is to promote a peaceful settlement of Kashmir disputes without necessarily sitting in judgement and denouncing those guilty of violating the rules of international conduct. Even the lowliest don't suffer from any sense of inferiority. Pakistan discovers, in terms of Kashmir issue, where the one ends, or where the other begins. Pakistan's peculiar sort of anti-India hate slogans on Kashmir issue ignites them. She belongs wherever she wants to go in their respective spheres of religious fanaticism, producing a soppy Islamic society and disordered imagination on the question of Kashmir issue.

All bodies of Islamic terrorism emit radiation or vibrations of anti-India hate slogans. This emission remains constant in India. When Pakistan is empowered with nuclear power, she is bigger than Kashmir problem rather than a victim to a self-regulated Islamic terrorism.

The word, FEAR, defines the mood of Pakistan's personism. The spectre of Islamic terrorism is haunting the world. Today, in the age of atom, the world is afraid not only of nuclear weapons, but haunted by Islamic fundamentalism. In fact, Pakistan, built by pestilential religious chauvinism, is herself in the grip of fear. Pakistan is afraid of many things, of India, of Afganistan, of the United States, of Israel, of disarmament, of the European Nations themselves, of the United Nations, and last but not all the least, of the awakened nations of Asia.

In the event of a third World War, fought with nuclear weapons, whatever may happen to the rest of the world, Europe, east and west, will be the first part of the earth to blow up in flames. Europe knows this as well as the United States and Russia themselves; the British white paper has admitted that in the event of nuclear war, there will be no defence for Great Britain.

Now time has come full circle. Out of the colonial world has emerged, in the course of two hundred years, a country to which most of Europe is today economically mortgaged and on which the whole of it is militarily dependent for its survival as Pakistan today on the United States for her own survival. Out of the 'Sleeping Orient' is now emerging nation after nation, nourished on the best cultural traditions of Europe, to whom Europe means colonial rule and exploitation. Today, Pakistan is a tinderbox of world terrorism.

The present atmosphere of crisis in Pakistan has been carefully built up by a systematic propaganda motivated by their usual violent prejudices animus against India, in order to create an atmosphere of Islamic terrorism for their own political ends in Kashmir. Why? Since Paksitan has no democratic constitution, it is perhaps understandable that its Govt. should not be able to appreciate the normal functioning of democracy in any other country. By handing over about 2,000 sq.miles of the territory of the Indian Union Territory of Jammu and Kashmir to China, Pakistan has deliberately and unilaterally destroyed all possibilities of implementing the U.N. Commission resolution on Jammu and Kashmir. Even Pakistan, embarking upon an irresponsible and dangerous course, has held out a threat of force by the so-called Azad Kashmir forces, which are under the operation control of ISI and the Pakistani Army, so as to spread out unlawful tentacles across the border and indulge in subversive activities.

On the contrary, over the past sixty years, tormented by opression and hunger, refugees, from that part of Jammu and Kashmir which continues to groan under the Pakistan's unlawful occupation, have been seeking security and opportunities for honourable living and employment in the area directly administered by the Jammu and Kashmir Govt.

As is well-known, J & K is a constituent State of the Indian Union and, therefore of the Indian Union Territory, Pakistan has no locus standi in this territory, having occupied a part of the territory by aggression.

In Pakistan, if you really go into 'who wants to know about anti-India hate slogans' they 'who' will disappear because there is truly no 'who'. 'Who' is to worry about the consequences? Mary McCarthy, American writer, says : "In violence we forget who we are." The working mind is not concerned with the future. If one is not ready to be awake, then one blocks another; if everyone in Pakistan is disciplined, the process becomes smooth. If not, Pakistan will never see the sanity of harmony and order in her own country. The moment you brand India 'Kafir', you will see only the label. And you miss seeing the person.

The tragedy of the year 1948. After the January 6 holocaust in Karachi when a large number of Sikhs coming from the interior to be shipped to India were killed, and roughly Rs. 2 crore worth of Hindu property looted, the Hindus of Sind numbering about a million and a half started migrating. A reference was made to Gandhiji and his sad death at the Pakistan Assembly not long afterwards. The Prime Minister, Liaquat Ali Khan, the Chief Minister of Sind, Mr. Khuro and other speakers paid glowing tributes to Gandhiji, repeatedly referring to him as Mahatma.

Mr. Jinnah was presiding. At the end, in the few words that he uttered he did not mention Gandhiji's name. He is believed to have not wanted to call him Mahatma and did not know what other appellation to use when his own colleagues in Govt. had called him Mahatma. So he referred to Gandhiji as merely 'he' and said that he served his community as he thought best, and that he (Jinnah) would convey to the Governor General of India the feelings of the House at an appropriate time.

He was keen on saying that Gandhiji served his community. If it is correctly said, the letter that went to Lord Mountbatten, India's Governor-General at the time, was over the signature of Jinnah's Secretary, and not unnaturally, the reply conveying thanks was sent to Mr. Jinnah by Lord Mountbatten's Secretary also.

It is indeed curious how while Hindu India seemed to think that Gandhiji favoured Muslims, and even in those terrible days following partition, they thought that the sufferings of the Muslims affected him more than the sufferings of the Hindu, and that he was more worried on hearing of the destruction of the smallest mosque during the riots than taking place all around, than the desecration of the bigger temple and gurdwara. Mr. Jinnah himself regarded as Enemy No. 1 of the Muslims. Those who knew him told that he had earlier aimed at being the undisputed leader of the country, and that Gandhiji's coming on the scene and capturing the hearts of the people very greatly disturbed Mr. Jinnah's plans. *It was the embryonic stage of Kashmir issue. It was developed in privacy. Was Jinnah really suffering from a morbid fear of Gandhiji? What an androphobia!*

In the beginning for some time, Gandhiji and Jinnah seemed to have worked together, but they soon parted. Gandhiji 's ways and ideas repelled Jinnah, while a suspect of ordinary Muslims because of his own ways of life. Mr. Jinnah became their undisputed leader. In their game of divide and rule, the British supported him. The unfortunate Hindu-Muslim controversy arose and that created Pakistan. And Kashmir issue, a by-product of partition, has begun to spread out its deadly wings of ingrained animosity all over this sub-continent. And time and the hour runs through the roughest day.

It is very hard to define the difference between the intellectual and a highbrow. Why? Because the highbrow is an intellectual with hiccups. There is, however, a fundamental difference between the highbrow and the intellectual on the one hand and the angry and the beat on the other.

All is in the name apparently. The fashion is Islamic terrorism. But it does square with the cult of personality. From Hitler to Mussolini via Paksitan, it has been and is the leader's personality and the follower's hero-worship, that has conditioned and tutored what is variously described as Islamic terrorism or Islamic jehad or crusade. There seems much truth in a sceptic's observation that all the cynicism resides in leaders and all the sentimentalism in followers.

Following the beaten track of Mr. Jinnah, the Islamic leaders of Pakistan today have derived from the same source, the eccentric. They are like the Dionysian revellers. Moreover, it must never be forgotten that every Islamic ruler on Kashmir issue is something of a practical joker. Why? He delights in pulling the chair from behind the chair from behind the complacent, the pompous and the smug. The Qur'an does not mention that killing is the staple food of jehad in the name of Islam. But the word 'jehad' is referred to 199 times in the Hadith which was written two centuries after the death of the prophet. Murad Ali Baig says in an article 'Revisionists Hijack Islam', "The Wahhabis interpreted jehad to mean a holy war even though it had actually meant a striving and Mujahideen was no holy warrior but only one who strives. For Muhammad there were two jehads and the greater one meant a struggle against one's own weakness while a lesser jehad was to fight against injustice. But there were strict rules and an authority of widely accepted repute could only declare jehad ... Muslim clerics should go back to the words of their Prophet instead of following the words of the revisionists who have hijacked the faith." (TOI Aug. 9, 2007).

The moment the word accepts a set of values, a code of ethics, a philosophy of life on Kashmir issue, in this sub-continent, comes along Pakistan and says this is all wrong. G.B. Shaw's satan is the person we all know, the hearty backslapper, the futile merry-maker, always the first to open a conversation as to end it, loud-mouthed, brassy, boring.

Islamic terrorism is the victim of a conspiracy at character-assassination. The trouble is that the trend today is to laugh at yesterday's inhibitions and fears. The Devil is very very passe. It may well be the beatnik who will put God on his throne and the Devil back in hell. Pakistan is a nation that has gone directly from barbarism of terrorism to degeneration without any interval. And it is governed by a mob. A nation of orgiastic character is controlled by militaristic nationalism.

A dictatorial regime is certainly under no such compulsions. It can decide on war or peace with claims of unanimous popular support at home without ever caring to direct vulgar endorsement of the kind a democratic Govt. cannot do without. A dictator can make politics of his people's fears and predilections. But even he cannot make of them the sinews of war. Pakistan is inherently terror-loving Islamic country. Pakistan Govts. are answerable to the meanest and the craziest of their constituents. They have compulsions behind their resignation to the present stalemate in Kashmir. The stink of a stalemate is there for all to inhale. Scandal breeds hatred; hatred begets division; division makes faction, and faction brings ruin. Pakistan does not know what they say between 'Dear Sir' and 'Sincerely Yours'. Those who have neither character nor honour may be wounded in a very tender part. Thieves are never rogues among themselves.

The biggest menace to the strength and stability of Islamic life consists in the almost universal habit of drinking religious fanaticism. Why? Because it acts as a constant and heavy drain on the human and physical resources. To be ignorant of one's ignorance is the malady of ignorance. With the majority of people living on the marign of subsistence, millions having no opportunity to work and the population increasingly nurtured by anti-India hymns of hate slogans, Pakistan can do with nothing less than an all out effort. The fact is generally recognised and indisputable in Pakistan that the ideas of cross-border terrorism in and out of Kashmir are gripping the minds of people everywhere stronger and stronger. In bowing to the inevitable, the security-minded must be applauded for their vigilance; like a Hamlet they have a pretty shrewd appreciation of the slings and arrows of outrageous future. Trule speaking, they have allowed themselves to be prisoned.

HOPE FOR THE KASHMIR SOLUTION : XI (UNCERTAIN GLORY)

Why is hope one of the three cardinal virtues? It is enough that it should have great practical value, that it should give men daring and help them to win when odds seem against them. Virtues that make for success may be exercised in evil enterprises and therefore are not cardinal. Besides, there is insincerity in the valuing of hope for the Kashmir solution because it makes for success; there is a self-hypnotism in being hopeful so that India may win, which, though it may help India to win in one particular case, is as dangerous as drug-taking to the reason. Hope, in fact, is not one of the cardinal virtues in Pakistan that she hopes so that she may win. It is a cardinal virtue when it is hope not about alone is proof against despair and cannot be destroyed by particular disappointments.

Islamic theology is not philosophy and the arguments which appear cogent and respectable in theology are perhaps worthless from the point of view of philosophy. Do they know the difference between a cat and a comma? A cat has its claws at the end of the paws, a comma has its pause at the end of a clause. So many agreements and pacts have gone into a dreamland of nightmares, in between comma and clause.

Who would escape a whipping if he had his deserts? That was Hamlet's question ... and Freud's too. Freud went far beyond the wall of darkness that separates our day and he knew how hard it was to get at the truth of man's mind. "Whoever undertake to write a biography," he worte, "binds himself to lying, to concealment, to hypocrisy, to flummery and even to hiding his own lack of understanding." The truth could not be had, and in any case it could not be told.

Hope is easily confined with Islamic faith. Pakistan may be certain in a gloomy faith; she cannot be certain in a gloomy hope; and if she has both faith and hope for the Kashmir solution, her faith cannot be a nightmare. In Pakistan, faith and hope run diametrically opposite. The distinction can be clearly seen in the faith of Pakistan, for they have a faith which, though it be faith in themselves about Islamic terrorism in Kashmir and their own triumph and destiny, is founded on despair and hypocrisy. They cultivate hope in religious fanaticism and Islamic theology because they think it will help them to victory; but their hope is based upon an Islamic belief. They believe the universe is morally wrong according to the deepest values of Muslim community. They have discovered that fact; they have denied the highest hopes of Indian people; and their triumph will prove the truth of their victory. It is rather Pakistan's preoccupied fallacy. Thus their hope of victory is inconsistent with hope. Their life, they say, is a struggle in which virtues of other religions are vice. Paksitan is left with Islamic faith alone of the three virtues ... militant extremism, religious fanaticism and global Islamic terrorism. They would find themselves masters of an ugly world and favourites of an ugly God. They think that God is on the side of those who are most aware of his ugliness; and their victory over the Kashmir question would be their consolation for unpleasantness of the truth.

Do you know Pakistan, plagued by insurgency and the worst-ever economic crisis, has been named among the "top 10 failed states" by the US-based Foreign policy journal? Pakistan, bracketed along with countries like Somalia, Afganistan and Sudan, has improved its position only by a notch. It is placed 10th in the index published in the July-August issue 2009, in the magazine. India is ranked 87th, showing an improvement over the previous year. Sri Lanka is placed 12th, Bangladesh 19th and Nepal 25th, using 12 indicators of State cohesion and performance. It is a sobering time for the world's most fragile country like Pakistan-virulent economic crisis, countless natural disasters and government collapse.

In this critical phase of economic bankruptcy and miscarried political judgement, Pakistan is sanguine about her victory over the Kashmir question. Why? Because she despairs of the nature of the Kashmiri people. When all in Pakistan are slaves, they have deserted from men's ideals of reality and will receive the reward of their desertion. If a man has suffered an intolerable wrong, we do not exalt ourselves above him by telling us home truths about the people of Kashmir are themselves men and share the common folly which they proclaim; they cannot escape from it by confessing it for others. The sixty years of independence finds Pakistan inured to disappointments, weary of self-flatteries and distrustful of sanguine promises. Who will hope for Kashmir solution?

Talkers and futile persons are commonly vain and credulous withal; for he that talks what he knows will also talk what he knows not. This habit of secrecy is both in politics and moral. It creates a grasping void.

Hope for the Kashmir solution! There is a lack of leadership. What is leadership? Leadership is an art and if you do not know the how of it, it is better for you to say, "Excuse me", than to say, "I can," when you really can't; and make a blind leader out of yourself. "If the blind lead the blind, both shall fall into the ditch," wrote Mathew two thousand years ago.

Capabilities of our Indian leaders are limited not so much by heredity and poverty as by their own vision of themselves.

Most of our leaders are sometimes looking at themselves through a magnifying glass, and they appear so big that they do not love or care for others. At times they are looking at themselves through a condensing glass and they appear too small; and they throw up their hands and say "no use". If our leaders are willing to sacrifice a portion of their mental anatomy on Kashmir solution, we believe they can see their way to leadership. Whereas our leaders are pre-occupied with foolish ideas and ideals which have robbed them of their strength. Party offices are the holy of holies to criminals and political terrorists.

Our leaders make grandiloquent speeches and self-denying gestures on Kashmir issue. They do for the sake of their country. With the creation of Pakistan, the fight of Muslims in India as a religious group has become anachronistic, and that they will remain a rigid communal group in the country only so long as they themselves choose to remain so as a self-segregated people. Indeed, it seems flagrantly self-contradictory. The defects of the understanding, like those of the face, grow worse as we grow older. The worm of conscience is the companion of the owl. The light is shunned by sinners and evil spirits only.

Hope for the Kashmir solution! In the middle of our bustle, the religious fanatics of India have so suppressed their religious romance in themselves, and tend to treat it with such intellectual snobbery that when it finally appears it takes the strongest forms like SIMI etc. The spark of religious romance still kindles communalism. A clump of trees becomes a forest, daring the hero to further conquests. But in the heart of each of them, beneath the veneer of culture lies the primeval lust for power, that same irresistible urge that we nowadays call Islamic globalisation. A man becomes a king at the wheel of his car. They have forgotten in the spirit of misadventure and lust for power that makes them feel they are monarchs of all their movements in India. Religiously divided and politically uncertain of the future of Kashmir, they can hardly help to come to grip with a fast-changing situation which demands not only realism but vision. In this situation, it can hardly hope to pull itself out of the morass in which it finds itself. With a ruthless sense of purpose, Pakistan is exploiting it for ends that have nothing to do with reducing tensions in this sub-continent. Her reassurances, however, by her very vehemence, betray a certain uneasiness over the possibility in future Kashmir. And she is engaged in skillfully exploiting the intense desire for peace in Kashmir. The talent of turning men into ridicule and exposing to laughter is the gratification of little minds. Even our country has committed a succession of blunders in the last sixty years ... a fire of stultifications and a fury of grievous miscalculations. The source of all opportunistic twists and turns lies in her profound isolation from the people. The entire purpose of Indian diplomacy has been to convey by every means possible the suggestion that the world can live at peace with its current problems.

The scenic splendour of Kashmir has no equal. Kashmir is completely encircled by mountains. On the southern side of the valley a mountain range seems to extend in unbroken continuity from Baramula in the west to Banihal in the east. This mountain range which is mostly snow-capped is known as the Pir Panjal. The range encloses many meadows and contains many lakelets. The principal lake is Konsarang which is located in the east. Aharbal waterfalls also lie in this range. These mountain meadows and lakes provide the best mountain excursions. What is known as the 'Kashmir Valley' really consists of many valleys and each of these has its own attractions, peculiarities and capital centres. Truly speaking, Pahelgaon has the appearance of a balcony and is situated in the lap of Pir Panjal surrounded by dense forests and steep mountains.

It is an undeniable fact that the Kashmir valley presents nude nature in a dazzling form revealing the new charms at new seasons of the year ... an earthly paradise of murmuring brooks and impetuous streams, crystal clear lakes, snow and cypress-clad mountains and uphill and downdale panoramic landscape.

From our military point of view, it has a tremendous strategic value. Now the question is : who is responsible for swallowing up the all-embracing panoramic landscape? A leadership or policy? Who will become a leader?

If we study the lives of great leaders, we will find that they had many of the same leadership qualities. Jesus was a great leader of whom it was said, "He was a blessing wherever he went." Was Gandhiji a great leader on the question of partition of India? Was Nehru a great leader on the question of Kashmir problem? Why? Because both the leaders had not been freed from the prevailing fallacies about themselves. Why? Their capabilities were limited not so much by heredity and poverty as by their own vision of themselves on the partition of India and on the Kashmir issue. George Bernard Shaw says : "When a stupid is doing something, he is ashamed of, he always declares that it is his duty." (Caesar and Cleopetra). Partition is a holiday of fools.

Nehru was sometimes prone to false reasoning, especially when he refused to Pakistan's error in Kashmir. He seemed to have been extremely disturbed over the unfortunate happenings in Kashmir. He had to realise that he was partly responsible for the ugly episodes in Kashmir. First of all he should not have allowed the division of the country on a linguistic basis. Linguism is another form of communalism. Apropos the translation of Mr. Nehru's foreward to R.D. Sinha Dinkar's book 'Sanskriti Ke Char Adhaya," may point out a flaw in Nehru's reasoning. He seemed to imply that the split personality between wide catholicity and narrow sectarianism that India has been suffering from has been with us throughout historical times. Such a view is erroneous. In fact parochialism has been natural to our soil. Broadmindedness was never a positive asset with us. The most vital periods of our history lauded us in fratricidal wars. The seeming catholicity of our outlook was nothing but an indifference born out of the enervating influence of climate as also the iron rod of a series of foreign rules. Linguism has raised its ugly head. Both Gandhi and Nehru were devoid of all reasons and calm judgements, the qualities specially belonging to a leader.

If at all there has been schizophrenia between catholicity and parochialism, it is of recent origin of Congress. The insurgent nationalism and neo-Hinduism launched by westernised Indians has been an auto-hypnotisation in a desperate bid to regain freedom. The tragedy of Mr. Nehru is that in his discovery of India he was extremely overlooking this fact. All religions of the world have eulogised the virtues of self-sacrifice and self-denial when they are meant for a common cause.

Our system of Govt. is our layered comprising democracy, aristocracy, mobocracy and autocracy each acting as a check and counter-check upon the others. Hope for the Kashmir solution!

So the result is lawlessness in a calculated disregard for the rule of law and the machinery of Govt. A country, it is true, gets several kinds of politicians ... half-baked politicians, pseudo-politicians, arm-chair politicians, hypocrite politicians, criminal-sponsored politicians, dissident politicians, double-dyed politicians, corrupted politicians, secular politicians, terror-prone politicians and so many politicians having no basic education of politics. They have rooted their bases in and around Kashmir in the name of democracy. Some of them are fifth columnists. Who will solve the Kashmir issue? They get the people they deserve. It is of no use to blame the other, though on the principle that the leaders must not set pace and pattern, the politicians are more to blame than the people. Majority of them rely on Muslim votes, sidetracking all terrorist activities in India. Their ideologies lie in between compromise and begging. Our politicians are like mosquitoes. Are mosquitoes religious? Yes, they first sing over you and then prey on you. Who will hope for the Kashmir solution? Like mosquitoes, they see among the masses hate, revulsion and scorn.

Our constitution, we are assured by our political leaders, is a sacrosanct document. Now the question is : How many times in the past sixty years has this sacrosanct document been tampered with for the purpose of inserting amendments to suit the powers that be either for the Kashmir issue or for Islamic terrorism in India or for the pretentious politicians of opportunism and spoonerism? The tragedy is that in the process they bring the constitution also into contempt. Those who complain most are most to be complained of. Terrorists are blamed for instilling fear and causing violence. Whereas our politicians create a pyromaniac climate of violence. They do not admit to their wrong-doings, creating a chaotic situation in our families, working places, in our neighbours and friends and in our environment. Dishonesty and foolishness are contagious. They practise the mechanical and pretentious use of political phraseology.

This process still goes on in Indian politics either on Kashmir issue or on any other vital issues. If the law of the land does not permit of certain official actions, the remedy is the rule of ordinance. "They forget," an eminent Grand Moghul of India is reported as saying "that the Govt. of India can override such laws as hamper it. We have the power of ordinance, the authority of Aurangazeb." So it has. But the Govt. of independent India which today occupies the seat of Grand Moghul, which citing historical precedents forgets the lessons of history. Today laws follow a supine submission to wrong and injustice. Now the question is : How long did the Moghul Empire survive the death of Aurangzeb?

The civil services, from the highest to the lowest, particularly on the Kashmir issue, also seem to be losing their grip and morale. It is really depressing, frightening and full of pathos.When it comes to a stop, the administration must collapse. Like our leaders, they have a saintly manner without a saintly character.

The very crowds, either in the valley or in other parts of India, do not hesitate today to decorate the portraits of our yesterday's politicians with garlands of old shoes and black flags. Our hypocrite leaders must realise this depressing truth today. It is almost as old as time. When ignorance enters, folly is at hand. Surrender your ego. Then the second door opens. Because our political leaders must not have the courage to be unpopular. They are the inferior and more mercenary, as the thimblerig gambler.

The craving for popularity is a malaise which has infected and percolated our emotionally unstable leaders, not only on the Kashmir issue but on other serious problems. Today a political leader might echo the lines of the old music-hall favourite, "I dreamt that I dwelt in marble halls." So a general spirit of indiscipline afflicts our country like a creeping paralysis. Unfortunately, while they do the 'doing', others do the 'dying' as we see in Pakistan today. Are they not thorough-going scoundrels?

From the time of has beens, our political leaders, in Kashmir, have been mesmerized by the cheers and applause of the multitude ... a dangerous game of complacency which is false and misleading. Mr. Nehru was right in deploring the generally poor calibre of India's ruling race. But might the fault not really lie higher? Might it not even lie at Mr. Nehru's restive feet? This political ditherism runs deeper into a dither of extreme vacillation. They are more politically untutored than socially ignorant.

Hope for the Kashmir solution! Pakistan's point of allegation is that India is trying to reduce the Muslim majority in the valley of Kashmir into an ineffective minority by the settlement of Hindus there. Whereas India's point of allegation is that delightfully provocative thoughts can keep infiltrating an endless but far more stimulating journey into a wilderness of history of destructive follies. Infiltrators are prepared to take pains and find it painless.

The Indian Constitution is a clumsy document. There are certain constitutional impediments in the Indian Constitution. So, Kashmir question is still alive. Any attempt at sabotage of the party by forming groups within the party is a clear picture how our Constitution is a photocopy of the 1935 Act. With this consititution, the frontiers of secularists and communalists are ever contracting and more and more States are being drawn into the vortex of this national struggle for power. So, Kashmir question due to follies and foibles of our Constitution is a source of Pakistan's threat to peace. It does not sound to New Delhi like the funeral bell of the whole family in the vale of Kashmir. One funeral makes enemy.

Hope for the Kashmir solution! The history of partition attempts to establish the psychology of nations. A mature mind's enmity is preferable to a callous youth's friendship. It is an old oriental adage. People whose physical growth is stunted are a dead loss to society. But unfortunately, the number of mental and emotional Muslims is proportionately much larger in the world than that of dwarfs and all unripe minds encased in the adult bodies are highly dangerous as they possess the power of translating the fatal immaturities into action with disastrous results. Fools and bairns should never see half-done work.

As in the vegetable and animal world, plants and animals find their fulfilment in attaining ripeness, similarly man's salvation lies in maturity. Authoritarianism in Pakistan, on the Kashmir issue, whether in politics or religion, is the enemy of growth as it takes the form of increasing dominance of the mosque or the provincial govts. in the life of the individual, and he ceases to think for himself, takes things on Islamic faith. Despite the fact that Muslim is influenced by Islamic customs and cultural institutions, there is sufficient margin in him for initiative. By overcoming immaturity, jehadis may be ushered into wisdom which will root out race prejudices and make the whole world one community, strengthening the spiritual foundations of life.

The religion of the Teacher would vanish completely when the image had sunk out of sight altogether. Islamic jehadis have systematically destroyed Islamic structures, cut down and burned the sacred tree of the Koranic message. Behind and beneath these disquieting developments in Pakistan is a sinister pattern wherein the Chinese hand obtrudes. Communism like terrorism owes allegiance to one God alone, happily for us, Indian pseudo-communists have moved from monotheism to polytheism. But whatever be the god or gods of communism, all good Marxists genuflect in one direction. The Mecca of the Marxists is China. It is heard round the Tower of Babel.

Islamic virtues, like essences, lose their fragrance in Kashmir when exposed. They are sensitive plants that will not bear too familiar approaches. He who learns and makes no use of his learning is a beast of burden with a load of books. Because Pakistan has deceived herself, since the cradle-song of partition. The Muslim world should know that the world is moving fast. However mighty you may be, you cannot stand alone without the help of the countries of the East. If Pakistan thinks so, she is mistaken on the Kashmir question. The ever-growing clash of warring ideologies is eating into the soul of humanity in Kashmir. The world is divided politically into East and West. Another conflict is still with us. It is another division. Now the division is uncompromising between the Islamic and the non-Islamic hemisphere marshalled away by the Christian communities. The former beckons a new dark age of modern terrorism. The liberty in the Islamic world has degenerated into license to make the world a prison house of Babylonian delights under the Islamic rule.

Hoping for the Kashmir solution! What is Kashmir? To India, Kashmir is the sacred place where the soul can lie down to a sweet sleep of peace, where we warm our poor hearts, and where all the sweet tones of the soul-life are heard. To Paksitan, Kashmir is the complex mechanism of Islamic civilisation. A spirit of Islamic fanaticism. He that never changes his opinion never corrects his mistakes, and will never be wiser on the morrow than he is today. Whatever name we may give to the Indo-Pak conflict, it is undoubtedly the initial phase of a decisive tug-of-war between two conflicting ideologies both of which struggle for supremacy in the vale of Kashmir. Pakistan has launched a calculated campaign for liberating the Kashmiri Muslims from the clutches of India. America, to which nothing looks more dangerous and detestable than Communist China, is determined to use every ounce of her strength and resources to check its spread, around the Indian sub-continent.

A disastrous third world war there looks inevitable, if not imminent. In this context, the question naturally arises as to what India's attitude should be. India has obviously one choice and that is to side temporarily with America either by Nuclear deal or by any other means.

Hoping for the Kashmir solution! Look at this Urdu couplet of a Pakistani poet : "Aa gaye soo-e-haram wa'iz ke bahkaney sey ham/ Warna razi ham sey butkhana the buthkaney se ham" (Misled by religious sermonisers in this mosque we did assemble/ Otherwise the temple was happy with us and we with the temple). We see how an Indian Muslim poet feels : "Na janoon mein yeh sab kya hai na Bangladesh na Pakistan/ Mujhey chahiye apney bachpan ka poora poora Hindustan" (I don't know all this, no Bangladesh, no Pakistan/ I want back my childhood day's total Hindustan).

Both the poets ascertain the same value and make the same vision that Paksitan is polluted from within. Indo-Pak conflict! The loss of a friend is like that of a limb; time may heal the anguish of the wound, but the loss cannot be regained.

It was a gloomy but bewildering night of the 15th August, 1947. It was a night of magic and enchantment. It was a night of unreality filled with drama. And the dark smudge along the rim of the moon hanging above New Delhi seemed like a whim, a vagary, the creation of a fanciful, abstract artist.

The setting of freedom movement was too ingenious, too beautiful, and too extravagant. The moon was the true one and the slight darkness over the valley of Kashmir which maimed its perfection was the shadow of partition. For this was a prophetic night, the night of political eclipse.

Who was willing to allow the moon to be swallowed by a demon? Who could resist the warning inherent in that weird and melancholy chant of partition? That subtle combination of threat and promise hangs ominously over the valley of Kashmir. When the eclipse of freedom movement passed at midnight there was a stunning silence. Only the faint nagging memory of the uncanny cry could be recalled. The lights in the houses all around the country, even in Kashmir, were switched off one by one. Mr. Jinnah's invaders slipped into the valley. Bemused by the witchery of Jinnah, hundreds and thousands of Kashmiri Hindu pundits got out slowly through the deserted streets of Kashmir.

An intangible nervousness begins to pervade the atmosphere of Kashmir. And invaders were being automatically dazed by a strange and unseen force. Even a blood-letting violence rushed frantically from house to house to get support for the jehadis and co. sauntered along, quickly chatting, one wondered what they might be saying to each other. They might have the same feeling as John Milton when he wrote : "In dim eclipse, disastrous twilight/sheds/ On half the nations, and with fear of change perplexes monarches."

Hoping for the Kashmir solution! If the British encouraged communal divisions, they did it for political reasons. The divide-and-rule eventually culminated in the two-nation theory of the Muslim League. Who was behind the screen? Leaders have already washed their dirty hands. Aligarh University in the pre-partition days came to be associated with the politics of the Muslim Leauge.

Today the people of Kashmir compel the Gandhi-Nehru and Co. to raise questions which the public by tacit consent responses ... why are we in the valley of Kashmir? Do we come from some other place? What is free will? Can it be reconciled with the laws of providence? What do I, or ought I, to become? How am I to become an individual? Answer of each question has left hastily.

INDO-AFGANISTAN TIES AND PAKISTAN : XII

The politician realises that it is easier to square a circle in Pakistan than to get round a mathematician. Mathematics and politics lie poles apart. Proficiency in mathematics requires high intelligence combined with infinite pains; but according to R.L. Stevenson, politics is the only profession for which no preparation is necessary. Our leaders are patients to the point of martyrdom.

Inconsistency is the guiding force in politics. Exaggeration, underestimation, deliberate misleading and half-truths are the very life and blood of politics. The tools of the game of Kashmir politics are the 'election promises'. A politician plays the game when he struggles to win the election. The rules of the game of mathematics are the laws of logic, whereas the rules of the game of Kashmir politics are the absence of laws. So the use of undefined terms is made deliberately vague by the votaries of Pakistan politics so as to satisfy their own ends. All the committed infamies of our leaders have produced in an adequate sense of horrors.

After sixty years of independence, has Pakistan changed much? No, but she thinks she has. In what way? Pakistan persists in talking about what a fool she used to be. The truth is that every party in Pakistan, not the least the Muslim League and Pakistan's people's Party, has been guilty of gross corruption, opportunism, showing the trump card of Kashmir. Their missions as well as visions on Kashmir issue are characterised by two shades of density; a dark central umbra surrounded by a light penumbra. Actually, there is no darkness in Pakistan, only a comparative difference in brightness of Islamic jehadi slogans with adjacent areas. All jehadis are like magnetic fields in themselves.

At a time when men and women are unjustly imprisoned, the place for just men and women are also in prison. Stillness of person and steadiness of features are signal marks of good breeding ... Vulgar persons can't sit still, or, at least, must work with their limbs or features. These peculiar features are featured by Pakistan on Indo-Afganistan ties and on Kashmir issue.

From the earliest period of history, an intimate dialogue has been going on between India and Afganistan. The land of the Hindu-Kush bears some of the richest evidences of Hindu and Buddhist culture. Since India's independence, the traces of violence and distrust which tainted the pages of earlier history of Indo-Afghan relations have been wiped out and the two countries have come very close to each other. In historical times, Afganistan has provided the gateway for all the conquering armies that marched down upon India from the barren steepes of Central Asia.

When India became independent in 1947, the past centuries of her relations with Afganistan offered no guidance of friendly relations due to Pakistan's gross and calculated interference in Kashmir. Whereas the Congress had, of course, endeared itself to the Afgans by its determined struggle for freedom and its sympathetic and friendly attitude to the Pathan tribesmen.

But the North-West Frontier province now belonged to Pakistan whose leaders have still now applied their propaganda machinery to incite the tribesmen to take up arms against India on Kashmir issue. A large number of these tribesmen has been induced by Pakistan-sponsored terrorist groups to invade Kashmir under the direction of ISI and Pakistani officers and equipped with Pakistani or Chinese arms. They compel them to ask pointedly the very questions which most engage the public. What are the roots of our frustration and despair living with an uncanny and spell-binding atmosphere in Kashmir? What prevents us from being ourselves? Why do we not dream of a fuller life and work for it? Do we have the right to our human inheritance? The Kashmiris know that if they are not individuals and do not have self-determined history, it is not because there is some evil in their blood and bones but because circumstances weigh too much with them. The threatening and portentous sign of partition is often the refuge of the injured and the defeated. The Nehru and co. was not concerned with the ills of Kashmiri people whose life is deadened by a dreary routine of terrorism and the edge of whose misery lies in its boredom. The metaphor of Indian leaders is a rhetorical flourish as well as a gesture of self-defiance. The use of a war-like metaphor is a decoy in Kashmir. The whole Kashmir is our fanatical asylum, lying between dishonest romance of peace-making process and cunning silliness. Political ghosts start queueing around the valley. The Kashmiris have no quarrel with anyone. Their only quarrel is with the decaying constitution.

There is no denying the fact that the bloodshed would drive Pakistan towards an Islamic revolution — Pakistan's thousands of religious schools are used as sanctuaries of extremism and terrorism. The blood of martyrs will bear fruit. Because the mosque is fanning out terrorism.

Hoping for the Kashmir solution! It is an obscure speculation involving fanciful thinking. And the enigmatic mystique of Pakistan characterised by theological dryness, wrinkling of religious faith and progessive political deterioration has abandoned the valley on a desolate island of religious fanaticism. Political hindsight of our leaders has made much about nothing. Because their energy is frittering away in petty squabble over the Kashmir issue.

Indians are the product of a richly religious and philosophical culture which provides amply assurances to questions on matters of fact and issues of conduct.

Pakistan cannot look at the sky of Kashmir, at a field a green valley, at a montage of faces, and not feel. The stretch of blue sky over the valley stabs at her heart. The poppies produce strange echoes in her mind. The faces stir up a whole crowd of memories. Pakistan cannot but feel and also think. She can't look at the insulted and the injured in the face and not ask what has caused the injury. Even Pakistan can't see her 'dreams' turn into a cactus bush and not try to understand the dialectic of the change in her country. And she cannot think about human sorrow and not want to do something to redeem that sorrow. Pakistan cannot yet learn real patience and tolerance from Islam.

Do you believe calls for jihad against India and US were made in Pakistan's National Assembly on 7th August, 2007 by a Parliamentary Secretary for defence? He argued that the dispute over Kashmir would be settled in 'one month' if jihadis were allowed free entry into areas under Indian control. He also argued that Quranic concepts should be allowed to guide foreign policy since in the case of Kashmir. He also reflected a deeply held belief in Pakistan that jihad was the only answer to ending Indian 'occupation' in Kashmir and that this task could be carried out by freedom fighter-jihadis. Hoping for the Kashmir solution! Pakistan does not know her tomorrow as well as her today. A condemned criminal who looks on the sunset through the bars of his cell knows on the morrow, not knowing the sun will rise for him for the last time. What a tragedy! A stream of lies, after independence, began to flow from Karachi towards Kabul, and India was accused of harbouring imperial ambitions against Pakistan and against the Muslim world generally.

Afganistan found Pakistan following the imperial frontier policy framed by the British. The rulers in Karachi, refusing to concede to the Paktoons of the North West Frontier their legitimate of self-determination, soon alienated Afghan sympathy. The political conflict took on wider aspects. Land-locked Afganistan has no outlet to the sea. Her foreign trade must flow through her neighbours. She has her longest land frontiers with Pakistan, good part of it undefined and in dispute. Her next longest border is with the then Soviet Union. On the West she is flanked by Iran, while, along the Hindu Kush, mountain passes link her with China.

After partition, Pakistan, on Kashmir issue, was playing such a role in her relationship with ISI and China. By hobnobbing with communist China, her new friend with whom she has already established a secret lie of entente cordiale. On Kashmir issue, Pakistan is standing on the burning deck of Afganistan. It is the epitome of idiocy. Why? Because everybody has left the burning deck and Pakistan has been doing no conceivable good by remaining there with the help of Taliban and is unwilling to pay lip-service to her idiotic episode.

The judgement is like a pair of scales and evidence is like the weights, but the will holds the balances in its hand; and even a slight jerk will be sufficient, in many cases, to make the lighter scale appear heavier. A million Muslims and Hindus were killed in the Punjab bloodshed in 1948. The Mahatma had stopped another massacre in Bengal. Kingsley Martin says : "The Mahatma discussed with me the communal problem raised by the fighting in Kashmir, and the next day I sat at his feet in a desecrated Muslim holy place while he preached reconciliation and forgiveness to the frightened audiences of Mussalmans. Two days later he was murdered by a fanatical Hindu because he had pleaded for fair play and tolerance for Muslims and, by another fast, had collapsed Sardar Patel to pay the last rupee that India owed to Pakistan." (India Revisited : Kingsley Martin, TOI April 6, 1958). So his death inaugurated a period of communal race. The 43 million Muslims in India had their local and personal grievances in the discrimination in the matter of jobs. British firms operating in India followed the example of Hindu firms and seldom appointed Muslims. In general, Hinduism is a tolerant religion. It was a measure of the difficulty that Muslims in India then opposed to any concession to Pakistan has intensified the communal fightings in Kashmir with the help of Afganistan jehadis. *Communal fighting was only one of the disasters prophesied by old British hands who thought that, once the steel frame of British rule was removed, India would be 'balkanised' ; the princely States would fight for their independence; the public service would sink into decay and corruption.* Communalism would flourish, and India would turn against Britain and the commonwealth. No picture could have been more falsified by events. New Delhi is the capital of bureaucrats, washing the dirty linen of each other's departments. From the beginning of our partition, our country has been afflicted with compromise as Pakistan with ISI and Afganistan jehadis against India on Kashmir issue.

Good lives make dull reading; bad lives make good reading. Or so one might think. But the Eichmann saga taught us better. Some bad men lived very dull lives indeed. This is the case with Pakistan and its leaders, crippled away with political ideologies, paralysed by spinal cord polio of crude Islamic die-herds, unhallowed by the anti-India hymns of hate and holier-than-thou-attitude, and largely dictated by the dictatorial passions of terrorist feelings up and about the Indian sub-continent — a syndrome of political paranoia and idiotism.

Why did so many of the leading Nazis — Hitler, Goering, Goebbles, Himmler, Eichmann — come from the catholic minority (one third) of the German nation? The answer is : Nazism was a revolt of the neo-nationalist periphery — Austria, Bavaria, the Rhineland — against the effete, Prussian aristocratic centre. These regions are, in fact, largely Catholic. It was they felt most urgently the need to prove themselves good Germans. Likewise, most of the Pakistani rulers have always been loyal to the subservience of Islamic dogmatism, leaving away all the doors of progressive outlook. They have all botched the Indo-Pak relations disastrously. For years, collusion is a dirty word, an ugly whisper, an insubstantial rumour. Pakistan's politics on Kashmir are chapter and verse of the clandestine comings and goings of loyalty to Islamic fanaticism. Never bid the Devil good morrow until you meet him. Religious fanaticism and terrorism in Kashmir go by destiny. And terrorism in India has come like a thief in the night.

Factional upheavals are a normal feature of Pakistan politics. And the successive upheavals have weakened the fibre of Pakistan's political parties and there are growing signs of internal disintegration. And her patriotism for Kashmir corroded by violence, untruth and corruption is at once sickening and sad. Any human destroyer, however ruthless, from Herod to Hitler, is preferable to the bomb. So far the great thinker appears to be on firm philosophical ground. But one is not inclined to share his optimism when he tries to derive confront from history. The Mongols were in the time of Chengis Khan utterly cruel and abominable; whereas in the time of his grandson Kubla Khan they became the most civilised, humane and charming people in the world. Whatever the personal charm of this great Khan, there is no doubt that with his other grandson Holague, and his remotest descendent Tamerlane, the Mongols reverted to type and repeated the horrors and devastations of Chengis. So the rulers of Pakistan may come and go, but their political characters are same. Is Pakistan as black as she is painted? Cynicism is no answer to Pakistan's malady.

"The fool who knows that he is a fool is for that very reason a wise man; the fool who thinks he is wise is called a fool indeed." (Dhammapada 63).

Pakistan suffers from a dire disease of political dualism. Why? To know when one does not know is best. To think one knows when one does not know is a dire disease. Being misdirected is part of Pakistan's daily experience. And the Kashmir episode being misdirected inlcudes diverse experiences. Even after a great deal of sad experiences, New Delhi persists in the delusion that the leaders of Kashmir Liberation Movement are the best men to consult about the right direction on the Kashmir question. Does New Delhi know those leaders afflicted with psychotic delusions are delusive in a demagogic manner of popular prejudices and false claims and promises, championing the cause of political bailiwick in Kashmir? Does New Delhi know these cultured viruses may lead to a set of confusion and uncertainty sometimes with feelings of anxiety about the Kashmir issue? Does New Delhi know these crotchety leaders full of whims and crankiness have prolonged the Kashmir issue implying a disorderly political vendors and tumultous crowd of militant jehadis for violence and cross-purposes in the valley? Does New Delhi know there is always a delusive method and meaning in their delusively propagated movement? The obvious motive behind this crotchety is to boost jehadis and terrorists, who have gone to the length of propaganda declaring even if there is a war between India and Pakistan, they would support and fight for the latter. They look upon India as a traitor to their country. How would we regard an Indian who makes a similar declaration? How would we feel if the militant jehadis of liberation movement go out of their way to celebrate the birthday of Sheikh Abdullah?

Who was Sheikh Abdullah? In 1950, when Prime Minister of Kashmir, Sheikh Abduallah, maintained that the ties between Kashmir and India could never be broken since they were born of the free-will of the Kashmiris. But in 1958, he was telling mosque audiences that the present Govt. of Kashmir consisted of traitors, goondas and infidels and that Kashmir's accession to India was temporary. He also accused the Indian Army of massacring hundreds of Kashmiri Muslims. Then the cries of 'Pakistan Zindabad' were being heard in Kashmir. He unveiled his great pretences. And his false-faced soothing words had never had sound promises.

The peace in Kashmir has entered the lion's den of Islamic jehad and still been at stake, braving all hazards and spurning the odds. The present explosions and riots in Kashmir seem to be a by-product of Sheikh Abdullah's grim warnings of the shape of thing to come. He seemed to provide a playground for his band with a particular boorish and crass-class of yahooism. He was the blunt monster with uncounted heads.

Truly speaking, a relentless and unremitting subjection to annoyance is implied. Ignorance, when voluntary, is criminal. Talking and eloquence are not the same. To speak and to speak well are two things. A fool may talk, but a wise man speaks.

Our old leaders and young leaders! Old wives are much less troublesome than young. Whatever makes the past or future predominates over the present, exalts us in the scale of thinking beings. Was not Sheikh Abdullah a political tub-thumper for creating a disorderly agitation and a milling about a crowd with uproar and confusion of jehadi voices all around Kashmir? Was not his tumultuous impetuosity attended by riot and lawlessness? Was he a protagonist of pure democracy in which the power is exercised directly by the people rather through representatives? He had always wronged the Kashmiri people with a religious display of verbal pyrotechnics? But the Kashmir question still remains unsolved. Was he a vociferous supporter of today's terrorism?

So greater damage on Kashmir issue follows from lack of decision as a result of which absolutism gets done. If inefficiency and dishonesty are condoned at the top then discipline and patriotism in Kashmir can hardly be expected to be found at lower levels. Discipline does not grow from the bottom. So Kashmir issue still remains unsolved. Can our tyrannous heart ever think of it?

Like all heroic harangues, Pakistan's advice on Kashmir solution sounds splendid ; but it is a bit difficult to comprehend and still more difficult to put into practice. Pakistan, on Kashmir solution, gives an authoritative decision blind-folded. Then the bargaining starts. To talk of dignity and generosity in the context of terrorism and other weapons of mechanised mass killings sounds as ironical as preaching the doctrine of Kashmir solution to wolves and tigers in the midst of a flock of a sheep. Pakistan's continual slanders had stuffed the ears with false reports.

Why accession? Kashmir accession to India was an inherent aspect of Jammu and Kashmir's movement for freedom from feudalism, landlordism and the Jagirdari system, and ideals of communal brotherhood and faith in socialism and welfare state. When the matter of accession was considered in 1947 and decided in favour of India, India only befitted her people. Was there any other alternative of accession to Pakistan? The other alternative of accession to Pakistan was incomprehensible. Why? Today landlords would have continued to suck Kashmiri people's blood. Because Pakistan stood for landlordism and the Jagirdari system where the poor were bleed for the benefit of the rich and the privileged few. A friend to everybody is often a friend to nobody; or else, in his simplicity, he robs his family to help stronger, and so becomes brother to a beggar. The entire affair is an example of Pakistan's hypocrisy and the stratagem whcih ascribes to India a crime of which Pakistan is itself guilty is of a piece with the well-known traditions of anti-India hymns of hate. And Islamabad has traditionally rehabilitated itself in the very image of its former master. A straight line is shortest in morals as well as in geometry. Pakistan still goes on camel carts.

The sage who coined the adage about the last straw which broke the camel's back quite obviously never sat on one. (On a camel's back, that is ; he might have sat on straws quite often). Having sat on a camel's back, Pakistan is convinced beyond doubt that no straw can break it, last or otherwise. Why? Because she lives in great infamy.

As is well-known, the camel is the most unsymmetrical beast in the whole animal world, going in where other animals come out, and up where they come down. In keeping with his general physical layout the camel is wicked, vile-tempered, uncooperative, vicious, revengeful and grumblesome, and strongly objects to people sitting on his back. Pakistan, like uncooperative, has never been advised by any learned counsel. Why? Pakistan knows it well.

In a blinding flash of faith a childhood belief in the efficacy of prayer is resuscitated and you pray earnestly for a speedy end to the ride. That is all you can do.

Who will teach Pakistan on Kashmir issue? The main object of teaching is not to explain meanings but to knock at the door of the mind. What is distressing in Kashmir is that when the 'real needs' of the Kashmiri people are expressed by a leader, he is apt to be dismissed as a dangerous radical. Apology is a kind of mental lethargy.

Either on Kashmir or on Afganistan problem, Pakistan is a nation of anarchy leavened by assassination. Defeated nations are always greeted with abuse. Pakistan is itself fiction, and stranger than truth. A nation of political satire, growing up in a rough-and-tumble religious atmosphere of fanaticism is treating the Kashmir issue in a boisterously rough manner. Pakistan is so dull, so dead in look and so woebegone that darkness will be the barrier of the dead.

Who is father of Islamic bomb in Pakistan? Who is Abdul Quadeer Khan? The nuclear ambitions and activities of other Islamic nations, especially Iraq's, as also their interaction with Israeli intentions are the basic purposes of Pakistan's nuclear weapon. But the Pakistani programme has naturally received the greatest attention. It is also thematically central, for Z.A. Bhutto had presented it as a common Islamic undertaking, which apparently helped him in securing Libiyan financing. In his last days, he recalled how he had been on the point of giving the Islamic civilisation what the Christian, Jewish and Hindu civilisations already possessed. Now the question is : Would he have derived any comfort from the knowledge that his work would not be given up by the man who was going to him hanged?

While the exact stage of Pakistani preparations must necessarily be a matter of conjecture, there seems little doubt that Islamabad has acquired both the technology and the basic materials for the Islamic bomb. But much of the preparation was completed within a few years of Z.A. Bhutto's assumption of power at the end of the Bangladesh war. In fact, the Pakistani bomb, when complete, would largely be the result of Bhutto's determination. It would be ironic if President Zia ul Huq had benefited from it, for Bhutto had died convinced that the USA had helped zia ovethrow him because of his nuclear ambition.

But undoubtedly the most exhaustive account, based on independent research on Pakistan's Islamic bomb, has been provided by Steve Weissman and Herbert Krosney, on 'Islamic Bomb'.

Both the researchers begin with an account of a secret meeting convened by Bhutto in Multan in Jan. 1972 where he first announced his decision to start work on the Islamic bomb; apparently the story was obtained from his former press secretary who had been present. There is a variety of information, mostly in Europe. There is a little information extracted directly from Pakistan; the authors must have been aware of how a British journalist had been badly beaten up in the course of his efforts to meet the man in charge of the Uranium enrichment plant, how even a western diplomat had been similarly treated for merely driving past the heavily walled plant. They had a quite uninformative interview with Munir Khan, the Chairman of the Pakistan Atomic Energy Commission, though his professor, I.H. Usmani, who had left for the United Nations, was much more forthcoming.

From others they gathered that Munir Khan is a 'patriot' who would do anything to acquire nuclear capability for his country. Who is Munir Khan? Steve Weissman and Herbert Krosney, in their book, 'The Islamic Bomb', say : "To those who know a man of charm but lacking in candour, often tricky and at times ruthless. As a scientist, he is said to be competent, but by no means brilliant." Pakistan only knows the definition of 'patriot'.

Another man is Abdul Qadeer Khan, father of Islamic Bomb in Paksitan. His wife was originally believed by the Netherlands Security Service to be Dutch but was later discovered to be a Dutch-speaking South African with a British passport. There is a great deal to say about the Dutch connexion of Abdul Qadeer, the Uranium enrichment man.

When it became known how Abdul Qadeer Khan had, by clandestine means, obtained details of the enrichment process from a multinational plant in Amsterdam and taken it home to start Pakistan's most important project in aid of the bomb, a British newspaper described him as 'the most successful nuclear spy since Klaus Fuchs and Alan Nunn May took their secrets to the Kremlin'. The account of this man's background and of his acitivities in Amsterdam is among the most riveting parts of their research. Security was clearly lax, for several of his colleagues had seen him going round key facilities and taking notes in a foreign script. Even more gripping is the story of Pakistani purchases, some clandestine but mostly open though with false statements about their purpose of vital components and materials from a variety of foreign sources. This is the general rule of Pakistan's hypocrisy and clandestine means over Islamic bomb. Pakistan is equipped at birth with the weapons of vilest means, full of lust for power. Those who cannot be accusesd of treason will be accused of ambition. This ambition shall have organised their tyranny over the Kashmiri people. Word, words, words. A plentiful lack of wit, having no reason and sanity, grows old as Pakistan is. Religious sickness and political impotence suffer much extremity for love of terrorism. Every night in Pakistan is unwholesome and ungracious. Elders and betters are in disgrace.

When the scandal broke, the Governments concerned were obliged to intervene. But the transactions did not stop immediately ; in fact, supplies appear to have continued even after they were officially banned. Weissman and Kronsey suggest that the authorities, especially French, cannot be entirely absolved of responsibility, not only for the successful Pakistani preparations but also for supplies to West Asia without much regard for the danger of nuclear arms proliferation. But the record cannot be set straight without mention how the Israeli bomb programme is said to have been aided by sources in fools. Becuase the blindness of men serves its own interests.

Do you agree a great political vaccum leads to strain in Pakistan? Because the continuing political crisis in Pakistan either on Kashmir issue or on the U.S. intervention in Afganistan or war on terrorism has revived the oft-raised debate about the basis of the country's nationhood ... whether it is an Islamic or terrorist country or a country of the psychic activity of man. Intellectuals and writers in the country agree that Pakistan's nationhood always came under strain whenever there is a political vacuum. They ascribe the separation of East Pakistani, in 1971, to Gen. Yahya Khan's rule and the current resurgence of subnationalism in Sind and Baluchistan to the continuing martial law rule of Gen. Zia-ul-Haq. Military rule and humours of shake hands. Compromise goes on.

Now a situation is emerging wherein a Sindhi leader does not know a Punjabi, a Punjabi leader is not familiar with a Baluch leader and, a Baluch with a Pathan. In this myriad-fold of abnormal crisis, Pakistan has lost her identity and integrity. *If Pakistan breaks up again, it would be because of this undemocratic system. 90% of the Army and 90% of the bureaucracy is made up of Punjabis. Others are like orphans.*

Underworld gang warfare and terrorism in India arc two sides of a coin, overlapping each other. Underworld gang warfare is not an uncommon phenomenon in what is a haven of Mumbai criminal activities. The cosmopolitan criminal activities of Mumbai are the breeding ground of terrorists, fighting away mostly from the eyes of the public, in the shady by-lanes and the labyrinths of shanty colonies.

A series of Mumbai blasts demands the cruellest facts of Pakistan-sponored terrorism in India. The gangs flourish and crave out their domains in a comsopolitan metropolis where a large number of people from outside and the State settles down. The field is fertile for filmdom and for such heinous activities. Political connexion also pays a nefarious role in destroying the morale of the police. Slumlords, who bully and control thousands of human dwellers, are created, encouraged and protected by local councillors, legislators, parliamentarians, irrespective of their party affiliations. Muslim-dominated Bollywood is not to be a missing link. These very slumlords often double up as gang leaders of terrorism in Mumbai. Goondaism assumes the massive proportion of a sophisticated and organised mafia-type operation in the city. Mumbai has a long history of such violence. Everything is proved upon the oaths of misjudgement and shameful cunning.

Even in Kolkata and other States, there are gangs and gang-wars. Guns are being used when there is a single target. And the smuggling lords are far more organised in Kolkata. They are fighting for their survival. Rulers know everything but pretend to know nothing. Tyrants do not tackle those who are strong. So Kashmir question remains unsolved. Why? Because underworld criminals, smuggling lords, and our political leaders are in league with each other; and their well-knitted nexus has been founded upon the ignorance of democracy. This nexus is the most dreaded of all terrorist activities. *Kashmir issue*!

The argument will deceive only those who pretend to be innocent or wish to be deceived. It is a common knowledge that to the Indian communists or Islamic terrorists no art is real and no culture worthwhile. Why? It does not serve and advocate the cause of their party. It is also a common knowledge that functions such as this are organised and utilised by them only as snares for indoctrinating the innocent Afganistanis and duping the unwary of Kashmiri Muslims on Kashmir issue. Partisanship in favour of one party will in the long run do more damage to the people of J & K.

Pakistan is responsible for the tumultous situation in Afganistan and Kashmir by raging gunbattles and a series of daring attacks of suicide bombers. Jalalabad of Afganistan, a former Taliban stronghold and capital of Nangarhar province, the heart-land of the Taliban and the major producer of the opium poppy, has always been in the news for funding the insurgency. Do you know the Taliban in NWFP during their five year tenure banned music, musicians and singers, and even music in buses and public places, shutting down Peshwar's only theatre, Nishtar Hall, and removing all billboards carrying pictures of women? Consumption of alcohol is a religious offense in Malaysia. But in Pakistan, religious fundamentalism, alcohol and terrorism dwell in the same house. Words are rascals as daylight discovers not more. Criminals smile in presence of our leaders.

When Pakistan got independence, Islamic nation wrote: 'Paradise lost in Kashmir'. When democracy died, Islamic terrorism wrote : 'Paradise regained in Kashmir'.

Pakistan is as guilty in the case of Afganistan as in that of Kashmir issue of deliberately supplying substantial quantities of arms in conditions that are liable to cause more instability than even before. The U.S. scolds the world for not sufficiently helping Pakistan invest in noble causes like nation-building. After all, talking about mullah sloshing its way about Pakistan's extremist houseguests is hogwash. Is not Pakistan's all-expenses-paid mission to nail those very houseguests? Besides, freedom-championing America has been a benefactor to militarily-marshalled Pakistan for so long that breaking-up must be hard to do. What a solemnised marriage de convenience between a free-wheeling democracy and the world's most formidable terrorist country! an unprecedented chimera! Today Pakistan is locked in death-grips. Terrorist organisations snarl defiantly at Islamabad. Even in Gojra, a shabby town in central Pakistan, where the tiny Christian minority has now been in a precarious situation. Words are so false that bonds disgrace them. And Kashmir issue is the corrupter of words.

Politics in Pakistan is traditionally a dirty game and no aspect of it is dirtier than the stab in the back of Islam. In the struggle for power which is the mainspring of all religious activity, no holds are barred and today's secret plotters in Pakistan will become the legitimate rulers of tomorrow, no matter if they adopt cross-border terrorism in India or plant a bomb under a dictator's conference table or hang him upside down in the main square where he is on the run. Agreements or pacts, like women, as fair flower as roses, once displayed, fall that very hour.

In the pre-independence era, any political executions that took place in India were of confirmed terrorists who had indulged in assassinations — and — violent methods. One of the instances may be cited here. The British tricked many nationalists to the scaffold. When Warren Hastings was Governor-General, he managed to have Nandakumar convicted and executed through the help of his friend, Mr. Impe, who occupied the position of judge in that notorious case. Was Nandakumar a terrorist? Had he indulged in violent methods? Thousand and thousand of sighs never saved Nanda Kumar.

Today, whether our political leaders are in the midst of pseudo-nationalists or pseudo-democrats, the sneer on their faces is as fixed as the simple on the face of Mona Lisa. Even the sight of death of a duped terrorist does not put them off. Today the Congress is a tear dropped from the heart of suffering humanity. The image of a tear several tons in weight is funny. If people refuse to say funny things, funny things can always be put into their mouths. Our leaders, on Kashmir issue, smile with airs of mystery. It is just of mystery — nothing less, nothing more — that sells the story of Islamic terrorism in and around Kashmir. They know they will not like the look of a terrorist but may be curious to know whether they used a knife and a fork to eat their dinner with jehadis in a secluded place. They are all as hungry as the sea.

Do our pseudo-nationalists and pseudo-secularists know had the army not been in the North-East (Nagaland, Manipur, Mizoram, Tripura, Meghalaya and Assam), it would have been another Cambodia? Why should not they think of it? They always play with some Jewel!

Even after sixty years of independence, Pakistan has not yet changed its foreign policy on Kashmir issue. Even she will rake up her demand for an independent Kashmir for long-lasting peace in South Asia. So, Pakistan wants an independent Kashmir to be resolved in accordance with the wishes of the people. Now the question is : Will this be the first indication to the Govt. of the India that they are not moving decisively to tackle terror? Are not the Al Quaida, Let and other militant groups all in different names doing their work in tandem for the same purpose to create havoc and destabilise India? Is not Pakistan quite ignorant of what they are doing in the name of Islam? Ignorant is he who says, what I say and know is true; others are wrong. In 'Sutra-kritanga 1.1.50, it says : "Those who praise their own doctrines and disparage the doctrines of others do not solve any problem." It is an axiomatic truth. Why? Because they see only one side of a thing — Islamic terrorism.

In the language of thermodynamics, Pakistan has always been in equilibrium with the surroundings of anti-India hate slogans where a particular view is right or a particular view is wrong. So, Kashmir issue still remains unsolved. And Kashmir solution makes a good voyage of nothing.

Today, Pakistan, geographically and politically, has suffered from a slow but steady internal haemorrhage. Baluchistan is bleeding heavily throughout the country. Pakistan's biggest province (covering 40% of it) is Baluchistan, the wrost governed and most neglected. It is to Pakistan a brain-teaser very difficult to solve. Unrest in Baluchistan began fifty years ago when Pakistan was hammering away at Kashmir issue. But the situation has worsened. What do Baluch nationalists want? They want autonomy, a greater share of revenue from oil and gas, to end wanton military operations against them. Even more ambitious insurgents want independence from Pakistan. Why? Because Baluchistan, a hotbed of tribal unrest and jihadi activity, is rich in uranium, copper and oil. It produces more than one third of Pakistan's natural gas. Islamabad uses Baluchistan as leverage of cross-border terrorism, particularly in India.

Its strategic importance is vulnerable not only to India but to China also. It is located on the Arabian sea and close to the strait of Harmuz. Baluchistan lies to the east of Iran and south of Afganistan. Any gas and oil pipelines from Qatar, Iran or Turkmenistan will have to pass through Baluchistan to reach either India or China.

The Baluchistan Liberation Front mainly operates from Kandahar. Pakistan accuses India and Afganistan of supporting the Liberation Army with funds. You are a terrorist, because you terrorise; you are a strong believer in anti-India hate slogans, because you are religiously fanatic. Where is the proof of your claim to be Islamic nation? Anyone arrogating superiority to himself, says Nanak in 'Adi Granth', shall be disillusioned.

Candour is a dangerous quality. Anyone who tells the plain truth, tells it at his own peril. In politics, especially, one must not call a spade a spade. If you are fighting in alien Govt. and some of your own people seem to be against you, suppress the impulse to call them as liberals. Call them moderates. If you like hiss these words through clenched teeth to make it quite plain, the liberators and moderators of history are not among your heroes. But stop there. Pull back the reins of candour with the head of discretion. If you do not, you are likely to get into the type of trouble in which Pakistani rulers are now finding themselves in Kashmir. Unless Pakistan gives up its irrelevant political posture, a final settlement will yet be stalled. Only gunboat diplomacy has undramatically gutted out democracy in Pakistan. Does Pakistan know no road is too long to the men who advance deliberately and witout undue haste; and no honours are too distant for the man who prepares himself for them with patience? A cat that has fallen into hot water will dread cold water too.

The essence of newspaper is news. But on Kashmir issue, knaves write newspapers and fools read them. The newspapers are the palladium of the people's civil, political and religious rights. Today newspapers constitute to mislead and confound the first three.

The man who has no land needs patch which he can call his own. The man who has no work needs a job. The man who has no hopes needs a spark of belief. The little man lost in a big world wants to belong. The man whom work has made into drudge needs leisure. The individual reduced to a tiny cog in the vast social machine wants to regain his humanity. A nation that is not bored of violence and terrorism needs not a sense of purpose. Who will answer to the needs of all? So precarious is the existence of Pakistan that its days of futurity are gone, even so is the life of men. In the Quran, 17. 18-19, it says : "If any do wish for the transitory things of life, we readily grant them such things as we will, to such persons as we will. But in the end we have provided hell for them; they will burn therein, disgraced and rejected.." Kashmir issue ought to be an eye-opener to our people. It is most unfortunate that even our topmost leaders think and speak of minorities, religions, and racialism, as if they were there by some divine right. Perhaps they do not know the sinister significance of the term 'minorities, in relation to a nation's existence. Do they know this term was extensively used for the first time for the Armenians in the Turkish Empire a century ago, and the Christian powers of Europe made full use of it as a powerful weapon against Turkey? Since then this term 'minorityism' — an abnormally benign and malignant mass of political issues — has always been used for creating divisions and schisms among a people inside and outside Kashmir. Few countries can have suffered so much from it as India. It forced partition on us. To talk of minorities should be considered an offence against Kashmir issue and the unity of the people of India. Merit merits an award only when the world is told about it — that is the truth and all the rest is untruth. In democracy, society is the master and the State the servant. But in Pakistan, the State is the master and society the servant. Pakistan is on the brink of anarchy. What is Paksitan today either on Kashmir issue or on Indo-Afgan relations? Pakistan means lawlessness and nothing can be achieved by anarchy, except destruction. Decay of a sense of law, along with a decay of the sense of religion, is the root of all evils in Pakistan. So Kashmir question still goes on and remains unsolved. Anarchy is the life-blood of Pakistan. Laws are useless unless people are taught to respect them. Pakistan belongs to the chattering classes where rascality of words makes them wanton.

Kashmir is the blackest chapter in Indian history. Though the dusk-to-dawn curfew, fanaticism is still running amuck and its latest manifestation is a new message of terror, delivered through thousands of leaflets to European and Hindu homes, warning them to quit the valley or be prepared to be liquidated. To the Kashmiri Hindu pundits, instructions are clear; whenver we see you, kill you and plunder your properties. So, Pakistan has been practising behaviour to her own shadow for the love of mockery.

Almost in desperation, it seems, the National Assembly of Pakistan, which has been the scene of many battles, both wordy and otherwise, has given into what it describes a new fundamental right — the right of making long speeches on Kashmir issue. This art of verbal pyrotechnics will make her a contemplative idiot.

On several occasions in the past, Jinnah has impressed upon the members the value and importance of short speeches. The longer you plead, the greater is your chance of losing the case. But the members remained impressed and now view with one another is the length of their speeches on Kashmir issue and Islamic terrorism. Pakistan, for over sixty years, has pleaded for Kashmir issue to the United Nations. Whereas India has impressed upon the members of the Security Council the legality of Kashmir's accession to India. The effect was dramatic. Finding no alternate way, Pakistan has started out terrorism in Kashmir in the name of liberation movement. Pakistan will learn what history teaches that 'by union, the smallest states thrive, by discord the greatest are destroyed.'

Terrorism in Pakistan is not absolutely unexpected. Many impartial observers have warned the West that the Islamic rule in Pakistan is sitting on a volcanic rock. The regime of the strong man is only a facade, a false screen over a seething mass of discontent and despair. Terrorists are desperate for their master's love.

Gen. Musharraf proceeded by suppressing every political party which had the courage to oppose his policies. He, treading the footsteps of his predecessors, lacks the shrewness of a politician. He vacillates too much and thinks too often. He ruled the people as a dictator with an indifference to their opinion that verged on contempt. The Islamic terrorism under his guidance is a Himalyan blunder — a grievous wrong which must be undone. It has shocked the conscience of the world. Gen. Musharraf is a down-the-line fascist. His romance of terrorism in Kashmir is full of suspense.

Use transformational vocabulary. Use empowering language. Use words wisely. Try and understand others' points of view instead of branding and labelling them as something or other. You will feel positive energy flow through you. And Kashmir issue will remain solved.

Metamorphosis of a language! Language is one of the major mysteries of life, and its relationship to our daily life an absorbing subject. Uncouth, barbarous, interlarded with Jehadi words and strangely inexpressive, original language in Pakistan is considered unfit as a Medium for polite intercourse, whether oral or written, Urdu or Arabic being used instead, whereas learned as serious works continued to be written in English. Exalted, lurid, macabre and erotic, language in Pakistan is impregnated with a tragic dualism and double-barreled foreign policy, and tended towards sensationalism. Kashmir story has so far been written in a series of interrupted sentences and fresh sandwiches of compromise. It has no continuity, no predicate, only razzle-dazzle and the resolution of survival. Boredom is a dragon. Kashmir fights unceasingly with every breath. Millions of words have been written on it, but the last word has not been written yet, and probably never will be.

13

INDO-PAK RELATIONS ON KASHMIR : A Whirlwind Romance of Midsummer Madness

Kashmir debate is pregnant with much tangential talkathon without any issue. Doubt is the disease of inquisitive, restless age. In these quiet situations, with tension and tempers of double-dualism and double-whammy, when potential damage from a single nuclear bomb is so easily created ... who knows that mistakes may be made. In making a position of weakness, a show of strength is often useful. It is the peculiar bouquet with one hand and brickbats in the threatened shape of nuclear missiles with the other may only have added to New Delhi's discomfort, and distracted vitally from the relevance of Kashmir solution. Democracy in Pakistan will have a precarious existence so long as the Govt. claims the rights and prerogatives of a democratic regime and at the same time refuses to be answerable to the people.

Does the USA have committed a blunder under the Eisenhower administration to pursuing a foreign policy of enlightened self-interest on Pakistan? Therefore one must seek in this curious country particular reasons for our concern.

Karachi, a great jerry-built town, seems far removed from us with its innumerable crows, its yellow-cheeked chattering myna birds, its hideous kites wheeling in parsee burial towers, its rubber-tired carts drawn by padding camels with belled legs. Its Karakul caps recalling the Mughal conquerors.

On the map Pakistan is an absurdity. Much more than half the population lives in Bangladesh (East Pakistan) ... one thousand miles across the Indian subdiet is fish and rice and the language is Bengali. Its inhabitants are descendants of lower caste Hindus converted to Islam. Geographically and climatically, it belongs to South-East Asia.

West Pakistan is a land of camels, mullahs, militant jehadis, devotees of anti-India hate slogans, veiled women and a proud fighting tradition of religious fanaticism. Its climate is hot and dusty. They are meat eaters and speak Urdu. They belong to that great stretch of Western Asia known as the Middle East.

America's particular interest derives largely from the fact that this weird geography gives Pakistan a special significance in political strategy, in both Middle Eastern and South-East Asian planning.. And Pakistan is being used for its symbolical value by Washington's policy makers to give appearance of strength to coalitions.

The three-storey building of ISI headquarters on Khyber road leads to the gateway to Afganistan and Central Asia through which the ISI pushes in combatants, weapons and explosives for years to help its erstwhile ally, the Afgan, Taliban, finally capture Kabul in 1996.

The relations between India and Pakistan are like North Pole and South Pole. No one does believe one another. What India thinks, Pakistan thinks reversely. For example : when the First Amendment Bill was passed on the Press Bill, newspapers in India had almost universally opposed the bill. Newspapers in America and Britain had condemned the move as a step towards totalitarianism. But there was one newspaper in the whole wide world which had indirectly welcomed restrictions on speech and expression in India. It was 'Dawn' of Karachi. Why? It believes that the constitution can be relied upon to help in the direction of curbing propaganda against Pakistan.

Mr. Nehru treated national and international issues in broad human terms. Not for him the stunted jargon of diplomacy and the anaemic evasive abstractions. For his press conference, on 9th February (Wednesday), 1955, for an hour, he dealt with questions which sought information, questions which were 'loaded' and questions which were plainly silly without the slightest sign of irritation.

Mr. Nehru preserved the air of the disarming amateur who did not know all the professional tricks from beginning to end. He started by asking appealingly, "How do I begin? What happens?", and the questions rained on him from Formosa to Kashmir to Goa and again to Formosa. "Could you say something about Goa?" he was asked. "Certainly, if you like," replied Mr. Nehru shaping like a tired but fond parent helping his children with the homework. "Goa, to begin with geography, is a part of India ...." came back the questioner "Did what he say about Goa apply to Gibratlar?" "So far as I know, "said Mr. Nehru quizzically, "Gibraltar is not a part of India."

Well then did Nehru consider Pakistan as geographically a part of India? "Certainly" Nehru said with a promptness that sent a thrill of anticipation around the packed hall. "But", and in his tone there was just the slightest tinge of apology as though he sensed that this was going to disappoint, "We separated by agreement and, what is more, Pakistan is ruled by Pakistanis and not by the Portuguese." A sharp tongue is the only edged tool that grows keener with constant use. Did Nehru know tongue is a savage beast, leave it freely, it will wound you? Strange to say, this person was entrusted with a charge of Prime Minister of India. Kashmir issue still remains unsolved. The longer you talk, the longer your client will stay out of prison.

There are so many 'Barons of Billingsgate', voicing forth the vilest of phraseology, in Parliament, not only the Parliament debate over Kashmir but irretrievably on any important issue. It has been goiong on for over 60 years. 'Billingsgate' has simply been translated into 'machu-bazar' (fishery-market of fish-mogerism) in national language. So, Kashmir issue remains unsolved.

Nowadays, Parliamentarians are those who speak loudest against any Bill in Parliament, either on a Kashmir, or a Terrorism Bill, or anything else, vote fastest for it. They are like so many chorus girls.

All his life Mr. Nehru had been a hero on Kashmir issue. His was the problem of riding two horses at the same time ... Partition of India and Kashmir dispute. This is the root cause of day-to-day deterioration of Kashmir issue. The conflict fundamentally is one of power politics and not of ideologies. India fails to study Pakistan. If you study your enemy, you will be wise.

Parliamentary dictionary! It consists of the vilest of phraseology of uncouth parliamentarians today. Kashmir issue does not matter to them.

Believe those who are secking for the truth. Doubt those who find it. Pakistan is like a woman. When she looks into the mirror, either it is a mirror or a scandal or a window-shop or a conspiracy.

The religion of nature is one of the oldest and most intractable dilemmas of the religious mind. In theological terms, it is the conflict between the idea of an omnipotent and benevolent God and the apparent chaos and brutality of a great part of the universe ; thus defined, the subject has an almost inexpressible atmosphere of tedium : the ground has been traversed many times and shown to lead nowhere. A perennial dilemma of this kind, both in India and Pakistan, needs ruthlessly restating from time to time. The religion of nature is extravagant. It will not remain under the influence of romanticism.

The human race today can be divided into the active, the passive, and the theorists those who do things, those who are done by, and those who observe and criticise. The second category is, the enormous majority. The first and the third together add up to well under 10% of mankind; but they are overwhelming minority in practice. In whatever community it may be, the doers and the theorists are the same sort of people : they go to the same universities, they speak the same language, they belong to the same clubs, they read the same periodicals. And in all these respects, they differ from the second category, the vast majority of mankind, those who are simply done by and put up with it. But in one vital respect, the doers and the theorists continue to differ. They do not think the same thoughts ; in fact, the theorists often doubt whether the doers think at all. Such is the gulf between responsibility and the lack of it.

One of the most widely recognised problems of today is that of establishing two way contact between thought and action, so that those who think may effectively influence those who act. It is a perennial problem. One of the things that makes it more intractable today is the fact that those who do things are generally too busy either to think or to listen to those who have time to think. But another is that the latter are so relentlessly determined to be influential, whether they have anything real to say or not.

Pakistan belongs to the latter. In Pakistan, the twin pillars of idealist and instinct psychology in the service of the reaction have been shattered; philosophy of the great Koran has been eliminated at the hands of plutocratic Govt., and Islamic terrorism has triumphed. Language, Pakistan has ever used on the Kashmir question, exists by virtue of her distinctions. Homonym, homograph, homophone give rise to daily embarrassment. When every word is equally another, language dissolves away. When languages merge on the solution of Kashmir question, there are no languages, the characteristic tones of Liaquat Ali Khan down to the present ruler, and even the tones of Nehru and his followers being lost even more rapidly than their meanings, like the flavours of different foods unsuitably combined and over-cooked, even they are eaten. Agreements will need more adequate notes, a more detailed index, a less chatty and quite uncontentious words.

A strong and proud professional middle class in India is a barrier against State tyranny, and even against Pakistan-sponsored militancy over the vale of Kashmir. It is not yielding in open competition with other classes. J.Korbel in 'Dangers in Kashmir', says about Sheikh Abdullah's decision-making approach on behalf of all Kashmir : "In Kashmir we want a people government. We want a government which will give equal rights and opportunities to all men ... irrespective of caste and creed ... It will be a joint government of the Hindus, the Sikhs, and the Muslims. That is what I am fighting for". Whereas Pakistan has hitherto been meretriciously functioning a treacherous and insidious game of mockery for the liberation of Kashmiri Muslims. Is she trying to throw dust of camouflage in the eyes of Muslim World?

What is delusion? And what are delusions of grandeur over the vale of Kashmir? It is a great question to the present world now. Delusion is the mechanism that explains the inability of the lover to appreciate the obvious imperfections of his lady: he cannot see them because his mind will not see them, the disturbing facts are not allowed to come into act with his passions and the opinions which result therefrom. In a similar way, the people of Pakistan presume the traditional beliefs of childhood, whatever contradictory facts their experience may subsequently have presented to them over the Kashmir question. Conflict arises, because beliefs and facts live in a logic-tight compartment of their minds and are never permitted to come face to face in the field of consciousness. Honest introspection will no doubt furnish them with copious examples from their own mental life. But Pakistan must pass on into the sphere of the abnormal, and endeavour to discover whether dishonestly cooked-up principle is evident in the phenomena of insanity totally deluged by their own self-created delusions of grandeur. The general picture of Pakistan on the Kashmir question is ugly and disheratening, indeed. The final impression is that Pakistan, claiming for the liberation of Kashmiri Muslims, after independence, is ruled by selfish, not very intelligent, and not very brave men. Whereas India herself emerges as a vain, impulsive, vacillating nation of feeble political judgement and limited intelligence and without courage. So Kashmir question is an eventful episode of double-dealing, broken promises, sham honour and sham loyalty in high places. The general picture of Islamisation over the vale of Kashmir, through the vehicle of terrorism, is one of the cowardice, and treachery and, above all ineptitude. Parliament attack showed the real valour and greatness of a nation's religious fanaticism and succeeded in proving that the infamy of the fanatical period is only darkness at night ... the darkness of an all-enveloping mad, and terrible Walpurgis night.

We find, as a matter of fact, that Pakistan plays a very large part in those phenomena, and that she renders unintelligibly a whole group of facts, generally regarded as peculiar characteristic of the insane. She, like a patient, who believes herself to be a queen, but who nevertheless cheerfully and contentedly carried out her daily task of scrubbing the word of jehad, is not perturbed by the incongruity between her beliefs on Islamisation and conduct on the vale of Kashmir. The conflict between the two is avoided by the process of not allowing any allegation to confront one another in the field of conciousness; the delusion is preserved in logic-tight compartments secure from the disturbing influence of hard facts. By this means the complex Pakistan has had underlying the delusion, complexes whose nature the world should study at a subsequent stage of their investigations, succeed in obtaining expression inspite of the incompatible processes present in the remainder of the mind.

In his memoir, 'In the Line of Fire', General Musharraf confesses to turning tragedy sometimes into what is light and comical. He now argues that the tragedy of his tinpot dictatorship has gone completely astray. How unhappy the great ruler of Pakistan has been through his ignorance and jealousy-ridden insanity; all of his views on the solution of Kashmir question is fanciful and chimerical, without any uniformity, without any foundation in truth. His memoir is perfect fairy land. He belongs to the Sunni. He is well aware of the death toll of the suicide bombing in different revered shrines, either in the Shia pilgrimmage city of Karbala or in the city of Karachi. He knows Karbala is a site of pilgrimmage for Shias from around the world. Even he knows the firing of artillery barrage at Kashmiri Hindu pundits. Islamabad in Pakistan, Anbar in Baghdad, Kashmir in India, Pok and others are Sunni-insurgent strongholds. He pulls everything behind the curtain. His misfortune is that he cannot mellow.

Instead, he has grown harder and more aggressive against India on the Kashmir question. Imposing terrorism is the tragical part of his life and is plainly none other than a bloody farce, without salt or savour. He, being a soldier, should be like other soldiers of our acquaintance. But he is a close, dissembling, false, insinuating rascal at the hands of Islamic priesthood and terrorism. He should be open-hearted, frank, plain-dealing soldier, a character constantly worn by them for some thousands of years. But he does not conform to the rule of decorum whether it is Kashmir question or not. It is based on his final folly. Unfortunately, he retains also a tendency to rely unduly on verbal ingenuity. He cannot resist the kind of supererogatory cleverness on the Kashmir question as our former Prime Minister, Mr.Rajiv Gandhi on the question of demolition of Babri Masjid. Gen Musharraf was running through the remarkable jugglery with transported phrases in Kashmir or never. Fear, greed and frustration make the Islamic rulers rude and vainglorious. Brooks Adams says in 'The Law of Civilization and Decay' : "Fear, which, by stimulating the imagination, creates a belief in an invisible world, and ultimately develops a priesthood; and greed, which dissipates energy in war and trade." Dissipating energy in war and terrorism over the vale of Kashmir and criss-crossing diplomacy of kashmir politics through negation and despair are the domestic architecture of Pakistan's politics over the Kashmir question. Mrs. Benazir Bhutto, former Primer Minister of Pakistan, is a royal Cinderella of Pakistan. Beneath the towering shadows of such a celebrated figure, she herself was scarcely visible on the Kashmir question. She was vain and idle to work out the problem. She might be used as a rival claimant to Musharraf's throne, if she had a powerful husband prepared to conspire against him. She has still been badly treated, the will to live up with dignity has not gone from her.

In the context of mounting economic distress of the masses after having been branded as an Islamic nation of being a Banana Republic, it is an urgent need for Pakistan to make friendly relations with India as regards best known to herself, begun to emphasize that Kashmir is absolutely necessary for her prosperity. The war preparations, the jehad now about sixty years old and the border raids may be a prelude to dangerous things happening in Kashmir. Pakistan has gained a strategic victory in the Security Council by inducing some of the powerful nations of the world to believe that Kashmiris are to a man eager to throw in their lot with Pakistan and they are being held down by force. But the Kashmiris would on no account transfer their allegiance to Pakistan.

The vivisection of India, Hari Singh's allegiance to India, 1965's Indo-Pak war, liberation of Bangladesh after being separated from West Pakistan, the Kargil war, and so many other political defeatism have made Pakistan bewildered and desperate as she knows what the verdict of the people is likely to be. 'Now or Never' seems to have become the watch-word of Pakistan, boggling about her self-created delusions ranging from ruthless gangsterism to more sympathetic criminals and tough reckless dogmatists endowed with a romantic appeal for peace with India. She does practice of strengthening the body of jehadi groups and enlarging the muscles of fanaticism by the exercise of her voice-worn phrases of anti-India slogans. It is now crystal clear that if India does not yield to Pakistan the whole of Kashmir, force and terrorism will be used and the preparations for war, the massing of denaturalised Pakistani troops along the borders of Bangladesh, Kashmir, and the Punjab are a clear indiction that terrorism is going to be used. *An unsophisticated foreigner may wonder that Pakistan which is a much smaller country than India and with resources altogether inadequate, should dare to challenge to a war. Can there be any doubt that Pakistan has been encouraged in her attitude not only by the Security Council but by some of the Commonwealth countries*? Already Pakistan's war-mongering attitude has had a serious reaction on the minority population in Bangladesh. So the mounting tension may lead to a catastrophe at any moment for the denouement of Kashmir drama. Pakistan's fanaticism, on the Kashmir question, is like a rope whip with many knotted lashes of jehadi groups having ephemeral catchwords of religious intonations. It is an expanding industry.

The Indo-Pakistan tension continues mainly because of the Kashmir question. If once the Kashmir question is solved, then, it is said, there would be amity between India and Pakistan. This is said mostly by people speaking for Pakistan. But the fact of the matter is that the Kashmir question itself has arisen because of the utterly communal outlook of Pakistani leaders. It is the root of the matter. If that changes, things would become far clearer. If that were not there, the talk of jehad ... religious war would not have arisen. It is true that the Kashmir question is the most important one in connection with Indo-Pak relations. Even after sixty years of independence, very few can plead ignorance today about the Kashmir question. Most know something of it. Some know much about it. Even the Ministers hardly know about it. But it is natural that very few know everything about it. They don't do penance for their penitential acts.

Pakistan has been steadily pursuing a deliberate policy of creating trouble over the sub-continent. Her strained relations with Afganistan are well-known. Afganistan is an Islamic State. The Paktoons, whose legitimate political aspirations have evoked the sympathy of Kabul, are good Muslims. Pakistan, which claims to be the greatest Islamic State, in the world, cannot establish cordial relations with Afganistan and Paktoons. Today Pak-Afgan border has been an invulnerable citadel of Al Quaida and Taliban style of terrorism. Extreme need makes survival impossible.

The terrorist movement is essentially religious and the leader was Gen. Musharraf, inevitably, because he was the young men's font of spiritual inspiration. Islam has founded a universal brotherhood. Many of the politically and socially conscious working men are angrily writing off theology as a part of the machinery for keeping them down. The Islamic socialists are determined to break up the image of Islamic fanaticism and replace it by one of a society-based Islamic brotherhood instead of the non-human values of the laisser faire economists. The great adventure of Islamic socialists today is over. But there is a distinction between the reasons for which a policy of Islamic fanaticism is adopted over the Kashmir valley, and the consequences of the policy ... a consequent weakness for flogging dead horse. Pakistan must have a fresh eye, unblurred by the emotions, prejudices and commitments of the time. Whereas Saddam Hussein had never done in the field of cooperation, which in many cases he feared as a system. And Gen. Musharraf has hit the line of realistic development, although it has taken him away from the original conception of cooperation. His general ideas as his predecessors are force today.

There is a thrilling dramatic age to the establishments of Islamic jehadis who first gave practical meaning to the magic word 'terrorism' at World Trade Centre. And Pakistanis made the first boisterous games of religious fanaticism, camping down a discordant catcalling at the U.S. Many roads seem to lead to Islamabad, from Afganistan as well as from Iran. History of Pakistan is commonly of aristrocratic or clerical background. Pakistan's dream of Kashmir is only a dream.

India should not be static in dynamic age. Our Parliamentarians go off at a tangent, leaving the critical issue embroiled in the cold but shambolic logic of their own position on Kashmir question. Most of them are involved in an octopus of crime. The sluggishness of courts is partly responsible for the increase in crime. They plug up a loophole in a law. When a new law is passed, lawyers usually leave a door ajar. Their career is most important. The temple, the Church, the mosque, the synagogues, even the human relationships are used for their possible benefit to personal ambitions. The position of a Parliamentarian wife in the family has diminshed. Various institutions have taken over the functions she has as a mother in bringing up the child. She may help her husband's career, but she remains restless, energetic, destructive, driven out by boredom.

As in India, even in Kashmir also, there were in the beginning two bodies fighting for political rights against the ruling dynasty there. One was based on communalism while the other was built upon the basis of nationalism. Though in the earlier days, Sheikh Abdullah, the leader of the National Conference of Jammu and Kashmir, was inclined to support the Muslim Conference in that State, he soon found out that he must build on the foundations of nationalism as against communalism and on the basis of democracy as against autocracy.

This was the beginning of the National Conference and its leader Sheikh Abdullah. Soon enough the National Conference aligned itself with the States People's Conference in India which was organisedly separated but working on the same line as the Indian National Congress. The States People's Conference worked for the establishment of democracy in the 562 and odd Indian States. If the Indian National Congress had stood firm and time to two principles more than any other, there had been nationalism free from all communals, racial and religious considerations, and peaceful methods free from violence of any kind over the vale of Kashmir. Even a fool can sometimes give good advice.

On account of our preoccupation with the relations between India and Pakistan, we often-times think more of them and their views and attitude and totally neglect the fact that in Kashmir itself there exists in its own right an actively conscious, growing and progressive community which has fought for its democratic rights for the last sixty years. The history of the movement for democracy in Kashmir is as full of thrills and sufferings and martyrdoms and as romantic. Any theoretical solution, therefore, which ignores this fact and tries to impose something from outside India or Pakistan or the Security Council, would neither be just nor fair to that living democratic community.

The National Conference in its long history had to fight not against British imperialism or against foreign power, but against the unbridled autocracy of the reigning dynasty. Hence it strengthened itself by spreading among the people the principles of democracy and the necessity to do away with the monarchial and autocratic rule. But in basic principles both the National Conference in Kashmir and the National Conference in India had been one and had worked along the same lines. Thus it came to pass that Sheikh Abdullah and Nehru became the spearheads of nationalism and democracy both in India and Kashmir. This is the history behind 'democracy' in Kashmir.

In Kashmir, the ruling dynasty happened to be Hindu. To Sheikh Abdullah and his National Conference, this did not at all matter. He would have fought the monarch and autarchy as fiercely even if he had been a Muslim. But it is interesting to note as to what was the attitude of the Muslim League and of Mr. Jinnah in the fight that Sheikh Abdullah urged against monarchy. It should be noted that Mr. Jinnah and the Muslim League did not support the National Conference and its fighters in this cause enthusiastically because they were allied with nationalistic forces in India. The League tried to encourage the Muslim Conference which was but a weak and isolated body without men of calibre who would fight the battle of democracy.

The Kashmir question is like the Delphic Oracle both to India and Pakistan that treat the problem with wary reticence. It poses problems which are inconvenient and often insoluble. The roots of the Kashmir question like the Oracle lay back in the past when religion and political action of both India and Pakistan were aspects of the same indivisible relationship between the human and the divine. Both the countries in their early agreements come down pretty decisively against the theory of deliberate fraud. But a verdict of Pakistan is implicitly contradicted by her incidental judgements throughout the discussion which, again and again, are those of hard-headed sceptics, whose staple theory of the Kashmir question is deliberately a political manipulation. On the Simla Pact, Pakistan is introvert, emotionally strained, intellectually tortuous, slow moving and deep and expressing herself in a style which may be rich, but is turgid and obscure. Such delusions of grandeur have enriched Pakistan's hypocrisy over the Kashmir question, to cast out fear by freedom. It raises the uneasy suspicion that 'Security' can become an obsession among the state functionaries anywhere in Pakistan. Pakistan has got private army in Brownshirts as Hitler once had. If she knows other countries' secrets, too many of the others know too many of Pakistan. It is all the more convincing, and the picture is odious. The then ruler of Pakistan feels lonely because ... like Hitler ... he is incapable of friendship and trusted no one; like Hitler, he sows discord at home and abroad in order to retain power ; like Hitler, he brands all criticism as enmity. He has other faults besides. He is greedy and mean over the Kashmir question, like his predecessors, often complaining that Pakistan is taxed too heavily. Her picture on the Kashmir question is megalomaniac, hectoring towards most people, but toadying to the White House.

Everyone in Kashmir agrees that democracy is the best but the only possible form of Govt. for any civilised state. It is certain that Pakistan is a mixed Govt. and the perfection of her constitution consists in this, that the dictatorial, the fanatical, the aristocratical and the democratical forms of Govt. are mixed and interwoven so as to give the people of Pakistan all the advantages of each without subjecting them to the dangers of these functionaries. And India's prosperity seems to be bound up with inequality of income and liberty with inequality of property. Kashmir is reasonably a typical group of holiday adventure.

General Musharraf, like his predecessors, has already lost himself. Partition of Kashmir along the cease-fire line was not to him a practical solution. Its practicability is evident from the despatch of foreign office dated 10 February, 1950. It is noted that "Although members of the security council and India and Pakistan are at present all committed to the idea of a plebiscite as a result of which the whole of the State of Jammu and Kashmir should go either to India or Pakistan, it is extremely doubtful whether the accession of the state of India or Pakistan as a whole is a practicable and permanent solution. All indications point to partition as the only workable solution but the difficulty is that any suggestion of partition at this stage would be extremely unpalatable to Pakistan." (R.H. Scott, New Approach).

This strange enigma of such a country still walks in history of lawlessness, deceptions and transient aliases. Whereas the Deputy High Commissioner, Lahore, despatched the following report on 20 April, 1950 : "Intelligent opinion in Lahore was now solidly in favour of partition on the Chenab as a compromise. Now that Pakistan is sure of herself and of her cause she is beginning to take a less emotional and more balanced view of the practical possibilities of the Kashmir question. The time seems to have come to treat the plebiscite as unworkable solution and turn to partition as a practical and immediate alternative." So, on Kashmir question, Pakistan has betrayed astonishing ignorance about many matters as she tells lies, many of them purposeless, some such as must injure her own cause. Quite often she has behaved with the irresponsibility of a small child with a delight in nonsensical mystification.

Scruples, human dignity, pity are but a monstrous fake in Pakistan whose mocking laughter would ring in her ears in her last instant of life.

Gilgit and Hunza, in the Northern areas, were once a part of Hari Singh's Kashmir. They are known a part of Pakistan. So political non-conformism must be punished by death. It means the abolishment of the last vestiges of freedom and legality. It reverts to the total dictatorship of thought.

Behind the background of hypocrisy of secularism, the bloody drama is played in Kashmir that remains in lifeless theatre-set induced by crude torture or sleeplessness or false promise of triumphant wickedness. Violence under the B.J.P. rule at the centre was fine delight, a blind delight, crying in brutal rage. Sunset marks the ever-changing hour of noon. Escaping infiltrators are being sheltered nightly in the mosques where the older was treacherously and barbarously murdered by the younger who was nephew. We may aptly call it a Frankenstein's monster : fear menacing its creators who cannot now control it, where subjugation is felt to embarrass self-respect of Kashmiri Hindu pundits, and seeks to console illusion for its own advancement. "Squeeze their hands till they yelp" replied Bertrand Russell with an unquenchable vitality, when somebody suggested that on shaking hands a celebrity should let his hand go limp. Throughout the ages, India has squeezed hypocritical and dogmatic ideas until Pakistan yelped and the world has got to know how stupid and disastrous Pakistan is. Cutting through the verbal maze of evasion and ugliness of ignorance, Pakistan has woven out a new dogmatic slogan. P.D. Ouspensky in 'Fourth Way' says : "A man must do nothing that he does not understand, except as an experiment under the supervision and direction of his teacher. *The more a man understands what he is doing, the greater will be the results of his efforts ... The results of work are in proportion to consciousness of the work.*" It brings about the inner change in man. It is waking from the sleep of life. What is its use in case of Pakistan? Nothing.

It does not raise the general level of her awareness and a constant struggle with the automatic functions, in herself, which keep her asleep in bed of terrorism. The same thing is true of her attitude to war with India, to international relations, to the proliferation of atomic weapons, to relations with western powers or to the Islamic mosques. Pakistan is disappointingly silent on the crucial, and the very real question facing parts of Kashmir and Pak-occupied Kashmir. The old ideas of Paternalism and trusteeship are becoming irrelevant in the large sections of the conitnent where the white man is now not a guardian but a guest. But Pakistan does not touch on the actual political problems confronting the Islam in a multi-racial state. But any political party in Pakistan must be concerned, not just with vague such as citizenship, but with firm matters of Muslim rights, voting qualifications and European protection.

If the country like Pakistan, on Kashmir question, is at one and the same time coming to be regarded as an instrument of immorality and functioning in such a way as to weaken all the natural fabrics of society ... between Lahore and Karachi, between Sind and Lahore, between Islamabad and Paktoonistan, and, the worst of all, between the Shia and the Sunni, it is not surprising that Pakistan herself should display the symptoms of disruption like Iraq. Politicians, limited as they are, are still the only people who can do nothing effective to check the trends. If the theatre of social disruption is still irresistible, the reason is largely because Pakistan has made it so on the Kashmir question. The archaic procedure of religious fanaticism is elevated, in fact, to the status of a platonic lie, preserving the much of justice over the Kashmir question with the best possible intentions. 'Opportunism' and 'realism' are very much the same thing, and both fail because they are based on the short-term insular view.

Intelligence, like journalism, must be produced at the right time, often by working against the clock. If the Director of Intelligence in India is familiar with the Kashmir problem, and can check the reasoning by which a solution to it is offered, he has to present that solution to a higher authority, outside the intelligent community, and his brief must be clear and concise, defining the problem itself, the conclusion arrived at and the main links in the chain of reasoning.

Pakistan's commitment to a long term military, political and economic alliance with U.S.A. will also be the signature of her death-warrant. One stroke of the pen will convert the Pakistan-sponsored terrorism from a European to a European menace. It is fact. The seeds of destruction are already to be found in 1950s. The entrenchment of U.S. privileges had rendered Pakistan powerless and crippled to deal with the Kashmir problem. These problems are racial, not parliamentary.

The European (and Western) picture of the Muslim world has been ever-changing : a succession, as it were, of 'stills' some in mudgy monochrome, others in a studied and deliberate blaze of colour, which as evidently aspires to as it rarely achieves the 'glorious'. Throughout the centuries of a contact between Europe and Islam which has been as inescapable as proximity could make it, these pictures have been remarkable for their incompleteness ... depending as each has usually upon a series of generalisations about a single point and the Arabs have each attracted an attention which has demanded and received the composition of a generalised background.

Pakistan's ever-changing breathing over the Kashmir question is hypocritical. According to Sanskrit proverb : "For breath is life, and you breath well you will live long on earth." Because Pakistan, on the Kashmir question, was born to be a clever causist, fanatically devoted to the dogmas of her faith. Besieged by an assiduously cultivated intellectualism, conditioned in a sanctum sanctorum of Islamic scholasticism, Pakistan cannot kill the racial trait of emotionalism. In the Middle East, it is the Arab over the jew, and on the Indo-Pak sub-continent, it has customarily been the Muslim over the Hindu. There is a tendency to build up a mystique about these single peoples who are felt to be loveable and loyal. It is much difficult to guess how Pakistan will dole out the blame for her failure to bring about demilitarisation. The end of any peaceful mission over the Kashmir question will shortly mark the beginning of an intensified campaign of vilification against India. Gen. Musharraf's failure confronts Islamabad with a greater test than of mere intensification of mudslinging against India. Propaganda across the border has been proclaiming from house tops that the failure of the Musharraf's mission would provide the green light for the full-scale unleashing of long-advertised holy jehad. The paramount question is : will tribal drums beat again at the bid of Islamabad as it was before at the bed of Karachi? The sixty year old Pakistani campaign of bluff now faces its toughest challenge. Musharraf's clenched first had its first major crisis.

Progressive Kashmir rejects medieval ideology. In 1944, the National Conference in its general annual session adopted its famous plan of 'New Kashmir'. Andante reactionaries and their retainers pronounced it as a leaf from the volume of communist socio-political theory. Their opinion was mostly based ... particularly such was the case with certain foreign observers ... on the red colour of the cover of the booklet. At any rate the authorities of the time found it convenient to dub this plan as being communistic, to justify the repressive measure they adopted to suppress the ever-growing popular movement for the attainment of democracy. But as time passed on and its true significance dawned on the people for whom this plan was devised, the following of Sheikh Abdullah increased in geomatric progression. Now the political language the people talked and the manner in which people of all sections endeavoured to identify themselves with one another, made it difficult for anyone to sort out people of Kashmir as Hindus and Muslims. A Sikh, without his external distinction, thought and behaved, after the general nationalist pattern which was popularised by the All Jammu and Kashmir National Conference. On all sides one heard the demand being made for the establishment of a constituent Assembly and responsible Govt. as expounded in the 'New Kashmir' plan.

To a weary Kashmir, torn asunder by suspicion, threatening, horrors, strife and hatred, Pakistan unhesitatingly brings out an ephemeral message of love and peace and harmony. A Prophet of love abounding was born in Mecca. His spirit hovers over the Holy Land, but it is now in shambles. His all-embracing message of love and peace has distracted, and his followers are engaged in a deadly strife poisoning the atmosphere of the world. Racial hatred and religious fanaticism have succumbed to the Great Koran which has taught and inscribed in unforgettable words coloured today by jehadis' murderous slogans. His followers stride across the world with a message of religious extremism; the crusaders trying to discover a mooring for revitalised national life has culminated in a conflagration.

The history of crusaders shows how religion was exploited for secular purposes. The Church itself became to some extent a political organisation. Even the Mosque has become an awe-inspiring haven of terrorist-cum-jehadi organisations. It is, more or less, an admitted fact of history that religious systems under modifications as they pass from people to people, or from country to country, and it cannot possibly be denied that these variations are primarily to be attributed to racial and environmental causes that we have witnessed now in Kashmir.

The civilisation of the West is largely Christian in origin. It has long ceased to be Christian in spirit and even in complexion. Racial and environmental causes, reinforced by ever-accelerating complications of political and economic life, have triumphed over the elemental simplicity and charity of the prophet's message. What the West has gained materially it has lost spiritually in this sub-continent; and today a grave menace confronts the civilisation of which it boasts. An unending confrontation between Islamic civilisation and Christian civilisation comes close to each other. It is an axiomatic truth. Islamic terrorism like atom bomb threatens to wither away the magnificent structure of Western civilisation. The Eastern nations have been the first victims of militant crusaders. Can the Muslim nations escape the devastating impact of religious fanaticism they have created? The economic structure in Pakistan built up by U.S. dollar diplomacy is in disquieting fissures. Pakistan has now been conditioned in the name of religious fanaticism and terrorism.

Today the West dominates the world, but its civilisation is in a process of dissolution. Whereas Pakistan, under the guise of law and humanity in Kashmir, is causing unrevealed tremor in the hearts of western statesmen. Life in Pakistan has lost its moorings under the stress of long-accumulating inner contradictions. For her mad rush for power in Kashmir and in Afganistan, the jehadis have begun to sail across the uncharted seas. The port left behind is lost to sight : the destination is beyond the horizon. At such critical hour perhaps it is wise to remember once more the vitalising messages of the Koran and the Bible. The message of Mohammad may restore equilibrium in an unbalanced stage and harmony in our distracted Kashmir.

A Prophet, it is said, is not honoured in his own land. No wonder, both Jesus Christ and Mohammad failed to elevate their own people into a new moral atmosphere. No wonder, the Near East, the ancient battle ground of nations, that sombre and awe-inspiring grave of militant empires refused to be impressed by the soft and mysterious voice of an obscure man. But a Prophet's message travelled triumphantly across deserts and mountains and rolling waves : it found appreciation, after long travail, in the mightiest and most civilised empire of the world. External Rome grew into majority and power and cultural efflorescence under the shadow of mysterious and lascivious paganism, and her close contact with the decaying Greek world made it more picturesque and romantic, if less spiritually fruitful and morally stimulating. Like the Roman empire, the long but dramatic collapse of the imposing fabric of Islamic culture has precipitated a moral crisis. Just as the legions and Praetors and laws of Rome had failed to respond to the needs of a changing world, so also the mosques and boisterous Muslim festivals have failed to satisfy the spiritual aspirations of Islamic nations so long as they are submerged under the unceasing flood of blood. Islamic countries have met this frightening crisis. Mohammad disciples have not yet offered to the bewildered crusaders of Kashmir a new ideal of reconstruction. Treading the footsteps of the great Koran, they are trying to conquer the vale of Kashmir through the red carpet of death and destruction instead of love and sufferings. A big steps, small leaps.

Nobody will deny that India became free at a very difficult time. Our leaders, having hatched out a new wave of freedom struggle for country's independence, had never thought that they would have to fall upon stupendous problems like Kashmir question. It is to them a Byzantine complex. Perhaps no country in the world had ever had to face such sisyphean problem after winning freedom. Pakistan was followed by mass migration and this in it turn led to the monstrous but towering problem of rehabilitation and re-settlement of the refugees. There were the problems of Kashmir in the north and Hyderabad in the South. Perhaps the greatest and most difficult of these is the economic problem. India's economic distress is a legacy of the war.

Some say that the partition of Kashmir is regarded as a desirable solution of the problem. The partition of India has created new problems without solving the old ones. The proposal to partition Palestine has intensified the conflict. So partition is not a panacea for any political conflicts.

It is generally said, and perhaps believed, that Sir Mohammad Iqbal first started the idea of Pakistan in his presidential address at the Allahabad session of the Muslim League in 1930. This is not at all correct, as such a proposal had been made by some leaders, both Hindu and Muslim, long before that year. Lajpat Roy was one of them. When it became clear to him, that the Muslims could not give up their separate electorates, he felt that such separations would inevitably lead to a separate Muslim state, particularly because there were in India certain Muslim majority areas, both in the Punjab and Bengal. He wrote accordingly in 1925 :

"Let those who demand communal representation, with separate electorates in all the representative institutions of the land, honestly confess that they do not believe in nationalism or in a united India. The two things are absolutely irreconcilable. Mr. M.A. Jinnah is the latest recruit to this party, and I really cannot understand how he calls himself a nationalist still. My suggestion is that the Punjab should be partitioned into two provinces, the Western Punjab with a large Muslim majority area to be a Muslim-governed province; and the Eastern Punjab with a large Hindu-Sikh majority to be a non-Muslim governed province". A cock-eyed conspiracy started out with all plots hatched. Being a strong advocate of the creation of separate Muslim states, but united with Hindu states under a national federal govt., Lajpat Ray went on to say :

"*Under my scheme the Muslims will have four states*:

1. *the Pathan province, or the North-West Frontier;*
2. *Western Punjab*

3. *Sind and*
4. *Eastern Bengal*

If there are compact Muslim communities in any other part of India, sufficiently large to from a province, they should be similarly constituted. It means a clear partition of India into a Muslim India and a non-Muslim India."

Now the question is : who had entrusted Lajpat Ray to deliver such comment? But, nobody, including the Muslim Leaguers and even Mr. Jinnah could not give any serious thought to Lajpat Ray's proposal. Why? The Muslims were obviously at that time, more or less sufficiently attached to the conception of India, as a whole, as their country, and had not enough courage to envisage a separate political existence, and to fend for themselves. Little thieves are hanged, but great ones escape. Why Lajpat delved into and spanned for the division of India? Lajpat Ray should have known that there was a remedy for everything except partition. He should have known 'there is a time and place for everything.' So, Pakistan has got a rewarding dividend on the partition of India and even on the Kashmir question. Today India is the purgatory of unrecognised political terrorists who are more and more vulnerable than the recognised terrorists. Whereas Pakistan is the paradise of terrorists and the hell of fundamentalists. What a carry on! Jinnah got pleased like a cat that's got the cream. However, *Matubul Hassan in his book on Mr. Jinnah asserts that it was Lajpat Ray who heralded the idea of partition of India*, such as was carried out, in an even larger measure, in August, 1947. *Neither Mr. Jinnah nor any Muslim Leaguer was the propounder of the theory of the partition of India.* So Mr. Jinnah and his followers had insisted upon and successfully brought about the partition of India, after following the statement of Lajpat Ray.

Another frightening suggestion of Lajpat Ray made the Kashmir situation worse and worse. He said : "If there are compact Muslim communities in any other part of India, sufficiently large to form a province, they should be similarly constituted ..." Mr. Jinnah had also taken this rewarding dividend from an Indian leader as a trump card on the question of Kashmir ... a Muslim majority area ... after the partition. Why did Lajpat Ray Chime in with those plots and conspiracies? Who will be responsible for this stuck-up and snobbish proposal?

Of the numerous publications on the subject, perhaps the most ambitious and the most pretentious is a book, written by Prof. Nafis Ahmed, called 'The Basis of Pakistan'. Unfortunately, his book labours under a grave disadvantage. The last page had been printed off on 5th Feb. 1947 ... that is nearly four months before the scheme of partition, as agreed to, was announced on the 3rd June, and more than six months before it was actually carried out on the 15th of August of that year, under the terms of the Radcliffe Award (National Press Syndicate, India, Nov. 2, 1948).

After the partition, the propagandists have started out their propaganda on the Kashmir question. In the history of the human race, the propagandists have always played a prominent part. The art of propaganda on Kashmir issue was well-understood and widely-practised. As the economic fabric of the society became more complex, so the necessity and outlets of propaganda increased on the Kashmir problem. Today propaganda is a world force of inestimable power; inestimable because at least two of the principle manifestations are ingeniously camouflaged as entertainment, news, or interesting pictures, political or semi-political propaganda. Truly speaking, a fool gets a lot of publicity. Disguised propaganda of Pakistan over Kashmir is difficult to control. So, Kashmir issue is like a phoenix rising from the smouldering ashes of partition.

A burning example can be cited here on the chemistry of disguised propaganda and fatwa to execute the apostate Salman Rushdie by Ayatollah Ruhollah Khomeini, Iran's supreme religious leader, 18 years ago, after the publication of the allegedly blasphemous 'The Satanic Verses' for the highly insulting and vilifying manner in which he portrayed early Islamic figures and doing harm to the Muslim world. It has outraged the Muslim world, and even the root of global terrorism has now been up in arms to kill Rushdie. Rushdie, who was born into an Indian Muslim family in Mumbai, could have avoided years of living in fear of his life. And Britian has decided to bestow a knighthood on him for services to literature without reigning a controversy in Pakistan that, 18 years ago, swept through the Islamic and Western world. Why? Because 'The Satanic Verses', which many Muslims consider blasphemous and believe ridiculed the Quran and early history of Islam, was first published in Britain five months before the February 12 bloodshed in Islamabad. Such blasphemous propaganda has heated up the monstrocity of jehadis who are wedded to the root of global terrrorism, leading to the inter-faith work and community cohesion work of the Muslim world.

At this juncture, Pakistan was emerging from a decade of military dictatorship under Mohammad Zia-ul-Haq, whose policies of Islamisation are often blamed for sowing the seeds of Islamic extremism and militancy. That month, the Soviet Army retreated from Afganistan, after a 10-year war with mujahideen guerrillas launched from Pakistan and covertly paid for by the United States and Saudi Arabia.

The echoes of history resound two decades on, as religious conservatives and liberals struggle for the helm of this volatile Muslim nation. No other Islamic country is as invulnerable as Pakistan in respect of Islamic extremism and militancy.

Ironically, the demonstrators 18 years ago began their march from Lal Masjid to spread out their Taliban-style movement, under another military ruler, Pervez Musharraf. 1.5 billion Muslims of the world have already flared up their anger and the Madrassa-based Islamic culture in Pakistan has boiled with indignation and blown its top of puritanism, breathing fire and fury with growing impatience. The Devil can quote scripture for his own ends. Hundreds and thousands of Muslims across the world, afflicted with such disguised propaganda, criticised the blashphemous attitude of Rushdie. The crowd chanted in one of the Pakistan capital's main bazaars, "Cut off the head of Salman Rushdie:" Such sentiments are the roots of global terrorism.

No evil, no wrong, no injustice can last long unless it is propped up by brute force. When Pakistan shouts hoarse about wreaking vengeance upon India, her voice is only the echo of the Pentagon. Truly speaking, Pakistan is the fulcrum on which the leader of American military might is planned to be applied in order to overthrow the Saddam Govt. in Iraq and the Taliban style of terrorism in Afganistan. They are all despicable pariahs in the eyes of the U.S., simply because it is broadbased upon the support of a goodwill of the people. The minatory attitude of the U.S. and the queer utterances of Pakistani rulers are not only painfully incompatible but brought out clearly their cold indifference to the cause of peace in Kashmir. And jehadis have started crying out with magic words 'open sesame' in Kashmir.

Pakistan is hankering after peace in Kashmir. Such disguised peace-lover with sham modesty can be gratifying to the albinocracies but it cannot change the historical basis of her pretentious attitude over the valley. The Islamic rulers in Pakistan want to digest Kashmir question without causing either an intellectual diarrhoea or a moral constipation.

The last sixty years of independence are rung out today with almost a total bleakness in Kashmir, flushing out anger and bridling up with fanatical crusade. Both the countries have failed to welcome the doleful knell announcing the departure of violence and sound of religious fanaticism over the vale of Kashmir. And man, the eternal dupe of tomorrow, eagerly looks forward to the fresh-born relationship between India and Pakistan for a better and brighter order of things than the past sixty years now dead. Standing at the confluence of the past sixty years and the coming of the new wave of terrorism, the people of Kashmir indulge in delightful dreams of peace and happiness in the valley amidst the depressing gloom. The blood-shot eyes of the past sixty years continue to cast a swell of Islamic fury, looking like thunder, at the present and the future across the man-made frontier of cross-border terrorism.

The age long experience of both Muslims and Hindus of India should not make them forget that we have paid dearly, as every other country has done, by calling in the aid of foreigners to settle our disputes. Even if we can't agree, let us fight out the matter. That is for better than outside intervention. History has taught that lesson. Letters of blood have inscribed that lesson on the pages of Indian history. Gandhism has not become a living force in the vale of Kashmir.

Slinging-mud at India has ever been the favourite game to Pakistan. The year 1948 is a landmark in the history of tank warfare in the world. Why? Because for the first time in the world, the Indian army used tanks over such heights as 12,000 to 13,000 feet above the sea-level and launched the big offensive from Zojila Pass, the eastern gateway of Kashmir valley towards Dras in the raider-held parts of fuzzy and frigid Ladakh. Moving from Zojila

Pass (11,500 ft. high) to Gumri Plains, 4 miles from the pass itself, was a singluar achievement of its kind in the world.

Kargil is an important trade and communication centre, and situated on the track leading to Skardu in the north, Dras and Srinagar in the west and Leh in the east. It is about 85 miles north-east of Srinagar.

It is important to note that from May 1948, there has been considerable enemy activity in this area when a large number of raiders using Gilgit-Skardu-Kargil route infiltrated into the interior of the Ladakh valley and the Zojila Pass regions, imperilling the safety of the Ladakh and Kashmir valleys.

The truth has to be told and is told only when it cannot be concealed. To threaten an all-out war by the rabble-rousing militant groups with all the resources of the Pakistan Govt. is nothing but a bluff. Why? Pakistan's all available resources have been and are being fully employed to get the Kashmir issue settled either by force of arms or by a plethora of terrorist activities to the hot passion of distempered blood. Pakistan is quite unfit to hear moral philosophy. Let their blood be their direction till their death. All the arguments to Pakistan, on the solution of Kashmir issue, are considered to be a cuckold and a whore. This is the example of her ill-disposed juggling and knavery. Pakistan is a fool positive on the Kashmir question. Her conduct has always been untruthful and dishonourable to India, even from the very beginning. And Pakistan, our neighbouring nation, takes advantage of our half-hearted decision and half-cooked-up military strategy with thousand doubts. We fear the tyrant, who either by public war or private treason. India should know that a stranger and distressed nation can never love your sweet words of peace and harmony in Kashmir.

Pakistan has nothing to do with Kashmir. It can't advance any argument, either on the score of geography or any other. On the solution of Kashmir, once the ruler of Hyderabad was a Muslim and that was enough justification for Mr. Jinnah to interfere in the Indo-Hyderabad dispute. Why? His Govt. had taken large sums of money from the State Treasury ; some of his officials deposited the Nizam regardless of any scruple. Even after 60 years of independence, the Muslims know in their heart of hearts that if Kashmir is saved, it can be saved only by the Govt. of India. The Muslims of Kashmir have come to realise who their friends are. The non-liberated part of that country will know, sooner or later, what freedom is, and what a hell it has so long been for the people, Muslims and Hindus.

It should be realised that Kashmir is not a piece of cheese to be cut into convenient pieces. India stands committed to protect the Kashmiri people from the demoniac clutches of Pakistan-sponsored terrorism. That pledge must be honoured at all costs. India's complete victory in Kashmir might engender long-term political troubles, domestic and international. We do not believe that surrender of a part of Kashmir to Pakistan will never solve our troubles and frowning gesture of hard fate. The partition of India has not yet spelt out the Arab-Jewish problem. Why should we believe that partition of India will be for a better and brighter order of things than the past sixty years just now dead? The blood-shot eyes of the past sixty years continue to cast a malevolent but funereal looks of Islamic jehadis incriminated with feudal-based Islamic country like Pakistan. Tyranny, hatred, falsehood and all the vices that degenerate the divinity in Islamic culture and embitter the relationship between the Hindus and the Muslims are as predominant in Kashmir today as they were before. Mr. Jinnah's mellowed and mild successors were apparently prepared to forget old scores, keeping religious bacteria at a suitable temperature.

Kashmir is invincible and unconquered, and should be unharmed. Why? It is the central point of world attraction, the navel; it purifies the heart wholly. It communicates through words and gestures, against 'corruptor of the world'. The term 'corruptor of the world' is taken from the Quran, and ranks among the highest on the scale of an individual's criminal offences.

Pakistan has got used to practising terrorism, lying almost prostrate under the successive blows of man-made racialism and sectarianism, with the message of religious fanaticism, especially in the vale of Kashmir. The people of Pakistan, suffering, as they do, from a million-fold multiplied means of ills and deadly sins, have not yet lost that power of fanaticism which has sustained them through innumerable periods of storm and stress in the history of Pakistan. Pakistan-sponsored terrorism in Kashmir is the living embodiment of this undying power of mountebankism, and from Islamabad the drooping heart of frustrated jehadis will imbibe afresh that moral strength. Even the suicide attacks can be traced to bibilical times. What is suicide attack? It is attack on a military or civilian target. The attacker knows that he will also die. Suicide attacks have an old ancestry. Even in bibilical literature, there is reference to Samson, who brought down the temple of Dragon, crushing him and many more philistines. In the second World War, Kamikez pilots from Japan carried suicide attacks on Allied ships. The Japanese army also used Kaiten, or suicide torpedoes to destroy allied ships. After the Second World War, Vietnamese death volunteers used this method. But in modern times, the first suicide attack took place in Lebanon in 1981, when a sole suicide attacker hit the Iraqi embassy in Beirut but the term came to international attention when Hezbollah's suicide bomber used a delivery van to kill 63 people in the American embassy in Lebanon in April 1983, followed six months later by another similar attack which killed around 300. During the period between 1980 and 1990, suicide-terrorism was mainly witnessed in Lebanon, Kuwait and SriLanka, but now it has become a global phenomenon, with incidents taking place in Israel, India, Pannama, Algeria, Pakistan, Argentina, Croatia, Turkey, Tanzania, Kenya, U.S.A. and U.K. Hezbollah was the first extremist group to employ this tactic but LTTE Black Tigers are considered as one of the most lethal suicide groups in the world. Their victims include former Indian Prime Minister, Rajiv Gandhi and Sri Lanka President Ranasinghe Premdassa. The biggest incident was the destruction of the twin towers in New York on Sept. 11, 2001, along with the attack on the Pentagon.

Pakistan has sponsored three types of suicide attacks, focussing her attention on the Kashmir question. The most common is a human-borne explosives, known as the human-bomb. The Rajiv Gandhi's assassination was carried out by such means. The second is vehicle-borne explosives, in which motorized vehicles carrying explosives are used. Examples of this mode are the 1983 Beirut barracks bombing in which trucks were used, and the 1996 Sri Lanka Central Bank bombing where a lorry was used. The third type is an aerial attack, in which air plane, glider, mini-helicopter etc. may be used, as in 9/11 attack. In most of these cases improvised explosive devices (IEDs) may be used. Apart from these common methods, terrorists also employ other ways, like the 1989 Tel Aviv-Jerusalem bus massacre, in which a Palestinian terrorist seized the steering wheel of the bus and crashed it over a steep precipice.

And the most important purpose of the suicide attack is to cause high casualties and maximum publicity at low cost. These attacks have a high media impact and they create a cacophony of fear-stricken world. And Military historians see suicide bombings as a symptom of asymmetric warfare, where one side lacks the means to engage in conventional war but alters the balance of victims through unconventional tactics. Who are potential terrorists and suspects? Most of them are mobile professionals. Rudyard Kipling says : "If you can meet with triumph and disaster/And treat those two imposters just the same..."

Pakistan's Madrassas, cockpits of modern style of suicide attacks, are accused of their linking to attacks not only in Kashmir but all over the world also. What is Madrassa? Like no human being can survive without water and air, no Muslim society can survive without Madrassa. Radical Madrassas, particularly in Pakistan's violent tribal areas, have been accused of training fighters for the Taliban insurgency there. General Musharraf's misrule is responsible for the rise of Islamic extremism in Pakistan. His stratocratic Govt. only provides a false sense of security and western support for the military only reinforced regional instability. Why? Because Pakistan's military on the Kashmir question is complicit in the worsening security situation, terrorism in Kashmir, and the growth of jihadi extremism and capabilities. So there is little sympathy for Pakistan's military ruler for massacre at the Mosque. Creator is a devourer. This worsening but alarming situation in Pakistan is that Pakistan-sponsored 'Inter-Services Intelligence (ISI)' coordinates foreign, domestic and military intelligence and has in the past been accused of helping to train Taliban and foreign fighters. So, I.S.I. is the epicentre of all terror-cells of home-grown Muslim extremists planning attacks either in the vale of Kashmir or other parts of the world. All the extremist groups are separately tutored by the I.S.I. in carrying out explosions by grinding and mixing different household materials. Hydrogen peroxide is mixed with organic material. The I.S.I. is said to have a unique insight into the terrorist camps... in North Waziristan, a tribal area of senior Taliban and Al Quaida leaders, in Dhamial, near the sprawling city of

Rawalpindi, and in Lahore. Iran has been bluntly accused of supplying arms to Taliban fighters either from Iranian revolutionary guard corps or being linked directly to the Govt. of Iran. Traditionally, the Shia-based Iran has always been inimical to the Sunni-based Talibanism. So, the Taliban is altogether hostile to Iran, triggering away sectarian bloodshed.

Planning of terrorism and suicide plots : The leaders of the 7/7 and 21/7 suicide plots are both thought to have planned their attacks in the foot-hills of the Hindu Kush mountain range of Pakistan's border with Afganistan. Al-Quaida-inspired plotters have always linked with Pakistan's 'Inter-Services Intelligence (ISI) to detonate explosives filled knapsacks in India. Many infiltrators, in the vale of Kashmir, born in Pakistan, have lived in and around the villages of Kashmir, and even in Turturk, a town close to LOC.

Pakistan's policy of Kashmir is undertaken as a desperate measure to pacify the hungry tribes of the north-west by providing them with easy opportunities for plunder, rapine and drug trafficking. Now Pakistan finds herself in a morass from which escape is very difficult. So, propaganda counts, but hard facts cannot be pushed off the scene by mere soft eloquence. If their befogged minds have cleared a bit, solutions to many difficult questions may have been found.. The moving finger writes, and having writ, moves on; and no man's eloquence nor wit can cancel out a line of it. Sentiment thrusts Pakistan into dry constitutional questions. Once again the bloody past haunts the creators of the future. Neither U.N.O. nor western powers nor commonwealth nor democracy nor any frightening gesture would deflect Pakistan from her resolve a world-devastating terrorism. The showdown may be delayed. The question of Muslims and non-Muslims on the Kashmir issue are unequivocally is a vexed but alarming nomenclature. *The term non-Muslims as applied to the majority community in India, along with minorities other than Muslims, has placed Hindus in an anomalous position.* Pakistan has obviously prioritized to this consideration. She has cast a separate light into the spectrum of colours, through a transparent prism of Kashmir. It is as if a capital sum as distinguished from the interest of Kashmir. And Pakistan has allowed her foreign minister as a privilege to gain an advantage over it. In no country of the world, the original inhabitants of the soil are given a name whereby their real identity is lost. The Hindus, after whom the sub-continent is known as Hindustan, lived here from time immemorial and thousands of years before the Muslims came and settled on the land. And they are being called non-Muslims under the existing constitution! The term non-Muslims presupposes that Muslims from the main population of India and all others represent either foreign element or minorities in the population of the country. Politicking of the political leaders is the best use of weapon on the question of Muslims and non-Muslims. It is a grave injustice to call the majority community by that name and thus treat them as aliens in their own motherland. Why this anomaly? This anomaly, which was the result of British imperialistic policy in India, is still being perpetuated by the Indian Govt. presumably to appease the Muslims and for no other ostensible reason. *There might be a justification for calling Hindus as non-Muslims in Pakistan after the partition. But how can our Govt. be justified in using the said term for the majority community in their original homeland, and even in Kashmir? The grave wrong done by foreign rulers has not yet been rectified by any of our Govts.* Justice demands that this long-standing grievance of the majority community in India be renamed and necessary change be effected now. The word "Hindus" for the majority community and 'non-Hindus' for all minorities including Muslims in India. Divide et impera has borne fruit in Kashmir. Hope for the best and prepare for the worst. Naturally, we have been worried and anxious. Grievous words stir up anger.

Religious beliefs and moral convictions become dominating forces throughout western Europe. Whatever ulterior motives, the present fashion of Pakistan on the Kashmir question may attribute to the men of the religious wars; there can be serious doubt that many of them are moved by the most passionate sincerity. This supercharge of inspired-irrationality gives the crusaders to the Kashmir events an explosive and incalculable quality which cannot be explained merely in social cacophony, economic unrest and tumultous religious age.

Those who have accepted the name of Pakistan as a symbol for close designs and crooked counsels have not always read her as a terrorist state. Thoughts and ideas of Islamic rulers, lying either at Islamabad or at Karachi, are so widely and slanderously disseminated at second and third hand that those who mostly religiously repudiated them often do so in ignorance of what they have actually taught. All they are domestic anarchists, ratcheting up tension and combining the revolutionary terrorist into a web of well-developed matrix. All they are cunning and adventurers on the Kashmir question.

Power has superseded authority as the main theme of political thought. Power today in this haunted sub-continent might be defined as anything which enables one man to control the actions of another without his consent. Both in India and Pakistan, if a man is forcibly propelled across a room, he is the object of an exercise of power in its crudest and most elementary form. He is being treated, as a thing, not a person. He is being neither commanded nor threatened but simply shifted. If, on the other hand, he is ordered to march at the point of a bayonet, an assault is being made not on his body but on his will. He may dislike marching more than anything else except dying, but in accepting the order, he makes an act of choice, and may accurately, though perhaps pedantically, be described as a free agent. But in an Islamic country, for an action is not unfree simply because it is taken under the influence of a powerful emotion deliberately stimulated by someone else. When a Govt. threatens its subjects with punishment if they do not conform to its wishes it is trying to control their behaviour by influencing their feelings as we see in India and other Islamic countries like Pakistan. In this respect, Govt. by force, does not differ from Govt. by rhetoric. Both make an assault on emotions, though one appeals to fear and the other may appeal to anything from pride to love. Both constitute exercise of power..

Dated back to the partition of India, individualists, in the vale of Kashmir, have thought of the good citizen as the repository of a rational intelligence, protected so far as possible from pressure by his fellow men, subjecting his feelings to the discipline of a rational will, unencumbered by prejudice and undisturbed by emotion. In 'Faith and Duty', N.H.G. Robinson believes that any adequate theory must cover three points : "that natural man is completely sinful, that his sinfulness is not entirely unrelated to a greater or less degree of moral imperfection, but that, none the less, no one is the subject of total moral corruption." If these three points can be held, it is possible to see how man can have an unconditional need of divine grace and also be able to accept it when it is offered. But India's carefully thought out and well-argued presentation over the Kashmir solution has long puzzled Pakistani theologians. It is good for Pakistan to follow an argument so well considered and so ably set forth. An estrangement between Hindus and Muslims, like old sins, casts long shadows over the valley. Jehadis are good servants but bad masters.

At this juncture, modern totalitarianism in Pakistan, either in communist or in Islamic colour, is the ultimate perversion of nationalism and the reduction and absurdum of individualism. It stems from the jehadi revolution, not from the ancien regime. Why? The reason for this transformation is that individualism contained within itself the seeds of a fatal contradiction over the Kashmir solution. We see the present history of Pakistan as a perennial conflict between men who live by the use of their minds and men who live by the sword of fanaticism; between technology and commerce which flourish in peace, and the bluff stupidity and the feudal arrogance of an aristocracy which owed its existence to war and maintained itself by force. The same instinct which has led the jehadi revolutionaries to hate-power as a supreme expression of irrationality later led them to use it in its most extreme form that we may call it 'global terrorism'. But the tragic fact remains that a western nation has contrived to conduct itself on the Kashmir issue in a more evil fashion than almost any other nation in human history. Why? Some of the chief reasons for this terrible aberration can be traced to contradictions which have existed and do exist in the west at large.

Why the Crusade? Rome and Persia had confronted one another for so many centuries, that it seemed that world order depended upon eternal action and reaction between them. It was the end of an epoch of more than 1000 years, and the eve of a new period of history to which crusades belong. Then at last, in the early seventh century, the equilibrium of the ages was shattered by the irruption of the new enthusiasm from the desert, the conquering creed of Islam. Heracluis was defeated by the sea of Galilee in 636, and Jerusalem fell after a siege of more than a year; at Kadesiah in 637 and Nekhavend in 638 the ancient Persian Empire was overwhelmed. The religion of Zoroaster gave place to the new uncompromising monotheism. But the balance of power in the Middle East very soon reverted to its immemorial lines.

The Caliph slipped into the seat of the Great King; and for 400 years, two refined civilisations, polarised upon Constantinople and Baghdad, learnt mutual respect in their continual antagonism, and often seemed to have more affinity with one another than either could feel with any denizens of the ocean of European and Asiatic barbarism in which they were islanded. The violence of the Caliph Hakim in the early eleventh century was an aberration that shocked even more than Christendom. Steven Runiman in his book 'A History of the Crusade', says : "In the middle of the eleventh century, the lot of the Christians in Palestine had seldom been so pleasant. The Moslem authorities were lenient; the Emperor was watchful of their interests. Trade was prospering and increasing with the Christian countries overseas. And never before had jerusalem enjoyed so plentifully the sympathy and the wealth that was brought to it by pilgrims from the West."

By this time, the hegemony of the Muslim world passed to the Fatimid Caliphate in Egypt. What ended the halcyon period of Christian-Muslim relations was the breakdown of the outer barriers that separated their combined dominions from the barbarian wilderness beyond their way.

Indian politicians as Pakistan, on the Kashmir question, are conceited, long-winded and often boastful, but with an engaging talent for telling ever-flowing lies full of pretensions. They have not yet concerned themselves more with social diagnostics and clinical analysis on the Kashmir question and trust rather than in the old traditional methods.

Had Gandhiji been alive today, what would have happened to Kashmir? It might be a question today. Being a pacifist, Gandhiji actively helped the South African Govt. in two wars and the Indian Govt. in the first world war. His reply to his friends who pointed his inconsistency was that as a member of the British Empire it was his duty to help it in war. It seems to be a flimsy excuse. His war efforts were painful to him as a pacifist and harmful to him as a politician, but he chose to be honest : "It would be madness for me to sever my connexion with the society to which I belong." (The Life of Mahatma Gandhi) This and many similar utterances quoted by Louis Fischer show how unfounded is the idea that Gandhiji was an enemy of the British Empire. He had, on the contrary, a great love for it, and a great faith in its ideals. Only in his later life, after events had made him despair of India's achieving Dominion States, did he wish to sever his connexion with the Empire? Nor did he conceive of Indian freedom in a narrow spirit, nor hesitate to point out to his countrymen the flaws in the Indian way of life. Had Gandhiji been alive today, what would have happened to the Kashmir question. The Kashmir question would have been more and more critical. Gandhiji was a good linker in the chain of freedom movement. A chain is no stronger than its weakers link. What is Kashmir question? It is a pattern of psychological awareness, of acute tension, of neurosis, of frustration, bewilderment and guilt of angst and the age of anxiety. The cries of anguish amongst the Kashmiri Hindu Pundits, alarm and despondency which have arisen, between India and Pakistan, on this irretrievable question, from

Islamabad to New Delhi, in all the matters including cross-border terrorism, culminating in the deep and distressed baying that has resounded through the religious fanaticism, might lead one to suppose that in angst, frustration, bewilderment, guilt and general distaste for Kashmir solution, we have nothing to do. Our predicament and our age of anxiety on this question are categorically sixty years ago. Do authors of terrorism and jehadi slogans, those tough, vivacious beings, really go about in dread of a fate, which they regard as worse than death, sexual sterilization by atomic bomb?

Kashmir ... a gardenful of flowers ... has now become a gardenful of Islamic militants. Kashmir–scented gardens still cling to us. Some of its names are part of our common speech. Its fragrance floats across the centuries. The gap between now and then seemed once impassable. Jehadi slogans, all along the valley, are still too often conceived of as a sudden opening of tight-closed door. The flowers have lain neglected when they are thrown. Their seeds have not yet been sown, after the Kashmir question emerges. Unnumbered generations of their offspring have flowered and faded in their turn; and the generations of men have looked upon them and seen their beauty. The apprehension of it ... something more than admiration ... has never been absent from the human mind, while buds have burst, colour has come back with spring, and bees have explored the blossoms as the air grew sweet with summer.

Less known are the numerous gardens in Kashmir still to be found in Kashmir. Some of them are one bombed sites. Others are in the burial grounds of Kashmiri Hindu Pundits, or innocent men, women and children or Islamic militants or Hindu temples burnt down in the great inferno of the fires of Islamic terrorism. The stuff of history is in their sites and names, but there is more than that. Kashmir is in our history, our own poetry, our trapestries and illuminations; it is the queen of our world gardens. It has become a nosegay and we may bury our faces in it .... an integral part of India. The valley of Kashmir travels in space, as its poetry travels in time. Memories cling to both from all this voyage. But the jehadis have failed to draw from it something kindly and gentle note of sweet phrases of love.

Terrorism catches not only in India but in the world at large. Pakistan suffers from political illness. Political illness catches Kashmir. Illness does not come from without. Man creates it for himself as India creates Kashmir problem for herself. And Pakistan uses the Security Council and the outer Islamic world as the useful instrument of controversy with which India makes herself ill. In a mass-produced society that rare bird, the eccentric, is to be cherished for his own sake, regardless of the value of his particular eccentricity. It is significant that Pakistan, a haven of terrorist-producing country is the breeding ground of so many spiritual eccentrics. If an Islamic country is to endure it must have some other and more powerful ideal to act as a driving force. Like communism, absolute, ideal Islamic society is a failure.

The more definite the religion, the more successful the community. Intellectual curiosity leads Pakistan to a question of Islamic globalisation, some of them induced very questionably, upon which utopia of Kashmir question is founded. Utopia can be built only with Fanaticism. Utopia has little room for Pakistan and none at for culture ... Pakistan will look in vain for highly educated, refined, cultured or elegant men and women in Pakistan society.

Winning over the anti-India hymns of hate by propaganda, the pattern of power politics in Pakistan has changed. The U.S. is losing ground on a number of fronts in the fight against the terrorists who have been significantly strengthened over the past twenty years. Why? Because it is Islamabad that has brokered a ceasefire with tribal leaders in an effort to drain support for Islamic extremism in the N.W.F.P. and other mountainous territories along the Afghan border. It is a worrisome malady for Pakistan. The scale of the infiltration by the terror network has led the Indian military officials to believe several members of the gang are still at a large and the threat of an atrocity remains high. Truly speaking, Pakistan-sponsored terrorism is sending ripples across East and West with the hardline religious parties.

In Kashmir, political ideology is as pernicious as erroneous. In India, for over sixty years, political activity comes first, and political ideology follows after. This practical conundrum is found in tradition. In Kashmir politics, the right determination both of ends and means springs not from pure empiricism and not from an ideology, but from a traditional method of behaviour. The warmth engendered in pleading a cause, and especially a cause which is felt to have differed unwarranted neglect, may excuse a certain amount of onesideness. Some foreign policy makers are eager to persuade us that the hen precedes the egg have sometimes seemed to ignore the equally valid proposition that the egg precedes the hen. But our political thinkers, on Kashmir question for over sixty years, have undoubtedly been guilty of the absurdity of supposing that political ideologies are generated by pure thought unsullied by practice in a political vacuum. By divorcing ideology from tradition, and by insisting on the primary of tradition over ideology, one may easily jump out of the ideological frying-pan into something much worse. Maureen Dowd says in New York Times : "While the U.S. administration lavished billions on Pakistan, including $750 billion in a risible attempt to win 'hearts and minds' in the tribal areas where Al Quaida leaders were hiding and training, President Musharraf had helped create a quiet mountain retreat, should be openness." Religious fanatics and communists are prejudiced mentors of the world, wrapped up in a narrow-doctrinal frameworks of worn-out ideologies. They are all pseudo-opportunists. Their jehadi-infested ideologies at the hands of radical groups are spread out of Kashmir and Tibbet. Islamic clerics should learn something from Dara Shikoh, the eldest son of Shah Jehan. "He would spend long hours in his library in today's Kashmiri Gate in Old Delhi, striving to understand a consciousness which dreamt of universal brotherhood ... Dara Shikoh's spiritual longing and quest for reality or haqiqat and unity or tawhid led him to study the Upanishads, 52 of which he translated from Sanskrit to Persian in his Sirr-i-Akbar the Great Secret. Focussing attention on the 'treasure of monotheism' found in the

Upanishads, Dara Shikoh draws remarkable parallels between concepts elucidated in the Holy Quran and the Upanishads with respect to tawhid ... "(Pranav Khullar, Times of India, Nov. 5, 2007).

Pakistan today is allowed to go unchallenged and spells greater darkness for a whole sub-continent. Islamabad has turned Islamic State into a warfare state of terrorism. The truths of fact are contigen and their opposite is possible. It remains unabated. And Afganistan has been made a scapegoat, causing much concern to the Middle-East. Death is so permanent ... drive out terrorism. Positive views of truth and beauty are those that impress the mind and lead to action; negation dwells mostly in cavil and denial.

Millions of words have been written so far on the Kashmir question, but the last word has not been written as yet, and probably never will be. There can be no conflict between religion and science. Faith, in contrast to superstition, is never irrational, nor is reason wholly devoid of faith. Religion seeks to reveal the truth, and so do science and philosophy; and the truth is all-inclusive and ultimately one. Both ... science and religion ... claim total allegiance and both penetrate every detail of our lives. But Islam and Islamic terrorism are self-contradictory. It has encountered so many other difficulties. And the prayers and hymns of Islamic philosophy are not, of course, written for the benefit of illogical positivists of Islamic terrorism in the valley of Kashmir and other parts of the world. So it is possible to convert a Muslim into a fanatical zealot, ready to torture and destroy and to suffer a mutilation and death for an obscene faith, baseless in fact, and morally monstrous. Pakistan is lost in the ordinary street of jehadi slogans. Half-hearted, she knocks at the peeling door. Pakistan is indifferent to danger where real danger exists. Rulers are the market place loungers of Islamabad. And the voice of the intelligence in Pakistan is drowned out by the roar of terrorism. It is hissed away by hate and extinguished by anger.

Gen. Musharraf is a famous and infamous figure in his day, relished and hated, kindly and vituperative, amoral rather than immoral, redoubtable and nearer to be ignored. He is the most unsparing culmination of his time. A self styled satirist. He gets used to roaring and making a noise of humour. He scourges pretentiousness and bumptiousness because he himself is pretentious and bumptious. Only one man in a thousand is a leader of men, the other 999 follow women. He is not true to himself. So he cannot be true to others. Theocracy in Pakistan is a divine lie, the judiciary the human lie and the military rule in Pakistan a half lie, with a heart of adamant and a sceptre of iron. And the net contribution of military rule in Pakistan to the outcome is obscurantism, distrust and retardation at every point where it touches the fortunes of Pakistan and of Kashmiri Muslims. The makers of Kashmir issue today are condemned as injudicious or corrupt. With pretended patriotism, they are basically impostures. Truly speaking, the people of India and Pakistan have been pillaged by the greedy cupidity of a privileged class. Don't reason with them.

Kings and rulers are always important people ... at any rate to themselves.

But in countries where democracy is but little known, where politics, fanaticism and personalities are practically synonymous, where the king or the ruler is of lineal descent from the most ancient and holy of families venerated by millions in the lands of the prophet or the dictator; then his words must be heard understood, for he speaks with the voice of history. Mr. Liaquat Ali Khan, Prime Minister of Pakistan, once said in Sept 12, 1950," Pakistan would never rest until she succeeded in securing for Kashmir Muslims the opportunity of deciding their fate independently and freely." Even after sixty years of independence, this funereal but frightening picture still exists in the voice of stratocratic rulers in Pakistan. In the mountains of lies, Pakistan's searching for truth is guilty of a kind of treachery after the imposition of terrorism. It is a constant stimulus to suspicion and ill-will.

With the pre-occupation of the Govt. with political issues and the problems like Kashmir issue created by the partition of the country, there was little nation-building activity. Whatever was undertaken had borne little fruit. Why? Because of the character of the bureaucratic administrative machine and of the pseudo-secularists. Nehru himself was not quite happy over the term 'secular state' and fetishism of secularism is a history of repeated injuries worm-eaten by the political insects to secure a mileage over a particular community. This administrative machine was designed for a police state. It could not function effectively for a Welfare State. The fear of the foreign master gone; corruption, bribery, nepotism are on the increase. The promises made by Mr. Nehru and Co. remained unfulfilled. The result is nation-wide depression, and frustration not only in the valley but in other areas of India. Bereft of this, Nehru could not effectively perform his action in Kashmir or influence public oppinion. According to the Bhagawad Gita, "Those who seek to enjoy the fruits of their work are verily unhappy because one has no control over the results." Everything has risen from nothing.

After independence, ominous signs had appeared in the valley. These were causing uneasiness among thoughful congress leaders. The threat was more dangerous as it came from some of the trusted Muslim leaders in Kashmir. The masses in the valley have ever been steeped in poverty and ignorance. And the Congress organisation at the centre was transformed into a totalitarian organisation entirely in the hands of a clique with a powerful person behind the Kashmir issue, speaking in a deceptive manner.

If democracy is throttled in the valley, with the help of administration, it would be dangerous for the centre to keep the valley normal. The ruling clique, backed by a powerful personality entrenched in the Nehru Govt., throttled all opposition first in the organisation and then in the country. To talk of neutrality is to deceive oneself. A conspiracy of circumstances may enable to maintain stranglehold in the valley for some time despite its revenge, and no consistency can prevent the people from asserting themselves and having a Govt. which answers their needs. Because the longer the delay in the change after it has become due, the greater is the violence of terrorism with which it comes about.

Who misleads whom focuses public attention on a matter of Kashmir issue. The strange combination of heterogeneous political and religious forces which have for many years been using the student community as a catspaw for meeting their ends and means has succeeded in overruling the views of the reasonable sections of the student community in Kashmir. The tales the terrorists tell are all of the disaster to the people of India. The whole of the valley is in a ferment. The most dangerous 'SIMI' is in the hands of the militant groups and there are bands of armed infiltrators swaggering through the villages of Kashmir. Truly speaking, the valley has been deserted except for the kites and the crows and the scavenging pariah dogs, and a sickly-sweet stench of corruption, hypocrisy, and a sweet compromise with religious fanatics has hung over the valley in a cloud of conspiracy almost as tangible as the clouds of bleated flies that buzz above the dead. The noise outside the valley seems to come from very far away. Therefore half-deemed democracy in Kashmir remains silent, writhed and groaned in terror but New Delhi does not move. Because its mind is entirely blank. The innocent men, women and children hear dimly the crack of the riffle-fire, but they do not move. The Kashmiri villagers look wildly about them, jaws dropped and even staring in disbelief; the villagers have known the terrorists for several years but the habit of their obedience is strong. Because their eyes are cold and unpleasant and with the speed and violence of a thunderbolt of Islamic fanaticism, the smashed knee of our democracy is a painful thing.

The terrible clanking file of terrorists and religious fanatics have still marched away across the border in the merciless sunlight and summoning up their comrades with a clarion-call "Save Islam for Islamisation in the valley'. Is this justice? Hush! Nonsense! These fools need a sharp lesson. Their taunts and jeers have driven out the Kashmiri Hindu pundits from rage to a murderous frenzy. Pakistan's hysterical assertion over the Kashmir question is received with scandalized horror. The San Francisco Chronicle said in an introduction to an article headlined 'Friend or Foe' : "Washington hailed Musharraf as an ally in the war on terror, but critics make a case that Pakistani leader is a terrorist." Even Adrian Levy and Catherine Scott-Clark, co-authors of Pakistan's nuclear proliferation and her blackmailing other nations on the pretext of her war on terrorism in India, Afganistan and elsewhere, write : "He (Musharraf) has always given the impression that he and his troops west-leaning moderates. However, the real Musharraf is far more complicated and a good deal of the time we have paid the general to stand by us, he has been cosseting the forces that are bent on undermining the West." Such a plain-speaking statement of theirs makes Musharraf a 'thug', a 'sonofabitch', and now a 'terrorist'. The newspaper of three British journalists expelled from Pakistan has called Musharraf a 'sonofabitch'. *Truly speaking, Musharraf is an American-sponsored 'Gangster' who believes in gangsterism in the valley of Kashmir where the bodies of the dead and dying are littered with deep blood.* The heat of the valley rises until it becomes difficult to breathe. It is worse than civil war, rebellion and anarchy. Hey presto! what a thunderous explosion of Islamic terrorism where the darkness lies beyond the moonlight in the valley! The excited crowd of Kashmiri students gets used to staging a most unruly and indecent agitation. They only want the immediate fulfilment of the impossible and absurd demands. They are being used as a tool manoeuvring politicians who are only interested in undermining the structure of the valley. Even the jehadi groups take advantage of this gesture and use the opportunity to whip up disorderly demonstration abetted by the aberrant religious leaders.

The partition of India caused deep wounds in the political, economic and emotional life of the country. Passions are roused and many unfathomable problems have cropped up, leading to continuing tension and ill-will between India and Pakistan. That Kashmir is a breeding ground of ill-will and religious insolence. Delay in solving the problem has been a constant source of distress and frustration to a vast number of Kashmiri Hindu Pundits. Rudyard Kipling says : "If you can meet with triumph and disaster/And treat those two impostors just the same."

Dacca, now the capital of Bangladesh (East Pakistan), had initiated a virulent campaign for a 'war of liberation' in Kashmir on Sept. 20, 1950, aided and abetted by Jinnah's Muslim League and by the tacit approval of Pakistan Govt. A militant body of speakers repeatedly warned India with the saying : "The people of the entire Islamic world are determined to liberate Kashmir against any opposition that imperialist India may offer .... No mountain or river barriers can stand in the way of their march on Kashmir. In every crucial test of history, Muslim strength has won." Their speeches, even after sixty years of independence, are punctuated with vociferous but provocative slogans like 'nare-taqdir' and 'larkey lange Kashmir'. So the terrorist groups today have taken up arms for the liberation of Kashmir.

A serious ideological conflict has made its appearance in the ranks of leaders of militant Islamic organisations in Kashmir, and inspite of protestations of it all being a family quarrel. Unless the conflict is faced squarely and that soon, these organisations may disintegrate. It is a favourite saying that the sum of the parts of a whole does not constitute the whole. This is more than true of India, when one set of doctrinaire, power-mad people would devise salves of universal application and would thrust their pet foibles and fancies on the rest of the country, ignoring the fact that other ideologies, other cultures and other ways of life have flourished in India and achieved marvels which have not been dreamt of in all the philosophies of the Hindu culture.

Man is an animal physically and not a very different one from many others. He is structurally a rather generalized member of the order of mammals to which he belongs. His skeleton contains exactly the same number of bones as that of a gorilla or chimpanzee. Gen. Musharraf, an Idi Amin of Uganda, a Joseph Stalin of the Soviet Union and other arbitrary rulers, was lacking in the human brain. His brain is of the gorilla or chimpanzee. He is a disciple of terrorism. He, standing like a Chinese Wall, did not care anybody else on the way of his invincible but irretrievable character as a military ruler. He shares political apocalypse with the great Idi Amin or Stalin, or Hitler. The ghastly thing about Islamic fanatics at the dawn of this century is their ignorance. If they could be compelled by law to read ethics and philosophy at university level, before they were allowed to embark upon their hateful experiments ... if only we could be sure they had heard of a few people like Plato. They might be dissuaded from torturing Kafirs to death in the interests of their beastly discoveries. As a consequence of this first step, they may even go forward to suppressing their methods of destroying themselves. The two treacheries are bound together in the same attitude of recklessness, imprudent curiosity on the question of Kashmir issue.

Between pain and nausea, Gen. Musharraf's fate has indeed been kind to him. Pakistan is a land of surprises ... a dreamland of nightmares. The adventures of Gen. Musharraf and his predecessors, in the valley of Kashmir, read like the most uninhibited type of historical romance, culminating in a mock duel and an abduction behind the snow-covered mountains in the valley. His book 'In the line of fire' is a delightful exploration of one of the oddest and most romantic by-paths of the history of rulers' hypocrisy over the valley. After partition, the violence of Pakistan's language, sometimes of her conduct and the abuse that she hurls at New Delhi have left an ugly stain on her memory. Inspite of Musharraf's great services to religious fanaticism carrying Islamic organisations in the non-Islamic countries, we may coin a good word for him; we accuse him of rancorous insolence. Even his political virtue on the Kashmir question is in someway counterfeit. Pedant, bigot and brute as he is, he has got good qualities. He obeys, whatsoever U.S. dictates. He does whatever and whenever U.S. commands. At the command of Washington, the potential law-breakers and trouble-shooters are sent to prison. It has never happened in the history of Pakistan.

As a military ruler, in the whirlpools and hidden currents of jehadi slogans within the country, his name is hateful to all the realms of Islamic world he prides in. A more disorderly mind than that of any other rulers in Pakistan has been gifted with less power of analysing common words on the Indo-Pak agreements. But the very disorderliness is his strength and virtue in the shaping of an all-embracing religious fanaticism in the valley. The echoes of his mighty roaring shakes the throne to its foundations. He has lacked restraint and balance on the removal of Chief Justice of Pakistan, and accepted bewildering and unsympathetic comments in place of a recognisable portrait of democracy.

It is Nehru who alone of them all found a definite joy in abandoning the pain and delight of the dream of partition and for self-destructive action after the Kashmir issue to the Security Council. He positively revelled in conflicts of power both at the centre and in the valley; and he was at his best in fixing things and persons, basically political hangers on, around the peripheries of the various conflicts arisen in Kashmir, most of which he had created and witnessed the strange, colliding roles in electioneering campaign, either in

Kashmir or in the party. He was, in big things that failed in Kashmir issue, a good loser, but horribly spiteful and petty-minded over little failures on communal question or opposition. He was inordinately vain and a great showman of Kashmir politics ... the greatest show on earth ... and he did not fail to do his own turns in the ring. Mr. Jinnah was well aware of his passion and his ignorance of the Kashmir issue. Kashmir started shivering violently, looking down into the wide valley. It knows nothing of these men. At the sound of it the passionate spell broke and dissolved before the cold inrush of reality, shaking with rage and shame and the shock of a sudden revelation. It loses itself in the sound of the distant singing and flicks away into the shadows of political hypocrisy and religious fanaticism.

Why Kashmir? In 1949, Sheikh Abdullah initiated a series of land reforms. M.Brecher, in his book 'The Struggle for Kashmir', says in a comprehensive but reflective way of his thinking : "A century of dogra rule had resulted in the ownership of most of the 2,200,000 acres of cultivable land in the hands of a small class of landlords-chakdars. The owners were Hindu, the tillers Muslim. With the reforms, the maximum land holding was limited to 22.75 acres : the remainder was distributed among the peasantry. The vast majority of Kashmiris have benefited from these reforms and many of those interviewed expressed the fear that in Pakistan, where no comparable land reforms have taken place, the land given to them might be returned to the landlords ..." He continues, "Kashmiris are essentially pre-Kashmiris, not pre-India or Pre-Pakistan, and that this feeling is tied up with the universal admiration for Sheikh Abdullah and his programme for reform ... the overwhelming majority who have benefited from these social and economic reforms favour the continuation of the present pre-Indian Govt. of Jammu and Kashmir."

So the fact is that the Kashmiris have not yet opted for union with Pakistan. Why? Because the Islamic clerics in Pakistan are insensibly led into a dangerous no-man's-land. They are all employed by unscrupulous politicians to dupe the credulous. So Pakistan's policy over the Kashmiris and the Kashmir question, without moral judgements of any kind, is not only impossible but completely meaningless. And their incidental judgements on the making of agreements are those of hard-headed sceptics, whose staple theory is deliberately a political manipulation over the Kashmiris. To them, Islamabad is often opportunistic and courteous to terrorism and terrorists whose purpose is the settlement of class conflict between Hindu and Muslim, and between shia and sunni, through dictatorship. It appears to have always leaned heavily to the clerics and oligarchic side. To them, the delphic oracle of Islamic terrorism over them has now become the religion. Not only that the delphic utterances of Islamabad, with much of their speculative theory and plain crankiness are surely an impasse to the solution of Kashmir question. Though a thicket of misleading irrelevancies, Pakistan's often obscure and always oblique pronouncements have turned upside down all promising agreements and treaties. Several other fancies are fancies and nothing else.

To the Kashmiris, it was jinnah who faced death and absolved himself from the historical responsibility of having plunged his country into religious fanaticism by unconstitutional and fraudulent means. Whereas Nehru himself was often in a mood of panic without understanding what was happening in the valley. He warmed the very sickness in his heart. But the trick over the Kashmir question can well become an obsession, and the obsession can become involuntary and irreversible. The combination of mischief and carelessness has characterized Congress policy over the Kashmir issue. If you want to know what the foreign policy of the country will be in next twenty or thirty years, find out what the Dissenting minority are saying now. In other words, the outraged clamour of Dissenters has more than once provided foreign secretaries with an excuse for abandoning an embarrassing policy over the Kashmir question to which they were otherwise committed, or for adopting one which they know to be right but unacceptable to their orthodox supporters. This is true. Whereas, on the Kashmir issue, there is a great deal of what might be termed honest inaccuracy and genuine self-deception. New Delhi's main task thus becomes an analysis of the illusions of the political and military leaders of Pakistan. Our foreign policy makers have thought it better to keep us absolutely in the dark about what they are plotting about the rumblings of cold war or proxy war in the valley.

Not only in India, a time of strained and breaking loyalties all over the world ... in politics, nationalities, religions, moralities and families, and even in religious fanaticism ... is certainly a time of trouble. That secular religion which once to be the hope of half the world has equally become a delphic oracle and a prey to conflicts of loyalty, nationalism and morality or familiar nation-states are being hustled.

In this troublesome century, the byzantine complexes of secularism, communalism, sectarianism, provincialism and democracy amidst autocracy and dictatorship of some Islamic nations like Pakistan are the biggest challenge to the familiar ways. In this sub-continent, this century opens with established religions under the weather and the eyes of youth upon collectivism as the day-star of new millennium. What has happened in Pakistan is probably more than responsible than anything else for the deep disillusion and hopelessness in Kashmir, which have come to rule not only the hearts of communalism and heads of perennial hypocrisy in the valley. Saudi Arabia is the most coveted passport. Something never defined, possibly undefinable, but known as 'freedom' or 'the open society' or 'democracy' or 'secularism'.

To discover what is going on, not only in Kashmir but beyond this sub-continent, we need a thoroughgoing study of loyalties. We need to know what leads Pakistan and who lies behind the Kashmir problem, to rupture the secure, comforting the bonds of custom and familiarity, to cut themselves off from the group in which we have grown up. If tensions and disloyalties, treasons and treacheries explode on both sides of two rival countries — India and Pakistan

— what is going on, which is common to them?

What real threat, or what conjured fear, causes such an all-Indian psychosis? Mercurial, volatile and mass motivated Kashmir is in disarray. The most disturbing effect is the impression, they create, of utter dismay, almost of hysteria in the Indian press and public at a time, in party politics, and above all in the precincts of justice. The rot has gone far, to produce that neurosis in Congress and courts alike. Our real problem today, either in Kashmir or in other parts of India or Pakistan in any other parts of this world, is rather the millions, in our society, who are without loyalty to any ideology are apathetic and anesthetic. The citizenry in the valley will suffer a kind of schizophrenia on the other hand, as a human-natural-defence-mechanism, they will decry and debunk any form of social activity, for that would identify them with the powers-that-be and imply acquiescence in the various forms of deployment of those powers. Thus a sort of traitors or infiltrators in the name of terrorists arises; not very many real, political or military or religious traitors, but a vast number of non-citizens ... citizens of nothing, attaching no positive value what to their community and its administrative state, having no emotive affection for it, living as atoms in it, fulfilling the barest minimum of obligations to get by, and generally betraying an 'I couldn't careless' mood. This is the scenario as we see in the valley today. All human societies are in the same flux, controlled by the same tensions. The rulers at the centre perversely push their worst characteristics into a shop window. They do not follow others who understate, or keep things out of their windows.

Riveting all our attention to the valley, we, in and around Kashmir, are caugth in the social dilemma. If social tensions, predatory, party politics and frustrated minorities erode the social position of Islamic society in Pakistan what would make a modern Industrial society? That requires a leadership. What we singularly lack is leadership. Only very bonding material would be put in that place. So the Kashmir question has still been alive in world politics. Why? Because it is decently glossed and masked in practice as well as among other Europeans, Asians, and even Islamic nations.

The ageing ruler, like Gen. Musharraf, felt lonely because ... like Hitler ... he was incapable of friendship, and he trusted no one; like Hitler he sowed discord at home and abroad in order to retain power and to teach India a lesson on the Kashmir issue. Like Hitler, he branded all criticism as enmity. He had other faults besides. He was greedy and mean, often complaining that he was out and out mentally taxed in the midst of political wind, currents of religious fundamentalism and terrible tides of Kashmir issue. Everything had merely irritated him, inspite of the warnings of Washington. He says : "Elections alone do not mean democracy." In 60 years of independence, democracy in Pakistan lives up with dignity only for 25 years. Why? Because Pakistani rulers believe in the dictum : what rights you have and what rights you have not, the thoroughgoing forms of political-religious mysticisms have always ended in nemesis, in the attempt to achieve immunity from rational criticism of the social order by imposing a fraudulent rationality upon the Kashmir question. The dilemma remains, how to establish a reverence for prejudices by the use of reason, an instrument inimical to prejudice. If a man's digestion is out of order, it will not serve him to become rationally acquainted with the physical function which the digestion is supposed to perform. Islamic communities in Pakistan are kept together by exciting the affections for anti-India slogans, and affections are natural forces which reason can authorise or condemn, but which have their source outside reason. So the Kashmir question remains unsolved.

Gen. Musharraf becomes the sole master of the whole terrorist machine. This thrillerish monster is Gen. Musharraf. Opportunism and realism are very much the same thing, and both fail because they are based on the short-term insular view.

We have to sort out the problems for the making of Kashmir question. Since independence, Pakistan has suffered from some uncurable diseases like Militarism which plays a significant role in Pakistan. Millions of Pakistanis are in a state of military slavery and don't dare to be singular and let the administration sleep. According to Jug Suraiya, a well-reputed columnist, says, in Times of India Nov. 30, 2007: "The army plays an indispensable role in Pakistan not because of the perceived 'India threat' or internal revolt in the provinces. The army is an essential agency for maintaining the status quo in a society where only 2% of the population owns over 90% of all national assets, including land. (Both Benazir and Sharif belong to this exploitative and currupt feudal elite. This means that there is virtually no real middle class in Pakistan, and as a result or a concomitant civil society worth the name. Both these are necessary for a true democracy to flourish. And both these are conspicuously lacking in Pakistan, particularly as compared with India." Pakistan has burst out the orthodox bounds of 'Islamic dream' in Kashmir when Pakistan overcomes her fear of a satanic fall by plunging Islam into the abyss, and she has developed from the means of appropriating for man the god-like power over the one risk hitherto in esoteric and exoteric religion. That once exercises, Pakistan's dream would be for ever vindicated as the mystical vision of a satanic messiah. Even Jinnah hid behind the self-depreciating pose of the inveterate dreamer. The creation of Pakistan was a deliberate piece of Machiavellian planning to weaken India. The British statement of policy in 1942 played unnecessarily into Jinnah's hands. The Congress made mistakes which had exactly the same results. Partition in magnitude, significance and consequences, dwarfs any other episode of the second world war. Who are the exorcists of the partition and of Kashmir question? A question of half-empty or half-full.

Historically, the religion of nature has meant many different things. It has meant the notion that the created universe is a parable of the divine purpose, expressing spiritual truths in an outward and visible form. It has meant the recommendation as a form of religious discipline or as a psychological therapeutics of the humble observation of the mysteries of the natural universe. All these beliefs when put in religious terms imply a purposeful creation, and theology has always wrestled with the problem of reconciling this theory with the apparent purposelessness or malignity of many of the forms of nature. The problem is that God has allowed the whole of nature to be infected by human sin. But to the non-theological mind of Islamic priesthood the margin left by such theories does not seem to be wide enough to compromise all those phenomena which cannot be properly included in the category of things bright and beautiful. So the religious fanaticism has silenced the critical intellect. And no therapeutic dose can be applicable thereagainst.

If the country like Pakistan is at one and the same time getting to be regarded as an instrument of immorality, and functioning in such a way as to weaken all the natural bonds of Islamic World, it is not surprising that the Islamic Society would display the symptoms of disruption as we see inside Pakistan as well as Kashmir. Politicians, limited as they are, can, for a start, look at the people they are governing and find about a little about them. They will find them not quite so different from their grandfathers as the conventions of Islamic classes suppose them to be. They find, no doubt, many real sources of social and political tensions and upheavals, which it is prudent to respect and to fear, but they will also have found many ghosts.

Anxiety and consternation have swept over India when Mrs. Indira Gandhi, former Prime Minister of India, died and the fears about Pakistan's sponsored-terrorism sound unbelievable to us. Why? Because Pakistan has been accused not merely of an extravagance but of terrible designs. One rumour was that Pakistan had threatened the streets of the valley would run with a cesspool of blood. Pakistan's love letters of peace-making mission over the valley are an important ingredient in this ectoplasmic synthesis, being taken verbatim into some of her works on Indo-Pak agreements. It is out and out insulting to the Kashmir question. If you can't ignore an insult, top it; if you can't top it, laugh it off; if you can't laugh it off, it's probably deserved. Promise not to destroy Pakistan but to send her back to religious fanaticism. Gen Musharraf really was something of a perverted military ruler, shaping all that surrounded him to his own needs, and mastering creditors of terrorism. The language of jehadi slogans, weapons, machines, politicians, with a singlemindedness and self-confidence that never failed. He has lived up to his pretensions in Kargil War.

The contrast between the rapacity of terrorism and religion over the valley is the central theme of Pakistan's foreign policy. The good are so good, the wicked so dependable in their wickedness. So a double patriot can be credited with twice the normal quantity of patriotic fervour. And it is with double patriots of fifth columnists in India whose activities have moulded the national policy of India on the Kashmir question through secret societies, Army pressure groups, and quasi-mystical propaganda during the last sixty years. Few leaders remain a wholly shadowy figure. The smouldering resentment of grinding poverty in the shadow of a great Kashmir question has blazed up at the signs of corruption and oppression of egoistic values within the forces of secularism which are now immeasurably stronger than they were in the old days. According to Chinese proverb : "He that takes medicine and neglects diet, wastes the skill of the physician." Watch your food of thought ... just watch it.

India is governed by a narrow but disunited oligarchy, susceptible to various pressures, especially from what is considered to be public opinion. The disgraceful advice on the Kashmir question is proferred by the timid elder statesmen, by the misguided leaders and by the selfish industrial magnets. This is India swinging between Kashmir question and Kashmir solution. So the Kashmir crisis remains unsolved.

The history of ways of looking at the history of Kashmir question has become an important part of contemporary historiography to which able historians have devoted much of their energies. The main task of the historian is to reveal the origins of his own ideas and preoccupations. History is more like psychoanalysis than it is like anatomy. Like many other military rulers in Pakistan, the present ruler, like a Machiavelli, is merely formulating what was already being practised in the valley which was, after all, an ego so paradoxical that Mr. Jinnah could become a main target of all Kashmir questions. The rules of Muslim behaviour had constantly been broken by earlier rulers, but the sinfulness of such a breach had up to them been regularly recognised. The makers of terrorism are doers not thinkers. They ruin away the great work of Islamic philosophy. And the intellectual world of Pakistan is a world, ignored by the orators, soldiers, murderers, fanatics, rascals, pseudo-prophets, of the great breaking of barriers. Islamic terrorism in Kashmir is an exterior event in history, as dramatic, as engmatic, but not part of Islamic tradition. Unforging and uncharitable, the Pakistani rulers have continued to assail all opponents to the views unrelenting hatred. All the supporters of Kashmiri Hindu pundits are denounced as liars and fools, braggarts and traitors of Muslim interests in the valley. All these fanatical hatreds can be attributed to a consuming love for Kashmir. The rulers fall foul of many former political friends who did not do their extremist attitude over the valley and alienate others by violence. And the Islamic clerics remain the idol and the oracle of successive generations of Pakistan. In deep water lies the truth of Islamic terrorism in the valley where men and women are not treated as individuals. The shackles are not gently being released.

What is the origin of the name Kashmir? According to A.P. Venkateswaran, "The origin of the name Kashmir can be traced to the ancient Indian sage, Kashyapa, who had founded the Kashyapa Gotra of the Hindus. In fact, Kashmir stands for Kashyapa Mir or the land of Kashyapa. When the Adi Shankaracharya travelled on foot three times around India, before he passed away at the very young age of 32 years, just as Christ also did, he had specially set up a shrine in Srinagar which stands there to this day for all to see." Now the question is : How can anyone make a serious claim on Kashmir on the plea that a majority of muslims live there? Such marginalised claim over Kashmir is a figure of fun, which hides Pakistan is in an embarrassing situation. Truly speaking, our so-called unrestrained but politically perverted rulers of Pakistan refuse to get through the Kashmir question with a fine-toothed comb. Now she is in the firing line of Machiavellian hypocrisy, and is found guilty of crime. Mr. Venkateswaran says : "Islam itself was founded by the prophet in the 7th century and had spread to other lands only much later." (A.P. Venkateswaran, The Tragedy of Kashmir, New Approach).

On October 26, 1947, the instrument of accession was signed in by the then Maharaja, Hari Singh, and was accepted by the Governor General of India. A personal demi official letter having the following important but significant words : "...it is my government's wish that, as soon as law and order have been restored in Kashmir and its soil cleared of the invader, the question of the state's accession should be settled by a reference to the people ..." was given to Maharaja Hari Singh by the then Governor General, Lord Mountbatten.

The following two statements have got a far-reaching effect on the question of a common Governor General of both India and Pakistan.

In the words of Prof. Khan Zaman Mirza, Institute of Kashmir Studies in Muzaffarabad : "It is clear from the overall conduct of Lord Mountbatten that, had the Muslim League accepted him as the common Governor General of both Hindustan and Pakistan, it would surely have signed the death warrant of an Independent State of Pakistan even before it had come into existence on 14th August, 1947 and would have resulted in some sort of confederation." Mr. Mirza did not mention any word of 'partition'. in his statement.

Whereas, a devious design of 'Partition Plan' has been cited on June 3, 1947, by the All India Congress Committee resolution of June 14, 1947. And the Declaration of the Committee is : "Geography and mountains and the seas fashioned India as she is, and no human agency can change the shape or come in the way of her final destiny. Economic circumstances and the insistent demands of international affairs make the unity of India still more necessary. The picture of India we have learnt to cherish will remain in our minds and heart."

Truly, we live in a strange period when unknown politicians become known. On the other hand, many a famous politician is unknown because countless flash-in-the-pan reputations distort our scale of values not only in the valley but all over India. This is a dilemma that transcends the crude division of society into East and West, and is far more serious than any mere failure or neglect of terrorism. It is the freebooters on the flanks, those wild and solitary raiders, who are in danger of critical crisis. The genuine outsider is all too hastily hauled inside.

Failure in Kashmir solution is a formidable argument against a policy ; again, it is not a decisive argument; a failure may be merely apparent, a disaster may be an inevitable part of the process by which Kashmir question is driving Pakistan to a knowledge of where their peace lies. Pakistan hankers after a hypothetical gain.

The echoes of fanatics' mighty roaring shake the non-Islamic throne to its foundations. But there lies real passion of democracy and its ultimate integrity. Whereas Islamic countries much regimented to their ideologies have accepted unsympathetic and confused comments in place of a recognisable and rounded portrait of healthy society. Because they are and have always been irrational. and full of faults.

The Rule of Law is a natural phenomenon. Men are inhibited from doing certain things, and offened when such things are done by reason of shared feelings as to what is right and proper upon these feelings, the content of which changes over time but the nature of which is unchanging, rests the possibility of social cooperation. The actions of individuals in Kashmir, puny or powerful, the decisions of those in office, and enacted laws by themselves, are subjected to these deep-lying convictions. That such convictions should be held strongly in Kashmir, and that they should be shared, constitutes the essence of the Rule of Law in the valley, which is actualised by the expression of moral approval or disapproval. This is certainly no new idea : it is perhaps the oldest of political ideas. But the problems in Kashmir are of extreme urgency. How can it be resolved?

Campaign of Islamic terrorism in Kashmir is without purpose. It can be argued that the Islamic dictatorship in Pakistan has evolved — and perhaps still involves — an unacceptable and intolerable subordination of means to end, a tragic sacrifice of the tangible present to a remote and unattainable future. People living in Pakistan are in comfortably organised liberal Islamic societies and find it natural to condemn fanaticism in pursuit of ends as one of the roots of evil not only for the Kashmir question but for this sub-continent also. Islamic terrorism is an epitaph of world Islamic philosophy. So, what Pakistan has done so far a nationalist brand of authoritarianism has made Pakistan what Hitler developed in Germany. It is a predestined liability to disaster.

Our sullen and ill-tempered politicians, preoccupied with moronism, have got a natural habit of compiling dictionaries or encyclopedias of political terms which serve as vehicles for the propagation of their ideas. And their ideas have made the Kashmir question more and more critical. Almost all really new ideas have a certain aspect of foolishness when they cannot be forgiven. It is called hypocrisy. The only foes that threaten India on the Kashmir question are the enemies at home. They are all indistinguishable in spirit from the practices of gangsterism. Who are they behind the curtain? So the Kashmir issue remains unsolved. Political wretchedness and unremunerative toil of relgious fanaticism are mingled with Kashmir question. They are not sufficient in number. They perjure themselves, cheat, steal and mislead the Kashmiri people.

A statesman must see that his suppliants are seated near the door so that they may be disposed of with the least possible embarrassment ; but a statesman must also discipline himself with as much rigour as a priest against the corrupting and enervating effects of anger, and remember always that his power is grounded in humility. In India, they are all lacking in their qualities.

Why the Kashmir question has not yet remained solved. Because, in India , a politician's mind is still in part formed by those inmates with whom he converses in his leisure hours; it is not cynicism but common sense to urge him to choose them with discretion and with a proper regard for the profit, in the largest meaning of the Kashmir issue, to be derived from their companionship. On peace-making process in Kashmir, the statesman cannot dispense with the science of pleasing, and his usefulness and honesty are injured when convention requires him to pretend that he can. Today hypocrisy of political leaders around Kashmir surrounds public life. Ordinarily this hypocrisy arises not from the need to conceal base policy and political behaviour but from the attempt to impose on politics naive and inappropriate standards a mass electorate can easily comprehend. In Indian communities whose affairs are arranged by discussion a statesman's role is to rule by pleasing. And the image of the incorruptible patriot cannot be deflected from his course by fear or favour. If the Kashmir valley is so satisfying, why try to lure down old friend or old enemy ... anybody for the sake of the friendly face? A more or less familiar odor permeates the whole Kashmir valley.

The habitual mistake of Indian democratic leaders on the Kashmir question is to underestimate the power of the enemy and to overestimate their own strength on the comfortable assumption that freedom or superior productive power, or a bigger stockpile of nuclear missiles, is bound to win. In this situation, multiplying evidences of trouble will point to serious internal strains within India. Symptoms of widespread 'unreliability' within the ruling party will drive the satellite Govt. to extremes of repression. These symptoms must worry and exasperate New Delhi.

There is another avalanche, starting along the Pak-Afganistan border. It is only a snowball, launched in other provinces of Pakistan with malice afore-thought, but it will descend upon us soon — tons and tons of it. There are some millions of guillible and misguided Muslims who do not see that they are getting into an Islamic garden of terrorism and Bonapartism. Between dogs and babies the choice is easy.

The trickery game of turning down all agreements on Kashmir solution is mystical. The United States has spent more than $ billions in a largely failed effort to bolster the Pakistani military against Al Quaida and the Taliban. The Bush administration and military officials believed that much of the US money was not making its way to frontline Pakistani units. Money has been diverted to help finance weapons systems designed to counter India, not Al Quaida or Taliban. The US has paid millions of dollars in inflated Pakistani reimbursement claims for that ammunition and other costs. The 5 billion dollar is provided through a programme known as *Coalition Support Funds* which reimburses Pakistan for conducting military operations to fight terrorism. Under a separate arrangement, *Pakistan receives 300 million dollar per year in traditional US military financing that pays for equipment and training*. The US must be aware of its aid. Cowardice is not synonymous with prudence. It often happens that the better part of discretion is valour.

On the Kashmir question, Pakistan has always been a good boss of terrorism and a good servant of jehadi groups but a bad master. Why? Because the military ruler need not learn anything from the West how to stop terrorism. Gen. Musharraf said : "... don't teach me...". He told it in a wide-ranging interview with the 'canadian Globe and Mail' on May 23, 2007. He said : "The uniform is part of my skin." On the same day, the New York Times in its blistering editorial observed," Washington is afraid, and entirely, not without reason, that nuclear armed Pakistan's next ruler could be even worse." Beast knows beast.

Pakistan may be termed as "Hamlet of Asia". This portrays an exasperation because Pakistan in particular and Asia in general refusee to view her Asiatic policy from her perspective. In these critical hours, resurgent Asia is in no mood to be tied to the apron-strings of any foreign country. Asia desires that foreign intervention in this Continent should be strictly limited to helping Asian countries in tackling various problems like militant terrorism, the inconsistent policies pursued by USA are responsible for provoking so much Asian resentment at their actions. Now the war clouds have engulfed the sky everywhere and drums of terrorism are being heard near our country. The mind that is cheerful at present will have no solicitude for the future, and will meet the bitter occurrences of life with a smile. "There is a disease", wrote Berbard Shaw many years ago, "to which plays as well as men become liable with advancing years. In men, it is called doting, in plays dating." Judging from this point of view, Pakistan has raised the Kashmir drama to new heights and opportunism, even if characteristically enough she chooses to express herself almost entirely through comedy of blunders. Most of the rulers are national-born mountebanks. What a gallery of characters Pakistan has directed so far in Kashmir drama with a variety of themes and political hyperboles. She wears masks in this drama of masquerade. In the preface of partition, her purpose as a playwright is to put Kashmiri Muslims right when it sees that they are going wrong. Her buffonery is rarely near tears but always close to laughter. She has already broken many idols with the impact of her Islamic ideas in Kashmir. Time defeats the strongest. In this highly competitive world, Kashmir has always to be in the lead or Pakistan has no future. Moral leadership is important : it cannot be all-sufficing. There must be strength as well. And if there is one lesson, the pressure of terrorism on this sub-continent has taught us that military strength of Pakistan is a broken-reed without U.S. dollars. Most people in Pakistan and other Arab countries lead a dull life of political slavery just as under the ancient despotisms of Asia. Terrorists daily defile the beauty of Islam that surrounds him and makes vulgar the tragedy. To get at everything hammer and tongs with back-channel diplomacy.

The Pakistani rulers are so anxious to expose the distortions of Kashmir issue, its subservience to political propaganda, that they all into the very errors they denounce. The authors of religious extremism oversimplify their task by lumping together popular pot-boilers, political propagandists' pamphlets and articles from encyclopedias and from the daily press.

We need clarity more than heat, and judgement more than polemical advocacy masquerading in the robes of justice. Rob Islam to terrorism for Pakistan.

Every remark of M.A. Jinnah on Kashmir issue is cheap; so probably inaccurate that it must throw suspicion on the whole argument. Imperialism is stated to be morally disreputable, purely selfish in motive, purely evil in its results. Nehru's policy on Kashmir question has been just shabby, deceitful, cowardly and vindictive. Mr. Jinnah is a ruthless and crude imperialist on Kashmir issue. Gen. Ayub Khan and Z.A. Bhutto are metamorphosed into good democrats under the guise of reaching a fair judgement on Kashmir. Gen. Musharraf is a terrorist, perjuring himself while straining the truth. *What Jinnah says is perfidious; what Nehru and Gandhi say is insincere and diplomatic illness*. They can never be content with enough. Someone ought to study why the political cartoon can be so much more persuasive than the political pamphlet.

If you are angry and sore, your tone is likely to become malicious and sour, and then your case may go by default. This ends by destroying all emphasis whatsoever and the result is muddle. Muckraking can indeed afford entertainment sometimes. There are gradations between the intention to deceive and unwillingness to be misunderstood. What seems virtuous in one's own good cause tends to seem venal in another's mouth.

The illusory self-righteousness of Pakistan quickens the sense of grievance that all other Islamic countries are being assailed by the persistent efforts of other political bag of tricks. Because Pakistan's formula on Kashmir is theoretically mistaken and politically harmful. Quite evidently, she has been having a long argument on the Kashmir issue with other religious leaders. If wrinkles must be written upon our brows, let them not be written upon the heart. Pakistan-sponsored Jehadi groups theoretically have much lesser powers than in the old days. In practice, they usually remain far higher than their theoretical status, and if it were undermined the whole system would be impaired or collapse. Pakistani leaders elsewhere have recognised that help and guidance of fanatical crusaders need to be continued. There is a double fallacy in such a thinking. The great Qur'an says : "The life of the world is but play and diversion and pageantry, and boasting among you, and rivalry in wealth and children; as the likeness of vegetation after rain, the growth whereof dumbfounds the sowers ..." (Lvii.20).

On the Kashmir question, Pakistan is more duped than her neighbours by her own nature. Her religious vanity and political romanticism are all her vanity. Tolerance is above all a rational value. It demands intelligence and discrimination in its exercise. If the obituary notices of a headmaster recall that he was intolerant of slackness in his pupils, we applaud; but if we read of a military General like Gen. Musharraf that he is a broad-minded man who tolerates a form of legalised terrorism, they are scandalised. Pakistan is used to singing out a song with the *jehadis* in Kashmir,' I can't tell why I love you, but I do' may savour of convincing sycophancy. But what song is a judge most likely to sing? The nation is now slowly beginning to divide vertically rather than horizontally. Mrs. Indira Gandhi was a great lady who had never felt fear on the question of Bangladesh liberation. This superlative lady was playing a part like the rest of us. There were many men who walked in purgatory in the war and yet contrived a mask so that they were accepted as imperturbable and were given the Govt. of their kind. Her courageous stand on Kashmir issue was a thought-out thing, that she had attained a peak of control which is beyond our reach. She was ninety percent fearless and only ten percent courageous. Her threshold was so high that she appeared to be insensitive to danger against the U.S. backed Pakistan aggression in East Pakistan (now Bangladesh) and passed for a time as men who did not know what fear was. No man can go on for ever in modern war. Sooner or later all men feel fear.

The sequel is not happy for Z.A. Bhutto. Mr. Bhutto, it seems, while not regretting his decision, then lives hidden, in fear of his life, a nervous invalid. He tasted the traditional pleasure of U.S. support like a homicidal maniac. The idea of Pakistan's policy on Kashmir has now lost its glamour, forfeited a nation's honour, and risked an Islamic country's reputation. Gen. Musharraf : He has also felt and thought no shame, made himself cheap to the world, while dragging through the mire of terrorism in Kashmir and bringing shame upon Pakistan. Men who seize power are effectively more intolerant and ferocious than men who inherit power. Powerful intellects as well as generous hearts are often fired by hopes all desperately mediocre. The governing class, however, had been deservedly scared, reacted with a reign of terror and mortal trepidation, but not with liberation of Bangladesh, fault-finding and hypercritical. They are combined with the spirit of unclassified thoughts, with a vast pleasure in doing small things perfectly. They are accompanied by reactionary superstitions and romantic custodians of Kashmir mystry, looking with hostility and contempt upon the patient work of India in the valley. Their quirks and mannerisms, their captious subtleties and teasing tricks, their cunning but often abstruse puns are at their best as intriguing and conspiratorial as the solution of a difficult crossword clue. Public feeling seems to be exploding in a climax of resentment against Pakistan. It is gentlemen's disagreement. Partition makes Pakistan, politics makes religious extremism.

A mob can be a dictator, if it is unrestrained and unashamed, as well as — or rather as ill as — Hitler.

A gardener must not be slothful and work-shy but full of zeal continuously. Pakistan does not like gardening in the valley, but she makes the gardens of terrorism. And she strongly suspects she is not alone in this pleasure ground. That others conceal in a corner of the toolshed, a dark distaste for the whole pursuit. She murmurs rebelliously as she returns to the double-trenching of treachery for the religious wolfishness in the valley. Why this wolfishness? Because this is a great gain of Islamic fanatics, but nothing is more perilous than to think it is the whole of the truth. Relaxation of tension has dangers as well as benefits for the west. Whatever the Simla Agreement signifies militarily, it records no kind of truce in the battle of interests, policies and creeds across the Indo-Pak border. Certainly no one in India can be happy when drawing up a negative balance sheet of events and policies, during the last sixty years. A stubborn colonial dispute seems almost incapable of Kashmir solution. The threads to be unravelled are delicate and complex. Pakistan is now writhed with political atmosphere and vibrated with religious shivers; and whatever is done in Kashmir will make its impact felt elsewhere. The power of Islamabad rests more on the psychological influence of fanaticism than on constitutional instruments. The people of Pakistan will ultimately work out a synthesized way of life of their own. That at least is a consistent and intelligible line.

Islamabad is a tough customer. The prospect of being beaten by the Taliban-Al-Quaida gangsterism is certainly galling and mortifying; the part of Goliath is never an easy one and the younger the David the harder the part. Islamabad must not too obviously let David win for that is an insult and a piece of bad manners. Even to play a kindly cat and mouse with Pakistan is dangerous. Kill the boy if you can. But there is one thing Goliath like I.S.I. must never do; it must not scratch.

The ravages of factious provincialism, married up with an ill-conceived pursuit of parochialism and tribal interests, have already damaged the spirit and unification of Pakistan, sustained by truly Islamic principles of social justice. Why? Because a cardinal principle of Islam is in the indivisible unity of people, in their essential oneness and in their strong feeling of brotherhood.

All these ills, deplorable in themselves and especially on the eve of any conference on Kashmir issue, with a power that hides its own troubles behind a monolithic front of terrorist groups, may not be overcome with care and time. And there will be grave dangers in Pakistan in trying to impose a system of parliamentary democracy upon the solid ground of religious fanaticism still largely communal, sectional as well as Siachen outlook. According to Confucius : "Things that are done, it is needless to speak about."

New Delhi has always had a political schizophrenia on the Kashmir issue. Mr. Nehru has done a disservice in pinpointing the Kashmir issue that we Indians talk in terms of high ideals and act in a completely opposite way. Political evasions are the common shelter of the hard-headed, the false, and the impotent ideologies. In every country, there is always a wide gulf between theory and practice, but in India, in the name of diplomatic dualism, this gulf is abysmal not only due to political ignorance but also to our natural inclination intoxicated by high-flown words and sentiments over the Kashmir issue. To achieve any kind of progress in Kashmir, it is not enough to be armchair politicians and 'parlour priests' of political parties. Why? Political leaders and their ideologies are just like a relationship between a deceiving wife and her deceitful husband. No political leader can ever be noble who thinks meanly or contemptuously of himself, and no political thinkers can ever be noble that think first and only of themselves.

Political and economic discontent simmers in the territory controlled by Pakistan and even the preference of democratic administration has been given up. Islamabad now rules the territory with an iron hand, and loud protests are heard against 'Punjabi colonialism'. If an important duty of Asian national is to right the wrongs of the past, its first loyalty nevertheless is to the cause of Kashmir peace. Solutions by force will solve nothing and can lead to further bitterness and frustration. It is Asian nationalism which clamours for the early elimination of all pockets of colonialism that continues to survive.

The trouble goes farther than that. Bangladesh is a cold acquaintance, a lukewarm friend. Her speech dribbles from her in reluctant mono-syllables, mechanically uttered and stripped off all feelings. She is a soul filled with lurking suspicion and cultivated distrust. The burden of a staunch, give-and-take friendship is to heavy for India to bear. And so she lives on ...a stranger to human benevolence ... a slave to the reticence that carries her even further along the path of loneliness as Pakistan.

A great lie is a great fish on dry land; it may fret and fling, and make a frightful bother, but it cannot hurt you. You have only to keep still and it will die of itself. Truly speaking, it is not so important to know everything as to know the exact value of everything, to appreciate what we learn, and to arrange what we know. Boris Pasternak, Nobel Laureate, says in 'Doctor Zhivago, "Gregariousness is always the refuge of mediocrities .... only individuals seek the truth, and they shun those whose sole concern is not the truth." Religiously doctrinated bureaucratic administration in Pakistan has sown the seeds of a terror-ridden atmosphere in Kashmir where great individual thinkers may dwell in a general atmosphere of mental slavery. Despotism instead of liberation movement crushes individuality amongst the Kashmiri people. It only generates fear for one's life and chills the spine in a terror crazed atmosphere. Kashmir issue is not very complicated knot. It should not be a Pandemonium of common gossip and idle gossip.

Failure to agree in good faith does not remove the possibility of subsequent agreement over the Kashmir issue. Failure, however, in bad faith will once again close the door to future negotiations. If the danger of a war has receded considerably so has the prospect of genuine coexistence and so long as the latter is unachieved, the former will remain as a threatening possibility. The crucial points of difference are simply enough and need not be complicated by the various time-table proposals and counter-proposals.

God in his wisdom has ordained that man's ambition for wealth and power should vary directly in proportion to their stupidity. The greater a man's desire for money and power, the more foolish he is as a rule and vice versa. As things stand today, in India, it is unlimited. It is not wealth, nor ancestry, but honorable conduct and noble disposition that should make the demoralised leaders great to the Kashmir issue. The liberation movement of the Kashmiri Muslims to curtail freedom in thought and action of others, in ways, however subtle or honourable, is not at all liberation. The Buddhist tradition dating beyond Christianity has shown no religious intolerance. There has never been any religious crusade. Why Islamic crusade over the valley of Kashmir? They have exploited one another in the name of love and Islamic brotherhood. 'Freedom to proselytism' does not certainly include freedom to run down the religious and culture of this ancient land. Doing nothing is the most tiresome job in the world because you cannot stop and rest. Conversion of ignorant and poverty-ridden tribal or backward people to Christianity on a mass scale is open to objection on the very same grounds. Out of the desire to save the world arises the seeds of terrorism. This is a heartening spectacle, in the valley of Kashmir. Pakistan, on the Kashmir issue, is an infidel in a true sense of that word. It is the mark of a psychic disease. It is a satanic pride on the throne of terrorism. Climatically, culturally and historically, Pakistan has perhaps a stronger claim to be headquarters of Islamic terrorism. Even crusade in the valley is appallingly disconcerting. In political parleys, Pakistan is quite unwise to lay too much store by the religious statements and gestures of Islamic leaders. Ernest Hemingway, Nobel Laureate in literature, says in 'Notes on the Next War' : "The first panacea for a mismanaged nation is inflation of the currency ; the second is war. Both bring a temporary prosperity; both bring a permanent ruin. But both are the refuge of political and economic opportunists." For very often external appearances prove completely deceptive as a cog in the Islamic-sponsored machinery of terrorism in the valley. Like the most omnipotent villain, Pakistan fills up chronicles of villainous misleader.

The verb 'to nap' sounds like an etymological freak and 'caught napping' has almost a semblance of derogation. In this world of nerve-raking tensions, political napping on the Kashmir issue has almost a medico-religious value. There must be a crusade to highlight its merits. Religious sleeping in Kashmir looks, like a hardened state of inanimated exercise, almost a voluntary, painless torture. Theological grandmasters nap at the religious camps without being detected or chagrined by infiltrators, possibly in the manner of Pakistani sorcerers who can fall into a graduated trances at will. Political napping is a much refined quality of relaxing which is unmolested by Kashmir nightmares or rather daymares. If New Delhi sleeps with that idea, the sleep will not be sweet at all. And this Sub-Continent is to be converted into a human zoo. The amputation and amalgamation of States are bound to develop centrifugal tendencies. Conflicting loyalties and personal rivalries will arise. And Pakistan is a past master at the intricate art of political napping in the valley of Kashmir. He is a traitor who preaches the pernicious view. The world is groaning under the weight of blood and gore in Kashmir — a sullen ground of Roman Holidays.

Kashmir is undoubtedly India's best window to the outside world and its disintegration in any form will undoubtedly be undesirable and unfortunate as it will upset the whole structure of India. And Pakistan wastes her efforts in a maze of inconsistencies. The words that a father speaks to his children in the privacy of home are not heard by the world, but, as in whispering galleries, they are clearly heard at the end, and by posterity.

All experiences have shown that mankind is more disposed to suffer, while evils are sufferable, than to right themselves by abolishing the forms to which they are accustomed. Because power politics is certainly the game suited to Islamabad's cards. The reason they give for this attitude — of all things — is their conviction that they have some highly questionable motive up their political sleeve on the Kashmir issue. Such is the irony of Pakistan, and such is the paradox of her politics. Even the avowed champions of the multi-racial ideal among the Pakistanis on the Kashmir issue look upon the Indians as nothing more than a necessary evil. Strong brick makers are those who spurn their best straw.

Like energy and emotion, the commanding performance of Madrassa-based theology and the free-for-all are packing in seperate compartments. Charm is elusive enough to be felt but can neither be described nor easily borrowed. Its possessor keeps getting away with murder, the dull one not even with suicide. The charmer can smile and gush to order as well as freeze his victim with a look more penetrating than any observation that falls from his lips during stolen moments freed from captivity. We know that a cat does not look at the world in the same way as a shrimp. It has different eyes. But does New Delhi see the Kashmir issue in a different way from an American or a Chinese or a Pakistani? Is it possible to disentangle the personal element in her vision from what is Indian and what is alien?

Pakistan's stock-in-trade in Kashmir is charm, and she can switch it on and off with greater ease than a flash-bulb.

Like a trade union, the Pakistani show business of terrorism in the valley of Kashmir has its own conventions and unwritten code. Any false sense of shame has no place in the show business, for the halo and its reflection can be easily confused. When the sun rises, the sunset is forgotten. Sunshine can never compete with moonshine, when moonglow itself is pursued by glow-womb.

Political idleness is the gate of all harms. Pakistan, a nation of idle nationalism, is like a house that has no walls; the devils may enter on everyside. Why? Because quarrels would never last long if the fault was only on one side.

Those who imagine that silence between friends is not calculated to the growth of their friendship are indeed mistaken. Silence suggests sympathy, genuine understanding, latent power. This is without doubt the best variety of friendship — friendship based strictly on waving terms. Best, most enduring, and endurable. Here in Kashmir, small indeed are the chances of friction, of misunderstanding, of a break. For it is speech that is to blame for the breaking of most friendship in between India and Pakistan. When a word is spoken, there is no going back. There is no return, no second chance. India or Pakistan cannot call back the spoken word or the accomplished deed any more than him who is dead.

Indo-Pak friendship will blossom and flower into a poem of peace in Kashmir which is to be welcomed however mixed the metaphor. Friendship only spreads fertility over the barren landscape and bids the choicest fruits and flowers spring up and flourish in the valley of political thorns and religious briers. Kashmir overburdened by many seemingly insoluble problems has been afflicted by another. Size is not grandeur, and territory does not make a nation.

Pakistan is quite bereft of realism and stark practicability. Idealism and realism are the two great forces moulding human progress, and real progress in Kashmir is made possible by the proper mixture of these two important ingredients. The soundest nations have realism and idealism mixed in proper proportions. A nation like Pakistan should have high ideals but should at the same time be practical minded, otherwise she will bump her head against the stone-wall of reality and harm herself. Success produces confidence; confidence relaxes industry and negligence ruins the reputation of an Islamic nation like Pakistan.

Laughter of Pakistan-sponsored Islamic terrorists in Kashmir is Pakistan's most characteristic function as an Islamic nation. The Jackass and the hyena are known to be capable of noises uncomfortably similar to those of Pakistan-sponsored militant groups. The laughter of Islamabad is the glee of the very devil; that of others is a gross and fleshly snicker; that of still other jehadis is a goat like inanity. Laughter of our leaders is the perfection of inanity ... an outward and visible sign of an inward, spiritual void, nothing reacting to nothing. Dictators rarely laugh. Jinnah strongly disapproved of laughter. Some estimable politcians of Kashmir, from the time of has beens, react death-rattle. Some parliamentarians hava a sibilant laughter ; others cluck; pseudo-secularists croak like as raven; other double-dyed secularists gurgle; there are gobbling laughters among the communalists. There are sniggering laughters among the communists at someone's mistakes.

Laughers, who simmer and simper in the cabinet, have two distinct operations. Some neigh like horses, or grunt like pigs as ISI does, snuffle like asthmatics. Laughter of bureaucrats also may have inwardness; it may be sinister, naughty, bibulous, satirical, bilious, hectic, simian, hysterical, abandoned, profane, exalted, Rabelaisian, Homeric or Shavian. There are tittering laughters among the people having been nervous about the terrorists invited.

The self-centred politicians laugh seldom, for, once again, egoism is a kind of insanity. Nehru suffered from this egoism. Why? Because Nehru's systematic selfishness of being a leader and self-opinionatedness on Kashmir has centered entirely upon his own interests or feelings. Such egregious blunder is as shocking as outstandingly bad. His copious outpourings of unrestrained flow of praise on China is shamelessly insolent, giving off bubbles of his self-delusion. And a frightening silence overshadows the valley. His China visit was a Himalayan blunder. Because he suffered from self-delusion. The laughter of religious fanatic all around the valley is preter-naturally serious, for the same reason.

Laughter of Gandhi had undiluted contempt for gestures. The stupidest usually laugh with the least discrimination especially when they are in a crowd. Partition to Gandhi was always simple like a dream wish or a curse or laugh tinged with irony. But he received thunderous applause. The arrogant man has everything to lose; for arrogance has always to deal with envy. And Kashmir involves in the agony of those who frame policies or those who are its victims by our leaders' ignominious and disastrous failures. Policies have to be firm and enduring, but statesmanship is usually bankrupt. An effective and coherent opposition in a faction-ridden Kashmir is unimaginable without a fusion of ideologies. Patriots are born fifth, columnists are made. The latter walk in the night, changing a dozen of political shirts.

Opportunity and merit have their incentives and rewards for Kashmir solution.

Do you know the vast majority of mankind wants peace for selfish reasons? Do you know peace becomes a prostituted word? Who will solve the Kashmir issue?

If we distinguish between Indian political leaders and the Indian animal, we see the Indian animal has proved to be a more reliable than our leaders.

Our leaders are inferior to domestic servants. Both of their efficiency is a rare quality in the class of people. Both are shabby in manner, slothful in taking decision, cantankerous while talking to others, gluttonous and are given to thivery. The worst about them is that they can't be found at the time of need. Both exploit each other as they can — the former the householders and the latter the people. Without domestic servants, the middle class families are inactive. And without middle-class families' support, our leaders can't win over the election. The domestic servants have self-respect, whereas our leaders don't have. The former are accountable to the house-holders, but our leaders not to the people. Both of them don't believe in age of retirement.

No difference between the rabbit and our leaders. The rabbit has a charming face. Its private life is a disgrace. Most of our leaders belong to disgraceful rabbit class of society.

14

Pakistan And History of Terrorism : Well-fed Romanticism of Fanaticism

Do people love truth? Do they love justice for themselves? Do they love peace wandering amid the phantoms in a sacred channel of life?

In the shark-filled waters of crime in which Pakistan swims, only terrorists are more intimidating. The days of liberty and science in Pakistan succeed to the gloomy night of ignorance and Despotism where the legislators have already resigned their functions to ecclesiastical powers and their perogatives to Islamic priests. Terrorism is like a scorpion that will finally sting itself to death. Why? Because a horde of political knaves rules Islamabad. A treacherous phantom rules the valley of Kashmir in the name of religion. Handshake still goes on for a definite agreement, through a vicious circle.

On September 13, 1993, President Bill Clinton stood between Israeli Prime Minister Yitzha Rabin and PLO Chairman, Yasir Arafat. The two long-standing foreign foes had just signed an agreement at the White House to end a generation of violence and bloodshed in the Middle East. The question in everybody's mind : Would Rabin shake Arafat's hand? Hand-Shake! Only a small part of a much layer problem. A histrionic show of grief.

Three thousand spectators waited in suspence on the White House lawn, with a great anxiety. Around the globe, millions were riveted to their TVs. Both the rival leaders were keeping a sharp eye on each other. Anxiety dotted about the viewers. Rabin paused for a split second before extending his hand to his longtime adversary. He was noticeably uncomfortable, but managed a small smile as the crowd roared its approval.

Hand-shakes in the world of politics are a mixture of cold-war and warmongerism full of sharp practice and craftiness. Clinton's high-stakes political theatre had gone well. A 25 year old fanatic Yigal Amir, was outraged that the two leaders had shaken hands. On November 4, 1995, Amir assassinated Rabin. The New York Times carried the headline "With a Handshake, Rabin's Fate Was Sealed." In India, parliament is the dreadful war-club, while proposal of hand-shake going on.

From Nehru down to the present ruler, hundreds and thousands of deceitful but flattering handshakes have so far played a deep game through our slippery border. It is the easiest of gestures. The headlines of handshakes tell the news of peace in Kashmir. The pictures of handshakes tell the news of friendship between India and Pakistan behind the curtain of cross-border terrorism. The subheads and subtitles tell the news of the fear of death in the valley, which is worse than all the rest. The devil's allies are the neutral men in and outside the border, under a cultural exchange programme. Skulls and crossbones mark a warning of danger.

Handshakes over the Kashmir issue are to grant Islamic terrorism to sow the Dragon's teeth. The outbreak of terrorism will bring no peace to the valley. It will, on the other hand, intensify discord by balancing the opposition forces and stocking unhealthy political rivarly. Artificially generating tension and distrust between the communities as the politicians are now busy in doing in the valley is, however, hardly the way to harmonious progress. Smacks of communal are to sin against the secular constitution. The greatest of faults is to be conscious of none. Savage border raids and reprisals in the valley are the first fruits of what must be described as a deliberate attempt by Pakistan to ferment hostilities and suspicions between India and Pakistan. The Western powers themselves have been guilty in the past of an arms traffic to Pakistan that could hardly be conducive to peace and stability in Kashmir. Pakistan-sponsored terrorist activities are creatures of habit. Why do the wicked always form groups, whereas the righteous do not? Because the wicked, walking in darkness, need company, but the righteous, who live in light, do not fear being alone. Pakistan's night of ignorance comes with quickened pace, to a satirical sketch.

Pakistan-sponsored terror vending machines want more blood, more shame and more brutalities not only in Kashmir but in other parts of India.

LASKHKAR-E-TAIBA :–

Origin : Formed in 1990 in Afganistan, Let's 'Political' wing Jama' at-ud-Da' awa is based at Muridke near Lahore. Prof. Hafiz Mohammad Saeed is the organisation's Amir.

Agenda : Restoration of 'Islamic rule' over all of India and union of all

Muslim majority regions surrounding Pakistan. Active in Jammu and Kashmir and elsewhere is biggest terror outfit in India.

Followers : Comprises cadres mostly from Pakistan and Afganistan. Sprinkling from Sudan, Bahrain, Central Asia. Funded, armed and trained by ISI. Has a little over 750 cadres in Jammu and Kashmir.

Areas of operation : Active in Jammu and Kashmir. It has carried out attacks in New Delhi, Mumbai, Banglore, Hyderabad, Varanasi, Kolkata, Gujrat. It has a network of sleeper cells, links with several Islamic extremist organisations. Works at the instance of ISI to expand frontier of violence. Has training camps across Pakistan and POK in Muzaffarabad, Lahore, Peshwar, Islamabad, Rawalpindi, Karachi, Multan and Quetta.

Training : Churns out both militant cadres and Ulema. The outfit collects donations from Pakistanis in middle east and UK, Islamic NGOs. It receives financial, material and other assistance from ISI.

Characteristics : No personal humility or even love of the true.

JAISH-E-MOHAMMAD

Origin : JEM has been formed, controlled and manned by Pakistan. Launched on January 31, 2000 by Mohammad Masood Azhar in Karachi after his release during hijacking of IA Flight IC 814. Assisted by ISI, Taliban osama bin Laden.

Followers : Mostly drawn from Pakistan and Afganistan. Links with fraternal Islamic outfits in Iraq, Central Asia and Phillipines. It also has links with Indian outfits like SIMI. Known to cooperate with Let and HUJI and Sunni terrorist outfits in Pakistan.

Agenda : Use of force to secure withdrawal of Indian security forces from J & K. Its offices in Pakistan serve as schools of Jihad. Speaking after his release, Masood Azhar said JeM would not only 'liberate' Kashmir, but also wrest Babri Masjid in Ayodhya, Amritsar and Delhi.

Area of Operation : Jaish has often confined its operations to J & K. However, several of its cadre have been arrested or killed by security forces in states other than J & K. It has launched joint operations with LeT.

Training : Specialists in attacking security camps dressed in army fatigues, though shoes are usually a giveway. Use suicide bombers without compunction, its cadre was behind attack on Pakistan President Pervez Musharraf. Cadre trained in internet use has arms training in camps in Pakistan and POK.

Characteristics : Errors and exaggerations do not matter. What matters are boldness in thinking with a strong pitched voice of extremism. Under any pretext kill his fellow man. Truth on the Kashmir issue is often eclipsed.

HARKAT-UL-JIHAD-ISLAMI (HUJI)

Origin : HUJI was launched in 1980 as part of the Pak-based jihad network against Soviets in Afganistan. After several changes over two decades it has spread out activities to J & K and other parts of India and Bangladesh. Major presence in Bangladesh, behind attacks in Varanasi, Kolkata. Spreads out network through Kolkata.

Followers : Drawn from 'Azad' Kashmir. Punjab and Karachi. In Bangladesh, home-grown Islamists, particularly in Chittagong, are part of cadre. Recurits also drawn from Deobandi madrasses from India and Kashmir.

Agenda : Strives to ensure secession of J & K through terrorist violence. In other parts of India, it aims to spread terror and undermine internal security. Alliance with SIMI.

Area of Operation : HUJI terrorists entered J & K in early 1992. In Bangladesh it aids terrorists in India's north-east and extremist and criminal forces. HUJI recruits fighters in Kashmir under Harkat-ul-Mujahideen. Several hundred trained in Afganistan. Part of Deobandi extremist network in Pakistan receives support from ISI.

Training : Basically physical training. Indoctrinated to carry out attacks against India. Special training in Pakistan for shooting, commando training, mortar training, rocket launchers and other items used in war. Special training for six months. Train children for jihad in schools and madrassas. Explosive training in secret places. Send people to Pakistan for training.

Past Experience : In Bihar, Hyderabad and Bangalore. And finally Jaipur.

Ultimate Target : Their ultimate target is the Arakan region of Myanmar.

Characterisitcs : At crowded public places like railway stations. Use modern methods.

SIMI

Origin : Founded in UP on April 1, 1977, emerged as on offshoot of Jamaat-e-Islami Hind, Its national general secretary Safdar Nagori and 12 other leaders were arrested in 2008 near Indore for running terrorist training camps and for involvement in attacks.

Followers : Has some 400 Ansars or full time cadres and 20,000 ordinary members. Its wide network is also aimed at school children.

Agenda : Propagation of 'correct' Islam and devotion to Jihad. Aims to establish a Shariat-based Islamic rule through 'Islami Inquilab'. Does not believe in a nation state or the Indian Constitution. Against 'anti-Islamic cultures.' Has emerged as supplier of foot soldiers to LeT, Jaish and HUJI.

Areas of Operation : SIMI has established links with terrorist outfits and attempts to incite communal feelings. Strong bases in UP, Delhi, Madhya Pradesh, Gujrat, Kerala, Maharastra, Andhra Pradesh and Assam. In Kerala SIMI behind 12-odd front organisations.

All these terrorist organisations are likely to establish during the Congress regime under different rulers. India's security neither has the wherewithal nor any national policy to combat terrorism within the country. For example, 'Parliament Attacks'. National Security Council (NSA), Research And Analytic

Wing (RAW), and Intelligence Bureau have proved the continued erosion of their security apparatus. Why? All these agencies have already bowed their heads to our corrupted leaders who are basically trained in dual diplomacy. India loses more lives to terror than any other country in the world except Iraq (August 27, 2007) looked at the toll of terror. Our political leaders on terrorism live in mental confusion or moral anarchy and seek vaguely for truth and beauty and moral support from the Western Powers. Why? When they are deluded and disillusioned, cynicism and confusion follow. Their comments are a good deal of rubbish. All they survive when pension rights guaranteed by the constitution. They are safeguarded. Inconsistency is the quality of their stagnant mind. An unhappy, cross-breed, the mule of politics engenders nothing. They make no preparation for our future generation. Reason is progressive but slow reason feebly climbs. Why then are not the pseudo-communists of India so loud in raising the slogans of peace and co-existence in Kashmir? Why do the politically prostituted leftists of the world, not start a third global war which according to them would liberate millions of people from the curses of capitalism and imperialism? Because they are all the clutches of capitalism.

According to terrorist experts, attacks on soft targets such as public places where innocent people are the victims are invariably carried out by sleeper cells of terrorist groups. We have failed before we have started. Confidence is deluded by corruption. Sixty years of failures. Appeasement runs high. There are two kinds of failures ... those who thought and never did, and those who did and never thought, Through our borders, friends may come and go, but enemies accumulate. And our political leaders are thinking of their own security instead of opportunity. Why? They seem to be more afraid of life than death. Their political theatricalism and extravagant display of secularism are sordidly exposed.

A terrorist, a superior unsocial animal, is not afraid of death. But there are animals of the jungle which are not — at least, so some of them know when they are going to die; some of them are known to have a fixed place for death to which they repair at a speed which hardly betrays the end is coming. Is there any terrorist who knows when he will die and where?

A terrorist is a superior unsocial animal. Why? Because he abuses his intellect, religious faith and puts his talents to sinister use. He is a superior unsocial animal. Why? Because he can ensnare the innocent or poach the other races, and use some others as beasts of burden to satisfy his love for fun. A terrorist in his heart of hearts believes in free love of 'theater of the absurd' but has created the unnatural ring-face of matrimony with theology and complexities of bureaucratic bungle. Theology makes him sinful. In this respect, he has to maintain a double face all his life. The camel or the elephant or the lion is not as proud of its form and figure as a terrorist. They are not as happy and contented in their respective spheres and situations as terrorist is in the Valley of Kashmir.

Islamic radicalism runs wild across schools and colleges, and even through the down-trodden areas of Pakistan. And these areas have become a refuge to Taliban and Al Quaida. So, Islamic fundamentalism totally rests on Pakistani young people. All Public Schools remain closed. Because the Poorest Pakistanis prefer to send their children to madrassas where radical agendas are staple food of education. Whereas the Turkish schools, under the portrait of Mustafa Kemel Ataturk, Turkey's founder, prescribe a strong-western curriculum, with courses taught in English, from mathematics and science to English literature and Shakespeare, Shelley, Keats, and Byron. Why? Because their parents want their kids to be capable of competing with the West without losing their indentities to it. They do not teach religion beyond the one class in Islamic studies. Whereas in Pakistan, a lump of earth, a stone and gold are all the same. A Sindhi proverb says : "The man who cannot distinguish gold from mud is either a mad man or a citizen of a mad country". Even the U.S.A. is going to buy food from farmers in Africa instead of offering food as aid. It is a protectionist policy, translating her thoughts into policy. And Pakistan is sabotaging her Islam and translating Islamic thoughts into terrorism. Pakistan needs a therapeutic treatments.

So the Kashmir issue has developed a missile race between two rival countries in this sub-continent. It would not be an exaggeration to say that the Kashmir episode is a poorly rewarding story of the ill-starred romance between an Islamic nation and half-Islamic terrorist organisations. These roles are flawlessly played by Islamic priests and Islamic rulers of Islamabad, both of whom bring a rare sensitivity and deep understanding to their roles on the theatrical ground of Kashmir. Matching the gossamer delicacy of Islamic spirit behind the Kashmir story are the unobtrusive production values of ISI. And these grand production values have been deplorably mauled by the White House. ISI appears to be the vicarious authority behind all off-the-record terrorism.

Which kind of Islam, Pakistan wants? The world says that Pakistan is extremist. Pakistan is dubbed as a nation of theocracy. According to Pakistan, the Pakistani rulers have to decide whether they want a liberal and moderate Pakistan or a terrorist or extremist Pakistan. If it be so, Pakistan must have an ISI-sponsored terrorism in India as well as in Kashmir today. A dangerous situation, as perilous as treacherous, is brewing up as the economic situation of the country is very fragile. Even the armed forces and ISI have played a key role in pressurising the Govt. to go back to place the notorious spy agency under the control of the interior ministry. To Gen. Musharraf, ISI is the first line of defence. Pride is the master sin of the Devil. Truly speaking, Pakistan has replaced the old totalitarian system of social hardship and violent crime, in the grip of turbulent economic situation. Alexander Solzhenitsyn, a Nobel Laureate on Literature, in 'The Gulag Archipelago', has voiced forth against the plight of Russians, attacked the Govt. for policies that, he said, drove the nation to poverty and scolded his compatriots for greed and venality. He, who as an outcast under communism, had been a beacon for thousands of marginalised people. Pakistan's theocratic rulers have ploughed in the same view as Alexander Solzhenitsyn viewed in Soviet Union.

Theology-based administration is a precept. Why? Because precept is instruction written in the sand. The tide flows over it, and the record is gone. Example is graven on the rock, and the lesson is not soon lost.

WHAT IS IT ABOUT 'SIMI' AND ITS NOMENCLATURE?

INDIA MADE...INDIAN TERRORIST GROUP

GUILTY OF ASSOCIATION?

How it Began?

Mohamamad Abdullah Siddiqi, now a professor of mass communication at Western Illinois University in the US, founded the 'Students' Islamic Movement of India (SIMI) at Aligarh, in April 1977, with a mission to liberate India from western culture influence and convert it into an Islamic society.

What is its Ideology?

Influenced by Deoband school of thought, SIMI aims to counter in India what it believes is the increasing moral degeneration, sexual anarchy and 'insensitiveness' as a result of following the 'decadent' west.

How it became Controversial?

SIMI originally emerged as a student wing of the Jamat-e-Islami. But the alliance was short-lived as Jamat disapproved of SIMI's extremist line. It has stepped up its subversive activities and is involved in almost all major explosions, communal violence and circulation of inflammatory material across the country.

Who are their Activists?

Its activists are highly educated technocrats, chartered accountants and doctors, many of whom have received training in explosives and arms and ammunition abroad and are adept at using technology to avoid detection. Availability of advanced and sophisticated technological means to the highly educated and motivated cadres from beyond the borders would also render it impossible to place hard evidence before a court or a tribunal.

Nomenclature of Its Subversive Activities

* West Bengal has been on SIMI's radar. In 2002, Hasib Raja, a SIMI activist, was arrested with RDX. Raja's intention was to blow up the Howrah Bridge. In 2003, five people, including two SIMI activists, were arrested while trying to remove clips of railway slippers on the Kumardubi Barakar line. In different states of India, where SIMI activists have been arrested with guns, explosives and blueprints of their terror plans.
* SIMI has managed to survive under the cover of a slew of Islamic outfits. Some of its operatives may have found way into the mainstream political parties as well.

* Most of its activists cool their heels in jails and face cases related to distributing fundmental literature.
* SIMI has become very strong in central India from where it has been spreading its tentacles to other regions.
* SIMI came into existence on April, 1977, at Aligarh Muslim University as a front organisation of Jamayit-e-Islami-Hind (JEIH) aims to utilise students/youth in propagation of Islam and offer support to Jihad.
* The organisation emphasises on the formation of Shariat based Islamic rule through Islam Inquilab. It does not believe in the nation state, as well as in the Constitution, or the secular order; it regards idol worship as a sin and its holy duty to end such idol worship.

The defects of understanding between our intelligence agency and the Govt. of India, like those of the face, grow worse as we grow old.

Apparently, Pakistan was the child of violence, but factually, it was the child of illiberal forces that had gained ascendency during the British rule. The realisation came upon Indian leaders at a very late period that the synthesising influence of Indian culture was not strong enough, to eliminate the separate tendencies between Hindus and Muslims. Thus the birth of Pakistan was thus a declaration of that lamentable reality. And the responsibility for the creation of Pakistan was not wholly one-sided.

Apart from the factual matter, a good conspectus of the three distinctive schools of Islamic thought in India may be given :

1. the orthodox school;
2. the Iqbal school with its idealist sympathisers and stress on action, and its conviction that the gate of interpretation was not once for all closed, and
3. the modernist school, initiated by Sir Syed Ahmed Khan, of which Maulana Abdul Kalam Azad was one of the principal leaders then.

To Step up Infiltration into Kashmir

He, who imagines, he can do without the world, deceives himself much; but he who fancies the world cannot do without him is still more mistaken. To infiltrate terrorists into Kashmir by Pakistan is to deceive herself much and is still more mistaken. G. Parthasarathy, former Indian High Commissioner to Pakistan, says : "Pakistan's new policies on Kashmir will involve strong backing for the separatist leadership and particularly for the hardliner Islamist, Syed Ali Shah Gilani." Infiltration into Kashmir is an ambrosial nectar to the Pakistan-sponsored hardliners in the valley. Why infiltration? G.Parthasarathy has categorically replied : "Infiltration is set to increase with a view to promoting violence and disrupting and discrediting the forthcoming state assembly elections ... New Delhi's response to these developments has been timid ..." ISI 's role has always been in favour of terrorism. Our lives in Kashmir are not determined by uniform process. Why? Human behavior in the valley is very complex, nonlinear and unpredictable. The Brave New World in the valley is far away. Why? Because Islamic theologians are hardliners not to decide controversial issues like Kashmir. Infiltration into Kashmir is the base-line of Islamabad's indpendent thought. G. Parthasarathy says again : "The move was also evidently intended to please the radicals in Nawaz Sharif's Pakistan Muslim League, whose views on Jihad and India are not very different from those of the military." ('Watch The Border, TOI, Aug. 13, 2008).

So, it is difficult to draw a clear line of separation between the abuse and the wholesome use of peace-making process in Kashmir. A good deal of lives in Kashmir must be sent in the act of being approached from all sides with varying degrees of resistance and surrender. But there is all the difference between demanding and arousing a response when it comes to measuring its quality. One is made to order, the other is spontaneous, and the distinction can get blurred if it comes to be treated with indifference.

The direct approach operates on symptoms, uses sanctions behind authority, exploits the fear of displeasing and the temptation to please at any cost. It can exact obedience and impose loyalty without the need to arouse respect and confidence. Any agreement on the Kashmir issue has neither the patience nor the inclination to understand an unfamiliar situation, but is anxious to score a bull's eye while thinking that tomorrow is another day. No wonder, any agreement on Kashmir is sometimes reminiscent of 'Gone With Wind'. In matters of conscience, first thoughts are best; in matters of prudence, last thoughts are best. Why? Thought is deeper than speech; feeling deeper than thought; souls to souls can never teach what to themselves was taught. So Pakistan-sponsored infiltration of jehadi groups are born with a nose and ten fingers, but no one was born with a knowledge of God. Infiltrators run across to the National Assembly from the babbling mob of ISI-paid scoundrels. Jihad is a word more used than understand.

All men dream : but not equally. The Pakistani rulers are the dreamers of the day. They are dangerous men. Why? For they may act their dreams with open eyes, to make it possible, with glossy slogans and slick stories soon forgotten.

An All India level of SIMI runs out its activities in India in different fronts : Tahreek-e-Ehyaa-e-Ummat, Tehreek-Talaba-e-Arabia, Tehrik Tahafuzz- Sha' aire Islam and Wahadat-e-Islami. Officially they are unknown. SIMI carries out, with these organisations and its allied organisations, activities for fund raising, instigating Muslims for riots and circulation of provocative CDs/ cassettes, including the collection of funds, circulation of literature and regrouping of cadres. It is an undeniable fact that all terrorists appear to be Muslims. All they are funded by Saudi Arabia and trained by Islamic countries. To fight terrorism, unjust laws still exist in India. Why? Terrorists have confounded the very essence of our laws and falsehood of our constitutional amendment. The wise man requires no law. All beings have their laws, the beasts their laws, but it is the mystic foundation of laws in India to fight terrorism. Why? Because there is a plenty of laws at the end of a night stick.

Pakistan-terror Designs In India

Pakistan-sponsored terrorists in India use the smuggling of the explosives involving a long chain of couriers. And the Jehadi outfits have made a significant change in bomb designs. In the modus operandi of jihadis, they have shelved the use of RDX and replaced it with locally available fertilisers and TNT and intended to mask Pakistan's signature from the explosives.

The mix of ammonium nitrate and RDX is more lethal and has a larger impact involving mass caualty at the blast as seen in the Sarojini Nagar blasts in New Delhi and those at Malegon, Mumbai and Varanasi. The use of ammonium nitrate mixed with TNT is low in strength.

If the blasts are orchestrated in a serial manner, in a crowded market, the impact remains the same. It was done in Jaipur and Ahmedabad.

RDX? It is available in European countries and Pakistan, the variety smuggled by terrorist outfits in India is of a particular quality that has Pakistani signature on it.

The bomb-making manuals are easily available on the internet on the terrorist friendly sites:. It is much easier for a home-grown terrorist to download the know-how and assemble bombs with locally available ingredients. The blasts in all cases are triggered by timer devices. For the serial blasts, the terrorists are local elements who know the place and are easily mingled with the crowd. The SIMI cadres work along with terror outfits like LeT, JeM and HUJI. Pakistan has fallen in love of terrorism, and not remained angry, frustrated, and piqued. So Pakistan has to talk a lot of inflammatory nonsense, and finally driven her to blustering and apoplectic indignation. A Frankenstein's monster is knocking at the doors of Pakistan from on all fronts.

Even the area where Benazir Bhutto was killed is known to be dangerous. There is a dead threat. So, Pakistan now has so far too many ungovernable, no-go areas. The trouble with normal is : it always gets worse.

And the Pakistani Army tries to act aggressively along the Line of Control (LOC) in Jammu and Kashmir. The ceasefire, along the 198 km. International Border in J & K, the 778 km. LOC and the 110 km. Actual Ground Position Line in the Siachen-Saltoro Ridge region, has been largely held since it came into force in November 2003. And the Pakistani troops are generally indulged in heavy cross-border firing during an infiltration bid in the different sectors of J & K like Bimbergalli, Gurez, Mendhar, Tangdhar and others. It is their old strategy of providing 'covering fire' to militants trying to sneak into J & K.

Who has assigned an innocent Muslim to be a terrorist? Who has assigned him the top place in the kingdom of mass destruction? How can a terrorist alone be made in the image of Allah? Is it not all fake or make-believe? Can Islamabad deny that a terrorist can change colours like a chameleon? What an excessive adulation for a terror-monger.

So, a terrorist can do everything unmanly and get away with the label of Allah's best creation. A cobweb is as good as the mightiest cable when there is no strain upon it.

Historical and geograpical factors have impelled the Pakistani people, as they have other Asian States, to adopt a policy of terrorism on which all the major parties are agreed. This alone contains some promises of a minimum degree of political instability which will not enable Pakistani leaders to concentrate on the planned consolidation of the State. It shows in what way the cancerous cells differ from healthy cells. Terrorism only destroys the true philosophy of Islam without damaging the other. The real question is : To whom does Pakistan belong?

Terrorism may be termed as the daughter of Pakistan, the sister of mullocracy and the parent of an Islamic country like Pakistan. It invites the Jehadis. Justice is as strictly due between neighbour nations as between neighbour citizens. A highwayman is as much a robber when he plunders in a gang as when single; and a nation that makes an unjust war is only a great gang. The Saudi Binladin Group is a construction and engineering company that has expansive holdings in the Middle East. Osama Bin Laden once owned a small stake in the company. Victims and survivors of September 11, 2001 were plotted by the Saudi Binladin Group along with numerous banks, charities and individuals worldwide. They provided material support and assistance to Al Quaida before September 11. So, a terrorist hardly seeks by contemplation and self-surrender to obtain Islamic unity or identity with the ultimate reality of Islam. Truly speaking, a terrorist is an infectious but fatal viral disease in Islam, causing an atmosphere of mystery and an abnormal tendency of mythomania. Everything is trapped inside the hermetic ISI scheme.

The people of Kashmir have had a bad deal since partition. They have been made the chattels of big power politics. Nothing has been done purely in the interests of the local people since Mr. Nehru put forward his scheme to the Security Council. After partition, India and Pakistan are together with the areas under dispute. The partition, therefore, hits the Kashmiris in three ways. It is inconvenient socially and economically. The disputed area will be unable to share in the liberation movement of some Kashmiri Muslims. Since the partition took place, the Pakistan administration has been harsher than that to which the Kashmiris were accustomed under Hari Singh. The impression is left that the Pakistan Govt. have been bending backwards in their anxiety to be fair to the Kashmiris, but in doing so have they been quite fair to the Kashmiris? The territories concerned are undoubtedly under Indian population. The Kashmiris are pastoralists and their characterisitic social pattern is that the areas that they inhabit and graze should be under one administration, not others.

The Kashmir issue is smothered in a cloud of black-channel diplomacy. What a hostile world, it seems, lurks behind those unwilling half-opened doors, through which come a ray of light and a smell of cooking-up conspiracy! It is a dreary job, and one cannot wonder that there are no political canvassers of peace in that turbulent valley. The apparatus of democracy in Kashmir will get down. Political medicine makes Kashmir issue ill. 'Non-Muslim' Jammu and Ladakh are considered as victims simultaneously of Islamic terror and State discrimination in favour of Kashmir. The districts of Jammu, Kathua and Udhampur are Hindu-majority areas. The Hindu fundamentalists always whip up 'Hindu Pride'. Why? To translate into votes for them.

We have to study and explore the root cause of terrorism in order to exterminate it and not to justify it. According to Pakistan, yesterday's terrorists are today's freedom fighters, while mentioning the names of Bhagat Singh and Nelson Mandela. Why? According to Pakistan, Bhagat Singh was branded as a terrorist by the British but India hails him as freedom fighter and has issued a stamp in his honour. And Nelson Mandela was also branded as a terrorist some years ago. It is a racy mixture of juicy hand-shake diplomacy.

A soft answer turns away wrath. There is no shield against so wrongs so effectual as an unresisting temper. Sensing the motive behind the Pakistan's proposal, former Attorney General, Soli Sorabjee, an expert member at the meeting, in Geneva, of the United Nations sub-commission on human rights on the Kashmir issue, lodged a protest to the names of freedom fighters being equated with terrorists. Sorabjee said : "Bhagat Singh and his friends did not shoot innocent pilgrims in an obvious reference to the killings of Amarnath pilgrims." He also added : "Mandela and his partymen did not go to a marriage party and shoot down innocent civilians. The claim of terrorism sought to be justified under the label of fight for freedom or the slogan of self-determination is spurious." Pakistan hardly knows little leaks sink the ship.

Why militants kill Muslims in Jammu and Kashmir? The Pakistan-sponsored terrorists play their role according to Pakistan's plan. To dissociate the Kashmiri Muslims from casting their votes in the elections makes it clear that the whole Kashmir is involved in insurgency. The terrorists and their mentor, Pakistan, are always desperate to mar the polls. Arun Joshi, in Hindustan Times, Aug, 26, 2002, says, "... the militants, by killing Muslims, are seeking to achieve a political objective." Not only that ISI is planning to change the Hindu majority demographic character of Jammu region. The demographic change has already helped militants to set up their bases and hideouts in Jammu. And the Pakistani infiltrators sneak into the Indian territory from the Pakistan-occupied Kashmir. Infiltrators are replenishing the ranks of militants. Most of them are veterans of the Afghan war and committed jehadis. They take advantage of the fortified caves and elude the expanded patrol of the Indian troops. The Army should use helicopter gunships in the hilly belts of the State to strike at their escape routes.

Stephen P. Cohen says in his book 'India : Emerging Power' that there are three weak points for India to be accepted as a responsible great power. One, India needs to clean up a basic contradiction of wanting a nuclear deterrent. Two, India's foreign policy making institutions desperately needs an overhaul. Three, India needs to move beyond a policy of 'no concessions, no talks' when it comes to Kashmir. Cohen is pessimistic and sees a continuation of the hurting stalemate of the past several years. Finally, India needs to work out a new relationship with the U.S. Cohen admits the Pokhran II nuclear tests, along with India's hi-tech successes and the Indian American community, helped catch Washington's attention in the 1990s. The Pokhran II nuclear tests, during the Bajpayee regime, seem only marginal to the larger story of India's global power. According to Cohen, India had insurrections in two states, a nuclear armed Pakistan, a ruined Soviet arms machine and a disastrous military intervention in Sri Lanka to show for all that effort.

Asghar Wajahat, a master of satire, takes on the present establishment of political and social dilemma. The dialogues between Gurudev and his disciple, Hariram, are acerbic :

Hariram : Gurudev, what will the simple do if he sees two hungry dogs fighting over a bone?

Guru : He will try to mediate between them.

H : And what will the clever do?

G : He will run off with the bone.

H : And what will the poitician do?

G : He will let loose two more hungry dogs on the scene

(Asghar Wajahat : Lies : Half Told)

In a swirling sea of facts and interpretations on the Kashmir issue, the dialogues give a fascinating survey of Indo-Pak and western powers. And the people of Kashmir are trapped in the towers of political camouflage. Muslims around the world believe that they are the main casualty of Washington's war on terror in the midst of rising anti-Islamic sentiment and perceived Western bias against their faith. Muslims are feeling that they are on the receiving end everywhere. So, there is a feeling of alienation in the Muslim world and this will lead to further alienation. Indonesia's biggest mainstream Muslim organisation, the 40 million strong Nandlatul Ulama strongly opposes any US attack. Striking against Iraq has unleashed a fresh turmoil in the Islamic World by widening a gulf between Muslims and the West. It is fact. The western powers have equivocated the Kashmir issue endlessly and quibblingly.

Faced with virtual rebellion by its leaders in the Ladakh region against attempts to flare up communal tension in the region, there are several organisations in the Leh region which are not in favour of separating from Jammu and Kashmir. Too many people of Kashmir are thinking of security instead of opportunity. Why? They seem to be more afraid of life than death. Another reason is that the Pakistan-sponsored terrorism dangerously pours into the valley across the border. G. Parthasarathy, former Indian High Commissioner to Pakistan, says : "The ISI-backed, Muzaffarabad-based, United Jihad Council joined the chorus proclaiming continuing jehad against India. There are indications that large numbers of jehadis are being readied close to Pakistani army posts along the LOC. This has been accompanied by the shootouts in Samba. New Delhi will have to prepare for increasing terrorist violence ..." He also says, "Moreover, the ISI pretends to be supporting the Americans in Afganistan even as it continues to provide shelter and assistance to Taliban leaders ... If support for the Taliban does not effectively end on Pakistani soil, the Americans, facing continued attacks on their forces in Afganistan, will inevitably strike on Pakistan territory." (Times of India, May 16, 2008).

Pakistan can live without her friends but can't without her neighbours. Pakistan's administration is entirely engrossed in patriarchal politics of surrogate leaders representing the role of women in Pakistan. Truly speaking, Pakistan is challenged by misinterpretation of Islam. Why? Because Islamic terrorism is limitless, invisible and full of Byzantine complex. It cannot be seen, heard, touched and smelled and is beyond the power of human comprehension. Pakistan's dream of democracy has now become a nightmare. Pakistan is considered to be a pyramid of hard-core priesthood. This pyramid is of religious bricks, each one depicting mischievous fanaticism, unfair extremism and untrue propaganda against India. For the propagandists of Islamic terrorism in Kashmir are in a virtual form of harakiri. Mr. Jinnah, who emerged with the greater credit from his lop-sided policy, did one thing which his racial chauvinists conspicuously overlooked. He refused to be cowed down by the threats and tantrums of his opponents.

Genocide in Kashmir

* 4,00,000 Kashmiri Pundits, constituting 99% of the total population of Hindus living in Muslim majority area of the Kashmir valley, were forcibly hammered out of the valley by Muslim terrorists, trained in Pakistan, since the end of 1989. They have been forced to live the life of exiles in their own country, outside their homeland, by unleashing a systematic campaign of terror, murder, loot and arson.
* Genocide in Kashmir and of Kashmiri Pundits have reached a climax with Muslim terrorism succeeding in 'CLEANSING' the valley of this ancient ethno-religious community.
* This peace-loving and culturally-rich community with a history of more than 5000 years, is fighting a grim battle to save itself from becoming extinct as a distinct race and culture.

Main Camp Sites in Jammu

The following camp sites in Jammu are the seething hotbed of all-powerful terrorism in the valley.

* Muthi Camp, Jammu
* Transport Nagar, Jammu
* Purkhoo Camp, Jammu
* Stadium Camp, Jammu
* Jhiri Camp, Jammu
* Nagrota Camp, Jammu

* Mishriwala Camp, Jammu
* Battalbalian Camp, Udhampur

Kashmiri Pundits :–

(a) Representatives of glorious heritage and legacy of Kashmir.

(b) Symbols of Brotherhood and Peace :

  * Kashmiri Pundits have always been devoted to spiritual and academic pursuits.
  * They have, during their history of more than 5000 years, nurtured values of peace, co-existence and tolerance.
  * They are original inhabitants of Kashmir.
  * Kashmiri Pundits are progenitors of Kashmir Shaivism—the philosophy of oneness of mankind.
  * Hinyan and Sarvastivadin sects of Buddhism found highest expression in Kashmir and Kashmiri Pundits spread their message to China and Central Asia.
  * Kashmiri Pundits have contributed immensely to the evolution of human thought by contributing to almost all fields of creative human endeavour like literature (mainly Sanskrit, language, science and philosophy from times immemorial).
  * Since the advent of Islam in 14th century, Kashmiri Hindus have been subjected to extreme persecution. To escape religious fanaticism in the form of forced conversions to Islam, they had either to embrace death or leave Kashmir more than once during the last six hundred years.
  * Present exodus of Kashmiri pundits is fourth mass exodus in the history of Kashmir since the advent of Islam in this part.

Atrocities on Kashmiri Pundits (A fact sheet) :–

* Educational institutions burnt, damaged forcefully occupied : 105
* Religious and cultural institutions destroyed/burnt/damaged : 103
* Shops, factories looted/burnt/occupied : 14, 430
* Agriculture dependent families deprived of their resource : 20,000
* Horticulture dependent families deprieved of their resource : 12,500
* Houses burnt : more than 20,000
* Houses looted : 95%
* Torture killings of Kashmiri pundits in the valley : more than 1,100

Terrorist Violence On the Kashmiri Hindu Pundits :–

* Terrorism in Kashmir is an ideological struggle with specific political commitments which are fundamentalist, religious extremism and communal in character.
* Terrorist violence is aimed at achieving the disengagement of the state of

Jammu and Kashmir from India and its annexation to Pakistan. It is the continuation of the Islamic fundamentalist struggle for the homeland of Pakistan which claims Jammu and Kashmir states on account of the Muslim majority character.

* The major dimension of the terrorist violence in Kashmir is the terrorists' commitment to the extermination and subjugation of the Hindus in the state because Hindus do not subscribe to the idea of separation from India, nor do they expect to be governed by the authority of the state which derives its sanction from the law and precedent of Islam. Kashmiri Pundits (Hindus) have always been in the forefront of the struggle against secessionism, communalism and fundamentalism. Hence this peace-loving minority with a modern outlook became the main victim of terrorist violence.

The strategies involved in the terrorist's operation against the Hindus in Kashmir include :

* The extermination of Hindus.
* Subjecting Hindus to brutal torture to instil fear among them in order to achieve their submission.
* To engineer a forced mass exodus of Hindus from the land of their ancestors and birth by way of issuing letters, kidnappings and torture deaths on non-compliance of the terrorists' dictates and ensure the destruction of the secular and pluralistic character of the socio-political fabric of the Kashmir society.
* Attacks, molestations, kidnappings, gang rapes of the women folk of the Hindus in order to instil fear and humiliation in them.
* Destruction and burning of the residential houses of the Hindus who leave their homes in looking out for safety. Looting of their properties and appropriation of their business establishments to ensure that they do not return.
* Attachment of their landed property.
* Destruction of the social base of the Hindus by the desecration and destruction of their places of worship.
* Appropriation of the property of the Hindu shrines and its attachments with the religious endownments.

Religious Sadism :–

Religious sadism of the Pakistan-sponsored terrorist groups goes at the peak of their religious fanaticism. Even the political ghosts are running behind the religious exorcists.

* Killing of Hindus in Jammu and Kashmir by terrorists clearly depicts extreme sadism. All victims have been subjected to extreme torture and terror.
* Torture deaths have been brought about by such inhuman practices as :

(a) Strangulation by using steel wires.
(b) Hanging
(c) Impaling
(d) Branding with hot irons
(e) Burning alive
(f) Lynching
(g) Bleeding to death
(h) Hacking out vital organs
(i) Dismemberment of human bodies
(j) Drowning alive

* Terrorists have frequently indulged in barbaric acts like performing 'death dances' after killing their target.
* Many a time, dead bodies were not even allowed to be properly cremated.

Kashmiri Hindu Pundits

In 'Koshur Samachar', P.N.K. Bamzai categorically and graphically picturises the ethnological character of Kashmiri Hindu Pundits.

The valley of Kashmir is known among the Kashmiri Pundits or Saraswat Brahmins of Kashmir as Saradapeeth or the Abode of the Goddess of Learning and Fine Arts. During their five thousand years of history, they have made colossal contribution to world civilisation in the field of Religion, philosophy, Sanskrit, Literature, medicine, history, aestehtics etc. As models of non-violence, they have never handled lethal weapons or spoken harsh words. Devoted to the study of Vedas and other Sastras in all their aspects, the essence of their studies has been coursing in their blood-stream from generation to generation. In peaceful or turbulent times, they were protected under their spiritual umbrella by a large number of highly advanced sants and sages who flourished in the valley from time to time.

No wonder, they preferred death to change in their religion and withstood stoically the ruthless masters for five hundred years of Muslim rule.And when pushed back to the wall, they migrated to places of safety in the not plains of India.

This process has been repeated in 1990 but on a vaster scale. Threatened with annihilation by Islamic fundamentalists and gun-toting terrorists, the hapless Brahmins migrated en masse to Jammu and other places in the hot plains of the rest of India, leaving behind their hearths and homes, movable and immovable properties, their jobs and business, even the education of their children. The treatment they received from the State and Central Governments is perhaps the most bitter instance of this nature in the world. As refugees in their own country, their governments treated them with disdain. Instead of giving them comfort and solace, their attitude towards them was callous and inhuman.

How and wherefrom did the Kashmiri Pundits or Vedic Aryans enter and settle in the valley is an interesting episode in the early movement of the people from place to place. The main theory about the Aryan settlement in Kashmir as advanced by Dr. Grierson was that they formed a part of the stream of Indo-Aryans from Central Asia, but did not share the migration to India via the Kabul River valley to settle in the Punjab. They broke away from the mainstream while crossing the Hindukush and entering the valley via Dardistan settled there. Dr. Grierson's theory was errorneous.

But after deep research, they came to the valley from the Punjab centuries after the first settlement of Aryans there.

Kashmiri Hindu pundits and Kashmir question are inter-related and overlapping each other. Briefly speaking, the earliest stream of Aryans who entered India found the banks of the River Saraswati in the Punjab fertile and conducive to easy cultivation, and settled there.

The waters of the river spread prosperity all around, the settlers passed centuries there in peace, building well-planned town and cities to live in. The Aryan society was by and by stratified into classes according to the kind of their work and profession or varna. But as ill luck would have been, the life-giving river changed its course several times and ultimately dried up. Known as Saraswat Brahmins, Kshatriyas and Vaisas, they were in search of equally good if not better land in the rest of the sub-continent. An enterprising batch went back to the mountains in the north to reside in the valley of Kashmir of whose beauty and salubrious climate they had heard from their forefathers who used to go there during summer. They sought the protection of Nila, the Lord of the Nagas and begged his permission to settle in the valley permanently as his subjects.

Nila listened to their tale of woe sympathetically but promised the requested permission on condition that they conformed to the social usages and customs of the Nagas. The Saraswats agreed to these conditions when the Naga chief permitted them to reside permanently in the valley.

Described in the Rig Veda as 'the mother of rivers', scholars have debated for centuries whether Saraswati is a myth or has been a reality at some distant point of them.

Fortunately, a team of archaeologists, geographers and historians, led by the famous archaeologist, Dr. V.S. Wakankat, began their quest of the river in 1985. Armed with high-tech facilities like landsat and multi-spectoral scanner (MSS), his team began the quest from the believed source of the river at Adi Badri in the Shivalik Hills in Amabala. They sieved through the whole area notably 150 prominent sites along the route in the Thar Desert ending at Somnath in Gujrat.

At the end of it all they had solid evidence to prove the existence of a highly developed culture on the banks of a mighty river which they say was Saraswati.

Apart from this evidence, the existence of a mighty river, matching the Vedic description of Saraswati has been scientifically proved. The multi-spectoral Scanner (MSS), a widely used and relied upon equipment in archaelogy, indicates various channels of the river in the region.

According to MSS observations of various channels, Sutlej was the main tributary of Ghaggar (the present name for Saraswati, now in Pakistan). But tectonic movements forced Sutlej to flow in different directions (at right angle to its original channel), thus leaving Ghaggar dry.

A study of landsat imagery of Ghaggar (Saraswati) reveals that the river had a constant width of six to eight kilometres from Satrana in the Punjab to Marot in Pakistan.

Aryan Entry into the Valley

At what point of time this important immigration into the Valley of Sarswat Aryans (comprising Brahmans, Kshtriyas, Vaisas, and Sudras) took place is not possible to say. However, the beginning of the Saptarshi or Laukika Era seems to be the time when the Sarswat Aryans entered into and settled in the valley, after getting permission from Nila, the lord of the Naga tribe who were already settled there. The beginning of this era nearly coincides with Mahabharat war. The date of the coronation of King Yudhishtir is given as Kaliyug Samvat 633. Kalhana too begins the Rajatarangini from this time as is evident from the description of the installation of Krishna of Queen Yasomati on the throne of Kashmir as the guardian of her son, King Gonanda II.

The Saptarshi or Laukika era is still in current use among the Brahmin population of Kashmir. Buhler was the first to prove from the extant tradition of Kashmiri Brahmin and other evidence that the commencement of the Laukika Era is placed on the Caitra Sudi, of Kali Samvat 25 (expired) or the year 3076-75 B.C. Since his discovery current accounts of the Laukika reckoning are to be found in all handbooks of Indian chronology.

That the Kashmiri Brahmins have held on to and followed this calender tenaciously for the last 5066 years is a strong point in favour of assuming their entry in Kashmir valley round about the beginning of this era. The various exigencies of time and division of labour gradually differentiated the priestly Brahmins from other castes. And when the Sarswat Aryans entered the valley, the Brahmins were in a dominating position and laid down rules and regulations for the other castes to follow in accordance with Nagas. From that time begins the emergence of Kashmiri Pundits or the Sarswat Brahmins of Kashmir as a distinct community in the all-embracing comity of people called Hindus.

Profoundly learned, it was only the Kashmiri Pundits who were capable of expounding the Vedas, the Vedanganas, the Itihasas, the Puranas and the Mimamsa. They were well-versed in the various orthodox and heterodox philosophic systems. Jurists, astrologers, mathematicians, poets and philosophers were from this community. Even the less educated among them did fairly well, for they could act as Kathavaoaks or reciters of sacred stories and performers of various domestic rites. Sanskrit was their mother tongue and both men and women spoke it fluently.

Society took good care of the Brahmins, for they received land gifts and money. There is a mention of many grants or agraharas in literature and epigraphs. Villagers were transferred to the Brahmins with pastures for cows with lands, water and trees, fruit bearing or otherwise.

A class that helped in the preservation of Dharma and contributed much to the cultural progress, naturally enjoyed some privileges in a society dominated by it. Smritis and the Puranas speak of the Brahmins as being exempt from taxation and capital punishment. The ancient Dharmasastras lay down that a Brahmin should not be given any corporal punishment. Many other Smritis speak of exile as the maximum punishment for a Brahmin.

Education

The Saraswat Brahmins of Kashmir were models of simplicity, purity, truthfulness, ascetic tendency and compassion. All these traits of the highest human culture were built up by Rishis and Maharishis who, in their secluded ashrams, performed austere penances and at the same time taught a large number of students who stayed in the ashrams and led a life befitting Brahmin Brahmachari. Thus the Guru-Shisha parampara was established. The children of a house-holder lived with Acharyas (teachers) in the latter's home. There they used to serve their teacher by gathering fuel for homa and offered morning and evening prayers. The recitation of the Vedic hymns with their proper accents, preceded by the syllable OM took place at day-break. Early morning was the time set apart for studies.

Consequently, Upanayan Sanskara, which literally means taking the child to the Guru, was the most important in one's life. The Brahman, the Khatriya and Vaisa boys were initiated when they were 8, 11 and 12 years respectively. This initiation of a boy into three R's took place on an auspicious day in a festive atmosphere. Gods were propitiated, feasts arranged and presents offered to the teacher before entrusting the student to his care. A very disciplined life was laid down by the medieval digests for students receiving Brahmanical education. By the time the boy attained the age of sixteen years, he was expected to be the master of all sciences and arts ....

In later times, a special sect were devotees and worshippers of Sakti ... the manifestation of power and energy of Siva ... came into prominence and were known as Saktas. Their rites and rituals and the mode of their performance differed basically from the mainstream of the Kashmiri Pundits.

The snow-capped mountain peaks around the valley evoked the image of Siva with Ganga coming out of His locks and gushing down in streams to the plains below, spreading all around. Hence, Kashmir has, from time immemorial, been known as the Land of Siva (Sivapuri). The worship and the study of Saivism is, therefore, a predominent theme in the the religious and philosophic practices of the Kashmiri Brahmins. Though the Tikka philosophy popularly known as Kashmir Saivaism took shape in the 8th century A.D. Sivasana or Sivagama, that is saivism as such, is far older than this date. Indeed we can trace its beginning in the Vedic Revelations.

Kashmir problem has been used as a point of dissension among the peoples of Asia by certain powers. China has done everything to capitalise this dissension and to fan out the flames of tension and bitterness between India and Pakistan. Is this conducive to the cause of peace in Kashmir?

The most influential Chinese philosopher, Confucius, says in the most reliable source of his teachings 'Lun Yu' (Conversations) : "If there be righteousness in the Heart, there will be Beauty in the character. If there be Harmony in the Home, there will be order in the Nation. If there be order in the Nation, there will be peace in the world." Pakistan is quite dissociated from the ethics of these qualities. Given independence and patriotism, neither of which is lacking in Pakistan, the Provinces of Pakistan are more than capable of safeguarding their security interests. It is Pakistan that pursues fame with pseudo-claims over Kashmir, trusts her happiness to the winds of Kashmir, but is an Islamic nation that endeavours after Kashmir by false merit, has to fear, not only the violence of terrorism, but the leaks of her diplomatic vessel. And those rulers who stand on the periphery of Kashmir question are anxious to get inside but admission is restricted which causes a great deal of heart-burning among the religious firebrands, who are then forced to form their own vicious circles of religious fanaticism. The political circles in Pakistan on Kashmir are very noisy, and radiate vulgar health. Literary circles are snobbish and aloof. They find the mounting of alien words of terrorism and the sound of their Jehad slogans, enchanting. A circle of this kind encourages world terrorism.

It was Keats who said that Newton had destroyed the beauty of the rainbow by dividing it into the colours of the spectrum. If this is true then surely the religious fundamentalists have ruined the circle of world peace by religious terrorism. Faulty punctuation on Kashmir policy can cause amusement, consternation and sometimes trouble. Political mishaps are like knives that either serve us or cut us, as we grasp them by the blade or the handle.

The Inter Services Intelligence Agency (ISI) plays a major role on the creation of the Islamist Taliban Movement, which took control of Afganistan in the 1990s and harboured Al Quaida until it was forced from power by US led forces in the wake of the September 11 attacks. The intelligent network of a country has been under military rule for half of its 60 years of independence. Neighbouring India and Afganistan have often blamed the ISI for masterminding acts of terrorism in their countries. The Practice of ISI is hermetically mysterious and willfully veiled and indirect.

History of Rocket Launchers : In the Sub-continent

The first use of rockets in the sub-continent predates the establishment of the British Raj. Tipu Sultan used rockets in the battle of Guntur in 1780 and the battle of Seringapatam in 1792 against the British.

Two of the rockets fired by Indian troops in 1792 are on display at the Royal Artillery Museum in London, modern missile programme started in the late 1950s with the development of anti-tank missiles. The Indian missile programme, which initially started with technology, gathers and reverses engineering, subsequently matured into the competence to build full-fledged series of operational missiles when India successfully tested and deployed the Prithvi and Agni ballistic missiles and the Brahmos cruise missile. While India continues to build its arsenal keeping in mind regional and extra-territorial security concerns like narrowing the gap with China and keeping a check on Pakistan, Pakistan's military programme is almost solely on India specific.

Most of their nuclear capable missile projects like the Babur (Hatf VII), and Ra'ad (Hatf VIII) are about increasing their payload and offering them a greater combat radius to act as a deterrent to India.

With Chinese and North Korean help, the Pakistan Atomic Energy Commission and the Khan Research Laboratories are pursuing medium range ballistic missile programmes. This also signals Pakistan's attempts to diversify suppliers in ballistic and cruise missile technologies.

India indigenously developed the Prithvi and Agni series of ballistic missiles and the Brahmos Cruise missile with Russian collaboration. Prithvi is a series of short-range ballistic missiles, which has three versions. India has also developed Dhanus, a naval version of Prithvi capable of being launched from ships. Agni is an advanced missile system that includes a short-range ballistic missile (SRBM) like Agni-I (700-800 Km), a medium-range ballistic missile (MRBM) Agni-II (up to 2500 km), the intermediate range ballistic missile Agni-III (3500-5000 km), and the under development Agni-IV, an inter-continental ballilstic missile (ICBM) ranging over 6000 km. India also has the Brahmos supersonic cruise missile ranging up to 290 km and is developing Nirbhay, a subsonic cruise missile with a 1000 km range. India has also developed Akash, which is a medium range surface-to-air missile and Nag, a 4-7 km ranging anti-tank missile based on fire-and-forget technology. Focusing attention on the Kashmir issue, both the countries — India and Pakistan — are fighting over missile competition in this sub-continent. Force alone is no answer to problems which affect people politically and psychologically. That is the lesson of our independent movement on the Kashmir issue, and the remembrance calls for a reappraisal of our attitude to others in and outside of our frontiers. Trifling troubles find utterances; deeply felt pangs are silent.

Now the question is : what missiles do Pakistan have? The answer is : The first indigenous ballistic missile developed by Pakistan was Hatf-1, which was developed in 1989. Ranging between 60 and 80 km, it was capable of carrying a 500-550 kg payload. It was subsequently modified to Hatf-1A with a 100 km range and later Hatf-2, which have a throw-weight of 500 kg and range between 290 and 300 km. However, it is unclear if the missiles have been modified for nuclear delivery. Pakistan has also developed the Hatf-III and the Hatf-IV with Chinese technology. Both can carry nuclear warheads. Nuclear warfare is prevailing over this sub-continent, and religious fanatics run a shadow government in Pakistan to train, recruit, regroup and resupply their movement. The advantage of that haven in Pakistan, even the lawless tribal realms, has allowed the Taliban leadership to exercise uninterrupted control of its insurgency through the same clique of mullahs commanders who ran Afganistan under theocracy until they were driven from power in December, 2001. ISI (Inter-Services Intelligence) is technically supposed to be under the PM's control but has traditionally functioned as a part of the influential army.

The Indian Muslims are now at the crossroads of Muslim scholars from Deobandi as well as other theological schools. Deobandi! It is one of the influential theological schools in South Asian Islam. The Darul Uloom Deoband, Saharanpur, Uttar Pradesh, is said to have inspired the Taliban ideology. Now it has passed strictures against terrorism as anti-Islamic. SIMI and other terrorist organisations have already hijacking Islamic tenets, and been fully abetted by a small group of ideological extremists different from Islamic school of thoughts. They contradict themselves. A horde of ideological extremists is guilty of soliciting to murder, providing unaccountable terrorist training camps relating to inflammatory speeches, and possessing terrorist articles. They fear no one except Allah. They will not change their ways. They are proud to be Muslims.

To counter terrorism, our double-dyed politicians are quick to promise to weed it but are generally slow to perform. They translate their promises into hypocrisy and lies, under the contradictions of their promises. To counter cross-border terrorism, our pseudo-secularists are weary of taking concrete steps. Why? Because they are the Brand Ambassadors of Secularism to the Western world as Pakistan seems to be the Brand Ambassador of Islamic terrorism and religious fanaticism to the Islamic world. Our leaders like to have a kiss-and-make-up meeting with other western powers on Kashmir issue. They transmit romantic ideas and romantic political notions about a kiss-and-make-up meeting on it. They like having the mealtimes more than the meals. And Kashmir has still been the hot-house of political camouflage. Our leaders are free to move on every meandering way in a whirlpool of political sabotage on Kashmir issue, getting an advantage over the electioneering campaign. They are like a newborn child, freed from the womb, be free to move on every path. Our glamorous often mysterious leaders get used to displaying theatricalism on Kashmir issue.

The worst carnage occurred in 2006 in Iraq, at the important Shia Golden Dome Shrine in Samara, north of the capital, Baghdad. Thunderous explosions and dense black smoke swirled through the centre of Baghdad, setting off dozens of secondary explosions and killings. According to the Muslim lunar calender, the Iraqi Government observe anniversary every year for a 15 minute period of commemoration for the bombing of the Golden Dome shrine. The worst carnage was executed by the Islamic extremists against the Muslim world. Are they considered to be staunch Muslims? The staunch Muslims of Islamic world are those who pray, who are fasting, who go Haj, who give Zakat, and perform other rituals. The extremists are generally in minority. Pakistan has got diplomatic association with Taliban and other extremist groups. Islamic terrorism is a sensitive issue to the world now and has the potential to destroy Pakistan .... a nightmare to a nation of religious fanaticism. We argue about how many tens of thousands of innocent people died at the hands of Islamic terrorist groups over the Muslim countries. Pakistan has left intact a system of blanket control of terrorism over the people. After partition, there are so many glorious pages of military coups, bright examples of political çant over the Kashmir issue and incurable racialism in Pakistan. Not only that but Islamabad-controlled television shows romantic serial blasts about the exploits of India's domestic and security agents, and a lavish party with an orchestra playing western music.

It is Islamabad where the rulers have formed one of the most powerful clans under the leadership of Gen. Musharraf. Pakistan is afflicted with a peculiar kind of optical delusion of her consciousness. Why? Because Pakistan dreams inward from each centre of compassion. But India is a pluralistic and mutilingual society. Whereas the terrorist societies of Pakistan hardly know every flicker of Islamic thoughts and feelings. Even after a serial of blasts, a thunderous applause represents the banners of crescent moon throughout the jehadi camps in the valley. Thus and thus the religious fanatics rattle sabre of jehadi slogans and tremors of Islamic terrorism all over the country.

Jamiat Ulama-i-Hind (JUH), the largest Muslim organisation in India, has decried and politically lambasted the azadi movement by separatists in Kashmir, saying the Valley is constitutionally an integral part of India. And its integration (with the rest of India) is in the larger interest of the Muslim community. Why? Because Pakistan-based Deobandi outfits .... Jaish-e-Mohammad, for instance ... have declared a jihad to 'liberate Kashmir'. JUH believes in the one-nation theory right since independence and that it is right to introduce communalism in the land-transfer issue. Why? Because that would lend weight to the two-nation theory. Because Muslims across the country are being portrayed as anti-nationals and terrorists. But our Govt. play double standard while dealing with terror and are soft on hardline Hindu outfits such as Bajrang Dal and VHP.

The jehadis use to run cyber-cum-computer training centres from mobilising funds to choosing the blast sites to recruiting those who plant bombs on cycles shortly before the blasts.

Almost every summer, the border firing and infiltration attempts happen, along the 198 km International border (IB) in J & K, the 778 km LOC and the 110 km. Actual Ground Position Line in the Siachen-Saltoro Ridge region. All these unwanted happenings are still very much relevant. Because Pakistan-sponsored terrorists manage to sneak in by cutting the barbed-wire fencing along the LOC. This indicates that infiltration is generally facilitated by Pakistani rangers posted nearby.

Kashmir issue is one of the world's toughest and worst-handled problems ... a record of unfulfiled promises, broken pledges and half-hearted measure. It is as dangerous a drift in this sub-continent as Arab-Israel war. As the Arabs have never been at peace with Israel, so Pakistan with India. To make human minds more energetic and passions more aflame.

India's decision to abolish interment terrorist camps — surely a euphemism for concentration camps of fanatical crusaders — has coincided with the consideration by the western powers. More than this will nevertheless be required to convince those who feel that terrorist camps and general paraphernalia of coercion are inseparable from the system of religious extremism. Political coercion and mobilsation of religious fanatics for Kashmir purpose are the moral techniques of Pakistan's totalitarianism. The only requirement of political gamesmanship over the Kashmir issue is that the skin of the wild animal shot becomes Govt. property and trophy cannot be displayed by the hunter. It will enable the extremists to shoot dangerous game. So, Pakistan is engaged in party manoeuvres and political squabbles and wrangles, and playing herself in the religion-based political cauldron.

Islamabad is the mother of all militant activities. The United States has not a rewarding dividend on the Kashmir question. Madrassa-based Islamic culture has hardened up and is the most brain-damaging circle of concern to the Islamic rulers. It is more vulnerable than the consequences of alcohol abuse and alcoholism. The rulers have hoarded up millions and millions of U.S. dollars for terrorism. So, the hollowed-out-Islamic thoughts have outreached the crudest form of terrorism.

Madrassa-based Islamic culture is a by-product of religious puritanism. The unrecognised political terrorists in India are more vulnerable than that of recognised terrorists. They all have enjoyed their encouraging style of strait-laced moral standards. The Devil can quote scripture for his own ends. So, the Kashmir issue remains unsolved.

Our shame-faced political leaders, totally shambolic in political shambles of Kashmir, have not yet reasoned out the solution on Kashmir problem. More than 600 Hindu temples have already been destroyed or demolished or desecrated outrageously either by the monstrocity of jehadis or by our political terrorists who are wedded to political criminals. More than 3,50,000 Kashmiri Hindu pundits have already been cleared out of Kashmir. But for the political interference, militant groups have not yet been obliterated from the valley. It is a back-channel diplomacy of our unbranded leaders not weakly and effusively sentimental.

Nearly 2,00,000 pundits have been displaced by the insurgency and around 60 percent of them have already settled in the Jammu region. The world community has got to focus on the long-ignored plight of the Kashmiri Hindu pundits. The Pundits, who are the Hindu community of Kashmir, have an ancient and a proud culture. Their roots in the Kashmir valley run deep. The pundits have been amongst the most afflicted victims of the Pakistan-supported campaign of terrorism in Jammu and Kashmir. Virtually, the entire population of 3,00,000 Kashmiri pundits have been forced to leave their ancestral homes and property. Threatened with violence and intimidation, they have turned into refugees in their own country. Our leaders remain silent in our moth-eaten politics.

This is the true face of insurgency in Kashmir. The militants have transformed a peaceful, secular state in India, one which happens to have a predominantly Muslim population, into a killing field as part of the goal of turning the state into an area under strict Islamic rule. From the stand-point of international stability, this would be a disaster.

The Jammu and Kashmir Government and Government of India have failed squarely to protect the Kashmiri pundits against Islamic terrorism. Jammu and Kashmir being the only Muslim majority state in whole of India, the protection of minorities and their living peacefully in their homeland is crucial for India to remain as a secular Democratic state. Ethnic cleansing of Kashmiri pundits (Hindus) from Kashmir valley is the crucial failure for Indian State to uphold its commitments to people of India as enshrined in Indian Constitution which provides right to live with dignity and honour to every citizen irrespective of caste, creed, religion or colour.

Within the narrower ambit of the administrative machinery, New Delhi has been in dilemma to cover the brand of self-consciousness. It is Kashmir debate that is easy to inflame local and communal passions but difficult to extinguish them. Often enough in the past has this lesson been learnt by our people but no sooner is it imbibed than it is forgotten. Crying wolf is a dangerous game in itself. Kashmir is a grim warning. For over 60 years, violence has griped the heart of the valley. Curfew orders have been defied repeatedly, public property has been set on fire and many innocent men, women and children have been attacked. To take a parochial view of the compromise is not only to keep the old hatreds alive but to question the credentials of Parliament, the highest authority in the land. The psychologically perverted and politically naked politicians who have incited the mobs to mobocracy and elsewhere during the last 60 years must bear the responsibility for the deaths of innocent citizens killed in the firings and for a calculated attempt at subversion of democracy. But no Parliamentarians have the rigth to disturb the public peace and to incite people to violence. Yes, we live in an age of irony. This midwifery of our leaders assists in bringing forth political terrorists with a regular recurrence.

It is a curious phenomenon to the world people whether Pakistan-sponsored terrorism has been inspired by early history of terrorism or early origins of terrorism or the 19th century terrorism or by the history of biological terrorism?

WHAT IS AN EARLY HISTORY OF TERRORISM?

1. Terror in Antiquity : Ist-14th century AD

The earliest known organisation that exhibited aspects of a modern terrorist organisation was the zealots of Judea. Known to the Romans as Sicani, or dagger-men, they carried on an underground campaign of assassination of Roman occupation forces, as well as any Jews they felt had collaborated with the Romans. Their motive was an uncompromising belief that they could not remain faithful to the dictates of Judaism while living as Roman subjects as we see in between Shia-based Karachi and Sunni-based Lahore in Pakistan. Eventually the zealots' revolt became open and they were finally beseized, and committed mass suicide at the fortification of Masada.

Even though both the zealots and the Assassins operated in antiquity. Strange to say, both are active even today. Their modus operandi is different today.

(a) Forerunners of modern terrorists operate in aspects of motivation, organisation, targeting and goals.

(b) Although both were ultimate failures. But today they are remembered hundreds of years later. They demonstrate a deep psychological impact in our society.

2. Origins of Terrorism : (14th-18th century)

Before the advent of terror, the Assassins were the next group to show recognisable characteristics of terrorism. A breakway faction of Shia Islam called Nizan Ismalis adopted the tactics of assassinations of enemy leaders. Why? Because the cult's limited manpower perverted open combat. Their leader, Hassam-i-Sabbah, based the cult in the mountains of Northern Iran. Their tactic of sending a lone assassin to successfully kill a key enemy leader at the certain sacrifice of his own life (the killers waited next to their victims to be killed or captured) inspired fearful awe in their enemies.

From the time of the Assassins (late 13th century) to the 1700s, terror and barbarism were widely used in warfare and conflict, but key ingredients for terrorism were lacking. Until the rise of the modern nation state after the treaty of Westphalia in 1648, the sort of central authority and cohesive society that terrorism attempts to influence barely existed. At that time, communication gap was tremendously wider and wider. And the causes that might inspire terrorism — religious schism, insurrection, ethnic strife — typically led to open warfare. By the time kingdoms and principalities became nations, they had sufficient means to enforce their authority and suppress activities such as terrorism.

It was the French Revolution that provided the first uses of the words 'Terrorist' and 'Terrorism' in full swing. Use of the word 'Terrorism' pitched in 1795 in reference to the Reign of Terror initiated by the Revolutionary Government. The agents of the Committee of Public Safety and National Convention that enforced the policies of 'The Terror' was referred to as 'Terrorists'. The French Revolution even provided an example to future States in oppressing their populations. It also inspired a reactionary loyalists and other opponents of the Revolution who employed terrorist tactics such as assassination and intimidation in resistance to the Revolutionary agents. The Parisian mobs played a critical role at key points during and after the Revolution. Such extra legal activities as killing prominent officials and aristocrats in gruesome spectacles started long before the guideline was first used.

Entering the Modern Era : (The 19th century)

During the late 19th century, radical political theories and improvements in weapons technology spurred the formation of small groups of revolutionaries who effectively attacked nation states. Anarchists espousing belief in the 'propaganda of the deed' produced some striking successes, assassinating heads of state from Russia, France, Spain, Italy and the United states. However, their lack of organisation and refusal to cooperate with other social movements in political efforts rendered anarchists ineffective as a political movement. In contrast, communism's role as an ideological basis for political terrorism was just beginning and became much more significant in the 20th century.

The terrorist group from this century onward that serves as a model in many ways for what was to come was the Russian Narodnya Volya (Peoples Will). They offered in some ways from modern terrorists, especially in that they would sometimes call off attacks that endanger individuals other than their intended target. Other than this quirk, we see many of the trails of terrorism here for the first time; clandestine, cellular organisation, impatience and inability for the task of organising the constituents they claim to represent; and a tendency to increase the level of violence as pressures on the group mount.

Judging from the present political situation, it may be said that an unprecedented violence and terrorism of Islamic fanaticism are fearsome predators. Pakistan has already missed some profound philosophical significance of the great Quran. why? Because Pakistan develops religious eccentricities and becomes cranks. It is as hot as the nether regions and just uncomfortable. On the other hand, Carlyle, recalling Shakespear's trenchant comment in 'The Merchant of Venice' on persons who are temperamentally averse to rejoicing or listening to the concord of sweet sounds observed in 'Sartar Resartus' : "The man who cannot laugh is not only fit for treasons, stratagems and spoils but his whole life is already a treason and a stratagem".

There are some political double-dealers, afflicted with diplomatic illness and pathological lying, who are surrounded by racks of massive volumes of Kashmir question, thinking seriously by the hour. Time was when the bathroom was part of an unmentionable vocabulary. But things have changed. Gandhiji declared publicly in his 'Harijan' that his lavatory was his library. Were the great ideas of partition born in his lavatory or nearabout or by the splash of water and the sound of the bathroon shower?

Terrorism is some compensation for great evils. What barbarians the terrorists are! The cannibal-like terrorist exclaims in horror "to kill without any real purpose" Thanks to the constant interest shown by a highly curious and vigilant western press, and by our neighbouring country, we, as a nation, are getting used to the process of the mirror being held up to us. Indeed, we are developing a thick skin and learning to laugh at ourselves and even at the ignorance of some of our critics. Our cracking at India's non-violence complex falls into the last category. Is India, proud of her ancient and being wedded to non-violence, ashamed of her nuclear proliferations? Yet there is definitely an element of guilt complex about the attitude of New Delhi. We have, however, known in this country of instances where idealistic fanaticism has routed forces of reason and realism by just invoking the name of Mahatma Gandhi! We should change our attitude. Why? Because attitude is a little thing that makes a big difference. Why? Because the only thing we can do is to play on the one string we have, and that is our attitude. What we think is 10 per cent but 90 per cent our attitude. Attitude can be produced by striking stone against stone. It is the most perversive of all elements.

The Muslims of Islamic country like Pakistan delude themselves by supposing that they can alter their anti-India slogans by a stroke of the pen. They err by thinking it is plan and not people that shapes education, that when they have difficulties and want a Kashmir solution it is enough just to have a scheme. Boys stay with Madrassa-based education only because of the intangible web of theology that is built up through the haphazard criss-cross of the threads of the human relationships.

Those boys are emotionally frozen and incapable of forming relationships with the people of behaviourism. They have lost their hold. Certainly they avoid like the plague of antagonisms of 'We' and 'They'.

Such an act can be real crime for terrorism in India. It is like stealing or like running through a field of lambing ewes or disturbing beastling pheasants. Without bitterness, one has to divide the Islamic virtues by 10 and multiply the vices by 100 to get a realistic idea of the Islamic views of what they are and do. When there is so much to mislead and divide the Islamic society by Shia and Sunni, a passion for Islamic truth is needed which will detect falsehood of Islamic terrorism and free people to be in a right relation to each other. The people of Pakistan have not been set free. Only those who have been set free can free others. Because only the loved can love. Pakistan's tragic descent into civil war and bloodshed is only too strangely in everyone's minds due to irresistible adventure of terrorism. Tombs are the clothes of the dead; a grave is but a plain suit, a rich monument is an embroidered one.

We know culture is a nebulous word and has a variety of meanings. To the cannibal the white man appears uncultured whilst to us the cannibals are barbarians. Judging from this angle, when we educate the masses, raise their standard of living and open a more varied life to them we are at the same time promoting their culture. When the Government becomes the arbiter of the arts, faiths, philosophies and morals of the people it cuts the soul out of these activities. It is the individual, his tastes, his ideas, his philosophies that matters.

A terrorist prides himself on being a slave, on being indistinguishable from what he himself calls the lower animals. His profound misapprehension that his slavery is a superior virtue leads him to attempt to impose it on others, to know it for what it is. He would fain infect others with the disease that afflicts him and they may well succeed in doing it for his own disaster. We are threatened with the disease even now. It would be wise for our Govt. to take necessary steps for quarantining those who show symptoms of it, before it is too late.

Why? To catch the affliction means that we lose all the joy of being; and that means that we are incapable of any worthy act. Esteem cannot be where there is no confidence; and there can be confidence where there is no respect.

According to 'Indo-Asian News Service', the Kashmiri Muslims have encouraged the return of Kashmiri pundits, in the valley, who had fled due to the insurgency raging for the last 20 years. Kashmir is incomplete without the pundits and the Kashmiri Muslims want them to return to their roots with dignity and honour. Nearly 2,00,000 pundits have been displaced by the insurgency and 60 percent of them have settled in the Jammu region. The Minister of Food and Supply, J & K, said, "My organisation is an apolitical venture and will work in the villages of Kashmir. NGO's priority is in working with Hindus displaced from villages as they have suffered the maximum and needed the most help. Previous governments had generated a kind of fear psychosis which prompted the pundits to flee the valley. Compared to the 96,000 Muslims who have lost their lives to the gun, only about 100 pundits have died."

Falsehood has an infinity of combinations but truth has only one mode of being. What of Pakistan's dreams? And her psychoses and complexes? Is her difficulty misanthropic, neurotic or religiously erotic on Kashmir issue?

Much of her trouble is directly due to her misguided attempts to suppress one or more sides of her being an Islamic country. The only way to solve these problems and pathological diseases is to choose ... choose between two or more preferences. Pakistan has lost with the craze for unified fundamentalists of Islamic terrorism. The trouble is that Pakistan has suppressed her natural pluralities into uninteresting unities. As things are, an atmosphere of stinking bad blood has been needlessly created in Kashmir. Robert Louis Stevenson wrote of Dr. Jekyll and Mr. Hyde, ".... one of the darker aspects of the matter .... Today, fortunately, everything is out in the open."

The mill of the mind grinds on. Kashmir is really a dark episode of frightening horror on the psychology of defeat and of the anguish born of a crisis in which Pakistan, an Islamic country, as well as men of religious fanaticism loses her identity. But they are never allowed to hear the cries of the victims. The big noise smothers the cries. The hypocrite rulers in Islamabad drink their morning coffee in peace. The horror of Pakistan is abstract. Pakistan has always been treated as status offender as our leaders.

Pakistan blunts the edge of her irony. She looks at a particularly bright side : terrorism is greater than any whammy of words. What is life to Pakistan on Kashmir question? We ask. Dogs fight for a bone. They fight for values. What are these? Pakistan is silent. She can't define. What is fulfilled is only her slow march of terrorism to Kashmir with a wry face that forebodes sure disaster to her office bearer. Why? Because she refuses to look in the face the victims of her cruelties in the valley. Because she runs into a carrier with the germ of an inner rot. Conceals more than it reveals.

Half a truth received by the jehadis, while the corresponding half is unknown or rejected by them, is a practical falsehood. Whereas our leaders smile confidently and are unabashed. We know the value of the voices of the voiceless. We tolerate terrorism and everything. Why? Because we believe nothing. If we utter one single syllable of protest, our mysterious leaders start all over again and begin the assault. The freedom and self-respect of the recipients should be surrendered in return. It is as hard for the good to suspect evil, as it is for the bad to suspect good. It is a full understanding of good and bad. Who will suspect them in our chattering society?

History of Terrorism : Terrorist acts or the threat of such action have been in existence for millennia. Despite having a history longer than the modern nation-state, the use of terror by governments and those that contest their power remains poorly understood. While the meaning of the word 'terror' itself is clear, when it is applied to acts and actors in the real world it becomes confused. Part of this is due to the use of terror tactics by actors of all levels in the social and political environment.

Biological Terrorism : It has a much longer history than bombings. And 'Biological warfare or Germ warfare' is the use of harmful bacteria as weapons. As far as sixty century 'Before the Common Era' (BCE), various people poisoned wells and used powerful herbs and infected corpses as tools of biological warfare. We know that Pak-Afghan border is the epicentre of terrorism. Scandals, slings and communal based vote-bank politics are the resultant effects of terrorism in India.

The first recorded use of biological agents was by the Romans, using dead animals to foul the water supply of their enemies. This had the dual effects of decreasing enemy numbers and lowering morale. The idea behind this kind of attack is that a weakened enemy is easily defeated The Tartars had the idea of infecting the enemy by catapulting bodies infected with bubonic plague over the walls of the city of Kaffa. Some historians believe that this event was the cause of the epidemic of plague that swept medieval Europe killing 25 million.

A more recent use of biological weapons involves the British and was suspected of being on the side of the French. As an "Act of good will" the British gave blankets to the Indians, but the blankets came from the hospital that was treating smallpox victims and, consequently, smallpox raged through the Native Americans greatly outnumbered the British and were suspected of being on the side of the French.

The followings are some examples of how biological warfare and terrorism has been used in the past. There is no doubt numerous other anecdotes of historical use of biological weapons not covered here.

6th Century B.C.

Assyrians poison the wells of their enemies with rye argot. Also Solon of

Athens poisons the water supply with hellobore (skunk cabbage) an herb purgative during the siege of Krissa.

1346 : During the siege of Kaffa, the Tartar Army hurls its plague-ridden dead over the walls of the city. The defenders are forced to surrender.

1422 : At the battle of Carolstein, bodies of plague-stricken soldiers plus 2000 cartloads of excrement are hurled into the ranks of enemy troops.

15th Century

It has been said that during Pizarro's conquest of South America, he improved his chances of victory by presenting it to the natives, as gifts, clothing laden with the variola virus.

1710 : Russian troops hurl the corpses of plague victims over the city walls of Reval during Russia's war with Sweden.

1763 : Captain Eouyer of the Royal Americans, under the guise of friendship, presents to the native Americans two blankets and a handkerchief contaminated with smallpox.

1767 : During the French and Indian war, the English General Sir Geffrey Amherst, gives blankets laced with smallpox to the Indians loyal to the French. The epidemic decimates the tribes of north-east America.

1797 : Napoleon attempts to force the surrender of Mantua by infecting the citizens with swamp fever.

1860-1865 : W.T. Sermon's memoirs contain an account of Confederate soldiers poisoning the ponds by dumping the carcasses of dead animals into them.

1914-1917 : Allegations are made against the Germans that during the World War I, they attempted to spread cholera in Italy, plague in St. Petersburg, and biological bombs over Britain.

1915 : Allegedly, a German-American, Dr. Arten Dilger, grows cultures of Bacillus anthracis (anthrax) and pseudomon as mallei glanders, supplied by the German Govt. in his Washington D.C. home. The agents and an inoculation device are given to sympathetic dockworkers in Baltimore to infect 3000 head of horses, mules and cattle destined for the Allied troops in Europe. It is also alleged that several hundred troops are additionally affected.

1931 : According to Prince Mikasa of Japan, Japanese military officials attempted to poison the League of Nations investigation commission who was researching Japan's siege of Manchuria. They poisoned the fruit with cholera. No one fell ill, however.

1940 : On October 4, the Japanese releases plague bacteria at Chuhsein resulting the deaths of 21 people. On October 29, plague is dropped by Japanese plane at Ninpo, resulting in 99 deaths. Japanese planes drop biological bombs at Chinhua. But there are no deaths.

1941 : In January, plague is introduced by the Japanese in Suiyuan and Ningshia provinces. A serious epidemic follows.

1950s : Mau Maus of Kenya use plant toxins to kill livestock.

1972 : Members of the right-wing 'Order of the Rising Sun' are arrested in Chicago. They possess 30-40 kg of typhoid cultures that are to be used to poison the water supply in Chicago, St. Louis, and other mid-west cities. The 2 arrested are betrayed by recruits. It was felt that had the detailed plan succeeded, it would have caused no problem due to chlorination of the water supplies.

1978 : On September 7, Bulgarian exile, Georgi Markov, in London, is injected in the leg with a steel ball impregnated with nicin via a speedy conducted umbrella. He is admitted into a hospital 36 hours after the attack where he is found to be febrile, tachycardic and with swollen lymph glands near the injection site. He died days later. This represents, in recent history, the first example of state-supported bioterrorism. The assassination is carried out by the communist Bulgarian Govt. with technology supplied by the Soviet Union.

1981 : An environment extremist group deposited packages containing anthrax contaminated soil outside a chemical weapons research facility and near a political party conference in Great Britain. The group, who called themselves the 'Dark Harvest Commandos' claimed to have obtained the material from Gruinard Stand, whose contamination they were protesting.

1984 : On August 29, Indian religious Rajneeshee cultists give water laced with Shalmonella to two country commissioners. Both get sick, 1 hospitalised in September, the Rajneeshee cult contaminates the sald bars of the Dates, OR and Wasco country, or with Salamenella. Over 750 are poisoned and 40 hospitalised. The purpose is to influence the outcome of a local election. It is only discovered a year later when members of the cult turned informants. Sheela, the chief of staff for Bhagavan Shree Rajneesh serves $2^{1/2}$ years and then is deported.

1995 : It is reported that on at least 10 occasions Ayum Shinrikyo attempted disperse anthrax, botulinum toxin, Q fever, and Ebola against the mass population and authority figures in Japan. No reported infections occur but below are five examples :

* **4/90 :** Outfitted car to disperse botulinum toxin through an exhaust system and drove car around parliament building.
* **6/93 :** Attempted to disrupt the wedding the Prince Naruhito by spreading botulinum in downtown Tokyo via car.
* **6/93 :** Spread anthrax in Tokyo via a sprayer system from the roof of a building. Done over 4 days.
* **3/95 :** Planted 3 briefcases designed to release botulinum in a Tokyo subway. The attack was averted when a cult member substituted a non-toxic agent instead.
* **1995 :** Members of Aum Shinniko cult release sarin nerve gas in Tokyo's subway system. The attack kills twelve and renders thousands sick.

2001 : Anthrax-laced letters sent through the mail killing 5 people. Seventeen others developed symptoms, but recovered. Most of the cases are linked to mail passing through NJ, NY or Washington or D.C. An estimated 10,000 people were placed on antibiotics. Attorney General John Ashcroft released the text from the anthrax letters sent to Daschle, Brokaw and the NY post. The letters dated Sept. 1 contain the phrases "Take Penacilin (sio) now", "Death to America", "Death to Israel", and "Allah is Great". Homeland Security Director Tom Ridge reported that the anthrax sent to Daschle's office was highly concentrated and designed to be disseminated and inhaled more easily.

In New York Times News Service, Thomas L Friedman, raised a question after the Bombay carnage : "So what can we expect from Pakistan and the other Muslim world after Mumbai?" It seems to him that the Pakistani Govt. which is extremely weak to begin with has been taking this mass murder very seriously, and, for now, no official connection between the terrorists and elements of Pakistani security services has been uncovered. He also raised a pertinent question why Pakistan has done in murdering defenceless men, women and children. Does it have not brought shame on us and on them? Why should Pakistan do that? The answer is simple. Because Pakistan knows that she cannot have a healthy society that tolerates in any way her own sons going into a modern city anywhere, and just murdering everyone in sight including other Muslims — in a suicide murder operation, without even bothering to leave a note. Because the act is their note, and destroying just to destroy is their goal. Mr. Friedman has categorically said : "We know from the Danish cartoons affair that Pakistanis and other Muslims know how to mobilise quickly to express their heartfelt feelings, not just as individuals, but as a powerful collective." That is what is needed here — Because this kind of murderous violence in the Bombay carnage on 26th Nov. 2008, is a powerful collective purpose — all the good people in Pakistan, including the community elders and spiritual leaders who want a decent future of their country, declares, as a collective, that those who carry out such murders are shameful unbelievers who will not dance with virgins in heaven but burn in hell. Truly speaking, Pakistan is in a state of Islamic bondage, pseudo-spiritual leaders and unbelievers chained by religious superstitions and anti-India hidebounds. The Mumbai carnage is a sincere expression of religious outrage by an individual Pakistani.

Ahmed Rashid, author of several books on the theatre of insurgency in Pakistan and Afganistan, and an expert in Islamic terrorism says in a co-authorised article with New York University's Barnet Rubin for the January issue, 2008, of 'Foreign Affairs' : "Al Quaida has established a new safe haven in the tribal agencies of Pakistan, where it is defended by a new organisation, the Taliban Movement of Pakistan." Rashid warns : "If the two countries mobilise their forces against one another, they will be walking straight into the trap laid for them by Al Quaida." Washington has been blamed for adopting a 'flawed and limited' policy on terror.

Who was behind the Mumbai carnage? Who controls the city's underworld business? Who smuggles petrol diesel, drugs, arms and other contraband with impunity? If anyone needs to do is to strike a deal with a particular underworld criminals. Why? Because he enjoys the patronage of powerful but influential politicians known to be business partners of those underworld barons. But our pseudo-secularist Govt. is completely reluctant about it or not. Everybody knows it but not our Govt. What a political hoax with the people! An astronomical amount of money is needed via the hawala route for any terrorist operation either in Kashmir or in any other part of India. An interesting but engrossing feature of the Mumbai carnage is that there is a joint probe by the IB, Enforcement Directorate (ED) and Directorate of Revenue Intelligence (DRI) revealed out a cracking report that one Hasan Ali had handled hawala transactions worth a whopping **Rs. 35,000 crore, much of it belonging to two Maharastra politicians. Not only that a laptop also revealed out details of vast amounts slashed away in Swiss bank accounts.** Now the question is : Are not our politicians worse than a banana republic like Pakistan? Democracy! where terrorists come by boat, and our morally degraded leaders come by vote. Most of them are ideologically prostitutes and ethically bastards. There is no shadow of doubt. How to solve the Kashmir issue is fundamentally an open question to all and sundry. Sir Creek, a narrow 99 km stretch of marsh-land, lying partly in Pakistan's Sindh province and partly in Gujrat off the Rann of Kutch, is an invulnerable area between India and Pakistan; and this disputed area is where the marine boundaries of the two countries are extremely hazy. The estuary is also where trawlers from both countries jostle for a good catch in brackish water. Sir Creek is one of the biggest sources of infiltrations coming across the border. Fishermen generally fish in these troubled waters of Islamic terrorism in India. The estuary is rich in fish.

Tao Te Ching, says in a message, LXXVI, : "The tree whose wood is the hardest is cut down. The mighty and the strong are thus cast down. And the humble and low are set on high." The hardest doctrinal framework of Pakistan sponsored Islamic terrorism would easily be cut down. Because the best part of our knowledge is that which teaches us where knowledge leaves off and ignorance begins.

Pakistan is the most stupid of all the Islamic countries of the world. Islamic terrorism the world over is very much in the doldrums. The United States must view with dismay the witches' cauldron they have brewed for themselves and their confused henchmen have a habit like the ghost in Macbeth of inconveniently reappearing. India proves that Pakistani leopard cannot change its spots. A real internationalist is one who brings his sympathy and recognition up to the point of practical and maximum help in support and defence of his own country by very means and in every possible form. This is the holy duty of every honest politician everywhere. Is not Pakistan guilty of spreading unfounded, terrorist-benefiting propaganda and media-cooked-up concocted news to discredit the United States? Has not Pakistan proved herself to be an instrument of world terrorism either in India or in other parts of the world? Does she have not surreptitiously engaged in behind-the-scene manoeuvres to defeat the purposes she viws? Certainly, very serious questions as to her intentions are raised on the Kashmir issue. Two things ought to be the object of fear, the envy of friends and the hatred of enemies.

Pakistan has brought terrorism forcibly to the country. The ISI has brought hatred, fear and want into every Muslim family of India. Islam is not process of transformation into Islamic terrorism. Islam has always been alive at the sight of the virtuous compassion and sympathy for the afflicted. Islam looks on the loveliness of the world and shares its sorrow. But today Islam begets illegitimate fear and anxiety. Terrorism is a combination of crude Islamic intolerance and religious ignorance locked up in anger and jealousy.

Comparison with Pakistan is inevitable; for both Pakistan and Islamic militants have at their best the same gift of Islamic irony, the same ability to turn accepted ideas upside down and inside out, the same love of verbal fireworks. This stepping stone is delightfully solid and unwobbly. Aggressively self-assertive to the point of religious arrogance, Pakistan has branded herself as an immature nation.

The National Assembly of Pakistan is divided sharply and distinctly into two camps. For purposes of identification. Those who belong to the first camp are full of guile and cunning about Islamic terrorism in the world. And those who belong to the latter, though numerically inferior, hold their own unimpecable political morals. They demand peace and cooperation at any cost in Kashmir. Not to be outdistanced in the arms race, the opposition pore over ancient files and collect evidence of Pakistan's Himalayan blunder made by their rivals on the Kashmir issue. The list is intimidating. In this maelstrom of plots, counterplots and ruthlessly-manoeuvred plans over Kashmir, Islamabad remains aloof and maintains a sham-modesty of neutrality. So, an inferno of the fires of antagonism and rivalry are kept alive by the satellites. In any major issue, they line up behind the Jehadis. Hot words ensue. Voices are raised. The result is that there has been very little or pure Islamic thought in Pakistan. What a shambles of political caesarism in Kashmir!

Both ISI and Islamic terrorism look exactly alike, we don't really know which is which. Sometimes ISI appears beside Islamic terrorism, but more often than not it is alone. It may show just a head with a beady eye.

Partition was done through compromise. It is : to love, to nourish and to perspire. Haste and rashness are storms and tempests, breaking and wrecking business.

Pakistan Prime Minister, Mr. Suhrawardy, once declared in Lahore, on Dec 2, 1956, that Pakistan would continue to seek alliances — military and otherwise — as long as there was even a remote danger from India to the country's safety and integrity. He categorically said that Indians as a whole had not accepted Pakistan's existence, and there was every possibility of a leadership arising in India which might work for a greater India by undoing partition and annexing Pakistan. Never join with your friend who abuses his wife.

India is a land of millions. The real strength of a country lies in her internal strength when the people of this world are torn by jealousy, hatred and violence; and armaments are being piled up. Whereas the communal character of Pakistan to the manner born is deplorable and her continued adherence to the two-nation theory is an anathema to the country's progress. Pakistan's prestige has suffered in this sub-continent. Why? In this topsy-turvy world of a weak bundle of bones in every way physical, mental and others, no one can keep isolated. Pakistan is seeking different paths of Islamic jehad against India on Jammu and Kashmir. When these paths conflict, clashes arise. Everywhere events are moving fast.

Among all the diseases of the mind there is not one more epidemical or more pernicious than the love of flattery. Most of the Pakistan rulers have not studied well about the Kashmir document. Having had a double-dyed diplomacy with superficial knowledge, their ignorance tingles our blood, benumbs our feet and freezes the Kashmir question like an apple.

Nehru seems to think that what he says is the truth and what anybody else says is propaganda. He also seems to imply that all propaganda of any kind is unworthy and that truth has no use for it. It is an unvarnished truth that throughout history propaganda has been used extensively by the deceitful persons for their nefarious purposes. Why? Because propaganda can be misused, however, it would hardly be justifiable to condemn all propaganda. There is nothing inherently wrong in propaganda and it can be put to just as many good users as bad.

After the 14th August, 1947, Nov. 11, 2000 is the most significant day in Pakistan's calender. That day of days saw the redrawing of the map of Pakistan's global terrorism vis-a-vis other million-fold multiplied means of terrorist activities throughout the world, showing the cards of religious fanaticism in Kashmir. What does it mean? It means 'one language' of Isalmic fanaticism and the people of Pakistan speaking in one language will be in one Islamic unit and split up their advantage and clubbed together piecemeal with fanatics speaking another language of death and destruction. Truly speaking, Kashmir is the incubator of Islamic terrorism.

Listen not to a tale-bearer or slanderer, for he tells you nothing out of goodwill.

The United States must necessarily be a coalition power to fight against Pakistan-sponsored Islamic terrorism. This coalition which has to be with countries separated by vast oceans, must be based on a correct understanding of the minds of the partners. One of the tragedies of the post-war decade has been the lack of an independent American policy for Asia. There was a hopeful beginning at the time of the Indonesian war. But since then, with the collapse of Chiang-Kai-Shek and the communist victory in China, American policy has been either largely negative or hopelessly tied to the apron-strings of the European colonial powers. For the first time, there is in Asia an awareness of the real character of Islamic terrorism.

An English essayist once said that the best way to defend ourselves is to attack others. Our security suffers a lack of coordination and in some places corruption is rampant.

The Military dictators of Pakistan with their pomp and theatricality have a strong upstart streak on them. Mussolini liked to watch his visitors walk over miles of gleaming marble before they reached his desk. Hitler thought nothing of hailing himself ... and did so at the slightest provocation. So the Islamic dictators of Pakistan have got used to exercising the same manner as Hitler and Mussolini did. And the bankrupted leaderships in Asia make room for the United States. And Pakistan is a mystery, a puzzling Islamic nation of our Muslim world.

The story of Islamic terrorism in India makes sad reading. No one can deceive himself with the hope that the small and unarmed population of the victimised areas can by itself forge effective sanctions to expel the occupation forces of SIMI. But if the past is any guide, the protest can hardly be expected to make any expression on Pakistani rulers who understand only one language — that of terrorism.

The Indian Leftists have got a suspicious character. Why? Because they do practise a political gamesmanship of democracy-damaging slogans inside and outside the parliament. Even on the Kashmir issue. They are political filibusters, playing on poorly-sounding sepulchral tones full of anti-national symphony. The treacherous, unexplored areas of the world are not in continents or the seas, they are in the minds and hearts of men. They are like a rusty iron machinery hiding in the undergrowth. All filibusters are linked together as a family. A good book is never exhausted. But our pseudo-Indian communists, like Islamic terrorists, do not perfume and give weight to democracy. Their slogans are always exhausted. They are political blackmailers and scars. Communism is a snake pit of betrayal. Like the terrorists, our pretentious as well as suspicious communists betray each other's families, they betray their wives and lovers. They are not those characters in movies. Emerson once remarked that "the curse of a country is eloquent men." The tempo of life has speeded up. There was when Edward Gibbon could write five volumes on the 'Decline and Fall of the Roman Empire'. Those time-worn days are useless and uninteresting. Who can tell today's terrorists and pseudo-communists will not be yesterday's social traitors? Why? Because the worse grows unchecked all the time by the perfidy of others. Nehru once declared the Indian communist party as '*the stupid of all the communist parties of the world.*' It is easier to build a governing class than to develop a class of governors. Two things ought to be the object of our fear, the envy of friends and the hatred of enemies.

Strange to say, religion is good but religious fanaticism, riding the Trojan-horse of unhealthy religious ambition, can lead Pakistan to a terrorist country. Local Jingoism is good but it can be apocalyptically damaging if it forgets to love the nation. Intolerance towards other countries' economic development is crude and rough gratified by another's sufferings for a vigorous campaign in favour of Islamic cause. Even the Islamic crusade flummoxed by the double-dyed religious teachers for religious ends of Islam is secret, mysterious and enigmatic. Pak-occupied Kashmir, a well-furnished incubator of terrorist organistaions, is nurtured in its infancy, uttering a deep hoarse sound of anti-India slogans instigated by the sinister influence of religious crusaders. Pakistan has now been at the acme of religious crippledom.

Both crusaders and crusade in the valley of Kashmir have now been under the spell of hypnotic inertia of religious dualism. The first crusade (1096-9) resulted in the capture of Jerusalem and the establishment of Crusader States in the Holy Land, but the second (1147-9) failed to stop a Muslim resurgence, and Jerusalem fell to Saladin in 1187. The third (1189-92) recaptured some lost ground but not Jerusalem, while the fourth (1202-4) was diverted against the Byzantine Empire, which was fatally weakened by the resultant sack of Constantinople. The fifth (1217-21) was sidetracked to Egypt, where it accomplished nothing, and although the sixth (1228-9) resulted in the return of Jerusalem to Christian hands the city was lost to the Turks in 1244. The seventh (1248-54) ended in disaster in Egypt, while the eighth and last (1270-71) petered out when its leader Louis IX of France died on his way east, and the Holy Land was left in Muslim hands until the 20th century. Although undertaken in a religious cause, the Crusaders were carried on like most other medieval wars and were generally badly organised and indecisive.

Today, Islamic terrorism in the name of crusade is frantically dangerous. Islamic faith among the terrorists is threatened by three encumbrances, namely, false outlook, limitless desires and deception. It vitiates the simplicity and dignity of Islam throughout the world. It spells disaster. Why? Because deception is the biggest encumbrance to attaining liberation of mind. An Islamic nation that is without Islamic knowledge, without Islamic faith and of a doubting nature perishes. So, the gist of Islamic development is not only crooked but also limited in growth and expansion.

The Mumbai terror-strikes are a domestic issue but not India's 9/11. It only ignites a backlash against Indian Muslims. It is not the triumph of ideology of extremism over democracy. The most effectual hitherto found is the freedom of terrorism. And it is the foundation stone of Pakistan's military rule. Pakistan lets the greater felon loose. The pattern of the Mumbai attacks is fundamentally different from preceding terror attacks on Indian soil. Why? Because earlier attacks had seen crude explosive devices by timers or mobile phones. The difference is : The Mumbai terrorists were armed with Kalashnikov assault rifles, hand grenades and huge quantities of sophisticated explosive. Viewing through Kashmir's nightmare, it is clear that the real problem lies within Pakistan, Afganistan and Bangladesh. Why? Because the most nefariously violent anti-India campaign of extremists in these vulnerable areas is against liberal, democratic values. Why? Because the extremists' commitment, endorsed by the coterie of Islamabad-ISI-religious extremism, to the establishment of an altered world order is based on their exclusionary religious beliefs, putting the entire world at grievous risk. And our country offers itself as an immediate and symbolically potent target. The world realises the problem through the Kashmir prism. But the miserable, despised and ideologically-rotten political leaders, dying and forgotten in the social shambles of terrorist activities, give us howling inside and outside the Parliament and their naked savagery with the Pakistan-backed underworld criminals. And the police are the handmade of our so-called political bastards. Terrorism in India is created by the behind-the-curtain political barons linked with underworld criminals. It is fact. No one can deny it.

We have only one Mother India but she speaks with myriad tongues. If this goes on, the advocates of crusade or terrorism will begin to set them as disruptive forces. They will be traitors to Islam. The more terrorist organisations in Pakistan nourish, learn and know, the prouder she feels as an Islamic nation. A magnificent mixture of Islamic triumph and tragedy.

Secrecy that is widely published is no secrecy. 'Strategy' to fight against terrorism is a wrong word to use ; 'tactics' to combat terrorism is more to the point, for tactics applies to all manoeuvres to win small advantages. There can be tactics of retreat but a strategy of retreat makes no sense. To receive favours from the unworthy is to admit that Pakistan's selfishness is superior to her pride.

Now, aggression has come, from the western world, and from the champions of Islamic countries in Asia. Americans themselves are growingly conscious of the failure of an Asian policy backing the European colonial powers. The United States has to use its influence more strongly to speed up the process of transition to independence in the areas where Islamic terrorism and religious extremism still exist. The danger at Pakistan's door-step is more real, if only more imminent. The bankrupt leaderships in Asia make room for the United States. When time holds up the mirror, Pakistan finds her own sin revealed. She can consider vice with all her baits on Kashmir and seeming pleasures, however noble the Koran. Why? Terrorists are made to be slaves. They know it and do not much mind. They live by their beliefs in Islam and die when their beliefs in Islam pass over into Himalayan blunder; when peace in Kashmir is disturbed by theological quarrels, they will continue to commit atrocities. The Kashmiri Muslims seem to rejoice in caste-related sentiments of the common people. Religious bigotry is a common disease of extremism in Pakistan. It is a never-ending series of Islamic passion. Such a deterring effect is distasteful to the entire Islamic world. Not only that Islamic nation has been mortgaged up to the hilt of Islamic terrorism and has gangrened the Islamic society in a humiliating way of moss-grown foreign policy over India and other foreign nationals. Not to be subdued by severities and penance for her moronic passion of violence over the innocent people, Pakistan's dual diplomacy against terrorism, the extra-ordinary secrecy, religious sorcery, and political deception on every front of Kashmir question suggests only among other things that the Islamic world has been confronted with unexpected consequences of other Islamic countries. In this moribund phase of political criss-cross, clouds have been gathering over Islamabad. Violence has already been used as an instrument of political pressure and every young and comparatively inexperienced Govt. in Pakistan faces its most severe test. Pakistan's foreign policy on Kashmir is just like a music without charms. A single unvaried tone of anti-India campaign. Disease knows no frontiers.

Riddled with failure, incompetence, evasion and social disaster, Pakistan — a ragged disreputable Islamic nation furiously angry and violent — has planned to liquidate democracy with irritating laughs and all those who do not shake hands the way she wants them to Islamic management. Islamic clergymen, with overmastering passion of religious mania, get into loud guffaws of merriment on seeing democracy in an awkward situation. And the noisy and riotous Rulers of Pakistan play rough and practical jokes on Kashmir issue, raking up the past habits and ranting out propaganda with empty declamation. To the rulers, the desire for solitude is something morbid and melancholy. Educational propaganda, in order to yield good results, must have a proper climate, the lack of which has been the primary cause of indiscriminate damage to primary Islamic education. As carriers of fanatical seeds and killers of Islamic message, Pakistan helps maintain a socio-religious balance in the valley of Kashmir. Terrorism represents something even bigger than the Islamic nation itself. As land is improved by sowing it with various seeds so is the mind by exercising it with different studies. We should be as careful of the books we read as of the company we keep. The dead very often have more power than the living.

Mr. Nehru's letter of Sept. 3, 1953, is instructive. He wrote : "The resolutions of the United Nations Commission are based on the recognition of the de jure authority of the State administration over even the areas now occupied by Pakistan, and the Constitutional right of the Govt. of India to safeguard the security of the State. There can be no question whatever of Pakistan or any outside authority sharing, in any way, in the administration of the State. The whole basis of the U.N. approach in its resolutions, and subsequently through Dr. Graham, has been the recognition that there is a difference between the status of the two countries in this and other matters." The letter goes on : "It is the Govt. of Jammu and Kashmir State that is recognised throughout; there is no recognition anywhere at any time of any Govt. in the areas of Kashmir State occupied by Pakistani forces .... the right and responsibility of the Govt. of India to maintain a certain minimum number of troops, such as might be required for the security of the State, have throughout been recognised."

The basic fact form which all else follows is that Pakistan is the aggressor in Kashmir and that aggression has continued even after sixty years in the face of U.N. resolutions on the subject.

Pakistan and the Case for Kashmir

There comes a perennial problem of Kashmir which Pakistan plans to bring up. Since the roots of the matter are lost in the mist and miasma of the past 60 years, it is pertinent to unearth them. India has no reason to be apologetic over Kashmir. Indeed, if anything, she has sound reasons for being aggrieved. The defensive and different so often assured by a good few Indians on this matter stems largely from ignorance of the facts of the case.

What are the facts? When Pakistan took place in August, 1947, the so-called princely states comprised over 565 units of varying size and resources. Of these, Kashmir, in area almost as large as Great Britian, covered before the Indo-Pakistan cleavage some 84,000 sq.miles.

The Indian Princes, as is well-known, were bound in special treaty relating with the British crown which exercised its domain over them under the doctrine of Paramountcy. This doctrine certainly conceded no independent status to any prince as Lord Reading made clear to the Nizam of Hyderabad in 1926. It could not, therefore, fairly be expected of the Indian successor Govt. that it should automatically accept a position which its predecessor had rejected for good reason.

Mr. Jinnah, realising that the overwhelming majority of 562 princely states were in Indian territory, sought to fish in troubled water and make trouble for India by encouraging, even inciting the Indian princes to declare their independence. Had they done so, they would have established over 500 independent islands or islets of territory within India whose unity and stability had already been precariously weakened by partition. Happily, patriotism and commonsense prevailed with all of them save three ... Kashmir, Hyderabad and Junagadh. With the latter two we are not concerned here.

A month before partition Lord Mountbatten, addressing the princes for the last time in his capacity as the Crown Representative, had advised them that practical considerations left them only with the choice of accession either to India or Pakistan subject to certain considerations which necessarily had to be taken into account. Among these considerations was geographical contiguity.

The Radcliff Award

Truly speaking, Pakistan is with jealousy as with the gout; when such distempers are in the blood, there is never any security against their breaking out, and that often on the slightest occasions, and when least suspected.

The Radcliff Award, which partitioned the Punjab and Bengal, gave India a frontier with Kashmir along the Gurudaspur district. Pakistan has also a frontier with Kashmir running along a much-longer line. But both countries could claim territorial contiguity with Kashmir unlike the cases of Hyderabad and Junagadh neither of which enjoys territorial contiguity with Pakistan. Why? Because of this, the case of Junagadh is in no way with that of Kashmir.

On Kashmir, India throughout has behaved with scrupulous rectitude and care. "We have, indeed, been over scrupulous in this matter so that nothing may be done in the passion of the moment which might be wrong," Nehru declared after Pakistan's aggression.

In June 1947, two months before partition, Mountbatten visited Srinagar and with the full authority of the newly created States department in India headed Sardar Ballabhai Patel advised the Kashmir Maharaja that he was free to accede to either India or Pakistan. This matter is on record.

"Ascertain the will of your people by any means," Mountbatten counselled Hari Singh, "and join whichever Dominion your people wish you to join by August 14 this year."

It was Kashmir's misfortune that in the Maharaja it had a ruler congenitally incapable of making up his mind and foolish enough ... as was Sheikh Abdullah later ... to believe that Kashmir could retain an independent status. Hari Singh hoped to triumph by delay, in the meanwhile entering into a Standstill Agreement with Pakistan under which that Govt. undertook to continue to run the communications, postal and telegraph services. The Maharaja offered a similar agreement to India which New Delhi refused for the valid reason both India and Pakistan would confirm the Maharaja in his separatist dreams.

Earlier in the spring of 1949, a no-tax campaign in Poonch was suppressed with great brutality by the Maharaja's Dogra forces. India had nothing to do with this. In Jammu province also many muslims lost their lives. Wedged in the underbelly of Kashmir was divided Punjab and when partition came the flames of the communal conflagration seeped into the State as Hindus, Sikhs and Muslims poured from the two wings of divided Punjab into Jammu and Poonch. Meanwhile Pakistan sought to force Kashmir into accession by with vital supplies such as salt, sugar, petrol, cloth and other consumer commodities.

In explanation and excuse, Karachi pleaded disruption of communications and traffic. If that were so, how could Pakistan explain the simultaneously organised incursion of tribesmen from the areas across the North-West Frontier into Kashmir?

Most of the equipments these men carried were obviously supported by Pakistan comprising as it did rifles, bren and sten guns, two and three inch mortars, anti-tank rifles, Mark-V mines and man-packed walkie-talkie sets. Moreover, the invaders were provided with motor transport and railway trains, given petrol, food and accommodation and rendered every possible aid and comfort on their way to Kashmir. Md. Zafarrulah Khan blandly denied these charges before the U.N., but when 'On-looker' paid to visit to Peshwar in August 1953 the Pir of Manki Shariff along with other frontier notabilities openly admitted that they had organised and helped the tribal raids and even took 'On looker' to some frontier villages and introduced several of the ex-raiders to him. Zafarrulah also repudiated the accusation that Pakistan army personnel had actively assisted the raiders but when on the U.N. Commission's first visit to Karachi in July 1948, it was no longer possible to conceal their presence in Kashmir, Karachi suavely admitted the fact.

What followed is comparatively well-known. By mid-October when a considerable part of the Poonch and Mirpur areas was in the possession of the invaders, even the Kashmiri Maharaja was sufficiently perturbed to protest on the one hand to Pakistan and on the other to appeal to India. Had the tribesmen not dallied at Baramulla, 55 miles from Srinagar, the Kashmir story might well have been different. By October 24, even Hari Singh's chronic indecision had given place deep-seated alarm and to a real concern for his own personal safety. He asked for New Delhi's armed assistance an appeal which was supported by Sheikh Abdullah. But the Govt. of India realised that it would be impolitic and improper to give military aid unless Kashmir first acceded to India insisted on as a prerequisite to the despatch of troops. This the Maharaja did in a letter dated October 26 and on the morning of October 27 a battalion of Indian troops flew out from Palam to Srinagar. It was this battalion which temporarily checked the invaders and as reinforcements came and helped to save the situation.

During the two following months, Mr. Nehru was in correspondence with the then Pakistan's Prime Minister, Mr. Liaquat Ali Khan, and in the course of this correspondence the Govt. of India, while its earnest desire from allowing the tribesmen to use Pakistan territory as a base for the invasion of Indian territory. No reply was received from Karachi to three communications from New Delhi, and on Dec. 30, 1947. India referred the matter to the Security Council of the U.N. Under articles 34 and 35 of the Charter, according to which any member may bring any situation whose continuance is likely to endanger the internal peace and security to the attention of the Security Council. Mr. Nehru also promised that the Maharaja's act of accession, which was endorsed by Sheikh Abdullah, should later be endorsed by a plebiscite, but this promise, it is important to note, was conditional on certain factors. These stipulated that peace and order would have to be established and the raiders driven out of Kashmir or themselves withdrew before the issue of a accession was decided by a plebiscite or referendum.

As the Prime Minister described it at the time, India's reference to the Kashmir issue to the Security Council was "an act of faith". India had nothing to conceal. In appealing to the Security Council, she urged that the primary duty of that body was to put a stop to the fighting by calling upon the invaders to withdrow and by requesting Pakistan to desist from letting her territory be employed as a base for invasion and attack. It must be noted that when the ceasefire was declared in January 1949, Kashmir was by no means completely free of the invaders. On the Pakistani side of the ceasefire line lived some 9,00,000 people with about another 1,00,000 centred in the northern area including Gilgit. Kashmir is also not free of the military invaders for both Pakistani troops as well as the so-called Azad Kashmir forces occupy large tracts of what is legally Indian territory.

The issue before the Security Council was simple and its hesitation in the known circumstances of the case to brand Pakistan as aggressor created legitimate suspicion in the Indian minds. The Security Council had once condemned Yugoslavia, Albania and Bulgaria for giving assistance to the rebels fighting the Govt. forces in Greece. What prevented it from condemning and compelling Pakistan to make the tribal invaders withdraw. Later in June 1950, when the North Koreans crossed the 38th Parallel Line, the Security Council was again to pronounce the North Koreans as invaders. But if the North Koreans had invaded South Korea, so had Pakistan invaded Kashmir. Truly speaking, the Security Council has always been ranked with grossly offensive rascality, seizing and carrying away the vitals of Security Council Charter. It has already bartered away its qualitative and synthetic approach to world peace. The basic fact from which all else follows is that Pakistan is the aggressor in Kashmir and that aggression has continued even after 60 years in the face of the U.N. resolutions with much-saturated and self-styled political depravity. India knew Pakistan once a servant of Machiavellian success in the book of pharisee.

Some other points made by Pakistan are equally revealing. It is : "The right of the Muslims of Kashmir to secure freedom from Hindu domination as we have done in Pakistan" smacks of the two-nation theory which has been utterly disproved in Pakistan itself. The two-nation theory is dead and attempt to revive it over Kashmir must render suspect Pakistan's bona fides in this matter. Does Pakistan feel Kashmir a home away from home?

It is interesting to note that it is Pakistan that rejects India's continuing offer of a no-war declaration between the two countries. Why? Because Pakistan is prepared to enter into such a pact only after the Kashmir issue has been settled to Pakistan's satisfaction and not before. Unfortunately, many responsible Pakistani leaders appear to have been inciting in the past and even today Pakistan has started out playing on a stringed musical Islamic instrument of jehadi with unrhythmic verses. This real politik stands no reasons.

China is no threat : Because China still has 23 million people living in poverty. China's very goal in its development is so that its 1.3 billion people can eat their fill, dress warmly and live well. Why could China threaten? They don't have the ability. China does not and will never threaten anyone. Why? Because anti-China sentiment runs high in China. There is a big difference with rich cities such as Beijing and Shanghai. As the butcher takes away the calf, so does her anti-china sentiment take away the shallow-rooted communism.

Whereas our neighbouring country, Pakistan, having been armed with outworn religious dogma and outrageously violent in her anti-India campaign, is quite different in all respects from India. So many differences lie in between the two countries.

The fly in the Kashmir oinment is, of course, Pakistan. Why? Pakistan serves primarily as a spring-board for terrorist designs. Undue solitude at this stage for Pakistan will only inflame India's suspicion. Depending on the good grace and military strength of U.S. is strictly not a pact but a mortgage deed.

She has already been branded with 'Banana Republic'. This is tantamount to entering Asia militarily by the backdoor of Afganistan and Iraq, a procedure which can only bring war — cold or hot — nearest to Asia's doorstep. Secondly, a military pact has validity only among equals.

The Americans are the most civilised people but not cultured. The Pakistanis are grossly uncivilised people and sordidly uncultured. Because there is a partnership of Islam and terrorism. Because there is Islam in their room and Islamic terrorism under their bed. Because the Pakistani rulers and the devil are dividing the Islamic souls in the cemetery. Stealthily approaching the graveyard, the two heard a voice saying, "One for you and one for me." Truly speaking, Pakistan describes the Kashmir issue with the enthusiasm of a salesman of Islamic terrorism, groaning and fuming furiously. The final revelation has to wait. Stripped of holiness, the shroud of Islamic nation holds a mystery.

What is culture and what is civilisation? Are there no cultured people among all nations although these people may be poor and without even a high-school education? But they observe the laws of God and nature better than the so-called people? Did the Chinese have the freedom of thought and expression for all this long period of 3,000 years? Were they not war-torn by the ancient kings and warlords? Even so can it be said today the Chinese are really people?

Pakistan : A country that has no history cannot be said a nation of cultured people. A country that has been inflicted with a narrow-doctrinal framework of high-voltage religious passion, saturated with rapaciously greedy and graspingly predatory Islamic sentiment, and mortified with wretched political hypocrisy over the Kashmir issue cannot be said an Islamic nation devoid of all Islamic ideologies and culture. So, Islamic terrorism must be there.

The United States is a champion of democracy, but it turns a blind eye to all the atrocities committed in Kashmir. Maybe she is compelled to do so due to the exigencies of the world situation. Similarly, India has to tolerate many other evils like terrorism.

Here in India, we boast of our places of pilgrimage, our civilisation and culture. Religion is a personal affair, unique and complex, and religious instruction if loosely imparted in schools and Madrassas would accentuate fanaticism and worn-out prejudices in a world of growing inter-dependence. A loosely instructed religious teaching in Pakistan cannot thrive best in a vibrating atmosphere of bloodshed and violence where each citizen does not strive to help the other and live bravely in the here and now. If he sees wrangling religious teachers and puny intellectuals scrambling mightily for a little limelight, then surely no amount of theoretical religious instruction can broaden their outlook or form their Islamic character under the pangs of unhappy ending. Even the growing religious indiscipline among the SIMI adherents and their disregard for Hinduism are the result of the neglect of religious education. The real roots of terrorism lie in Muslim-oriented areas of India. They know the thunder of terrorism, still dream the nightmare of Islamic globalisation. It is an Islamic trick of the jihadi trade, trading upon their religious fanaticism.

Is there a crisis of culture? But no one in Pakistan wants to raise this awkward question." O dark, dark, dark, amid the blaze of noon" ... what's the use of crying their heart out like Samson? Even if there is a crisis, let them learn to live with it.

Pakistan today : From defeat to defeat to defeat, Pakistan looks backwards. Partition was a beginning and terrorism will be a destiny.

Islamic terrorism : Is it the fever in their brain? What is a crisis of culture? It is a crisis of Islamic values. The old values and old beliefs no longer answer the new needs. Are they quite sure what values they are trying to create through Islamic terrorism? They have the image of the crisis of their culture in the faces of their millions. Who are broken down by their circumstances? They are not responsible for the want, the misery and the fear in which so many live. It is a crisis of colonialism or semi-colonialism, a crisis of acquisitive societies — they know what they are striving for. Who are the offenders that are to be examined?

They know only too well the evils of terrorism, of religious extremism, of colonialism, and of want and misery in the midst of shameless and unblushing sevility to Islamic theology. They fist for compliments and show their paces from their neighbouring Islamic nations. They are physically and mentally choked. That is certainly a symptom of a dangerous crisis in Pakistan, what are the roots of this moral suffocation? They are tortured and their ribs are broken under the pangs of grasping Islamic rule. Where are the roots of this cruelty and this degradation? The people of Pakistan are told lies — lies about events to which they are a witness and yet they do not question about these lies. Where are the roots of the lies and craven fear? Are we to look for them in the neurosis of a single man? Terror in Kashmir : They remain silent and when they spoke they denied there was any terror in India. Where the roots of this silence? Is their dialectical innocence or in their anxiety to save their own skin from the big powers? This silence is composed and framed of treachery.

There are symptoms of crisis. The people in Pakistan are told they are free when they are really not free — that their standard of living is rising high when they know at their breakfast table that it is not. Is there no crisis of Islamic culture when a whole people are made to live on a diet of lies and a romance of pathological lying full of diplomatic illness? Everything is now explained away by the word 'mistake'. 'Mistake indeed :' When Islamabad lies, I.S.I. plays a deceptive role; Islamabad lies deliberately to deceive the other. When a militant spills the blood of innocent men, women and children, either in Kashmir or outside Kashmir, an extremist does not commit a mistake. Confucius, Chinese philosopher, says : "If justice goes astray, the people will stand about in helpless confusion." Terrorism does not help comfort them tomorrow. Yesterday to Pakistan is foul words. Today to Pakistan is foul wind. Tomorrow is foul breath. All are noisome.

When Islamabad tries to convince the other not by reason but by persecution, it is not because Islamabad believes that physical torture over the Kashmiri Hindu pundits is the most effective argument but because Islamabad fears that reason is not all on its side. When the fear of reason and of truth becomes so widespread as it does in India and other foreign countries, isn't it time to find out if there is a crisis of Islámic culture? If there were no crisis of culture, so many poets and philosophers would confess that for years they believe in chimeras and that when the chimeras rally, one dies slowly of a broken heart. Would they beg for the bread of freedom and the bread of reason from excruciating clutches of religious serfdom?

The point is that the crisis of Islamic values is not confined to Pakistan. The pattern is new in every moment. And every moment is new and shocking. They know that Pakistan has not withered away but has grown new tentacles. There will be always the danger of terror. They also suffer from schizophrenia of religious dualism. They know that the prosperity of so many Muslim Leaguers is based on the exploitation of Hindu property left at the time of partition. So many of them have two sets of morals — one at home and another abroad. Even their poets sometimes succumb to the anonymous power of the market. It is the fear of failure that is the killer of Pakistan. A mighty stream of Jehadi slogans gushes out from the Pak-occupied based terrorist camps — their sole is the source of power. So Pakistan has to cram all religious feelings into her mind. If you create an external disharmony, you create an internal disharmony also.

Apart from the cases of Pakistan on Kashmir issue, China has stepped up incursions by its troops across the *Line of Actual Control (LAC)* into Sikkim at both the military as well as diplomatic levels. It is believed '*Finger Area*' — the so-called 2.5 km the northern most tip of Sikkim — has caught the fancy of the Chinese. Why? Because the terrain is flat — a parity in Sikkim, and 'tankable'. A road between Gir and Takshang Gang, near the Khamba Dzong in Tibet, runs close to the '*Fingertrips area*'.

If democratic India and totalitarian China are the world's two rival political experiments, so are Pakistan and Afganistan are on a larger scale. Pakistan suffers from the formidable armed gangs of terrorists masquerading as religious sects and smashes the anti-Islamic elements in a resolute and courageous drive in which the armed forces of militant organistaions and the civil services zealously cooperated. At one stroke, gambling, prostitution and opiumdens of drug-barons are rampant inside and outside *the Crescent Triangle and the Golden Triangle... the most popular drug-producing areas of Pakistan under the patronage of hard-boiled Pakistani rulers*. A musical comedy between rulers and I.S.I., an Islamic fungus in the world of terrorism. Inevitably, anti-India line is very loud in the Govt's policies. Pakistan is adept in the art of cheating the conscience. She decides the Kashmir issue by spinning coin. This gives both sides a sporting chance of terrorism and peace-making process in

Kashmir. In the 'Evening Star' of London, Earl Attlee writes on Nov. 20, 1956 : "*Kashmir has definitely opted for Union with India.*"

The fact that Pakistan has been accepted as a terrorist country is a good news to the world. And the bad news? She is going to pay for it. She enters the gates of hell and is immediately set upon by a dozen of religious demons. The band-leader, I.S.I., is her fiance poking Islamabad with pitchforks. Whenever Pakistan commits a blunder of cross border terrorism, people say, "What a foolish nation:". And if a terrorist commits a blunder, people say, "He is so foolish:" *Religious publicity means public shame and humiliation. The elephant dips his trunk in the muddy river.*

Kashmir is not a communal but a political question. India has always contended this. But the trouble is that Pakistan's claim on Kashmir is intrinsically communal. She nonchalantly rattles the bones of religious fanaticism over the stones of Kashmir; and she unwittingly releases a series of weird events.

She has brought the set of bones from the jehadi store. Who is the proprietor of those bones? Who is the preserver and pursuer of lofty but impracticable ideas? Pakistan flashes out a quizzical smile, having a quiver full of terrorists. A traitor to Islam. *To remain in the middle is difficult.* Why? Because the pendulum goes to the right, then it goes to the left; then again to the right, and again to the left.

History of Pakistan is the unfolding of miscalculation, having nit-picking allegations over India on Kashmir issue. So many cavernous conferences have been held so far. Pakistan's silence over terrorist activities is artificial. Born in a tempest of anti-India slogans, when partition died, Islamic fanaticism is a lasting storm.

Our political leaders should tell their problems to people who don't like them why they are in league with the underworld criminals to fight against terrorism. Because they are the only ones who want to hear them. They don't do so because of their quizzical look. The hollow man — the naked man — the man in anguish — the revolutionary — the lonely — the neurotic — the man who is to face to face with his debacle. We know them all. Their ideological dogmas burn in the fires of lust and hate and glamour and who is he that puts them out? The paradox remains. The sufferings of our democracy inside the Parliament are bound up with ego-asserting nature of parliamentarians. They prefer not to answer questions. Why? Either because they are irrelevent or because no words can cope with them. To air their criticism and complaints does no service to the country. It is much as if a ship in distress keeps firing at her rescuers. After partition, our political monsters lead the way of democracy.

We don't know how far we can go. Our leaders in the name of fighting against terrorism cannot control and subjugate the popular masses; therefore in some cases they try to halt any further estrangement on Kashmir issue. The Congress party at the centre, for over decades, have fostered soullessness and cynicism in the ruling circles and fed obstinacy and arrogance among the rulers, using its monopoly of political power in the service of reaction and for bolstering up reactionary policies in Hindu-Muslim community. It has permeated every pore of the Govt. with festering corruption and unbelievable inefficiency to wage war on terrorism. It has encouraged the authoritarian trends of Kashmiri Muslims who spell serious threats to our democracy. It has hardened bureaucracy and enabled it to spread its deadening influence at all levels of public administration in Kashmir. It has even stifled the voice of those who stand against Islamic terrorism. And finally, this monopoly of political power has provided incentives for mass destruction, wanton police firing and various other sinister methods of third degree. Our political monsters! Howling monsters! drunken monsters! ignorant monsters! religious monsters!

If one likes to write a biography of Pakistan after partition, writing her life-history would be an eye-opener to many. An illiterate man in Pakistan would not be a bad one to recite his experiences to tell the beadroll of the pains and pleasures that fell to his lot in his sojourn through life. Most men's lives are depressingly dull and are not worth going. Who is the protagonist of SIMI? He is with all his virtues and vices in bold relief. He cares not for any Hindu community, for applause from the pit and stalls, nor does he appeal to the gallery in a last desperate attempt at mock-shows of religious fanaticism and make-belief in Islamic terrorism. He is not talking at posterity. He is cunning with an intimate, a friend in his retreat to whom he may whisper 'Terrorism is sweet'. Jihadis are so woefully misunderstood that they appear to be complex. Islamic terrorism is now a perishable product. Why? Because it is easy to fool yourself. It is possible to fool the people you work for. It is more difficult to fool the people you work with. But it is almost impossible to fool the people who work for you.

How sad is the story of the partition! The political and defence problems between India and Pakistan continue as a running sore and a heavy drain on the resources of the two countries.

So, Islamic terrorism is a kernel of the forbidden fruit which still sticks in the throat of Pakistan, sometimes to the danger of her chocking.

Pakistan's crisis has now reached its boiling point. Who was behind the curtain? It was Gen. Musharraf who headed a military dictatorship. The authoritative 'Financial Times' On May 15, 2007, dolefully editorialised : "He is now in danger of forfeiting western support — His re-elected president led him into a political blind alley." Not only that he dismissed Chief Justice but he wanted to be a more obedient figure at the head of the judiciary. He deepened instability in Pakistan, reeling from bloody political riots over the year in Karachi. It appeared to be the work of an Islamic militant.

The Persian word 'Khurasan' is often used in militant videos to describe Afganistan. Peshwar is the capital of NWFP, a region bordering Afganistan where pro-Taliban and Al Quaida-linked militants are active. Nothing exists for Pakistan. Everything else is opinion. She looks into space of limited dimensions.

It is the ISI that communicates its wishes to the orchestrated battle plan of Islamic terrorism in and around Kashmir by whistling, singing and making gestures of sporadic violence. It becomes a part of Pakistan's history. It is supposed to be an Islamic secret. Pakistan is torn between pride and anger — a replica of her darling perversities hallowed by tradition.

It is dangerous evolution of anti-India terrorism, siphoning off funds for terrorist activities. Jihadi groups are also collaborating with other terror groups and entering into partnership with criminal syndicates for carrying out kidnapping for high ransoms and bank robberies. As part of its plans to hollow out the Indian economy. Pakistani agencies are dumping counterfeit currency in India. Large amounts of high-quality fake Indian currency are detected and the normal route is Nepal and Bangladesh. Very critical to defeat global terrorism. We have to turn searchlight inward relentlessly to weed out all the parameters of our political leaders and their hangers-on who are in league with underground criminals. Why? Our leaders' political solecism is a disease. They have as many friends as enemies.

LEWIS CARROLL in his immortal 'Alice's Adventures in Wonderland' writes about a whiting asking a snail to join him in a Lobster Quadrille : "Will you, won't you, will you, won't you, will you join the dance?" The world seems to be asking Pakistan a similar question. Will she, won't she, will she, won't she stop cross-border terrorism in and around Kashmir? Pakistan is quite similar to that of Carroll's snail. Pakistan, harping on the same string as usual, says that she "would not , could not, would not, could not, would not join the dance." It is not surprising that Pakistan is considered to be an 'official militant', inhailing hashish of religious fanaticism. She has had to bite the dust. Being once politically gangrened, no one is then respected.

Belligerency and hostility rather than tolerance have marked relations between religions almost throughout history. But not satisfied with over-simplified explanations, latter-day historians have been suggesting that it was not religion alone that led to bloody and prolonged conflicts in many parts of India and of the world. Racial and economic factors also played their part. This may be true, but what is disturbing in Kashmir in other parts of this continent is that even today the followers of separatist movement of one faith are not always friendly towards those of others and that old antipathies come out at the slightest provocation. 'Rouge' Islamic militants are beyond Pakistan's control and, therefore, can't be stopped from infiltrating into India is an easy way out of taking responsibility. Pakistani rulers' high-sounding verbosity, while speaking into the microphone, and carrying out cosmetic raids on terrorist outfits do not amount to much if one runs with the hare and hunts with the hounds. They are never tired of stating that surely cross-border terrorism and infiltration would show no startling ups and downs. Truly speaking, they hinge on support from the mujahideen lobby — a group that knows whose side Pakistan is really on. Pakistan has long been maintaining that all talk of militants being trained and funded in Pakistan and POK is a figment of India's imagination. This chilling response has echoed around the world. It is simply the revival of Islamic culture over the Kashmir issue. Because her secret is a canny fusion of aesthetic and themes of global terrorism. The stylised action sequences are bound up with such Old Hollywood concerns as duty and morality. Pakistan does not learn from her experience or from the experience of others who teach us valuable lessons. Pakistan's knowledge usually witnesses a spike in infiltration and violence levels. Pakistan seems to be a perennial youth in the garden of religious fanaticism, working hard at doing nothing and changing not their frame of mind. Terrorism is a sequential event after partition. A dictatorial mark of peremptory challenge.

Many ghost companies have taken initiative for terrorist-raising funds operating through our stock exchanges. Terror groups operating with the support of Pakistan have resorted to carefully charted manipulation of Indian stock exchange through ghost companies to raise millions of dollars for planning and carrying out strikes against India. The operation to play stock exchanges aims to allow outfits like Lashker-e-Taiba, Hizbul Muzahideen and Al-Badr to tap funds through an ostensibly legitimate route, only that the companies, often with addresses in the Middle East, are fronts for Pakistani agencies or exist only on paper.

Stock exchanges in Mumbai and Chennai have, on occasions, fictitious or national companies which are engaging in stock market operations. I.S.I. carries out the plot for economic subversion. There is a complex mix of funding routes through stock exchanges, banking channels, ordinary ATMS and hawala trails as well as operation of legitimate businesses like hotels and transport, used by modern terrorists to sustain and launch their operations. The Jihadi plot against India's atomic facilities has revealed that stock exchange operations are being used to fund terror. Some of the fake companies are running bogus businesses.

A horrifying aspect of the use of 'legit' means to provide funds for terror is the use of banking channels from destination like Dubai and UAE. The money accessed by terrorist outfits is also being ploughed into legitimate businesses like restaurants, real estate and shipping to generate fronts and provide funds for anti-India operations without attracting attention. LTTE, Tamil separatist group, has a very well-established network of legitimate business, which provides funds and logistics. M.K. Narayanan, former security adviser, spoke at a conference on international security at Munich, in February, 2007 : "These businesses are a plausible cover for operatives, and the combination of conventional money laundering techniques with the hawala route to transfer money made it is a very difficult task for security agencies to track funds for terrorist purposes, since no audit or paper trail is available."

LeT, Hizbul and Al Badr are richly patronised from across the border. Shared objectives like the 'low intensity conflict' in Kashmir and elsewhere from the rationale for Pakistani support. Mr. Narayanan said : "A tentative estimate of funds made available to terrorist outfits annually is in the region of a few million dollars."

Pakistan-sponsored terrorism is like the mosquito that flies among applause. She develops an Islamic allergy to the world. She is just as a nation without dignity is a flock of sheep, individuals without it are slaves. Terrorists are irreligious parasites of Islamabad and bondmen to ISI. The back of the elbow is called the funny bone. Why? Because it borders on the humerus, the upper arm. Terrorist are treated like a funny bone. No one can differentiate between a car and a donkey cart. Because Pakistan has no sense of Islamic terrorism which is a potent lingua franca based on the great equalisers of Islamic melodrama and militant adventure. The embryonic form of terrorism has become big business. Because terrorism knows no borders.

We, in India, have seen religious divisions plaguing the entire life of the country, creating near-civil war conditions and finally resulting in partition. A major force in breaking the bonds of religious bigotry has been nationalism. It is nationalism which has had to contend with ideas of religious revivalism and separatism based on belief. After its formation, Pakistan has had to face a clash between two sects of Muslims. Since then different tendencies have been gaining ground and the country's jehadi based regime is more concerned with religious disputes than with political and economic development. In West Asia, Arab nationalism has gained ascendency over religion and in most areas there is little difference between Muslims and others where participation in the larger life of the community is concerned. The question is Israel and Jews is there, but it is treated more as a political problem than a religious one.

Pakistan's claim over Kashmir is like a thief finding fault with the Kotwal. Even Ayub Khan once said that Kashmir was a question of life and death for Pakistan. He also said that while India was extending its hand of friendship to Pakistan, there was no reciprocality from the other.

Pakistani leaders are still repeating what they said earlier about Kashmir which had no basis, no reality, and no truth. Kashmir has been the victim of aggression from Pakistan first, and now it is a victim of aggression from Islamic terrorists. It is not just the border of Kashmir which is violated but it was the strategic border of India first.

Today, Pakistan, driven by hypnotic inertia of remorse, wants Islamic terrorism to profit from her mistakes. A tough combination of blood and bloodshed, of religion and fananticism and, of fascism and dictatorship. There is a lot of hurricanes popping up. A complex process produces a cracking sound of terrorism. Islamic terrorism is a state secret of Pakistan.

Pakistan today looks at the tree of democracy every morning, but it does not seem to be growing at all. She stops looking at it except religious fanaticism. And her steady going has now become monotonous. And Kahsmir to her is just a fig leaf of her imagination. The sign was a full stop, not a comma. Pakistan will one day weep over the valley of Kashmir, pray over it but the wounds will be far from healed. Why? Because she tore a parent apart and created agonizing conflicts between the grown children. Pakistan is as hypocritical to the troubles of a social inequality as mysterious for self-created self-annihilation. It is Islamic misfortune. The genesis of this campaign is not hard to find.

The mystery which life was no longer a mystery. Marxism seemed to solve all the riddles behind the Kashmir issue, resolve all the dilemma arisen between Hindu-Muslim unity and reconcile all the contradictions between India and Pakistan. The cliches of Marxist thought as Islamic doctrinaire have acquired the aura, the enchantment of creative ideas. There is nothing which we cannot explain in terms of materialistic interpretation of history.

If a young Muslim drinks deep at the well of fanatical Islamic rule and pamphlets, the more he drinks, the greater will be his craving for the heady wine of Islamic terrorism. He will cry for "madder music and stronger wine". In the first flash of adolescent love, he will be intoxicated as the young Marxist or young Muslim terrorist. A delerious ecstasy of a new passion will seize him. The message of Islamic brotherhood through the vehicle of Islamic terrorism may electrify him, transform him and lift him high in the clouds of religious bewilderment. The hectic days of Pakistan aggression after partition did not last long. And the spring of Islamic fanaticism will be followed soon by the winter of despair, of weariness, of dis-illusionment, of loss of faith, and of cynicism. Political stragglers, being non-political beings, escape from the world of strife and struggle to a dreamland of their own creation. Martial law and communism can never exist where the courts are open.

Treachery of our political leaders on Kashmir issue has achieved political prosperity with the stragglers, the defeatists, the opportunists creeping back to the fold of the parties.

Treachery : (A Rough Road to Go As You Please) Two hundred fifty years earlier in 1757, there was another although in reality it was won only through treachery. A foreign power enchanted itself in Bengal by treacherous means and betrayal of some Indian themselves. Betrayality! Some political leaders are very much intoxicated with this world. Why not terrorism in India? Long is the way of treachery in India. Terrorism and treachery are almost equally pressing. They now talk glibly of democracy.

Vacuums have been created and are being created in our social and political integration. Vacuums cannot exist for long. Wherever there is a vacuum, danger arises. Pakistan has filled up this vacuum with terrorism, corruption and treachery. Why other leaders are so apathetic? Or is it that they are bored? You do not keep the wolf away from the door by taking away the door.

Such a vacuum has been filled by the western powers through their strength, European unity and progress. And Pakistan seems to be allergic to the term 'vacuum'. The so-called power vacuum has been fraught with the greatest danger not only to the peace of Kashmir but to the peace of the world. Our so-called political leaders, fully neurotic in words and hypnotic in deeds, have created rotten boroughs, leading to corruption, treachery and creation of religious institutions, popular and democratic only in name. And rotten ideologies are at a premium. Tomorrow it will be dangerous. Whereas Pakistan's religious leaders have no religious clairvoyance beyond fanaticism. The Quran says : "... And who, I hope, will forgive me my faults on the Day of Judgement?" (The Quran 26.77-82) Different neighbours with different ideologies within Pakistan. A fusion of long-term contamination, inside a laboratory of jehadis, gyrates an atmosphere of rife with conspiracy theories. An outcome of militancy has never been in their control. The Atharva Veda says : "Life without goodness, good thoughts, good actions and good words is like the sky in the night without the moon or stars."

Pakistan's dazzling growth of violent attitude over Kashmir and other parts, and her authoritarian government have effectively masked the plethora of problems that plague the Islamic administration. The jehadi chickens have come home to roost as Waziristan, Swat, and other provinces. Like Hamlet, the indecision whether to pick up the gauntlet against such extremism and radicalism remains part of Pakistan. For example, General Musharraf was a Pakistan made Gorbachev. The much-maligned Musharraf had imposed two military coups — one in October, 1999 and the other in November, 2007. Truly, Pakistan is now impregnated with high illiteracy and a strong Islam-bound society. Hundreds of pro-Taliban militants and their radical cleric leaders have been flushed out in the scenic Swat Valley, in the north west of Peshwar. Even Pakistan tribal areas along the border with Afganistan have long been regarded as safe havens for Al Quaida and Taliban militants who fled US-led forces hunting them in Afganistan following the September 11 attacks in 2001. The United States has spoken darkly about serious consequences, including a possible World War III, if Iran continues its pursuit of nuclear weapons.

Mass movements in Pakistan in the past have forced dictators to pass on the reins of power to elected officials in Pakistan. Zulfikar Ali Bhutto, his daughter Benazir and Nawaz Sharif himself were beneficiaries of the Pakistani people's preference for democratic leaders over army officers, who are in league with ISI. Since independence, Pakistan has always slipped into chaos while religious fundamentalists have begun to threaten the very existence of democracy. Why? Because fundamentalists don't like a vibrant civil society. Because fundamentalists get through the mechanics of pleasure and imagination of global terrorism. A marriage between military bosses and religious fundamentalists. So, the Kashmir issue remains unsolved. The root cause of everything is ignorance. This sets a dangerous precedent. All these are ingredients of treachery.

Is Pakistan an Islamic State in the real sense of the term? Islam does not believe in terrorism. An Islamic State does not mean a state of theocracy. Pakistan believes in democracy. But that democracy will be punctuated with Islamic values and principles. It is a paradox. Can love and hate live together? Today, Islam breaks the silence of the valley, rattling a thunderous ear-splitting jehadi slogans throughout the valley. Those slogans awake the echoes, awake the dead.

Who is responsible for this crisis-ridden phase in Kashmir? Today, the Congress, on the Kashmir issue, takes a long spoon to seep with communalism, sitting behind the curtain. Indeed, it is such compromises with principles and such glaring discrepancies between Congress professions and practice that are corrupting the soul of the Congress, of Kashmir politics and of Indian politics. It has packed the organisation with chorus-singers, since independence by the thousands. And Kashmir is buzzing with factional intrigues, casteist and communal bargains. We have more than suspicion that Mr. Nehru's initial hesitancy to take a clear stand regarding Kashmir is attributable to his dependence on the United States. Following the footsteps of Congress dynastic rule, Kashmir has been up with the fruits of the twin evils of casteism and factionalism, a deadly double-whammy that is sapping political life not only in Kashmir but in almost the entire country.

The Pakistani Frontier corps has been heavily infiltrated and influenced by Taliban militants. The London 'Observer', on June 22, 2008, says : "The extremists in Pakistan are getting safe havens to rest, recuperate and retool in Pakistan and come across the border. The concerns have been conveyed to the Pakistani authorities."

Terrorism is a mindset problem of Pakistan. What is mindset? Ego creates mindset. Pakistan mindset is a protective mechanism of self-defence. Why? Because they are scared of what others think about their notions and beliefs. So mindest is self-destructive and they have quite often experienced this since independence. For example, a simple discussion between India and Pakistan, either on Kashmir issue or war on terrorism or peace in Kashmir or any other diplomatic problem, develops into an argument and leads to a verbal fight, and can get more intense. Why? Because of mindset.

What makes their mind hard and closed? This is an automatic, front-line defence mechanism for the protections of their belief systems based on their state of ego. A hard mind offers immense resistance. Action and speech determine the quality of Pakistan's internal character and these come from the mind. This religious illusion leads to sorrow.

Terrorist threat is not abstract. It is real. The apparent motive is hatred. Al Quaida-affiliated Sunni Muslim group with roots in Uzbekistan called 'Islamic Jehad Union' is believed to have trained in Pakistan. The only thing Pakistan can do is to play on the one string. That is their attitude. Winston Churchill says : "Attitude is little thing that makes a big difference." So Pakistan accepts this attitude and displays the narrowness of mind. Judging from this point of view, it may be said that Pakistan-engineered hatred leads ultimately to the destruction of Islamic faith in religion itself. This is the destruction of religious bigotry. So, Pakistan mindset develops antagonisms based on religion. Their mindset is superior to their sense organs.

The coordination between the powers of a civilian government on foreign and defence and ISI shapes the foreign and defence policies of Pakistan. This limited democracy is quite comfortable to the U.S. This method will have to weaken the stability in Pakistan. Islam is compulsory in Pakistan. This basic principle constitutes the primary factor of Islamic terrorism. Fire can be produced by striking stone against stone. Pakistan without terrorism is just like marriage without sex. Terrorist-based Pakistan and clowns-based Indian politics are on the same platform with different ideologies. Both are vampires frantically obsessed with their common interest. Both have struck deep roots in corruption and poorly-showing dogmas. So, Kashmir question remains unsolved.

The following is the story of A.Q. Khan, father of the Islamic bomb, and Al Quaida leader, Osama bin Laden who offered to supply atomic weapon barely a month before the 9/11 terror attacks. This story, written in a book of 414 pages by two investigative journalists, Douglas Frantz and Catherine Collins, is as calamitous to land Pakistan in trouble as disastrous to threaten the Islamic nation to supply nuclear weapons for mass destruction to a globe-trottering terrorist organisation. According to the book, '*The Man From Pakistan: The true story of the world's most dangerous nuclear smuggler AQ Khan*', two Pakistani nuclear scientists, said to be close to A.Q. Khan, met Al Quaida leader, Bin Laden, and went to Taliban headquarters in Kandahar in mid-August 2001 spent three days with him who was keen on acquiring weapons of mass destruction. A.Q. Khan, father of 'Islamic bomb', was the mastermind behind a vast clandestine enterprise which sold nuclear secrets to rogue states like Iran, North Korea and Libya. Before leaving, Osama had told his fiendishly preverted followers that "something great was going to happen, and Muslims around the world were going to join them in the holy war." A couple of weeks later, the twin towers in New York were brought down. What is more revealing is that a year before they met Osama in Kandahar, set up a non-profit organisation, Ummah Tameer-e-Nau, to carry out relief work in Afganistan, including advising the Taliban on scientific matters. Several Pakistani army generals are very much sympathetic to the Taliban cause.

It is a well-orchestrated terrorist plan of Pakistan to maintain good ties with three deadly wings .... The Taliban, ISI, and the Defence. ISI is more a political ideologue and physical supporter to the cause of Taliban. Many continentals think life is a game; whereas Pakistan thinks terrorism is a game. Today Pakistan is like Hollywood glittering gaily with the false sheen of baubles in a dim shining world of unreality. She develops a flair for emotional religious incantation which accounts for the highly spiritual flights of imagery noticeable in her subsequent works of terrorism.

Born in a family of four brothers ... ISI, Military rule, anti-India hate-slogans and Mosque-oriented religious fanaticism ..., Pakistan is the only one Islamic nation in the terrorist profession. Known for her hypocrisy and political somersault on Kashmir issue, Pakistan started out to be an Islamic fanatic and still remains to teach Islamic terrorism. The vampire wanders about after dark, seeking whom it may devour and returning to the ISI-den before dawn. If sensuality were happiness, beasts were happier than us. Most of the Islamic leaders who had come to power after World War II had been purged or assassinated. They were replaced by a group of hand-picked puppets who enjoyed power at theocratic rulers. It was no longer inspiring the masses but was rather the object of popular hatred and contempt. Look at Pakistan. No longer has the Islamic world a Master, to guide, direct, lead. Pakistan that Mr. Jinnah left behind used to stretch from Lahore to Karachi via Pak-occupied Kashmir. But the loss had been more than compensated by the blind and unquestionable loyalty of religious extremists. And she now emerges as the leader of religious orthodoxy at this period of ideological cross-currents. To combat terrorism, laws are effectively toothless in India. As the gifts are a precondition of marriage, so are the gifts of hypocrisy and dual-diplomacy on Kashmir issue a precondition of partition. In these circumstances, our planning and execution are shockingly poor. What a treachery!

Pakistan believes in advertising of fanaticism to educate the grown-up young generation and thereby creates a greater consumer demand of terrorism, in respect of political designs and skillful display of religious merchandise from Asian to European countries. So, Pakistan is crowded with ghosts of fanaticism, and there is hardly a village of any age which cannot point to some house, hall, manor, mosque which is not haunted by anti-India slogans.

Infiltrators and terrorists are two sides of a coin, overlapping each other. One side is destructive, and the other side is destructively parasite of ISI. Many terrorists infiltrate into Kashmir from the Keran sector of Kupwara district, from different areas on the LOC, in Machi sector, in the Ranjwar sector, in Teetwal operating in Jammu and Kashmir. But infiltration across the border continues unabated.

The militant infrastructure across the LOC, Poonch and Guraz valley, with a major cache of arms and ammunition, grenades, explosives and other deadly weapons has always been active. These explosives are generally trans-shipped through the higher reaches of Gurez valley. What is the importance of the Gurez valley? It is a safe haven for terrorists and their couriers to trans-ship arms, ammunition and stores for sustenance of terrorists in depth areas of Kashmir valley. And POK ... a drawing-room of militants as well as a warming pan of terrorists camps ... is a bastard of political gamesmanship and of religious delusion. Why? To undermine the ongoing peace process and to deceive the army patrolling and searching in the jungles and areas astride the LOC. It is fact that former General Musharraf had told the terrorists not to cross the LOC and wait for further instructions from the Pakistani army. So, ISI + Pakistani army = Pakistan Civil Administration. Routes of infiltrators are very much porous to pass through slowly.

But the U.S. public opinion is different. Is Pakistan totally without brains? Is Pakistani administration politically disillusioned and religiously grievous? The U.S. has helped Pakistan on many occasions, and this is the way the U.S. repays her generosity by allowing the most evil in the world to live his life in peace in Pakistan. Pakistan's deal with Taliban militants in Waziristan region is a replica of Islamic bankruptcy and a holy horror of tomorrow's politically adulterous generation. Such non-worshipping and non-practising religious groups not only harden the Islamic heart but sin against the light of Islam. This devil-worshipping thought and shamanistic witches' cauldron of Islamic jehad only lay ghosts of Aladdin's lamp. Certainly, there is a confusion among the U.S. strategic community and the media about a Faustian bargain between Paksitan and terrorists. They have been regarding Pakistan's motives and bona fides in arriving at a deal. Benazir's murder shows that democracy in Pakistan under the violence of jehadi extremism and fundamentalists, vibrating highly with emotions of religious crucifixion. There is a mutual exclusiveness between the West and the Islamic world on strident anti-Islamic propaganda and on religious propaganda of jehadi extremists. Will Pakistan be a great beneficiary after treading the footsteps of a desert culture of 1400 years ago when Islam was completely divided and an ever-growing thirst for revenge, religious mischievousness, severance of relations and political squabbling went high at the lofty dome of violence and destruction? Will not Pakistan learn a lesson when antagonism runs against all other groups on the question of religious, political and social dissensions?

Why? Because the Pakistan Army leadership ovre the last six decades has developed a supreme confidence in itself to rule the nation supporting the terrorist activities in Kashmir and other parts. Because they have managed to retain the bulk of U.S. assistance which has given a great mileage to instal the Taliban Govt. in Afganistan. Under the pretext of a moderate Muslim State in Pakistan, the rulers have already siphoned off billions of U.S. dollars after using the jihadis for the purpose of their foreign policy in Kashmir and in Afganistan. In these circumstances, they underestimated the jihadis. Consequently, the triumph of Islamic jehad has started in the Pakistan-Afganistan border — a safe haven for Pakistan-sponsored terrorists. The fact is that it is ISI and the Army that have led Pakistan to the brinkmanship of world terrorism.

A.K. Doval, former Director of Indian Intelligence Bureau, says : "Fears of Pakistan becoming a failed state have heightened, and worsening internal security could prove the route to the dangerous eventuality — the threat of Pakistan sliding into a free-for-all chaos is much bigger, as instability in a radicalised society could result in the unchecked release of destabilising in a radicalised society which can impact the whole is now as vulnerable as frontier tribal areas — a distinct possibility is that democracy may not continue at all."

Since independence, Pakistan has so far failed to plant a good harvest of democratic set-up in her land. The Spanish proverb says : "He that has a good harvest must be content with a few thistles." Truly speaking, Pakistan has never granted the sower to live to see the harvest of democracy. Whereas Pakistan spreads her benefits of religious fanaticism in Kashmir and thrives for them. Because she has already encapsulated the resultant effect of terrorism at the World Parliament of Islamic Jehad, in the face of today's tremendous challenges.

And the chances of whistle-blowing for democracy are getting lower and lower. India should learn a lesson from the Bible which says : "If you wait until the wind and the weather are just right, you will never plant anything and never harvest anything." But our leaders have not yet learnt anything.

In what way would it be possible to abolish the oldest profession of political and religious prostitution from the world immediately? What are the causes of religious prostitution of Pakistan-sponsored religious extremism? There is a bewildering variety of guesses. By barring a dissatisfied religious thought from taking another unwanted scurrilous dogma of blood-letting violence and terrorism, it drives him to a militant. In practical life, prostitutes are no more so for selling their bodies for money. The shedding of this false morality among our leaders is a pure prostitution. Kashmir issue suffers from this psychological change. It is a risky profession. It demands no mathematical formula. So Pakistan's formula of Kashmir policy is also like saying that Hamlet's celebrated and enigmatic indecision is a case not of existential angst but of algebra. And terrorism is the mechanism of Pakistan's sub-conscious mind when she starts confronting with India.

The high rates of suicide bombers and the growing depression of Pakistan's civil govt. truly arise from a loss of sense. Is there anything stronger than terrorism? It is political and religious delusion. The beginning of peace-making process in Kashmir is easy but continuing is hard. Is there anything stronger than delusion? It is the thoughtlessness of ignorance from which Pakistan suffers. So the thoughtful barbarities of religious fanaticism appear with a deliberate and multilateral approach of jehadi militants. A pall of gloom hangs over Pakistan. The FATA (Federally Administered Tribal Areas) serves as a staging area for Al Quaida's attacks in support of the Taliban in Afganistan as well as a location for training new terrorist operatives for attacks in Pakistan, West Asia, Africa, Europe and the United States. There appears to be a real danger of Pakistan passing on nuclear technology to terrorists. With about 85 nuclear bombs in its arsenal the risk that, that radical Islamic-Al Quaida or Taliban may gain access to nuclear material is real.

It is not easy to differentiate between indigenous Muslims and illegal Bangladeshis destabilising the social equilibrium. With huge amounts of money being pumped into the North-East by the Centre, much like Jammu and Kashmir, the survival of militancy has become a vested interest for some political parties. The vote-bank politics over the Bangladeshi settlers suits the designs of ISI and Bangladesh's DGFI (Directorate General of Forces Intelligence). Our leaders, as vampires that cast no shadow, are not reflected in social mirrors.

Even the Chinese have been very much active in supplying weapons and explosives to the north-eastern insurgent groups. The trade routes in the region are fluid, particularly where the Myanmar and China borders meet. Even they have increased the flow of funds into these groups, in collaboration with the Myanmer army to smuggle arms into India. So Kashmir issue remains unsolved and terrorism remains unabated.

Have you heard the Black Widow militants? Who are they? The Black Widow militants are the anti-talks faction of the Dimasa tribal militant outfit in Assam. They set up the ambush so as to catch the policemen in enveloping fire. To combat terrorism! Everything is lost in our political gamesmanship.

Pakistan's Kashmir policy is a large trade of 'small profits and quick returns'. Whereas Indian policy is a trade of 'large profits and slow returns'. And POK is a deep miry place of Islamic depression ... a slushy sediment of irreligious dogmas falling into a fitful slumber. And the sounds and words of jehadi slogans run into one terrorist camp to another, making insinuations against the non-Muslims of India. The progressive disease is caused by a virus-like SIMI and other Islamic organisations that multiply slowly in the host organisms of secular Indian society and have a long incubation period. The operation uses more rapid explosives.

Poverty and outdated social customs are probably the one of the greatest causes of religious fanaticism. 'Anti-India slogans' continue to sway Pakistan and are battened upon the well-established prejudices in Pakistan. So, the rulers depend upon the spontaneous or all-out military support and keep the terrorist machinery alive. Even the brusque manner of our Kashmiri leaders has lost many diplomatic battles and their oratorial talent often tempts them to run away on the impulse of words. Others see in them a symbol of bellicosity alternately waving the olive branch and belching fire and brimstone. Mr. Jinnah as the Moses of the Muslim League led his flock through the valley of Kashmir. So the diseases of religious fanaticism flourish most when man is submerged in poverty and the masses live in sub-civilised conditions, in slums and squalor. It is just a smack of religious superciliousness. The higher the sun arises, the less shadow does it cast; even so the greater is the goodness and sham modesty of Pakistan behind the curtain of politically dressed-up treachery and religiously woven-up make-believe-diplomacy, the less does she cover praise.

Many funny things happened during and at the conclusion of the partition of India. And we know the vital part that a horde of pathologically debased political leaders played in the intrigues leading up to that wicked vivisection. Islam-based modern Pakistan has a pinchbeck angularity and cerebral appearance which follows that Islamic vein is dry.

Why do they practise terrorism? Any resolution on Kashmir issue has certainly put Pakistan in cold storage and regarded their demands as obsolete and impracticable. This under-current of pessimism is evident in Pakistan's anti-India demonstrations. Although noted for their noise, obscenity and hooliganism, the demonstrations for over sixty years have totally lacked in mass fervour. Even Pakistan's shaking hand with India has already betrayed her treachery on Kashmir. Why do they practise terrorism? Breaking all rules and conventions of protocol, the Govt. of Pakistan totally boycotted the Republic Day celebrations by the Indian High Commissioner in Karachi and elsewhere in Pakistan in 1956-57. When Pakistan was nurtured in her cradle of chorus singing and cramped up in a narrow-doctrinal frame-work of Islamic priestcraft, a crack of jehadi slogans with mischievous harshness or malicious change in pitch, ranted the air of Kashmir and encouraged the Kashmiri Muslims. Basking in the ill-feeling belligerency and irreconcilable pet aversion, they have started fighting for liberation movement. So they are fraudulently wrong in a similar experiment with communal feelings. This impression has gained ground rapidly in Kashmir and harmed the prestige of the Govt. of India. Why not? An offensively noisy chattering can't be consumed with anger.

Why do they practise terrorism? Who can deny that Pakistan has kindled the flame of religious fanaticism and wanted to show to the world now that terrorism is the saviour of mankind? Hitler may have massacred a large number of innocent jews, but he carried out that heinous job in his own country. Stalin's record of mass murders both inside and outside his country lies unbeaten. His followers today, in the name of Islam, are killing the innocent men, women and children by the thousands, crushing under the religious wheels of deadly juggernaut, inside and outside the country. Is there any difference between Stalin and Pakistani rulers sitting at the helm of religious fanaticism? The people of Pakistan are bound to realise what has been done cannot be undone; and neither vile abuse nor mob violence can reopen the question of Kashmir's future which has been settled once and for all by the people of the State themselves. Finding no alternate way, the then President of Pakistan asserted that "the real masters of the situation now, as always before, are the people of Kashmir themselves." The tragic irony of Pakistan's demand has been lost. Because blurred memories sound indistinct.

The world has had to condemn this butchery belatedly. But Pakistan has not had a word of sympathy for the innocent people. Nevertheless with such bitter memories, Pakistan is our guest for compromise. It is despondency. Because despondency is the vexation and despair of a cowardly pride; nothing is worse. The people of India will not submit to blackmail. Terrorism and anti-India slogans, like some of our political ideologies, were born on the wrong side of the blanket.

What good has Pakistan derived from carrying out this terrorism? Because they do not play to this tune. Behind the curtain, there is someone who is smiling enigmatically and smirking revoltingly at others. All romantic possibilities are instantly exhausted. Fate, over game for a spot of fun at the expense of jilted lovers, mocked the fellow with a circumstance that bore the deceptive look of an opportunity.

The Islamic violence and Indo-Pak conflict on the question of Kashmir issue are categorically an Islamic dramatisation of its inner violence of world Muslim community. Why? Because the poisonous fumes of their inner turbulence seep through the collective consciousness of Islamic community. Why? Because they have already robbed them of their sanity of outlook, and at the same time they are endangering their survival. Because ideological differences are at the root of their violence. Because Pakistan's civil society and media have been silent on Islamic terrorism in the world. Even the strands of the Middle East crisis are so knotted up that it would be quite impossible for any Islamic country to unravel the crisis-ridden phase of world Muslims. Undoubtedly, Pakistan is a Robin Hood of Islamic terrorism. Because Pakistan has been cursed with blessed nuisance on Kashmir issue.

Do you believe that the takeover of the Ziarat marble quarry — the mountain of white marble shines with such brilliance that it looks like snow in the sun — is a coveted national asset of Pakistan and one of the boldest examples of how the Taliban have made Pakistan's tribal areas far more than a base for training camps of jehadi mililtants or a launching pad for sending fighters into Afganistan or into the porous areas of Indo-Pak borders? Do you believe that the marble in the tribal aeas is one of the most highly prized for use in expensive floors and walls in Pakistan and in limited quantities abroad and in harnessing the resources of a region where there are plenty of other mining operations for coal, gold, copper and chromate? Do you believe the Taliban stay there running a full swing business and offer within Taliban or Taliban within Pakistan? It is a paradox of today's Pakistan. Is Islam a faith which promotes tolerance and harmony? Is Pakistan a terrorism-based Islamic nation or Islam-based terrorist nation? How long will it be gyrating within a framework of parochial thoughts? Do they not know they are in extremis? Do they not feel ashamed or stupid and lose the respect of other people, beating their deadly wings of horrors very fast and making a continuous high-sounding slogans of jehad? All the hullabaloo is a hypothetical question.

The Taliban-running quarry has extended its reach through more of the rugged territory in northern Pakistan known as the Federally Administered Tribal Areas of FATA. Today the Taliban not only settle disputes in their consolidated domain but they also levy taxes on every truck that ferried the treasure from the quarry, smuggle drugs and other contraband, and impose their self-regulated brand of rough justice, complete with courts and prisons. The quarry operation in the Mohammad district, strategically situated between the city of Peshwar and the Afghan border is a great mileage to the Taliban. Why? Because they deploy their fighters and suicide bombers in two directions. One against NATO and U.S. forces over the border in southern Afganistan, and the other against Pakistani forces — police, army and intelligent officials — in major Pakistani cities. So the Taliban are using their income they exact to strengthen their hold and turn themselves into a self-sustaining fighting force. Pakistan's hope in Islam is dead Pakistan sleeps within the shadow of religious extremism.

The secret intelligence agencies are always alert but those are not always trustworthy, regarding illegal wiretapping, burglaries and money laundering to make public. It is a game of conspiracy of conspirators against national security. For example, the Watergate Scandal is the most famous annoying source in American history. W.Mark Felt was the No. 2 official as associate director of the Federal Bureau of Investigation and fought the President Nixon's effort to obstruct the FBI's investigation of the Watergate break-in. Without Felt, there might not have been a Watergate ... shorthand for the revealed abuses of presidential powers in the Nixon White House. "We know what's leaked, and we know who leaked it," Nixon's chief of Staff, H.R. Haldeman, told the President in October 1972, four months after a team of washed-up CIA personnel hired by the White House was caught trying to wiretap the Democratic party's national offices at the Watergate Complex. Have our leaders throats to answers?

Whereas in India, our political leaders for political advantage, suppressing the cause of national interests, have always been misusing the investigating reports. Democracy for whom? Through constant vigilance, our leaders shed fear, while sitting on the throne. They fail to recognise the distinction between public money and national interest, because of their basic confusion directed towards satisfying bodily requirements alone and achieving the goal of lasting happiness. At the centre is the accumulation of wealth enough for their lifetime and their descendents. Who will solve the Kashmir question? Because they remain unfulfilled from the sway of craving, greed and anger. Most of them are financial terrorists, braver than any other Islamic terrorists. So, today's terrorists may be tomorrow's heroes. All the financial terrorists make severe blow to our economy as well as to our Indian consumer. Wire-tapping to our leaders is like great triumphers.

Is the terrorist an individual with a pathological psyche? Is political leukemia seducing the blood cells of our democracy? Pakistan has already multiplied and spread out those seduced cells. It may be a tell-tale sign of political conspiracy. Do you know Pakistan is in the midst of serious but grave internal security threat from a collective organisation of Taliban, Al Quaida and J & K terrorist elements to take over the country? Do you know a steady infiltration of Taliban and Al Quaida elements in Pakistan's biggest cities of Lahore and Karachi, ringing alarm bells with a plethora of posters and leaflets and trying to oust the govt? Do you know fear-stricken Talibanised Pakistan has been under a great threat? Is India concerned about Taliban-making inroads into urban areas and cities of Pakistan located close to the border? What are the causes of these problems? The basic cause of problems is in self, family, society and nature to find resolutions of inner conflict. Paksitan needs a rigorous self-examination of the veracity of Islam-based democracy. It is not battery-operating game. The terrorist is made by the social system. Is it not important to synchronise efforts to check the new breed of jehadis who have technology and are extensively using the internet to coordinate their terrorist operations? Our Govt. is quite indifferent.

So, Pakistan looks attractive for any conference on Kashmir issue with fashionable clothes of anti-terrorism outfits. But no one can apprehend that resources in Pakistan are used for the dastardly attack in India. This is the picture of a 'failed State'.

What are the geographical peripheries of this sub-continent? Harbans Mukhia, Prof. of History, JNU, says : "The geographical distribution of the density of population in the subcontinent flies in the face of the notion that the medieval Indian state could have been even the chief agency of conversion. The highest density is located in four geographical peripheries of the subcontinent : the Kashmir valley in the north, Pakistan in the west, Bangladesh in the east and in the Malabar region down south. That is where the Muslims are, and where, in a majority." As per his opinion, these were also the political peripheries of the Medieval Muslim state. Kashmir has turned to Islam long before the medieval Indian state reached there in Akbar's reign. West Punjab was a land where the hold of the medieval state was forever disputed and tenuous. East Bengal was seldom under the control of Delhi or Agra and the Muslim state reached never extended to Kerala anyway.

On the other hand, the heartland of the Muslim empire — Bihar, U.P. Delhi and East Punjab — for nearly six centuries the Muslims never exceeded around 15 percent of the total population. Significantly, the massive conversions of the population — occurred between the second quarter of the 19th century and 1941, the last census before the partition, when the British ruled here. And overall, a fraction less than 25 percent of the population had recovered from the arrival of Islam in India to about the time of partition.

Prof. Harbans Mukhia says : "The Muslims inhabiting the Indian subcontinent comprises the largest concentration of the community in the world — conversions were effected by the might of the medieval Muslim state in India over the six centuries that it ruled." (TOI, Dec. 20, 2008).

Why Secularism? Was it not a dastardly manoeuvred pre-destined decision by our so-called and well-branded pseudo-secularists for securing their vote bank politics, knowing everything for the present situation? Have not our secularist forces been weakening the democratically woven social infrastructure of India? Is it not a very torid time to India to understand the tortuous process of negotiations offered by Pakistan on counter-terrorism? Is not Pakistan too much pride in her own appearance sidetracking all allegations levelled against her? Thinking is essential but worrying is unnecessary. Because suicide bombers are the atomic weapons of Muslims. Why? Because Muslims do not have the latest weapon to fight enemies who are committing atrocities against Muslims. So jehad has become compuslory for all Muslims. And Pakistan will have to be kind and merciful enough to terrorists. Even South Waziristan tribal district bordering Afganistan is under the hegemony of Taliban militants. The domestic constituencies of Pakistan have been paralysed. The establishment of a Caliphate in south and central Asia — LeT's self-proposed goal — has little to do with Kashmir. India's secularism is extremely pleasant and enjoyable word to Pakistan. Terrorists get delighted.

We are aware of the evil influence of Islam which irreligious faiths have produced when they have become institutionalised. The history of sixteenth century Europe will reveal what heinous crimes were committed in the fair name of christ. The sisterly touch of Pakistan's romantic endearment with Islamic priesthood — an undying gratitude of her dying beloved — has preserved in a militant cobweb of genuine hide. In politics and jobs, and in private life of Islamic theology, Pakistan seems to breed hundreds and thousands of political snobs accused of shoddy workmanship in the name of Islam in Kashmir. Pakistan wanted a reign of plutocracy and terror, and the massacre and the wholesale genocide of the non-Muslim population of the state on which the Maharaja of Jammu and Kashmir did not seem to be lenient. The Maharaja secured the services of the Indian Army to crush the resistance movement designed by Jinnah.

Lord Mountbatten asked the commonsense question of how Mr. Jinnah could be responsible for withdrawing the tribesman, if he had no control over them to which Mr. Jinnah replied : "If you do this, I will call the whole thing off." Truly speaking, Pakistan has been consciously misleading the people of Pakistan with regard to her true intentions. Pakistan that sets for an Islamic saint is sure to be a sinner, and a man who boasts that he is a sinner is sure to have some feeble, maudlin, snivelling bit of saintship about him. It is enough to make Pakistan an Islamic nation of playing terrorism divided into a number of parts and shown on different days. And Pakistan is very much careful of her ministrations while terrorists are in trouble.

Not only that Pakistan's religious sophistication has sales value among the Muslim community whether they are the learned or not. A plain mystical diet is not good enough for the modern palate. It is proved to be a cunning cook when a young man of 24 sets out to prescribe a cure for the sickness of Pakistan, we are apt to be a little sceptical. The truth is that the people of Pakistan are all sick. Sick of what? It is no ordinary disease. They suffer from ennui. They are bored. They are nauseated. They have a feeling they do not belong to terrorism. Why? Because terrorists are outsiders. They are outsiders ... that's all. They pull a sad face. We recall the poet's words : "I turn round/Like a dumb beast in a show/Neither know what I am/Nor where I go." And Pakistan says : Terrorists are outsiders and outsiders. All of them are not dumb. The trouble with some of them is : they feel too much, brood too much and speak too much. There indeed is the secret of their method. They can spot their illness better than we could.

Pakistan knows all the evil outsiders and she would like them to know them, too. She sees there is nothing for her to do, no mission to fulfil. She peers through the keyhole of ISI. She sees nakedness. She sees death. And she can't get over it.

Nietzsche, Dostoevsky, Camus or Sartre all are outsiders to Pakistan. Why? Becuase she does not have to listen to their words. Because she must try to become a saint. She is sure the philosophers they have quoted were outsiders.

Pakistan is the same for every outsider. It is a country without values. Because there are outsiders and outsiders. All the jihadis or the militants or the fanatics are all outsiders. Some seek refuge in reason in the lap of ISI or the defence ... some in POK. For the intellectual outsider it is a question of being nothingness. For the emotional, it is a question of absolute love for Islam. Pakistan cocks up her ears.

Today, our political leaders, drowning their corruptible practices and treachery in a conundrum of anti-national feelings, have achieved political prosperity, living in the islands of religious and caste-ridden luxury within a matrix of pent-up communalism. All they now feel uncomfortable on Kashmir and terrorism. So Kashmir question remains unsolved for their behavior that is extremely pathological and quite uncontrollable. The stragglers, the defeatists, the opportunists, again creep back to the fold of the parties.

In an article, entitled 'Congress Position', Gandhiji wrote on January 27, 1948, three days before his death, "the Congress can only die with the nation. A living organism ever grows or it dies." The Congress has won political freedom but it has yet to win economic freedom, social and moral freedom. These freedoms are harder than the political if only because they are constructive, less exciting and not spectacular." It is fact that identification of a party and Govt. would lead to the degeneration of both. It would weaken the roots of the Congress and wither the tree of its organisation.

Today, the Congress, like a mammoth tree, shrivelling within itself, has assured a deceptive and wrong-headed canopy of leaves, and beneath this umbrella shelters a lot of treacherous leaders, and opportunists, and squats a miscellaneous brood eager to pluck the fruit from the branches even before it ripens. Down with Kashmir question! Within the Congress the centre of gravity has shifted from Kashmir.

Many accuse the Congress of being monolithic party. In fact, as it functions today, the party is highly amorphous compound of many miscellaneous elements with only one focal point ... the Gandhis. To fight against terrorism and terrorists is not the pivotal role. The primary aim is to offer incense at the shrine with a few acolytes behind the high priests, and a way off in the dim distance stand the hoi polloi worshipping reverently from afar. Blasts are going on and on. But the pattern is reflected in the country. And Kashmir question stands alone in wilderness as it was before. So secularism is the open sesame to the Congress. Today it is hemmed in on all sides of pseudo-secularists horsing about terrorism. They sit at each other and keep changing from self-defeating problems to self-contradictory opinions.

The 62- year old religious maestro like Pakistan, best known to the wildest body of terrorist lovers as conductor of a symphony orchestra of terrorism, has created for Islam and climbed to the summit of orchestral achievements of religious fanaticism. Pakistan loves music of jehad extremists better than the message of Islam and takes to selling her Islamic thoughts to young generation with evil means. She uses the trans-shipped money, either by hawala or by any other means, to buy music of authoritarianism.

In the pursuit of learning everyday something is required. But in the pursuit of learning religious fanaticism, everyday something is given away. Pakistan has now become defenceless against themselves.

Kashmir is not an issue to India. But it is a Himalayan issue and a question of prestige to Pakistan. Why? Pakistan only knows it. Because terrorism seems to be a nomenclature of religious extremism. When agreements fail, terrorism is the best weapon. When hand-shaking diplomacy fails, political dualism begins. When political dualism fails, cross-border terrorism begins. This process is going on and on. So terrorism is a name used by Pakistan instead of Islamic nation. The lowest of the low. Pakistan is a blood-sucking nation that spreads the disease of terrorism ... a monologue of today's Pakistan.

Like a wise man, India should not trust anybody. Be always on the alert. Step carefully in your walk, supposing everything to be a snare. The heedful do not die. And the heedless! They are like into the dead. I Ching says, in Great Commentary : "Danger arises, when a man feels secure in his position. Destruction threatens when a man seeks to preserve his wordly estate. Confusion develops when a man has put everything in order. Therefore the superior man does not forget danger in his security, not ruin when he is well-established, nor confusion when his affairs are in order." (Great Commentary 2.5.9) In sharp contrast, Pakistan's political record of spinning a double-dealing attitude and belligerency on Kashmir issue is clear, as documented in detail by evidence on file at the United Nations. She has ever been accused of not cooperating with India, much more degrading, defying, detaining or endangering the lives of Kashmiri people. She has never tried to comply with every India's resolution and has ever been accused of launching a single major military attack, of invading the demilitarised areas and of occupying those areas. No nation, anywhere, has ever defied the U.N. member nations, the General Assembly, the Security Council, their resolutions, their official representatives and the United States itself, so consistently, so blatantly, so flagrantly as has Pakistan. Pakistan has ever had aggressive tendencies towards Kashmir. A great injustice and inexcusably murderous act has so far been committed against India on Kashmir issue. So Pakistan's policy is aggressive and expansionist. After every aggression or terrorist activity, Pakistan appears to be a gentleman. Who is a gentlemen is a model of virtue and benefactor and a symbol of good example, walking humbly with one's God, fighting the good fight and shaming the devil with well-spent life and good conscience. Whereas Pakistan has steeped in vice, sunk in iniquity, sin-laden morality and misleading infernal desire with an unspeakable orgy of violence. Why? In profound silence, the druggist packed some quinine pills when both sides of Islamabad and POK are in deep ferment. Because Pakistan skims the cream of everything she earns. An astoundingly fanatical spirit infuses Pakistan's life and work. A good conductor of terrorism respects the vice of every religious note and interprets the jehadi slogans with a strictly stoic fidelity. The plants of her infidelity are taller and more sturdy, after sitting on the Chinese red-carpet with the warmth lapping luxuriously done about the Chinese leaders. So, the fires of religious fanaticism start cracking cheerfully in the living room of POK, gradually spreading its warmth all along the world. Terrorism is so heavy and thick on top of Islam that it absorbs no true colour of Islam from the diabolical and shambolic thoughts of Islamic theology. To Pakistan, whatever is unjust in Kashmir may be powerful and whatever is powerful may be unjust.

When is Pakistan true to herself? The answer is when they are not being lived by others, when they think their own thoughts and feel their own feelings, when their loves and hates are their own. Is it always possible to say how far their loves and hates are their own and how far the result of the circumstances of their birth and upbringing, the fears and anxieties imposed by the conditions of their life and the ideas absorbed in their chance encounters with men and books? The people of Pakistan have won their freedom from all that imposed on them, can they be sure who are they? Do they find out which of these persons is fake and which real?

The same dilemma confronts them when they meet others or non-Islamic people of the world. The question before them is : If they cannot even know what is authentic in them, how can they sense what is authentic in others? Do they know they have been described often as a clinging vine? Who is the real ruler in Pakistan? Do they know the real ruler is lapping up the pheasant, bone, feathers and all of western powers, without caring to ask how long they will have been hanging on tenterhooks of country-made terrorism? Do they know the path that misleads them from moral standards to Islamic terrorism is strewn with their dead selves? There is no end to those questions.

So they are in a spider's web of poisoned chalice either by the United States or China. Perhaps it cannot be helped. Human life is shot with ambiguity through and through. For they know that most of them do not live their own lives ... that they cannot decide for themselves. They dig their own death-trap. Because they have chosen to do so but because they have no choice.

If today in Pakistan, there is no bird to put a song into the throat of morning, it is because the morning is misty with the smoke of religious fanaticism. This peculiar mode of expression is as necessary to Pakistan as it is the belly-band to a fat man.

When T.S. Eliot, Nobel Laureate, speaks of the evening spread out against the sky "like a patient etherised upon a table", the imagery of Pakistan may appear cold. Why? Because Islam at the hands of Pakistan does not settle the quality of the drink as bad or the mixing as dangerous. And Pakistan's story of Kashmir has such a hollow ring that is the natural result of speaking with an empty stomach. So, the Kashmir issue still remains unsolved. Because India has a heritage of perverted leaders. Pretension mingles with compromise.

Pakistani attack on Kashmir is a great moral crime and an unIslamic act. All that Pakistan wants is to grab Kashmir in the name of holy Islam, which gives the message of peace to human beings living on this earth, no matter what faith they profess. Why? Because Pakistan has a heritage of murderous violence ... the most earth-shattering amphictyonic association of jihadis militants ... of which she can justifiably be proud. It deserves to be remarked that practically all the old practices of gross robust Islamic humour with an extravagance of religious carricature of violence are today in a very moribund phase, if not already a defunct state. Years of neglect through want of patronage has made these deadly practices of violence suffer; most of them are today languishing and struggling for existence; some of them are already dead. For example, a camp-follower of a murderous band of terrorists strangled a Kashmiri Hindu pundit to death and buried him. It is to them an old practice of violence. Kashmir is choked with bloody and invisible hand in between our mistrust and their mistrust.

Both Gandhiji and Jinnah had long noses. The nose, besides being an index of national and personal character, also serves as a clue to one's internal state. Jinnah's nose was sharper than that of Gandhiji's. Jinnah had a trick of turning red under the effect of certain emotions and stimulants on the question of partition. The nose is a symbol of character and curiosity. Take the nose away, and what remains of the human face divine?

Long the noses have made history, and the longer the nose the stranger the story. For example, Mrs. Indira Gandhi on her comprehensive but dynamic decisions on the liberation of Bangladesh, the Simla Pact, and so many other remarkable decisions. "Give me a man," said Napoleaon, "with plenty of nose". Most big men had long noses ... Caesar, Cromwell, Wellington and so many others.

Nose-rubbing among Polynesians was a form of greeting to shaking hands. Mr. Ballavbhai Patel is reported to have rubbed his nose while taking any decision. That form of greeting, however crude and grotesque, it might seem to us, certainly marks the earliest beginnings of the importance of the nose amongst our political leaders on the question of political problems. Our leaders certainly feel pretty when they are led by the nose. Very rare is the sharp nose among our present leaders. Has anybody heard of the noseless celebrity, male or female? Longer nose goes by favour.

To a foreigner, India is synonymous with the Taj Mahal. And to him, Pakistan is synonymous with Islamic terrorism. Why? To create a national awareness and a patronage for it. A man who does not trust himself is not to be trusted by others. When young we trust ourselves too much; and we trust others too little when old. Rashness is the error of youth; timid caution of age. Manhood is the isthmus between the two extremes — the ripe and fertile seasons of action when, we can hope to find the head to contrive, united with the hand to execute.

What irks Pakistan? As the Security Council debate on Kashmir draws nearer Karachi was mounting a familiar offensive against India purporting to see in Kashmir a dagger pointed at the heart of Pakistan. Once again the old cry of India's aggressive intentions was raised as a smoke screen behind which to flourish the equally old gambits of tribal raiders straining at the least, of peace-loving Pakistani leaders vainly attempting to restrain the material order of their camp-followers, the press and radio raised preconcerted voices in a concentrated hymn of hate. Hissing hate and spitting vitriolic anti-India campaign threatened all manner of dire consequences to 'Bharat which is India'. Bharat which is India can take care of herself. Can Pakistan?

For plainly, these frenzied efforts to mobilise hate against a neighbouring country are no more than a diversionary tactic to draw attention away from Pakistan's own internal ills. A belley-ache does not put a man in the best of tempers. And of frantically digested religious belley-aches, Pakistan unfortunately has had more than most. Yet it is as illogical to blame India for these belley-aches as it would have been for old Mother Hubbard to blame her poor dog because the cupboard was bare. Pakistan, by birth, is a political wheeler-dealer, stinging America for U.S. dollars.

Before Buddha, many seers and saints had stated that the root of all misery was man's ignorance of the nature of reality. A good heart, benevolent feelings and a balanced mind lie at the foundation of character. The strength of Pakistan's Civil Govt. does not lie in the clarity or popularity of its policies. Indeed, so far as major policy issue on Kashmir are hardly distinguishable from the lie taken by other groups belonging to mullocracy. Life begins with pain. We come into the world without our permission. When the accoucheur smacks us shrewdly at our bottom it is with pain. Sorrow and reluctance that we give tongue to our loud and persistent buzzing sound. Then, on through life in a frantic endeavour to be absent when the things are uncomfortable and amongst those present when life is pleasant. And always there are mistakes. We get the lines mixed. We are present when we should have been absent. And when one's name is finally called by Dante's 'Inferno of the fires' ... from yet unknown depths of darkness, the human spirit emerges to a new and unwilling consciousness and falters : Religious fanaticism. An accretion of hypocrisy is slowly added to treachery.

False happiness is like false money. Lying is like trying to hide in a fog. If you move about you are in danger of bumping your head against the truth. And as soon as the fog blows away you are gone anyhow. Pakistan needs a regenerative medicine, replacing terrorism without fear of rejection. Pythagoras says : "There is geometry in the humming of the strings, there is music in the spacing of the spheres." It should be with full depth and dimension. It must be from inside. Otherwise — Pakistan will be in a death-trap of terror iceberg. Agreements! Cancel and tear to pieces that make great bond!

What is Pakistan today? What does she feel for her own unscrupulous ends? Pakistan wants to live deep and suck out all the marrow of life, to live so sturdily and Spartan-like as to put to rout all that was not life, to cut a broad swath and shave close, to drive their indiscipline life into a corner and reduce it to its lowest terms. Sucking the marrow out of life does not mean choking on the bone. A breath of hate, jealousy, anxiety or fear lies at the bottom of her heart. An article of religious delusion and political dualism does not give a straight answer to any question. Pakistan needs a social geometry.

Take the political set-up. In the last 60 years of social turbulence, political calamities and religious fanaticis, bringing religion to political fermentation and sectarianism, Pakistan has had no less than ten Prime Ministers and many a tyrannical military coup. Of these Prime Ministers some were assassinated. During the first ten years, Pakistan had no less than five Prime Ministers, and of these one was assassinated, one pre-emptorily dismissed, one stayed in the saddle, while of the remaining two, one ex-Prime Minister succeeded another ex-Prime Minister as an ambassador abroad. In the last 60 years, ministers, coming and going, in a swiftly changing kaleidoscope, are a dime a dozen. Today the Swat valley, once known as the Switzerland, has fallen to an invincible terrorist group like Taliban. The terrorists in Pakistan and Afganistan have already posed a grave threat to the global security. This is the central front of terrorism and extremism sponsored by Pakistan.

Even after the downfall of imperial Govt. in Nepal, the Limbu community is demanding a separate state for itself. The Limbus are of Mongoloid origin and can also be found in Sikkim, Darjeeling and Kalimpong in West Bengal and Bhutan. They follow the Kiranti religion, which predates Hinduism and based on ancestor worship. This distressing phase of religion is as dismal as mutual. How effortless is the everyday farewell of religion given by the fanatical family. Their motive is their existence; bread of religion for their children and for the world Nepalese. Observation more than books, experience rather than persons, are the prime education. Confucianism ventured dictatorship, persecuting Laoism, Moism, Buddhism, Nestorianism and Christianity through drastic and even blood methods called 'religious liberty'. Throughout the whole history of China, cruel wars raged in the country in every century. In this way, the Chinese absorbed the many many non-Chinese people against their will. In the meanwhile, Confucianism became mummified and was abandoned by the Chinese themselves before they turned 'Red' because Confucianism failed to improve the condition of life and was unable to make the poor people, who were tormented by the war-lords, happier. They do not look for the objective factors which have cramped their individuality, restricted their choice and the possibility of what shall I become. And Pakistan is only as a mere terrorism-based Islamic nation that can experience existence in the world today or tomorrow. A passing fancy may impel them to cut chrysanthemus instead of cutting roses. It is the tension and the ambiguity of their life which make them respond to Hamlet's words.

Ishtiyaque Danish assesses the influence of international Islamist radicalism and says : "Indian Muslims are as divided as any other socio-religious group. There are the Sunnis and Shias, Deobandis and Brelvis, Hanafi and Salafi, among others. This list does not include fundamentalist Islamists. Then there are several religious socio-cultural and political organisations such as Jamat-e-Islami Hind, Tableeqhi Jamat, Jamiat-e-Ulema-e-Hind and Jamiat-e-Ahle Hadith, which command a large following. Then there is Sufi Islam, which appeals equally to the secular and the religious, as well as the educated and the illiterate. Those known as Wahhabis, especially the ones with Jihadist tendencies, are mere fringe elements." He also says : "Jamat-e-Islami is a revivalist religious organisation. Cadre-based, the closely-knit formation wields considerable influence but has never been a mass movement. Both Deobandis and Brelvis are critical of some of Jamat's ideas. The Jamat-e-Ulema Hind waged India's struggle for freedom alongside Mohammad Ali Jinnah's two nation theory, it has an all-India presence and is influential. Its religious beliefs are similar to those of the Tableeghi Jamat and Deobandis. Many Indian Muslim youth seem to be influenced by Sayyid Ahmed Shaheed, but in a way that could only be the result of a selective of his life story ... "(The Insider-III, TOI, October 6, 2008).

The fact is that the birth of Pakistan has shaken the very foundation of the life of Indian Muslims, and nothing but complete extermination awaits them if they do not cease being mere passive spectators to the great developments taking place around them. The Passive attitude on vital Kashmir question has given encouragement to the enemies of India and even weakened their case before others. And they naturally wonder as to how Indian Muslims, for whose ultimate good they are making so much sacrifice, can adopt such a passive and indifferent attitude towards Kashmir.

Their passive attitude so far has encouraged Pakistan to believe that the Indian Muslims are a source of strength to it. They must, however, come out and declare that they are the greatest source of Pakistan's weakness and India's strength. The very first step, therefore, which Indian Muslims should take is frankly to tell Pakistan that they do not look to it for support and they will even be compelled to look upon it as their greatest enemy if by foul actions. Pakistan jeopardises the positions of Muslims not only in Kashmir but in other parts of India also. Paksitan makes their life miserable. Why are we expected to have a double-standard of morality regarding Pakistan-sponsored terrorism in Kashmir and U.S. dollar imperialism? The blood-stained record of religious extremism and blood-spilling episodes of racialism in Pakistan are all too familiar. But are not well-cooked up jehadi slogans accompanied by terror and dictatorship? Do they not devour their children? General Musharraf was no saint like Tukaram, but neither was Hitler nor Mussolini. If Pakistan had been a liberal democrat, modern Pakistan would have been like modern Germany. But who will usher it in?

There is a certain number of sloppy sentimentalists in every country. Give them a grievance and they will worry it like a dog with a bone. We are suffering from now. The cracks are running amock. Hardly Kashmir in the worst form is the common accompaniment of terrorism. The humanitarians in Kashmir raise their hands in horror and denounce Pakistan who believes in the birch as brutes as saddists.

Sentimentality and logic are poor bedfellows; and the Parliament wrings its hands in horror at the jehadi slogans harshly yelling out for Kashmir and indulging in large scale banditry. (During the freedom movement, millions of men were taught violence and practised violence as a national duty, and that inevitably weakened the respect for law. Again, as the freedom movement was getting on, the bonds of parental discipline in the home were relaxed.).

The foreboding shadows of Pakistan have fallen across the vale of Kashmir after the downfall of Bangladesh. Pakistan is an Othello as powerful and as passionate as Z.A. Bhutto's pervading Bangladesh is a Desdemona as beauteous and as unsophisticated. The tragedy of today's Pakistan is based on two themes ... the themes of racialism and of religious passion.

Religious zest as typified by jehadis is one of Pakistan's policy and totalitarianism as exemplified by Islamic rulers is the other. Distress is a normal concomitant of Pakistan's economic scene. Atrocity stories of terrorists, either in Kashmir or in Pakistan, always cause anger and hatred, and untrue atrocity stories seem to us pernicious in the same way as pornography, and their purveyors as dangerous to society as pornographers.

Persons do matter but anxious questioning never yielded the right answer. We have known a period or a country where the hour did not bring forth the man; though there have been occasions when great men have outlived their period of usefulness.

Majority of our political parties has got a secularist bias. But secularism in India is different from secularism elsewhere. It has been a puzzle to many who hold less adventurous opinions. It has no value without a vote-catching idea. They may sound it in times of opposition. Sometimes they border on the ridiculous. Flattering is our national conscience, whatever may happen in Kashmir.

While discussing the Kashmir issue either in Parliament or elsewhere about terrorism, our leaders prefer to rest on their oars and there is so much hero-worship and lack of foresight that they have to behave like a dictator as if running the whole issue. After the blasts, they are merely a lame duck limping on one leg that is secularism. It is quite meaningful inasmuch as it betrays bankruptcy of statesmanship. Incapacity to fight terrorism meets the same punishment as crime.

How much of Gandhism does the Congress think survives in India and even in Kashmir today? The answer of this question is very little. Kashmir issue is a living example. Mendacious publications, deliberate falsehood and distortion of facts for political and personal ends have made the Kashmir issue worse and worse. The gospel of separatist movement comes as easily to some lips of secularists and communalists as the gospel of Gandhism. Shying away from all constructive thoughts, the Congress advocates the use of narrow parochialism and casteism. This is a strange 'tamasha' of keeping the people in a cage like animals.

Once pseudo-leaders succumb, they start slipping down the descent. Only he falls more suddenly and the consequences to him are more painful. "The mask falls, the man remains and the hero disappears," as Rousseau said. Why?

They are obsessively preoccupied with what it may be possible to prove shoddy and diseased. All heroes have come to bore us. So we take them down, one by one, anatomise them and drag before the public gaze the contaminated limbs with a malicious chuckle, a gleeful smacking of the lips. For over sixty years, it is quite clear to us that our political heroes and their self-styled ideologies are exposed and denounced by the State. It seems shocking to us that a public personage, idolised for years as an eminent revolutionary, should become overnight a deviationist, an imperialist stooge, a tool of a foreign capitalist clique, a treacherous hyena.

The only victors in the next world war will be the worms. The object must be not to win it but to avoid it. It is a challenge to political, not to military strategists.

Failure in democratic set-up is a common heritage of Pakistan even as the dyer's hand is subdued to that it works in. Some of her vaunted successes can be proved to be not successes at all. To be a failure need not be a catastrophic calamity. There may be a far worse fate in store for Pakistan than that. To fall in everything else is Pakistan's birthright. Why? Because she is still nursing the unconquerable hope and still clutching the inviolable shade. Religious extremism is worthy of her hire. Here is a fame for Pakistan : In every branch of human speculation, this is continually happening.

What phantoms they are and what phantoms we pursue. He that dies a martyr proves that he was not a knave but by no means that he was not a fool; since the most absurd doctrines of religious fanaticism are not without such evidence as martyrdom can produce. A martyr, therefore, by the mere act of suffering, can prove nothing but his own faith.

Having gone up like a rocket in world terrorism Pakistan will come down like a stick. There is sudden disillusionment which is reflected in the abrupt end of the middle.

Politics in India owes their origin to King Dasaratha when he surrendered to the artful Kaikayee.

No man was ever endowed with a judgement so correct and judicious, but those circumstances, time, and experience, would teach him that of these things with which he thought himself the best acquainted with, he knew nothing; and that those ideas which in theory appeared the most advantageous were found, when brought into practice to be altogether impracticable.

Partition began in a minor way, but most things of consequence have small beginnings. Pakistan is merely seeking an opportunity to live up to her reputation as a blood-sucking nation full of jehadi slogans. We found dead bugs in our pillows, under our counter-panes and strewn with literally among our clothes. But now that the scourge is over, Pakistan takes a few deadly bugs of religious militancy in our stride. Terrorism has descended on us, and the people of Kashmir sleep disturbed and annoyed day by day. There are the everyday noises in the turbulent valley. There are the others. A hundred voices in discordant unison of jehadi slogans. Revivalism of such murderous slogans is an equally significant point to the danger of vulgarisation.

In World War II, if you shot down 10 percent of the enemy's bombers you had done well. If you did it three nights running you had scored a victory, and the enemy probably had to change his tactics. But what would it be to shoot down 10 per cent of an attacking air fleet carrying the biggest nuclear weapons?

The danger of nuclear weapons! The main reason why the danger has decreased is because an aggressor has virtually no chance of escaping disastrous loss by retaliation with the same weapons. If the victim of aggression is strong and well prepared, he cannot be prevented from striking back with catastrophic effect. Therefore, it is the nations possessing nuclear weapons themselves which have at the same time the best power of defence against them ... the power of retaliation.

There has been much speculation as to how long a nuclear war would last. The popular view is that it would be short. It is correct. Why it should be a matter of hours. It might be as long as two or three weeks.

It is well-known that the most powerful nations set great store by them and have carefully studied their effects in manoeuvres, with and without troops. Nuclear weapons have introduced into the world such potentialities of black-mail as have never been conceived in international relations. So, nuclear war is the retaliatory power of nuclear weapons directed by missile throwing appliances. Pakistan has always been blackmailing India through this process.

Agreements between India and Pakistan on Kashmir issue are empty phrases or diplomatic catchword or a stunt slogan. Terrorism is the art of destruction. The unending and seamless terror and terror sanctuaries are flourishing across the western border. Why? Islamabad's use of terrorism is an instrument of state policy. Every attack is controlled from Pakistan; and her war-rhetoric will result in short-term gains but not yield any positive result in the long run. And every pattern of terror suggests an increasingly Pan-Indian and trans-national aspect to the attacks on India. It is the gift of Islamic terrorism, lying in ISI's blessings. But as the early Christians said, "If the sun were not hung so high, someone would have claimed it long ago." Pakistan usually considers walking on water or in thin air a miracle. War is the very anti-thesis not merely of peace, but of all freedoms, individual and social. Pakistan's progress cannot flourish under these circumstances. Why? Because war-hysteria is a terrible epidemic which seizes men's needs, and terrorism is the virulent bacilli of fear that carries the infection. War never solves any problems.

Pakistan has passed broadly through the different but critical phases of lunatic fringe, lumbering together with so many unwanted but extravagantly and romantically chivalrous ideas. The first phase saw a political hoax done to burlesque embroidered with glamourous anti-India hymns of hate among the growing generation and exposed peculiar oddities. The second phase saw a strange and comical identity of an Islamic nation done with amused perplexity.

The third phase saw a double-dyed diplomacy on Kashmir issue and political dualism on the liberation of Bangladesh. The fourth phase Pakistan failed to read the Kashmir question like a book and found the nation on a razor-edge of tinpot dictatorship. And the fifth phase sees Pakistan has started out emitting rays of Islamic violence, beaming with joy of fanaticism and extremism, diverging from a focal point of true Islamic philosophy and stirring up a contemptible set of mass-murdering terrorist outfits in agitation for social and political change in Kashmir rabbling on about a Roman Holiday in Kashmir. This rabble-rousing process of terrorism shivers the world at large. So, Pakistan is a good dealer and mathematical researcher of Islamic terrorism.

In these circumstances, political authority of each and every Govt. in Pakistan is fragile and the ruling coalition is continually wrecked by differences. Every attack in India is planned, coordinated and executed by elements in the ISI. Do you know it was the ISI, backed by millions of covert dollars from the CIA, that ran arms to guerrillas, fighting Soviet forces in Afganistan in the 1980s? Do you know the ISI connections have helped the terrorists of Kashmir retain the safe haven in Pakistan? Do you know since 2001 the Taliban fled Afganistan have steadily grown in strength and boldness? Confronted by religious extremism and financial bankruptcy, Pakistan is losing her self-confidence. The crisis-ridden Pakistan is bound by teething troubles and dead weight of mischief-makers, sidetracking all ethical way of living. Does Pakistan have ever heard of the Delphic oracle 'know thyself and know the world and the gods? The Delphi was the holy centre of ancient Greece. When written in Chinese, the word 'crisis' is composed of two characters — one represents danger, and the other represents opportunity. The gods cannot help those who do not seize opportunities. And Pakistan has come to the edge of all opportunities last. Why? Because of selfish dependence on dollar diplomacy.

Do you know the parents of Pakistan name their babies after Laden, terror don? Do you know the parents of Italy also name their babies after wartime fascist dictator Benito Mussolini or his wife Rachele, and even the bonus applies to babies born in 2009 in villages where birthrate is low? No comment. Will it hurt anyone? Will it improve on the silence? Fill the day with terrorism and end the day with terrorism. The tide of Islamic radicalism has swept across the globe with all fascist nature. Messy surroundings. Pakistan is sunk as she has lost touch with the people, making a power-sharing deal with the militants. So, Kashmir issue remains unsolved as it was before.

Indo-Pak deal on Kashmir issue has always been riddle in word-puzzle. A deal of compromise! Is there any perseverance for the foundation of all knotty problems? All have some daring singularity, maintaining their attitude of their own principles. Deal for whom? Jehadi slogans are the ogreish exclamation to frighten the subcontinent felicitating the other fellow terrorist groups in high feathers. Pakistan seems to be a pasture of the Taliban. Deal! Where ISI's indulgence in amorous advancement of SIMI is like the vassal's fidelity to his feudal lord. Pakistan believes in a proverbial saying : "Fast bind fast find."

Lewis Carroll, in Alice in Wonderland, picturises the way of deal in a humorous way : "Would you tell me please, which way I ought to go from here?' 'That depends a good deal on where you want to get to' said the cat. 'I don't much care where,' said Alice. "Then it doesn't matter which way you go," said the cat." The trick of deal lies in always breathing and connecting breath of jehadi groups to the Islamic sensation in the ISI hands throughout the session in Indo-Pak deal on Kashmir issue. 'Deal' means dark clouds gathering overhead.

Do you know Mahatma Gandhi, the Father of the Nation, who used truth and non-violence in the fight for India's freedom, donned an army uniform? Do you know the Father of the Nation wore the British Army's uniform in 1899, as a member of a voluntary ambulance unit during the Anglo-Boer war? This little known fact is reported in the magazine 'Sainik Samachar' (Soldier's News), formerly called 'Fauji Akhbar' has been archived in the coffee-table book 'Soldiering On' released on January 2, 2009 in the centenary year of the magazine.

Why Navjuvan Trust was unwilling to ask the Govt. of India to extend the copyright? Why Navjuvan Trust, since its inception, has published some 300 volumes of Mahatma Gandhi's works including articles, letters and speeches, apart from translations of his autobiography? So, freedom movement, partition, and Kashmir problem have been confronted with a permutation and combination of riddles in different political objects by variation of religious colours. Some of our intellectuals take pride in their intellect. Scorn the intellectual as much as the world esteems it. They want to escape the past and acquire a new political profile. Their political alliances are often built not on the basis of shared ideology but for the sake of gaining office. They think this is a morality play. Their logic is limited by the boundaries of petty politics. Let's not fool ourselves. The facts behind Kashmir issue are where we have agreed to let investigation cease. We know partition comes out like a lion and goes out like a lamb, leaving Kashmir issue and Hindu-Muslim feud.

WHAT WRONG WITH OUR PUBLICITY SERVICES?

The answer is : So much for Kashmir which has highlighted the melancholy deficiencies of our publicity machinery. On the broader plane, the same defects are noticeable, and arise largely from the same causes. It is not that we lack publicity but that the publicity is to a considerable extent misconceived and misdirected. The purpose of publicity is to win friends and influence people. India has failed to convince, and where necessary, to convert.

Why? Because of the veil of illusion by which he is concealed. Why? Because of her propaganda that goes round and round by various tortuous paths. What is basically wrong with our publicity is that those who direct it are too much concerned with the impersonal machinery and too little concerned with the human factor around the Kashmir issue. And yet it is the human factor both at the giving and receiving ends which vitally matter. It is the calibre and training of publicity officers to counter terrorism and Pakistan's lies and sham modesty at one end and the impression they and their publicity have not yet made on human beings at the other end which alone counts. Without question they will be the greatest losers. India on Kashmir issue will be as happy as she decides to be, not depending on outer or worldy circumstances. Happiness and sadness are the internal states of a Kashmiri. So, requirement is not in New Delhi, not in military strategists. The well digger should only connect the external world with the inner springs, distinguishing between obligation and non-obligation. There is no place for arrogance and frenzy in the behavior of a religious person. Our religious leaders, quite distrustful of their ability and opinion, suffer from morbid thoughts and hesitant shyness. They shut off from the Kashmir issue in a lazy nonchalant manner.

Here much of the propaganda material on Kashmir and terror-based Pakistan, and on cross-border terrorism is potently misconceived and ineffectual. Often it is badly written, or stated bristling with over-statement and over emphasis so that a terror-victim has the feeling that anti-terror propaganda is being shouted at him. If the facts are sound and good, let them speak for themselves with no frills and furbelows.

Are we doing enough of our propaganda publicity on Kashmir issue, particularly through the Asia and African worlds? Sickened by strong emotion and mentally unsound by sadistic jokes, our media is badly outclassed in publicity.

In films, propaganda publicity has a persuasive vehicle. It should be suitably dubbed in the more important Asian and African languages. It should be capable of yielding impressive dividends of goodwill against Pakistan's cross-border terrorism. Kashmir will present an ideal subject for the films, explaining the foreign policy of India for an intelligently-conceived films. The Voice of America increasingly demonstrates the vehicles of propaganda for several reasons.

The basic issues should be simply and succintly executed. For example, is it fair or equitable to allow the aggressor or the jihadi militants to secure the fruits of a continuing aggression or terrorism in India and to turn a deaf ear to the victims warning that Islamic terrorism today would mean a reversal to the holocaust and upheavals of 1947, and of communal repurcussion? Or is not terrorism a Pakistani-sponsored vitriolic passion for global terror before the world?

What is wrong with our propaganda on Kashmir and Pakistan-sponsored anti-India campaign? Everything. It is wrong at the fount and wrong in the channels through which it is purveyed. Our propaganda on Kashmir should not plead a cause. The smacking of especial pleading on Kashmir is always unconvincing. Here Pakistan has scored heavily against us for by seizing on the principle of self-determination and pinpointing the Kashmir issue. She has put the issue out of focus. And India has already a large sector of world opinion by reducing the issue to a simple syllogism. And Pakistan with false syllogism. That this State ignorance has existed even after sixty years of independence. Whereas Pakistan has successfully prejudiced the atmosphere against India on Kashmir, unleashing a period of virulence against India and Indians. Here we fall dismally. And the valley of Kashmir stands quiet still: so still that it realized where it was that it has seen itself. What is the reason?

The reason is that our policy on propaganda is determined primarily by bureaucrats seated at their secretariat desks and surrounded by files. Able and competent though they are, few know the world outside India to which our propaganda publicity is directed, and even fewer have any practical knowledge of journalism through which propaganda is largely purveyed. *Propaganda is the vital organ of foreign policy.*

The file mentality puts premium on hand-outs. To the bureaucrat, everything sacred must be committed to paper and an individual inured to finding all the answers in his files likes to think that the most popular recipient of such hand-outs is the waste-paper basket. For, Pakistan has gained more mileage over Kashmir and terrorism than India. And India suffers heavily from Kashmir issue. Our country is now in doldrums, not to distinguish between men of the right calibre and right person. Do our secretaries exercise a wholesome discretion?

The tyranny of propaganda mesmerises men at every level of our propaganda machineries. The British attitude towards Kashmir is less than one of fair play and particularly damaging to relations between the two countries because of the implied doubt of Indian integrity. The British Govt. has not been shaken by the strength of reaction produced in India. The most significant of secretaries in this vital field is the discovery of India's position in Asia, increasing conscious comprehension.

Today, communal arithmetic and the bogey of communalists have threatened to be a country-wide rebellion of 'ticket-jilted' congressmen in Kashmir against the organisation. So, the Kashmir question still remains unsolved. They are jubilant because they have at last attained their much-cherished objective of forging a united front of communal groups under their leadership. Fumbling, hesitant BJP has succumbed and has taken the inevitable jump forward to the slogans of 'Hindus for Hindustan'. And the Muslim organisations have taken the risk of cracking up under the stresses and strains of the pronounced ideological differences between the coalescing groups. From the errors of others,a wise man corrects his own, our country has not yet learnt this lesson. The polling booth is now the common goal, where everyone is master of his fate. A monopoly of political power can corrupt even the best of parties.

Pakistan on Kashmir solution says that she is not prejudiced at all. She is going with a perfectly open and unbiased mind to listen to what she is convinced is pure rubbish. Pakistan's crime is that they dream about more freedom in Kashmir. If corruption continues to flourish, the fault lies with the Kashmir administration as much as with the people. Today Kashmir is the refuge of political scoundrels, fools and cowards.

There is an unhappy tradition of Congress bossism on Kashmir issue. Discussion among the Congress leadership is a perennial topic of backchat among officials which has a deleterious effect on the morale of the Kashmir administration. The people of Kashmir regret the State of affairs in a region where there is such a heavy backlog to work out, politically, economically and socially, and so little time to waste on political manoeuvrings. Lies and perfidy in Kashmir remain in a state of wretched barbarity.

The factionalism prevailing in Kashmir can only be matched with its economic backwardness, while the political inexperience of leadership has to be set against the lack of emotional and administrative cohesion in the valley where the Hindus and the Muslims have been isolated from each other and in varying stages of political and administrative evolution. The ruling Govt. in the State is a house divided against itself.

What twists the knife in the wind is the realisation that something was rotten in the State of Kashmir.

The people of all classes want to travel, to read, to think, to listen to the wireless wit jamming; to go to universities in other countries; in short to mix the rest of the world. The Islamic terrorists and hide-bound communists are simply ridiculous with their absurd rules and idiotic regulations. Their hatred and ill-treatment to the intellectuals and leaders of all the professions and upper classes has led to the ruination of each subjugated country.

Even in Pakistan, the people are asking what kind of creed it is that makes half of Pakistan little better than a prison camp of horror. The Islamic priests are to blame for all this as the communists. The Islamic priests are the locust of Islamic nations with their creed of hate, violence, terror and subversion of all kinds as communists do. Through their looting and despoliation of industries and educational institutions — of which they know nothing — their confiscation of properties, their transportation of whole factories, goods and edibles to other terrorist camps — they have starved off and ruined the economics of a country. The terrorists are the most hated people in the world today.

Salafism, derisively called Wahhabism in Pakistan, is a historical movement, which demands that Muslims return to Islam as it was practised in the early period when the deviations we see today were non-existent. What is Salafist ideology? The Salafist ideology seeks to restore the 'Islam' practised by the Prophet, his companions and their immediate followers. This is the 'Islam' the great classical jurist Imam Ahmad Ibn Hambal sought to establish. The Salafis or Ahle Hadith group in India are, in fact, unitarians. With Saudi help, they are well-organised but do not command a huge following among Indians. Through a countrywide network of madrassas, Deobandis greatly influence Indian Muslims.

Every question Pakistan answers on Kashmir issue leads on to another question. If war is an extension of policy then abuse is an extension of argument. When arguments exhaust themselves, people try to indulge in abuse. That is what Pakistan is trying to do in advancing Pakistan's case on Kashmir. These things cannot help Pakistan. Islamabad blows hot and cold in the same breath. On the one hand, it says that Pakistan does not want to embark upon a war and desires to have peace with India, while on the other, it asks its lieutenants the Fakir of Ipi and other Islamic priests and jehadi groups to declare a holy war on India. How can we now trust the sincerity and honesty of Pakistan's leaders? Islamabad dances willy-nilly to the tunes the pipers it appointed choose to play.

We say we love flowers, yet we pluck them. We say we love trees, yet we cut them down. And people still wonder why some are afraid when told they are loved.

Pakistan should discover what is true behind Kashmir issue. Reason, reason alone, should determine their opinion.

What is more miserable than discontent? partition. What is more than distrust? Kashmir. Today, labouring spider weaves tedious snares to trap enemies. Pakistan is more busy than labouring spider. Why? Because Pakistan's pale-faced fear always keeps with the mean-born partition.

Kashmiri Hindu Pundits stare at our authority with sad unhelpful tears. So mighty are our vowed enemies that we seek after compromise, compromise, compromise.

Do our rulers know wolves are gnarling at their entrance? Will you bring a burden of dishonour home? People are blind with weeping and sick with groans. And our rulers! They are crowned with infamy.

One ideology, one programme and no opposition — that is Pakistan's political credo. Need it be told that it bears a family resemblance to that of Hitlerite Germany, which had its brief day of splendour and is now no more ? The similarity is not merely of a surface nature—it is very much real. In Hitler's Germany, there was the domination of the myth of the Nordic blood and in Pakistan it is that of the Islamic faith. In the former, all else than having pure German blood were destined either to go out or live the helot's life. prominent Pakistan's spokemen are never tired of bragging that they are out to establish the noblest brand of democracy in their country. But the leaders are out to bluff the world. Muzzling of the opposition is surely undesirable but mudslinging and vapid opposition would be no less so. In India, parliament is a secret league between the parties for exploiting the masses. Everyone knows that Nehru was the last person to do political harakiri by kowtowing to Karachi as directed by Liaquat Ali Khan. There is now a revival of the old Jinnah tactics when India was undivided — misrepresentation, breach of confidence, obstruction and chest-beating— which ill suits the needs of international diplomacy, in particular fouling the channels of communication and discussion between two independent states.

Nepal should turn to India for advice and guidance and follow her lead in matters that are of vital importance not only to herself but to resurgent nationalism in Asia as a whole. The liquidation of colonialism in Asia is creating a vacuum which would be dangerous to allow to continue for long. India cannot step in to bridge the gap and take over the role played by dying colonialism. A sort of hyphen should be bound by forces of friendship. It has to be recognised that if Asia is to escape the ravages of a global war, she must emerge out of the cesspool of power politics of the west.

Why terrorism ? There is a wide gap of communication between the security and freedom. The reproductive capacity of our mentally-aberrated leaders weakens the strength and freedom of our country. Who are ministers ? A Chinese fable says a Chinese poet provided everyone of his sons with a job but there was one incompetent for any profession. He made him a minister. If we apply the Chinese wisdom to this Chinese fable, we will have the explanation for most of our failures in India on Kashmir issue. The epidemic of corrupted leaders is also progressing. The result is that many who have been counted may have to be discounted. But the trouble is where we revitalise one set the other set will feel devitalised.

Whether cold war strategists have really any hand in the developments of Kashmir problem behind the curtain is a highly intriguing question. For the moment all that we are given to see is the engrossing spectacle of fleeing ambassadors and rolling heads in between India and Pakistan; and this can be realised only with a vigorous dose of Machiavelli. That prince of diplomats laid it down that no power could, for good or ill, tolerate its avowed enemies and rivals; he who establishes a tyranny without killing Brutus, or a republic without killing the sons of Brutus will not last long. On both sides of the curtain, Kashmir issue is an exciting gamble on the question that lasts out long. A good diplomat like a good military leader will have an inborn sense of humour and can crack a joke even in the worst of situations.

Any military strategy is as threatening as trouble brewing. And the fatal reaction is as desperate measures as perilous in disguise. The world of terrorism is as courting disaster as the growing danger of drug -addiction. Both spring out from a lonely world of mental frustration, false happiness and sickness. So, Pakistan's religiously addicted Islamic terrorism is as the deadly fear of going back to the ghastly slavery of Islamic law as the deadly slogans of the Devil. Falling in this unsolved dilemma and unshakeable faith, Pakistan is in a state of complex processes of possible explanations, in between evasion and sophistry. When there were rumours in 1969 that Beatle Paul McCartney was dead, Pakistan will have to follow McCartney who issued this denial:

"I am alive and well and concerned about the rumours of my death. But if I were dead, I would be the last to know." Only Pakistani rulers will have to be the last men to know the death-knell of their country's existence.

There is a Yiddish proverb : "Don't approach a goat from the front, a horse from the back or a fool from any side."

And Kashmir issue, like pendulum, swings forward and backward in between unanswered questions. It is not hard problem. It could be solved just after partition. But our leaders[1] uncanny insight — What a premature death! premature death is like accepting defeat without having been defeated. Cold words and hot words make the issue worse and worse. It dies from religious blindness and political errors and betrayals. Cold words and hot words still go on. French scientist and philosopher Blaise Pascal says-

"Cold words freeze people, and hot words scorch them, and bitter words make them bitter, and wrathful words make them wrathful. Kind words also produce their own image on men's souls; and a beautiful image it is. They soothe, quiet and comfort the hearer."

Remember : The digit '7' represents a significant historical breakthrough in Indian history. The year 1757 (the battle of plassey), the year 1857 (the sepoy Mutiny or the first war of independence), the year 1947 (India's independence). Hypothetically, we can assume that the year '2017' or '2027' may be another historical event in Indian history. If it be so, Pakistan's geographical position will be in a question mark.

To reach the conclusion connected with this adjective chapter, we can safely say that Pakistan lays great emphasis on the importance of the individual, and speaks of education and legislation for freedom, but it is still not clear exactly what sort of freedom Pakistan means. Most of her prescriptions are negative : she wants education to teach children how easy it is for them to be taken in by appeals to their emotions, and legislation to protect them ... or adults ... from being insidiously attacked by subliminal persuasion or won over when in a state of high suggestibility. Above all, they should be taught a proper respect for facts on Kashmir issue and for the language she uses in expressing them. But Pakistan goes on to speak of education in values. Here her new alternative to the new Islamic World is in some ways an improvement on her predecessors. Not only is the individual to be allowed a free choice but this choice is to be restricted by preventing him from imposing his preferences on others ... a very necessary corollary. But there are still two conflicting objections. In the first place, Pakistan's proposal for 'education in values' is a phrase to set the shivers running down any good liberal spine. In the second place, what is to be done if the people, with their eyes wide open, conscious of their own freedom, nevertheless choose a conformist, manipulated Islamic society?

This is a very old liberal dilemma in a new guise. Is Pakistan allowed to force people to be free? This question has perplexed the political philosopher and the social prophet, but practical politician often remains curiously unworried. For the answer lies not in a crusade or in a Jehadi slogan or in Kashmir solution but in a compromise.

Pakistani leaders are men of the herd. By their very intolerance of the eccentric it is unlikely to surrender to an Inquisitor. They may drift into an untidy and ill-directed imitation of the fanatic Islamic World, but they will not let themselves be dragooned purposefully into the real thing.

The prophet of doom is so eloquent that Pakistan may even defeat her own ends, by tempting the Muslims to despair too easily.

So, everything on Kashmir solution is uncertain shifting contradictory full of nightmarish dreams and ungentle games in between 'reality' and 'Dream'. Why? Because it seems obsessed with the haunting experiences of the immediate post-partition period, and with the cruel loneliness of children who feel they have nothing in common with the fictitious hollow orderliness of their parents' world.

BIBLIOGRAPHY

R.H. Scott : New Approach
Dr. B.R. Ambedkar : Thoughts on Pakistan
The News Chronicle Zamindar Cavalcade (1948)
Friends Not Masters : Ayub Khan's political Autobiography
Titus Andronicus : Shakespeare
The Emergence of Pakistan : Chowdhury Md. Ali
Fourth Way : P.D. Ourpensky
Plots and Conspiracies : Andrew Shirley
Basis of Pakistan : Nafis Ahmed
Faith and Duty : Robinson
A History of the Crusade : Storen Runimen
The Life of Mahatma Gandhi : Louis Fischer
New York Times
In The Line of Fire : Gen Musharraf
The Struggle for Kashmir : M.Brecher
The Gita
The Upanishad
Ramkrishna Kathamrita
A.P. Venkateswaran : The Tragedy of Kashmir
Canadian Globe and Mail : 2007
Boris Pasternak : Dr. Zhivago
Ernest Hemingway : Notes on the Next War
Dr. Arnold Toynbee : A Study of History
Eugen Kogon : The Theory and Practice of Hell
Kalidasa : Ritusamhara
Edgar Snow : People On Our Side
Jagmohan : Bogey of Kashmir Autonomy
Omar Khayyam

Mark Twain : Mark Twain in Eruption
Jean Paul Sartre : Troubled Sleep
Lt. Gen. K.S. Brar : The Role of the Army in Kashmir
Time in India
George Bernard Shaw : Caesar and Cleopetra
The Koran
Amrita Bazar Patrika : 1892
SomPrakash : 1872
Bharatbasi : 1886
Dainik : 1886
Albert Camu :
Shakespeare : Hamlet
Kingsley Martin : India Revisited
Murad Ali Baig : Revisionists Hijack Islam
The Athrava Veda
The News : 2009
George Orwell : Animal Farm
A. Enock : This War Business
F.A.E. Crew : Must Man Wage War?
Manchester Guardian (London) : 1955
Stephen P. Cohen : India-Emerging Power
Jay Luvaas : Education of an Army